ACCOUNTIN[illegible]
FINANCE [illegible]SS

ACCOUNTING AND FINANCE FOR BUSINESS

Geoff Black and Mahmoud Al-Kilani

PEARSON

Harlow, England • London • New York • Boston • San Francisco • Toronto • Sydney
Auckland • Singapore • Hong Kong • Tokyo • Seoul • Taipei • New Delhi
Cape Town • São Paulo • Mexico City • Madrid • Amsterdam • Munich • Paris • Milan

PEARSON EDUCATION LIMITED

Edinburgh Gate
Harlow CM20 2JE
United Kingdom
Fax: +44 (0)1279 431059
Web: www.pearson.com/uk

First published 2013 (print and electronic)

ISBN: 978-0-273-77394-8 (print)
978-0-273-78934-5 (eTxt)
978-0-273-77396-2 (eBk)

British Library Cataloguing-in-Publication Data
A catalogue record for the print edition is available from the British Library

Library of Congress Cataloging-in-Publication Data
Black, Geoff.
Accounting and finance for business / Geoff Black and Mahmoud Al-kilani.
pages cm
Includes bibliographical references and index.
ISBN 978-0-273-77394-8 (pbk.)
1. Accounting. 2. Managerial accounting. 3. Business enterprises – Finance. I. Al-kilani, Mahmoud. II. Title.
HF5635.B66167 2013
657–dc23 2013008126

10 9 8 7 6 5 4 3 2 1
17 16 15 14 13

Print edition typeset in Minion Pro 10.5/13
Print edition printed and bound by Rotolito, Lombarda, Italy

NOTE THAT ANY PAGE CROSS REFERENCES REFER TO THE PRINT EDITION

Brief contents

Contents

ACCOUNTING AND FINANCE FOR BUSINESS ONLINE

A wide range of supporting resources are available at:

MyAccountingLab

Register to create your own personal account using the access code supplied with your copy of the book,* and access the following teaching and learning resources:

Resources for students
- **A dynamic eText** of the book that you can search, bookmark, annotate and highlight as you please
- **Self-assessment questions** that identify your strengths before recommending a personalised study plan that points you to the resources which can help you achieve a better grade
- **Flashcards** to test your understanding of key terms

Resources for instructors
- **Instructor's manual**, with additional questions, complete and fully worked solutions, as well as case study debriefs
- **PowerPoint slides**, containing figures from the book

For more information, please contact your local Pearson Education account manager or visit www.myaccountinglab.com.

*If you don't have an access code, you can still access the resources. Visit www.myaccountinglab.com for details.

Preface

Our aim in writing this book has been to make your study of accounting and finance as interesting and enjoyable as possible. Such adjectives might not be those that immediately spring to mind when embarking on this subject area, but we hope that you will come to find this a fascinating and rewarding area of study – and of particular benefit to your future career.

Our use of QR codes throughout the book is a particular feature. By downloading a QR reader app to your smartphone or tablet computer, then opening it and pointing at the code, you will be taken within seconds to an essential resource related to a relevant chapter: perhaps a company website or pdf file of a document such as an annual report. We believe that this will greatly enhance your learning experience.

In addition to the core chapters, a number of revision exercises and practice examination papers are included to help you consolidate your knowledge. Also, a case study – the business adventures of Marvin the Magician – chart his career from a humble beginning in Chapter 1 through to his developing an international manufacturing and media empire in later chapters. Many 'news clips' have also been included which illustrate real-life business situations as recorded in news media – particularly the *Financial Times*.

In writing this book, we particularly want to thank our publishers and editors at Pearson, including Lucy Winder, Katy Rowlands, Gemma Papageorgiou, Louise Hammond, Priyadharshini Dhanagopal, Brian Burge and Linda Dhondy. Our special thanks are due to our family members and Professor Stuart Wall and Eleanor Wall for their support, and specifically to Rachel Black for invaluable help in preparing the PowerPoint slides which are available to lecturers.

We are always interested in receiving feedback on your experience of using the book, which can either be made by e-mail to **commentonbook@googlemail.com** or directly to the publishers.

Guided tour

MyAccountingLab is an online assessment and revision tool that puts you in control of your learning through a suite of study and practice tools tied to the online eText.

Why should I use MyAccountingLab?

With more than 300,000 registered students using MyAccountingLab each year, you can be confident that this is the most effective and reliable learning solution for accounting available today.

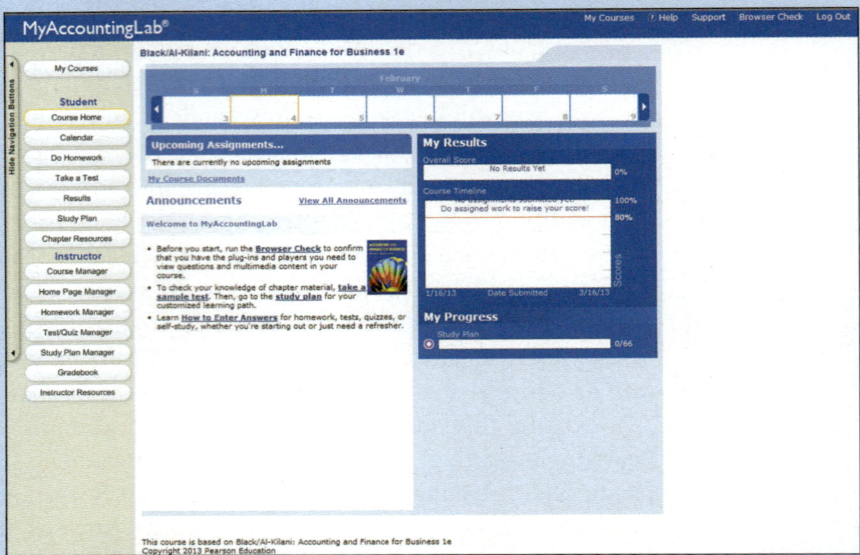

We recently polled 10,000 student users of MyAccountingLab from around the globe:

- 92% of students said that MyAccountingLab learning aids helped them while completing homework and/or preparing for exams.
- 89% of students said that MyAccountingLab helped them earn a higher grade.
- 92% of students would recommend MyAccountingLab for future courses.

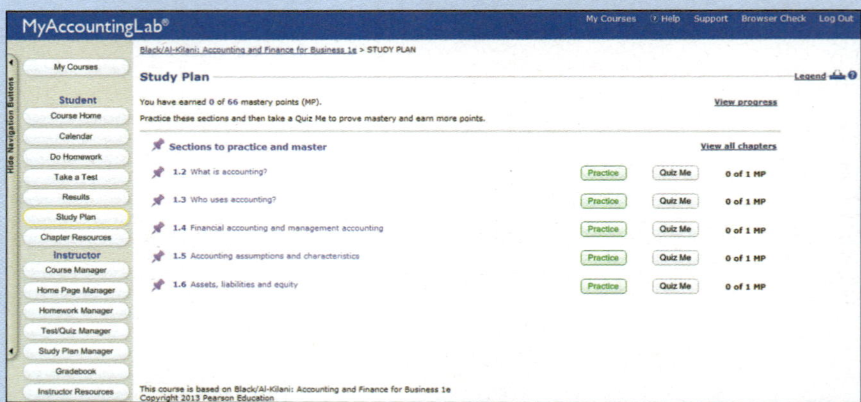

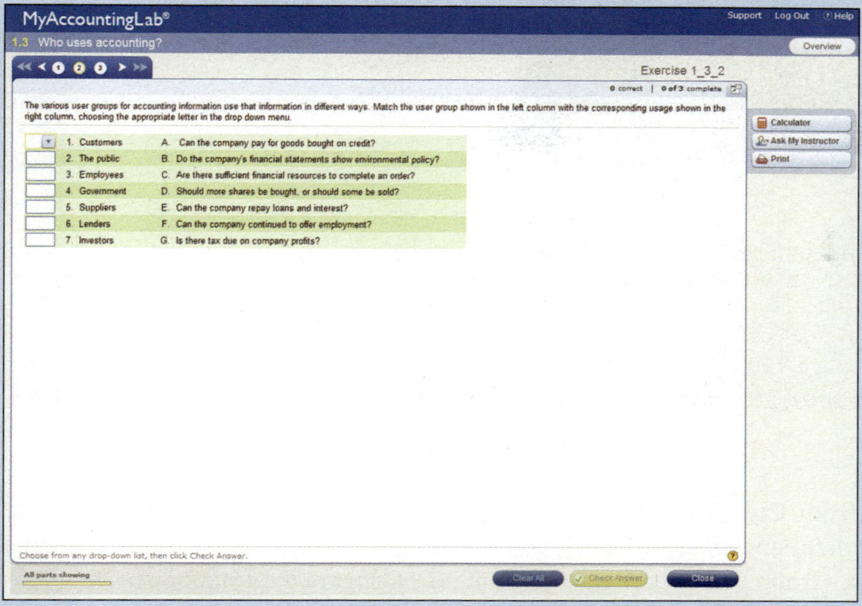

How do I use MyAccountingLab?

Practice tests for each chapter of the textbook enable you to check your understanding and identify the areas in which you need to do further work.

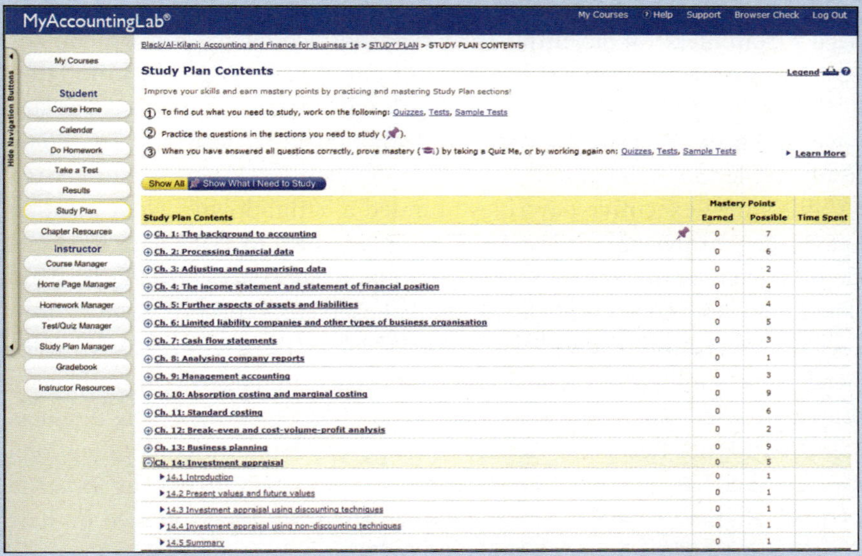

Based on your test results, we create a personalized **Study Plan**. This highlights areas where you still need to revise, allowing you to focus on weaker areas and study more efficiently. It also links to the eText, so you can re-read sections in topics you have not yet mastered.

We also provide step-by-step solutions to exercises, so you can see how to get the right answer.

Lecturer training and support

Our dedicated team of client service managers offer personalised training and support for MyAccountingLab, ensuring that you can maximize the benefits of MyAccountingLab.

For a visual walkthrough of how to make the most of MyAccountingLab, visit www.myaccountinglab.com

To find details of your Pearson account manager, go to www.pearsoned.co.uk/replocator

Acknowledgements

We are grateful to the following for permission to reproduce copyright material:

Cartoons

Cartoon on page 110 from *Introduction to Accounting and Finance*, 2e, Prentice Hall (Geoff Black 2009) 101, Pearson Education Limited

Figures

Figure 4.2 from Compass Group plc, http://annualreport11.compass-group.com/pdfdownloads/financial/cgplc_2011_cfs_independent_auditors.pdf; Figure 5.4 from The Alumasc Group plc, Report and Accounts 2011; Figure 6.4 from SuperGroup plc; Figure 17.1 from Forest Stewardship Council, http://us.fsc.org/

Text

Extract on page 7 from Elektron plc, http://www.elektron-technology.com/wp-content/uploads/2012/02/Elektron-plc_Annual-Report_2011.pdf; Box on page 152 from James Halstead plc, 12 January 2011; Article on page 270 from Baker gets fingers burnt as cupcake deal proves too tasty. Website discount was 'worst business decision', *The Times*, 22/11/2011 (deBruxelles S.), ©deBruxelles S., NI Syndication, 22/11/2011; Activity 16.2 from Vince Cable's new executive pay rules branded a 'climbdown', *The Gaurdian*, 20/06/2012 (Syal R.), Copyright Guardian News & Media Ltd 2012 The Financial Times Article on page 6 from Going concern, *The Financial Times*, 11/02/2010 (Lex), FT.com, © The Financial Times Limited. All Rights Reserved; Article on page 77 from Auditor quits Chinese group Boshiwa, *The Financial Times* 16/03/2012 (Cookson R.), © The Financial Times Limited. All Rights Reserved; Article on page 151 from Peugeot launches €1bn rights issue, *The Financial Times* 06/03/2012 (Reed J.), © The Financial Times Limited. All Rights Reserved; Article on page 155 from Silicon Valley hype machine blows a gasket, *The Financial Times*, 20/06/2012 (Waters R.), © The Financial Times Limited. All Rights Reserved; Article on page 162 from Line softened on hard copies of annual reports, *The Financial Times*, 01/09/2011 (Jones A.), © The Financial Times Limited. All Rights Reserved; Article on page 183 from GENERAL RETAILERS - Game administrators cut jobs and close shops, *The Financial Times*, 27/03/2012 (Felsted A., Sakoui A.), © The Financial Times Limited. All Rights Reserved; Article on page 217 from Report urges FA to overhaul debt levels, *The Financial Times*, 29/07/2011 (Hammond E.), © The Financial Times Limited. All Rights Reserved; Article on page 324 from When there's no Plan A, *The Financial Times*, 21/05/2010 (Moules J.), © The Financial Times Limited. All Rights Reserved; Article on page 373 from Supply chain: Tsunami, floods and storms move logistics up the agenda, *The Financial Times*, 21/01/2012 (Wright R.), © The Financial Times Limited. All Rights Reserved; Article on page 389 from No easy formula for success as companies face scepticism, *The Financial Times*, 29/05/2012 (Murray S.), © The Financial Times Limited. All Rights Reserved; Article on page 394 from Barclays suffers executive pay backlash,

The Financial Times, 27/04/2012 (Jenkins P.), © The Financial Times Limited. All Rights Reserved; Activity 16.3 adapted from Accounting: Fooled again, *The Financial Times*, 19/03/2010 (Hughes J.), © The Financial Times Limited. All Rights Reserved; Exercise 16.3 from UK retreat on accountancy standards, *The Financial Times*, 30/01/2012 (Mundy S.), © The Financial Times Limited. All Rights Reserved; Article on page 411 adapted from Calls for corporate disclosure of social impact, *The Financial Times*, 17/06/2012 (Crooks E.), © The Financial Times Limited. All Rights Reserved; Article on page 413 from Puma to kick leather into touch, *The Financial Times*, 22/06/2012 (Clark P.), © The Financial Times Limited. All Rights Reserved; Article 17.1 from US companies urged to put natural capital in accounts, *The Financial Times*, 24/06/2012 (Scot M.), © Mike Scott, Carbon Copy Communications Ltd.; Article 17.1 from Apple agrees to China pollution audit, *The Financial Times*, 15/04/2012 (Nutall C.), © The Financial Times Limited. All Rights Reserved; Exercise 17.2 from Puma releases 'true' carbon emission cost, *The Financial Times*, 17/05/2011 (Marsh P.), © The Financial Times Limited. All Rights Reserved

In some instances we have been unable to trace the owners of copyright material, and we would appreciate any information that would enable us to do so.

Chapter 1

The background to accounting

Objectives

When you have read this chapter you will be able to:

- Explain what is meant by 'accounting'
- Distinguish between financial accounting and management accounting
- Identify the main users of accounting information
- Understand the concepts and principles on which accounting is based
- Distinguish between assets, liabilities, equity, income and expenses
- Understand the basic 'accounting equations'

1.1 Introduction

The major global economic upheavals of recent years have created an atmosphere of mistrust of those professions working within the financial sector. Bankers, investment analysts and accountants have all suffered in terms of damage to their reputations due to the public's perception of them being subject to weak regulations leading to, and possibly encouraging, illegal or unethical behaviour by large corporations. Although not immune from such criticism, accountants would claim that they have made tremendous strides in recent years to put in place a set of standards that are 'fit for purpose'. They would also argue that their role is not to portray a financial picture which is unique in its perfection, honesty and reliability. What they do attempt to achieve is the presentation of often highly complex data that can be relied upon as a *reasonably* truthful and fair summary of financial events.

This chapter introduces you to the whole area of accounting – what it is, who it is for, and who makes the rules and regulations that govern it. Accounting has a number of divisions, two of which are *financial accounting* and *management accounting*. These are explained in this chapter, as well as some of the key concepts and principles that underpin accounting. The chapter also introduces some key terms: assets, liabilities, equity, income and expenses, and how they are linked within a number of key accounting equations. These equations help us to understand the logical basis of accounting and see how the financial affairs of even the most complex organisation can be summarised and analysed.

1.2 What is accounting?

You may think that you know nothing about accounting, but consider this conversation:

> 'Ted wrote his car off last week. He'd gone into the red to pay for it, but – would you credit it – the car wasn't insured. There's no accounting for some people. The bottom line is – you need to protect your assets!'

You may be surprised to learn that this contains six separate accounting references (wrote . . . off; into the red; credit; accounting; the bottom line; assets). Most of the terms are so familiar that they are used without thinking where they came from. One respected broadcaster even went so far as to say: 'it is rather intriguing that the origins of writing, which has led to so much romance, history and philosophy, should have begun with accountancy'![1]

The origins of accounting can in fact be traced back to ancient times, with the need for accurate records of trading transactions. A logical system of recording financial information, known as double-entry bookkeeping, was in use in medieval Italy, and the first published accounting work, *Summa de Arithmetica, Geometria, Proportioni et Proportionalità*, was written in 1494 by a Venetian monk, Luca Pacioli. The principles of double-entry bookkeeping are still in use today, even where all financial data is processed by computers, and an introduction to how it works is given later (in Chapter 2).

[1] 'In Our Time: The written word', Melvyn Bragg, BBC Radio 4, 2 January 2012.

Scan the following QR (Quick response) code with your smart phone's QR reader (downloadable free – just Google QR reader) to take you to the website of the American Accounting Association:

Accounting can be defined simply as the recording, summarising and interpretation of financial information. A classic and more detailed definition is that offered by the American Accounting Association (1966), as follows:

> The process of identifying, measuring and communicating economic information about an organisation or other entity, in order to permit informed judgements by users of the information.

Let's explore the words *identifying, measuring and communicating* within this definition. Key areas of the accountant's work involve:

- *Identifying* the important financial components of an organisation, such as assets, liabilities, equity, income, expenses and cash flow.
- *Measuring* the monetary values of the important financial components in a way which gives a faithful representation of the organisation.
- *Communicating* the financial information in ways that are useful to the users of that information.

Scan the following QR code with your QR reader to take you to the website of the Association of Accounting Technicians:

Although anyone can call themselves an 'accountant', long-established professional accountancy bodies set rigorous qualifying examinations. Only their members can describe themselves as, for example, Certified Public Accountants, Chartered Accountants, Certified Accountants or Management Accountants, and action would be taken if unqualified accountants claimed to belong to these organisations. They impose strict rules of conduct on their members, and play an important part in developing and enhancing a viable set of rules and regulations for the accountancy profession. Technician-level qualifications are also available for those employed in an accounting function. For example, the Association of Accounting Technicians (AAT) has more than 120,000 members in over 90 countries.

1.3 Who uses accounting?

Scan the following QR code with your QR reader to take you to the website of the International Accounting Standards Board:

The International Accounting Standards Board (IASB) was formed in 2000 with the aim of developing accounting standards that 'require high quality, transparent and comparable information in financial statements and other financial reporting to help participants in the world's capital markets and other users make economic decisions'. In 2001 the IASB adopted a *Framework for the Preparation and Presentation of Financial Statements*[2] ('The Framework') which sets out certain concepts that underlie financial statements – we look at these later in this chapter. The Framework is gradually being updated, with the first phase having been completed in 2010. It contains the following as the objective of *general purpose financial reporting*:

> The objective of general purpose financial reporting is to provide financial information about the reporting entity that is useful to existing and potential investors, lenders, and other creditors in making decisions about providing resources to the entity. Those decisions involve buying, selling, or holding equity and debt instruments and providing or settling loans and other forms of credit.[3]

[2] International Accounting Standards Board (2001) *Framework for the Preparation and Presentation of Financial Statements*. London: IASB.

[3] International Accounting Standards Board (2010) *Conceptual Framework for Financial Reporting*. London: IASB.

The 'existing and potential investors, lenders, and other creditors' referred to above are further described as 'primary users' (see Figure 1.1), as they rely on general purpose financial reports for much of the financial information they need to make rational financial decisions. In addition to these primary users, several other user groups can be identified, including:

User group	Information needs
Management	Financial information necessary to be able to run the enterprise with maximum efficiency
Employees	People will be interested in their employer's stability and profitability, in particular of that part of the organisation (such as a branch) in which they work. They will also be interested in the ability of their employer to pay their wages and pensions
Customers	Customers who are dependent on a particular supplier or are considering placing a long-term contract will need to know if the organisation will continue to exist to complete the contract
Regulators	Reliable financial data helps governments to assemble national economic statistics which are used for a variety of purposes in controlling the economy. Specific financial information from an organisation also enables tax to be assessed
The public	Financial statements often include information relevant to local communities and pressure groups such as attitudes towards environmental matters, plans to expand or shut down factories, policies on employment of disabled persons, etc.

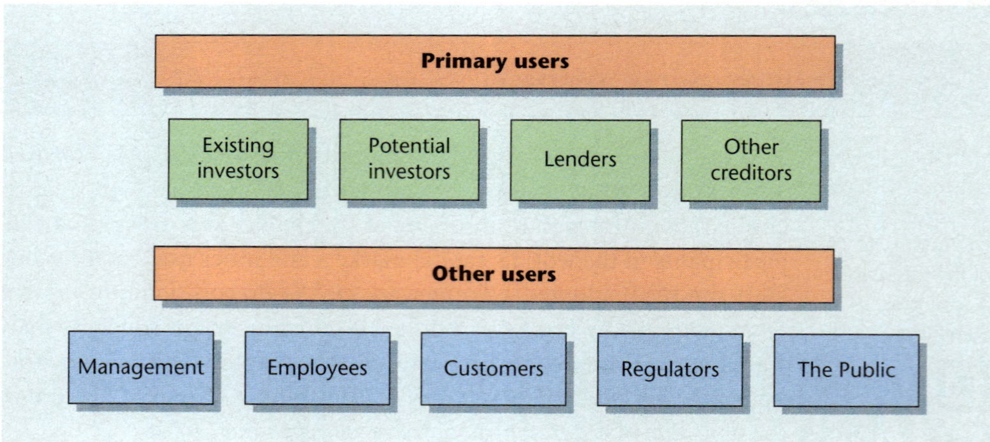

Figure 1.1 Primary and other users

1.4 Financial accounting and management accounting

Accounting information can be classified broadly between financial accounting and management accounting.

Scan the following QR code with your QR reader to take you to the website of the Chartered Institute of Management Accountants:

Did you know?

The Chartered Institute of Management Accountants, founded in 1919, has over 172,000 members and students in 165 countries, and is the world's largest professional body of management accountants.

Financial accounting is the day-to-day processing of an organisation's financial transactions and the summarising of those transactions to satisfy the information needs of the primary and other user groups listed above. It is sometimes referred to as meeting the *external* accounting needs of the organisation, and as such is subject to many rules and regulations (a regulatory framework) imposed by company legislation, stock exchange regulations and financial reporting standards.

Management accounting is sometimes referred to as meeting the *internal* accounting needs of the organisation, as it is designed to help managers with decision making and planning. Unlike financial accounting, it often involves estimates and forecasts, and is *not* subject to the same regulatory framework as financial accounting. Later (in Chapters 10–16) we explore some of the management accounting areas such as marginal costing and break-even analysis.

1.5 Accounting assumptions and characteristics

Accounting procedures and practices have evolved over many centuries and are now known by the acronym GAAP (Generally Accepted Accounting Principles). The Framework refers to two underlying assumptions when preparing financial statements:

1.5.1 Underlying Assumption 1: The accrual basis

When preparing financial statements (other than cash flow information), the effects of transactions are recognised *when they occur* even if the resulting cash is received or paid in a different period. In practice, this means that we not only consider money paid and received in a particular time period, but also money *owed to and by* the business.

Stop and think

The alternative to the accrual basis is simply to record cash flows, where businesses only summarise cash received and paid in a particular period ('cash accounting'). For example, a small car sales business may have received cash of £70,000 for the sale of 30 cars in 2014, which had been bought and paid for in the same year for £40,000. If the business had paid £10,000 expenses during the year, then it might be argued that the business made a profit of £20,000 (£70,000 − [£40,000 + £10,000]). However, there are many unanswered questions that cast doubt on whether this presents a reasonable picture of the business's performance. For example:

- Did the business have any unsold cars either at the start or the end of the period?
- Did the business have any amounts owing to suppliers at the start or end of the period?
- Had any cars been sold during the period which hadn't been paid for?
- Did the business have any assets such as land and buildings, computers etc. which were bought prior to 2014? What was their value of the end of 2014?
- How much value had the owners invested at the start of the year, and how had that value changed by the end of the year?

Simple cash accounting might make life easier for very small businesses, but it is not acceptable as a means of making a faithful representation of an enterprise's financial position and performance.

1.5.2 Underlying Assumption 2: Going concern

Financial statements are normally prepared on the assumption that the business is a *going concern* (i.e. a business that can 'keep going' for the foreseeable future). This means that someone reading a financial report would not need to assume that there was a major financial problem, unless they were specifically alerted to such a fact. In a financial recession, the decision as to whether or not a company is a going concern can be problematical, as this article shows:

News clip

FT

Going concern

Every company that has ever existed has failed – except for the ones still around. This might seem obvious but it highlights a criticism of the "going concern" principle – the assumption that a business will continue to operate for the foreseeable future. It is short-sighted to assume that companies will exist forever. After all, only half of new companies are destined to survive for five years. And it is not just start-ups that suffer. Last week, the auditors of accountants Vantis and of the holding company for British record label EMI questioned the ongoing viability of the businesses. This doesn't mean bankruptcy is imminent but it puts stakeholders on notice that something is badly wrong. In spite of its faults, the assumption of longevity is essential to ensure that banks continue to lend, suppliers send provisions, and employees feel secure or simply don't jump ship: just saying a company might not be a going concern can become a self-fulfilling prophecy. The problem, though, is the presumption of innocence. In other words, directors and auditors have to find a reason why a company should not be a going concern rather than why it should be. If the burden of proof was reversed, investors might gain a greater insight into their company's health.

Source: Lex, *The Financial Times*, 11 February 2010

The following is a short extract from the 2011 annual report of Elektron plc, an engineering company, explaining how the company's directors justified their reasons for adopting the going concern basis when presenting the financial results:

News clip

FT

The Directors have reviewed current cash flow projections for the coming twelve months taking account of reasonably possible changes in trading performance, borrowing facilities, and forecast covenant compliance. The Directors have no reason to believe that any of the existing borrowing facilities might be withdrawn or that there would be any other material change in the current financial projections of the Group. As a result the Directors formed a judgement when approving the financial statements that there is a reasonable expectation that the Group has adequate resources to continue in operational existence for the foreseeable future. For this reason, the Directors continue to adopt the going concern basis in preparing the financial statements.

Source: Elektron plc Annual Report, 2012

In addition to the two underlying assumptions, the Framework also lists a number of *qualitative characteristics* (QCs) of financial statements which make the information provided useful to the user groups, of which two (*relevance* and *faithful representation*) are described as *fundamental* QCs, and a further four (comparability, verifiability, timeliness and understandability) are described as *enhancing* QCs (see Figure 1.2.)

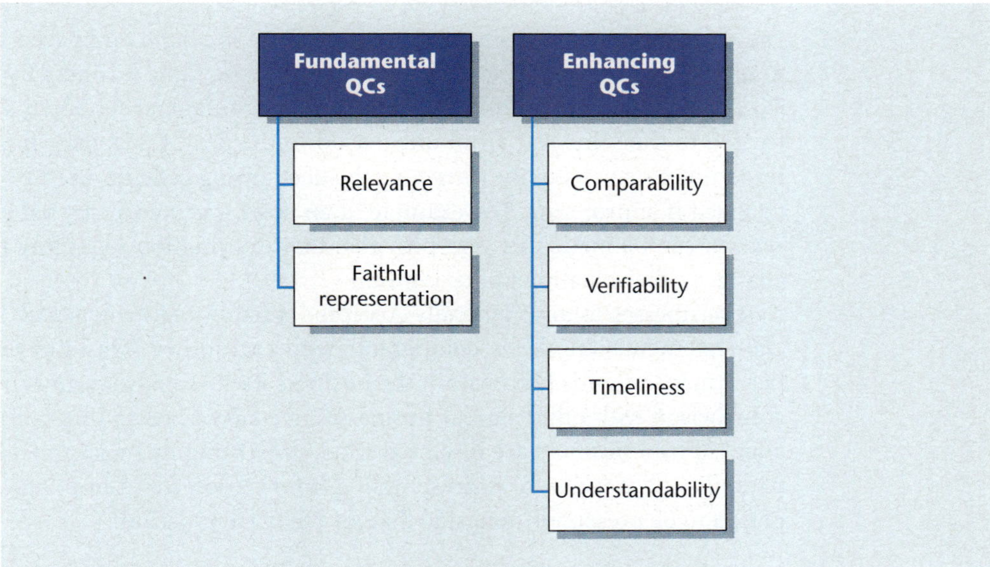

Figure 1.2 Qualitative Characteristics (QCs) of useful financial information

1.5.3 Fundamental QC 1: *Relevance*

Financial information is relevant if it is *useful* to users for making a decision, and it has a *predictive* value, a *confirmatory* value or both of these. Information has predictive value if it can be used in making predictions about the eventual outcomes of past or current events. It has confirmatory value if it provides feedback about previous evaluations.

For example, by including information about sales income for 2014, you might be able to predict sales income for 2015 (the predictive value of the information), or else confirm a prediction of 2014's sales income that might have been made in 2013 or earlier (the confirmatory value of the information).

Another aspect as to whether financial information is relevant is whether it is *material* – if you left it out, would it matter when making your decisions? An example of this could be a large multinational corporation stating its results to the nearest £ million, rather than showing every single pound. Otherwise users could be overwhelmed with irrelevant information.

1.5.4 Fundamental QC 2: *Faithful representation*

The overall aim of the financial statements in an ideal world should be to present a view of the business's financial position and performance that was complete, neutral (unbiased) and free from error. Realistically, it would be hoped that the preparers of the financial information make every reasonable attempt to maximise the qualities of completeness, neutrality and freedom from errors.

For most large businesses, there is a requirement to appoint an independent auditor who comments on whether or not the financial statements give a faithful representation (also known as a 'true and fair view') of the enterprise's financial position and performance. In the event of the auditor finding that the statements do *not* give a faithful representation then full details of why they have reached this decision must be given.

1.5.5 Enhancing QC 1: Comparability

Information about a business is more useful if it can be compared with similar information about other businesses, and also about the same business from another period. To enable this comparability, items within the financial statements should usually be treated in the same way from one period to the next. Obviously, financial information must not be consistently *wrong*, so the accounting policies used by a business can be changed if appropriate. For example, if an asset was incorrectly valued last year, a correction can be made this year provided that information regarding the reasons for the change in the valuation policy is given.

If businesses follow Generally Accepted Accounting Principles (GAAP) their financial statements should be comparable with each other. This allows users to establish performance trends both within the business itself (e.g. over a five-year period), and by comparison with other similar businesses. Details of accounting policies that have been adopted by a business are disclosed when presenting financial statements. To aid comparability, it is usual for corresponding information for at least one previous financial period to be presented alongside that for the current period.

1.5.6. Enhancing QC 2: Verifiability

To achieve a faithful representation, financial information should be capable of being verified. For example, direct verification could be obtained by physically counting cash or inventory to ensure that any values included within the financial statements are matched by an actual asset. Sometimes *indirect* verification is used, for example confirming the closing amounts payable to suppliers by investigating opening balances, invoices received and payments made.

1.5.7 Enhancing QC 3: Timeliness

For financial information to have maximum benefit, it should be made available as soon as possible to enable users to incorporate it in their decision-making. Generally, the older the information, the less useful it is.

1.5.8 Enhancing QC 4: Understandability

Information provided in financial statements should be presented clearly and concisely, though it is also recognised that some financial activities are inherently complex and cannot be made easy to understand. Financial reports are prepared for users who have a reasonable knowledge of business and economic activities and a willingness to study the information with 'reasonable diligence'. However, at times even the most well-informed and diligent users may need expert advice to understand information about complex financial activities!

1.6 Assets, liabilities and equity

Much of the work of financial accountants consists of summarising financial information in accordance with generally accepted accounting principles. This information is largely derived from a transaction processing system which will be explained in detail later (in Chapters 2 and 3). The system is based on the relationship between the three key components of *assets, liabilities* and *equity*.

1.6.1 Assets

A definition of assets, as contained in the IASB Framework, is 'a resource controlled by the entity as a result of past events and from which future economic benefits are expected to flow to the entity'. Typical business assets are divided between non-current assets,[4] which are expected to be retained by the business for at least a year and are of significant value, and current assets, which might change frequently during the course of the business's activities.

Typical examples of non-current assets are:

- Land
- Buildings
- Motor vehicles
- Machinery
- Computers.

Nearly all non-current assets will be subject to *depreciation* (a loss in value due to factors such as usage or ageing), a topic dealt with later (in Chapter 3). Another term used to describe the acquisition of non-current assets is *capital expenditure*, i.e. expenditure on long-term assets contributing to the accumulation of capital by the organisation.

---

[4]Also known as 'fixed assets' in some countries.

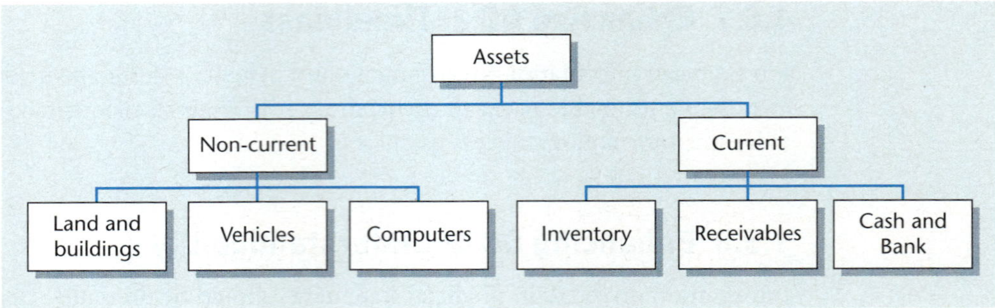

Figure 1.3a Classifications and examples of assets

Typical examples of current assets (see Figure 1.3a) are:

- Inventory of unsold goods
- Trade receivables (the amounts owed to the business by customers)
- Prepayments (amounts paid in advance for items such as rent)
- Bank balances (cash in the bank – also called 'cash-equivalents')
- Cash balances (cash held by the business, but not in the bank).

Activity 1.1

Make a list of any assets you own, with a rough estimate of their total value. You could start by considering what you are wearing!

Answer

Your answer might include non-current assets, such as a car, motorbike or bicycle, clothes, jewellery, etc., and current assets, such as cash and bank balances. Make a total of their estimated value.

1.6.2 Liabilities

The definition of liabilities contained within the Framework is 'present obligations of the entity arising from past events, the settlement of which is expected to result in an outflow from the entity of resources embodying economic benefits'. Typical business liabilities are divided between *current liabilities*, which are expected to be paid within one year, and *non-current liabilities*, which are expected to be paid after more than one year.

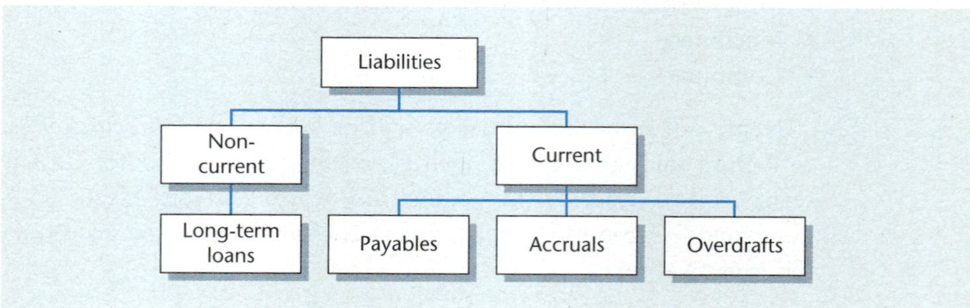

Figure 1.3b Classifications and examples of liabilities

Typical examples of current liabilities (see Figure 1.3b) are:

- Trade payables (the amounts owed by the business to suppliers of goods)
- Accruals (estimated amounts due for expenses such as electricity, where the bills have not yet been received)
- Bank overdrafts.

A typical example of a non-current liability is:

- A loan due for repayment in more than one year's time.

Activity 1.2

Make a list of any liabilities you have, with a rough estimate of their total value. Do you have a bank overdraft or a student loan?

Answer

Apart from an overdraft or a student loan, you might owe a credit card balance, rent, mobile phone bills, etc.

1.6.3 Equity

Equity is also sometimes referred to as 'capital' or 'ownership interest', that is, the value which the owner or owners have invested in their business. The Framework defines equity as 'the residual interest in the assets of the entity after deducting all its liabilities'.

Activity 1.3

Deduct the total value of your liabilities which you found in Activity 1.2 from the total value of your assets found in Activity 1.1.

Answer

If your assets exceed your liabilities, you have *positive* equity (lucky you!). If your liabilities exceed your assets, you have *negative* equity – owing more than you own.

1.7 The accounting equation

As we have seen, we find the value of the equity by deducting liabilities from assets.

Assets − Liabilities = Equity

Accountants prepare a key summary, known as a *statement of financial position*,[5] which lists the values of the three components at a specific date. Assets and liabilities are split between those that are 'non-current' and those that are 'current'. In some countries the equation might be rewritten as Assets = Liabilities + Equity, but otherwise the information is identical (See Figures 1.4a and 1.4b). We shall be looking at statements of financial position in detail later (in Chapter 4).

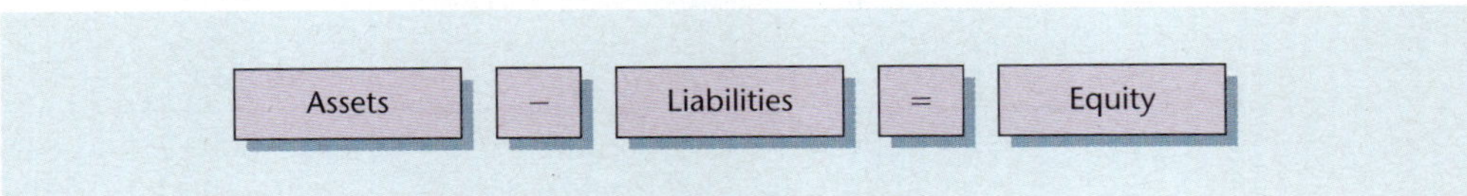

Figure 1.4a The accounting equation – version 1

[5] Known as a *balance sheet* in some countries.

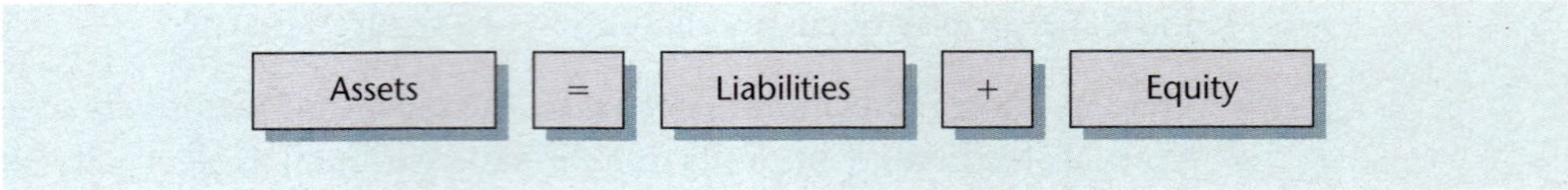

Figure 1.4b The accounting equation – version 2

Now attempt Activity 1.4.

Activity 1.4

For each of the following transactions, show the effect (as pluses and minuses) on assets, liabilities and equity. The first has been completed for illustration.

		Assets	Liabilities	Equity
		£	£	£
1	The owner starts the business with £3,000 paid into a business bank account on 1 April	+3,000 (bank)		+3,000 (equity)
2	The business buys machinery with a bank payment of £800 on 2 April			
3	The business buys an office computer for £800 from Dart Tech on 4 April and agrees to pay in May			
4	On 5 April, a bank lends the business £10,000 which is paid into the bank account on the same day			
5	The business pays Dart Tech £800 by bank transfer on 1 May			
6	The owner takes £100 from the bank for personal spending money			
	Summary (overall change)			

Answer

		Assets	Liabilities	Equity
		£	£	£
1	The owner starts the business with £3,000 paid into a business bank account on 1 April	+3,000 (bank)		+3,000 (equity)
2	The business buys machinery with a bank payment of £800 on 2 April	+800 (machinery) − 800 (bank)		
3	The business buys an office computer for £800 from Dart Tech on 4 April and agrees to pay in May	+800 (computer)	+800 (trade payable: Dart Tech)	

		Assets	Liabilities	Equity
		£	£	£
4	On 5 April, a bank lends the business £10,000 which is paid into the bank account on the same day	+10,000 (bank)	+10,000 (loan)	
5	The business pays Dart Tech £800 by bank transfer on 1 May	−800 (bank)	−800 (trade payable: Dart Tech)	
6	The owner takes £100 from the bank for personal spending money	−100 (bank)		−100 (equity)
	Summary (overall change)	+12,900	+10,000	+2,900

Stop and think

Applying the accounting equation, Assets − Liabilities = Equity, we see that the overall increase in assets (£12,900) less the overall increase in liabilities (£10,000) is matched by the overall increase in equity (£2,900).

1.7.1 How does the value of equity change?

The owner's investment will change for a number of reasons, most obvious of which is if more equity is contributed by the owner, or equity is withdrawn by the owner. However, the other main reason is the business making either a *profit* or a *loss* over a specific period. We calculate profit or loss by comparing a business's *income* with its *expenses.*

- If income exceeds expenses, the business makes a profit, and the owner's equity increases.
- If expenses exceed income, the business makes a loss, and the owner's equity decreases.

Income and expenses are defined as follows:

- **Income**: the revenue generated by the business by selling its goods or services, plus any sundry income such as bank interest received.
- **Expenses**: the expenditure made by a business related to the income generated within the same financial period. The cost of acquiring non-current assets is *not* considered as an expense, as the assets last for *several* financial periods. However, an estimate is made, known as depreciation, of the proportion of the non-current asset's value used up in the *specific* financial period. This loss in value is then treated as part of the expenses when calculating the profit or loss and is also deducted from the non-current assets value in the statement of financial position.

Remember that the accruals basis tells us to include *all* the relevant income and expenses for a period, not just cash received or paid in that period.

The comparison of income and expenses leads us to the equation shown in Figures 1.5a and 1.5b:

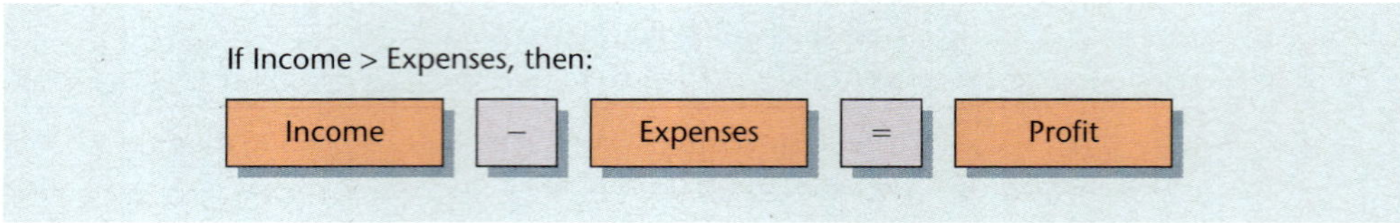

Figure 1.5a The profit or loss equation, where Income > Expenses

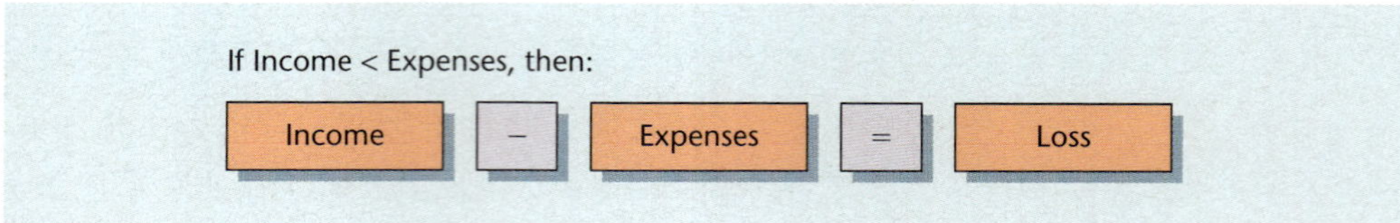

Figure 1.5b The profit or loss equation, where Income < Expenses

This formula forms the basis of a second key financial summary, the *income statement*, which we shall be looking at later (in Chapter 4).

Stop and think

If we combine the two accounting equations (A − L = Eq and I − Ex = P or L), we can see that the equity figure changes over a specific period (known, in algebraic terms, as from time zero to time one) depending on whether a profit or loss is made.

Equity at the start of the time period:	$A_0 - L_0 = Eq_0$
If a profit is made during time one:	$A_1 - L_1 = Eq_0 + (I_1 - Ex_1)$
Or if a loss is made during time one:	$A_1 - L_1 = Eq_0 - (I_1 - Ex_1)$

In other words, total assets at the end of time one minus total liabilities at the end of time one equal equity at the start (time zero) plus or minus the profit or loss (income less expenses) earned during time one.

The two key financial summaries which have been referred to – the statement of financial position and the income statement – reflect the five components of the two equations, as shown in Figure 1.6.

When, (in the next chapter) we see how financial transactions are processed by using accounting systems that follow double-entry bookkeeping, we are using a rearrangement of the five components, as follows:

$$\text{Assets} + \text{Expenses} = \text{Liabilities} + \text{Equity} + \text{Income}$$

We can call this the *double-entry equation.*

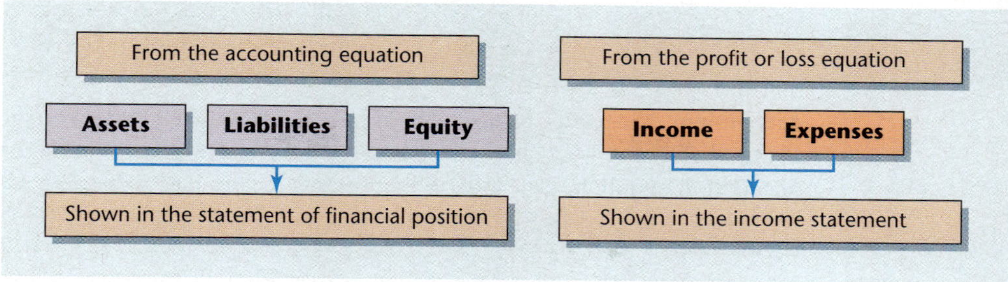

Figure 1.6 How the two accounting equations relate to the statement of financial position and the income statement

1.8 Alternative terminology

Most large businesses throughout the world follow the requirements of *International Financial Reporting Standards* (IFRSs) when presenting their financial information. However, many smaller enterprises are not required to comply with these standards, and might follow the rules and regulations laid down by their own country's regulators rather than using the international equivalent. As a result, financial terms that might be seen in the annual reports of large companies might be described in different ways in their smaller counterparts. Within this text, for consistency, and to reflect the increasing importance and influence of IFRSs, terminology used in IFRSs is used throughout where relevant. The following is a guide to IFRS and 'non-IFRS' terminology:

IFRS terminology	Non-IFRS terminology
Trade payables	Creditors
Trade receivables	Debtors
Non-current assets	Fixed assets
Non-current liabilities	Long-term liabilities
Statement of financial position	Balance sheet
Income statement	Profit and loss account (or 'P & L')
Inventories	Stock (of unsold goods and materials)

1.9 Summary

We have considered three equations in this chapter:

1	**The accounting equation**	Assets − Liabilities = Equity
2	**The profit or loss equation**	If I > E, Income − Expenses = Profit
		If I < E, Income − Expenses = Loss
3	**The double-entry equation**	Assets + Expenses = Liabilities + Equity + Income

1.10 Chapter glossary

Accounting The process of identifying, measuring and communicating economic information about an organisation or other entity, in order to permit informed judgements by users of the information.

Accounting equation The formula representing the relationship between a business's assets, liabilities and equity, expressed as Assets − Liabilities = Equity (or alternatively, Assets = Liabilities + Equity).

Accrual basis The underlying accounting assumption that when preparing financial statements (other than cash flow information), the effects of transactions are recognised when they occur even if the resulting cash is received or paid in a different period.

Assets A resource controlled by the entity as a result of past events and from which future economic benefits are expected to flow to the entity.

Capital Another term for equity.

Comparability Items within financial statements should usually be treated in the same way from one period to the next and in accordance with GAAP. This allows comparability from one time period to another and also between one business and another.

Confirmatory value Information that can provide feedback about previous evaluations of financial events. It is one of the aspects of *relevance*.

Current asset An asset whose value might change frequently during the course of a business's activities.

Current liability A liability expected to be paid within one year of the date of the statement of financial position.

Depreciation An estimate of the loss in value of a non-current asset.

Double-entry bookkeeping The system, first described by Luca Pacioli in 1494, which allows a logical record to be made of all the components of the accounting equation.

Double-entry equation The equation that allows financial information to be processed, using double-entry bookkeeping,

Equity The value of the investment of the owner or owners of a business, found by deducting all of the organisation's liabilities from all of the organisation's assets. Also known as 'capital'.

Expenses Expenditure made by a business related to the income generated within the same financial period. It includes goods bought for resale, and overheads such as light and heat, wages and salaries, and depreciation on non-current assets.

Faithful representation Financial statements should, as far as possible, be complete, neutral and free from errors.

Financial accounting The day-to-day recording of an organisation's financial transactions and the summarising of those transactions to satisfy the information needs of user groups in accordance with the regulatory framework.

GAAP Generally Accepted Accounting Principles.

Going concern An underlying assumption that financial statements are normally prepared on the basis that the enterprise is able to continue in business for the foreseeable future.

Income The income generated by the business by selling its goods or services. Also known as revenue.

Income statement A financial summary showing income and expenses for the financial period.

Liabilities Present obligations of the entity arising from past events, the settlement of which is expected to result in an outflow from the entity of resources embodying economic benefits.

Management accounting The internal accounting needs of an organisation, involving planning, forecasting and budgeting for decision-making purposes.

Non-current assets Assets that are normally expected to be retained by the business for at least a year and are of a significant value. Most are subject to depreciation. Also occasionally referred to as 'capital expenditure' or 'fixed' assets.

Non-current liability A liability expected to be paid more than one year after the date of the statement of financial position.

Predictive value Information that can be used for making predictions about the eventual outcomes of past or current financial events. It is one of the aspects of *relevance*.

Profit or loss equation A comparison of the income for a period with the expenses of the same period to calculate either a profit or loss for that period.

Regulatory framework The rules and regulations followed by financial accountants, imposed mainly by company legislation, stock exchanges and the International Accounting Standards Board.

Relevance Financial information is relevant if it is useful to users for making a decision and it has a predictive value, a confirmatory value or both of these.

Statement of financial position The financial summary of an enterprise's assets, liabilities and equity at a specific point in time.

Timeliness To be useful, financial information should be made available as soon as possible.

True and fair view An alternative term for a faithful representation of the financial statements.

Understandability Financial information should be presented as clearly and concisely as possible.

Verifiability To achieve a faithful representation, financial information should be capable of being verified either directly or indirectly.

Additional resources

Only accessible on Android-based devices

Now work through the various exercises and problems that you can find within the My Accounting Lab that are relevant to this chapter. Either use the QR code shown in the margin (if you use an Android-based device), or visit www.myaccountinglab.com for the log-in page.

Self-check questions

The answers to these questions are in Appendix 1.

1 Financial accounting is:

(a) Mainly concerned with forecasting the future
(b) Used only by the management of the business
(c) Used only by people outside the business
(d) Used by people both inside and outside the business

2 The key aspects of accounting are:

(a) Identifying, measuring and communicating economic information
(b) Processing, recording and publishing financial information
(c) Summarising, analysing and interpreting business information
(d) Conveying inside information about the company to the owners

3 Which one of the following is described as a 'primary user' by the Conceptual Framework for Financial Reporting?

(a) Employees
(b) Regulators

(c) Existing investors
(d) Customers

4 Which one of the following is an underlying accounting assumption?

(a) Relevance
(b) Going concern
(c) Comparability
(d) Timeliness

5 Non-current assets are assets which are:

(a) Likely to last at least a year and are valuable
(b) Not going to be depreciated
(c) Unlikely to last a year
(d) The unsold goods of the business

6 Current assets are assets which:

(a) Keep their value over at least a year
(b) Often change their value
(c) Are depreciated
(d) Always have very substantial value

7 Liabilities are usually divided between:

(a) Urgent and non-urgent
(b) Fixed and current
(c) Current and non-current
(d) Medium-term and long-term

8 A bank overdraft is usually classified as:

(a) A current asset
(b) A non-current liability
(c) A current liability
(d) Equity

9 The accounting equation can be shown as:

(a) Equity – Liabilities = Assets
(b) Equity + Assets = Liabilities
(c) Assets + Liabilities = Equity
(d) Assets – Liabilities = Equity

10 Which of the following will *not* result in a change in the owners' equity?

(a) A non-current asset bought by the business for £10,000
(b) A profit made by the organisation
(c) A loss made by the organisation
(d) The owners withdrawing £50,000 from the organisation

Self-study questions

Questions marked with this symbol (#) indicate that the suggested answers are available to lecturers only – other answers are in Appendix 2.

1.1 Using your knowledge of the accounting equation, fill in the white boxes for each of the ten separate businesses shown in the following table (all figures in £):

	Assets £	Liabilities £	Equity £
1	25,630	14,256	
2		23,658	15,498
3	619,557	352,491	
4	69,810		14,863
5		21,596	35,462
6	36,520		24,510
7		65,342	86,290
8	114,785	17,853	
9	212,589		146,820
10		63,527	201,581

1.2 (a) For each of the following transactions, show the effect (as pluses and minuses) on assets, liabilities and equity. The first has been completed for illustration.

		Assets £	Liabilities £	Equity £
1	Owner starts business with £10,000 paid into a business bank account on 1 May	+£10,000 Bank		+£10,000 (equity)
2	Business buys furniture with a cheque for £2,500 on 2 May			
3	Business pays £600 by cheque for a photocopier on 4 May			
4	Business receives an invoice on 5 May from Chambers Ltd for £2,000 for inventory			
5	Also on 5 May, the business buys inventory with a cheque for £600			
6	Owner takes £400 from bank for personal spending money on 6 May			
7	On 7 May, the business pays the invoice received from Chambers Ltd on 5 May			
8	On 8 May, the business receives an invoice for £4,000 for a motor van			
	Summary (overall change)			

(b) From the above table, complete the following:

Overall change in assets
Less overall change in liabilities ____________________
Overall change in equity ____________________

(c) What is the name given to the formula Assets − Liabilities = Equity?

1.3 The annual report of a major company included the following statement:

Going concern
The Directors consider that the Group and the Company have adequate resources to remain in operation for the foreseeable future and have therefore continued to adopt the going concern basis in preparing the financial statements.[6]

(a) Explain why the *going concern* assumption is of importance to a user of an annual report.
(b) Explain the meaning of 'accruals' as an underlying assumption when preparing financial statements, and the qualitative characteristic of 'comparability'.
(c) Explain why a 'faithful representation' is of particular importance when presenting financial statements.

1.4# A business has reported record profits and increased asset values, but has also disclosed that it is unable to be considered as a 'going concern'. Suggest three reasons why a profitable company might be in danger of financial collapse.

1.5# 'A business's financial affairs should not be disclosed to anyone other than its directors and owners'. Criticise this statement by reference to the 'user groups' identified in the Framework.

1.6# Write a brief report distinguishing between the key aspects of 'financial accounting' as contrasted with 'management accounting'.

1.7# Rohana is thinking of starting a business. She wants to make sure that she understands the financial implications of her enterprise, so has consulted an accountant, and asks the following questions:

1 How will I know if the company has made a profit?
2 What key accounting rules and regulations have to be considered?
3 What is the main objective of providing financial statements?

What answers is the accountant likely to give to Rohana?

1.8# Nickleby has summarised its key financial information for the past year, as follows:

	£
Total sales made in the year	840,000
Total cash received in the year from customers	735,000
Total costs, including goods for resale	240,000
Total cash paid for costs, including goods for resale	255,000

(a) What was the total profit which Nickleby made during the year?
(b) How can the 'total cash paid in the year for costs, including goods bought for resale' be greater than the 'total costs, including goods bought for resale'?

[6]Tesco plc Annual Report 2012

Case study

Marvin makes a career choice

Marvin always had an ambition to be a magician. As a child he took great delight in making his younger brothers and sisters disappear and he was often in demand to perform conjuring tricks at parties. It was a natural career choice for him when, at the age of 21, he decided to leave college on 1 July and make his fortune in the world, setting up in business as a magician. He made the following payments in his first week out of college:

On 1 July he paid £3,000 for a glittering costume with a top hat and cloak; on 2 July he paid £2,000 for a special edition of a book, *'The ancient secrets of magic*; and on 3 July he bought four packs of magicians' playing cards from Kazam Limited for £100 each. Marvin expected to use these items for many years. He paid cash from his own savings for the costume and the book, but he agreed that he would pay for the playing cards in a few weeks' time from the business bank account.

His first appearance as a magician was on 7 July at the National Magic Show, for which he was paid a fee of £750 by cheque, with which he opened a business bank account on the same day. He incurred £20 travel expenses which he again paid from his own savings.

Required

(a) Prepare a summary of Marvin's income and expenses for the week ended 7 July. Ignore any depreciation on Marvin's assets.

(b) Draw up a list as at 7 July of Marvin's non-current assets and current assets, then deduct any current liabilities from the assets. What is Marvin's equity at that date? Show how you can prove that the equity figure is correct.

Answers are in Appendix 3

Further research

The following organisations are of interest:

American Accounting Association: **www.aaahq.org**
American Institute of Certified Public Accountants: **www.aicpa.org**
Association of Accounting Technicians: **www.aat.org.uk**
Chartered Institute of Management Accountants: **www.cimaglobal.com**
International Accounting Standards Board: **www.ifrs.org**

Chapter 2

Processing financial data

Objectives

When you have read this chapter you will be able to:

- Understand how financial data is processed
- Record financial transactions within an accounting system
- Prepare a simple trial balance whilst appreciating its limitations
- Appreciate the advantages of computerised accounting software packages

2.1 Introduction

We have seen that the five key components of the accounting equation and the profit or loss equation are: assets, liabilities, equity, income and expenses. We also saw how a long-established system of recording financial transactions known as *double-entry bookkeeping* uses a rearrangement of these five components to form a third equation:

$$Assets + Expenses = Liabilities + Equity + Income$$

Records of financial transactions of the vast majority of commercial organisations are made according to this equation. The system is highly structured and logical and enables even the largest organisation to keep track of its financial position over time.

Figure 2.1 shows how transactions are sorted into the five key categories of financial information. When each transaction is recorded in the system, the relevant effect on assets, expenses, liabilities, equity and income is recorded. This is an endless process which continues for as long as the organisation is in existence.

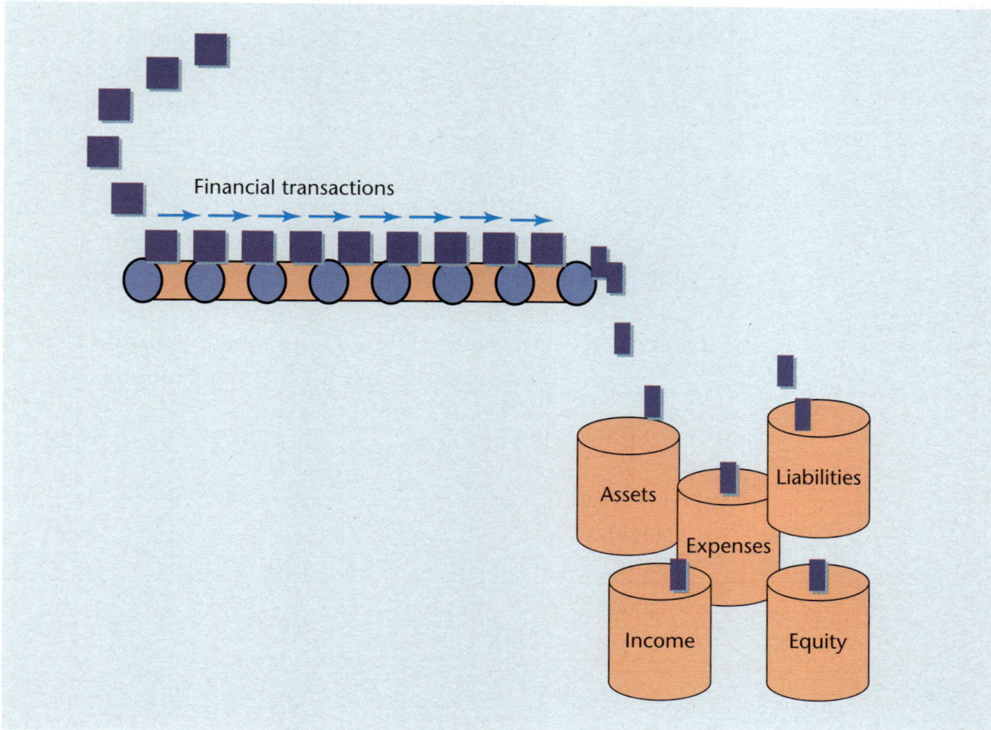

Figure 2.1 Sorting financial data using the double-entry equation

2.2 The dual aspect of transactions

As the name implies, *double-entry* bookkeeping requires each financial transaction to be recorded in *two* locations within the accounting records of the organisation. This is due to the recognition that each transaction affects the business in two separate ways: that the organisation both *receives* and *gives* value when the transaction is made. This is sometimes referred to as the *dual aspect* of transactions. For example, a business buying a machine with a bank transfer of £10,000 not only *receives* a machine costing £10,000 but also *gives* £10,000 from its bank account. In terms of the double-entry equation we can see that the increase in one asset (machine + £10,000) is matched by the decrease in another asset (bank balance – £10,000). Another example would be if the business sells goods for £4,000 to a customer who pays immediately, the business both *gives* goods valued at £4,000 and *receives* cash into its bank account for the same amount. The accounting equation stays in balance as the asset of the bank balance increases (+ £4,000) whilst income in the form of sales increases by the same amount.

Activity 2.1

Look at the following transactions of Andrew Rose. How will they affect the double-entry equation? Enter the changes to each component of the equation (as pluses and minuses) in the table below, and then show the overall effect on the double-entry equation. The changes relating to the first two transactions have been entered as an example.

1	**1 January**	Starts a business by opening a bank account with £4,000
2	**2 January**	Buys goods for resale with a bank transfer of £2,000
3	**3 January**	Sells goods for cash, £700
4	**4 January**	Pays wages £300 by cash
5	**5 January**	Buys stationery from Paper Products valued at £700. Andrew expects to pay for the stationery in a month's time
6	**6 January**	Buys a computer with a bank transfer, £1,000
7	**7 January**	Sells goods to Sarah Prince for £820. Sarah hopes to pay in two months' time
8	**8 January**	Andrew pays a lottery win of £1,000 into the business bank account
9	**9 January**	Andrew draws out £100 from the business bank account for his own use
10	**10 January**	Andrew buys goods for resale costing £1,500 from BiggaBuys, and intends to pay for them in a month's time

	Assets £	Expenses £	Liabilities £	Equity £	Income £
1	+ 4,000 (Bank)			+ 4,000	
2	– 2,000 (Bank)	+ 2,000 (Purchases)			
3					
4					
5					
6					
7					
8					
9					
10					

Overall effect:

Answer

	Assets £	Expenses £	Liabilities £	Equity £	Income £
1	+ 4,000 (Bank)			+ 4,000	
2	− 2,000 (Bank)	+ 2,000 (Purchases)			
3	+ 700 (Cash)				+ 700 (Sales)
4	− 300 (Cash)	+ 300 (Wages)			
5		+ 700 (Stationery)	+ 700 (Trade payables)		
6	+ 1,000 (Computer) − 1,000 (Bank)				
7	+ 820 (Trade receivables)				+ 820 (Sales)
8	+ 1,000 (Bank)			+ 1,000 (Equity increase)	
9	− 100 (Bank)			− 100 (Equity decrease)	
10		+ 1,500 (Purchases)	+ 1,500 (Trade payables)		

The overall effect of the ten transactions is:

Assets £	Expenses £	Liabilities £	Equity £	Income £
+ 4,120	+ 4,500	+ 2,200	+ 4,900	+ 1,520
= + 8,620		= + 8,620		

Stop and think

In transactions 1 and 8, Andrew is increasing the value of his equity, but transaction 9 reduces this value. When an owner takes out money or goods from the organisation, it is referred to as 'drawings'.

In transactions 2 and 10, because the goods are for resale, they are referred to as 'purchases'. Expenses such as stationery, fuel, etc. which are used up in running the business, are not classed as 'purchases', but might be entered as 'office expenses', 'motor expenses', etc.

In transaction 5, the stationery company is a trade payable (a liability), until Andrew pays the amount owing.

In transaction 6, the computer is a non-current asset, not an expense (see Chapter 1), as it is expected to last for more than one accounting period and is of significant value.

In transaction 7, Sarah Prince's amount owing to Andrew is classed as a trade receivable, Andrew's asset, until she pays the amount she owes.

The overall effect of the transactions is to confirm the double-entry equation, that the combined values of assets and expenses will *always* equal the combined values of liabilities, equity and income.

2.3 How the system works

The dual aspect applies to *every* financial transaction that needs to be recorded by the organisation, and the double-entry system reflects this.

Within the system, entries are made in *ledgers*, which contain individual records known as *accounts*. There is no limit to the number of ledgers or accounts which a business can open, but usually they tend to be grouped as follows:

Accounts grouped within:		
('Personal' ledgers)		**('Impersonal' ledger)**
Receivables Ledger	**Payables Ledger**	**General Ledger**
Contains the individual personal accounts of customers/clients who buy on credit terms from our business	Contains the individual personal accounts of suppliers from whom our business buys on credit terms	Contains accounts for every *type* of asset (other than receivables), liability (other than payables), income and expenses, as well as the equity account
		Cash Book
		Although part of the General Ledger this is a separate record containing the details of the bank account, cash account and petty cash account

Did you know?

The Receivables Ledger is sometimes referred to as either the *Sales Ledger* or the *Debtors Ledger*.

The Payables Ledger is sometimes referred to as either the *Purchases Ledger* or the *Creditors Ledger*.

The General Ledger is sometimes referred to as the *Nominal Ledger*.

Each account is split into two sides, a *debit* side and a *credit* side. The debit side is always on the left. The words 'debit' and 'credit' are often abbreviated to Dr and Cr. The accounting equation reflects these two sides, as follows:

Assets + Expenses	=	**Liabilities + Equity + Income**
Accounts with more debit entries than entries credit		*Accounts with more credit entries than debit entries*

An account, in its simplest form, takes the following format:

(Name of account)				
Date	**Details**	**Debit**	**Credit**	**Balance**

The 'balance' column shows the overall debit (abbreviated to Dr) or credit balance (abbreviated to Cr) after the entry of the transaction on the same line. Looking back at Activity 2.1, the first transaction, where Andrew Rose starts a business by opening a bank account with £4,000, would be shown in the Ledger Accounts as follows:

Bank account (part of the 'Cash Book')				
Date	**Details**	**Debit**	**Credit**	**Balance**
1 January	Andrew Rose: equity	4,000		4,000 Dr

Andrew Rose: equity account (a General Ledger account)				
Date	**Details**	**Debit**	**Credit**	**Balance**
1 January	Bank		4,000	4,000 Cr

Stop and think

The asset of the bank balance has increased. Therefore, based on the double-entry equation, the account is *debited*. The owner's equity has also increased, so his equity account is *credited*. It is vital that you understand how the entries in the bank account are shown. The rule is:

Money paid IN to the bank appears on the DEBIT side of the bank account
Money paid OUT of the bank appears on the CREDIT side of the bank account.

This is a mirror image of how you would see the details of the bank account shown on a statement received from the bank, because the statement shows the state of the business's bank account in the *bank's* ledger, not the business's. So every additional amount the business pays in increases the *bank's* liabilities, which are credits in the bank's ledger according to the accounting equation (i.e. the bank's payables have increased). This is often confusing to accounting students, as if we have money in the bank, it is normal English usage to say we have a 'credit balance', even though it shown as a *debit* balance in our ledger!

The ledger account entries for the next four of Andrew Rose's transactions are shown below. Where several entries affect the same account they are shown within that one account rather than separate accounts being opened for every new entry.

The next four transactions are:

2 January Buys goods for resale with a bank transfer of £2,000
3 January Sells goods for cash, £700
4 January Pays wages £300 by cash
5 January Buys stationery from Paper Products valued at £700. Andrew expects to pay for the stationery in a month's time

The entries (including the transaction on 1 January) will be:

Andrew Rose's business
Cash Book

Bank account (part of the 'Cash Book')				
Date	**Details**	**Debit**	**Credit**	**Balance**
1 January	Andrew Rose: equity	4,000		4,000 Dr
2 January	Purchases		2,000	2,000 Dr

Cash account (part of the 'Cash Book')				
Date	**Details**	**Debit**	**Credit**	**Balance**
3 January	Sales	700		700 Dr
4 January	Wages		300	400 Dr

General Ledger

Andrew Rose: equity account				
Date	**Details**	**Debit**	**Credit**	**Balance**
1 January	Bank		4,000	4,000 Cr

Sales account				
Date	**Details**	**Debit**	**Credit**	**Balance**
3 January	Cash		700	700 Cr

Purchases account				
Date	**Details**	**Debit**	**Credit**	**Balance**
2 January	Bank	2,000		2,000 Dr

Wages account				
Date	**Details**	**Debit**	**Credit**	**Balance**
4 January	Cash	300		300 Dr

Stationery account				
Date	**Details**	**Debit**	**Credit**	**Balance**
5 January	Paper Products	700		700 Dr

Payables Ledger

Paper Products account				
Date	Details	Debit	Credit	Balance
5 January	Stationery		700	700 Cr

Stop and think

Notice that the Paper Products transaction is on *credit terms* (Andrew's business isn't paying immediately, but is allowed some time to pay), so there's no immediate effect on either the bank or cash account.

Activity 2.2

Complete the following ledger accounts with the remaining entries (from Activity 2.1) required for the transactions up to January 10.
The transactions are:

6 January	Buys a computer with a bank transfer, £1,000
7 January	Sells goods to Sarah Prince for £820. Sarah hopes to pay in two months' time
8 January	Andrew pays a lottery win of £1,000 into the business bank account
9 January	Andrew draws out £100 from the business bank account for his own use
10 January	Andrew buys goods for resale costing £1,500 from BiggaBuys, and intends to pay for them in a month's time

Andrew Rose's business
Cash Book

Bank account (part of the 'Cash Book')				
Date	Details	Debit	Credit	Balance
1 January	Andrew Rose: equity	4,000		4,000 Dr
2 January	Purchases		2,000	2,000 Dr

General Ledger

Andrew Rose: equity account				
Date	Details	Debit	Credit	Balance
1 January	Bank		4,000	4,000 Cr

Computer account				
Date	Details	Debit	Credit	Balance

Sales account				
Date	Details	Debit	Credit	Balance
3 January	Cash		700	700 Cr

Purchases account				
Date	Details	Debit	Credit	Balance
2 January	Bank	2,000		2,000 Dr

Drawings account				
Date	Details	Debit	Credit	Balance

Payables Ledger

BiggaBuys account				
Date	Details	Debit	Credit	Balance

Receivables Ledger

Sarah Prince's account				
Date	Details	Debit	Credit	Balance

Answer

The following shows the completed ledger accounts recording *all* transactions (including those needed to complete Activity 2.2 above) from 1 January.

Cash Book

Bank account (part of the 'Cash Book')				
Date	Details	Debit	Credit	Balance
1 January	Andrew Rose: equity	4,000		4,000 Dr
2 January	Purchases		2,000	2,000 Dr
6 January	Computer		1,000	1,000 Dr

Bank account (part of the 'Cash Book')				
Date	Details	Debit	Credit	Balance
8 January	Andrew Rose: equity	1,000		2,000 Dr
9 January	Drawings		100	1,900 Dr

Cash account (part of the 'Cash Book')				
Date	Details	Debit	Credit	Balance
3 January	Sales	700		700 Dr
4 January	Wages		300	400 Dr

General Ledger

Andrew Rose: equity account				
Date	Details	Debit	Credit	Balance
1 January	Bank		4,000	4,000 Cr
8 January	Bank		1,000	5,000 Cr

Computer account				
Date	Details	Debit	Credit	Balance
6 January	Bank	1,000		1,000 Dr

Sales account				
Date	Details	Debit	Credit	Balance
3 January	Cash		700	700 Cr
7 January	Sarah Prince		820	1,520 Cr

Purchases account				
Date	Details	Debit	Credit	Balance
2 January	Bank	2,000		2,000 Dr
10 January	BiggaBuys	1,500		3,500 Dr

Wages account				
Date	Details	Debit	Credit	Balance
4 January	Cash	300		300 Dr

Stationery account				
Date	**Details**	**Debit**	**Credit**	**Balance**
5 January	Paper Products	700		700 Dr

Drawings account				
Date	**Details**	**Debit**	**Credit**	**Balance**
9 January	Bank	100		100 Dr

Payables Ledger

Paper Products account				
Date	**Details**	**Debit**	**Credit**	**Balance**
5 January	Stationery		700	700 Cr

BiggaBuys account				
Date	**Details**	**Debit**	**Credit**	**Balance**
10 January	Purchases		1,500	1,500 Cr

Receivables Ledger

Sarah Prince's account				
Date	**Details**	**Debit**	**Credit**	**Balance**
7 January	Sales	820		820 Dr

Stop and think

Each entry has the date, a reference to the name of the account which contains the 'other half' of the double-entry, the value and the overall balance (debit or credit) following the entry. Figure 2.2 shows a summary of the accounts, divided between the five key financial components.

2.4 Checking the maths

At intervals, we can perform a simple but essential check on the arithmetical accuracy of the entries we have made. This is known as a **trial balance**, and shows, at a specific date, *every* balance in every ledger account, listed under the headings 'debit' and 'credit'.

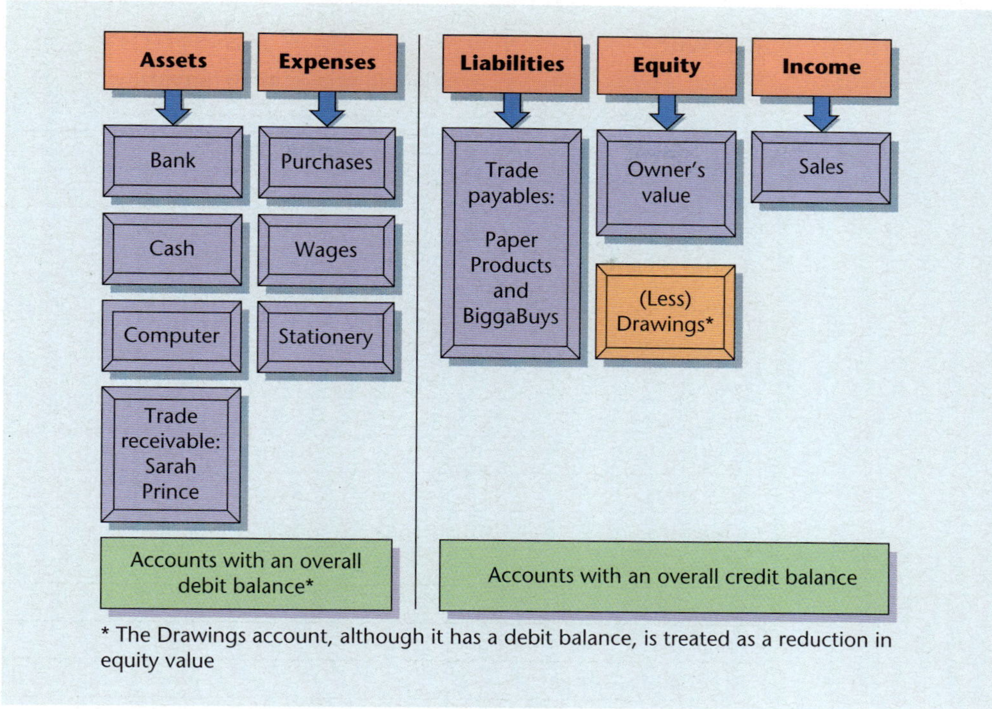

Figure 2.2 Summary of the ledger accounts contained in Activity 2.1

Activity 2.3

Prepare a trial balance for Andrew Rose as at 10 January, by entering every account balance from the ledger (in practice any accounts with zero balances are omitted). List the debit and credit balances in their respective columns. The first two balances have been entered.

Trial balance as at 10 January

Details	Debit	Credit
Cash Book:		
Bank	1,900	
Cash	400	
General Ledger:		
Payables Ledger:		
Receivables Ledger:		
Totals:		

Answer

Trial balance as at 10 January

Details	Debit	Credit
Cash Book:	1,900	
Bank	400	
Cash		
General Ledger:		
Andrew Rose: Equity		5,000
Computer	1,000	
Sales		1,520
Purchases	3,500	
Wages	300	
Stationery	700	
Drawings	100	
Payables Ledger:		
Paper Products		700
BiggaBuys		1,500
Receivables Ledger:		
Sarah Prince	820	
Totals:	8,720	8,720

Stop and think

This proves that all the debit entries equal the total of all the credit entries, as they should under the accounting equation. It is not a guarantee of accuracy, as we may have completely omitted an entry, reversed entries, entered the wrong amount in the correct accounts or the correct amounts in the wrong accounts! However, the trial balance is still an essential check to be made before proceeding to summarise the financial information (as explained in Chapter 4).

2.5 Optimising the system

The double-entry system, as we have seen, requires entries to be made within ledger accounts. Because of the mass of information generated by businesses, it is helpful to management to keep certain parts of the system within a number of self-contained areas, as follows:

- Bank and cash transactions within a cash book
- Small cash transactions within a petty cash book
- Invoices received or issued within Day Books
- Returns of goods within Day Books
- Specialised adjustments within a journal.

These are known as 'books of prime entry' (or *primary accounting records*) as they show the first stage of the data recording process prior to transferring the information into the ledger accounts (see Figure 2.3).

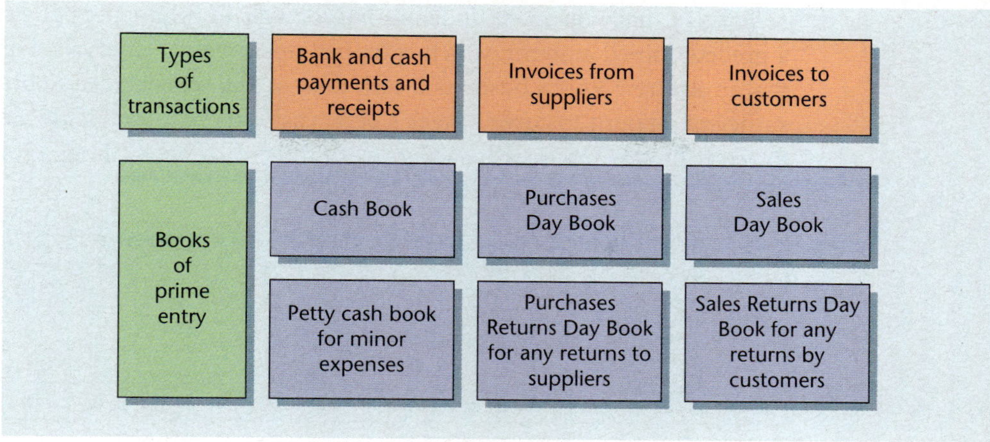

Figure 2.3 Books of prime entry (other than the Journal)

2.5.1 The cash book

In a small business, the cash book is used to record the transactions affecting both the business's bank account and also its unbanked cash (notes and coins), shown within a cash account. Often, the two accounts are shown in what is known as a 'columnar' form, with two debit columns and two credit columns. Andrew Rose's cash book could be shown as follows:

Cash Book							
		Bank account			Cash account		
Date	Details	Debit	Credit	Bank Balance	Debit	Credit	Cash Balance
1 January	Andrew Rose: equity	4,000		4,000 Dr			
2 January	Purchases		2,000	2,000 Dr			
3 January	Sales				700		700 Dr
3 January	Wages					300	400 Dr
6 January	Computer		1,000	1,000 Dr			
8 January	Andrew Rose: equity	1,000		2,000 Dr			
9 January	Drawings		100	1,900 Dr			

The advantage of this layout is that details of all the cash and bank transactions are within the same part of the ledger.

2.5.2 The petty cash book

Virtually all organisations spend cash on relatively low-value items such as tea and coffee, stamps, cleaning, etc. Such items are usually considered too insignificant to be recorded within the main cash account in the cash book, so they are given their own book within the system, known as the *petty* cash book.

Did you know?

The word 'petty' comes from the French 'petit', meaning small.

This is usually operated under an *imprest* system, where the petty cash has a 'float' of a predetermined amount, which is topped up at regular intervals. For example, assume that in Andrew Rose's business a cash float of £80 was decided upon on 8 January as a sufficient amount to cover a week's petty cash expenditure. Firstly, £80 would be transferred from the 'main' cash account within the cash book (though it may, alternatively, have been drawn out from the bank account):

Cash account (part of the 'Cash Book')				
Date	**Details**	**Debit**	**Credit**	**Balance**
3 January	Sales	700		700 Dr
4 January	Wages		300	400 Dr
8 January	Transfer to petty cash		80	320 Dr

The petty cash book is then opened. Using a 'typical' week's petty cash expenditure for illustration and assuming that the cash float is topped up back to £80 at the start of the following week, the petty cash book for Andrew Rose is as follows:

Petty cash book				
Date	**Details**	**Debit**	**Credit**	**Balance**
8 January	Transfer: Cash Account	80		80 Dr
9 January	Window cleaning		10	70 Dr
10 January	Tea and coffee		3	67 Dr
11 January	Travel tickets		5	62 Dr
12 January	Stationery		12	50 Dr
13 January	Postage		6	44 Dr
13 January	Stationery		15	29 Dr
14 January	Stationery		20	9 Dr
15 January	Transfer: Cash Account	71		80 Dr

During the week, £71 has been spent from the opening cash float of £80. At the start of the following week (15 January), the float must be 'topped up' by drawing £71 from the main cash account, and transferring it to the petty cash to again make up the £80. The imprest system is a useful control against fraud, as the person responsible for the petty cash would normally have to present evidence of the expenditure (vouchers, receipts, etc.) to a senior person controlling the main cash book when requesting the top-up for the petty cash float.

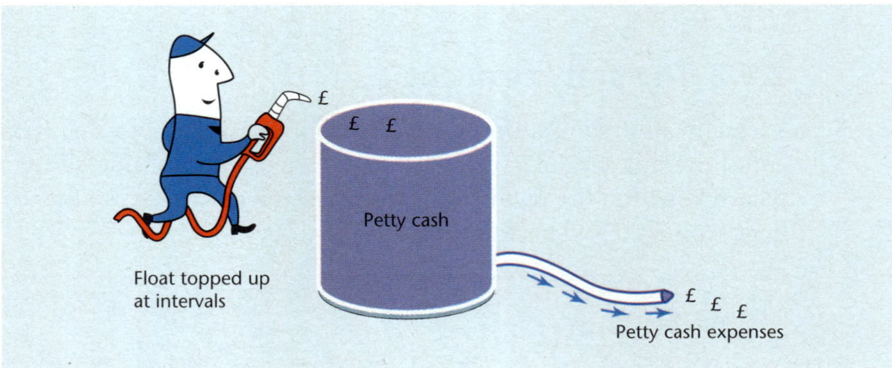

Figure 2.4 The petty cash imprest system

2.5.3 Analysed cash books and petty cash books

There can be a great variety of expenses paid out of the cash book and petty cash book, but they can usually be grouped into a relatively small number of categories. These can be shown in an extended version known as an *analysed* cash book or petty cash book. This makes it easier to complete the double-entry bookkeeping, by allowing totals for the period to be debited to their respective accounts in the General Ledger. For example, Andrew Rose's analysed petty cash book could be shown as follows:

Petty cash book									
Date	**Details**	**Debit**	**Credit**	**Balance**	**Cleaning**	**Travel**	**Postage**	**Stationery**	**Other**
8 January	Transfer: Cash Account	80		80 Dr					
9 January	Window cleaning		10	70 Dr	10				
10 January	Tea and coffee		3	67 Dr					3
11 January	Travel tickets		5	62 Dr		5			
12 January	Stationery		12	50 Dr				12	
13 January	Postage		6	44 Dr			6		
13 January	Stationery		15	29 Dr				15	
14 January	Stationery		20	9 Dr				20	
15 January	Transfer: Cash Account	71		80 Dr					
					10	5	6	47	3

The totals of each expenditure column can then be transferred to the relevant account in the General Ledger, rather than posting each individual entry. For example, £47 can be entered in the Stationery account, rather than the three separate payments.[1]

Activity 2.4

From the following details, write up the analysed petty cash book of Edgar Ramirez's business:

1 October	Petty cash book opened with a float of £100
2 October	Repair to office chair £14
3 October	Bought milk for office £8
4 October	Made cash donation to local charity £5
5 October	Paid £36 for a train ticket
6 October	Paid a car parking charge of £7
7 October	Paid a laundry bill of £19.
8 October	Petty cash float topped up to the original amount

Provide columns that summarise travel, laundry, repairs, refreshments and other expenses.

[1]Many businesses also have to record Value Added Tax (VAT) charged to customers or paid to suppliers. The books of prime entry for such businesses will contain columns showing the VAT received or paid; information that is needed to complete official returns sent at intervals to the taxation authorities.

Answer

Petty cash book									
Date	Details	Debit	Credit	Balance	Travel	Laundry	Repairs	Refreshments	Other
1 October	Transfer: Cash Account	100		100 Dr					
2 October	Chair repair		14	86 Dr			14		
3 October	Milk		8	78 Dr				8	
4 October	Charity donation		5	73 Dr					5
5 October	Train ticket		36	37 Dr	36				
6 October	Car parking		7	30 Dr	7				
7 October	Laundry		19	11 Dr		19			
8 October	Transfer: Cash Account	89		100 Dr					
					43	19	14	8	5

2.5.4 Day books

In Activity 2.1 (see page 24), only three of the transactions were on *credit terms*, where there was a delay between the date on which goods were bought or sold and the date of paying or receiving the amounts due. It is vital to keep individual personal accounts of trade receivables and payables (as seen with the ledger accounts for Sarah Prince – a receivable, and Paper Products and BiggaBuys – both payables), so that the business knows at any time the amounts owing by and to the business. However, it is usually unnecessary to show *every* individual purchase and sale in the Purchases and Sales accounts in the General Ledger. Even a moderately sized business may generate many hundreds or thousands of invoices over a financial period, so it makes sense to reduce the detail in these two ledger accounts by summarising the invoices in separate books known as *Day Books.*

There are four Day Books:

- Purchases
- Sales
- Purchases returns, and
- Sales returns.

Although individual invoices and returns are entered in the Day Books and then transferred to the personal accounts of customers and suppliers, at intervals, totals are transferred from the Day Books to the relevant General Ledger accounts (particularly the sales account and purchases account), so significantly reducing the number of entries shown within those accounts (see Figure 2.5).

The Day Books are also useful for resolving queries, as they provide a list of all invoices issued or received and goods returned to or by the business. They also have a role to play in the creation of control accounts (see Chapter 3) and in recording Value Added Tax (VAT) totals for official returns.

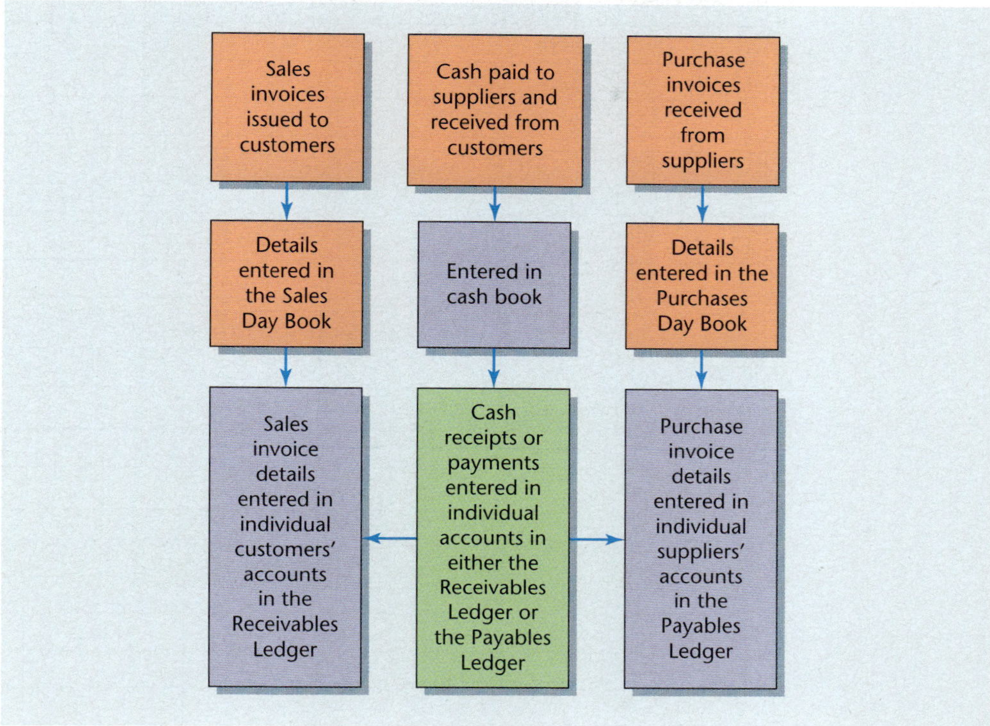

Figure 2.5 **Information flow into the Payables Ledger and Receivables Ledger**

Activity 2.5

Ted Craven's business recorded the following transactions during the period 7–14 July. Show how they would appear in the Day Books, the personal ledgers (Receivables Ledger and Payables Ledger) and the General Ledger.

7 Jul	Invoices received from T. Rogers £300, P. Cox £800, J. Wall £450
10 Jul	Invoices sent to L. Kenwood £790, A. Gardiner £980, L. Kerr £340
11 Jul	Invoice received from P. Cox £100, and invoice sent to L. Kerr, £490
12 Jul	Ted Craven returned goods worth £125 to P. Cox
13 Jul	A. Gardiner returned goods to Ted Craven which cost £50
14 Jul	Ted Craven paid the amount owing to P. Cox, and L. Kerr paid in full

Answer

Purchases Day Book		
Date	Details	£
7 July	T. Rogers	300
	P. Cox	800
	L. Wall	450
11 July	P. Cox	100
		1,650

Sales Day Book		
Date	**Details**	**£**
10 July	L. Kenwood	790
	A. Gardiner	980
	L. Kerr	340
11 July	L. Kerr	490
		2,600

Purchases Returns Day Book		
Date	**Details**	
12 July	P. Cox	125
		125

Sales Returns Day Book		
Date	**Details**	
13 July	A. Gardiner	50
		50

Payables Ledger

T. Rogers account				
Date	**Details**	**Debit**	**Credit**	**Balance**
7 July	Invoice		300	300 Cr

P. Cox account				
Date	**Details**	**Debit**	**Credit**	**Balance**
7 July	Invoice		800	800 Cr
11 July	Invoice		100	900 Cr
12 July	Purchases returns	125		775 Cr
14 July	Bank	775		–

J. Wall account				
Date	**Details**	**Debit**	**Credit**	**Balance**
7 July	Invoice		450	450 Cr

Receivables Ledger

L. Kenwood account				
Date	**Details**	**Debit**	**Credit**	**Balance**
10 July	Invoice	790		790 Dr

A. Gardiner account				
Date	**Details**	**Debit**	**Credit**	**Balance**
10 July	Invoice	980		980 Dr
13 July	Sales Returns		50	930 Dr

L. Kerr account				
Date	**Details**	**Debit**	**Credit**	**Balance**
10 July	Invoice	340		340 Dr
11 July	Invoice	490		830 Dr
14 July	Bank		830	–

General Ledger

Sales account				
Date	**Details**	**Debit**	**Credit**	**Balance**
14 July	Sales Day Book (total invoices)		2,600	2,600 Cr

Purchases account

Date	Details	Debit	Credit	Balance
14 July	Purchases Day Book (total invoices)	1,650		1,650 Dr

Purchases returns account

Date	Details	Debit	Credit	Balance
14 July	Purchases Returns Day Book (total returns)		125	125 Cr

Sales returns account

Date	Details	Debit	Credit	Balance
14 July	Sales Returns Day Book (total returns)	50		50 Dr

Cash Book

Bank account				
Date	**Details**	**Debit**	**Credit**	**Balance**
14 July	L. Kerr	830		830 Dr
	P. Cox		775	55 Dr

Stop and think

The Day Books take the detail out of the four General Ledger accounts shown, as only the *totals* of the invoices or returns are entered. It is vital that full records of individual suppliers and customers are still maintained within the personal ledgers. Note that the Day Book totals are transferred into the General Ledger at the last day of the period, 14 July.

2.5.5 The journal

Occasionally there may be adjustments or corrections to the financial information recorded within the ledger system. Journal entries show which accounts are to be debited and which to be credited (always in that order), with a simple explanation for the entries, known as a 'narrative'. Once the details have been entered into the journal, the entries are then made in the actual ledger accounts affected.

Activity 2.6

Assume that the following errors were made when entering the transactions of Ted Craven in Activity 2.5:

- The invoice (£300) from T. Rogers was mistakenly credited to P. Bodger's account.
- The invoice from J. Wall was incorrectly entered in the Purchases Day Book and J. Wall's ledger account as £540 instead of £450.

Answer

The Journal

		Dr	Cr
		£	£
Debit	P. Bodger	300	
Credit	T. Rogers		300
– Correction of error due to incorrectly recording an invoice from T. Rogers in P. Bodger's account			
Debit	J. Wall	90	
Credit	Purchases		90
– Correction of error in amount recorded in both the Purchases Day Book and J. Wall's ledger account			

> **Stop and think**
>
> The journal is not used very often, but is useful for explaining the reasons for making essential changes to ledger accounts.

2.6 Computerised accounting systems

As would be expected, most businesses use computers for some or all of their accounting needs. The data recording system described in this chapter forms the basis of accounting software programs. These programs give the following advantages:

- Speed
- Accuracy of calculation
- Integration of functions, avoiding duplication of effort
- Reduction in costs of professional accountancy services
- Provision of detailed financial reports for management
- Provision of summarised financial information complying with the regulatory framework.

Scan the following QR (Quick response) code with your smart phone's QR reader (downloadable free – just Google QR reader) to take you to the website of Sage Instant Accounts software.

References are given at the end of this chapter to the websites of a number of leading accounting software suppliers. Some might let you download 'demo' accounting programs for evaluation with no obligation to purchase them. Alternatively, try searching the internet for freeware or shareware accounting software, or browse for accounting apps for smart phones (scan the QR code in the margin to take you to one such site). If possible, download one of these programs and see how it works by entering Andrew Rose's transactions from Activity 2.1. There are many more features available on these programs than can be utilised by this simple example, but it should give you the confidence to explore these further.

The widespread use of computerised accounting packages has resulted in far less time spent on the processing of transactions and more on the control and evaluation aspects of financial management. For example, very detailed data can be extracted from the Receivables Ledger showing precisely the products or services purchased by customers and clients, the frequency of those purchases, changing trends in the popularity of different product lines, etc.

2.7 Summary

The ledger (*all* the accounts of the business) is divided into:		
Personal ledgers		Impersonal ledger
Receivables Ledger	**Payables Ledger**	**General Ledger**
Accounts for each of the customers who buy on credit terms	Accounts for each supplier of goods and services who allows a period of credit	Accounts for each *type* of asset, liability, income and expenses, as well as the equity account. Note that the bank and cash accounts are sometimes shown in a separate Cash Book, with 'petty cash' shown in a 'petty cash book'

2.8 Chapter glossary

Account The individual record contained within the ledger.

Analysed Cash Book or petty cash book A Cash Book or petty cash book with additional columns to enable similar payments to be grouped together to reduce the amount of bookkeeping entries needed.

Books of prime entry The location of the first stage of the recording process: the Cash Book, petty cash book, Day Books and journal.

Cash Book The record containing the bank account and cash account. Part of the General (impersonal) Ledger.

Credit The right-hand side of a ledger account. Liability, equity and income accounts have credit balances. Abbreviated to Cr.

Debit The left-hand side of a ledger account. Asset and expenses accounts have debit balances. Abbreviated to Dr.

General Ledger The impersonal ledger containing accounts for equity and types of assets, expenses, liabilities and income. Also known as the Nominal Ledger.

Impersonal Ledger The General Ledger.

Imprest system A method of controlling petty cash by keeping a 'float' which is topped up at intervals.

Journal A book of prime entry used to record the correction of errors and other adjustments between ledger accounts.

Ledger A collection of individual records known as accounts.

Nominal Ledger Another name for the General Ledger.

Personal ledgers The Receivables and Payables Ledgers, containing the individual accounts of customers and suppliers who trade on credit terms.

Petty cash Small items of expenditure, usually shown in a separate book.

Purchases The name of an account in the General Ledger which records goods bought for resale.

Trade payable A supplier of goods or services who is owed money by the business.

Trade receivable A customer or client who owes an amount to the business.

Trial balance A list of all the account balances, divided between debit and credit balances at a specific time. If the total debit balances equal the total credit balances, the trial balance is said to 'agree' and shows that the arithmetic of all the entries is correct. It is not a perfect check of overall accuracy.

Additional resources

Only accessible on Android-based devices

Now work through the various exercises and problems that you can find within the My Accounting Lab that are relevant to this chapter. Either use the QR code shown in the margin (if you use an Android-based device), or visit www.myaccountinglab.com for the log-in page.

Self-check questions

The answers to these questions are in Appendix 1.

1 A business sells goods for £1,000 paid into its bank account. The entries to be made are:

(a) Debit Sales account Credit Bank account
(b) Debit Inventory account Credit Bank account
(c) Debit Bank account Credit Sales account
(d) Debit Bank account Credit Purchases account

2 Goods bought for resale will be debited to the:

(a) Inventory account
(b) Office expenses account
(c) Sales account
(d) Purchases account

3 When the owner takes out cash from the business for personal use it is referred to as:

(a) Drawings
(b) Wages
(c) Equity
(d) Salary

4 Trade payables are:

(a) Customers who pay cash
(b) Customers who owe money to the business
(c) Suppliers who are owed money by the business
(d) Suppliers who have been paid by the business

5 Which of the following is a *personal* ledger?

(a) General Ledger
(b) Payables Ledger
(c) Cash Book
(d) Income statement

6 The cash book contains which of the following pairs of accounts?

(a) Petty cash and Bank
(b) Drawings and Bank
(c) Bank and Cash
(d) Equity and Cash

7 Which of the following is *not* a book of prime entry?

(a) The Purchases Day Book
(b) The Journal
(c) The Cash Book
(d) The General Ledger

8 The petty cash float of a business has been set at £100. During a week, £80 was paid out for petty cash expenses. The amount to be drawn out of cash to 'top up' the float is:

(a) £80
(b) £20
(c) £100
(d) £180

9 A trial balance is:

(a) A perfect check on the bookkeeping system
(b) A check on the accuracy of the bookkeeping entries
(c) A check on the arithmetical accuracy of the bookkeeping entries
(d) A way of proving that the business has made a profit

10 After preparing a trial balance, it is noticed that the total of the debit balances is £500 greater than the total of the credit balances. Which one of the following could have caused the difference?

(a) A duplication of a credit entry of £500, but only one debit entry for that amount
(b) A duplication of a debit entry of £500, but also a duplication of the credit entry for that amount
(c) A transaction of £500 that has been omitted entirely from the system
(d) A duplication of a debit entry of £500, but only one credit entry for that amount

Self-study questions

Questions marked with this symbol (#) indicate that the suggested answers are available to lecturers only – other answers are shown in Appendix 2.

2.1 The Annual Report of Pearson plc contains a Statement of Directors' Responsibilities. This includes the following paragraph:

> The directors are responsible for keeping adequate accounting records that are sufficient to show and explain the company's transactions and disclose with reasonable accuracy at any time the financial position of the company and the Group. This enables them to ensure that the financial statements and the report on directors' remuneration comply with the Companies Act 2006 and, as regards the Group financial statements, Article 4 of the IAS Regulation. They are also responsible for safeguarding the assets of the company and the Group and for taking reasonable steps for the prevention and detection of fraud and other irregularities.

1 Explain what is meant by 'adequate accounting records'
2 Why does the statement refer to 'reasonable' accuracy rather than 'total' accuracy?
3 What is meant by 'safeguarding the assets of the company'?

2.2 The following is a list of all the balances (in random order) in the ledgers of Vladimir Popov at 1 June 2014:

Name	Amount	Debit balance or Credit balance?
Receivable: J. Petrov	650	Debit
Rent and Rates	6,400	Debit
Machinery	25,680	Debit
Equity	?	Credit
Wages	18,630	Debit
Purchases	14,560	Debit
Advertising	1,500	Debit
Payable: P. Pavlov	960	Credit
Accountancy fees	350	Debit
Sales	32,510	Credit
Bank	5,000	Debit
Payable: L. Grigorvic	250	Credit

(a) What was the balance on Vladimir's Equity account on 1 June 2014? (show your workings)

(b) Rearrange all the balances (including the equity account balance) under each of the following headings:

Assets	*Expenses*	*Liabilities*	*Equity*	*Income*

(c) Total the balances that appear under each of the five headings in part (b) above, and then complete and prove the following formula:

$$\textit{Assets} + \textit{Expenses} = \textit{Liabilities} + \textit{Equity} + \textit{Income}$$

2.3 (This is a basic example, with neither a Payables Ledger nor a Receivables Ledger needed.) From the following transactions of Rachel Roberts, write up a cash book showing cash and bank transactions and ledger accounts for all other transactions. Prepare a trial balance at 7 October.

1 Oct	Started the business by paying £9,000 into the business bank account and also providing £100 as an opening cash balance
1 Oct	Bought goods for resale with a bank transfer of £4,000 and paid £60 in cash for stationery
2 Oct	Sold goods for £600 (paid by bank transfer) and £280 cash
3 Oct	Paid a cheque for £30 for advertising and a cheque for £45 for printing
4 Oct	Paid rent by bank transfer, £100
5 Oct	Sold goods for £700 (paid by bank transfer) and £130 cash
6 Oct	Paid wages £260 cash. Owner withdrew £400 from the bank for personal use
7 Oct	A customer was given a refund by cheque £40 for faulty goods returned to the business

2.4 (This is a more complex example requiring Day Books and all three ledgers.)

The following are the first week's transactions of George Andrews:

May 1	George started the business by paying in £4,000 into the business bank account
May 1	Bought goods for resale with a cheque for £2,000 and paid £30 by cheque for advertising.
May 2	Sold goods for £2,400, paid by bank transfer
May 3	Paid £80 by cheque for printing
May 4	Paid rent by bank transfer, £150
May 5	Sold goods for £800, paid by bank transfer
May 6	Paid wages £300 cash.
May 7	Bought goods for resale costing £2,100 on credit from Jupiter plc, and sold goods worth £250 on credit to Saturn Ltd

Enter all the above transactions into the bookkeeping records of George Andrews and prepare a trial balance at 7 May.

2.5 Tariq Ahmad's business recorded the following transactions during the week ended 7 May. Show how they would appear in the Day Books, the personal ledgers (Receivables Ledger and Payables Ledger) and the General Ledger.

1 May	Invoices received from C. Moss £630, J. Carter £419 and A. McKeane £330
2 May	Invoices sent to K. Palfreyman £199 and L. Patel £870
3 May	Invoice received from A. Iqbal £560 and A. McKeane £210
4 May	Tariq Ahmad returned goods worth £80 to J. Carter
5 May	L. Patel returned goods to Tariq Ahmad which cost £62
6 May	Tariq Ahmad paid the amount owing to J. Carter, and L. Patel paid in full
7 May	Tariq Ahmad returned goods worth £40 to A. Iqbal

2.6 Lara Kelly recorded the following petty cash transactions during the week ended 20 October:

14 Oct	Started the week with the normal cash float of £200. Paid £26 travel expenses
15 Oct	Paid £14 for window cleaning
16 Oct	Paid £18 for train fares
17 Oct	Paid £40 for new kennel for guard dog, and £19 for dog food
18 Oct	Paid postage £3
19 Oct	Made a loan of £10 to Hiram Decker, a member of staff
20 Oct	Paid £24 for window cleaning
20 Oct	The cash float was topped up to £200

Show the analysed petty cash book for the week (with columns for cleaning, travel, postage and 'other').

2.7 Joy Li runs an office in Singapore. She accounts for petty cash based on the 'imprest' system. The amount of the cash float is $600, and she restores the float on a weekly basis. The following were the payments from the petty cash for the week ending 12 June 2014:

Show the analysed petty cash book for the week (with five columns for cleaning, adverts, printing, postage and stationery, travel, and 'other').

Date	Description	Amount
8 June	Stationery for office	50
8 June	Advert in local newspaper	100
9 June	Tea and coffee for office	30
10 June	Postal charges	15
10 June	Printing, business cards	40
11 June	Wages to office cleaner	110
12 June	Fuel for car	100
12 June	Stationery	45
12 June	Petty cash float topped up to $600	

2.8 Show how the following errors would be corrected by means of journal entries in the books of Paul Pascoe:

(a) £400 received from Andrew Cheung which should have been posted to his account in the Receivables Ledger but was entered in Andrew Young's account.
(b) A cheque for £40 paid for stationery which was wrongly entered on the debit side of the bank account in the cash book and the credit side of the stationery account.
(c) An invoice for £200 for goods for resale received from a supplier, Dingle Dynamics, was omitted entirely from the books.

Case study: Marvin buys rabbits

Marvin the magician (see Chapter 1's case study) entered his second week of business and was offered fees to appear as an entertainer at three events during the week. Realising that he had no rabbits to pull out of his top hat, he contacted the United Rabbit Corporation, which agreed, on 8 July, to supply six white rabbits at a cost of £40 each. On the same day, Amalgamated Carrots plc supplied several sacks of rabbit food at a total cost of £250. Both companies sent Marvin invoices. Marvin built a rabbit hutch from scrap materials at no cost.

On 10 July, Marvin travelled to William Green's party, which was a success, and he was paid £100 in cash for his magic act. Travel expenses cost £15 cash. On 11 July he paid a cheque for £18 for cleaning his costume, which became dirty after handling the rabbits. On 12 July he paid £9 for a train ticket in cash, and travelled to Violet Cartwright's party, which was also successful, and he received a cheque for £120. On 13 July he performed at Jasper Peter's party which was only partly successful, since a child felt sorry for the rabbits and let them all escape. They were never seen again. Marvin gave an invoice to Mr and Mrs Peter for £250 for his magic act at the party.

On 14 July, he returned the unused rabbit feed to Amalgamated Carrots plc, which gave him a refund of £60. He paid the United Rabbit Corporation invoice by cheque and also paid Kazam Limited's account for the playing cards bought in the first week.

Required

(a) Enter the first week's transactions in a cash book and ledger accounts. Day books and a petty cash book are not required. The transactions (as shown in Chapter 1's case study) were:

1 July	Used his own funds (part of Marvin's equity) to buy a costume £3,000
2 July	Used his own funds (part of Marvin's equity) to buy an ancient book £2,000
3 July	Bought playing cards £400, by invoice from Kazam Limited
7 July	Received £750 for appearing in a magic show and opened a bank account. Paid £20 travel expenses, using own funds (also part of Marvin's equity)

(b) Enter the second week's transactions (as shown above) into the cash book and ledger accounts.

(c) Prepare a trial balance as at 14 July.

Answers in Appendix 3

Further research

Accounting software developers include:

Quick Books **www.intuit.co.uk**

Clear Books **www.clearbooks.co.uk**

Chapter 3

Adjusting and summarising data

Objectives

When you have read this chapter you will be able to:

- Understand the need to summarise financial information
- Understand the accounting adjustments for opening and closing inventory, and the basis of valuation of inventory
- Appreciate the need for accruals and prepayments
- Understand what is meant by 'depreciation'
- Understand the layout of a simple income statement and statement of financial position

3.1 Introduction

We have seen (in the previous chapter) how all but the very smallest businesses use a continuous financial data recording system known as double-entry bookkeeping. This ensures that the transactions are sorted according to their effect on the five key aspects of the business: assets, expenses, liabilities, equity and income. This system will be operational over the entire life of the business and is the source of such day-to-day information as who the business owes money to (payables) and which customers owe it money (receivables). The cash and bank records will help to avoid unforeseen banking difficulties caused by spending more cash than the funds available, and any account queries raised by customers and suppliers can usually be resolved by looking at the information in the Day Books and personal ledgers.

At intervals, something else is needed. It is necessary for the managers and owners to step back from the detail and take an overview of the business performance. In this chapter we explain the first stages in constructing two of the most important financial summaries, the *income statement*, which summarises income and expenses over the financial period to establish if the business made a profit or loss, and the *statement of financial position*, which shows the assets, liabilities and equity at the end of the financial period.

3.2 Financial periods

When first established, a business must decide which time periods are most suitable for summarising its financial information. Although the management of a large and complex organisation might require some key information produced on a weekly or monthly basis, a small business with an owner-manager might prepare summaries only once a year. External factors may also be relevant, as tax authorities will require at least annual information on profits, and legislation and stock exchange regulations might impose specific time periods on relevant organisations.

Regardless of these possibilities, it is expected that *every* organisation will produce at least a report covering its 'financial year'. The choice of date on which a financial year ends varies from business to business and might coincide with the calendar year (31 December), tax year (31 March in many countries) or simply a date convenient to the business which causes least disruption to its normal working (for example, a holiday company might choose 31 October because it is in the 'quiet season' for travel bookings).

Stop and think

Many companies choose to end their financial period on the last *working* day before the end of a month so that they have a complete number of weeks in each financial year. For example, the world's third largest retailer, Tesco plc, chose Saturday 25 February 2012 for the end of its financial year, to ensure a full 52-week period.

3.3 Accounting adjustments

The International Accounting Standards Board's Conceptual Framework for Financial Reporting includes the *accrual basis* as one of the two underlying assumptions when preparing financial statements (other than cash flow information). This means that *all* relevant financial information must be contained within financial summaries regardless of whether associated cash flows have taken place. In practical terms, this means that a number of important adjustments have to be made at the end of the financial period prior to summarising data within the income statement and statement of financial position. In this chapter we are looking at:

- Inventory adjustments
- Accruals and prepayments
- Depreciation.

Additional adjustments, including those relating to bad and doubtful debts are considered later (in Chapter 5).

3.3.1 Inventory adjustments

At the end of a financial year, a trading or manufacturing business is likely to have inventories of unsold goods, unused raw materials and possibly partly-completed items. These must be valued so that they can be *excluded* from the 'cost of sales' calculation needed when establishing the current year's profit. The inventory at the *start* of the current year will, however, be *included* in that calculation as it would be part of the cost of the goods sold during the current year. For example, a business buying and selling wind turbines might have had 10 at the start of its financial year, bought 80 during the year and had 20 left unsold at the end of the financial year. The income statement needs to show the overall cost of the 70 wind turbines (10 + 80 − 20) sold in the year.

In the statement of financial position (which summarises assets, liabilities and equity) at the end of the financial period the closing inventory valuation will be included as part of the business's current assets (the value of the 20 unsold wind turbines in the above example). The value placed on inventory has a direct influence on profit levels – the higher the value of closing inventory, the greater the profit. Because of this, it is vital that such values are as accurate as possible.

In the majority of cases, inventory is valued at cost price, i.e. the price paid when the goods or raw materials were purchased. Sometimes it is difficult to establish the cost price, particularly in the case of raw materials or goods bought at different dates and at different prices (e.g. liquids, chemicals, ingredients). It is usual in such circumstances to either take an average cost price or to value inventory on a theoretical 'First In, First Out' (FIFO) basis, where it is *assumed* that the first inventory into the business was the first inventory to be used, thus leaving the unsold inventory to be valued at the most recent prices. (This is explored further in Chapter 5).

Partly completed items (also known as *work in progress*) are valued according to the degree of completion, but again on the basis of cost price plus labour costs, etc. Inventory is never valued at the normal *selling* price, as to do so would be to include a profit which, by definition, is unearned, as the goods comprising the inventory are unsold. Occasionally, inventory has deteriorated, gone out of fashion or otherwise been devalued so that its anticipated selling price is actually *less* than its cost price. Only in these circumstances can the inventory be valued at what it could be sold for, less any expenses needed to be incurred to make it saleable (also known as the 'net realisable value'). The relevant International Accounting Standard (IAS 2) summarises this in the following way:

Inventories are required to be stated at the lower of cost and net realisable value

Activity 3.1

At the end of its financial year, a lady's fashion business has 500 green handbags which cost the company £10 each. The normal selling price of a handbag is £25, but due to fashion changes, no one wants to buy green handbags. The company is now only able to sell yellow handbags. The only chance of selling green handbags is to add a yellow strap at a cost of £2 per handbag and to reduce the selling price to £8 each. What is the closing value of inventory?

Answer

The closing inventory of green handbags would be valued at:

$$(500 \times £8) - (500 \times £2) = £3{,}000.$$

Note that neither the original cost price nor the 'normal' selling price are relevant to the calculation in this example.

3.3.2 Accruals

Accruals are additional expenses incurred during the financial period which have neither been invoiced nor paid by the end of that period. They do not include 'trade payables' which would have been invoiced in the normal way. Examples would include utility charges such as electricity, gas, water, etc. that have not been fully paid by the end of the year. If the utility companies send bills on a quarterly basis, it is likely that on the day chosen as the end of the financial year, some part of the year's utility charges will be unpaid. Such accruals must be added to the balance in the relevant general ledger account. For example, if a business's first financial year ends on 31 December and by that date only 10 months of mobile phone bills had been paid, then the final 2 months charges will have to be estimated.

10 months paid by the year-end + 2 months accrual
= 12 months expense for year 1

In each subsequent year, the total expense for the year will be calculated as follows:

(Total paid in the year – Opening accrual from previous year)
+ Closing accrual = 12 months expense

Activity 3.2 and Figure 3.1 explains this.

Activity 3.2

The electricity supplier to Athens Bakery always bills its final quarterly charge just after the end of the bakery's financial year. Its quarterly charge has risen from £400 per quarter in Year 1 (the first year of its business), to £600 per quarter in Year 2, to £800 per quarter in Year 3. What is the total electricity charge in each of the three years?

Answer

The total electricity charge to be included when calculating profits in each of the three years is £1,600, £2,400 and £3,200 respectively, as explained in Figure 3.1

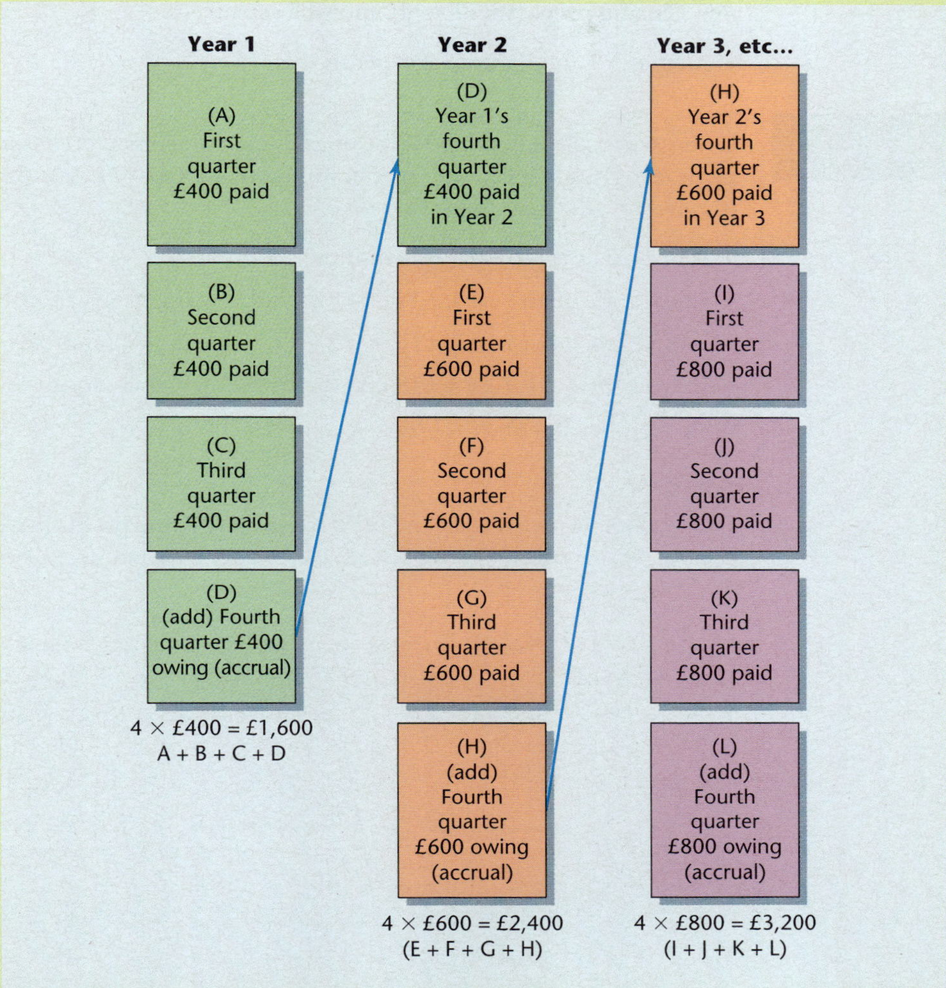

Figure 3.1 Accruals

3.3.3 Prepayments

Businesses will sometimes make payments within one financial period but all or part of the benefits are received in a future time period. These are known as *prepayments*. Examples include rent paid in advance and insurance premiums paid now but relating to the year ahead. For example, if a business had paid for 18 months rent by the end of its financial year, then six months of that rent is treated as being prepaid and must be deducted in arriving at the total rent charge for the year.

18 months paid by the year-end − 6 months prepaid = 12 months expense

In each subsequent year, the total rent expense for the year will be calculated as follows:

(Total paid in the year + Opening prepayment from previous year)

− Closing prepayment = 12 months expense

Activities 3.3 and Figure 3.2 explains this.

Activity 3.3

When Athens Bakery started its business, it paid the rental on its bakery buildings six months in advance. After that, it was required to pay 12 months in advance. Rent payments in the first three years were:

- Start of Year 1: £6,000 for six month's rent
- Halfway through Year 1: £14,000 for the following twelve months' rent
- Halfway through Year 2: £16,000 for the following six months' rent
- Halfway through Year 3: £18,000 for the following six months' rent.

What is the total rental expense in each of the three years?

Answer

The total rent expense to be included when calculating profits in each of the three years is: Year 1: £13,000, Year 2: £15,000, Year 3: £17,000, as explained in Figure 3.2.

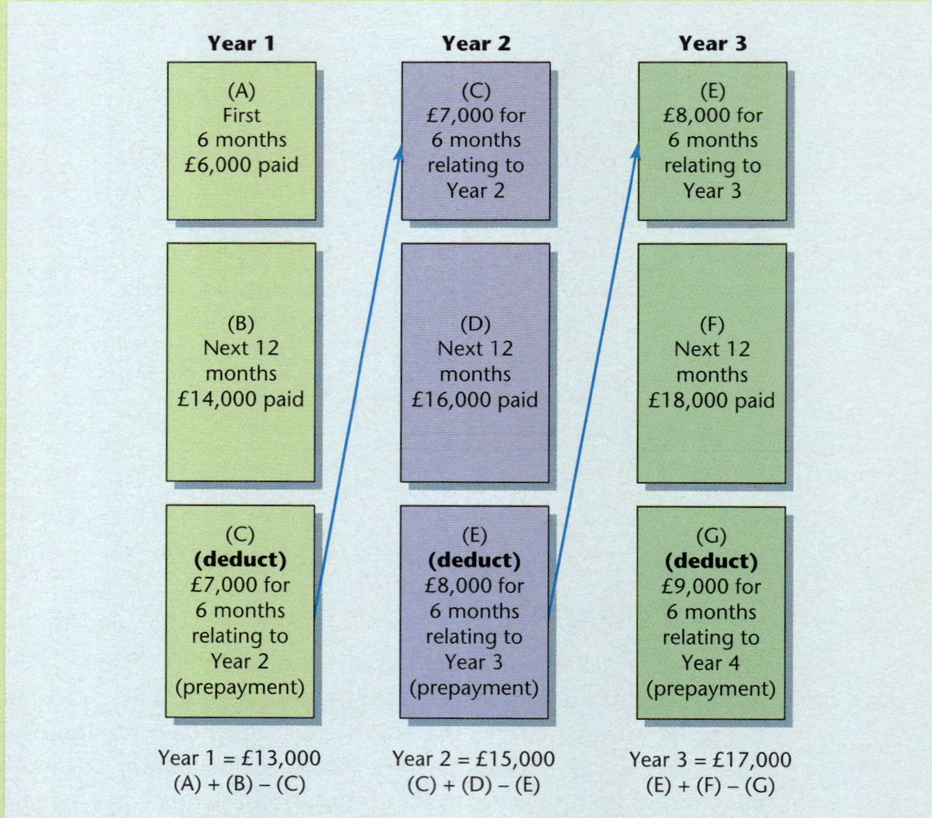

Figure 3.2 Prepayments

Stop and think

All we are doing by adjusting for accruals and prepayments is ensuring that the expenses shown in the financial summary cover *only* the required financial period, neither more nor less than that. If you are showing the results for a year, you can't just include *three* quarterly bills – you have to add the final quarter as an accrual. Similarly, you can't include *five* quarterly bills – you would have to omit the prepayment of the fifth quarter.

3.3.4 Depreciation

Non-current assets such as buildings, machinery, computers and motor vehicles are usually subject to *depreciation* – defined by International Accounting Standard (IAS) 16: Property, Plant and Equipment as *the systematic allocation of the depreciable amount of an asset over its useful life*. Most freehold land – land owned rather than leased – is *not* depreciated as its life is regarded as infinite (though land where value is extracted such as a mine or quarry *would* be depreciated). The *depreciable amount* referred to in the definition is the loss of value that the asset suffers due to factors such as wear and tear, passage of time and obsolescence due to changes in technology.

Did you know?

Non-current assets are sometimes referred to as being either *tangible* or *intangible*. Tangible assets are those which are physical (i.e. can be 'touched'), such as cars, machinery, buildings, computers, etc. Intangible assets have no physical presence, and include brand names, computer software and the values of patents and copyrights. Intangible assets might also lose value over time, in which case they are subject to *amortisation* – which works in exactly the same way as *depreciation*! There is a separate IAS (No.38) which looks at intangible assets.

Due to the underlying assumption of the accrual basis (see Chapter 1), all relevant aspects of the business must be included, not just those that result in a cash flow.

Consequently, an estimate must be made of the amount of depreciation incurred by the non-current assets during the financial period. This total is then included within the income statement as an expense when arriving at the profit or loss for the period. The depreciation estimate is based on three values, only the first of which is known with any certainty:

1 The *cost* of the non-current asset, which is easily determined if bought from an outside supplier. However, any installation costs incurred to bring the asset into a working condition should also be included as part of the cost. For example, if a factory wall had to be demolished and rebuilt to allow the installation of a large machine, the building costs would be included as part of the cost of the machine. If the non-current asset is built by the business itself, then labour costs and other directly attributable costs would be included as part of the cost of the asset.

2 The *useful life* of the asset, which is the estimate of how long the non-current asset will continue to provide economic benefits to the organisation.
3 The *residual value*, (also known as a salvage value) which is the estimate, based on prices prevailing at the date of acquiring the asset, of the value which the asset may have at the end of its useful life. In many cases, it is assumed that the asset will have *no* residual value.

Activity 3.4

A welding robot is bought by a car manufacturer for £200,000 on 1 January 2014. It costs £40,000 to install the robot and it is expected to be used for a period of 10 years, after which it is expected to be sold to an industrial museum for £4,000. What is the key information needed for depreciation calculations?

Answer

For the purpose of depreciation calculations:

- The cost is £240,000 (£200,000 + £40,000).
- The useful life is 10 years.
- The estimated residual value is £4,000.

A variety of methods can be used to calculate the amount of depreciation to be allocated to a specific financial period. The two most common methods are the *straight line method* and the *diminishing balance* method.

The straight line method

This assumes that depreciation occurs evenly over the life of the asset, so the asset is written off (reduced to its residual value) in equal instalments over its useful life. In fact, the straight line method is sometimes called the *equal instalment* method. Straight line depreciation is used by most businesses for the vast majority of non-current assets.

The following is an extract from the 2011 annual report of the global medical technology group Smith and Nephew plc, stating the company's depreciation policy:

Scan the following QR code with your QR reader to take you to the website of Smith and Nephew plc:

Accounting policies

Property, plant and equipment

Property, plant and equipment is stated at cost less depreciation and provision for impairment[1] where appropriate. Freehold land is not depreciated. Freehold buildings are depreciated on a straight-line basis over lives ranging between 20 and 50 years. Leasehold land and buildings are depreciated on a straight-line basis over the shorter of their estimated useful economic lives and the terms of the leases.

Plant and equipment is depreciated over lives ranging between three and 20 years by equal annual instalments to write down the assets to their estimated residual value at the end of their working lives. Assets in course of construction are not depreciated until they are brought into use.

The useful lives and residual values of all property, plant and equipment are reviewed each financial year-end, and where adjustments are required, these are made prospectively.

Source: Smith and Nephew plc Annual Report, 2011

[1] An impairment could be a further reduction in an asset's value caused by factors such as unexpected events such as natural disasters

The formula for calculating depreciation under this method is:

$$\frac{\text{Cost} - \text{Estimated residual value}}{\text{Useful life in years}}$$

The welding robot (see above) would be depreciated over 10 years at £23,600 p.a.:

$$\frac{(£240{,}000 - £4{,}000)}{10} = £23{,}600 \text{ p.a.}$$

Activity 3.5

Monteverdi Minerals bought a forklift truck for £30,000 on 1 March 2014. It was estimated to last for 5 years, when it would be worth £4,000. What is the annual depreciation under the straight line method?

Answer

$$\text{Annual depreciation} = \frac{(\text{Cost} - \text{Residual value})}{\text{Useful life in years}}$$

$$= \frac{(30{,}000 - 4{,}000)}{5} = £5{,}200 \text{ p.a.}$$

Did you know?

The depreciation rate under the straight line method can also be expressed as a percentage. For example, 20% p.a. straight line depreciation means equal instalments over 5 years, 25% p.a. straight line is over 4 years, etc.

The diminishing balance method

The diminishing balance method (sometimes called the 'reducing balance' method) assumes higher depreciation in earlier years than in later years and is used where it is clear that greater benefits are provided by assets when new than when they become older – perhaps as a result of general wear causing them to become more liable to break down or less capable of producing a high-quality product. The method works by applying a given (or calculated) percentage to the net value (i.e. cost less total depreciation up to the date of the calculation).

Activity 3.6

Terrapin Media Agency paid £12,000 for a car for a sales manager on 1 April 2013. The depreciation rate is 40% p.a. What is the depreciation for each of the three financial years ending on 31 March 2016, on a diminishing balance basis?

Answer

Year 1: £4,800, Year 2: £2,880, Year 3: £1,728

Workings:

Cost	12,000
Depreciation: Year to 31 March 2014 (40% × £12,000)	**4,800**
	7,200
Depreciation: Year to 31 March 2015 (40% × £7,200)	**2,880**
	4,320
Depreciation: Year to 31 March 2016 (40% × £4,320)	**1,728**
	2,592
etc. until sold or scrapped	

Stop and think

The Excel spreadsheet function DB can be used to generate the annual depreciation amounts under the diminishing balance method.

For example, assume that an asset with a five-year life cost £26,000 and has an estimated residual value of £1,000.

1 Open the spreadsheet.

2 Click on the Formulas tab.

3 Click on 'Insert Function', and put DB in the search bar.

4 Click Go.

5 The function DB should be highlighted under 'Select a function'.

6 Click OK, and you will see the screen shown in Figure 3.3.

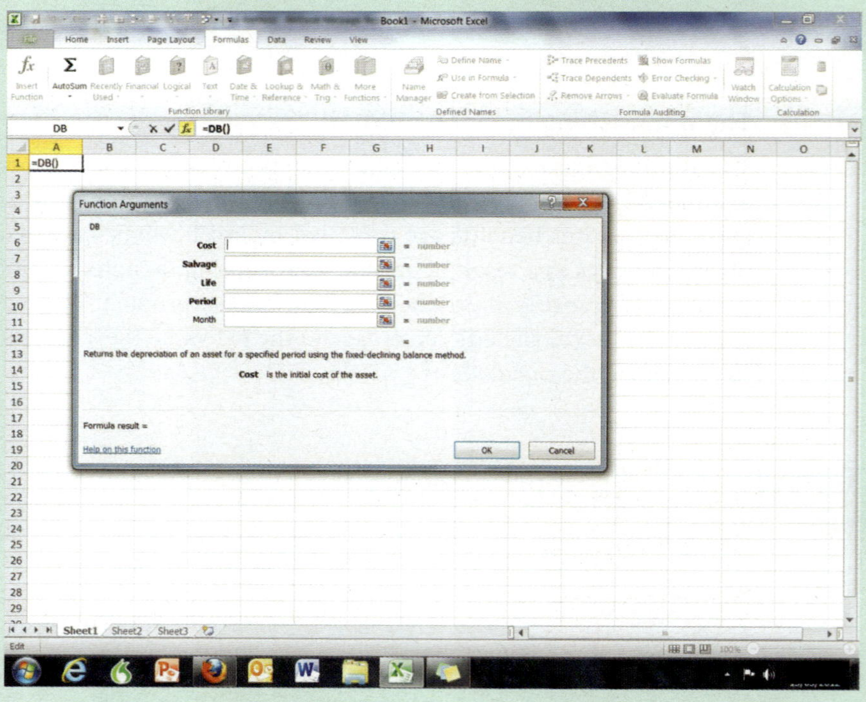

Figure 3.3 Excel DB function

Enter the values as follows (note that 'Salvage' is used instead of 'estimated residual value') – see Figure 3.4.

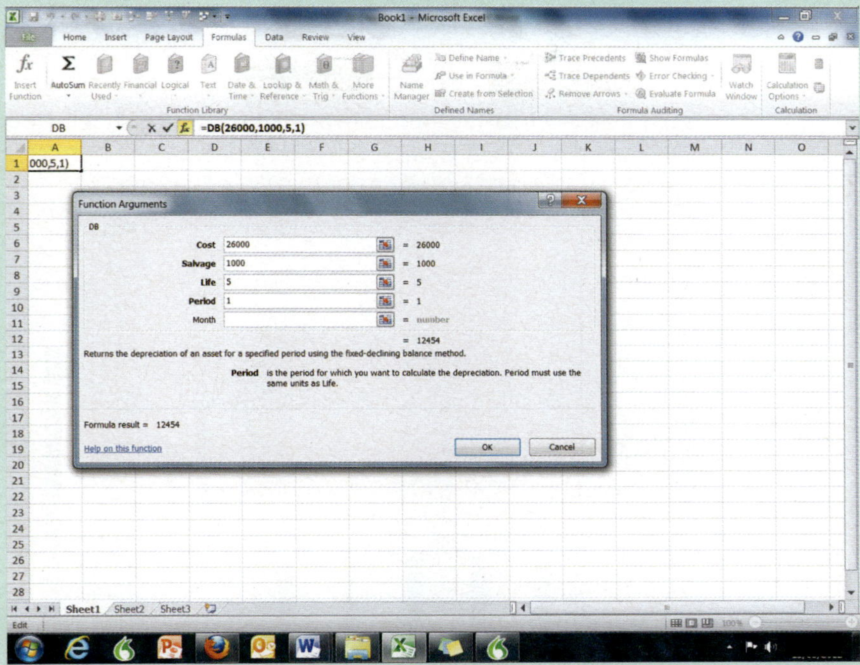

Figure 3.4 Excel DB function with data inserted

Figure 3.4 shows the first year's depreciation under this method (£12,454). Subsequent years' values can be calculated simply by changing the 'Period' value to 2, 3, 4 and 5. This calculates the values as: Year 2: £6,489, Year 3: £3,380, Year 4: £1,761, Year 5: £916.

The effects of using either the straight line or diminishing balance method of depreciation can be clearly shown by plotting bar charts. Let's look at the 'Stop and Think' example of an asset costing £26,000 with a five-year life and an estimated residual value of £1,000. Using the straight line method, annual depreciation would be £5,000 each year for five years ([£26,000 – £1,000]/5). The diminishing balance method, using the values from the Excel spreadsheet function, will show the following year-on-year calculations:

	£
Cost	26,000
Year 1: Depreciation:	12,454
Depreciated value at the end of Year 1	13,546
Year 2: Depreciation	6,489
Depreciated value at the end of Year 2	7,057
Year 3: Depreciation	3,380
Depreciated value at the end of Year 3	3,677
Year 4: Depreciation	1,761

	£
Depreciated value at the end of Year 4	1,916
Year 5: Depreciation	916
Final residual value after 5 years	1,000

Figure 3.5a shows the annual depreciation under each method; Figure 3.5b shows the closing net depreciated value at the end of each year.

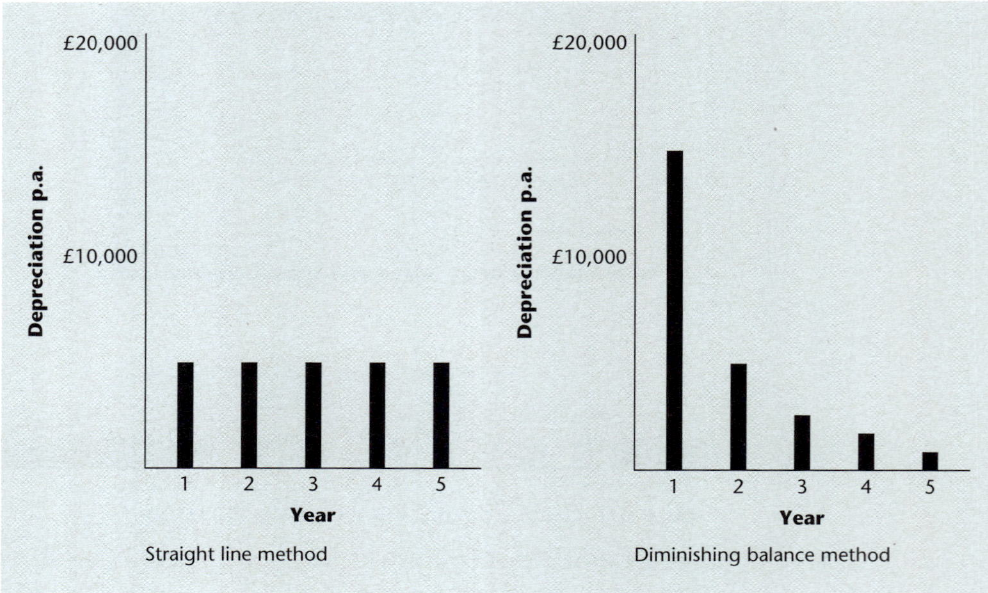

Figure 3.5a Bar charts of straight line and diminishing balance methods of depreciation

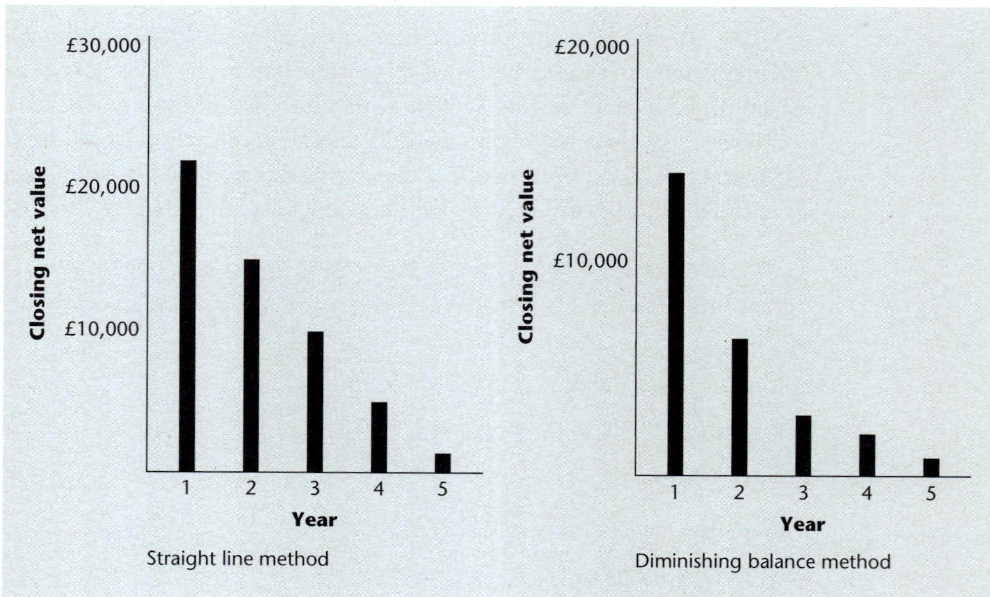

Figure 3.5b Bar charts of straight line and diminishing balance depreciation methods (using the same example as in Figure 3.5 (a)), showing the closing net value under each method.

> **Did you know?**
>
> In each method, the cost is £26,000 and the estimated residual value after 5 years is £1,000. The difference is how the depreciation of £25,000 is *apportioned* over the five-year period.

3.4 Basics of the financial summaries

Later (in Chapter 4) we shall be looking in detail at the two key financial summaries, the income statement and statement of financial position, but it is helpful at this stage to have a preview of the information they contain. Figure 3.6 recalls the steps we have taken to reach this point.

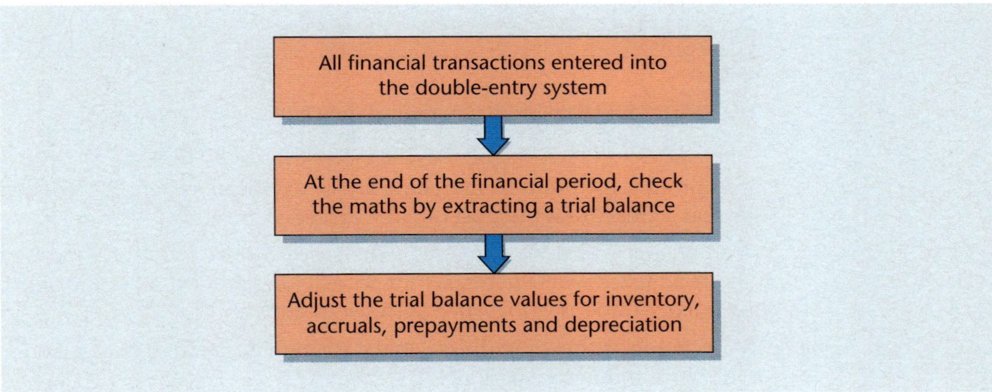

Figure 3.6 Stages before the production of the income statement and statement of financial position

3.4.1 The income statement

This is a summary of all the revenue and expenses for a financial period. For a simple trading business, it is shown in a two-stage format. The first stage starts with the Revenue (sales income) and then deducts the 'Cost of Sales' to arrive at a 'gross' profit. The second stage deducts all other expenses from the gross profit to arrive at an operating profit. Here is a (very) simple guide to the layout:

Revenue		A
Less Cost of sales		(B)
Gross profit (A – B)		C
Less Expenses		
Selling	D	
Administration	E	
General expenses	F	
(D + E + F)		(G)
Operating profit (C − G)		H

Using invented data, the income statement of Boston Burgers is shown below:

Boston Burgers
Income statement for the year ended 30 June 2014

	£	£
Revenue[1]		500,000
Less **Cost of sales**[2]		(200,000)
Gross profit[3]		300,000
Less **Expenses**[4]		
Selling	95,000	
Administration	25,000	
General expenses (including depreciation)[5]	45,000	
		(165,000)
Operating profit[6]		135,000

Notes:

[1] *All* the sales for the period, whether or not they have been paid for.

[2] Calculated by the formula ([Opening Inventory + Purchases] − Closing Inventory).

[3] *Gross* profit is the profit from trading *before* 'overhead' expenses are deducted. It would be shown as a gross *loss* if the 'cost of sales' exceeded 'revenue'.

[4] These are the 'overhead' expenses, which *exclude* the cost of the goods sold in the period. They are adjusted where necessary for accruals and prepayments and are often grouped for convenience into categories such as the ones shown.

[5] Depreciation as shown in the income statement is only that charged on non-current assets for the current financial period.

[6] *Operating* profit is the profit after *all* costs have been deducted. It would show as an operating *loss* if the total expenses exceeded the gross profit.

3.4.2 The statement of financial position

This is a summary of all the assets, liabilities and equity *at the end of the financial period*. There are a number of possible layouts, but the one shown below reflects the accounting equation of **Assets** − **Liabilities** = **Equity** (as referred to in Chapter 1). The statement starts with the depreciated value of non-current assets. The current liabilities are then subtracted from the current assets to give a *net* current assets total. Any non-current liabilities are deducted from the sum total of non-current assets and net current assets to give an overall value of total net assets. Finally, the value of the owners' equity is shown, which should result (because of the accounting equation) in exactly the same value as the total net assets. Here is a (very) simple guide to the layout:

Non-current assets		A
Current assets	B	
Less Current liabilities	(C)	
Net current assets (B − C)		D

(Subtotal) (A + D)	E
Non-current liabilities	(F)
Total net assets (E − F)	G
Equity	G

Using invented data, the statement of financial position of Boston Burgers is shown below:

Boston Burgers
Statement of financial position as at 30 June 2014[1]

	£	£	£
Non-current assets[2]			
Land and buildings			111,100
Motor vehicles			47,500
Fixtures			6,800
			165,400
Current assets			
Inventory		45,000	
Receivables		23,000	
Prepayments		4,000	
Cash equivalents[3]		2,000	
Cash		600	
		74,600	
***Less* Current liabilities**			
Payables	33,000		
Accruals	5,200		
		(38,200)	
Net current assets[4]			36,400
			201,800
***Less* Non-current liabilities**			(50,000)
Total net assets			151,800
Equity			151,800

Notes:

[1] The statement of financial position is always dated as the last day of the financial period, never 'for the year ended . . .'.

[2] The value *after* the total depreciation has been deducted (i.e. not just the current year's depreciation).

[3] This could be a bank balance.

[4] Also known as working capital.

Stop and think

Look very carefully at the way these two statements are presented (as the next chapter covers them in greater detail).

3.5 Summary

The financial data system at the end of a financial period shows:

- Information derived from opening balances at the start of the year
- Invoiced transactions during the year
- Cash paid and received during the year.

All are entered in accordance with the double-entry bookkeeping system.

In order to summarise *all* the relevant information in accordance with the accrual basis (one of the two fundamental assumptions of accounting explained in Chapter 1) the following items must be adjusted before preparing the income statement and statement of financial position:

Closing inventory	Closing accruals	Closing prepayments	Depreciation for the current period
Unsold goods at the end of the financial period, valued at the lower of 'cost and net realisable value'	Overheads incurred in the period but not yet invoiced	Overheads paid for in the period but relating in whole or in part to the following period	The estimated loss in value of a non-current asset caused by factors such as wear and tear and obsolescence

3.6 Chapter glossary

Accrual An expense owing at the end of a financial period where the invoice has not yet been received.

Amortisation The equivalent of depreciation, as applied to intangible non-current assets.

Depreciation The loss in value of a non-current asset over time.

Diminishing balance method A method of calculating depreciation using the assumption that the loss in value is greater in the early years than in the later years of the asset's life

Financial period The period, often a year, used as the time interval for summarising financial information.

Gross profit The difference between revenue and the cost of sales, before overhead expenditure has been deducted.

Income statement The financial summary which records the revenue and expenses for a financial period.

Intangible non-current asset A non-current asset that does not have physical properties, e.g. a brand name.

Inventory The value of unsold goods, unused raw materials and work in progress.

Operating profit The profit generated from the operating activities of the business after all relevant costs have been deducted.

Prepayment An expense paid in one financial period where the benefits are not received until some future period.

Residual value The estimate of value at the end of a non-current asset's useful life.

Statement of financial position The financial summary which records assets, liabilities and equity at the end of a financial period.

Straight line method A method of calculating depreciation using the assumption that the loss in value occurs evenly over the life of the asset.

Tangible non-current asset A non-current asset with physical properties, such as land, machinery, cars, etc.

Useful life The estimate of how long a non-current asset will be of use to the business.

Working capital Another term for net current assets, the difference between current assets and current liabilities as shown on the statement of financial position.

Additional resources

Only accessible on Android-based devices

Now work through the various exercises and problems that you can find within the My Accounting Lab that are relevant to this chapter. Either use the QR code shown in the margin (if you use an Android-based device), or visit www.myaccountinglab.com for the log-in page.

Self-check questions

The answers to these questions are in Appendix 1.

1 A financial period:

(a) Always ends on 31 December
(b) Can end on any date the business chooses
(c) Must always be of 12 months' duration
(d) Must always exactly match the official taxation year

2 A business bought 500 computer games at £10 each which it would normally sell at £25 each. However, a virus has caused the games to crash, and they are now worthless. How would the games be valued in a statement of financial position?

(a) £10 each
(b) £25 each
(c) Zero value
(d) At the expected profit of £15 each

3 Which one of the following is another term that means 'partly completed items'?

(a) Closing inventory
(b) Raw materials
(c) Work-in-progress
(d) Opening inventory

4 Which one of the following formulae is used when calculating the 'cost of sales' in an income statement?

(a) (Opening Inventory − Purchases − Closing Inventory)
(b) (Opening Inventory − Purchases + Closing Inventory)
(c) (Opening Inventory + Purchases − Closing Inventory)
(d) (Opening Inventory + Purchases + Closing Inventory)

5 Relating to the opening and closing inventory for a financial period, which of the following is true?

(a) Both figures are used to calculate 'cost of sales' in the income statement but only the opening inventory is shown in the statement of financial position
(b) Only the opening inventory is used to calculate 'cost of sales' in the income statement, but both figures are shown in the statement of financial position
(c) Both figures are used to calculate 'cost of sales' in the income statement but only the closing inventory is shown in the statement of financial position
(d) Only the closing inventory is used to calculate 'cost of sales' in the income statement, but both figures are shown in the statement of financial position

6 If a business owed £4,000 for advertising at the start of a financial period, paid advertising bills totalling £34,000 during the financial period and owed £3,000 for advertising at the end of the period, what will be the total advertising cost to be included within the expenses shown in the income statement?

(a) £35,000
(b) £34,000
(c) £41,000
(d) £33,000

7 A business paid a £720 subscription to a trade magazine on 30 June 2013, for the two years to 1 July 2015. The business's financial year ends on 30 November 2013. What relevant figures for subscriptions will be shown in the financial summaries for that period?

(a) £150 in the income statement, £570 prepayment in the statement of financial position
(b) £720 in the income statement, nil in the statement of financial position
(c) £360 in the income statement, £360 prepayment in the statement of financial position
(d) £1,440 in the income statement, £720 prepayment in the statement of financial position

8 A business buys a car which costs £15,000. This price includes £500 for insurance and £60 for car tax. The business's name was painted on the side of the car at an additional cost of £160. The car is expected to be in use for five years, after which time it will have an estimated value of £4,600. What is the annual depreciation if the straight line method is used?

(a) (£14,600 − £4,600)/5 = £2,000
(b) (£15,160 − £4,600)/5 = £2,112
(c) (£14,440 − £4,600)/5 = £1,968
(d) (£15,000 − £4,600)/5 = £2,080

9 A machine is bought for £18,000, plus £3,000 installation costs. It is to be depreciated on a diminishing balance basis using a rate of 60% p.a. What is the depreciation to be charged in the *second* year of the asset's ownership?

(a) £12,600
(b) £4,320
(c) £5,040
(d) £8,400

10 By the end of its financial year, a company has total revenue of £7 million, Cost of sales £5 million, and total expenses £3 million. Which one of the following statements is true about this company?

(a) It makes both a gross loss and an operating loss
(b) It makes a gross loss and an operating profit
(c) It makes both a gross profit and an operating profit
(d) It makes a gross profit and an operating loss

Self-study questions

Questions marked with this symbol (#) indicate that the suggested answers are available to lecturers only – other answers are given in Appendix 2.

3.1 Vonelle plc sells computer equipment. The company accountant asks your advice about the following two product lines:

- **20 tablet computers**: original total cost £9,000. They have been unsold for 3 years and the company sales manager believes that the only way of selling them would be to upgrade the memory (at a cost of £75 per machine) and sell them at £350 each.
- **10 laptops**: originally bought for £400 each to meet a special order, but the customer went out of business before delivery. Each machine is overprinted with that customer's logo. The machines could be sold for an estimated £600 each, but only if the logo was erased at a cost of £10 per machine.

(a) Explain what is meant by the phrase 'inventory should be valued at the lower of cost and net realisable value'.
(b) Explain, with reasons, how each of the two product lines should be accounted for in the financial summaries of the company.

3.2 Toronto Manufacturing commenced business on 1 January 2011. On that date it bought machinery costing £200,000. The machinery is to be depreciated on the straight line method over 10 years with an estimated residual value of £24,400. Operating profits after depreciation for its first three years were as follows:

Year ended 31 December 2011	£160,000
Year ended 31 December 2012	£190,000
Year ended 31 December 2013	£230,000

(a) Explain what is meant by *depreciation*.
(b) Calculate the annual depreciation charged on the machinery in each of the three years.
(c) If, instead of using the straight line method, they had used the diminishing balance method (using a 19% per annum depreciation rate) to depreciate the machinery over the same time period and to the same residual value, what operating profit after depreciation would have been recorded for each of the three years? Explain the results shown in your calculations.

3.3 A business property is rented at £2,500 per month. During the year ended 31 December 2013 the business paid 15 months rent, 4 months of which related to rent owing on 1 January 2013. One month's rent was owing on 31 December 2013.

(a) Explain what is meant by an accrual.
(b) What is the total of the rent expense to be shown in the income statement for the year ended 31 December 2013?
(c) What information relating to rent would be shown in the statement of financial position as at 31 December 2013?

3.4# A cosmetics company rents advertising space in a train station at £5,000 per month. On 31 December 2012 the business had prepaid 7 months of the 2013 rental. During the year ended 31 December 2013 the business paid a further 10 months' rent, part of which was prepaid for 2014.

(a) Explain what is meant by a prepayment.
(b) What is the total of the advertising expense to be shown in the income statement for the year ended 31 December 2013?
(c) What information relating to advertising would be shown in the statement of financial position as at 31 December 2013?

3.5# Pierre Dubois has been in business for many years, and his financial results (in no particular order) for the year ending 31 January 2014 were as follows:

	£
Trade receivables at the year-end	5,500
Administration costs excluding depreciation	34,000
Trade payables at the year-end	6,000
Non-current liability (bank loan) at the year-end	5,000
Non-current assets (net of depreciation) at the year-end	26,000
Revenue	142,000
Depreciation for the year	8,000

	£
Bank balance (asset) at the year-end	2,500
Cost of sales	56,000
Inventory at the year-end	6,000
Owners' equity at the year-end	29,000

From the above information produce Pierre's income statement for the year ending 31 January 2014 and his statement of financial position at that date.

Case study

Esmeralda appears, then disappears

Marvin (see previous case studies) was finding that as the year progressed he was in great demand. He felt he needed an assistant so decided to employ Esmeralda, who had previously been chief inventor at Kaboosh Limited, a company manufacturing equipment for magic tricks and novelties. As a leaving present, that company had given Esmeralda a 'disappearing lady' apparatus. Being unsentimental about such things, she promptly sold it to Marvin on 1 December for £2,000. Esmeralda started to appear (and disappear) as part of Marvin's magic act.

After two months in her new job, Esmeralda persuaded Marvin to diversify by buying in items made by her former employers and selling them at the children's parties to the parents and guests.

During the following January, Marvin received a letter from his bank, asking for financial summaries for his first six months in business. January is a quiet month for him, so he spent some time producing the following information:

	£
Cash and bank receipts	
Sales of novelties bought from Kaboosh Ltd	2,500
Appearance fees as entertainer	18,320
Cash and bank payments	
Kaboosh Ltd for novelties to be sold	1,500
Wages	1,200
Kazam Limited for playing cards	400
Travel expenses	2,600
Rabbits and rabbit food, less returns (expenses)	430
Cleaning	140
Esmeralda for 'disappearing lady' apparatus	2,000
Marvin's drawings	11,890
Other information	
Cash balance at 31 December	560
Bank balance at 31 December	120

	£
Total invoices received from Kaboosh Ltd up to 31 December	1,700
Inventory of unsold novelties at cost price at 31 December	80
(Note: there was no 'opening inventory.')	
Amounts owing from customers for novelties	350
Other non-current assets still owned at 31 December:	
Costume at cost	3,000
Magic book at cost	2,000
Opening equity (see case study in Chapter 2)	5,020

Notes

1 The costume, the magic book and the playing cards are to be grouped as 'Magician's equipment' and depreciated at 20% p.a. (that is, over 5 years), straight line method, with no residual value. Note that the depreciation period here is only 6 months.

2 The 'disappearing lady' apparatus is to be depreciated at 40% p.a. on the diminishing balance method. The full 6 months' depreciation is to be deducted, even though it was owned for only part of that time.

3 Marvin owed £100 wages to Esmeralda at 31 December, and had paid £50 in December for a train ticket which was going to be used in January.

Required

Prepare Marvin's income statement for the 6 months to 31 December, and a statement of financial position as at that date. Note that in the income statement, gross profit on novelties should be calculated first and the fees added to that before deducting the expenses.

Answers are in Appendix 3

Chapter 4

The income statement and statement of financial position

Objectives

When you have read this chapter you will be able to:

- Understand the different ways in which the income statement can be presented for various types of business models and organisations
- Be aware that limited companies publish financial summaries which must conform to specific rules and regulations
- Produce a detailed income statement and statement of financial position from a trial balance, adjusting for such items as accruals, prepayments and depreciation

4.1 Introduction

We saw (in the previous chapter) how the financial summaries reflect the application of accounting principles to financial information. The two key summaries we have already briefly encountered are the *income statement*, showing income and expenses for a financial period, and the *statement of financial position* showing assets, liabilities and equity at the end of the financial period (see Figure 4.1). In this chapter we look in more detail at these, showing how the statements can be made more meaningful for different types of businesses.

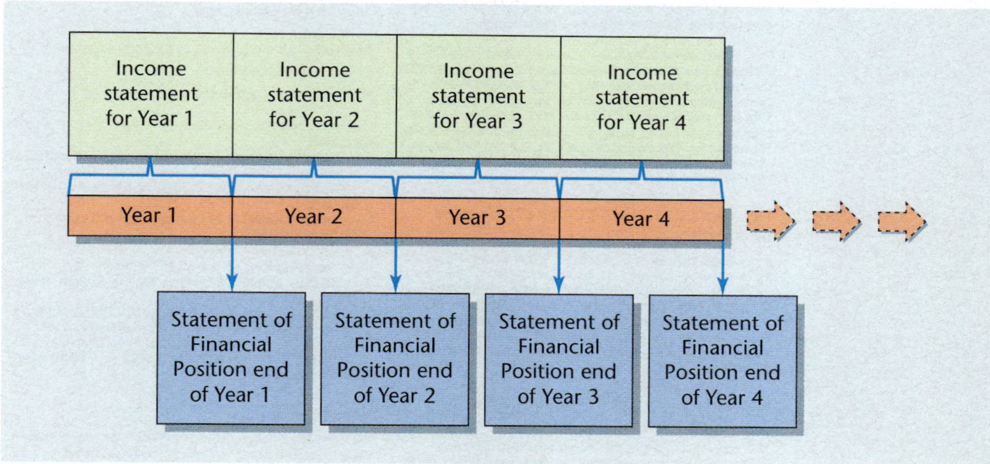

Figure 4.1 Timeline for summarising financial information

4.2 The income statement

The profit or loss as shown in the income statement is calculated by comparing total revenue with total expenses which, according to the underlying assumption of the accrual basis, must reflect *all* the relevant transactions for the financial period, not just those which represent cash inflows or outflows. Jokes are sometimes made about accountants who, when asked by a business owner what profit their business has made, would reply, 'How much would you like it to be?', implying that by skilful accounting surgery the final figures could be as high or low as suited the needs of the business. Because some of the information (such as depreciation) found in the financial summaries relies on estimates, it is true to say that accounting is not an exact science. However, in the past 30 years, and particularly since the formation of national and international accounting regulatory boards, rules have been tightened in a concerted attempt to overcome the real anxieties expressed by users regarding the reliability of information. All large businesses are required to appoint an independent auditor who reviews the organisation's published financial reports and comments on the degree to which they comply with the fundamental qualitative characteristic of *faithful representation* (see Chapter 1). The largest firms of auditors (known as the 'Big Four') are PwC, Deloitte, Ernst & Young and KPMG, and they number the vast majority of the world's

Scan the following QR code with your QR reader to take you to the website of Deloitte:

leading commercial organisations amongst their clients. Figure 4.2 is an example of one such auditor's report addressed to the members (owners) of Compass Group plc, a multinational catering company:

Consolidated financial statements

Independent auditor's report to the members of Compass Group PLC

Introduction

We have audited the Group financial statements of Compass Group PLC for the year ended 30 September 2011 which comprise the consolidated income statement, the consolidated statement of comprehensive income, the consolidated balance sheet, the consolidated cash flow statement, the consolidated statement of changes in equity, the accounting policies and the related notes 1 to 36. The financial reporting framework that has been applied in their preparation is applicable law and International Financial Reporting Standards (IFRSs) as adopted by the European Union.

This Report is made solely to the Company's members, as a body, in accordance with Chapter 3 of Part 16 of the Companies Act 2006. Our audit work has been undertaken so that we might state to the Company's members those matters we are required to state to them in an auditor's report and for no other purpose. To the fullest extent permitted by law, we do not accept or assume responsibility to anyone other than the Company and the Company's members as a body, for our audit work, for this Report, or for the opinions we have formed.

Respective responsibilities of directors and auditor

As explained more fully in the Directors' Responsibilities Statement, the directors are responsible for the preparation of the Group financial statements and for being satisfied that they give a true and fair view. Our responsibility is to audit and express an opinion on the Group financial statements in accordance with applicable law and International Standards on Auditing (UK and Ireland). Those standards require us to comply with the Auditing Practices Board's Ethical Standards for Auditors.

Scope of the audit of the financial statements

An audit involves obtaining evidence about the amounts and disclosures in the financial statements sufficient to give reasonable assurance that the financial statements are free from material misstatement, whether caused by fraud or error. This includes an assessment of: whether the accounting policies are appropriate to the Group's circumstances and have been consistently applied and adequately disclosed; the reasonableness of significant accounting estimates made by the directors; and the overall presentation of the financial statements. In addition, we read all the financial and non-financial information in the Annual Report to identify material inconsistencies with the audited financial statements. If we become aware of any apparent material misstatements or inconsistencies we consider the implications for our report.

Opinion on financial statements

In our opinion the Group financial statements:
- give a true and fair view of the state of the Group's affairs as at 30 September 2011 and of its profit for the year then ended;
- have been properly prepared in accordance with IFRSs as adopted by the European Union; and
- have been prepared in accordance with the requirements of the Companies Act 2006 and Article 4 of the IAS Regulation.

Opinion on other matters prescribed by the Companies Act 2006

In our opinion:
- the part of the Directors' Remuneration Report to be audited has been properly prepared in accordance with the Companies Act 2006; and
- the information given in the Directors' Report for the financial year for which the financial statements are prepared is consistent with the Group financial statements.

Matters on which we are required to report by exception

We have nothing to report in respect of the following:

Under the Companies Act 2006 we are required to report to you if, in our opinion:
- the part of the Directors' Remuneration Report to be audited is not in agreement with the accounting records and returns;
- certain disclosures of directors' remuneration specified by law are not made; or
- we have not received all the information and explanations we require for our audit.

Under the Listing Rules we are required to review:
- the directors' statement contained within the Business Review in relation to going concern;
- the part of the Corporate Governance Statement relating to the Company's compliance with the nine provisions of the UK Corporate Governance Code specified for our review; and
- certain elements of the report to shareholders by the Board on directors' remuneration.

Other matters

We have reported separately on the Parent Company financial statements of Compass Group PLC for the year ended 30 September 2011.

Ian Waller

Ian Waller (Senior Statutory Auditor)

for and on behalf of Deloitte LLP
Chartered Accountants and Statutory Auditor
London, United Kingdom
23 November 2011

Figure 4.2 Auditor's report

Source: Compass Group plc, 2012

Sometimes an auditor finds it difficult or impossible to comment on a company's financial reports. The following News clip explains particular problems that Deloitte found when attempting to audit several Chinese companies:

4.2.1 Format of the income statement

Regardless of the size of the organisation, an income statement will be produced at least annually. When incorporated within a detailed annual report it is likely to be presented in a highly summarised version but with comprehensive notes also provided. For example, the income statement of one of the world's largest oil companies, BP, shown on page 180

News clip

Auditor quits Chinese group Boshiwa FT

By Robert Cookson in Hong Kong

Deloitte has resigned as auditor of Boshiwa International, a Chinese maker of children's apparel that has licences for brands including Harry Potter and Manchester United, over corporate governance concerns.

Shares in Boshiwa plunged 36 per cent in Hong Kong on Thursday on the news before being suspended from trading.

Boshiwa is one of dozens of Chinese companies whose auditors have resigned in recent years amid concerns about corporate governance. In its resignation letter, Deloitte said it was unable to complete its audit of Boshiwa because the company's management had not provided enough financial information.

Deloitte said that it had "concerns about matters pervasive to the financial statements", including the existence and commercial substance of recorded prepayments amounting to Rbm392m ($62m) to a supplier of the group.

In a filing to the Hong Kong stock exchange, Boshiwa said it expected to be unable to publish its annual results as planned by the end of the month, which would put it in breach of stock exchange rules.

Boshiwa raised $321m in September 2010 through an initial public offering in Hong Kong arranged by UBS, Credit Suisse, and Bocom International. At the time, Chinese consumer stocks were strongly in favour with investors so the shares sold at the top of the price range.

Since listing, however, Boshiwa's shares have lost more than two-thirds of their value. Investors have grown more cautious about Chinese companies because of fears of a slowdown in the mainland economy as well as concerns about corporate governance.

Dozens of Chinese groups listed in the US, the UK and Hong Kong have been accused of fraud or accounting discrepancies over the past two years, often by shortsellers hoping to profit from declines in their shares.

Last year, Deloitte quit as auditor of Longtop after accusing the company of "very serious defects", including faking its bank statements. The software group, which raised $210m in 2007 via a New York IPO organised by Deutsche Bank and Goldman Sachs, delisted from the New York Stock Exchange last August.

Deloitte also last year resigned as auditor of Real Gold Mining, saying that the Chinese gold miner had failed to disclose material information involving related parties. Real Gold's Hong Kong-listed shares have been suspended since May.

Boshiwa said it was "disappointed" with Deloitte's decision to resign and would appoint a new auditor in due course. The company added that it is considering establishing a special committee to investigate the circumstances.

Source: The Financial Times, 16 March 2012

of a 300-page report, gave just *20* lines of information to cover the revenue and expenses of an organisation with an annual income in excess of $375 billion! However, highly detailed information on each of the figures within the income statement was also available within the report. When a business's own management needs to assess its performance it will produce a more detailed analysis of the income statement for its own purposes. The format of such an income statement will vary depending upon whether the organisation is:

- A manufacturing business (producing the goods they sell, for example a dairy company converting milk into cheese)

- A trading business (buying in goods for resale, for example an electronics retailer purchasing computers and televisions from Japanese manufacturers) or
- a service business (selling a service, for example an architect designing a new hotel to be built in Moscow).

There will be further differences depending upon whether the organisation has been structured as a:

- Sole proprietorship (a one-person business)
- Partnership (two or more owners of the business) or
- Limited liability company (a business with shareholders).

4.2.2 Manufacturing businesses

Companies which manufacture the products that they sell will have specific costs relating to the manufacturing process. They are divided between:

- *Direct costs*, which can be readily identified with the items being produced. For example, in a ship-building company, the cost of metal and the other fittings used to construct the ship, plus the wages paid to the metalworkers and fitters, are direct costs. In a chocolate factory, direct costs would be the cost of cocoa, sugar, colourings and other ingredients. Another name for direct costs is *prime* costs.
- *Indirect costs* are all other manufacturing expenses which cannot be directly associated with the items being produced. These could include the rent of a shipyard or factory, the wages paid to supervisors, the cost of running the staff canteen, etc.

More information regarding the classification of costs is given later (in Chapter 10).

Activity 4.1

During the year to 31 December 2014, Lars Anderson incurs the following costs in his factory, which produces cakes for sale to hotels and restaurants:

	£
Ingredients	102,952
Wages to factory workers	74,120
Wages owed to factory workers	6,300
Factory rent and rates	12,500
Factory light and heat	8,543
Wages to supervisors	26,100
Depreciation of factory machinery	3,910
Inventory of raw materials on 1 January 2014	12,400
Inventory of raw materials on 31 December 2014	11,500
Partly completed inventory (work in progress) on 1 January 2014	1,540
Partly completed inventory (work in progress) on 31 December 2014	640

Calculate the *cost of manufacturing* (for inclusion as part of the 'cost of sales' in the income statement) for the year ended 31 December 2014.

Answer

Lars Anderson
Cost of manufacturing for the year ended 31 December 2014

	£	£
Raw materials		
Opening inventory at 1 January 2014	12,400	
Add Purchases of raw materials	102,952	
	115,352	
Less Closing inventory at 31 December 2014	(11,500)	
Cost of raw materials		103,852
Other direct costs:		
Production labour (74,120 + 6,300)		80,420
Prime cost of production		184,272
Indirect factory costs:		
Rent and rates	12,500	
Light and heat	8,543	
Wages to supervisors	26,100	
Depreciation of factory machinery	3,910	
		51,053
		235,325
Add Opening work in progress	1,540	
Less Closing work in progress	(640)	
		900
Cost of manufacturing		236,225

Stop and think

This summarises all the factory costs for the period, dividing them between direct and indirect, and adjusting for opening and closing inventories of raw materials and work in progress. The final total – the cost of manufacturing – will be included in the income statement as part of the 'cost of sales' total when calculating the gross profit. The analysis of manufacturing costs provides extremely useful information which will be further considered later (in Chapters 10–12). For example, if the factory had produced 500,000 cakes in 2014 we can calculate the average cost of producing one cake as being £236,225 divided by 500,000 = 47.25 p

The income statement for Lars Anderson's business can now be completed. Assume that:

- Sales in the year totalled £684,500
- Opening inventories of finished products were valued at £42,380
- Closing inventories of finished products were valued at £65,190
- Selling expenses totalled £84,300
- Administration expenses totalled £65,160
- All other expenses (including depreciation) totalled £55,862.

Lars Anderson
Income statement for the year ended 31 December 2014

	£	£
Revenue		684,500
Less **Cost of sales**		
Opening inventory of finished products	42,380	
Cost of manufacturing (see previous calculation)	236,225	
	278,605	
Less Closing inventory of finished products	(65,190)	
		(213,415)
Gross profit		471,085
Less **Expenses**		
Selling expenses	84,300	
Administration expenses	65,160	
General expenses (including depreciation)	55,862	
		(205,322)
Operating profit		265,763

4.2.3 Trading businesses

If a business buys *all* the goods it sells (i.e. does not manufacture them itself) then the *cost of manufacturing* calculation as seen in the previous section is irrelevant. The income statement would be very similar to that of Lars Anderson as shown above, though 'cost of manufacturing' would be replaced by the 'Purchases' (the value of the goods for resale purchased in the year). Activity 4.2 shows an income statement where the business both manufactures *and* buys in the products that it sells.

Activity 4.2

Assume that Lars Anderson (see Activity 4.1), has an identical twin brother called Benni Anderson who runs another cake factory in another town which (miraculously) has recorded exactly the same financial information as Lars' business, with the one exception that in addition to his own manufactured cakes, Benni buys in and sells speciality wedding cakes from another manufacturer, the Icing and Splicing Wedding Cake Company. Benni provides the following *additional* information for the year ended 31 December 2014:

	£
Sales to hotels and restaurants for the year *(all products, including wedding cakes)*	710,200
Purchases from the Icing and Splicing Wedding Cake Company	25,670
Total inventory of cakes *(including wedding cakes)* on 1 January 2014	46,100
Total inventory of cakes *(including wedding cakes)* on 31 December 2014	69,700
Additional selling costs related to wedding cakes	10,000

Prepare Benni's income statement for the year ended 31 December 2014.

Answer

Benni Anderson
Income statement for the year ended 31 December 2014

	£	£
Revenue		710,200
Less **Cost of sales**		
Opening inventory	46,100	
Cost of manufacturing	236,225	
Purchases of wedding cakes	25,670	
	307,995	
Less Closing inventory	(69,700)	
		(238,295)
Gross profit		471,905
Less **Expenses**		
Selling expenses	94,300	
Administration expenses	65,160	
General expenses (including depreciation)	55,862	
		(215,322)
Operating profit		256,583

Stop and think

At what point can a transaction be *recognised* as revenue within an income statement? You may think that the answer would always be 'when a sale has been made', but consider the following sequence of events. At which one of the stages can we record a sale?

1 Initial enquiry from a customer
2 Estimate of price given to customer
3 Sample products requested
4 Customer places order
5 Product made
6 Product delivered
7 Product accepted by customer
8 Customer invoiced
9 Customer pays

It is only at stage 7 – the customer accepting the product – that the revenue can be recognised and included within the income statement.

4.2.4 Service businesses

A service business is one that, as the name implies, provides a service to customers and clients in return for payment. Examples include professionals such as lawyers, accountants and designers. In such cases neither 'cost of manufacturing' nor *gross* profit calculations would be appropriate. Instead, a relatively simple income statement can be drawn up that starts with the revenue earned from the services provided and then deducts expenses to calculate operating profit, as in the example of an architect (using invented figures) which follows:

Frank Wright-Lloyd, Architect
Income statement for the year ended 30 April 2014

		£
Revenue (fees from clients)		264,297
Less **Expenses**		
Office expenses	92,162	
Travel expenses	18,190	
General expenses (including depreciation)	55,862	
		(166,214)
Operating profit		98,083

The analysis of expenses can be much more detailed than in this example if required by the business. In the above example (and also for the Anderson brothers examples) only three categories of expense have been included, but a more detailed analysis could be provided.

4.3 Income statements of partnerships and limited companies

Later (in Chapter 6) we look in detail at the types of business organisations that have more than one owner. Commonly these are either partnerships or limited liability companies. In our example shown above we have kept things simple by looking at the income statements of one-owner businesses (sole proprietorships). In such cases, all the operating profit is added to (or operating loss deducted from) the equity when calculating the closing value of the owner's investment in the business, as shown in the statement of financial position. In the case of partnerships (which, by definition, have at least two owners) further detail must be added after the calculation of the operating profit (or loss) to reflect any financial implications of the partnership agreement. For example, in a two-person partnership you cannot assume that profits are split equally. Also, there may be specific terms, for example where one partner receives a fixed amount of profit, with the remainder being allocated according to agreed percentages. The part of the income statement that allocates profits or losses is sometimes called an *appropriation account*. For a business operating as a limited liability company, the appropriation account shows deductions for taxation liabilities and transfers to reserves. Activity 4.3 (part (a)) gives the outline layout of the income statement of a partnership, and Activity 4.3 (part (b)) gives the outline layout of the income statement of a limited liability company. These topics are covered in more detail later (in Chapter 6).

Activity 4.3

Income statements of partnerships and limited liability companies

Part (a) Partnerships

Assume that Lars and Benni Anderson (see Activities 4.1 and 4.2) decide to form a partnership on 1 January 2015 and they have agreed to share profits in the proportions: Lars 3/5, Benni 2/5. Their 2015 results are exactly the same as the combined data of the two individual businesses in 2014. Show the partnership's income statement for the year ended 31 December 2015.

Answer

The Lars and Benni Anderson Partnership
Income statement for the year ended 31 December 2015

	£	£
Revenue (684,500 + 710,200)		1,394,700
Less **Cost of sales**		
Opening inventory (42,380 + 46,100)	88,480	
Cost of manufacturing (236,225 × 2)	472,450	
Purchases of wedding cakes	25,670	
	586,600	
Less closing inventory (65,190 + 69,700)	(134,890)	
		(451,710)

	£	£
Gross profit		942,990
Less **Expenses**		
Selling expenses (84,300 + 94,300)	178,600	
Administration expenses (65,160 + 65,160)	130,320	
General expenses (including depreciation) (55,862 + 55,862)	111,724	
		(420,644)
Operating profit		522,346
Divided as follows:		
Lars Anderson (3/5)	313,408	
Benni Anderson (2/5)	208,938	
		522,346

Part (b) Limited liability companies

In a partnership or a sole proprietorship (one-person unincorporated business) the partners or owner are *personally* responsible for taxation on any profits. However, a limited liability company *itself* is responsible for tax on any profits, and this must be shown on the income statement. Any remaining profits can then be transferred to the company's reserves (part of the company's equity). Assume that on 1 January 2016 Lars and Benni Anderson transfer their partnership into a limited liability company (a separate legal entity with shareholders) named The Anderson Brothers Limited. Operating results were exactly the same as for 2015, except that directors' salaries were paid (Lars £150,000, Benni £100,000). A tax rate of 20% of the operating profit has been assumed. Show the income statement for the year ended 31 December 2016.

Answer

The Anderson Brothers Limited
Income statement for the year ended 31 December 2016

	£	£
Revenue		1,394,700
Less **Cost of sales** (details as in partnership example)		(451,710)
Gross profit		942,990
Less **Expenses**		
Directors' salaries	250,000	
Selling	178,600	
Administration	130,320	
General expenses (including depreciation)	111,724	

	£	£
		(670,644)
Operating profit before taxation		272,346
Less **Taxation**(20% × £272,346)		(54,469)
Retained profit for the year		217,877

Stop and think

Having looked at the *fictional* cake businesses run by the Andersons, Figure 4.3 shows an example of an *actual* bakery company (Greggs plc), which manufactures and retails a range of products including sandwiches, cakes and drinks.

Greggs plc
Consolidated income statement
for the 52 weeks ended 31 December 2011 (2010: 52 weeks ended 1 January 2011)

	2011 Total	2010 Total
	£'000	£'000
Revenue	**701,088**	662,326
Cost of sales	**(272,778)**	(252,651)
Gross profit	**428,310**	409,675
Distribution and selling costs	**(342,641)**	(321,261)
Administrative expenses	**(34,903)**	(36,049)
Other income	**9,665**	-
Operating profit	**60,431**	52,365
Finance income	**69**	158
Profit before tax	**60,500**	52,523
Income tax	**(15,997)**	(14,589)
Profit for the financial year attributable to equity holders of the Parent	**44,503**	37,934
	=======	=======

Figure 4.3 Income statement
Source: Greggs plc income statement (adapted), 2012

4.4 The statement of financial position

This is the summary of a business's assets, liabilities and capital, reflecting the accounting equation Assets − Liabilities = Equity. Such a statement can be produced at *any* time from the accounting system, but businesses are expected to produce, as a minimum, a statement of financial position at the end of their financial year. Although the main headings of *non-current* and *current* assets and *non-current* and *current* liabilities are universal, the 'equity' part of the statement varies according to whether the business is structured as a sole proprietorship, a partnership or a limited company.

Activity 4.4

Lars Anderson (see Activity 4.1 above) needs to produce his statement of financial position at 31 December 2014. At that date, in addition to the values of closing inventory (raw materials, work in progress and finished products) Lars advises you of the following information as at 31 December 2014:

1 The total depreciated value of non-current assets is £96,500.
2 Trade receivables totalled £18,300 and trade payables totalled £34,620.
3 Prepayments amounted to £900 and accruals totalled £2,300.
4 Cash equivalents (bank balance) are £2,100 and cash amounted to £670.
5 The business had a long-term liability of £45,000.

Show Lars Anderson's statement of financial position at 31 December 2014 from the above information.

Answer

	£	£	£
Non-current assets (depreciated value)			96,500
Current assets			
Inventory (11,500 + 640 + 65,190)		77,330	
Trade receivables		18,300	
Prepayments		900	
Cash equivalents (Bank)		2,100	
Cash		670	
		99,300	
Less **Current liabilities**			
Trade payables	34,620		
Accruals	2,300		
		(36,920)	
Net current assets			62,380
			158,880
Less **Non-current liabilities**			(45,000)
Total net assets			**113,880**
Equity			**113,880**

Activity 4.5

The partnership of Lars and Benni Anderson (see Activity 4.3a above) needs to produce its statement of financial position at 31 December 2015. For simplicity, assume that all the values shown in Activity 4.4 also apply to the partnership. The statement of financial position for the partnership would be exactly the same as in Activity 4.4, except that the equity value would be split according to how much each partner had invested, the amount of profit allocated and how much each had withdrawn from the partnership. For example, at 31 December 2015, if Lars had £64,200 invested and Benni £49,680, then the equity section of the statement would be rewritten as follows:

	£	£
Equity		
Lars Anderson	64,200	
Benni Anderson	49,680	
		113,880

All other details in the statement (assets and liabilities) would be unchanged.

Activity 4.6

The limited liability company set up by Lars and Benni Anderson (see Activity 4.3b above) needs to produce its statement of financial position at 31 December 2016. For simplicity, assume that all the values shown in Activity 4.4 also apply to the limited liability company. Although the vast majority of the information would stay the same, we would also need to show *taxation* as a current liability. Equity value would be split between the value of the share capital (shares bought by the owners, assume £10,000) and the company reserves (retained profits, assume £49,411). (Further details are given in Chapter 6.)

The Anderson Brothers Limited
Statement of financial position at 31 December 2016

		£	£
Non-current assets (depreciated value)			96,500
Current assets			
Inventory (11,500 + 640 + 65,190)		77,330	
Trade receivables		18,300	
Prepayments		900	
Cash equivalents		2,100	
Cash		670	
		99,300	
Less **Current liabilities**			
Trade payables	34,620		
Accruals	2,300		
Taxation	54,469		

	£	£
	(91,389)	
Net current assets		7,911
		104,411
Less **Non-current liabilities**		(45,000)
Total net assets		**59,411**
Equity		
Share capital	10,000	
Reserves	49,411	
		59,411

Did you know?

Some countries use the term 'balance sheet' instead of 'statement of financial position', particularly for smaller businesses, but they mean exactly the same.

4.5 Published income statements and statements of financial position

Scan the following QR code with your QR reader to take you to the annual report section of Glaxo SmithKline, a leading pharmaceuticals company.

Most sole proprietorships and partnerships do not have to make their financial summaries available to anyone outside the business itself – other than the tax authorities and possibly the business's bank. In such businesses, members of the public have no right of access to the information. However, those business organisations that have *limited liability* (where, simply, the owners' potential loss if the business fails is limited to the amount they have invested) must make their summarised financial information *available to the public* by way of published accounts. Small and medium-sized companies are required to reveal rather less financial information than larger companies, but as a minimum for even the smallest company, a statement of financial position would be put on the public record on an annual basis. Larger businesses – particularly those with shares trading on stock exchanges – are required to publish very comprehensive information, with the annual reports often extending over 200 pages. If you want to download a full annual report, use the QR code shown in the margin. This takes you to the website of Glaxo SmithKline, a leading pharmaceutical company.

We shall be looking in more detail at businesses with limited liability later (in Chapter 6).

4.6 Preparing the summaries from accounting data

Having taken an overview of the broad content of the income statement and statement of financial position, we can investigate the way in which these summaries can be constructed from the accounting data contained within the double-entry system.

Activity 4.7 presents a trial balance (a list of all active ledger balances at the end of the financial period), together with additional information that reflects the further adjustments required (inventory, accruals, prepayments and depreciation) to ensure that the information complies with the underlying assumption of the accrual basis, as discussed earlier (in Chapter 1).

Activity 4.7

From the following trial balance, prepare the income statement and statement of financial position of Carole Grey (a sole proprietor) for the year ended 30 April 2014:

	Dr £	Cr £
Bank	13,050	
Cash	250	
Electricity	4,000	
Equity at 1 May 2013		12,100
Loan (repayable 2025)		10,000
Motor cars – cost	22,000	
Motor cars – depreciation to 1 May 2013		13,200
Office fittings – cost	20,000	
Office fittings – depreciation to 1 May 2013		10,800
Opening inventory at 1 May 2013	90,000	
Owner's drawings	25,000	
Trade payables		27,600
Purchases	207,900	
Trade receivables	35,200	
Rent	15,000	
Revenue		420,700
Wages and salaries	62,000	
	494,400	494,400

Notes:

1 Closing inventory at 30 April 2014 was £110,000.
2 Electricity of £1,000 is to be accrued at the year-end.
3 Rent of £3,000 has been prepaid at the year-end.
4 Depreciation on the office fittings is calculated over 5 years using the straight line method, assuming a residual value of £2,000.
5 Depreciation on the car is calculated at 60% using the diminishing balance method.

Answer

As Carole is a sole proprietor her income statement follows the example shown in Activity 4.2 above. Before constructing the statement we need to follow a series of steps:

Step 1

Read through the trial balance items, making a mental note of possible problem areas – these could include the depreciation calculation and the adjustment for accruals and prepayments.

Step 2

Read through the notes, and write in the adjustments needed for accruals and prepayments against the relevant account names.

Electricity *(+1000)*	4,000
Rent *(–3000)*	15,000

Step 3

Using the information in Notes 4 and 5, compute the year's depreciation charge. The calculations are as follows:

Motor cars	
Cost	22,000
Less Depreciation to 1 May 2013	(13,200)
Depreciated value at 1 May 2013	8,800
Depreciation 60% × £8,800	**(5,280)**

Office fittings

(Cost − Estimated residual value)/5

= (£20,000 − £2,000)/5

= £18,000/5 = **£3,600**

Again, we can make a note on the trial balance of the two depreciation calculations:

Motor cars: depreciation to 1 May 2013 *(+5,280)*	13,200
Office fittings: depreciation to 1 May 2013 *(+3,600)*	10,800

Note that only the bracketed figures appear in the year's income statement, but the *total* depreciation of £18,480 (£13,200 + £5,280) and £14,400 (£10,800 + £3,600) will be shown in the statement of financial position.

Step 4

Start the income statement by writing the heading at the top of a new page, drawing two columns about 3 cm wide on the right-hand side. The first part of the summary ends with the gross profit. Remember the sequence **'Revenue − Cost of sales = Gross profit'**. Tick items in the trial balance as you enter them.

Step 5

Complete the summary by entering the remaining items of revenue and expenses, not forgetting the accrual and prepayment. Don't forget to include only the current year's depreciation. The completed income statement is shown below.

Carole Grey
Income statement for the year ended 30 April 2014

	£	£
Revenue		420,700
Less **Cost of sales**		
Opening inventory at 1 May 2013	90,000	
Add Purchases	207,900	
	297,900	
Less Closing inventory at 30 April 2014	(110,000)	
		(187,900)
Gross profit		232,800
Less **Expenses**		
Electricity	5,000	
Depreciation: motor cars	5,280	
Depreciation: office fittings	3,600	
Rent	12,000	
Wages and salaries	62,000	
		(87,880)
Operating profit		**144,920**

Stop and think

Having completed the income statement, the remaining information in the trial balance allows us to enter the details of assets, liabilities and the owner's equity onto the statement of financial position, as shown below. As Carole is a sole proprietor, the statement of financial position follows the example shown in Activity 4.4 above, but we can include some extra detail to show how we have computed the value of the non-current assets and the final equity value.

Carole Grey
Statement of financial position as at 30 April 2014

	Cost	Depreciation	Depreciated value
	£	£	£
Non-current assets			
Office fittings	20,000	14,400	5,600
Motor cars	22,000	18,480	3,520
	42,000	32,880	9,120
Current assets			
Inventory		110,000	
Trade receivables		35,200	
Prepayments		3,000	
Cash equivalents: Bank		13,050	
Cash		250	
		161,500	
Less **Current liabilities**			
Trade payables	27,600		
Accruals	1,000		
		(28,600)	
Net current assets			132,900
			142,020
Less **Non-current liabilities (loan)**			(10,000)
Total net assets			**132,020**
Equity			
Opening balance, 1 May 2013		12,100	
Add operating profit		144,920	
		157,020	
Less Drawings		(25,000)	
Closing balance, 30 April 2014			**132,020**

4.7 Summary

The key components of the financial summaries for manufacturers, traders and service providers are as follows:

	Manufacturer	Trader	Service provider
Cost of manufacturing	Required, showing direct and indirect costs of manufacture, as adjusted for any work-in-progress	Not required	Not required
Gross profit calculation	Required, including the cost of *manufacturing* as part of the 'cost of sales' calculation	Required, Sales *less* Cost of Sales = Gross Profit	Not required
Income statement	Required, showing Gross Profit *less* Expenses = Operating profit (or loss)	Required, showing Gross Profit *less* Expenses = Operating profit (or loss)	Required, showing Revenue from clients *less* Expenses = Operating profit (or loss)
Statement of financial position	Required. Note that current assets of a manufacturing business might include three types of closing inventory: raw materials, work in progress and finished goods	Required. Note that the only inventory figure included as a current asset is closing inventory of unsold goods	Required. Note that service providers do not usually have an inventory figure

The key differences and similarities between the income statement and statement of financial position of sole proprietorships, partnerships and limited liability companies are as follows:

	Sole proprietorship	Partnership	Limited liability company
Income statement	The operating profit or loss is transferred directly to the owner's equity account	The operating profit or loss is divided according to the agreement between the partners, and then transferred to each partner's equity account	Taxation is deducted from the operating profit, and the remaining profit is then transferred to reserves. Salaries to directors are included as one of the overhead expenses in the income statement
Statement of financial position	'Usual' format for assets and liabilities (i.e. divided between current and non-current). Equity represents the sole owner's investment	'Usual' format for assets and liabilities (i.e. divided between current and non-current). Each partner's share of the equity is shown separately	'Usual' format for assets and liabilities (i.e. divided between current and non-current). The company's equity capital is shown together with its reserves

4.8 Chapter glossary

Appropriation account An additional part of the income statement, inserted after the operating profit or loss, showing, for a partnership, the financial implications of the partnership agreement or, for a limited company, taxation and reserve transfers.

Auditor An independent accountant who reports on whether the financial summaries reflect a faithful representation of a business's affairs.

Cost of manufacturing The first part of a manufacturing business's income statement, showing all the costs, direct and indirect, of producing the products made in the period.

Direct costs Costs which can be readily identified with the items being produced, for example sugar in a biscuit factory.

Gross profit The profit before overhead expenses are deducted

Indirect costs All manufacturing costs other than direct costs, (e.g. the rent of a biscuit factory).

Loss An excess of expenses over revenue.

Operating profit or loss The profit or loss remaining after all overheads have been deducted from the gross profit

Prime costs Another name for direct costs.

Profit An excess of revenue over expenses.

Work in progress Partly completed inventory.

Only accessible on Android-based devices.

Additional resources

Now work through the various exercises and problems that you can find within the My Accounting Lab that are relevant to this chapter. Either use the QR code shown in the margin (if you use an Android-based device), or visit www.myaccountinglab.com for the log-in page.

Self-check questions

The answer to these questions are in Appendix 1.

1 Profit is calculated by:

(a) Comparing assets with liabilities
(b) Comparing assets with expenses
(c) Comparing revenue with expenses
(d) Comparing revenue with liabilities

2 An independent auditor is:

(a) An independent accountant who prepares the financial summaries
(b) An independent accountant who reports on whether financial summaries show a faithful representation
(c) An employee of a business who checks if the financial summaries of that business show a true and fair view
(d) An independent accountant who reports on whether the financial summaries are totally accurate

3 The income statement of a partnership which manufactures the goods it sells will include:

(a) Cost of manufacturing, gross and net profit calculations and an appropriation account
(b) As (a) but without an appropriation account
(c) As (a) but with a partnership account
(d) Only the appropriation account

4 For a soft drinks factory, direct costs could include:

(a) The cost of machinery used to liquidise oranges
(b) Depreciation of a bottle washing machine
(c) Factory rent
(d) Flavourings

5 Which of the following headings is *not* part of the 'cost of manufacturing' calculation?

(a) Prime cost of trading
(b) Total cost of manufacturing
(c) Raw materials
(d) Indirect factory costs

6 A company has opening inventory £3,900, closing inventory £2,800 and purchases £18,650. What is its *cost of sales*?

(a) £1,100
(b) £17,550
(c) £19,750
(d) £25,350

7 In a manufacturing company which also buys in completed goods for resale, 'cost of sales' is found by the formula:

(a) Openinginventoryofrawmaterials + Purchases + Costofmanufacturing − Closinginventory of raw materials
(b) Openinginventoryoffinishedgoods + Purchases + Costofmanufacturing − Closinginventory of finished goods
(c) Openinginventoryoffinishedgoods + Purchases − Costofmanufacturing − Closinginventory of finished goods
(d) Openinginventoryoffinishedgoods + Purchases + Costofmanufacturing + Closinginventory of finished goods

8 In which one of the following types of business organisation would taxation on profits be shown as a deduction from operating profit in the income statement?

(a) Sole ownership
(b) Partnership
(c) Limited liability company
(d) Sole proprietorship

9 At the end of its financial year to 31 December 2014, a business had charged £25,000 depreciation in its income statement. On 31 December 2013, the cost of its non-current assets were £140,000 and total depreciation up to that date amounted to £60,000. No non-current assets had been bought or sold in 2014. What relevant figures would be shown in the income statement for 2014 and the statement of financial position as at 31 December 2014?

(a) Income statement: £85,000 depreciation included as an expense, £55,000 shown as the depreciated value of non-current assets in the statement of financial position

(b) Income statement: £25,000 depreciation included as an expense, £80,000 shown as the depreciated value of non-current assets in the statement of financial position
(c) Income statement: £60,000 depreciation included as an expense, £140,000 shown as the depreciated value of non-current assets in the statement of financial position
(d) Income statement: £25,000 depreciation included as an expense, £55,000 shown as the depreciated value of non-current assets in the statement of financial position

10 Lee and Wong are partners, sharing profits and losses in the ratio 3:1 respectively. The partnership made an operating loss of £8,000 in the year. The opening equity balances were: Lee £20,000, Wong £10,000. During the year, Lee drew out £11,000 from the partnership, Wong drew out £5,000 from the partnership. What is the value of each partner's equity balance at the end of the year?

(a)	Lee	£3,000	Wong	£3,000
(b)	Lee	£15,000	Wong	£7,000
(c)	Lee	£25,000	Wong	£13,000
(d)	Lee	£20,000	Wong	£10,000

Self-study questions

Questions marked with this symbol (#) indicate that the suggested answers are available to lecturers only – other answers are given in Appendix 2.

4.1 From the following information (in no particular order), prepare detailed income statements for each of the three separate businesses.

Name:	Business 1: Amber	Business 2: Blue	Business 3: Cerise
Type of business:	Manufacturer	Trader	Service provider
Year ended:	30 April 2014	31 May 2014	30 June 2014
	£	£	£
Revenue	253,620	184,162	–
Closing inventory:			
Finished goods	13,671	10,700	–
Raw materials	9,641	–	–
Work in progress	32,040	–	–
Purchases (finished goods)	–	65,210	–
Raw materials purchased	52,450	–	–

Name:	Business 1:	Business 2:	Business 3:
	Amber	Blue	Cerise
Type of business:	Manufacturer	Trader	Service provider
Year ended:	30 April 2014	31 May 2014	30 June 2014
	£	£	£
Opening inventory:			
Finished goods	12,634	12,700	–
Raw materials	8,320	–	–
Work in progress	35,620	–	–
Fees from clients	–	–	85,400
Factory indirect expenses (excluding depreciation)	89,322	–	–
General office expenses (excluding depreciation)	34,600	54,923	21,500
Depreciation: factory	6,000	–	–
Depreciation: office	3,600	2,300	1,600
Production labour	47,653	–	–

4.2 From the following information (in no particular order), produce the income statement of Wesley Timpson, who buys and sells goods, for the year ended 30 November 2014:

	£
Closing inventory, 30 November 2014	16,822
Depreciation on office furniture for the year	2,500
Depreciation on computers for the year	900
Depreciation on motor cars for the year	4,500
Light and heat	5,230
Opening inventory, 1 December 2013	15,684
Postage and stationery	2,710
Purchases	124,100
Revenue	245,610
Sundry office expenses	3,571
Communication charges (mobile phones, e-mail, etc.)	1,499
Wages and salaries	47,231

4.3 From the following trial balance and notes relating to Betta Buys, a retail store (owned by a sole proprietor) prepare an income statement for the year to 28 February 2014, and a statement of financial position as at that date.

	Dr	Cr
	£	£
Bank	960	
Cash	250	
Shop fittings – cost	30,000	
Shop fittings – depreciation to 1 March 2013		10,400
Motor car – cost	12,000	
Motor car – depreciation to 1 March 2013		4,800
Revenue		425,000
Purchases	204,000	
Opening inventory at 1 March 2013	90,000	
Rent	15,000	
Electricity	4,000	
Trade receivables	35,200	
Trade payables		27,600
Wages and salaries	62,000	
Owner's drawings	25,000	
Equity at 1 March 2013		10,610
	478,410	478,410

Notes:

1 Closing inventory on 28 February 2014 is £70,000.
2 Electricity of £1,000 is to be accrued at the year-end.
3 Rent of £3,000 has been prepaid at the year-end.
4 Depreciation on the shop fittings is calculated over 5 years on the straight line method, assuming a residual value of £4,000.
5 Depreciation on the car is calculated at 40% using the diminishing balance method.

4.4 Helen Thorne, a retail jeweller, extracted the following trial balance for her business as at 31 May 2014.

	Dr	Cr
	£	£
Revenue		325,340
Opening inventory, 1 June 2013	35,750	
Purchases	168,220	
Insurance	7,420	
Wages	33,100	

	Dr £	Cr £
Phone and e-mail	5,200	
Light and heat	6,230	
Security guards' wages	12,400	
Repairs to premises	3,970	
Amortisation of leasehold premises to 1 June 2013		18,000
Depreciation of safe to 1 June 2013		4,800
Depreciation of shop fittings to 1 June 2013		10,200
Rent and rates	17,000	
Sundry expenses	3,940	
Leasehold premises, at cost	60,000	
Safe, at cost	12,000	
Shop fittings, at cost	34,000	
Trade receivables	3,400	
Trade payables		19,670
Bank overdraft		2,380
Cash	520	
Website maintenance expenses	1,430	
Publicity and advertising	9,740	
Loan (repayable 2026)		20,000
Opening equity, 1 June 2013		38,630
Owner's drawings	24,700	
	439,020	439,020

Notes:

1 Closing inventory at 31 May 2014, £27,880.

2 Security guards were owed £400 wages at 31 May 2014 and £200 was also owing for phone and e-mail.

3 £900 of the charge for maintaining the company website was paid on 1 January 2014 to cover a year from that date.

4 Depreciation is to be calculated as follows:
   - (i) leasehold premises are amortised in equal instalments over a 20-year period
   - (ii) the safe is depreciated at 40% p.a. by the diminishing balance method
   - (iii) the shop fittings are depreciated at 10% p.a. by the straight line method, assuming no residual values.

Prepare Helen Thorne's income statement for the year ended 31 May 2014 and a statement of financial position as at that date.

4.5# Alibaba sells kitchen equipment. Only part of the following information relating to Alibaba is relevant in calculating the company's 'cost of sales' to be included within the gross profit calculation for its financial year. The company both buys in completed products for sale and also manufactures goods for sale. You are required to calculate the cost of sales, showing your workings.

	£
Opening inventory of raw materials	58,630
Closing inventory of raw materials	62,152
Selling and distribution costs	65,240
Raw materials purchased in the year	358,260
Factory wages and other factory overheads	126,521
General administration overheads	205,360
Opening inventory of finished goods	12,390
Closing inventory of finished goods	9,520
Finished goods purchased in the year	140,750

4.6# Hansel and Gretel are partners, sharing profits and losses in the ratio 3:1 respectively. The partnership's operating profit for the year ended 30 September 2014 totalled £86,000, their equity balances at the start of the year were: Hansel £35,800, Gretel £17,600; and drawings of £48,200 were made by Hansel and £16,400 by Gretel. The 'total net assets' of the partnership at the end of the year amounted to £74,800.

(a) Prepare the section of the partnership's income statement showing the division of the profit between the two partners.
(b) Prepare the partnership's statement of financial position in as much detail as is possible from the above information.

4.7# Vermay Fashions Limited is a small business buying and selling dresses. Its trial balance as at 31 July 2014 is shown below:

Vermay Fashions Limited
Trial balance as at 31 July 2014

	Debit £	Credit £
Cash	531	
Shop fittings – cost	5,773	
Shop fittings – depreciation to 1 August 2013		1,959
Motor car – cost	10,997	
Motor car – depreciation to 1 August 2013		6,301
Revenue		126,743
Purchases	32,183	
Opening inventory at 1 August 2013	2,272	

	Debit £	Credit £
Rent	3,828	
Electricity	2,421	
Telephone	963	
Trade receivables	1,411	
Trade payables		795
Wages and salaries	18,299	
Director's salary	15,522	
Sundry expenses	445	
Share capital		10,000
Reserves at 1 August 2013		5,672
Bank balance	56,825	
	151,470	151,470

Notes:

1 Closing inventory is £2,669.
2 Electricity charges are to be accrued at the year-end, totalling £1,398.
3 Rent has been prepaid at the year-end, amounting to £213.
4 Shop fittings are depreciated by the straight line method (no residual value) over 5 years.
5 Depreciation on the car is calculated using the diminishing balance method at 30% per annum.
6 Taxation is to be provided at a rate of 20% of the operating profit (to the nearest £).

Prepare the income statement for the year ended 31 July 2014, and a statement of financial position as at that date. Show all workings.

Case study

Marvin makes magic

During the second half of his first year in business, Marvin (see previous case studies) decided to supplement his income by manufacturing and selling magic sets. This was in addition to his fees as an entertainer and any profit made by selling bought-in novelties from Kaboosh Limited. He rented a workshop on 1 March 2012 and employed his assistant Esmeralda's seven brothers and sisters as production workers. At the end of his first year of business, 30 June 2012, he produced the following trial balance:

	Dr £	Cr £
Appearance fees as entertainer		34,300
Cleaning	280	
Cost of machinery used in workshop	3,600	
Cost of magician's equipment	5,400	
Cost of disappearing lady apparatus	2,000	
Light and heat of workshop	2,400	
Other workshop expenses	4,100	
Production wages paid to Esmeralda's brothers and sisters	5,620	
Purchase of materials used to manufacture magic sets	15,621	
Purchases of novelties bought in from Kaboosh Limited	3,400	
Rabbit expenses	430	
Sales of novelties and magic sets		45,821
Marvin's drawings	19,720	
Opening equity		5,020
Trade payable – Kaboosh Limited		240
Travel to performance venues	5,510	
Bank balance	660	
Cash in hand	40	
Wages to assistant (Esmeralda)	12,400	
Workshop costs: rent and rates	4,200	
	85,381	85,381

At the end of the year, the following further information was provided:

1 Closing inventory of materials used to manufacture magic sets was valued at £6,320 and closing inventory of bought-in novelties was valued at £2,400. All the manufactured magic sets were sold in the year. There was no work in progress at the year-end.
2 £200 wages was owed to Grimstock, one of the workers on the production line, whilst £100 was owed for light and heat.
3 One-seventh of the rent and rates had been prepaid for the following financial period. Marvin was owed £200 at the year-end by Tanya Turner for a party fee. This had not been shown in Marvin's accounting records.
4 Depreciation for the year on the magician's equipment totalled £1,080, and depreciation for the year on the disappearing lady apparatus was £800. Depreciation on the workshop machinery was to be calculated on the straight line method over six years, assuming a residual value of £600. A full year's depreciation was to be charged, even though the machinery had been owned for less than a year.

Answers are in Appendix 3

Required

Prepare Marvin's income statement for the year ended 30 June 2012, and a statement of financial position as at that date.

Further research

Leading audit firms include:

Deloitte: **www.deloitte.com**
Ernst and Young: **ey.com**
KPMG: **www.kpmg.co.uk**
PricewaterhouseCoopers: **www.pwc.com**

Chapter 5 Further aspects of assets and liabilities

Objectives

When you have read this chapter you will be able to:

- Make adjustments when non-current assets are sold
- Understand and apply key methods of inventory valuation
- Understand why provisions for doubtful debts are needed and make adjustments for bad and doubtful debts
- Distinguish between current and non-current liabilities

5.1 Introduction

In this chapter we look at some further aspects of some of the key components found within the statement of financial position, answering such questions as 'what happens if non-current assets are sold?', 'how is inventory valued?' and 'what if customers don't pay their debts?' We look at these in the order in which the relevant items would be found on the statement of financial position: non-current assets; current assets; current liabilities; non-current liabilities.

5.2 Sales of non-current assets

We saw (in Chapter 3) how nearly all non-current assets are subject to depreciation ('amortisation' in the case of intangible assets such as computer software). Depreciation recognises the loss in value of a non-current asset over its estimated useful life due to various factors, including wearing out, usage or becoming obsolete due to changes in technology. When an asset reaches the end of its useful life, the business has the following choices:

- Scrap the asset, in which case it may have some value, for example an old machine may contain recyclable metal and components. If the asset has no value, then it is sometimes referred to as being 'written off'.
- Part-exchange the asset, where any value given for the old asset is used partly to pay for a replacement asset.
- Sell the asset at its market value.

Whatever happens to the asset, it will have a depreciated value in the business's ledger, which is usually the cost of the asset less all the depreciation charged to the date of sale. Sometimes companies do not depreciate assets in the year of sale, but policy varies from business to business. Whatever the eventual fate of the asset being disposed, a calculation must be made of the profit or loss, by comparing the depreciated value (cost minus total depreciation to the date of disposal) with the disposal proceeds. The balance is either a profit (where proceeds are greater than depreciated value), which is *added* to gross profit in the income statement, or a loss (where proceeds are less than depreciated value) – see Figure 5.1 – which is shown as an *expense* in the income statement.

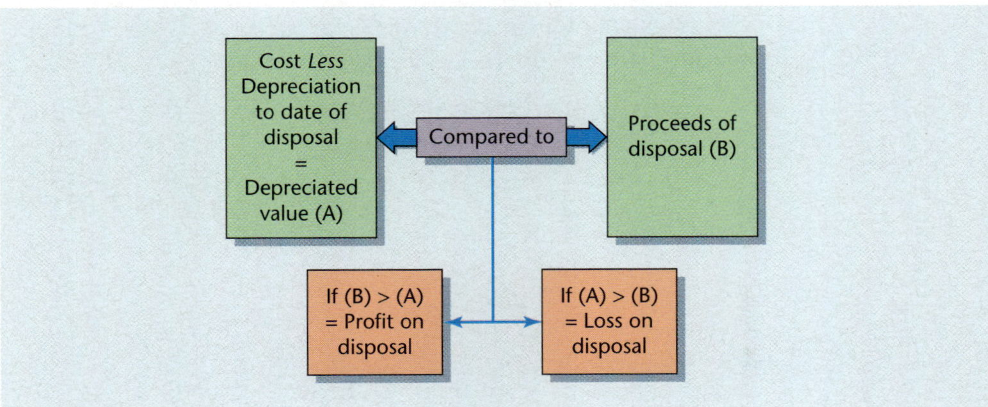

Figure 5.1 Profit or loss on the disposal of a non-current asset

Activity 5.1

Amy has been in business as a commercial photographer for several years. At 1 January 2014 her non-current assets and total depreciation balances were as follows:

	Cost £	Total depreciation £
Pintax camera	650	450
Tripod	135	100
Darkroom equipment	1,600	1,250
Luxus car	5,000	3,600

During the year to 31 December 2014, the following transactions occurred:

- The Pintax camera was exchanged for a Fujitsu 200XL costing £800. A £100 part-exchange allowance was given, and the balance was paid by cheque.
- The tripod was thrown away and not replaced.
- The darkroom equipment was sold for £200 and not replaced.
- The Luxus car was sold in March for £1,600. A Cougar estate car was bought in May for £7,000.

Cameras are depreciated at 10% p.a. straight line method and cars at 25% straight line method. It is Amy's policy not to depreciate assets in the year of sale, but to charge a full year's depreciation in the year of purchase, even if bought part way through the year.

Show the relevant extracts recording the above information in Amy's income statement for the year ended 31 December 2014 and her statement of financial position as at that date.

Answer

The profit or loss calculations are as follows:

- The Pintax camera had a depreciated value of £200 (£650 − £450) but fetched only £100 in part exchange, therefore a loss of £100.
- The tripod had a depreciated value of £35 (£135 − £100) but had no value when it was scrapped, therefore a loss of £35.
- The darkroom equipment had a depreciated value of £350 (£1,600 − £1,250) when it was sold for £200, therefore a loss of £150.
- The Luxus car had a depreciated value of £1,400 (£5,000 − £3,600) but was sold for £1,600, a profit of £200.

The overall loss on disposals was therefore (£100 + £35 + £150) − £200 = £85.
Depreciation for the year is calculated as follows:

Fujitsu 200XL camera £800 × 10% =	£80
Cougar estate car £7,000 × 25% =	£1,750
Total depreciation	£1,830

Income statement for the year ended 31 December 2014 (extract)

	£	£
Gross profit		(not known) £
Less Expenses (include):		
Loss on disposal of non-current assets	85	
Depreciation	1,830	

Statement of financial position as at 31 December 2014 (extract)

Non-current assets	**Depreciated value £**
Camera (£800 − £80)	720
Car (£7,000 − £1,750)	5,250
	5,970

Stop and think

The statement of financial position shows only the non-current assets owned at the end of the year (the new camera and car), the business having disposed of all other non-current assets. A summary of the changes of each category of non-current asset can be given as a note to the statement of financial position. This is shown as follows:

£	Cameras	Tripod	Darkroom equipment	Cars	Total
Cost, 1 January 2014	650	125	1,600	5,000	7,375
Additions in the year	800	–	–	7,000	7,800
	1,450	125	1,600	12,000	15,175
Less Disposals	(650)	(125)	(1,600)	(5,000)	(7,375)
Cost, 31 December 2014 (A)	**800**	–	–	**7,000**	**7,800**
Depreciation, 1 January 2014	450	100	1,250	3,600	5,400
Charge for the year	80	–	–	1,750	1,830
	530	100	1,250	5,350	7,230
Less Depreciation on disposed assets	(450)	(100)	(1,250)	(3,600)	(5,400)
Depreciation, 31 December 2014 (**B**)	**80**	–	–	**1,750**	**1,830**
Depreciated value, 31 December 2014 (**A**)–(**B**)	**720**	–	–	**5,250**	**5,970**
Depreciated value, 1 January 2014	200	25	350	1,400	1,975

5.3 Inventory valuation

5.3.1 The importance of the valuation

The key date for valuing inventory is the end of the financial period, as the valuation affects the cost of sales calculation in the income statement and also the current assets total in the statement of financial position. If inventory is *overvalued* it will increase this year's profit but reduce next year's, as the closing balance of one period is the opening balance of the next. The value of the 'total net assets' shown in the statement of financial position will also be distorted. How, then, should inventory be valued? The relevant accounting standard, IAS 2,[1] states that *'inventories shall be measured at the lower of cost and net realisable value'*. It also contains these definitions:

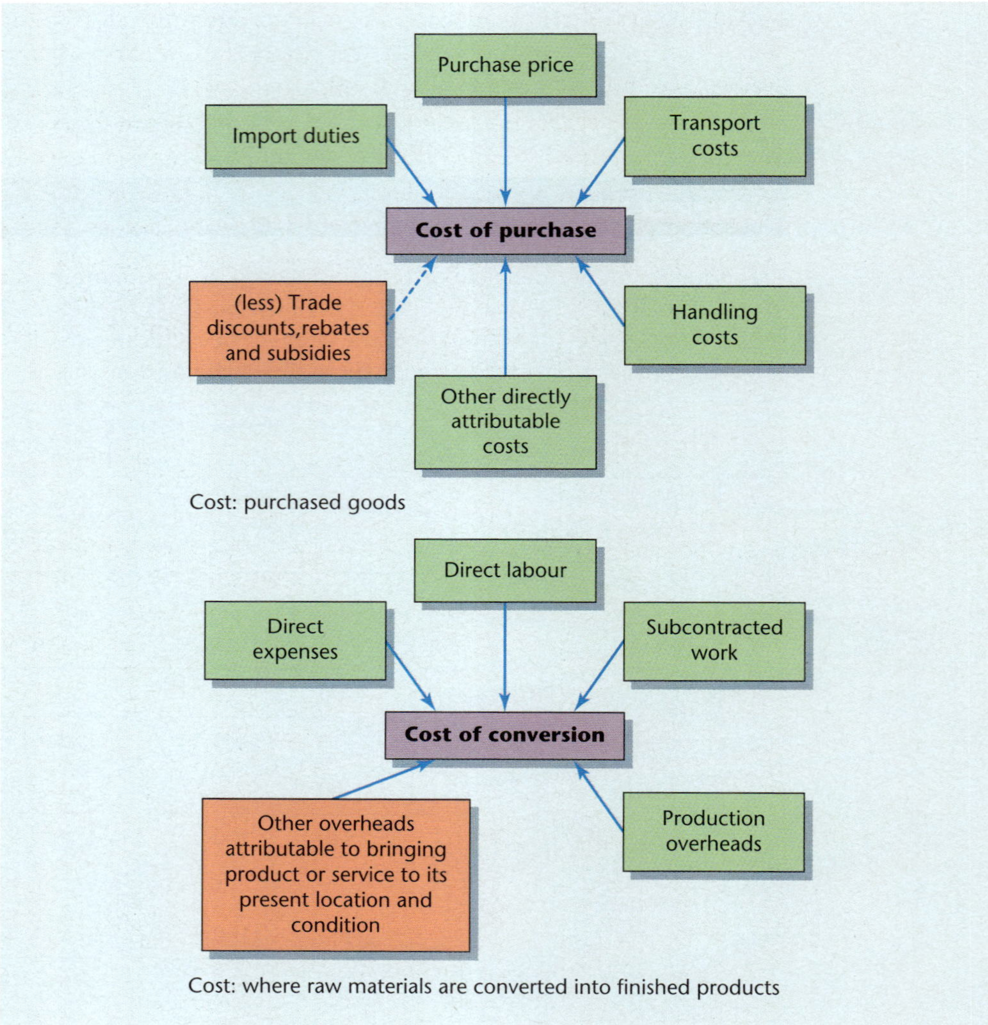

Figure 5.2 Cost of purchase and cost of conversion

[1]International Accounting Standards Board (2008) *International Accounting Standard 2: Inventories.* London: IASB.

- **Cost (of inventory)**: 'all costs of purchase, costs of conversion and other costs incurred in bringing the inventories to their present location and condition'. *Costs of conversion* refer to those costs incurred when converting materials into finished goods. They include direct labour and an allocation of other direct and indirect production overheads (see Figure 5.2).
- **Net realisable value**: 'the estimated selling price in the ordinary course of business less the estimated costs of completion and the estimated costs necessary to make the sale'.

The need to give a 'faithful representation' of the business's financial position and performance was explained earlier (in Chapter 1). One aspect of this is that in valuing assets such as inventory we would never *anticipate* a profit by valuing it at its normal selling price. For example, if a washing machine retailer had 500 machines unsold at the end of its financial period which it bought in at £100 each and would normally be sold at £300 each, it is against accounting principles to value the unsold inventory at 500 × £300. In normal circumstances the inventory would be valued at 500 × £100. The only exception is where the net realisable value (the likely selling price after deducting relevant costs to enable the inventory to be sold) is *less* than the cost price, in which case the IAS 2 definition is applied. This may happen in cases such as where inventory has deteriorated in some way or is unfashionable.

Another problem is deciding what can be included as 'cost'. It might be as simple as looking up an invoice and reading off the price paid: for example, the owner of a bicycle shop with four Speedwing Racers in its inventory is probably able to find their purchase price quite easily; but in many cases the price paid cannot be matched to actual goods, perhaps due to the physical nature of the inventory.

Activity 5.2

A retailer of pet fish looks in the fish tank at the end of his first financial year, 31 December, and counts 500 goldfish. All the fish are bought from the same supplier, but prices change frequently. Details of inventory purchases and sales are as follows:

	Number purchased (fish)	Cost of each fish (£)	Sales at end of month (fish)
1 Jan	350	2	–
1 Mar	600	3	300
1 Jul	800	4	550
1 Oct	700	5	1,000
1 Dec	650	6	750
31 Dec (Closing inventory)	500	?	

What value should be placed on the closing inventory?

Source: Introduction to Accounting and Finance, 2e, Geoff Black, © Pearson Education Limited 2005, 2009

Answer

We can't tell by looking at them! Goldfish do not swim around with price labels on them, and it would be very difficult to look at one goldfish and say with certainty when it was bought. What has to be done is to apply a *theoretical valuation method* such as FIFO or AVCO.

5.3.2 FIFO and AVCO

FIFO stands for First In, First Out, and *AVCO* for Average Cost. There is a third valuation method, *LIFO*, which stands for Last In, First Out, but this is not allowed to be used under the International Accounting Standard. Each of these methods of inventory valuation is theoretical and does not necessarily reflect the way in which inventory physically moves through the business, so a cake shop could use FIFO without getting into trouble due to selling stale products! AVCO can be either *periodic* or *perpetual*: periodic means that the average is calculated at intervals (for example, once a year or quarterly); perpetual requires recalculation every time a price change is recorded.

In times of rising prices, using FIFO will result in a higher inventory value than the other methods (the *latest* prices being applied to closing inventory).

Did you know?

If the LIFO valuation method was used it would result in the *earliest* (and almost certainly lowest) prices being used, probably bearing very little relation to current price levels. This would result in an unrealistically low inventory value, a low profit and consequently a low tax bill which is why most government tax authorities do not allow LIFO to be used for the calculation of taxable profits! Remember also that LIFO is not allowed under IAS 2.

Activity 5.3

Use the FIFO (First In First Out) method to value the goldfish at 31 December (see Activity 5.2).

Answer

Use a 'price grid' to establish which fish are, in theory, sold at which prices.

Purchase price	£2	£3	£4	£5	£6
January purchases	350				
March purchases		600			
Subtotal	350	600			
March sales (FIFO)	(300)				
July purchases			800		
Subtotal	50	600	800		
July sales (FIFO)	(50)	(500)			
October purchases				700	
Subtotal	–	100	800	700	
October sales (FIFO)		(100)	(800)	(100)	
December purchases					650
Subtotal	–	–	–	600	650
December Sales (FIFO)				(600)	(150)
December Closing Inventory	–	–	–	–	500

Closing inventory = 500 × £6 = £3,000

Activity 5.4

As a comparison, use the LIFO (Last In First Out) method to value the goldfish at 31 December.

Answer

Use another 'price grid' to establish which fish are, in theory, sold at which prices.

Purchase price	£2	£3	£4	£5	£6
January purchases	350				
March purchases		600			
Subtotal	350	600			
March sales (LIFO)		(300)			
July purchases			800		
Subtotal	350	300	800		
July sales (LIFO)			(550)		

Purchase price	£2	£3	£4	£5	£6
October purchases				700	
Subtotal	350	300	250	700	
October sales (LIFO)		(50)	(250)	(700)	
December purchases					650
Subtotal	350	250	–	–	650
December sales (LIFO)		(100)			(650)
December closing inventory	350	150	–	–	–

Closing inventory = (350 × £2 = £700) + (150 × £3 = £450), total £1,150

Activity 5.5

Finally, use the AVCO (Average Cost) method (perpetual inventory) to value the goldfish at 31 December.

Answer

Use a third 'price grid' to establish which fish are, in theory, sold at which prices.

	Fish £	Price £	Value £	Average £
January purchases	350	2	700	
March purchases	600	3	1,800	
Subtotal	950		2,500	
Average (£2,500/950 fish = £2.632)				2.632
March sales	(300)	2.632	(790)	
July purchases	800	4	3,200	
Subtotal	1,450		4,910	
Average (£4,910/1,450 fish = £3.386)				3.386
July sales	(550)	3.386	(1,862)	
October purchases	700	5	3,500	
Subtotal	1,600		6,548	
Average (£6,548/1,600 fish = £4.093)				4.093
October sales	(1,000)	4.093	(4,093)	
December purchases	650	6	3,900	
Subtotal	1,250		6,355	
Average (£6,355/1,250 fish = £5.084)				5.084
December sales	(750)	5.084	(3,813)	
December closing inventory	**500**	**5.084**	**2,542**	

Stop and think

Closing inventory valuations using each of the three methods are:

FIFO	£3,000
LIFO	£1,150
AVCO	£2,542

Can you see why LIFO has resulted in a very low valuation? This method values the fish at the earliest (and lowest) prices.

Activity 5.6

Calculate the gross profit for the year, using each of the three inventory valuation methods. Assume that each goldfish is sold for £10 and that no goldfish died during the year.

Answer

	FIFO		LIFO		AVCO	
	£	£	£	£	£	£
Revenue (2,600 × £10)		26,000		26,000		26,000
Less **Cost of sales**						
Opening inventory	–		–		–	
Purchases*	13,100		13,100		13,100	
	13,100		13,100		13,100	
Less Closing inventory	(3,000)		(1,150)		(2,542)	
		(10,100)		(11,950)		(10,558)
Gross profit		15,900		14,050		15,442

*(350 × £2) + (600 × £3) + (800 × £4) + (700 × £5) + (650 × £6).

Stop and think

Can you see why LIFO is not permitted under IAS 2? It results in unrealistic valuations and profit figures.

5.4 Bad and doubtful debts

The next current asset listed after 'inventory' in the statement of financial position is 'trade receivables', which is the total of all the individual customers' and clients' account balances within the Receivables Ledger at the date of the statement of financial position. Accountants, in order to show a faithful representation of the financial position, must be reasonably sure that the total shown in the statement of financial position represents *good debts* (that is, debts that *will* be paid by customers), as there might also be:

- *Bad debts* – where there is *no* possibility of the customer paying, and
- *Doubtful debts* – where there is *uncertainty* whether the debt can be paid.

Scan the following QR code with your QR reader to take you to the website of a leading US firm of debt collectors, Caine and Weiner:

5.4.1 Bad debts

Bad debts are the nightmare of any business – the customer has been sold goods or services and does not pay for them. It is an extreme step to consider a debt as bad, and is usually the end of a long-drawn-out process involving reminders, threats of legal action, lawyers' letters, etc. Once the decision has been taken, the debt shown within the customer's Receivables Ledger account is cancelled (*written off*) and transferred into a bad debts account within the General Ledger. At the end of the financial period, the total of all the bad debts will be included as part of the expenses shown within the income statement. With the amount of the debt having been cancelled, obviously it will not be included as part of the trade receivables shown within the current assets on the statement of financial position. Sometimes, miracles happen and a debt previously written off is paid. In that case, the amount is included within the income statement as a 'bad debt recovered'.

Activity 5.7

Tariq owed £650 to the Canberra Carpet Company. Despite many reminders and phone calls, Tariq refused to pay. The company has now heard that Tariq has left the area with no forwarding address and with many other unpaid bills. The company has reluctantly decided to write off the debt at 31 December 2014. Total trade receivables at that date (before writing off Tariq's debt), amounted to £6,950.

Show the relevant extracts from the financial summaries of the Canberra Carpet Company.

Answer

Income statement for the year ended 31 December 2014 (extract)

	£
Expenses include:	
Bad debt written off	650

Statement of financial position as at 31 December 2014 (extract)

	£
Current assets include:	
Trade receivables	6,300

The effect of writing off the debt is to decrease profit by £650 and reduce the company's assets by the same amount. Bad debts = bad news!

Activity 5.8

Two years later, on 1 December 2016, the managing director of the Canberra Carpet Company gets an e-mail from Tariq. It says: 'Made a fortune in the Icelandic Goldfields! Sorry about the unpaid bill! Money now transferred into your company's account!' What entries would be made in the company's financial summaries to reflect this happy event?

Answer

Income statement for the year ended 31 December 2016 (extract)

	£
(Added to gross profit)	
Bad debt recovered	650
(No relevant entries in the statement of financial position, other than an extra £650 in the bank balance)	

Stop and think

£650 has been paid into the company's bank account, representing unexpected income in the year, which is taken to the income statement as additional profit.

5.4.2 Doubtful debts

Some debts are neither good nor bad – instead there is an element of doubt as to whether they will be paid. Reasons for this include:

- Disputes over the quality of goods or services causing the customer to withhold payment
- Unresolved queries such as duplicated invoices
- Financial difficulties of a customer, raising doubts as to whether they will eventually pay
- Customers whose debts have been owing for a long period.

The major difference between *doubtful* debts and *bad* debts is that if a debt is considered doubtful there is still some hope that the customer will pay, so the customer's Receivables Ledger account is kept 'alive'. However, an amount of profit is transferred to a *provision* to recognise the potential loss if the debt eventually does become bad. This is adjusted up or down in future years, depending upon whether there are more or fewer doubtful debts to be provided for by the end of the financial period.

The provision can be either:

- Specific (relating to actual amounts owing by named customers), or
- General (an agreed percentage – based on past experience – of total receivables is provided for, after bad debts have been written off).

Did you know?

A provision is an amount set aside out of profits to cover a future loss, even if the exact amount is uncertain. Incidentally (and confusingly), a provision *for doubtful debts* could also be referred to as either a *provision for bad debts* or a *provision for bad and doubtful debts*! They all mean the same thing: *a provision against the future possibility of a debt becoming bad*. They must never be confused with 'bad debts', where all hope of recovery has been abandoned and the debt is written off as a loss.

Activity 5.9

Assume that the Texas Tea Company's doubtful debts were as follows:

2014 (no doubtful debts)

2015 Total doubtful debts = £6,900

2016 Total doubtful debts = £8,200

2017 Total doubtful debts = £7,800

What provision for doubtful debts would be needed in each year?

Answer

- In 2014 there is no provision.
- In 2015 a provision of £6,900 is created (show £6,900 as an expense in the income statement and *deduct* £6,900 from trade receivables in the statement of financial position).
- In 2016 the provision needs to be *increased* by £1,300 (show £1,300 as an expense in the income statement and *deduct* £8,200 from trade receivables in the statement of financial position).
- In 2017 the provision needs to be *decreased* by £400 (show £400 as income in the income statement and *deduct* £7,800 from trade receivables in the statement of financial position).

Note that there are no entries to be made in the customers' accounts in the Receivables Ledger.

Good, doubtful and bad debts are summarised in Figure 5.3.

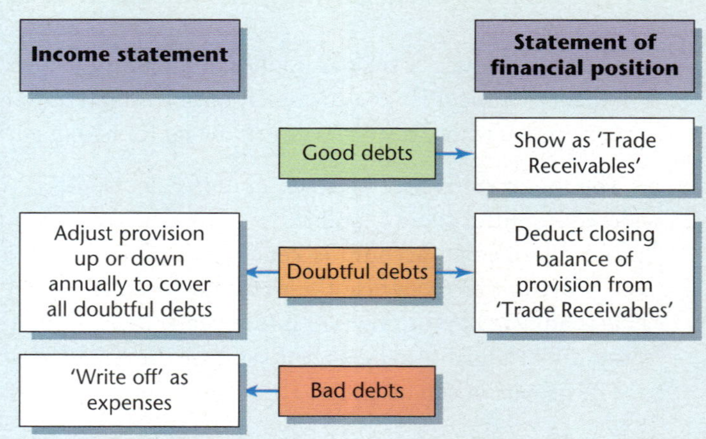

Figure 5.3 Good, doubtful and bad debts

Stop and think

Many students have difficulty understanding how provisions work. Look very carefully at the amounts either coming out of the income statement (2015: £6,900, 2016: £1,300) or going back into the income statement (2017: £400). What do you notice? Apart from the first year, you do not need to take out *all* the provision in each year – you are just 'fine tuning' it to make sure that the closing amount of the provision equals the total of doubtful debts at the date of the statement of financial position. Re-read the above activity and then see if you can apply its principles to the next one.

Activity 5.10

Barker Biscuits, a company which started on 1 January 2014, had identified the following balances on its Receivables Ledger:

As at 31 December:	2014 £	2015 £	2016 £
Total trade receivables including:	49,310	39,551	37,690
Bad debts:			
Alpha Inc	2,500		
Beta Ltd	560		
Gamma plc		630	
Delta Partners			1,700
Doubtful debts:			
Epsilon and Company	300		
Zeta Inc	2,600	1,600	1,200
Omega LLP		1,700	
Sigma plc			1,800

Show the relevant extracts from the financial summaries for each of the three years.

Answer

Income statement for the year ended 31 December 2014 (extract)

	£	£
Expenses include:		
Bad debts written off		3,060
Provision for doubtful debts		2,900

Statement of financial position as at 31 December 2014 (extract)

	£	£
Current assets include:		
Trade Receivables (£49,310 – £3,060)	46,250	
Less Provision for doubtful debts	(2,900)	43,350

Income statement for the year ended 31 December 2015 (extract)

	£	£
Expenses include:		
Bad debts written off		630
Increase in provision for doubtful debts (£3,300 − £2,900)		400

Statement of financial position as at 31 December 2015 (extract)

	£	£
Current assets include:		
Trade Receivables (£39,551 − £630)	38,921	
Less Provision for doubtful debts	(3,300)	
		35,621

Income statement for the year ended 31 December 2016 (extract)

	£	£
Added to gross profit:		
Decrease in provision for doubtful debts (£3,300 − £3,000)		300
Expenses include:		
Bad debts written off		1,700

Statement of financial position as at 31 December 2016 (extract)

	£	£
Current assets include:		
Trade Receivables (£37,690 − £1,700)	35,990	
Less Provision for doubtful debts	(3,000)	
		32,990

Stop and think

The Alumasc Group plc, a leading building and engineering products company, recorded a bad debt of £0.5 million in its 2011 annual report. Figure 5.4 shows the level of its 'credit risk' within its trade receivables, as shown within its annual report:

Credit risk

Group policies are aimed at minimising credit losses, and require that deferred terms are granted only to customers who demonstrate an appropriate payment history and satisfy creditworthiness procedures. Individual exposures are monitored with customers subject to credit terms to ensure that the group's exposure to bad debts is minimised. However, the group did suffer a net £0.5 million bad debt in its Facades business during the 2010–11 financial year, see page 21 of the Business Review for further details [not shown here]. Goods may be sold on a cash with order basis to

Scan the following QR code with your QR reader to take you to the website of The Alumasc Group plc:

mitigate credit risk. Some operating units purchase credit insurance where the cost is not excessive when compared to the risks covered.

At 30 June, the analysis of trade and other receivables that were past due but not impaired is as follows:

					Past due but not impaired	
Year ended 30 June 2011	Total	Not past due	< 30 days	30–60 days	60–90 days	> 90 days
	£000	£000	£000	£000	£000	£000
Trade receivables	17,343	13,603	2,428	719	269	324
Construction contracts	4,170	3,820	175	105	19	51
Other receivables	453	453	–	–	–	–
	21,966	17,876	2,603	824	288	375

Figure 5.4 Credit risk

Source: The Alumasc Group plc, Report and Accounts 2011

5.5 Current and non-current liabilities

Liabilities are described as 'current' if they are due for payment within one year of the date of the statement of financial position. It is considered useful to distinguish these from any liabilities that are repayable *after* more than one year (referred to as *non-current* liabilities). The main current liabilities found within the statement of financial position are:

- Trade payables, being amounts owed for goods or services
- Accruals, which are expenses owing at the end of a financial period where the invoices have not yet been received
- Bank overdrafts and other short-term borrowing
- Taxation due on the profits of limited liability companies (this is not relevant to sole proprietorships or partnerships as their *individual* owners are personally responsible for meeting any tax on profits).

Non-current liabilities are those creditors due for payment *after* more than one year from the date of the statement of financial position. They might comprise long-term loans (possibly referred to as bonds or debentures), pension liabilities and deferred taxation (where a tax liability might arise at some undefined future time).

5.6 Summary

In this chapter we considered the following:

AVCO	Average cost, a theoretical inventory valuation method that requires average prices to be calculated either continuously (perpetual method) or periodically to establish a value for closing inventory. This method *is* acceptable under International Accounting Standards.

FIFO	First In First Out, a theoretical inventory valuation method that assumes that the earliest inventory received is the first to be sold or used in production. This leaves the most recent (and usually the highest) values to be applied to the closing inventory. This method *is* acceptable under International Accounting Standards.
LIFO	Last In First Out, a theoretical inventory valuation method that assumes that the most recent inventory received is the first to be sold or used in production. This leaves the earliest (and usually the lowest) values to be applied to the closing inventory. This method is *not acceptable* under International Accounting Standards.
Bad and doubtful debts	Bad debts are irrecoverable and are 'written off' to the income statement. With doubtful debts there is still hope, so do not write them off, just make a provision against the possibility of a loss in the future.
Current and non-current liabilities	Current liabilities are those expected to be settled no more than 12 months after the date of the statement of financial position; non-current liabilities are those due for settlement more than 12 months after that date.

5.7 Chapter glossary

AVCO *Average cost*, a method of inventory valuation which applies average prices to value closing inventory. 'Perpetual valuation' requires constant updating of the average when prices change; 'periodic valuation' changes only at intervals, for example annually.

Bad debts Debts where there is no hope of collecting the amount due.

Bond A name sometimes given to a limited company's loan.

Cost of inventory Expenditure incurred on inventory to bring it to its present location and condition.

Current liability An amount due for payment within one year of the date of the statement of financial position.

Debenture A name sometimes given to a limited company's loan

Doubtful debts Debts where there is uncertainty as to whether the amount due will be paid, but the business has not given up hope of payment.

FIFO *First in, first out*, a method of inventory valuation which assumes that the earliest inventory acquired is the first to be used, resulting in closing inventory being valued at most recent prices.

Good debts Debts which are expected to be paid in the normal course of business.

LIFO *Last in, first out*, a method of inventory valuation which assumes that the most recently acquired inventory is the first to be used, resulting in closing inventory being valued at earliest prices. Not allowed under International Accounting Standards.

Net realisable value Selling price of inventory, after deducting all relevant costs to enable it to be sold.

Non-current liability An amount due for payment after more than one year of the statement of financial position date.

Provision An amount set aside out of profits to reduce the value of an asset, due to factors such as uncertainty of value (e.g. provision for doubtful debts).

Provision for bad debts Another term for a provision for doubtful debts.

Provision for bad and doubtful debts Another term for a provision for doubtful debts.

Provision for doubtful debts An amount of profit set aside to cover the possibility of some debts becoming bad in the future.

Theoretical valuation methods Inventory valuation methods such as FIFO and LIFO which assume that inventory moves through the business in a particular way.

Additional resources

Now work through the various exercises and problems that you can find within the My Accounting Lab that are relevant to this chapter. Either use the QR code shown in the margin (if you use an Android-based device), or visit www.myaccountinglab.com for the log-in page.

Only accessible on Android-based devices

Self-check questions

The answers to these questions are in Appendix 1.

1 A business sells an asset on 1 January for £8,000. The asset was bought exactly three years previously for £24,000 and depreciation was charged at 30% p.a. on the diminishing balance method. What is the profit or loss on disposal?

(a) £5,600 profit
(b) £232 profit
(c) £232 loss
(d) £16,000 loss

2 A profit on the disposal of a non-current asset is included within the financial summaries by:

(a) Including the profit as Income within the income statement
(b) Showing the profit as an Expense within the income statement
(c) Increasing the value of the non-current assets shown in the statement of financial position
(d) Decreasing the value of the non-current assets shown in the statement of financial position

3 What is the effect of overvaluing closing inventory on the current year's profit?

(a) Decreases the gross profit and operating profit
(b) Increases the gross profit but decreases operating profit
(c) Decreases the gross profit but increases operating profit
(d) Increases the gross profit and operating profit

4 Applying the FIFO method of inventory valuation in a period of rapidly rising prices will result in:

(a) Inventory valued at low prices
(b) Inventory valued at high prices
(c) Inventory valued at average prices
(d) Inventory valued at selling prices

5 Why can LIFO not be used to compute profits under accounting standards?

(a) It results in irrelevant and out-dated inventory values
(b) It would result in high profits, and the International Accounting Standards Board wants to discourage this
(c) It would mean that businesses would always have old inventory and the International Accounting Standards Board wants to discourage this
(d) It is a theoretical method, unrelated to actual prices

6 A company bought 50 dresses at £40 each. Normal selling price is £60 each but the dresses are now thought to be old-fashioned and have to be shortened at a cost of £5 each. What should be their total value as part of closing inventory?

(a) £2,750
(b) £3,000
(c) £2,000
(d) £1,750

7 What is a bad debt?

(a) A debt where there is some hope of getting paid
(b) A debt where there is no hope of getting paid
(c) A debt which is doubtful
(d) A debt where the customer has gone to a different country to live

8 Mumbai Limited is owed £400 by Bangalore plc. Mumbai Limited now regards Bangalore plc as a bad debtor. What will be the effect of 'writing off' the debt as bad?

(a) No effect on profit, but trade receivables decrease
(b) The bank balance goes down and the profits decrease
(c) Profit decreases, as do current assets
(d) Profit decreases, but no effect on the statement of financial position

9 A business starts its year with £800 in a provision for doubtful debts. At the end of the year, trade receivables total £12,000 of which £600 are considered doubtful. What is the effect on the income statement and statement of financial position?

(a) £200 is added to profit and the statement of financial position shows trade receivables less provision as £11,400
(b) £600 is deducted from profit and the statement of financial position shows trade receivables less provision as £11,400
(c) £1,400 is deducted from profit and the statement of financial position shows trade receivables less provision as £10,600
(d) £800 is added to profit and the statement of financial position shows trade receivables less provision as £11,400

10 A non-current liability is:

(a) A liability due for payment within 12 months
(b) The same as a prepayment
(c) A liability due for payment after more than 12 months
(d) The same as an accrual

Self-study questions

Questions marked with this symbol (#) indicate that the suggested answers are available to lecturers only – other answers are given in Appendix 2.

5.1 Straits Liners is a shipping company which at 1 January 2014 owned the following vessels:

- The Invisible, bought for £450,000 on 1 July 2009
- The Submersible, bought for £600,000 on 1 August 2010
- The Outrageous, bought for £900,000 on 1 March 2011

All the ships are depreciated over five years on the straight line basis, assuming a residual value of 25% of cost price, with a full year's depreciation in the year of purchase but no depreciation in the year of sale. During the year ended 31 December 2014, the following events occurred:

- The Invisible disappeared in the Bermuda Triangle and was considered lost.
- The Submersible was part-exchanged for a new ship, The Implausible, on 3 October. The cost of the new ship was £700,000. £200,000 was given in part exchange, with the balance paid by bank transfer.
- The Outrageous was still owned at 31 December 2014.

Show all the relevant entries in the income statement for the year ended 31 December 2014 and in the statement of financial position as at that date. Show all workings.

5.2# Martha started business on 1 October 2010 buying and selling memory sticks. Each year in October she placed an order for memory sticks with the Mystic Memory Stick Company. During her first four years of trading, Martha's purchases and sales of memory sticks were as follows:

Year ended 30 September	Purchases	Sales
2011	120,000 @ 70p	100,000
2012	120,000 @ 90p	100,000
2013	120,000 @ £1.10	140,000
2014	120,000 @ £1.30	100,000

(a) Calculate the value of inventory on 30 September 2014, using each of the following inventory valuation methods:
 (i) FIFO (first in, first out)
 (ii) LIFO (last in, first out)
 (iii) AVCO (average cost – perpetual method).

(b) Explain why, under accounting standards, FIFO can be used, but LIFO is not permitted.

5.3 Trimmings plc manufactures textiles which are sold to fashion designers to be made into garments.

Although the majority of textiles in inventory at 31 May 2014 were likely to be sold at prices significantly above the manufacturing cost, the company accountant is concerned about the following product lines:

1 Orange Lace. Manufacturing cost £9,000. This has been on a shelf since 2005. The accountant believes that the only way of selling it would be to shred and bundle it (at a cost of £500) and sell it as industrial cleaning wipes for an anticipated price of £2,000.

2 Saltypigs. Originally printed to meet a high demand for garments linked to a popular television series, there is no further demand for the textile in this country. The textiles cost £16,000, and the only possible source of revenue would be to export the material at a cost of £2,750 for use as sun shades in Chad. Administration costs to handle the sale are estimated at £2,650, and the sale price is estimated at £4,000.

(a) Explain what is meant by the term 'inventory is valued at the lower of cost and net realisable value'.
(b) Explain, with reasons, how each of the above product lines should be accounted for in the final accounts of Trimmings plc for the year ended 31 May 2014.

5.4 #

(a) Explain the circumstances where a *theoretical* inventory valuation method may have to be used to value inventory.
(b) A company in the building industry is about to value its inventory of steel bars. It has 5,000 steel bars in inventory on 30 September 2014, all of equal size and quality, which were delivered in lorry loads at 100 steel bars per lorry. During the financial year ended 30 September 2014, the price of steel bars fluctuated, as follows:

Quarter	Price per bar
October–December	£250
January–March	£280
April–June	£270
July–September	£290

Lorry-loads of steel bars delivered during the year were as follows:

Quarter	Deliveries
October–December	60
January–March	90
April–June	170
July–September	45

Steel bars used on contracts were as follows:

Quarter	Steel bars used
October–December	3,500
January–March	8,000
April–June	9,500
July–September	10,500

There was no opening inventory of steel bars.
The company values its inventory on the 'First In First Out' basis. Calculate the value of its inventory of steel bars at 30 September 2014.

5.5 Bickley Brothers sell luxury picnic hampers from their prestigious shop in London. When the firm's accountant drew up the list of Receivables Ledger balances at the business's year-end, 31 May 2014, the following information was revealed:

	£
Total balances	13,525
This *includes* £2,400 owed by Robin Taylor, now considered to be a bad debt, and a further number of doubtful debtors, amounting to £3,500.	
Bickley Brothers had an opening balance of £3,000 on its provision for doubtful debts at 1 June 2013.	

On 31 May 2015, the business had total Receivables Ledger balances of £17,630. Of that total, one customer, Moira Harris, owes £600 which is considered to be a bad debt. A further £3,200 of trade receivables is considered doubtful at that date.

(a) Explain the difference between bad and doubtful debts.
(b) Show the relevant extracts from the income statements for each of the years ended 31 May 2014 and 31 May 2015 and the statements of financial position ended on those dates.
(c) What would be the effect on the income statement for the year ended 31 May 2015 and the statement of financial position as at that date if on 4 December 2014 Robin Taylor pays the amount he owed?

5.6# The receivables ledger of Caraway plc included the following balances:

Total Receivables Ledger balances	£89,600
Bad debts included within that total	£2,700
Doubtful debts identified at the end of the year	£6,200

There was also an opening provision for doubtful debts of £4,700.
Show the entries relevant to trade receivables that would appear in the company's income statement and statement of financial position.

Case study: Esmeralda doesn't disappear, so Chiquita appears

As Marvin (see previous case studies) entered the second year of his business, things appeared to be going well. His fame was spreading and he was invited to appear on 1 July 2012 at the prestigious Gala Stars Show. As the highlight of his act was the 'disappearing lady' trick, he was highly embarrassed when, after saying the 'magic words' and tapping the correct number of times with his wand, the curtains drew back to reveal Esmeralda in a close embrace with a stagehand. Marvin was so furious that as soon as the show was over he not only sacked Esmeralda but also closed his magic set factory (thereby putting Esmeralda's seven brothers and sisters, the factory's only employees, out of work). Immediately, all the factory's inventory was sold at cost and the factory machinery was sold at its depreciated value.

During the six months to 31 December 2012, the following events occurred:

1. The disappearing lady apparatus was sold on 1 August 2012 for £1,000. Its depreciated value at 30 June 2012 was £1,200 (cost £2,000 less 40% p.a. diminishing balance depreciation). A further one month's depreciation is to be charged prior to calculating the profit or loss on disposal.
2. Marvin took on a new assistant, Chiquita, who was previously employed as a receivables ledger clerk at Kaboosh Limited. She was to perform in a new 'saw the lady in half' routine (for which a new prop costing £3,000 was bought on 1 September 2012) as well as supervising the collection of Marvin's trade receivables. She immediately prepared a report on the Receivables Ledger, showing that at 31 August 2012 he was owed £900, including £200 from Tanya Turner who was a 'bad' debtor, and £150 from Carlos Gonzales whose cheque had been returned by his bank three times marked 'no funds available' and was to be considered doubtful.

Required

(a) Calculate the profit or loss on disposal of the 'disappearing lady' apparatus.

(b) Explain the effect on Marvin's profit and assets of classifying debts as 'bad' or 'doubtful'.

Answers are in Appendix 3

Further research

There are many companies that offer to collect debts on behalf of their clients. Type 'debt collection' into your search engine to see the range of services offered.

Revision of Chapters 1–5

Introduction

Having got this far, you may be feeling rather overwhelmed by the amount of information and explanations you have had to absorb. This revision section is included to give you a chance to consolidate your knowledge. Answers to all the questions (other than the case study) are contained in Appendix 4.

Multiple-choice questions

1 Management accounting is:
   (a) Used to make the business more cost-efficient
   (b) Required by government legislation
   (c) Used only by people outside the business
   (d) Used to prepare a trial balance

2 Double-entry bookkeeping means:
   (a) There are two doors leading into the accountant's office
   (b) Every transaction is entered twice on the debit side and twice on the credit side
   (c) Transactions are entered in two separate parts of the bookkeeping system
   (d) All work is duplicated with no real benefit

3 GAAP stands for:
   (a) Generally Available Accounting Practices
   (b) Generally Accepted Accounting Principles
   (c) Government Authorised Accounting Principles
   (d) Give Accountants A Present

4 Which of the following is an underlying assumption of accounting?
   (a) Prepayment basis
   (b) Bad debts
   (c) Gone Concern
   (d) Accrual basis

5 Current assets include:
   (a) Inventory, trade receivables and prepayments
   (b) Inventory, trade receivables and accruals
   (c) Inventory, trade payables and prepayments
   (d) Inventory, trade payables and accruals

6 Depreciation is calculated because:
   (a) Most non-current assets tend to lose value over time
   (b) Money must be set aside to replace the assets
   (c) Every non-current asset loses value over time
   (d) The owners know exactly how much non-current assets lose in value over time

7 Non-current liabilities are those which:
(a) Are due for repayment in less than one year
(b) Are never repaid
(c) Are due for repayment after more than one year
(d) Will be repaid in one year's time

8 'Drawings' is shown on a sole proprietor's statement of financial position as:
(a) An addition to the equity account
(b) A deduction from the equity account
(c) A current liability
(d) A current asset

9 The double-entry equation can be written as:
(a) Assets − Expenses = Liabilities + Equity + Income
(b) Assets + Expenses = Liabilities − Equity + Income
(c) Assets + Expenses = Liabilities + Equity − Income
(d) Assets + Expenses = Liabilities + Equity + Income

10 Which of the following *will* result in a change in equity?
(a) A non-current asset bought by the business for £10,000
(b) A profit made by the organisation
(c) A payment received from a customer
(d) A supplier paid by the business

11 A grocer buys a delivery van from Homer Motors for £9,000 by bank transfer. The effect on the grocer's business is to:
(a) Increase a non-current asset (the delivery van) and decrease a current asset (the bank balance)
(b) Increase an expense (purchases) and decrease a current asset (the bank balance)
(c) Increase a non-current asset (the delivery van) and increase current liabilities (a trade payable, Homer Motors)
(d) Increase a current asset (the bank balance) and decrease a non-current asset (the delivery van)

12 Another name for the impersonal ledger is the:
(a) Payables ledger
(b) General ledger
(c) Receivables ledger
(d) Cash ledger

13 A petty cash float is:
(a) The amount of petty cash left after all the payments for a period have been made
(b) The amount of petty cash paid out during a specific period
(c) The amount drawn from the main bank account and paid into the petty cash, equivalent to petty cash payments made during a specific period
(d) An agreed amount of petty cash needed to cover typical petty cash payments for a specific period

14 'Trade receivables' are:
(a) Customers who owe money to the business
(b) Customers who buy goods for cash
(c) Suppliers who are owed money by the business
(d) Suppliers who have been paid by the business

15 A jam factory pays £3 for a stapler for use in its office. How would this be shown in the financial summaries?
(a) As a non-current asset in the statement of financial position
(b) As purchases in the income statement
(c) As stationery in the income statement
(d) As a current asset in the statement of financial position

16 The imprest system is used to control which of the following?
(a) The design of the company's advertising campaigns
(b) Petty cash expenditure
(c) The rate of pay of employees
(d) The amount of money the owner can take from the business

17 If a ledger account has debit entries totalling £450 and credit entries totalling £200, the balance on the account is:
(a) Credit balance £250
(b) Debit balance £250
(c) Debit balance £650
(d) Credit balance £650

18 During a month a business spends £195 on petty cash items and pays into petty cash a £5 note which the owner had borrowed in the previous month. There was a cash float of £200 at the start of the month. Using the imprest system, how much will be paid into petty cash at the start of the next month?
(a) £200
(b) £10
(c) £190
(d) £390

19 What is *amortisation*?
(a) The equivalent of depreciation for intangible non-current assets
(b) A system of controlling petty cash
(c) The process of controlling bad and doubtful debts
(d) The process of recording financial information in a ledger system

20 Which one of the following is *not* an acceptable stock valuation method?
(a) LIFO (Last In First Out)
(b) Invoice price
(c) FIFO (First In First Out)
(d) AVCO (Average Cost)

21 A company has 25 digital radios in its inventory which it bought for £50 each. Each radio is normally sold for £100, but due to a slight cosmetic fault, the company will have to reduce the selling price to £45 each. What is the total value of the inventory of the digital radios to be included as a current asset in the statement of financial position?
(a) £1,250 (25 × £50)
(b) £2,500 (25 × £100)
(c) £1,125 (25 × £45)
(d) £1,375 (25 × [£100 − £45])

22 Relating to the closing inventory for a financial period, which of the following is true?
(a) The value is shown only in the income statement (as part of the cost of sales calculation)
(b) The value is shown only in the statement of financial position as a current asset
(c) The value is shown in both the income statement and the statement of financial position
(d) The value is added to the 'purchases' total in the income statement

23 A business started its year owing £4,000 for electricity. During the year it paid electricity bills totalling £24,000 but owed £5,000 by the end of the period. What will be the figure transferred to the income statement for electricity?
(a) £33,000
(b) £15,000
(c) £23,000
(d) £25,000

24 A business installs a machine costing £40,000. The machine is expected to last for 5 years and have an estimated residual value of £4,000. What is the machine's depreciated value at the end of 2 years' ownership?
(a) £25,600
(b) £7,200
(c) £14,400
(d) £21,600

25 A car is bought for £16,000. It is to be depreciated on a diminishing balance basis using a rate of 40% p.a. What is the car's depreciated value at the end of 2 years' ownership?
(a) £9,600
(b) £5,760
(c) £12,800
(d) £3,200

26 For a pen factory, *indirect* costs could include:
(a) The cost of plastic to make the pens
(b) The cost of heating the factory
(c) The wages paid to the skilled workers making the pens
(d) The cost of velvet-lined boxes in which each pen is packaged

27 Which of the following headings appears when calculating the 'cost of manufacturing' for a manufacturing business?
(a) Cost of sales
(b) Gross profit
(c) Prime cost of production
(d) Operating profit

28 A company has opening inventory £6,900, closing inventory £7,800, purchases £33,650 and sales revenue £98,000 What is its gross profit?
(a) £49,650
(b) £109,050
(c) £65,250
(d) £123,970

29 Which one of the following types of business organisation has to show taxation as a deduction from its operating profit?
(a) Limited company
(b) Partnership
(c) Sole proprietorship
(d) Sole trader

30 A business sells an asset on 1 January for £12,000. The asset was bought exactly two years previously for £24,000 and depreciation was calculated over five years on the straight line method, assuming no residual value. What is the profit or loss on disposal?
(a) £7,200 loss
(b) £2,400 loss
(c) £12,000 loss
(d) £12,000 profit

31 A company starts business on 1 January. In that month it buys 300 grecks at £40 each, then 200 at £50 each. On the last day of the month it sells 400 grecks. If it uses FIFO to value inventory, what is the inventory value at 31 January?
(a) £4,500
(b) £4,000
(c) £5,000
(d) £5,500

32 A company selling designer watches bought 400 for £60 each. Normal selling price is £100 per watch, but a change in fashion has resulted in all the watches being saleable at only £30 each, after a different strap, costing £2 each, has been fitted to them. How should the inventory of watches be valued?
(a) £11,200
(b) £24,000
(c) £39,200
(d) £12,000

33 What is a doubtful debt?
(a) A debt where there is some hope of getting paid; even though payment is delaye
(b) A debt where there is no hope of getting paid
(c) A debt which is bad
(d) A debt where the customer has queried an invoice

34 At the start of a year, a business has £3,000 on its provision for doubtful debts account. By the end of the year, doubtful debts have increased to £4,200. What entries would be shown in the financial summaries?
(a) Expenses include £7,200 and trade receivables are reduced by £7,200
(b) Expenses include £4,200 and trade receivables are reduced by £4,200
(c) Profit is increased by £1,200 and trade receivables are reduced by £4,200
(d) Expenses include £1,200 and trade receivables are reduced by £4,200

35 If a bad debt is unexpectedly paid some years after it was written off, what would be the effect in the financial summaries for that year?
(a) Increase profit and decrease trade receivables balances
(b) Increase profit and increase the bank account
(c) Increase the trade receivables balances shown under current assets
(d) No effect

Exam-style questions

Question 1

Aneka Patel's trial balance at 31 May 2014 was as follows:

	Dr £	Cr £
Advertising	18,563	
Bad debts	5,835	
Bank overdraft		14,852
Bank interest paid	5,231	
Equity at 1 June 2013		100,000

	Dr	Cr
	£	£
Cash in hand	650	
Trade payables		24,510
Trade receivables	16,540	
Depreciation on fixtures and fittings at 1 June 2013		6,503
Depreciation on motor cars at 1 June 2013		26,800
Drawings	67,500	
Electricity	6,420	
Fixtures and fittings (cost)	24,210	
Insurance	2,640	
Loan interest (half-year)	2,400	
Long-term 6% loan (repayable in 2019)		80,000
Motor cars (cost)	65,920	
Provision for doubtful debts at 1 June 2013		2,000
Purchases	482,230	
Rent and rates	5,900	
Revenue		626,220
Inventory at 1 June 2013	87,355	
Sundry expenses	13,700	
Telephone	11,240	
Wages and salaries	64,551	
	880,885	880,885

Notes:

1 Inventory at 31 May 2014 was valued at £84,800
2 Depreciation is to be provided as follows: motor cars at 40% p.a. on the diminishing balance; fixtures and fittings at 10% on cost.
3 Revenue includes £2,000 from Wem Garage for the sale of a car which was bought two years previously at a cost of £6,000. No entries relating to the disposal of the car have been made, and the car has been fully depreciated for the two years prior to sale.
4 At 31 May 2014 £1,300 was owed for electricity, and £200 of the insurance was prepaid. The second half-year's loan interest is unpaid.
5 The provision for doubtful debts is to be increased by £500.

Required

Prepare Aneka Patel's income statement for the year ended 31 May 2014 and her statement of financial position as at that date. Show all relevant workings.

Question 2

From the following trial balance and attached notes, prepare an income statement for the year ended 30 September 2014 and a statement of financial position as at that date.

Felicity Frankton
Trial balance as at 30 September 2014

	Dr £	Cr £
Bad debts written off	500	
Bank balance	2,350	
Equity, 1 October 2013		15,940
Computers, at cost	3,610	
Depreciation on computers, 1 October 2013		1,850
Depreciation on motor cars, 1 October 2013		7,600
Drawings	16,900	
Light and heat	2,200	
Motor cars, at cost	16,500	
Opening inventory, 1 October 2013	16,520	
Proceeds of sale of motor car		1,500
Provision for doubtful debts, 1 October 2013		800
Purchases	32,410	
Rent and rates	3,200	
Revenue		105,800
Sundry office expenses	10,200	
Trade payables		13,600
Trade receivables	24,200	
Wages and salaries	18,500	
	147,090	147,090

Notes:

1. Closing inventory was valued at £14,560.
2. A car costing £7,900 on 1 October 2010 was sold during the year for £1,500. Depreciation to the date of sale was £6,000. No entries had been made relating to this sale, other than crediting the proceeds to a separate general ledger account, as shown in the trial balance.
3. £600 was owed for rent and rates at the end of the year, and £200 had been prepaid at the end of the year relating to sundry office expenses.
4. The provision for doubtful debts was to be adjusted to equal 5% of the closing trade receivables total.
5. Depreciation is charged as follows:

Computer equipment: over five years on the straight line basis, assuming no residual values
Motor cars: 60% p.a. on the diminishing balance basis, with no depreciation being charged in the year of sale.

Question 3

From the following trial balance and attached notes, prepare an income statement for the year ended 31 December 2013 and a statement of financial position as at that date.

Patrick Cooper
Trial balance as at 31 December 2013

	Dr	Cr
	£	£
Revenue		289,512
Purchases	132,950	
Opening inventory	5,820	
Bank interest	950	
Wages and salaries	39,540	
Drawings	22,000	
Administration expenses	55,500	
Equity at 1 January 2013		16,268
Trade receivables	6,300	
Trade payables		5,210
Provision for doubtful debts		300
Bad debts written off	250	
Selling expenses	37,790	
Equipment at cost	14,000	
Depreciation on equipment at 1 January 2013		2,350
Bank overdraft		1,600
Cash in hand	140	
	315,240	315,240

Notes:

1. Closing inventory was valued at £4,900.
2. There was an accrual of £300 for selling expenses and £150 of the administration expenses were prepaid.
3. An item of equipment bought for £600 on 1 January 2010 was sold for £100 on 1 January 2013. The proceeds are shown as part of 'Revenue'. Equipment is depreciated at 20% p.a. on the straight line basis, with no residual values.
4. The provision for doubtful debts is to be increased to £550.

Case study

Marvin's second birthday

Marvin (see previous case studies) celebrated two years in business on 30 June 2013. At that date, his versatile assistant, Chiquita, produced the following trial balance:

	Dr	Cr
	£	£
Appearance fees as entertainer		45,200
Cost of magician's equipment	7,700	
Cost of 'saw the lady in half' equipment	3,000	
Bad debt	200	
Purchases of novelties for resale	15,600	
Sales of novelties		35,900
Marvin's drawings	32,000	
Wages to assistant (Chiquita)	24,600	
Travel to performance venues	6,220	
Cleaning	1,320	
Loss on disposal of 'disappearing lady' apparatus	160	
Opening inventory of novelties	2,400	
Opening equity, 1 July 2012		18,300
Trade payables		480
Trade receivables	2,600	
Bank balance	5,160	
Depreciation on magician's equipment, 1 July 2012		1,080
	100,960	100,960

Notes:

1 At the very start of the year he closed down the manufacturing section, selling inventory of raw materials and machinery at their book values. There is no need to prepare a 'cost of manufacturing' section in the income statement.

2 Closing inventory of bought-in novelties at 30 June 2013 was £2,500.

3 Marvin owed £250 for dry-cleaning at 30 June 2013, but had paid £600 on 1 April 2013 for a rail season ticket lasting 12 months.
4 Depreciation for the year on the magician's equipment was £1,300. The 'saw the lady in half' equipment is depreciated over four years, assuming a residual value of 20% of cost price.
5 A provision for doubtful debts is to be created of 5% of the closing trade receivables total.

Required

Prepare Marvin's income statement for the year ended 30 June 2013 and a statement of financial position as at that date.

Answer to case study in Appendix 3

Further research

Look in your library for introductory financial accounting textbooks. Look at the way different authors write about the topics covered so far in Chapters 1 to 5.

Chapter 6

Limited liability companies and other types of business organisation

Objectives

When you have read this chapter you will be able to:

- Identify the characteristics of sole proprietorships, partnerships (including limited liability partnerships) and limited companies
- Appreciate the different long- and short-term financing possibilities for various types of business organisation
- Distinguish between rights issues and bonus issues
- Understand the meaning of 'published accounts'
- Give a basic definition of a 'group' of companies

6.1 Introduction

In the preceding chapters, the main emphasis has been on the recording and summarising of a *sole proprietor's* financial information. Many businesses, including the largest in terms of sales and profitability, are not sole proprietorships but are formed as either partnerships or limited liability companies. Limited liability companies (usually shortened to 'limited companies') themselves can be either 'private' limited companies (Ltd) or public limited companies (plc's). Many limited companies are *subsidiary* companies, owned by another company, in what is known as a 'group' of companies. All these have differing financial characteristics, some more complex than others. In this chapter we take an overview of these, with the emphasis on limited companies.

6.2 Sole proprietorships

Sole proprietorships are businesses owned by one person. Legally there is no distinction between the business and the owner (unlike limited companies, where the company has a separate legal existence from its owners). The advantages of operating as a sole proprietor are as follows:

- The owner has absolute control over the business.
- The business can be established without any legal formalities other than informing the taxation authorities
- Personal supervision by the owner may result in a better service to customers and clients.
- The owner does not have to reveal the financial results of the business to the public. (Contrast this with the two forms of limited liability business organisation, explained below, where results do have to be revealed.)

However, there are also disadvantages, including the following:

- The owner has *personal* liability for all the debts of the business, without limit.
- Total control and personal supervision usually require long hours and very hard work.
- There is no co-owner with whom to share the problems and anxieties associated with running the business.
- If the owner is absent from the business due to sickness or other reasons, this may have a serious effect on the state of the business.
- Future prospects for expansion are restricted, as they depend solely on the one owner's ability to raise finance.

The main sources of finance for a sole proprietor are:

- Equity introduced by the owner
- Loans from friends and family
- Bank borrowings, through overdrafts or loans (possibly secured against the personal assets of the owner)
- Profits ploughed back into the business.

Although many people prefer independence and quite happily continue as sole proprietorships, it is extremely difficult to expand a business without also increasing the number of people who own it. The main choice for sole proprietorships wishing to convert to or form multi-ownership enterprises is between a partnership and a limited company.

Scan the following QR code with your QR reader to take you to the website of the Department for Business Innovation and Skills

Did you know?

A UK Department for Business, Innovation and Skills statistical survey, *Business Population Estimates for the UK and Regions 2011,* found that there were an estimated 4.5 million private-sector businesses in the UK at the start of 2011 employing an estimated 23.4 million people with an estimated combined annual turnover of £3,100 billion. 62.4% of these businesses were sole proprietorships, 27.7% were limited companies and 9.8% were partnerships. Scan the QR code to take you to the website for full details.

6.3 Partnerships

A *partnership* is defined in the UK's Partnership Act of 1890 as:

> The relation which subsists between persons carrying on a business in common with a view of profit.

Partnerships are often formed by professional practices such as architects, accountants and solicitors. In fact, for many years, the rules of these professions prevented them from forming limited liability companies. Whilst the minimum number of partners is two, there is no maximum number, so major professional partnerships might have hundreds or even thousands of partners. The simplest partnership is two people setting up a business together, sharing profits or losses on a 50/50 basis, each contributing the same equity and effort. However, often one of the partners has more cash, time or experience than the other, so the partners agree perhaps a 60/40 split to recognise this. Partners can decide whatever arrangements they wish, provided they are legal, and it is important that all partners sign a formal partnership agreement (covering such matters as profit shares, partners' salaries and equity contributions) so that future disagreements are avoided.

Stop and think

A classic example of a partnership *disagreement* was the 1998 case of *Joyce v Morrisey and Others,* which related to a dispute regarding the profit sharing ratio of a successful rock band, 'The Smiths'. The band had four members including Mike Joyce, the drummer. The two lead members of the group, Morrisey and Johnny Marr, had allocated profits to themselves of 40% each and only 10% each to Mike Joyce and Andy Rourke (the remaining band member). Joyce and Rourke took legal action – though Rourke subsequently withdrew from the action – claiming that the profits should have been shared *equally* amongst all four members. There had been no written partnership agreement. After listening to all the arguments, the judge found in favour of the drummer, and required the band's profits to be split equally.

Did you know?

The accounting firm PricewaterhouseCoopers has approximately 9,000 partners worldwide.

The advantages of partnership include the following:

- The problems and pleasures of running the business are shared.
- There is access to greater expertise and financial input.
- Losses as well as profits are shared.
- The financial results do not have to be made public (unless it is a *limited liability partnership* – see section 6.3.5).
- Few legal formalities are involved, though a partnership agreement should be drawn up to avoid misunderstandings.
- The partnership can have a continuing existence (subject to the partnership agreement) even on the death of a partner in a two-partner firm if a suitable replacement partner can be found.

Disadvantages include the following:

- Personality clashes may threaten the business and ultimately cause the break-up of the partnership.
- In the vast majority of partnerships, there is no restriction on the personal liability of partners for the debts of the business (but see section 6.3.5).
- Generally, a partnership has less access to funding for expansion than a limited company.

The main sources of finance for a partnership are:

- Equity introduced by the partners
- Loans from friends and family of partners
- Bank borrowings, through overdrafts or loans, secured either on the partnership's assets or on the personal assets of individual partners
- Profits ploughed back into the business.

6.3.1 Accounting requirements of partnerships

In nearly all respects, partnership accounting is identical to that of a sole proprietorship. The only difference is that separate accounts *must* be opened for each partner showing the financial implications of the partnership agreement. These include details of:

- Shares of profits and losses
- Equity introduced and withdrawn by each partner
- Drawings made by each partner
- Whether any partners are to receive a guaranteed salary (for example, if only one partner works full-time for the partnership)
- Interest charged on drawings (to discourage individual partners from drawing excessive amounts)
- Interest allowed on equity balances (to reward those partners who have invested more than others).

6.3.2 Partnership accounts

As stated above, within the partnership, it is essential to have separate accounts (usually known as partners' capital accounts) for each partner to record their respective financial stake in the business. Starting with any initial equity contribution, this will increase over time due to profit allocations and decrease when the partner draws value out of the partnership. If these separate accounts were not maintained, it could cause severe problems if a partner died, retired or otherwise left the partnership, as it would be difficult, if not impossible, to establish the amount to be repaid to the partner or the deceased partner's family in such circumstances.

6.3.3 Partnership income statements

When preparing a partnership's financial summaries, the income statement will be produced in exactly the same way as that for a sole proprietorship. The only additional information comes in a separate section (often referred to as an *appropriation account*) after the operating profit or loss has been determined, as the profit or loss has to be divided between the partners according to their partnership agreement. If partners have also decided to pay themselves salaries or charge interest on drawings or allow interest on partners' equity, these items are also shown in this section.

Activity 6.1

Gilbert and Bufton are partners sharing profits and losses in the ratio 3:2. The operating profit for the year ended 31 December 2013 was £60,000. As Gilbert worked full-time whilst Bufton worked part-time for the partnership, Gilbert was allowed a salary of £12,000 p.a.

Show the 'appropriation account' section of the income statement for the year.

Answer

	£	£
Operating profit for the year		60,000
Divided as follows:		
Gilbert: fixed salary		(12,000)
		48,000
Gilbert: share of remaining profit (60% × £48,000)	28,800	
Bufton: share of remaining profit (40% × £48,000)	19,200	
		48,000

Stop and think

Gilbert's salary is not deducted as an 'expense' in arriving at the operating profit figure, unlike employees' salaries. It is part of the way in which the partners have decided to share the profit, so is shown as an 'appropriation'.

6.3.4 Partnership statement of financial position

The top part of the statement of financial position, showing non-current and current assets and liabilities, is identical to that of a sole proprietorship. However, the sole proprietor's equity account is replaced by details of each of the partners' capital accounts.

Activity 6.2

Assume that Gilbert and Bufton (see Activity 6.1) started the year with capital account balances of £25,900 and £15,750 respectively. During the year, Gilbert drew out £35,000 from the partnership and Bufton took £17,000.

Show the relevant extract from the partnership's statement of financial position as at 31 December 2013.

Answer

	£	£
Total net assets *(details would be provided)*		49,650
Gilbert's capital account		
Opening balance, 1 January 2013	25,900	
Add Salary	12,000	
Share of profit	28,800	
	66,700	
Less Drawings	(35,000)	
Closing capital balance, 31 December 2013		31,700
Bufton's capital account		
Opening balance, 1 January 2013	15,750	
Add Share of profit	19,200	
	34,950	
Less Drawings	(17,000)	
Closing capital balance, 31 December 2013		17,950
		49,650

An alternative way of showing the same information is to adopt a 'columnar' format, as follows:

	£	£	£
Total net assets *(details would be provided)*			49,650
Capital accounts	**Gilbert**	**Bufton**	
Opening balances	25,900	15,750	
Add Fixed salary to Gilbert	12,000	–	
Shares of profit	28,800	19,200	
	66,700	34,950	
Less Drawings	(35,000)	(17,000)	
Closing balances	31,700	17,950	49,650

Stop and think

No additional information is given in this format, but it looks a lot neater!

6.3.5 Limited liability partnerships

The vast majority of partnerships are referred to as 'general' or 'conventional' partnerships, to distinguish them from a relatively new form of business organisation, the *limited liability partnership* (or LLP). The LLP combines the organisational flexibility of a general partnership with the great advantage of limited liability. The owners of a LLP are (officially) referred to as 'members' rather than partners, and limited liability gives the members protection in the event of the LLP failing. Creditors of the LLP cannot require the members to use their personal assets to pay the LLP's debts. This is very similar to the advantage enjoyed by the shareholders of a limited liability *company*, which is referred to in section 6.5 below.

The accounting requirements for an LLP are virtually identical to that of a general partnership, but one major difference between the two types of organisation is that an LLP must *publish* its financial statements (though large LLPs publish more information than smaller ones). In the UK, this is achieved by submitting them annually to *Companies House*, which is the UK government's database of information maintained for every LLP and limited company on its register. Members of the public can gain access to this information through its website. Scan the QR code to take you to the website of Companies House (or see the reference at the end of this chapter).

Scan the following QR code with your QR reader to take you to the website of Companies House

Since the Limited Liability Partnerships Act was passed in 2000, many professional firms such as chartered surveyors, accountants and lawyers have converted their business organisation from that of a general partnership to a limited liability partnership. There are no taxation advantages or disadvantages that are relevant when making this change – the critical difference is the advantage that limited liability brings to the owners.

Did you know?

In February 2012, there were 51,000 limited liability partnerships registered with Companies House (out of 2.8 million businesses on its database).

6.4 Limited liability companies

Although there are many advantages in running a business as a sole proprietorship or a conventional partnership, these can be outweighed by the fact that the owner or partners have personal responsibility for meeting all the debts of their business. Whilst this may be of little concern to the proprietors of healthy, profitable enterprises, it can have a devastating effect on the fortunes of owners of failing or loss-making businesses, as they must meet the claims of creditors from their personal assets – possibly having to sell their homes – if the value of the business's assets are insufficient.

Another major disadvantage for ambitious business owners is the restricted scope they have for raising funds for expansion. To overcome these, many businesses are organised as limited liability companies (usually shortened to 'limited companies').

Their main features are:

- They are separate legal entities, able to trade, own assets and owe liabilities (including tax on their profit) in their own right independently from their owners.
- Ownership is (with rare exceptions) divided into shares ('the share capital') which can be bought and sold.
- The owners (known as shareholders or members) have limited liability for the debts of the company, so even if the company fails with considerable debts, their loss is restricted to the value of their part of the share capital.
- Management is in the hands of directors, who might own only a small part of the share capital. They are elected by the shareholders.
- Public limited companies (plc's) are allowed to sell their shares to the general public, which enables them to have access to virtually unlimited funds for expansion. Private limited companies (Ltd) cannot sell their shares to the public.
- Limited companies can raise money by issuing corporate bonds (also known as 'debentures'), being fixed interest loans usually secured on the company's assets, or by issuing convertible loan stock, meaning loans which can be converted into shares at a later date. *Neither of these are part of a company's share capital.*
- Employees can be offered shares in the company as an incentive to increasing their contribution towards increased profits.
- The company has perpetual existence, so even if an individual shareholder dies, the company continues.
- There may be tax advantages, particularly for highly profitable businesses, in structuring as limited liability companies.

Did you know?

In 2012, the directors of Tesco plc, one of the world's largest supermarket companies, owned just 8.4 million out of 8 billion shares issued by the company.

Limited companies do have a number of *disadvantages* when compared with other forms of business organisations:

- Lack of secrecy, as companies have to publish financial information, though large companies have to disclose more than small ones (see the previous reference to Companies House).
- Extra costs of complying with legislation: - for large companies this includes a requirement to appoint an auditor who is an independent qualified accountant responsible for reporting whether the published financial information shows a faithful representation of the financial situation.
- More formality – shareholders' meetings must be held to agree important issues, annual returns have to be completed and sent to the government, etc.
- Some shareholders might have no part in the day-to-day management of the company, yet will seek to exercise influence on the company and put pressure on the

directors, particularly in relation to the level of dividends (part of the company's annual profits returned to shareholders) that the company pays.

6.4.1 Accounting specifically for limited companies

Day-to-day financial recording for a limited company is identical in nearly all respects to that of sole proprietorships or partnerships. However, records are also needed of the following items which are specific to limited companies:

- Directors' salaries (also referred to as *remuneration* or *emoluments*) which are treated as an *expense* of the company, and therefore deducted when arriving at the operating profit or loss in the income statement.
- Auditors' fees (though most small companies do not have auditors).
- Taxation due on the profit for the financial period. Whereas the owners of sole proprietorships or partnerships are *personally* responsible to pay the tax on the business's profits, a limited company is treated as a legal entity *in its own right*, so the company itself has the responsibility for paying its tax rather than the individual shareholders. The tax due is deducted from operating profit in the income statement and is shown as a current liability in the limited company's statement of financial position.
- Dividends, which are rewards to the shareholders. These are usually expressed as 'pence per share' and might be paid once or twice a year (interim and/or final dividends).
- Reserves of profit (retained earnings), which are the remaining profits kept in the company after taxation and dividends have been deducted.
- Share capital and reserves, which are explained in the next section.

6.4.2 Share capital and reserves

Although the 'net assets' side of a limited company's statement of financial position is very similar to that of other types of business organisation, it is the information in the 'equity' section that shows major differences compared to that of sole proprietorships or partnerships. It is divided into two main parts:

1 **Share capital**, which is the total share capital issued to shareholders (see Figure 6.1). The vast majority of these shares are known as *ordinary shares* or the *equity capital* of the company. US companies refer to this as *common stock*. Each share carries an equal right to vote at company meetings and to share in any dividends, so the more shares owned, the more votes and dividends a shareholder has. Shares have a nominal value (also called a *par value*), for example 25p or 5p. Sometimes dividends are expressed as a percentage of this nominal value. The actual amount of share capital in the hands of shareholders is known as the *issued* or *called-up* share capital. Some companies, as well as having ordinary shares, issue *preference* shares, which carry a fixed rate of dividend and have priority over the ordinary shares in respect of the payment of their dividends and the repayment of capital in the event of the company's liquidation. These shares might be *redeemable*, which means that the company can refund the preference shareholders' capital (subject to certain rules to protect the overall capital of the company) after a specified time. Share capital is referred to as 'permanent' capital of the company, as it is not normally repaid to the shareholders

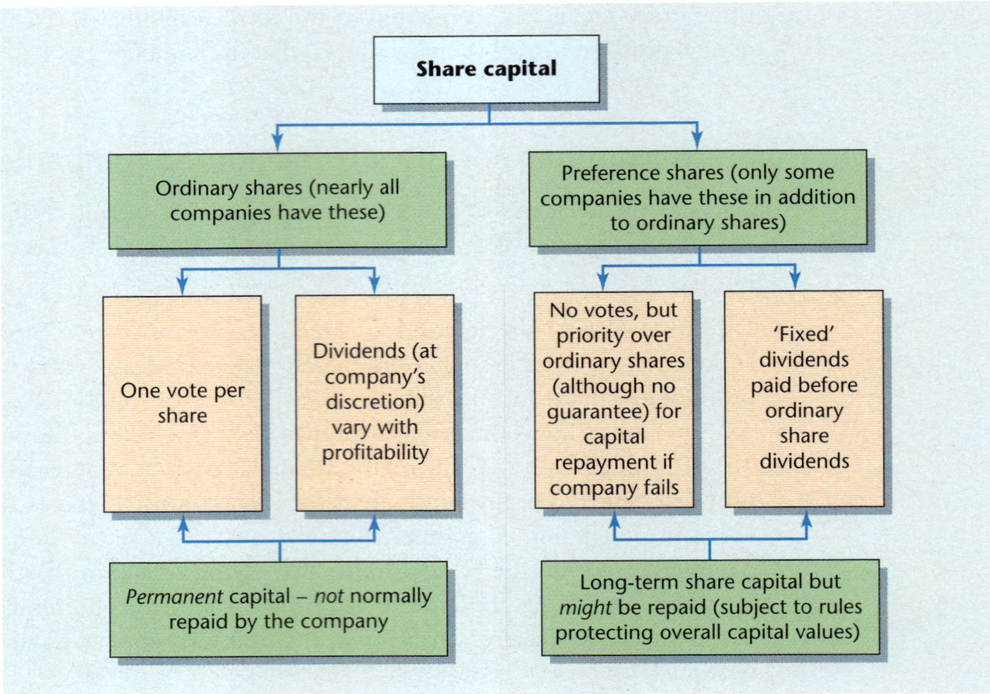

Figure 6.1 Share capital

once they have invested. This does not prevent one shareholder selling the shares to another person (for example, through a stock market in the case of a public company), though for small companies they are likely to need permission from the board of directors before a sale can be made.

Did you know?

Walmart Inc, the world's largest supermarket chain, had issued 3.5 billion units of common stock (the US equivalent of 'ordinary shares') at the end of its 2011 financial period.

2 **Reserves**, which are classified as either *non-distributable* reserves or *distributable* reserves (see Figure 6.2). The main distributable reserve is the retained earnings, which represents all the profits kept in the company after tax and dividends have been deducted, not just for the current year but since the company formed. Such reserves are known as 'distributable' because they can be used for company dividends (i.e. it is possible for the company at some future point to use some or all of these reserves to be returned to shareholders).

Did you know?

Walmart's retained earnings stood at $68.7 billion at the end of its 2012 financial period

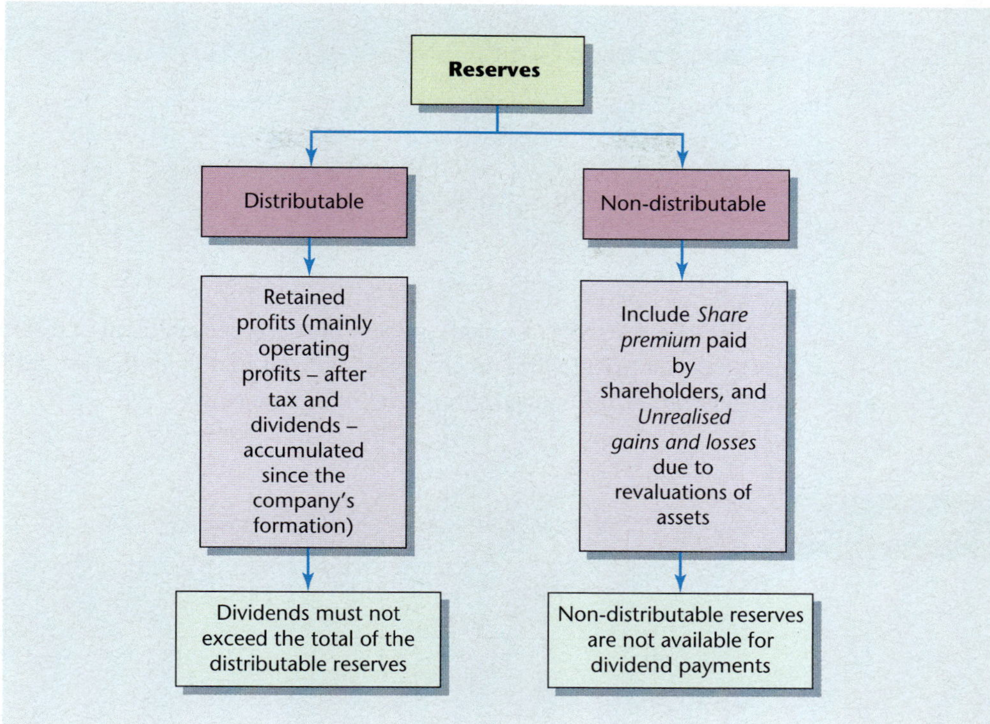

Figure 6.2 Reserves

The main *non-distributable* reserve is the share premium, which is the amount *above the nominal value* paid into the company by shareholders. For example, a company might sell its 25p nominal value shares for £2.75, in which case the 25p's go into the share capital section of the statement of financial position, whilst the remaining £2.50's are shown under a separate heading, 'share premium'.

Did you know?

Walmart's share premium totalled $3.7 billion at the end of its 2012 financial period

Another non-distributable reserve would arise if a company decided to *revalue* some of its non-current assets (particularly land and buildings). For example, if a plot of land bought several years ago for £300,000 is now worth £900,000, the company might wish to show this increase by adding £600,000 to the non-current asset value and creating an asset revaluation reserve for the same amount. The £600,000 is known as an *unrealised gain* ('unrealised' meaning that the land has not been sold), and is *not* included as part of operating profits in the income statement. However, the overall result is that the asset value shown in the statement of financial position is more realistic. It is important to note that such reserves are 'non-distributable' because they *cannot* be used to pay a dividend.

Stop and think

Bearing in mind that dividends are paid by the company to its shareholders, can you understand why 'unrealised' gains are not allowed to be used?
The answer, of course, is that the company has not sold any assets, so has no extra cash available with which to pay the dividend.

In the next activity, we shall prepare the income statement and statement of financial position of a private limited company, but not in a form that would be 'published'. We look at *published* financial summaries in section 6.6.

Activity 6.3

Salamanca Ltd's trial balance as at 31 May 2014 was as follows:

	Dr £	Cr £
Advertising	3,400	
Loan repayable 2025		40,000
Bank balance	20,000	
Sales delivery expenses	1,890	
Directors' salaries	77,300	
Non-current assets: depreciated value as at 1 June 2013	248,720	
Loan interest paid (finance costs)	1,900	
Dividends paid	5,000	
Office expenses	10,930	
Office salaries	26,200	
Opening inventory at 1 June 2013	23,500	
Retained earnings as at 1 June 2013		209,000
Purchases	117,620	
Revenue		345,000
Sales employees' salaries	36,640	
Share capital (25p nominal shares)		100,000
Share premium		140,000
Trade payables		86,200
Trade receivables	347,100	
	920,200	920,200

Notes:

1 Closing inventory at 31 May 2014 was £27,900.
2 Depreciation for the year totalled £8,350.
3 There were neither accruals nor prepayments at the year-end.
4 Tax on profits amounting to £16,000 was to be accounted for.

Prepare the company's income statement for the year ended 31 May 2014 and its statement of financial position as at that date.

Answer

Salamanca Ltd
Income statement for the year ended 31 May 2014

	£	£
Revenue		345,000
Less **Cost of sales**		
Opening inventory at 1 June 2013	23,500	
Add Purchases	117,620	
	141,120	
Less Closing inventory at 31 May 2014	(27,900)	
		(113,220)
Gross profit		231,780
Less **Expenses**		
Directors' salaries	77,300	
Sales employees' wages	36,640	
Office salaries	26,200	
Advertising	3,400	
Sales delivery expenses	1,890	
Depreciation	8,320	
Office expenses	10,930	
		(164,680)
Operating profit		67,100
Finance costs		(1,900)
Profit before tax		65,200
Less Taxation		(16,000)
Profit for the year, after tax		49,200
Less Dividend		(5,000)
Retained profit for the year		44,200

Salamanca Ltd
Income statement of finacial position as at 31 May 2014

	£	£	£
Non-current assets (248,720 – 8,320)			240,400
Current assets			
Inventory		27,900	
Trade receivables		347,100	
Cash and cash equivalents		20,000	
		395,000	
Less **Current liabilities**			
Trade payables	86,200		

	£	£	£
Taxation	16,000		
		(102,200)	
Net current assets			292,800
			533,200
Less **Non-current liabilities** (Loan repayable 2025)			(40,000)
Total net assets			**493,200**
Equity			
Share capital			100,000
Share premium			140,000
Retained earnings:			
Balance at 1 June 2013		209,000	
Retained profit for the year		44,200	
			253,200
Total equity			**493,200**

Did you know?

'Cash and cash equivalents' is the term used on a company's statement of financial position to indicate cash, bank deposits repayable on demand and any other investments that are readily convertible into known amounts of cash.

Stop and think

Of the £65,200 profit before tax, £16,000 goes to the government as taxation, £5,000 to shareholders as their dividend, and the balance of £44,200 is left within the company and added to the retained earnings as shown in the statement of financial position.

Note that the word 'reserve' is *not* the same as 'cash'. Reserves are represented by many different types of net assets, only one of which might be a cash balance.

6.4.3 Changes to share capital

A company's share capital might change for a number of reasons, including, for a public limited company, a new share issue sold to 'outside' investors or, for a private limited company, new shares issued to family, friends and known business acquaintances. Two other reasons for a change are as follows:

1 A *rights issue*, which is a further share issue to existing shareholders, in proportion to existing holdings (for example, a '3 for 2' rights issue gives the holders of two existing shares the 'right' to buy a further three shares, so if you hold 6,000 shares you could buy a further 9,000 shares). A rights issue is often the easiest way for a successful

company to raise more equity, and shares are usually offered at an attractive price to tempt investors. Obviously, a struggling company could have difficulties in attracting more investment from their shareholders.

News clip

Peugeot launches €1bn rights issue

FT

By John Reed in Geneva

PSA Peugeot Citroën on Tuesday launched a €1bn rights issue to fund its alliance with General Motors, which will pay €304m to take a 7 per cent stake in the French carmaker.

Philippe Varin, PSA's chief executive, said the company planned to use the proceeds of the share offer to launch a new low-CO^2 small-car platform and expand in emerging markets with its US partner.

Mr Varin told the Financial Times that the two companies were looking at working together in regions including Latin America, India, and Russia, but had not yet made any decisions. The joint platform will build small, lightweight "B" segment cars and be equally funded by the French and US manufacturers, he said, and launch its first cars "slightly after 2016".

The Peugeot CEO said the two carmakers had no plans for now to build cars at the same plants. "I don't think it is on the agenda today," Mr Varin said in an interview at the Geneva auto show.

Peugeot's offer, which will run from March 8 to March 21, is being made at €8.27 a share, a significant discount from the company's closing share price of just over €14 on Monday. For every 31 of the company's existing shares, 16 new ones will be issued.

GM and Peugeot's controlling family shareholders will between them take up about 31 per cent of the offer. The Peugeot family will pay €140m for its shares, and retain its position as the company's largest shareholder, with 25.2 per cent share of PSA's capital and 37.9 per cent of voting rights.

The proceeds of the share issue will be spent over three to four years. "€1bn is not going to be spent overnight," Mr Varin said.

Source: *The Financial Times*, 6 March 2012

2 A *bonus issue* (also called a scrip or capitalisation issue) is a free issue of shares to existing shareholders, again in proportion to their existing holdings, so a '1 for 4' bonus issue would mean that a shareholder with 1,200 shares would be given a further 300. This increase in the total number of shares has the effect of reducing the value of each share proportionally, so overall the effect is neutral (more shares but at lower value). Sometimes, a bonus issue is made simply to reduce a relatively high stock market share price so that investors are not deterred from investing. The 'Stop and think' box below describes such a situation, where the company's share price had risen to over £7, but following its '1 for 1' bonus issue, this was reduced to £3.50.

To cover the value of the bonus issue, the company makes an internal transfer from its reserves (distributable or non-distributable) into the share capital. If *distributable* reserves are used, the transfer into 'permanent' share capital obviously reduces the funds available for potential future dividends. This might not be welcomed by shareholders! Cynical commentators might argue that a bonus issue is little more than a 'public relations' exercise where a company is trying to persuade its shareholders that they are getting something for nothing, and relatively few companies in recent years have made bonus issues.

Stop and think

Bonus issue

At the Company's Annual General Meeting on 3 December 2010, shareholders unanimously approved a resolution granting the Company the authority to undertake a bonus issue of new ordinary James Halstead shares of 5p each ("Ordinary Shares"). Holders of Ordinary Shares as at the close of business on the record date of 13 January 2011 will receive one new Ordinary Share for every Ordinary Share then held.

James Halstead plc
12 January 2011

Source: James Halstead plc, Regulatory news announcement to the London Stock Exchange (extract), 12 January 2011

Activity 6.4

The 'share capital and reserves' section of Salamanca Ltd's statement of financial position at 31 May 2014 (see Activity 6.3 above) was as follows:

	£	£
Equity		
Share capital		100,000
Share premium		140,000
Retained earnings:		
Balance at 1 June 2013	209,000	
Retained profit for the year	44,200	
		253,200
Total equity		493,200

Assume that on 1 June 2014 a rights issue on a '3 for 5' basis was made at 80p per share. All the existing shareholders decided to take up their shares, and paid for them in full by 30 June 2014. Six months later, the company made a bonus issue on a '2 for 1' basis, the issue being paid up equally from the share premium and the retained earnings. Assume these are the only changes to equity which have been made in the period.

Show the revised 'Equity' section after the rights issue and after the bonus issue.

Answer

Statement of financial position (Equity section) after the rights issue:

	£	£
Equity		
Share capital[1]		160,000
Share premium[2]		272,000
Retained earnings:		
Balance at 1 June 2014		253,200
Total equity		685,200

Notes:

1 Original 400,000 shares (shares are of 25p nominal value, therefore £100,000 = 400,000 shares), plus 240,000 issued as '3 for 5' = 640,000 @ 25p nominal value = £160,000.
2 Original £140,000, plus £132,000 [240,000 shares × (80p – 25p)] share premium on rights issue = £272,000.

Note that the net assets will also total £685,200, as £192,000 will be added to the bank balance under 'current assets' (240,000 shares issued at 80p = £192,000).

Statement of financial position (Equity section) after the rights issue *and* the bonus issue:

	£	£
Equity		
Share capital[1]		480,000
Share premium[2]		112,000
Retained earnings[3]		
Balance at 1 June 2014		93,200
Total equity		685,200

Notes:

1 '2 for 1' trebles the previous share capital (an extra 1,280,000 shares @ 25p each = £320,000).
2 Half of the bonus comes out of the share premium (£272,000 – £160,000 = £112,000).
3 Half of the bonus comes out of the retained earnings (£253,200 – £160,000 = £93,200).

Stop and think

Note that the bonus issue has no effect on the statement of financial position total. It is £685,200 before and after the issue. The biggest change is that the bonus issue has resulted in £160,000 being transferred out of the distributable reserves (retained earnings) into 'permanent' share capital. From the shareholders' viewpoint, this could seriously reduce the level of future dividends.

6.5 Sources of finance

When a business is considering how it can continue and develop, it will have to make many vital decisions regarding alternative ways in which finance can be raised. Profitable businesses may be able to thrive by ploughing back profits into the company (known as 'internal financing'), but to expand, or cope with recessions and poor trading, additional external finance may be necessary. For short-term needs, bank overdrafts might be used, as they are the most flexible type of borrowing, but other possibilities exist, including debt factoring and invoice discounting. Occasionally, 'emergency' finance might be needed if all other avenues have been explored. For longer-term financing needs, ordinary or preference shares can be sold, or loans can be raised with fixed or variable interest rates which are repayable (or convertible into equity capital) at an agreed future date. As a way of avoiding large cash outlays, many businesses decide not to pay for non-current assets in one lump sum but instead enter finance leasing contracts, where smaller payments are made over a prolonged period. Efficient management of inventory, receivables and payables will also result in a more financially viable business. This section looks at these various financing possibilities, both long- and short-term (see Figure 6.3).

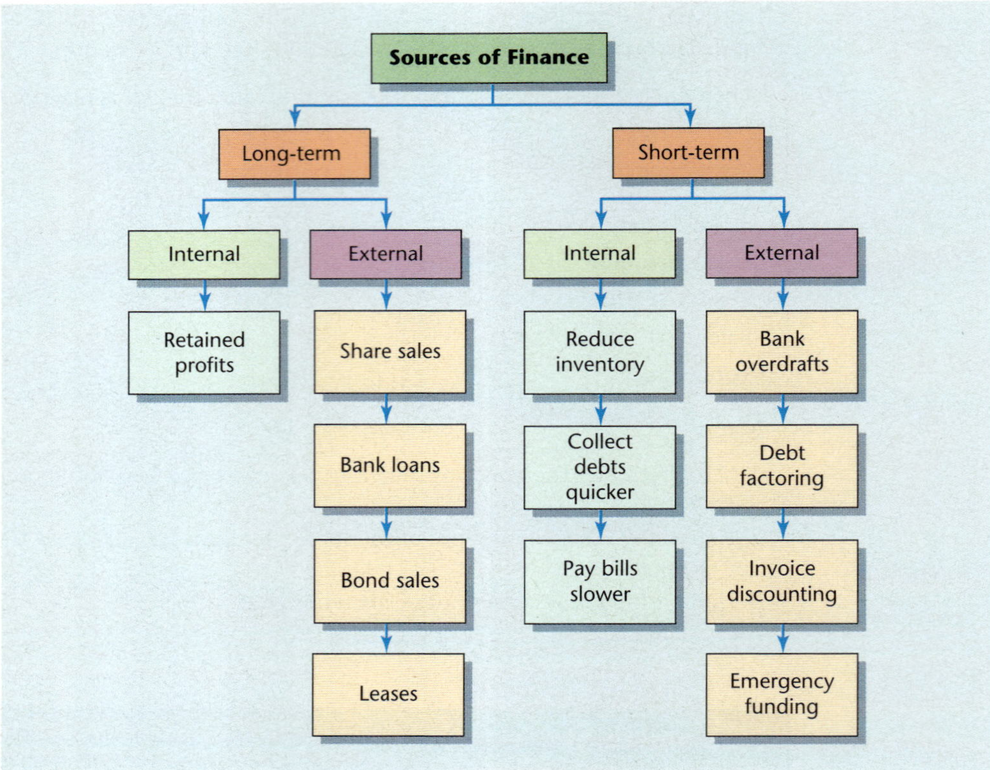

Figure 6.3 Long- and short-term financing

6.5.1 Long-term sources of finance: share sales

Private companies comprise the vast majority of limited liability enterprises, and are not allowed to offer their shares for sale to the public. However, they *are* able to sell their shares, but the people who buy are likely to be friends, relatives or business acquaintances of existing shareholders. A *public* limited company (plc) wanting to raise capital by means of a share issue will usually do so by an *offer for sale*, whereby the shares are sold first by the company to a financial institution (for example, a bank), which then offers the shares for sale to its clients or the general public by various means, including advertisements in newspapers and on websites. When a company offers its shares to the public for the first time, this is known as an initial public offering (IPO), and full details of the company and its reasons for raising capital are given in a document known as a *prospectus*. One of the largest IPOs of recent times was that of Facebook, the social network company, which raised $16 billion in May 2012, with individual shares sold at $38, a price which valued the whole business at $104 billion. There was massive publicity for the share sale at the time, which stoked up demand to a point where they hit $46 very soon after the float. However, the speculative bubble soon burst and before long they were trading at below $30. The 'News clip' below contains an article that appeared in the *Financial Times* in June 2012 which reflected on the speculative frenzy which seems to accompany some IPOs–particularly in new technology areas.

News clip

Silicon Valley hype machine blows a gasket

FT

By Richard Waters

Silicon Valley has patented a new class of momentum stock in recent years. What makes companies in this group different is that they don't rely on the usual Wall Street speculators to hype their prospects and pump up their share prices.

Instead, an ecosystem of opportunistic private investors with an eye for a quick return, along with the emergence of new and opaque secondary markets to trade the shares, has proved fertile ground for overheated speculation. Whether this can survive the fallout that is still spreading from last month's botched Facebook IPO is another matter.

It was this investment market for late-stage private companies – essentially, those with the potential to go public soon – that did more than anything to fuel the latest consumer internet bubble. Centred on Facebook, it included Zynga and Groupon, both of which made it to the stock market last autumn, as well as companies that are still private like Twitter and Dropbox, the cloud storage company that was recently valued at $4bn.

If the demand from private market investors were there, so was the supply of entrepreneurs who were more than happy to bide their time before making the jump to the public markets. Mark Zuckerberg's willingness to turn his back on the stock market far longer than the founders of other hot internet companies that came before has become a model for many other up-and-coming technocrats.

The hedge funds, mutual fund groups and others who had recently crowded into the business of investing in IPO candidates are now in retreat. That is the message from venture capitalists and investment bankers who are less prone to moving in and out of these markets as fashions change – though such generalisations should be handled with caution, since the investors who remain have every reason to boost their negotiating position with companies trying to raise money.

It isn't hard to see why the pre-IPO investment craze looks a lot less exciting than it once did. Anyone who jumped into Facebook's last big round of private financing – arranged early last year by Goldman Sachs and valuing the company at $50bn – has made a fair profit, though the low valuation of around $70bn hit earlier this month after Facebook went public yields nothing like the sort of windfall that many had anticipated.

For other companies, the picture can look a lot bleaker. At the peak of the pre-IPO craze early last year, for instance, social games company Zynga was valued in a private fundraising round at some $9bn – considerably more than the $4bn or so it is currently judged to be worth as a public company. Groupon, the daily deals company that spurned a $6bn takeover offer 18 months ago, was recently trading at a lower value than that on Wall Street – and only slightly above the level at which it raised money from private investors in early 2011.

If the late funding rounds lifted the valuations of these companies and stoked anticipation among eager stock market investors, a new group of private secondary markets, open only to experienced investors, added to the hype. It was these markets that put a peak price on Facebook earlier this year in the run-up to its IPO of $46 – considerably higher than the $31 or so that the shares now change hands for on the stock market.

For a time, the private momentum stock game looked like a winner for anyone who got in early. By the time the companies reached their IPOs, wide-eyed stock market investors were gagging for a piece of the action – and with only small floats of shares released to the public, the stocks enjoyed some early success.

If the public markets have wised up to this game – and if some of the speculative heat has left the pre-IPO business – then what does it mean for other companies that had been looking to ride the wave? After all, the ready availability of both capital and secondary market liquidity has helped companies remain private longer, while raising large amounts of cash and satisfying employees and early investors who want to sell some of their stock.

One answer came earlier this week from Facebook board member and early investor Peter Thiel in the form of a new $402m investment fund aimed at "growth" stage companies – the previously unfashionable segment of the venture capital market that sits between the earliest rounds of funding and the pre-IPO candidates. Mr Thiel wants to feed these companies the money to take bigger swings at new markets while digging in for a longer stay in the private world.

The Silicon Valley game of pumping up companies for quick IPO returns looks like it may be over – for now. But given how quickly venture capital fashions change, it is certain to return.

Source: *The Financial Times*, 20 June 2012

Scan the following QR code with your QR reader to take you to the website of SuperGroup plc, where you can download the entire prospectus.

It is very unusual for public limited companies to sell their own shares *directly* to the public. Where relatively small amounts are involved, one or more financial institutions might buy all the available shares off the company and then sell the shares to their own clients. This is known as a 'placing'. Most large share sales will be *underwritten*, which means that if insufficient shares are taken up by the public, 'underwriters' will buy the unsold shares at an agreed price, charging a commission to the company as their fee for taking the risks involved. The underwriters will then sell on their shares at the appropriate time through the stock market. The underwriting process guarantees that the company will sell all the shares.

Figure 6.4 shows details of SuperGroup plc's share offer, where it sold 25 million shares at £5 each.

Activity 6.5

Look at today's share price for SuperGroup plc. Has the share price risen or fallen since the share issue?

6.5.2 Long-term sources of finance: loans

The long-term loan capital of a company might comprise several different elements, including the following:

- *Bank loans*, which carry either a fixed or variable interest rate, and will usually be secured against company assets to protect the bank in the event of default. Repayments of both capital and interest are made over the loan period, which can be

THIS DOCUMENT IS IMPORTANT AND REQUIRES YOUR IMMEDIATE ATTENTION. If you are in any doubt as to what action you should take, you should immediately consult a person authorised under the Financial Services and Markets Act 2000 (as amended) ("FSMA") who specialises in advising on the acquisition of shares and other securities.

This document comprises a prospectus ("**Prospectus**") relating to SuperGroup PLC (the "**Company**") and has been prepared in accordance with the Prospectus Rules of the Financial Services Authority (the "**FSA**") made under section 73A of FSMA and has been filed with the FSA. This document has been made available to the public as required by the Prospectus Rules.

Application has been made to the FSA for all of the Ordinary Shares, issued and to be issued in connection with the Offer, to be admitted to the Official List of the FSA (the "**Official List**") and to London Stock Exchange plc (the "**London Stock Exchange**") for such Ordinary Shares to be admitted to trading on its main market for listed securities (together "**Admission**"). Admission to trading on the London Stock Exchange constitutes admission to trading on a regulated market. It is expected that Admission will become effective and that unconditional dealings will commence in the Ordinary Shares on the London Stock Exchange at 8.00 a.m. on 24 March 2010. All dealings in the Ordinary Shares prior to the commencement of unconditional dealings will be of no effect if Admission does not take place and such dealings will be at the sole risk of the parties concerned. No application has been made, or is currently intended to be made, for the Ordinary Shares to be admitted to listing or traded on any other stock exchange.

The Company and its Directors (whose names appear on page 19 of this document) accept responsibility for the information contained in this document. To the best of the knowledge of the Company and its Directors (who have taken all reasonable care to ensure that such is the case), the information contained in this document is in accordance with the facts and contains no omission likely to affect the import of such information.

Prospective investors should read this document in its entirety and, in particular, the "Risk Factors" set out on pages 10 to 17 when considering an investment in the Ordinary Shares of the Company.

The Company is offering up to 25,000,000 new Ordinary Shares ("**New Shares**") under the Offer. The New Shares will, following Admission, rank *pari passu* in all respects with the other issued Ordinary Shares and will carry the right to receive all dividends and distributions declared, made or paid, on or in respect of the issued Ordinary Shares following Admission.

SuperGroup PLC

(Incorporated and registered in England and Wales under the Companies Act 2006 with registered number 07063562)

Offer of up to 25,000,000 Ordinary Shares at a price of £5.00 per Ordinary Share and admission to the Official List and trading on the London Stock Exchange

Sponsor and Sole Bookrunner
SEYMOUR PIERCE LIMITED

Enlarged Share Capital immediately following Admission (assuming the Maximum Amount is raised pursuant to the Retail Offer)

Ordinary Shares of 5p each *Issued and fully paid*	
Number	*Amount*
79,000,020	£3,950,001

Seymour Pierce Limited, which is authorised and regulated in the UK by the FSA, is acting for the Company and for no one else in connection with the Offer and will not be responsible to anyone other than the Company for providing the protections afforded to customers of Seymour Pierce Limited or for providing advice in relation to the Offer or any matters referred to herein. Apart from the responsibilities and liabilities, if any, which may be imposed on Seymour Pierce by FSMA or the regulatory regime established thereunder. Seymour Pierce does not accept any responsibility whatsoever for the contents of this document or for any statement made or purported to be made by it, or on its behalf, in connection with the Company, the Ordinary Shares or the Offer. Seymour Pierce accordingly disclaims all and any liability whether arising in tort, contract or otherwise (save as referred to above) which they might otherwise have in respect of such document or any such statement. Seymour Pierce Limited has given and not withdrawn its consent to the issue of this document with the inclusion of the references to its name in the form and context to which they are included.

Investors should rely only on the information in this Prospectus. No person has been authorised to give any information or make any representations other than those contained in this Prospectus and, if given or made, such information or representations must not be relied on as having been authorised by the Company, the Directors or Seymour Pierce Limited. Without prejudice to any obligation of the Company to publish a supplementary prospectus pursuant to section 87G of FSMA and paragraph 3.4 of the Prospectus Rules, neither the delivery of this Prospectus nor any subscription or purchase of Ordinary Shares made pursuant to this Prospectus shall, under any circumstances, create any implication that there has been no change in the affairs of the Company of the Group since, or that the information contained herein is correct at any time subsequent to, the date of this Prospectus.

In the event the Company is required to publish a supplementary prospectus pursuant to section 87G of FSMA and paragraph 3.4 of the Prospectus Rules, investors will have a statutory right pursuant to section 87Q of FSMA to withdraw their application to purchase or subscribe for Ordinary Shares in the Offer before the end of the period of two working days beginning with the first working day after the date on which the supplementary prospectus was published. Investors who do not exercise their right to withdraw their application within the stated two day period will be deemed to have accepted the terms contained within the supplementary prospectus.

The contents of this Prospectus are not to be construed as legal, financial, business or tax advice. Each prospective investor should consult their legal adviser, financial adviser, business adviser or tax adviser for legal, financial or tax advice.

This document does not constitute or form part of any offer or invitation to sell or issue, or any solicitation of any offer to purchase or subscribe for, any securities other than the Ordinary Shares to which it relates or any offer or invitation to sell or issue, or any solicitation of any offer to purchase or subscribe for, such Ordinary Shares by any person in any circumstances in which such offer or solicitation is unlawful and is not for distribution in or into the United States, Australia, Canada or Japan.

The New Shares have not been and will not be registered under the US Securities Act or the applicable securities laws of Australia, Canada or Japan and may not be offered or sold within the United States, Australia, Canada or Japan or to, or for the account or benefit of, citizens or residents of the United States, Australia, Canada or Japan.

The contents of the Company's website or any website directly or indirectly linked to the Company's website do not form part of this document and investors should not rely on it.

Capitalised terms have the meanings ascribed to them on pages 178 to 185 of this document.

Figure 6.4 SuperGroup Plc share offer

Source: SuperGroup plc

of any duration agreed by the lender (though a minimum of 12 months is required for it to be regarded as a 'non-current liability' on the borrower's statement of financial position).

- *Bonds*, also known as debentures, are also likely to be secured against company assets and usually carry a fixed rate of interest. Bonds can be bought and sold by investors after issue, in the same way that shares are traded. The lenders are *creditors* of the company, not shareholders. As with shares, the market price will depend on supply and demand, but bonds are seen as a less risky investment owing to their security. However, lower risk also brings a lower reward in the form of a fixed interest rate, which remains unchanged regardless of how profitable the company becomes. Another aspect of lower risk is that the interest is payable to bond owners *before* any shareholders' dividends can be declared. Some loans (*convertible* loan stock) might be exchanged for ordinary shares at a date (or dates) stated in the bond deed, which may make them more attractive to investors. Some loans might even be termed 'irredeemable', meaning that there is no set repayment date.

Did you know?

Loan interest reduces the amount of profits that is subject to tax. This lowers the effective interest rate paid by the borrower. For example, a company paying 6% on a loan with a tax rate of 20% on its profits is paying a 'real' rate of interest of only 4.8%.

Figure 6.5 shows how Tesco Bank Bonds were advertised in a UK newspaper in December 2011.

6.5.3 Long-term sources of finance: finance leases

A *finance lease* is a means by which companies obtain the right to use assets over a period of time. The ownership of the asset never passes to the actual user of the asset. For example, a company (A) needs a machine costing £700,000 (see Figure 6.6). Rather than paying that amount, it may enter into a finance arrangement with a finance company (B), where B buys the machine and then leases it to A (referred to as the *lessee*), with A paying an agreed amount to B (referred to as the *lessor*) over a specific time period (for example, £150,000 p.a. over 5 years, including £50,000 finance charge). B retains ownership of the machine, makes a profit on the finance arrangement (£50,000 in the above example), and can sell it at the end of the lease contract. At the end of the lease term, A can replace the 'old' asset by entering into a new lease. A has the advantage of avoiding a large cash outlay for an outright purchase of the machine, enabling it to replace ageing or outdated assets in a cost-efficient way.

6.5.4 Short-term sources of finance: bank overdrafts

A bank overdraft is a flexible form of borrowing, usually secured on company assets. It tends to be used for short-term financing, but is often renegotiated annually, therefore becoming part of the company's long-term financial requirements. Temporary increases in the limit can be negotiated with the bank. The main drawback is that the overdraft

TESCO Bank

Tesco Bank RPI Linked 8 year Sterling Bond.

Tesco Bank is a wholly owned subsidiary of Tesco plc and offers a wide range of retail financial service products to customers predominantly located within the United Kingdom.

The new Tesco Bank Retail Price Index (RPI) Linked 8 year Sterling Bond is available for purchase until 9 December 2011*. The Bonds will be issued on 16 December 2011.

- Tesco Bank RPI Bonds can be bought and sold in multiples of £100 face value, but the minimum initial investment needs to be £2,000.
- Tesco Bank RPI Bonds pay interest twice a year – each interest payment being calculated on the basis of a 1% annual interest rate, adjusted for changes in the level of the RPI**.
- On maturity (16 December 2019) the Tesco Bank RPI Bonds will be due to be repaid at their face value, adjusted to take account of any overall increase in the RPI. If the RPI has fallen, the amount due to be repaid will be the face value.

Investors can buy and sell their Tesco Bank RPI Bonds at any time, during normal market hours and subject to market conditions, and check the price on the London Stock Exchange website. Further information can be found at www.londonstockexchange.com/newissues

The only way to buy the Tesco Bank Retail Prices Index Sterling Bond is through a stockbroker. Contact your stockbroker today, or any of those listed below, for more details.

Barclays Stockbrokers
www.barclaysstockbrokers.co.uk/Investment-Choices/IPO

Charles Stanley
www.charles-stanley.co.uk/newissuesdesk

Halifax Share Dealing
www.halifax.co.uk/sharedealing/bond-offer

Stocktrade (A division of Brewin Dolphin Ltd.)
www.stocktrade.co.uk

Killik & Co
www.killik.com/bonds

Redmayne-Bentley LLP
www.redmayne.co.uk/tescobond

Selftrade
www.selftrade.co.uk/tesco

Joint Lead Managers: Barclays Capital, Evolution Securities and Lloyds Bank Corporate Markets.

Important Information

In the event that Tesco Bank is not able to pay its debts in full or goes out of business, you may lose some or all of your investment. The market price of the Bonds could fall below their face value of £100 during the life of the investment, and you may lose some or all of your investment if you sell your Bonds before maturity. In the event that the RPI falls during the period, the interest rate on the Bonds may be less than 1% per year. If you are in any doubt as to the suitability of these investments for your circumstances, you should seek independent advice from a tax adviser or an investment professional and from your stockbroker regarding the ISA or SIPP eligibility of the Bonds. Contact your stockbroker or any of those listed above for further information regarding buying or selling these Bonds.*The date the offer closes, unless the offer is closed earlier.**Adjustment will be calculated by comparing the RPI figure as of the month 8 months before each payment date with the RPI figure as of April 2011. Please refer to the Information Booklet, the Offering Circular, the Drawdown Prospectus and the Final Terms relating to the Bonds. Tesco Bank is a trading name for Tesco Personal Finance PLC which is the legal entity that will issue the Bonds. References to Tesco Bank in this advertisement are references to Tesco Personal Finance PLC. Tesco Bank is authorised and regulated in the United Kingdom by the Financial Services Authority. This is an advertisement and is not a prospectus for the purposes of EU Directive 2003/71/EC or Part VI of the FSMA. An offering circular dated 16 August 2011 as supplemented by a supplementary offering circular dated 11 November 2011 ("Offering Circular"), the final terms relating to the Bonds ("Final Terms ") and a Drawdown Prospectus dated 29 November 2011 ("Drawdown Prospectus") have been prepared and made available to the public as required by Part VI of the FSMA. Investors should not subscribe for any securities referred to in this advertisement except on the basis of information contained in the Offering Circular, the Final Terms and the Drawdown Prospectus. Investors may obtain copies of the Offering Circular, the Drawdown Prospectus and the Final Terms relating to the Bonds from the website of the London Stock Exchange and inspect copies on request at the registered office of Tesco Bank at Interpoint Building, 22 Haymarket Yards, Edinburgh EH12 5BH. Before buying or selling any Bonds you should make sure that you fully understand and accept the risks which are set out in the Offering Circular and the Drawdown Prospectus, and you should determine whether the investment is appropriate for you on the basis of all information contained in the Offering Circular, the Drawdown Prospectus and the Final Terms relating to the Bonds. Tesco Bank do not provide legal, tax, accounting or investment advice in relation to the Bonds and are not responsible for any advice you may receive from any third party. You should be aware that the Bonds involve a variety of risks and you should seek independent advice if you are in any doubt as to the suitability of this investment for your circumstances. Tesco Bank and its affiliates, connected companies, employees or clients may have an interest in securities of the type described in this advertisement. The Bonds have not been and will not be registered under the United States Securities Act of 1993, as amended, and include Bonds in bearer form that are subject to certain U.S. tax law requirements. Subject to certain exceptions, Bonds may not be offered, sold or delivered within the United States of America or to, or for the account of or benefit of, U.S. persons.

Figure 6.5 Tesco advert

Source: Sunday Times, 4 December 2011

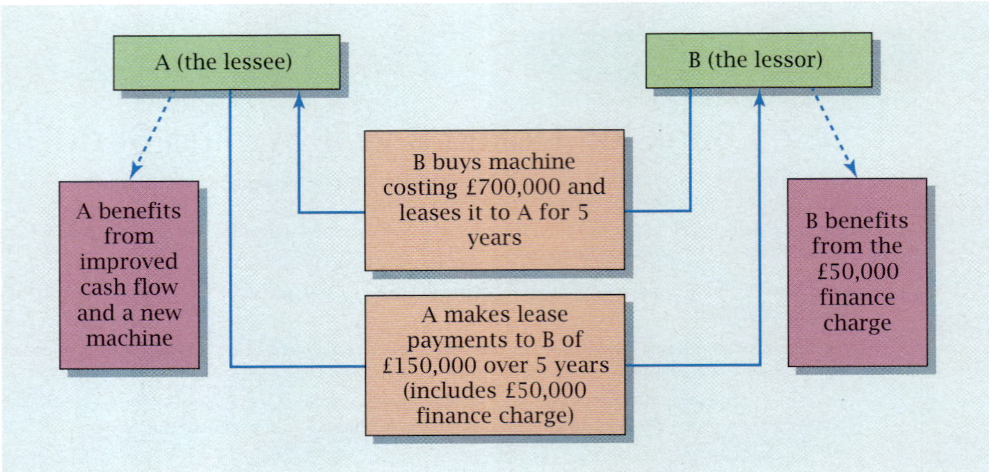

Figure 6.6 Finance leases

is repayable on demand, but this would only happen if the company was in extreme financial difficulties. Normally some repayment scheme can be agreed, with the overdraft being transferred into a long-term loan.

The overdrawn company pays interest on the *actual* balance, not the agreed limit, so that if it has used £400,000 of an agreed £500,000 limit, it is only charged interest on the £400,000. Most banks charge a flat percentage fee when an overdraft is arranged or renegotiated, so there is a financial disincentive in having a higher limit than is necessary.

6.5.5 Short-term sources of finance: debt factoring and invoice discounting

Uncollected debts from customers represent a significant problem for a company, and large amounts might be spent in credit control procedures. Some companies make use of specialised agencies that provide services, known as *debt factoring* and *invoice discounting*, that can dramatically improve cash flow from customers – though at a cost.

Scan the following QR code with your QR reader to take you to the website of Skipton Business Finance, a company that provides invoice discounting facilities.

- **Debt factoring** is where the operation of a Receivables Ledger of a company (let's call it A) is outsourced to a specialised financial institution (a *factor*, B), which then takes on the full responsibility of debt collection, and effectively 'buys' A's outstanding debts. This brings an immediate cash flow benefit to A and also lower future accounting costs. B will initially advance approximately 80% of the outstanding debts, and then pay the remainder, less a commission, to A when the debts are paid. The downside is that B will charge a fee (approximately 3% of A's turnover) for operating A's Receivables Ledger, and it may be seen by A's customers as a signal that A is in financial difficulty (see Figure 6.7).
- **Invoice discounting** is where the company (let's call it C) continues to operate its Receivables Ledger and collects all payments from invoices (see Figure 6.7). Copies of the invoices are sent electronically to the discounting company (D), which transfers a percentage of the amount (usually around 85%) owed to Company C into C's

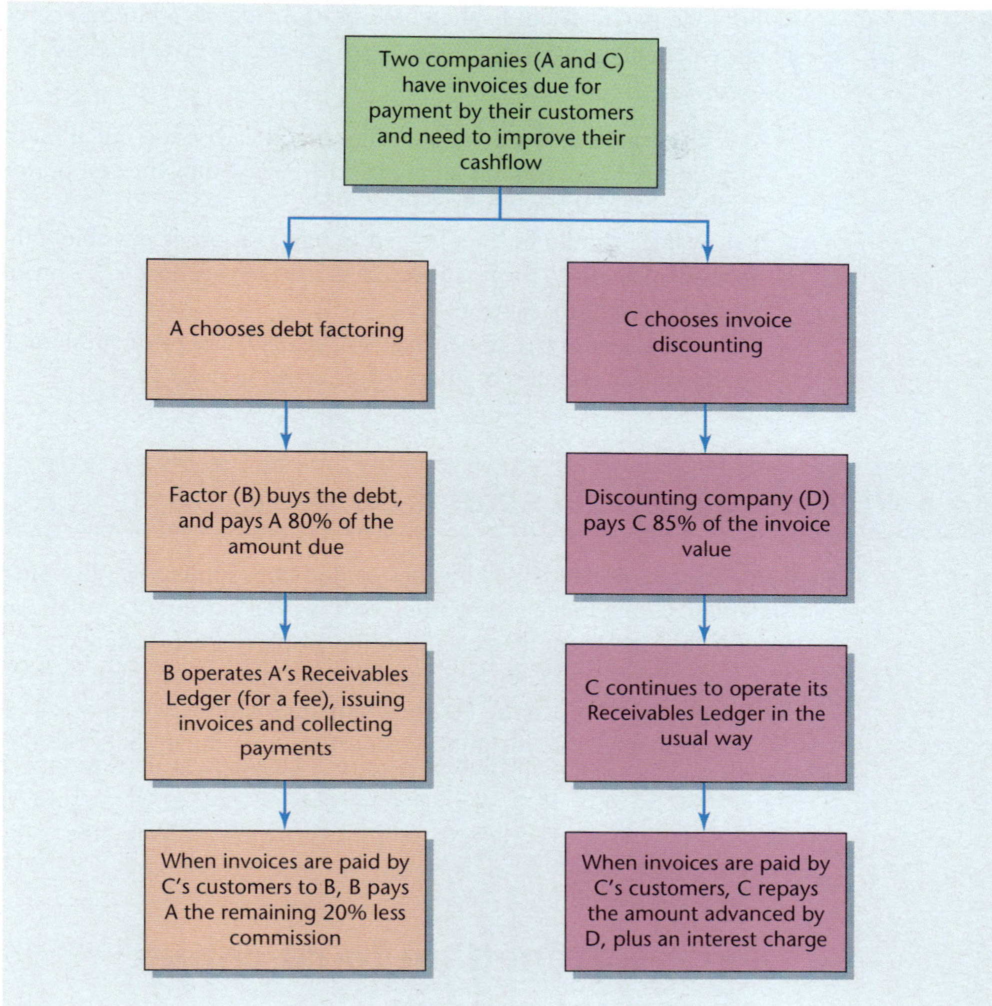

Figure 6.7 Debt factoring and invoice discounting

bank. This gives Company C cash inflow without waiting for the invoice to be paid. Eventually when the customer pays the invoice directly to Company C, C then repays the amount advanced by Company D. Company D charges interest on the amount advanced.

- **Emergency funding** is a last resort, where all other attempts at raising cash have failed. This should only be seen as a very short-term fix to a problem, as extremely high interest rates (e.g. 4,000% per annum!) would be charged, with dire consequences if the loans are not repaid by the agreed date. Look at the website of wongabusiness.com (or use the QR code in the margin) for an example of how such financing works.

Scan the following QR code with your QR reader to take you to the website of Wonga Business, a company that provides emergency funding:

6.5.6 Internal sources of finance

As well as the short- and long-term external finance sources listed above, there are several internal sources that can be used. Some are obvious – for example, retaining profit rather than paying it out to shareholders as dividends – but others relate to the efficient management of the *working capital*, as represented by inventories, receivables and payables, as follows:

- Inventory should be kept to a minimum, otherwise too much inventory may be held, resulting in high costs for storage and security, plus interest on overdrafts and loans used to pay for the inventory.
- Receivables should be encouraged to pay as soon as possible, otherwise inadequate control may result in uncollected debts (see section 6.5.5 on debt factoring and invoice discounting, above).
- The time taken to pay trade payables (the payables payment period) might be lengthened to take advantage of interest-free credit periods.

6.6 Published financial summaries

Legislation requires that all businesses that have limited liability must publish financial statements. For smaller companies, only a brief summary of their finances is required, but for the largest companies, including all plc's, a very detailed annual report must be prepared which is sent (mostly by electronic means – but see the 'News clip' below) to all shareholders and, in the UK, to Companies House, which acts as a store of company information available for public inspection. Key documents can be downloaded for a very small fee.

News clip

Line softened on hard copies of annual reports

FT

By Adam Jones, Accountancy Correspondent

Overwhelming opposition from investors large and small has defeated a proposal to allow companies to stop printing hard copies of their annual report and accounts.

The Financial Reporting Council, the accounting and corporate governance watchdog, said it had abandoned the plan after "concerns were raised that the removal of hard copy reports would disadvantage small shareholders, many of whom are elderly and/or have limited access to the internet".

Other proposals published by the FRC on Thursday included an obligation for companies to put their audit contract out to tender once every 10 years, or explain why they had not.

Earlier this year, Stephen Haddrill, the FRC's chief executive, described printed annual reports as an "enormous waste of paper and an enormous waste of time, and a waste of money".

The climbdown reflected complaints by investors and City professionals, many of whom had argued that, regardless of a reader's age, it was more difficult to read such long and complex documents on screen.

"For many investors, myself included, it is much easier to look through a printed book," said Simon Laffin, the former chairman of pub group Mitchells & Butlers, in a letter opposing the proposal.

Mr Laffin – who chairs the audit committees of Aegis and Quintain Estates &

Development – also cited the example of Argos, pointing out that the retailer still circulated printed copies of its catalogue as well as operating online.

"One key lesson of the digital economy is not that people want everything online, but that they demand information in a variety of ways to suit their lifestyle," he said.

The UK Shareholders' Association, a private investor body, echoed this, declaring: "There is no substitute for a printed document when a reader wants to refer rapidly from one page to another, compare related items, make comparisons with previous years and perhaps make notes in the margins."

Meanwhile, the Investment Management Association, which represents fund managers, had warned that online-only information could be changed after publication, making hard copies an important bulwark against manipulation.

Source: *The Financial Times*, 1 September 2011

Many plc's regard their annual report as an opportunity to show off the best of their company, in effect treating it as a public relations exercise. The glossy photographs of the company's products and exotic locations of major contracts can give some reports the style of a holiday brochure.

An examination of the typical elements that make up a large company's annual report reveals a mixture of statutory items, requirements of accounting standards, additional stock market regulations (for companies with shares 'listed' on a Stock Exchange) and voluntary disclosures. Tesco plc, one of the world's largest supermarket groups, published its annual report covering the year ended 25 February 2012 in May 2012. Its income statement and statement of financial position (called here by its alternative name, the *balance sheet*) are shown in Figures 6.8 and 6.9.

Group Income Statement
Year ended 25 February 2012

	2012 £m	2011 £m
Continuing operations		
Revenue	64,539	60,455
Cost of sales	(59,278)	(55,330)
Gross profit	5261	5125
Administrative expenses	(1,652)	(1,640)
Profits/losses arising on property-related items	376	432
Operating profit	3,985	3,917
Share of post-tax profits of joint ventures and associates	91	57
Finance income	176	150
Finance costs	(417)	(483)
Profit before tax	3,835	3,641
Taxation	(879)	(864)
Profit for the year from continuing operations	2,956	2,777
Discontinued operations		
Loss for the year from discontinued operations	(142)	(106)
Profit for the year	2,814	2,671

Figure 6.8 Tesco plc Group Income Statement

Source: Tesco plc Annual Report 2012 (adapted)

Group Balance sheet
25 February 2012

	2012 £m	2011 £m
Non-current assets		
Goodwill and other intangible assets	4618	4338
Property, plant and equipment	25,710	24,398
Investment property	1991	1863
Investments in joint ventures and associates	423	326
Other investments	1526	938
Loans and advances to customers	1901	2127
Derivative financial instruments	1726	1139
Deferred tax assets	23	48
	37,918	35,167
Current assets		
Inventories	3,598	3,162
Trade and other receivables	2,657	2,330
Loans and advances to customers	2,502	2,514
Derivative financial instruments	41	148
Current tax assets	7	4
Short-term investments	1,243	1,022
Cash and cash equivalents	2,305	2,428
	12,353	11,608
Non-current assets classified as held for sale	510	431
	12,863	12,039
Current liabilities		
Trade and other payables	(11,234)	(10,484)
Financial liabilities	(7,431)	(6,751)
Current tax liabilities	(416)	(432)
Provisions	(99)	(64)
Other	(69)	-
	(19,249)	(17,731)
Net current liabilities	(6,386)	(5,692)
Non-current liabilities	(13,731)	(12,852)
Net assets	**17,801**	**16,623**
Equity		
Share capital	402	402
Share premium	4,964	4,896
Other reserves	40	40
Retained earnings	12,369	11,197
Equity attributable to owners of the parent	17,775	16,535
Non-controlling interests*	26	88
Total equity	**17,801**	**16,623**

*Non-controlling interests relate to the proportion of total equity held in one or more of Tesco's subsidiary companies that are not owned by Tesco plc. For example, Tesco owns only 70% of its Malaysian subsidiary

Figure 6.9 Tesco plc Group Balance Sheet (equivalent to Statement of Financial Position)

Source: Tesco plc Annual Report 2012 (adapted)

Other major components of the annual report (other than the income statement and statement of financial position) include:

- Business review
- Corporate governance report
- Cash flow statement

- Reconciliation of movements in equity
- Explanatory notes to the financial statements
- Auditors' report.

The cash flow statement is considered later in (Chapter 8). Key aspects of the other listed components are as follows:

Business review

There is no statutory requirement for a business review but it is an important feature of corporate reporting, providing an opportunity for directors to set out a clear and objective analysis of a company's development, performance, position and prospects. A typical review includes:

- Commentary on the operating results
- Review of the group's financial needs and resources
- Commentary on risks and uncertainties.

For example, Tesco plc, in its business review contained within its 2012 Annual Report included the following paragraphs:

> It has been a year of significant change and one in which we took decisive action on some very important issues for Tesco: our reset of expectations for the UK for the forthcoming year, the announcement of our intention to dispose of our business in Japan, the focus on moving Fresh & Easy closer to profitability and the renewed focus on delivering a reliable Tesco Bank. As a part of this we made several key management changes during the year which have allowed some significant new appointments as we renew and reinvigorate the Tesco team.
>
> This has very much laid the ground for the future; a future where we will make sure that our capital and our talent are put to work where it benefits most our customers and hence our shareholders. The future Tesco will demonstrate greater innovation and creativity as we address the needs of consumers around our world – both in store and online.

Corporate governance report

This part of the annual report outlines the way in which the company governs itself. Specifically, it sets out such matters as the composition of the board of directors, the responsibility of the board and the frequency of attendance at board meetings by individual directors. It also outlines the company's risk management procedures and how dialogue with stakeholders is maintained and enhanced.

Reconciliation of movements in equity

This gives an overview of the various reasons (including the payment of dividends and transfers to and from reserves) for the changes in the 'total equity' as shown in the opening and closing statement of financial positions, and cuts through much of the fine detail presented elsewhere in the annual report. Figure 6.10 shows Tesco plc's statement, which, for 2012, indicates that the company's total equity increased from £16,623m to £17,801m, mainly as a result of the year's profit of £2,814m, less dividends of £1,180m.

Explanatory notes to the financial statements (including statement of accounting policies)

The information within the main financial summaries is supplemented by explanatory notes which serve to explain and expand each of the key items. The notes always

Group statement of changes in equity
25 February 2012

£m	*Share capital*	*Share premium*	*Retained earnings*	*Other*	*Non-controlling interests*	*Total*
At 26 February 2011	402	4,896	11,171	66	88	16,623
Profit for the year			2,806		8	2,814
Other net income			(393)	53	5	(335)
Issue of shares	1	68				69
Dividends authorised in the year			(1,180)			(1,180)
Other adjustments	(1)		(240)	126	(75)	(190)
At 25 February 2012	402	4,964	12,164	245	26	17,801

Figure 6.10 Tesco plc Group statement of changes in equity

Source: Tesco plc Annual Report 2012 (adapted)

commence with a statement of the accounting policies adopted by the company (a short extract is shown in Figure 6.11), and there then follow many pages of detailed information needed to comply either with relevant accounting standards and/or statute. It is unusual for companies to give more than the minimum requirements (as that might be to a competitor's advantage), but the auditors' report will confirm whether or not these minimum requirements have been met.

Tesco plc

Notes to the Group financial statements (extract)

General information

Tesco PLC ('the Company') is a public limited company incorporated and domiciled in the United Kingdom under the Companies Act 2006 (Registration number 445790). The address of the registered office is Tesco House, Delamare Road, Cheshunt, Hertfordshire, EN8 9SL, UK. The financial year represents the 52 weeks ended 25 February 2012 (prior financial year 52 weeks ended 26 February 2011). For the UK, the Republic of Ireland and the US, the results are for the 52 weeks ended 25 February 2012 (prior financial year 52 weeks ended 26 February 2011). For all other operations, the results are for the calendar year ended 29 February 2012 (year ended 28 February 2011).

The main activities of the Company and its subsidiaries (together, 'the Group') are those of retailing and retail banking.

Basis of preparation

The consolidated Group financial statements have been prepared in accordance with International Financial Reporting Standards ('IFRS') and IFRS Interpretations Committee ('IFRIC') interpretations as endorsed by the European Union, and those parts of the Companies Act 2006 applicable to companies reporting under IFRS. The consolidated Group financial statements are presented in Pounds Sterling, generally rounded to the nearest million. They are prepared on the historical cost basis, except for certain financial instruments, share-based payments, customer loyalty programmes and pensions that have been measured at fair value.

Discontinued operations

During the financial year, the Board approved a plan to dispose of its operations in Japan which is consistent with the Group's long-term strategic priority to drive growth and improve returns by focusing on its larger businesses in the region. In accordance with IFRS 5 'Non-current Assets Held for Sale and Discontinued Operations', the net results for the year are presented within discontinued operations in the Group Income Statement (for which the comparatives have been reclassified) and the assets and liabilities of the business are presented separately in the Group Balance Sheet. See Note 7 for further details.

Subsidiaries

The financial statements of subsidiaries are included in the consolidated financial statements from the date that control commences until the date that control ceases.

Intragroup balances and any unrealised gains and losses or income and expenses arising from intragroup transactions are eliminated in preparing the consolidated financial statements.

Joint ventures and associates
The Group's share of the results of joint ventures and associates is included in the Group Income Statement using the equity method of accounting. Investments in joint ventures and associates are carried in the Group Balance Sheet at cost plus post-acquisition changes in the Group's share of the net assets of the entity, less any impairment in value. The carrying values of investments in joint ventures and associates include acquired goodwill. If the Group's share of losses in a joint venture or associate equals or exceeds its investment in the joint venture or associate, the Group does not recognise further losses, unless it has incurred obligations to do so or made payments on behalf of the joint venture or associate. Unrealised gains arising from transactions with joint ventures and associates are eliminated to the extent of the Group's interest in the entity.

Use of assumptions and estimates
The preparation of the consolidated Group financial statements requires management to make judgements, estimates and assumptions that affect the application of policies and reported amounts of assets and liabilities, income and expenses. The estimates and associated assumptions are based on historical experience and various other factors that are believed to be reasonable under the circumstances. Actual results may differ from these estimates. The estimates and underlying assumptions are reviewed on an ongoing basis.

Critical estimates and assumptions that are applied in the preparation of the consolidated financial statements include:

Depreciation and amortisation
The Group exercises judgement to determine useful lives and residual values of intangibles, property, plant and equipment and investment property. The assets are depreciated down to their residual values over their estimated useful lives.

Impairment
i) Impairment of goodwill
The Group tests annually whether goodwill has suffered any impairment. The recoverable amount of the cash-generating units has been determined based on value in use calculations. These calculations require the use of estimates as set out in Note 10.
ii) Impairment of assets
The Group has determined each store as a separate cash-generating unit for impairment testing. Where there are indicators for impairment, the Group performs an impairment test.

Recoverable amounts for cash-generating units are based on the higher of value in use and fair value less costs to sell. Value in use is calculated from cash flow projections for five years using data from the Group's latest internal forecasts. These calculations require the use of estimates as set out in Note 11.

Property, plant and equipment
Property, plant and equipment is carried at cost less accumulated depreciation and any recognised impairment in value.

Property, plant and equipment is depreciated on a straight-line basis to its residual value over its anticipated useful economic life. The following depreciation rates are applied for the Group:

- freehold and leasehold buildings with greater than 40 years unexpired – at 2.5% of cost;
- leasehold properties with less than 40 years unexpired are depreciated by equal annual instalments over the unexpired period of the lease; and
- plant, equipment, fixtures and fittings and motor vehicles – at rates varying from 9% to 50%.

Assets held under finance leases are depreciated over their expected useful lives on the same basis as owned assets or, when shorter, over the term of the relevant lease.

Figure 6.11 Tesco plc Notes to the financial statements: accounting policies
Source: Tesco plc Annual Report 2012 (adapted)

Auditors' report

The auditors are required to report to shareholders ('the members') on whether the group accounts have been properly prepared, in accordance with accounting standards and relevant legislation, and whether they give a true and fair view of the activities of the company. Figure 6.12 shows Tesco plc's report. The auditors may qualify their approval of the accounts if they feel that the records have not been well kept or if all the

Independent auditors' report to the members of Tesco PLC

We have audited the Group financial statements of Tesco PLC for the 52 weeks ended 25 February 2012 which comprise the Group income statement, the Group statement of comprehensive income, the Group balance sheet, the Group statement of changes in equity, the Group cash flow statement and the related notes. The financial reporting framework that has been applied in their preparation is applicable law and International Financial Reporting Standards ('IFRS') as adopted by the European Union.

Respective responsibilities of directors and auditors

As explained more fully in the Statement of Directors' responsibilities set out on page 88 [not shown], the Directors are responsible for the preparation of the Group financial statements and for being satisfied that they give a true and fair view. Our responsibility is to audit and express an opinion on the Group financial statements in accordance with applicable law and International Standards on Auditing (UK and Ireland). Those standards require us to comply with the Auditing Practices Board's Ethical Standards for Auditors.

This report, including the opinions, has been prepared for and only for the Company's members as a body in accordance with Chapter 3 of Part 16 of the Companies Act 2006 and for no other purpose. We do not, in giving these opinions, accept or assume responsibility for any other purpose or to any other person to whom this report is shown or into whose hands it may come save where expressly agreed by our prior consent in writing.

Scope of the audit of the financial statements

An audit involves obtaining evidence about the amounts and disclosures in the financial statements sufficient to give reasonable assurance that the financial statements are free from material misstatement, whether caused by fraud or error. This includes an assessment of: whether the accounting policies are appropriate to the Group's circumstances and have been consistently applied and adequately disclosed; the reasonableness of significant accounting estimates made by the Directors; and the overall presentation of the financial statements. In addition, we read all thefinancial and non-financial information in the Annual Report and Financial Statements to identify material inconsistencies with the audited financial statements. If we become aware of any apparent material misstatements or inconsistencies we consider the implications for our report.

Opinion on financial statements

In our opinion the Group financial statements:

- give a true and fair view of the state of the Group's affairs as at 25 February 2012 and of its profit and cash flows for the 52 weeks then ended;
- have been properly prepared in accordance with IFRS as adopted by the European Union; and
- have been prepared in accordance with the requirements of the Companies Act 2006 and Article 4 of the IAS Regulation.

Opinion on other matter prescribed by the Companies Act 2006

In our opinion:

- the information given in the Directors' Report for the 52 weeks ended 25 February 2012 for which the Group financial statements are prepared is consistent with the Group financial statements.

Matters on which we are required to report by exception

We have nothing to report in respect of the following:

Under the Companies Act 2006 we are required to report to you if, in our opinion:

- certain disclosures of Directors' remuneration specified by law are not made; or
- we have not received all the information and explanations we require for our audit.

Under the Listing Rules we are required to review:

- the Directors' statement, set out on page 49 [not shown], in relation to going concern;
- the part of the Corporate Governance Statement relating to the Company's compliance with the nine provisions of the UK Corporate Governance Code specified for our review; and
- certain elements of the report to shareholders by the Board on Directors' remuneration.

Other matter

We have reported separately on the Parent Company financial statements of Tesco PLC for the 52 weeks ended 25 February 2012 and on the information in the Directors' Remuneration Report that is described as having been audited.

Richard Winter (Senior Statutory Auditor)
for and on behalf of PricewaterhouseCoopers LLP
Chartered Accountants and Statutory Auditors
London
4 May 2012

Figure 6.12 Tesco plc Auditors' report

Source: Tesco plc Annual Report 2012

information they require is not available. Such qualifications usually fall into two categories: (1) those relating to accounting policy, and (2) those relating to unsatisfactory levels of information.

The full detailed requirements needed to produce published financial summaries are outside the scope of this book, but Activity 6.6 shows how a basic set of published statements can be produced.

Activity 6.6

Prepare a 'published' version of Salamanca Ltd's income statement as shown in the answer to Activity 6.3

Answer

Salamanca Ltd
Published income statement for the year ended 31 May 2013

	£
Revenue	345,000
Less **Cost of sales**	(113,220)
Gross profit	231,780
Less **Expenses**	(164,680)
Operating profit	67,100
Finance costs	(1,900)
Profit before tax	65,200
Less Taxation	(16,000)
Operating profit for the year, after tax	49,200

Note that the 'published' statement of financial position will be identical to that shown in the answer to Activity 6.3, but with notes giving a detailed breakdown of items such as non-current assets.

Details of dividends paid in the year are shown separately within a 'reconciliation of movements in equity' (see Figure 6.10 earlier).

6.7 Groups of companies

Many companies are owned by other companies. This means that either all, or a majority, of the voting shares of the one company (the 'subsidiary' company) are held by the other company (the 'parent' company). This relationship is referred to as a *group of companies*, and special accounting requirements exist to reflect the finances of the entire group, as well as the individual companies comprising the group. Specifically, a *consolidated* (or group) income statement and a consolidated (or group) statement of financial position must be prepared. The procedures relating to group accounting are outside the scope of this text, but you are likely come across the word 'consolidated' or 'group' when you look at the annual reports of public limited companies. For example, the various Tesco plc extracts shown above all relate to the 'group' of companies, comprising the parent company and its 23 subsidiaries.

6.8 Summary

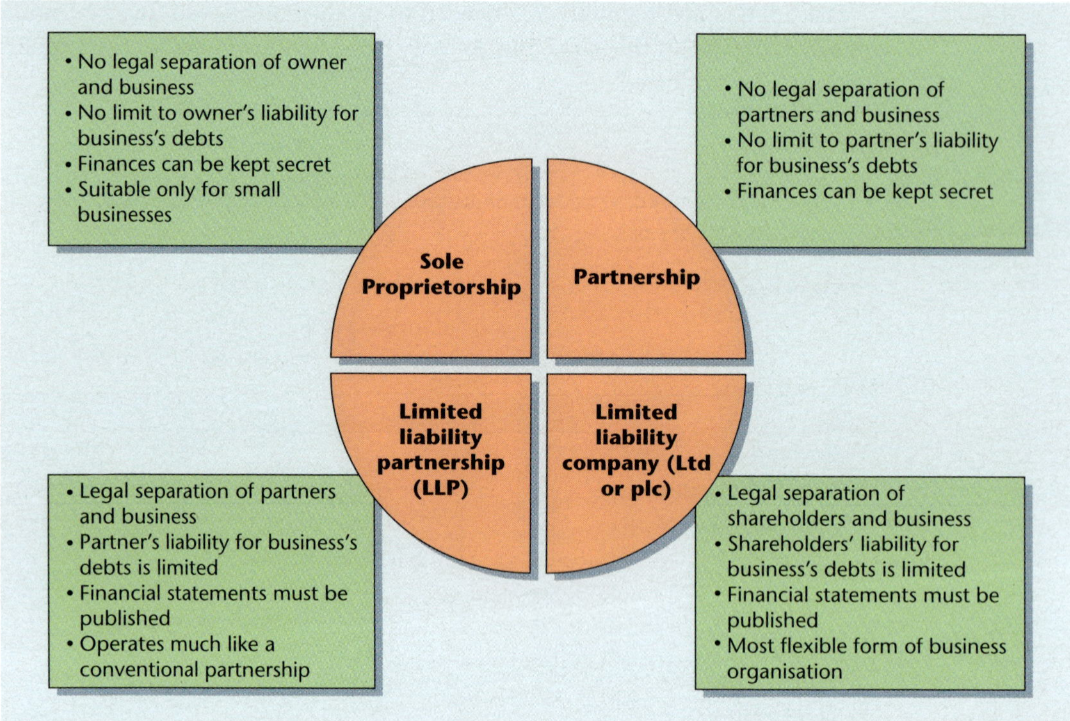

Figure 6.13 Summary of the main features of each type of business entity

6.9 Chapter glossary

Asset revaluation reserve A non-distributable reserve created when an asset (usually land or buildings) is revalued. It records an *unrealised* gain.

Auditor An independent qualified accountant who reports on whether published accounts show a true and fair view.

Bonds Loans raised by a limited company, usually secured on the company's assets.

Bonus issue Free shares given to existing shareholders to transfer part of a company's reserves to them without any cash changing hands.

Consolidated The accounts of a group of companies.

Convertible loan stock Loans raised by a limited company which may be converted into shares of that company at a future date.

Debenture Another term for 'bond'.

Debt factoring Where a financial institution takes over the credit control function of a company in return for a percentage fee. Debts are in effect sold to the factor to improve cash flow.

Directors The officers who manage a limited company.

Distributable reserves Reserves built up from retained profits via the income statement of a limited company. They can be used to pay dividends.

Dividend The reward on capital which shareholders receive from a limited company.

Equity capital The ordinary shares of a limited company.

Finance lease A legal contract enabling a company to use an asset without paying large sums to buy the asset outright.

Group of companies A situation where one company (the parent company) owns one or more other companies (subsidiaries).

Invoice discounting Where a financial institution advances cash against a company's outstanding invoices to help cashflow.

Limited company A business organisation whose owners have limited liability for the debts of their business.

Limited liability The restriction on liability of shareholders for the debts of their company to the amount of the capital which they have invested in the company.

Limited liability partnership A partnership whose members have limited liability.

Liquidation The end of a company's existence, whereby all its assets are sold and its liabilities paid, any surplus capital being returned to shareholders.

LLP Abbreviation denoting a limited liability partnership.

Ltd Abbreviation denoting a private limited company.

Members Another word for shareholders, but also used to describe the owners of a limited liability partnership.

Nominal value The 'face value' of a share, for example £1 or 25p. Also called par value.

Non-distributable reserves Reserves built up from shareholders' contributions (the share capital and the share premium) or through unrealised gains (asset revaluation reserve).

Ordinary shares The most common form of shares issued by limited companies. Each share carries equal voting and dividend rights. Also known as the equity capital.

Par value Another term meaning nominal value.

Partnership The relation which subsists between persons carrying on a business with a view of profit.

Partnership agreement The legal contract between partners that sets out their rights and responsibilities within the partnership.

Partnership appropriation account Part of the income statement of a partnership, showing how profits or losses are apportioned between partners according to their partnership agreement.

Partnership capital account The record of the capital of individual partners.

Plc Abbreviation denoting a public limited company.

Preference shares A class of shares carrying a fixed rate of dividend and giving the holders preference over equity shareholders regarding payment of dividends and repayment of capital in the event of the company's liquidation.

Private limited company A limited company which is prohibited from selling its shares to the public.

Public limited company A company which is allowed to sell its shares to the general public.

Published accounts The annual financial report of a limited company, produced in accordance with the Companies Act and other relevant rules and regulations laid down by accounting regulators or the Stock Exchange.

Reconciliation of movements in equity A summary contained within published accounts showing the changes to a company's equity during the financial period.

Reserves Funds set aside within a limited company, created from profits or paid in by shareholders. They are not the same as 'cash'.

Retained profits The profits left over after all appropriations (e.g. tax and dividends) have been made.

Rights issue The right given to existing shareholders to buy more shares.

Share premium The non-distributable reserve built up from amounts paid by shareholders for their shares, in excess of the nominal value of those shares.

Shareholders The owners of a limited company.

Sole proprietorship A business owned by one person.

Unrealised gain A surplus arising after the revaluation of an asset such as land, where the asset itself is not sold. It is treated as a non-distributable reserve.

Working capital The net current assets of an organisation.

Additional resources

Now work through the various exercises and problems that you can find within the My Accounting Lab that are relevant to this chapter. Either use the QR code shown in the margin (if you use an Android-based device), or visit www.myaccountinglab.com for the log-in page.

Only accessible on Android-based devices

Self-check questions

The answers to these questions are in Appendix 1.

1 Plc stands for:

(a) Private limited company
(b) Public liability company
(c) Public limited company
(d) Public limited corporation

2 Which of the following is a disadvantage of trading as a conventional partnership?

(a) Access to other people's expertise and finance
(b) Sharing of losses
(c) Privacy of financial results
(d) Partners usually have unlimited liability for partnership debts

3 Share capital is:

(a) The way in which capital is divided at the end of each year
(b) The way in which partners decide to divide profits and losses
(c) Another name for the stock exchange in a capital city
(d) The way in which the ownership of a limited company is divided

4 Payments to directors would be shown in the financial statements as:

(a) An expense in the income statement
(b) A dividend
(c) A current asset
(d) Part of share capital

5 The owners of a limited liability partnership (LLP) are usually known as:

(a) Directors
(b) Members
(c) Shareholders
(d) Limited partners

6 A bond is:

(a) Another name for share capital
(b) A loan usually secured on a company's assets
(c) A loan convertible into shares at some future time
(d) A preference share

7 If a new company has issued 200,000 ordinary shares of 20p nominal value at a price of £2, what will be the values of the share capital and share premium?

(a) Share capital £40,000, Share premium £360,000
(b) Share capital £40,000, Share premium £400,000
(c) Share capital £400,000, Share premium £360,000
(d) Share capital £400,000, Share premium £40,000

8 What is a major difference between a distributable reserve and a non-distributable reserve?

(a) Non-distributable reserves can be used to pay a dividend but distributable reserves cannot
(b) Non-distributable reserves can be used to pay company bills, but distributable reserves cannot
(c) Non-distributable reserves cannot be used to pay a dividend but distributable reserves can
(d) Non-distributable reserves all come from operating profits, distributable reserves all come from the shareholders

9 If a '5 for 3' rights issue is made at £1.90 per share, how much would a shareholder who owns 15,000 shares pay to the company to buy all the shares he is entitled to?

(a) £28,500
(b) £17,100
(c) £47,500
(d) £5,700

10 If a '3 for 2' bonus issue is made to a shareholder who originally paid £2 per share for 10,000 shares, how much would the shareholder pay for the bonus shares if the current market value is £4 per share?

(a) £30,000
(b) £60,000
(c) £45,000
(d) Nothing – the shares are free

Self-study questions

Questions marked with this symbol (#) indicate that the suggested answers are available to lecturers only – other answers are given in Appendix 2.

6.1 'A partnership is just a collection of sole proprietors.' Discuss this statement.

6.2 Disraeli and Gladstone are partners, sharing profits and losses in the ratio 2:1. They have agreed that Disraeli should receive a salary of £9,000 and that interest on both partners' opening capital of 5% p.a. should be allowed. Disraeli's opening capital was £20,000, whereas Gladstone's was £15,000. During the year ended 31 December 2013, Disraeli had drawings of £18,000 and Gladstone drew £14,000. Operating profit for the year was £40,000. No interest was charged on partners' drawings.

Show the relevant extracts from the partnership income statement for the year and its statement of financial position at the year-end.

6.3# The share capital and reserves section of Bantam plc's statement of financial position as at 31 December 2013 was as follows:

	£000
Share capital (5p nominal value)	240
Share premium account	200
Retained earnings	760
	1200

In view of the large balance of retained earnings, and in response to shareholder pressure, the company's chairman wants to make changes to the share capital and reserves, and has made the following *alternative* suggestions:

1 Pay a dividend of £200,000 by using the balance within the share premium account
2 Repay all the share capital to the shareholders
3 Use the retained profits balance to issue bonus shares on a 2 for 1 basis
4 Use the retained profits balance to pay a dividend of £200,000.

(a) Explain the extent to which each of the four alternatives is legally acceptable.
(b) What are the relative advantages from the *shareholders'* viewpoint of alternatives 3 and 4?
(c) What are the relative advantages from the *company's* viewpoint of alternatives 3 and 4?
(d) Assume that the company has decided to implement alternative 3 on 5 January 2014 and then, on 12 January 2014, it implements alternative 4. Redraft the statement of financial position extract as it would appear on *each* of these two dates. Assume that there were no other changes to share capital or reserves in the period.

6.4 From the following trial balance of Morse Ltd, prepare an income statement for the year ended 31 December 2013 and a statement of financial position at that date (not in a form suitable for publication).

	Dr	Cr
	£	£
Directors' salaries	59,200	
Wages of salesforce	65,230	
Office salaries	34,900	
Advertising and website charges	15,300	
Finance costs	2,502	
Sales delivery costs	632	
Office expenses	33,897	
Revenue		462,600
Opening inventory at 1 January 2013	14,900	
Purchases	140,800	
Share capital (50p nominal shares)		25,000

	Dr £	Cr £
Share premium		15,000
Dividends paid	5,000	
Bad debts written off	750	
Retained earnings as at 1 January 2013		17,600
Delivery vehicles, cost as at 1 January 2013	143,600	
Depreciation of delivery vehicles at 1 January 2013		27,800
Trade receivables	64,100	
Trade payables		32,711
Bond (repayable in 2020)		11,600
Cash and cash equivalents	11,500	
	592,311	592,311

Notes:

1 Closing inventory at 31 December 2013 was £17,650.
2 Depreciation on delivery vehicles is chargeable at 30% on the diminishing balance basis.
3 £800 was owing for office expenses and £160 had been prepaid for website charges at 31 December 2013.
4 Taxation amounting to £24,000 is to be accounted for on the year's profits.

6.5# A limited company's total equity in its statement of financial position was as follows:

	£	£
Equity		
Share capital		100,000
Share premium	75,000	
Asset revaluation reserve	140,000	
Retained earnings	330,000	
		545,000
Total equity		645,000

Note: share capital comprises ordinary shares of £1 nominal value each.

(a) To what extent is it true to say that reserves equal cash?
(b) Explain the difference between a distributable reserve and a non-distributable reserve and give one example of each from the above statement of financial position.
(c) What is a share premium? If the company had only ever made one issue of shares, what price was each share sold for?
(d) Explain why an asset revaluation reserve is created. What other item in the statement of financial position, not listed above, would have been affected when this reserve was created?
(e) Explain a way in which the company could return reserves to shareholders without paying cash to them.
(f) If the company, immediately after extracting the above statement of financial position, made a rights issue on a '3 for 2' basis at £2.40 per share, what effect would that have on the statement of financial position, assuming that all shareholders took up their rights?

6.6 Pembroke Limited was putting the finishing touches to its statement of financial position at the end of its first financial year, 30 September 2013. The only part of the statement of financial position left to complete was the 'Total equity' section. When the company was formed, it had ordinary share capital of £60,000, split into shares with a nominal value of 50p each. The shares were issued at a premium of 10p per share. The closing balance of retained earnings at 30 September 2013 was £82,000.

(a) Prepare the 'Total equity' section of Pembroke Limited's statement of financial position as at 30 September 2013.

(b) After a successful first year's trading, the directors of Pembroke Limited feel that they should be rewarded for their efforts. It has been suggested that they would benefit financially if the balance remaining on the company's retained earnings was used to issue *bonus shares*. Write a concise report to the directors explaining the nature of a bonus issue and the circumstances when it might be appropriate.

Case study Marvin and Chiquita make Machiq, but Esmeralda makes trouble

Marvin and Chiquita (see previous case studies) have been working very successfully together, so on 1 July 2013, the start of Marvin's third year in business, they decided to form a 'conventional' partnership (i.e. not an LLP), to be called Machiq Partners, sharing profits or losses in the ratio Marvin 3/5 and Chiquita 2/5. All of Marvin's assets and liabilities are transferred to the partnership at their depreciated value. This totals £17,570, which is transferred to Marvin's capital account. Chiquita pays in £10,000 as her capital. No payment was required for any goodwill built up by Marvin in the previous two years.

They agree that no interest should be charged on their drawings or credited on their capital balances. No salaries are to be paid to either partner. During a successful year together the partnership earned an operating profit of £58,800. Marvin had drawings of £32,850 and Chiquita drew £18,520.

Required

(a) Show the relevant extracts from the partnership income statement for the year ended 30 June 2014 (appropriation section) and its statement of financial position at that date.

On 30 June 2014, the partners received the following letter from Esmeralda, Marvin's former assistant:

Dear Marvin

My seven brothers and sisters and I have consulted legal advice and are going to sue you for £10 million as compensation for wrongful dismissal when you sacked us two years ago. We would have written sooner but it has taken us this long to recover from the shock of losing our jobs.

Hope you are keeping well.

Esmeralda

Marvin thinks (incorrectly) that the only protection from this claim is to immediately form a limited company, so Machiq Partners became Machiq Limited with effect from 1 July 2014. The company took over all the assets and liabilities of Machiq Partners at their book values, and had a share capital of 14,000 ordinary shares of £1 each. The shares, which were issued at a premium, were allocated to Marvin and Chiquita in the same proportions as their closing capital balances in the partnership. During the year ended 30 June 2015, Machiq Limited made an operating profit before taxation of £92,000. Taxation was to be provided on this amount at 20%, and a dividend of £2.25 per share was paid. Nothing further was heard from Esmeralda or her family during the year, although there were rumours that she had rejoined her former employer, Kaboosh Limited.

Required

(b) Show Machiq Limited's income statement (starting with the operating profit before taxation) for the year ended 30 June 2015, and the 'total equity' section of the statement of financial position as at that date.

Answers are in Appendix 3

Further research

The official website for Companies House: **www.companies-house.gov.uk**

The full annual report of Tesco plc: **www.tescocorporate.com**

Detailed statistics showing the number of businesses, employment and turnover in the UK: **http://stats.berr.gov.uk/ed/sme/**

Chapter 7

Cash flow statements

Objectives

When you have read this chapter you will be able to:

- Understand the relative importance of revenue (turnover), profit and cash
- Appreciate the importance of good working capital management to ensure liquidity
- Prepare a cash flow statement based on past transactions
- Be aware of the relevant International Accounting Standard relating to cash flow statements

7.1 Introduction

'Turnover is vanity, profit is sanity, but cash is reality'.

This (unattributed) business saying sums up the importance of cash as a critical component in the survival of any organisation. To deconstruct the quotation, firstly it is suggesting ('turnover is varity') that any business can exaggerate its revenue so as to flatter its overall performance. Imagine a managing director of a company whose sales last year were £1 million, who wants to double that figure in the current year. Probably all that is needed to achieve this is to launch a huge advertising campaign and slash prices down to a fraction of the previous year. Unfortunately, whilst the target of doubling sales might be met (which might be very good news for the director if he or she is on a sales-related bonus!), the company is *highly* unlikely to make any profit due to the cost of the adverts and the greatly reduced margin on revenue. As for the second part of the quotation, *profit is sanity*, you should know by now that a business's operating profit is calculated after *all* relevant expenditure has been deducted from revenue, regardless of whether an associated cash inflow or outflow has been received or paid. Although this is the most accurate and realistic measure of a business's operating performance (and in accordance with the *accrual basis*, which is one of the two underlying assumptions when preparing financial statements, as explained in Chapter 1), it is ironic that even a highly profitable business might fail, due to its inability to pay its bills owing to insufficient cash. Consequently, the third part of the quotation, *cash is reality*, reflects the sad but inescapable fact that a business that cannot pay its bills will not survive. After all, a supplier owed £20,000 is not going to be impressed by being told that, although the business made a profit of £100,000, the bank overdraft limit has been reached and no further cash can be paid out.

In our study of accounting so far, cash (which includes 'cash equivalents' such as bank current account balances) has perhaps taken a back seat when compared with profits; after all, accounting principles require us to adjust cash transactions for the effect of receivables, payables, accruals, prepayments, unsold inventory, depreciation and provisions when preparing the income statement – so we do not see 'unadjusted' cash transactions on the income statement. Even within the statement of financial position, 'cash and cash equivalents' is just one item appearing within the list of current assets, with no special importance.

If cash is 'reality', then it makes financial sense to give this asset a particular prominence within financial reporting. This has been recognised by the existence of an international accounting standard[1] that requires businesses to prepare *a cash flow statement*, which summarises the cash inflows and outflows over the previous financial period.

A former chairman of the International Accounting Standards Board, Sir David Tweedie, once commented that: 'Cash is the lifeblood of the business. If it dwindles the business will die. But it is also a very difficult figure to fiddle.' This relates to the widely held – though inaccurate – perception that, whilst the existence (or non-existence) of cash and bank balances can be proved with certainty, 'profit' can be

[1]International Accounting Standards Board (2008) *International Accounting Standard 7: Statement of Cash Flows*. London: IASB.

manipulated ('fiddled') in accordance with a business's requirements, unrelated to the underlying financial transactions. The vast majority of information contained within the financial summaries is based on objective, verifiable data, but there is scope for subjectivity as well, in such areas as the amount of depreciation to be charged, how inventory and other assets should be valued, and whether a provision for doubtful debts is needed. The publication of accounting standards has narrowed considerably the areas of individuality available to accountants and their scope for 'creative accounting'. Remember, also, that many limited companies must appoint independent auditors who report on whether or not the accounts give a faithful representation of the business.

7.2 Cash flows and working capital

If a business has sufficient cash to meet its liabilities as they fall due, it is said to have good *liquidity*. It can also be referred to as being *solvent* – particularly if it could quickly change assets into cash if the need arose, for example if it had investments such as deposit accounts where relatively short notice (around 3 months or less) could be given to gain access to the money. Surprisingly enough, it is also possible for a business to have *too much* liquidity: if it has excessive cash then it is not reinvesting it. Rather than hoarding cash it could be buying new non-current assets, taking over other businesses or using the cash to fund research and development projects. In this way the business can expand and become more profitable. The ideal business is both profitable and liquid, and (in the next chapter) we shall look at ways of analysing both these aspects of a company's performance.

From a practical point of view, companies need to have enough cash to meet their day-to-day requirements, so that they are not in the embarrassing (and potentially life-threatening) situation of being unable to pay their bills as they fall due. This requires good *working capital* management, which relates to the control of levels of inventories, trade receivables and trade payables. Working capital is defined as the relationship between a business's current assets and current liabilities, and its adequacy can mean the difference between survival and failure. Figure 7.1 shows how cash flows result from the process of buying inventory, selling the inventory, paying the supplier for the inventory and receiving the cash flow from the customer. The 'cash in' and 'cash out' amounts are not the same, as the supplier is paid the cost price whereas the customer is paying the (higher) selling price. Consequently, there will be a surplus of cash every time the cycle is completed, which goes towards the costs of running the business (such as wages), investing in non-current assets and rewarding the shareholders.

As the figure shows, apart from the four main components of the working capital cycle, other cash inflows and outflows occur from time to time such as loans being received and non-current assets being purchased. Working capital management, to be successful, will try and ensure as far as possible that the minimum inventory levels are maintained, trade receivables (debtors) pay their bills as quickly as possible, and trade payables (creditors) are paid at the end of any interest-free credit period, rather than being paid immediately. The consequences of having either too much or too little of each of the working capital components are as follows:

Working capital component	Too much?	Too little?
Inventory (unsold or unused stocks of raw materials, components or finished products)	Having excessive inventory might be caused by having unusable, unsaleable or very slow moving items. Some inventory is perishable or might become unfashionable in time. Remember that keeping inventory incurs costs such as storage, insurance, security, etc.	Insufficient inventory might cause hold-ups in production due to lack of parts. Customer orders might be unfulfilled, with the possibility of them going to competitors.
Trade receivables (amounts owed by clients and customers)	Giving credit to customers is a natural part of most business's commercial practice, but excessive money owed over long periods must be discouraged. An efficient credit control system should be in place.	This is only a problem if the business is losing customers by not offering a reasonable amount of credit.
Trade payables (amounts owed to suppliers)	If suppliers of goods and services are not paid within a reasonable time then there is a risk that they will withhold any further supplies until invoices are paid. Businesses can quickly get a reputation as a 'bad payer' resulting in a loss of goodwill.	Paying too quickly does not make commercial sense if the suppliers offer interest-free credit as part of their normal trading practice.
Cash and cash equivalents	Any surplus cash can be used to reinvest in the business (e.g. by purchasing new non-current assets), reward investors (e.g. by paying dividends) or repay debt	Insufficient cash may result in unpaid bills and loss of reputation. Increased borrowing might be needed with a consequent rise in finance costs.

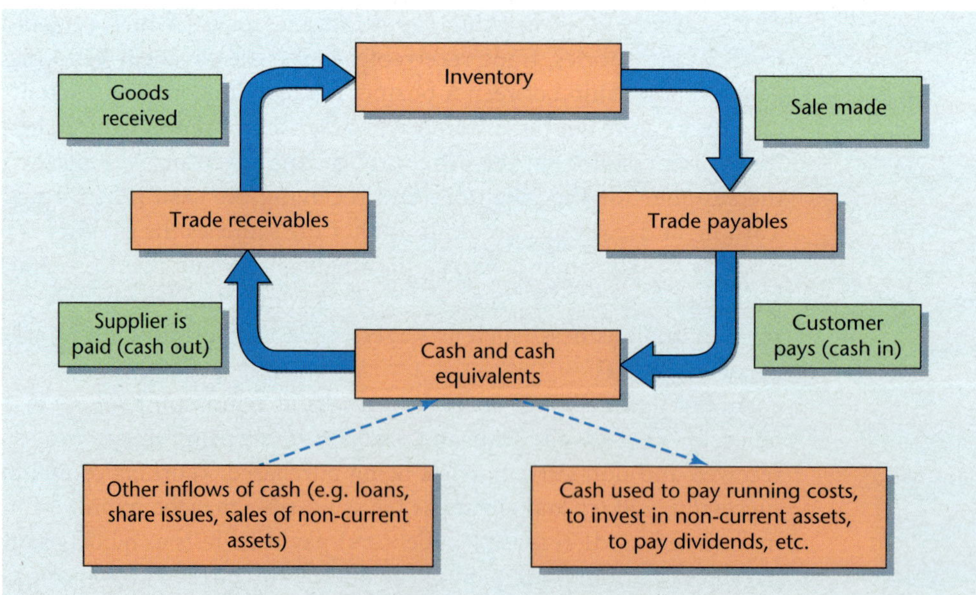

Figure 7.1 The working capital cycle; day-to-day cash management

The consequences facing a company with working capital problems are illustrated in the 'News clip' below. At one stage, Game Group plc described itself as 'Europe's leading specialist pc and video games retailer', but working capital difficulties meant that it was unable to pay its costs, and suppliers started to withhold new products from the company due to previously unpaid bills.

(This topic is explored further in Chapter 8).

News clip

Game Group enters administration

FT

By Andrea Felsted and Anousha Sakoui

Nearly half of Game Group's 610 UK stores are to close, with more than 2,000 jobs being lost, after the video games retailer was put into administration on Monday.

PwC, appointed as administrator to the chain, said 277 stores would close with immediate effect, with 2,100 staff to be made redundant this week.

The administrator said the remaining 333 stores, employing 2,814 people, would stay open as normal, as it raced to find a buyer.

Mike Jervis, joint administrator and partner at PwC said: "Our priority is to continue trading the business as normal as we continue to pursue a sale. The recent job losses are regrettable but will place the company in a stronger position while we explore opportunities to conclude a sale."

OpCapita, the private equity group that bought Comet for £2 last year, made an offer for the group's debts before Game put administrators on standby. It is still thought to be looking at the UK assets and some international operations, although people close to the situation said OpCapita had not been in touch with the administrator on Monday.

GameStop, the US video games retailer, also showed late interest, according to two people familiar with the situation, and is still looking at some of the group's international operations. It may be interested in the UK assets but is unlikely to want to pay a significant amount for them.

Hilco, the retail restructuring group, is also eyeing Game's international assets.

An issue for some potential buyers is that the UK business has heavy working capital requirements. There are big spikes in the amount of working capital needed when new video games are released.

"It needs to be someone who has access to appropriate working capital facilities," said one person with knowledge of the situation.

The option whereby Game's lenders – led by Royal Bank of Scotland and Barclays – roll over their £85m of debt into a new, slimmed down company, with new management, remains on the table. Under this scenario, they would then look to sell the business at a later date.

Peter Smedley, an analyst at Charles Stanley Securities, drew parallels with Jessops, the photographic equipment retailer acquired by HSBC in a debt-for-equity swap. However, he pointed out that because there were multiple lenders to Game, this could complicate any similar deal. The most probable option for PwC is to find buyers for the various parts of the business.

The appointment of PwC as administrator was delayed from Friday because of the falling due of a £21m quarterly rent bill.

Source: The Financial Times, 26 March 2012

7.3 The cash flow statement

Just as there is a particular way of presenting the income statement and statement of financial position, IAS 7 provides a format to follow for the cash flow statement. Although the statement is nothing more than a summary of cash (and equivalent) transactions over a financial period, the information is made more meaningful by grouping the transactions into key headings. These headings are set out in the accounting standard, though at this stage in your studies it is sufficient to understand a summarised version of the format.

For illustration, Tesco plc's cash flow statement (in an abridged version) for 2012 (with 2011's figures given for comparison) is shown in Figure 7.2.

Tesco Plc
Group cash flow statement for the year ended 25 February 2012 (£m)

		2012		2011
Cash flows from operating activities		5,688		5,613
Interest paid		(531)		(614)
Corporation tax paid		(749)		(760)
Net cash generated from operating activities		**4,408**		**4,239**
Cash flows from investing activities				
Purchase of property, plant and equipment	(3,374)		(3,178)	
Proceeds from sale of property, plant and equipment	1,141		1,906	
Interest received	103		128	
Dividends received	40		62	
Other (including acquisition of subsidiaries)	(1,093)		(791)	
Net cash used in investing activities		**3,183**		**(1,873)**
Cash flows from financing activities				
Proceeds from issue of share capital	69		98	
Increase in borrowings	2,905		2,217	
Repayment of borrowings	2,720		(4,153)	
Dividends paid to equity owners	1,180		(1,081)	
Other (including own shares purchased)	(440)		(75)	
Net cash from/(used in) financing activities		**(1,366)**		**(2,994)**
Net decrease in cash and cash equivalents		**(141)**		**(628)**
Cash and cash equivalents at beginning of period		**2,428**		**3,102**
Effect of foreign exchange rate changes		24		(46)
Cash and cash equivalents at end of period		**2,311**		**2,428**

Figure 7.2 Tesco plc group cash flow statement

Source: A bridged from *Tesco Plc Report and Financial Statements 2012*. Courtesy of Tesco plc.

The structure of the 2012 statement can be explained as shown in Figure 7.3:

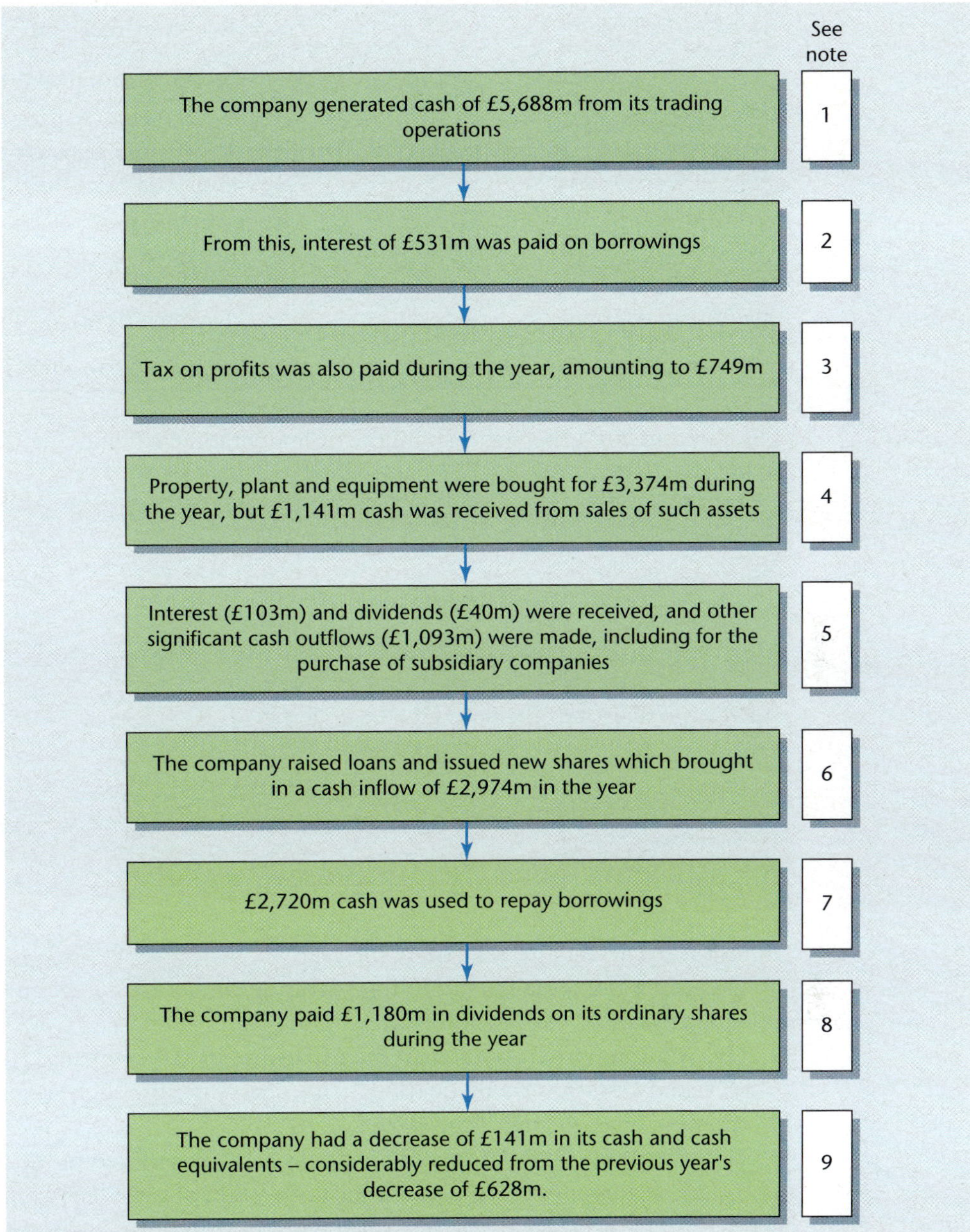

Figure 7.3 Structure of the 2012 statement (links to notes in the text)

Notes

1 This is not the same as the 'profit for the year'. To arrive at the figure, the profit as shown in the income statement has to be adjusted as follows:

(a) Add back any estimates deducted in arriving at the profit (particularly depreciation). This is because depreciation (and also profits or losses on the disposal of non-current assets), whilst included in the income statement, has no effect on cash flow.

(b) Adjust for changing inventories, receivables and payables values, as follows:

Increase in cash flow requiring amounts to be added back to profit:	
Change	**Effect of change**
Decrease in inventory	Less cash tied up in inventory
Decrease in receivables	More customers have paid their bills
Increase in payables	We owe more (i.e. we have held on to our cash)
Decreases in cash flow requiring amounts to be deducted from profit:	
Change	**Effect of change**
Increase in inventory	More cash tied up in inventory
Increase in receivables	Fewer customers have paid their bills
Decrease in payables	We have paid more to our suppliers

For Tesco in 2012, the 'net cash inflow from operating activities' figure was arrived at as follows:

	£m
Operating profit	3,985
Depreciation	1,498
Increase in inventories	(461)
Increase in trade and other receivables	(139)
Increase in trade and other payables	679
Increase in other adjustments	126
Cash generated from operations	5,688

2 This is the actual interest paid in the year.
3 This is the tax actually *paid* in the year, not the tax *estimated* on the profits for the current year.
4 This is an important pointer to the expansion of the company. Here, cash outflows exceeded cash inflows by nearly £2.2bn, showing how aggressively the company is investing in assets such as property.
5 This represents the interest and dividends actually received in the financial year, and the actual amount of cash paid for the acquisition of subsidiary companies.
6 The company raised a relatively small amount from the issue of share capital (£69m), but borrowings increased by over £2.9bn.
7 Whilst borrowings increased by over £2.9bn, the company also repaid over £2.7bn, leaving a net increase in borrowings of £175m. Contrast that with the previous year's significant net repayment of nearly £2bn.
8 These are the equity share dividends actually *paid* in the year. In practice it would represent the previous year's final dividend, plus any interim dividends paid during the current year.
9 The company finished the year with a decrease in cash and cash equivalents of £141m. Note how this compares with the year's reported operating profit of £3,985m. Overall, it can be seen that over the two years there has been a very

significant decrease in cash and cash equivalents balances, from £3,102m at the start of the 2010/11 financial period down to £2,311m by the end of the 2011/12 financial period.

Activity 7.1

The statements of financial position of Ampersand plc as at 31 May 2012 and 31 May 2013 are as follows:

		2013			2012	
	£000	£000	£000	£000	£000	£000
Non-current assets (depreciated value)			54,000			47,000
Current assets:						
Inventory		14,000			11,000	
Trade receivables		19,100			17,400	
		33,100			28,400	
Less						
Current liabilities						
Trade payables	14,200			15,500		
Taxation	14,000			13,000		
Bank overdraft	19,600			10,900		
		(47,800)			(39,400)	
Net current liabilities			(14,700)			(11,000)
Total net assets			39,300			36,000
Equity						
Share capital			21,000			10,000
Share premium account			7,500			17,500
Retained earnings			10,800			8,500
Total equity			39,300			36,000

The summarised income statements for the two years ended 31 May 2013 are as follows:

	2013	2012
	£000	£000
Gross profit	153,340	132,200
Less Expenses (including depreciation £3.2m)	(105,640)	(94,900)
	47,700	37,300
Profit/(Loss) on sale of non-current assets	(1,400)	2,800
Operating profit	46,300	40,100
Less Interest paid	(10,000)	(10,000)
Profit for the year	36,300	30,100
Less Taxation	(14,000)	(13,000)
Profit after tax	22,300	17,100

	2013 £000	2012 £000
Less Dividends paid	(20,000)	(11,500)
Retained earnings for the year	2,300	5,600
Retained earnings brought forward	8,500	2,900
Retained earnings carried forward	10,800	8,500

Notes:

1 A bonus issue was made during the year to 31 May 2013 by transferring £10m from the share premium account.
2 A summary of the company's non-current assets (at cost price) for the year ended 31 May 2013 is shown below (£000s):

	£
1 June 2012 Opening balance	87,000
31 May 2013 Additions	14,000
	101,000
31 May 2013 Sales*	(12,000)
31 May 2013 Closing balance	89,000

* The assets which were sold realised £2.4m, which represented a loss on disposal of £1.4m when compared with their depreciated value at the date of sale.

Produce a cash flow statement for the year ended 31 May 2013.

Answer

Step 1

Using the Tesco cash flow statement as our guide, we can start by calculating the net cash flow from operating activities.

	£000
Operating profit	46,300
Depreciation	3,200
Loss on sale of non-current assets	1,400
Increase in inventory (14,000 – 11,000)	(3,000)
Increase in trade receivables (19,100 – 17,400)	(1,700)
Decrease in trade payables (15,500 – 14,200)	(1,300)
Net cash inflow from operating activities	44,900

Step 2

We've done the hardest part, so we can now set out the cash flow statement as follows, starting with the net cash inflow from operating activities as calculated in Step 1:

Ampersand plc
Cash flow statement for the year ended 31 May 2013 (£000)

		2013
Cash flows from operating activities		44,900
Interest paid		(10,000)
Taxation paid (see note 1)		(13,000)
Net cash from operating activities		21,900
Cash flows from investing activities		
Purchase of non-current assets (see note 2)	(14,000)	
Proceeds from sale of non-current assets (see note 2)	2,400	
Net cash used in investing activities		(11,600)
Cash flows from financing activities		
Proceeds from issue of share capital (see note 3)	1,000	
Dividends paid (see note 4)	(20,000)	
Net cash from/(used in) financing activities		**(19,000)**
Net decrease in cash and cash equivalents		**(8,700)**
Cash and cash equivalents at 1 June 2012		**(10,900)**
Cash and cash equivalents at 31 May 2013		**(19,600)**

Notes:

1 The amount paid in the year (i.e. the previous year's provision).
2 This is from the information contained in the summary of non-current assets.
3 There was a bonus issue during the year. This is a *free* issue of shares so therefore does not involve a cash flow. The amount was £10,000 so the remaining part of the £11,000 difference between opening and closing share capital amounts must be due to a new share issue.
4 This represents the dividends actually paid in the year.

7.4 Summary

Key headings in a cash flow statement are as follows:

1 **Cash flows from operating activities.** The operating profit as adjusted for the year's depreciation and changes in inventories, trade receivables and trade payables between the start and end of the financial period.
2 **Interest paid.** Cash outflows during the financial period relating to finance costs.
3 **Taxation paid.** Cash outflows during the financial period relating to taxation payments.
4 **Net cash from operating activities.** The combination of headings 1 to 3 above.
5 **Cash flows from investing activities.** Cash flows relating to the purchase and disposals of non-current assets.
6 **Cash flows from financing activities.** Cash flows relating to the issue of shares or the receipt or repayment of loans.

7 **Net increase or decrease in cash and cash equivalents.** The figure resulting from the combination of headings 4 to 6 above.

8 **Cash and cash equivalents at the beginning of the period.** The values of cash and 'near-cash' assets at the start of the financial period.

9 **Cash and cash equivalents at the end of the period.** The values of cash and 'near-cash' assets at the end of the financial period.

7.5 Chapter glossary

Cash equivalents Short-term, highly liquid investments that are readily convertible to known amounts of cash and which are subject to an insignificant risk of changes in value.

Cash flow The inflows and outflows of cash through a business over a particular period.

Cash flow statement A summary of cash flows over a defined past period. When published it must be set out in accordance with the relevant accounting standard, IAS 7.

Liquidity The ability of a business to access enough cash and cash equivalents to pay debts as they fall due.

Solvency The ability of a business to pay its debts as they fall due. An *insolvent company* is one that has failed due to lack of solvency.

Working capital The current assets (inventory, trade receivables and cash and cash equivalents), less the current liabilities (trade payables and short-term liabilities such as bank overdrafts).

Working capital cycle The day-to-day cash flow movements relating to the components of working capital.

Additional resources

Only accessible on Android-based devices

Now work through the various exercises and problems that you can find within the My Accounting Lab that are relevant to this chapter. Either use the QR code shown in the margin (if you use an Android- based device), or visit www.myaccountinglab.com for the log-in page.

Self-check questions

The answers to these questions are in Appendix 1.

1 Cash has been described as:

(a) The lifebuoy of the business
(b) The lifeboat of the business
(c) The lifeline of the business
(d) The lifeblood of the business

2 'Cash and cash equivalents' includes:

(a) Only cash balances
(b) Only bank balances
(c) Stock Exchange investments
(d) Cash in hand plus bank current account balances

3 How can a profitable business fail?

(a) Because it can't pay its bills
(b) Because it has more current liabilities than current assets
(c) Because it has a bank overdraft
(d) Because it has too much cash

4 When adjusting an operating profit to calculate the 'cash flows from operating activities', an increase in inventories over the financial period would be:

(a) Added to operating profit
(b) Ignored
(c) Included in the 'cash flows from investing activities'
(d) Deducted from operating profit

5 The heading in a cash flow statement 'Cash flows from financing activities' means:

(a) The cash outflow due to loan interest payments being made
(b) The cash flow from share and loan issues and repayments
(c) Proceeds from the sale of non-current assets
(d) The change in the level of bank balances in the period

6 If 'Taxation' is shown on the cash flow statement, it is likely to be:

(a) The taxation paid this year on the current year's profit
(b) The taxation payable next year on this year's profit
(c) The taxation paid this year on last year's profit
(d) The taxation paid last year on last year's profit

7 Depreciation is added back to profit when arriving at the cash flow from operating activities because:

(a) Depreciation is only an estimated amount
(b) Depreciation does not affect profit
(c) Depreciation does not result in a flow of cash
(d) Depreciation affects only the statement of financial position, not the income statement

8 If operating profit before taxation and interest was £95,000, depreciation for the year was £17,000, inventory has decreased during the year by £7,000, trade receivables have increased by £11,000 and trade payables have decreased by £4,000, what is the overall cash flow from operating activities?

(a) £104,000
(b) £112,000
(c) £98,000
(d) £134,000

9 Working capital is defined as:

(a) Non-current assets less current liabilities
(b) Total equity
(c) Current assets less current liabilities
(d) Non-current assets plus current assets

10 Which one of the following best describes an *insolvent* business?

(a) One that can't pay its bills
(b) One with more current liabilities than non-current assets
(c) One that is dependent on long-term finance rather than short-term finance
(d) One that has to ask its shareholders to invest more cash into the company

Self-study questions

Questions marked with this symbol (#) indicate that the suggested answers are available to lecturers only – other answers are given in Appendix 2.

7.1 From the following information, calculate the missing figure in each column.

	A	B	C	D
	£	£	£	£
Net cash flow from operating activities	14,800	?	21,400	48,660
Interest paid	(5,800)	(2,900)	(6,000)	(2,950)
Taxation paid	(7,200)	(4,500)	(7,100)	(24,880)
Cash flows relating to investing activities	17,300	(2,970)	?	(6,520)
Cash flows relating to financing activities	(9,020)	(6,000)	11,380	?
Change in cash and cash equivalents	?	6,200	11,750	(9,450)

7.2 If cash is the 'lifeblood of a business', does that make it more important than profit?

7.3 'A company that regularly shows net cash outflows in its annual cash flow statements will inevitably fail'. Discuss.

7.4# Non-accountants don't understand jargon such as 'profit', 'assets' or 'equity', nor the various adjustments required by the accruals principle. They do, however, understand 'cash'. Why not save money by just issuing a cash flow statement instead of an income statement and a statement of financial position?

7.5# From the following information, calculate the cash flow from operating activities for each column.

	A	B	C	D
	£	£	£	£
Operating profit before interest	36,620	29,937		20,060
Operating loss before interest			22,660	
Depreciation	12,000	16,000	24,000	15,000
Increase in inventory	9,650			14,850
Decrease in inventory		5,840	5,622	
Increase in trade receivables			2,240	12,795

	A	B	C	D
	£	£	£	£
Decrease in trade receivables	7,980	6,722		
Increase in trade payables	3,380		9,713	
Decrease in trade payables		6,840		11,629
Cash flow from operating activities	?	?	?	?

7.6 The statements of financial position of Asterix plc as at 31 May 2013 and 31 May 2012 are as follows:

	31 May 2013		31 May 2012	
	£000	£000	£000	£000
Non-current assets (net book value)		43,000		32,000
Current assets				
Inventory	19,000		18,000	
Trade receivables	9,000		7,500	
Bank	–		2,800	
	28,000		28,300	
Less **Current liabilities**				
Trade payables	6,100		9,900	
Taxation	5,000		4,000	
Bank overdraft	5,700		–	
	(16,800)		(13,900)	
Net current assets		11,200		14,400
Total net assets		54,200		46,400
Equity				
Share capital		34,000		33,000
Share premium account		300		200
Retained earnings		19,900		13,200
Total equity		54,200		46,400

The summarised income statements for the two years ended 31 May 2013 are as follows:

	2013	2012
	£000	£000
Gross profit	46,100	38,900
Less Expenses (including depreciation £6m in 2013)	(17,000)	(20,900)

	2013	2012
	£000	£000
	29,100	18,000
Less Loss on sale of non-current assets	(3,200)	–
Operating profit before interest	25,900	18,000
Interest payable	(1,200)	(1,200)
Profit for the year	24,700	16,800
Less Taxation	(5,000)	(4,000)
Profit after tax	19,700	12,800
Less Dividends paid	(13,000)	(2,000)
Retained profits for the year	6,700	10,800
Retained profits brought forward	13,200	2,400
Retained profits carried forward	19,900	13,200

Notes:

1 A summary of the company's non-current assets for the year ended 31 May 2013 is shown below (£000s):

1 June 2012 Opening balance	76,000
31 May 2013 Additions	22,000
	98,000
31 May 2013 Sales	(8,000)
31 May 2013 Closing balance	90,000

2 The assets which were sold realised £1.8m, which represented a loss on disposal of £3.2m when compared with their depreciated value.

Produce a cash flow statement for the year ended 31 May 2013.

Case study

There's the profit, but where's the cash?

Machiq Limited (see previous case studies) was formed on 1 July 2014 and has been making increasing profits. By 30 June 2016 it reports the following summarised income statements and statements of financial position:

Income statements for the year ended 30 June

	2016	2015
	£	£
Gross profit	176,400	*133,260*
Less Expenses (includes depreciation £5,060 in 2016)	(58,600)	*(39,460)*
Operating profit for the year	117,800	*93,800*
Less Interest payable	(1,800)	*(1,800)*
Profit for the year before taxation	116,000	*92,000*
Less Taxation	(26,950)	*(18,400)*
Profit for the year	89,050	*73,600*

Statement of financial position as at 30 June

	2016		2015	
	£	£	£	£
Non-current assets (depreciated value)		165,980		*74,040*
Current assets:				
Inventory	32,650		*17,370*	
Receivables	30,950		*39,560*	
Bank	–		*6,240*	
	63,600		*63,170*	
Less **Current liabilities**				
Payables	46,080		*41,710*	
Taxation	26,950		*18,400*	
Bank overdraft	2,400		–	

	2016		2015	
	£	£	£	£
	(75,430)		*(60,110)*	
Net current assets/(liabilities)		(11,830)		*3,060*
Total net assets		154,150		*77,100*
Equity				
Share capital		24,000		*14,000*
Share premium account		31,000		*21,000*
Retained earnings		99,150		*42,100*
Total equity		154,150		*77,100*

Reconciliation of movements in equity

	Share capital	Share premium	Retained earnings	Total	2014/5
At 1 July 2015	14,000	21,000	42,100	77,100	*35,000*
Issue of shares	10,000	10,000		20,000	–
Profit for the year			89,050	89,050	*73,600*
Equity dividends paid	———	———	(32,000)	(32,000)	*(31,500)*
At 30 June 2016	24,000	31,000	99,150	154,150	*77,100*

The changes in the share capital and share premium account were due to a sale of shares to Trixie Richardson, who had recently left Kazam Limited after 10 years' service as chief accountant. Trixie was appointed managing director of Machiq Limited on 10 April 2016. During the year ended 30 June 2016, Machiq Limited bought two Mercedes cars for £48,500 each for Marvin's and Chiquita's use. No assets were sold in the year. Trixie is concerned that, whilst the company seems to be profitable, its cash flow appears to be poor.

Required

(a) Prepare a cash flow statement for the year ended 30 June 2016.

(b) Do you agree with Trixie's opinion of the cash flow? What have been the key cash inflows and outflows in the year?

Answers are in Appendix 3

Further research

Tesco plc's cash flow statement: **www.tesco.com/corporateinfo/**

Chapter 8

Analysing company reports

Objectives

When you have read this chapter you will be able to:

- Understand the need for public limited companies to publish information
- Undertake preliminary research prior to analysing company accounts
- Identify and appraise the key components of an annual report
- Distinguish between, and compute, a vertical and horizontal analysis of financial information and make an interpretation of the data revealed by the analysis
- Prepare ratios within five main groupings and analyse the data revealed
- Understand concerns regarding the validity of accounting information

8.1 Introduction

The published financial information of Tesco plc (as referred to in the previous chapter) comes in two versions:

1 The Annual Review and Summary Financial Statement, intended for users who do not require fully comprehensive financial information but need only the highlights of the company's performance. The most recently published statement contained 54 pages. Summarised versions of the income statement, statement of financial position, cash flow statement and various other items of financial data appeared on nine of these pages, the rest being devoted to general information about the company, with many full-colour photographs of stores, products, customers and employees. The QR code shown enables you to download this report.

2 The Annual Report and Financial Statements, which gives all the information required to be published by the Companies Act, Accounting and Financial Reporting Standards and the Stock Exchange. This contained 153 pages, including not only the key financial statements but also 46 pages of detailed notes to the accounts. The same QR code shown enables you to download this report.

Scan the following QR code with your QR reader to take you to the website of Tesco plc, where you can download annual financial reports

Tesco has several hundred thousand shareholders and the production of attractive full-colour reports with tempting photographs of foodstuffs and smiling shop assistants is used partly as a public relations exercise to keep shareholders loyal and maintain confidence in the company. Smaller companies might have very few shareholders and so the annual report, whilst still containing the key financial statements, will tend to be matter-of-fact documents without any frills. Financial information published for small and medium-sized limited companies would not be as comprehensive as that required of a plc.

Neither sole proprietorships nor 'conventional' partnerships are required to publish accounts (but limited liability partnerships must do so), and their financial summaries will normally be seen by only a handful of people: the owner or partners, the accountant who produced the information, the taxation authorities and possibly a bank manager. Any wider distribution is entirely at the discretion of the owner or partners.

8.2 Data for analysis

The purpose of this chapter is to *make sense* of the information contained in the financial summaries: to analyse, interpret and come to a conclusion. To illustrate the analytical process, we shall use the financial statements of a fictitious company, Brooklyn plc, for the years 2014 and 2013 as set out below.

Brooklyn plc
(published) Income statement for the years ended
31 December 2014 and 2013

	2014	2013
	£000	£000
Revenue	6,590	*4,350*
Less Cost of sales	(4,220)	*(2,820)*

	2014	2013
	£000	£000
Gross profit	2,370	1,530
Less Expenses	(700)	(470)
Operating profit	1,670	1,060
Less Finance costs	(60)	(70)
Profit before tax	1,610	990
Less Taxation	(450)	(270)
Retained profit for the year	1,160	720

Brooklyn plc
Statements of financial position as at 31 December 2014 and 2013

		2014			2013	
	£000	£000	£000	£000	£000	£000
Net current assets (net value)			6,200			5,320
Current assets:						
Inventory		2,200			680	
Trade receivables		550			500	
Cash and cash equivalents		250			200	
		3,000			1,380	
Less **Current liabilities**						
Trade payables	750			330		
Taxation	450			270		
		(1,200)			(600)	
Net current assets			1,800			780
			8,000			6,100
Less **Non-current liabilities**						
Bonds			(1,000)			(1,500)
Total net assets			7,000			4,600
Equity						
Share capital			3,100			2,500
Share premium			1,500			500
Retained earnings			2,400			1,600
Total equity			7,000			4,600

Additional information:

Inventory at 1 January 2013 = £640,000.

Stock market prices: end 2014 = 561p, end 2013 = 547p.

Share capital consists entirely of ordinary shares with a £1 nominal value.

Reconciliation of movements in equity

(£000)	Share capital	Share premium	Retained earnings	Total	2013
At 1 January 2014	2,500	500	1,600	4,600	*4,000*
Issue of shares	600	1,000		1,600	—
Profit for the year			1,160	1,160	*720*
Equity dividends paid			(360)	(360)	*(120)*
At 31 December 2014	3,100	1,500	2,400	7,000	*4,600*

Brooklyn plc
Cash flow statement for the year ended 31 December 2014

		2014 £000		2013 £000
Cash flows from operating activities		405		*765*
Interest paid		(65)		*(60)*
Tax		(270)		*(170)*
Net cash from operating activities		**70**		***535***
Cash flows from investing activities				
Purchase of non-current assets	(1,640)		(720)	
Proceeds from sale of non-current assets	380		400	
Net cash used in investing activities		**(1,260)**		***(320)***
Cash flows from financing activities				
Proceeds from issue of share capital	1,600		—	
Dividends paid	(360)		(120)	
Net cash from/ (used in) financing activities		**1,240**		***(120)***
Net increase in cash and cash equivalents		**50**		***95***
Cash and cash equivalents at beginning of year		**200**		***105***
Cash and cash equivalents at end of year		**250**		***200***

8.3 The first stage: preliminary research

There are many reasons for analysing financial statements, including the following:

- Investment – you may be an existing shareholder or considering investing in a business.
- Curiosity – you may have used a business's products or services and wish to find out more about what they do.

- Commercial reasons – you trade with the business or are considering trading with it.
- Lending decisions – banks and other financial institutions need to know if a business is capable of repaying loans or is in a sound position if loans are being requested.
- Self-interest – you may want to find out more about the company that employs you. For example, is it likely to continue trading and keep you as an employee?
- Business rivalry – how well or badly is a competitor doing compared with your business?
- Taxation – the taxation authorities may need to be satisfied that the accounts appear complete and trustworthy.
- Environmental factors – local communities and pressure groups may wish to find out more about local companies, including their employment and ecological attitudes.
- Economic analysis – business trends can be ascertained by analysing company results.

Those wishing to make the analysis may already know a great deal about the company, as shareholders, as workers or by virtue of publicly available information such as newspaper or website comment. The key background information which is needed prior to starting a detailed analysis of the financial statements includes:

- Type of trade – what does the company do?
- Competitors – who does it compete against? What share of the market does it have?
- Geographical spread – where does it sell its goods and services and which countries does it buy from?
- Management – who are the managers and how well qualified are they?
- Quality of products – how reliable are the products the company sells?

Much of this information can be gained from the 'non-financial' parts of the annual report, by accessing data via the internet or in libraries, or even by visual inspection of products, stores, adverts etc. All this preliminary research is useful in placing the business in an appropriate context prior to making any detailed financial calculations. Figure 8.1 shows some of those who might be interested in company financial information.

Figure 8.1 Who is interested in financial information?

Having obtained a good general impression of the scope and nature of the business, the analyst should then read through the annual report, making a note of any unusual or interesting items such as changes in accounting policies and businesses acquired in the year. By looking at the 'bottom lines' of the four financial summaries, an immediate impression can be gained of the business's progress in the year. For Brooklyn plc, this shows:

- Income statement: retained profit for the year has increased from £720,000 to £1,600,000.
- Statement of financial position: total net assets/total capital employed has risen from £4.6m to £7m in the year.
- Reconciliation of movements in equity: total equity has increased from £4.6m to £7m in the year
- Cash flow statement: cash has increased by £50,000, compared with an increase of £95,000 in the previous year.

By all four measures the company appears to have performed well even though the cash increase is rather less than 2013.

Activity 8.1

Obtain a copy of an annual report of a plc (see Further Research at the end of this chapter) and identify the sections listed above. Read through the auditors' report to see if the accounts show a true and fair view, and try to find out how many shares the chief executive owns and how much he or she was paid as a director. Look at the 'bottom lines' of the key financial statements (use group figures where there is a choice). How do you think the company performed in the year?

Answer

Obviously the answer depends on which company's report you are looking at, but as an illustration, Tesco plc's 2012 annual report showed a true and fair view according to the auditors, PricewaterhouseCoopers (see Figure 6.12). The company's chief executive, Philip Clarke, owned 1.8 million shares, and had options to purchase a further 4.3million. He was paid a total of £1.1m for the year. The company's financial summaries showed progress in terms of both profit and increase in net asset value, but a continuing decline in cash and cash equivalents balances:

Income statement (see Figure 6.8):	Profit for the year increased from £2,671m to £2,814m.
Statement of financial position (see Figure 6.9):	Total net assets/total equity rose from £16,623m to £17,801m in the year.
Cash flow statement (see Figure 7.2):	Closing cash and cash equivalents declined from £2,428m to £2,311m in the year.

Stop and think

Tesco plc had 8 billion shares in issue, so Philip Clarke owned under 0.02% of the company, and his total pay was 0.27% of the year's operating profits.

8.4 The second stage: horizontal and vertical analysis

Having gathered the background information, the next stage is to start the numerical analysis of the financial statements. Advanced mathematics is not required, but you should understand percentage and ratio calculations. Refresh your memory with the next activity.

Activity 8.2

Calculate the following:

(a) 6,815 as a percentage of 27,260.
(b) 3,720 as a percentage of 1,200.
(c) The increase from 3,120 to 11,232 as a percentage of the former figure.
(d) The decrease from 16,040 to 12,832 as a percentage of the former figure.
(e) The ratio of 5,541 compared with 18,470.
(f) The ratio of 46,000 compared with 11,500.

Answer

		Calculation
a	25%	$\frac{6,815}{27,260} \times 100 = 25\%$
b	310%	$\frac{3,720}{1,200} \times 100 = 310\%$
c	Increase of 260%	$11,232 - 3,120 = 8,112$ $\frac{8,112}{3,120} \times 100 = 20\%$
d	Decrease of 20%	$16,040 - 12,832 = 3,208$ $\frac{3,208}{16,040} \times 100 = 20\%$
e	0.3:1	$\frac{5,541}{5,541} = 0.3$
f	4:1	$\frac{46,000}{11,500} = 4$

Horizontal and vertical analyses are ways of comparing the relative size of individual components within the financial summaries. Horizontal analysis achieves this by calculating the percentage change from the preceding year to the current year, whereas vertical analysis expresses each income statement item as a percentage of the sales total, each statement of financial position item as a percentage of the total net assets, and cash flow statement items as a percentage of the net cash flow from operating activities.

Using the Brooklyn plc statements, the analysis will be as follows (figures have been rounded to the nearest whole number):

Brooklyn plc
(published) Income statement for the years ended 31 December 2014 and 2013

	2014	2013	'Horizontal' analysis	'Vertical' analysis 2014	'Vertical' analysis 2013
	£000	£000	% change	%	%
Revenue	6,590	4,350	+51	100	100
Less Cost of sales	(4,220)	(2,820)	+50	(64)	(65)
Gross profit	2,370	1,530	+55	36	35
Less Expenses	(700)	(470)	+49	(11)	(11)
Operating profit	1,670	1,060	+58	25	24
Less Finance costs	(60)	(70)	−14	(1)	(2)
Profit before tax	1,610	990	+63	24	23
Less Taxation	(450)	(270)	+67	(7)	(6)
Profit for the year, after tax	1,160	720	+61	18	17

Note that each percentage in the 'horizontal' column is calculated using the following formula:

$$\frac{(2014 \text{ value} - 2013 \text{ value}) \times 100}{2013 \text{ value}}$$

The statement of financial position and cash flow statement can be analysed in a similar way:

Brooklyn plc
Statements of financial position as at 31 December 2014 and 2013

	2014	2013	'Horizontal' analysis	'Vertical' analysis 2014	'Vertical' analysis 2013
	£000	£000	% change	%	%
Non-current assets	6,200	5,320	+17	89	116
Current assets:					
Inventory	2,200	680	+224	31	15
Trade receivables	550	500	+10	8	11
Cash and cash equivalents	250	200	+25	4	4
	3,000	1,380	+117	43	30
Less **Current liabilities**					
Trade payables	750	330	+127	11	7

	2014	2013	'Horizontal' analysis	'Vertical' analysis 2014	2013
	£000	£000	% change	%	%
Taxation	450	270	+67	6	6
	(1,200)	(600)	+100	(17)	(13)
Net current assets	1,800	780	+131	26	17
(sub-total)	8,000	6,100	+31	114	133
Non-current liabilities					
Bonds	(1,000)	(1,500)	−33	(14)	(33)
Total net assets	7,000	4,600	+52	100	100
Equity					
Share capital	3,100	2,500	+24	44	54
Share premium	1,500	500	+200	21	11
Retained earnings	2,400	1,600	+50	34	35
Total equity	7,000	4,600	+52	100	100

Note that each figure in the vertical analysis is expressed as a percentage of the statement of financial position total.

Brooklyn plc
Cash flow statement for the year ended 31 December 2014

	2014		2013		'Horizontal' analysis	'Vertical' analysis 2014	2013
	£000	£000	£000	£000	% change	%	%
Cash flows from operating activities		405		765	−47	100	100
Interest paid		(65)		(60)	+8	(16)	(8)
Tax		(270)		(170)	+59	(67)	(22)
Net cash from operating activities		**70**		**535**	**−82**	**17**	**70**
Cash flows from investing activities							
Purchase of non-current assets	(1,640)		(720)		−128	(405)	(94)
Proceeds from sale of non-current assets	380		400		−5	94	52
Net cash used in investing activities		**(1,260)**		**(320)**	**+294**	**(311)**	**(42)**

	2014		2013		'Horizontal' analysis	'Vertical' analysis 2014	2013
	£000	£000	£000	£000	% change	%	%
Cash flows from financing activities							
Proceeds from issue of share capital	1,600		—		—	394	—
Dividends paid	(360)		(120)		+ 200	(88)	(16)
Net cash from/(used in) financing activities		**1,240**		**(120)**	**+ 1,133**	**306**	**(16)**
Net increase in cash and cash equivalents		**50**		**95**	**− 47**	**12**	**12**
Cash and cash equivalents at beginning of period		**200**		**105**	**+ 90**	**49**	**14**
Cash and cash equivalents at end of period		**250**		**200**	**+ 25**	**61**	**26**

Note that each figure in the vertical analysis is expressed as a percentage of the net cash flows from operating activities.

8.4.1 Interpreting the analysis

It is obvious that Brooklyn plc has expanded in 2014. The horizontal analysis shows within the income statement how much the increase has been, and the major changes have been the consistent increases in both revenue and costs by approximately 50%, coupled with a reduction in finance costs (–14%) which has resulted from a part repayment of the bond as disclosed by the statement of financial position.

The vertical analysis reveals that amounts have remained fairly constant, apart from the halving of finance costs as a percentage of sales.

The statement of financial position's horizontal analysis reveals the first worrying statistic about the company: the fact that inventory levels have increased by 224% in the year, even though total net assets have increased by 'only' 52%. The 200% increase in the share premium shows that the shares issued in the year were sold at an amount considerably in excess of their nominal value. The vertical analysis of the statement of financial position again highlights the increasing amount of inventory held by the company at the end of 2014 and the reduction in its non-current liabilities.

The horizontal analysis of the cash flow statement again shows some areas of concern. Net cash inflow from operating activities has declined by 36%, with massive increases in net capital expenditure (non-current asset purchases less sales). However, sales of shares have financed this. Overall there was a 25% increase in the amount of cash and cash equivalents. The vertical analysis for 2014 shows that the cash outflow on capital expenditure was almost matched by financing changes (new shares being issued less bonds repaid) and also shows increasing tax and dividend payments.

8.5 The third stage: ratio analysis

Having established the percentage movements between the two years, and assessed the relative strengths of the component parts of the financial statements, the next step is to calculate specific percentages and ratios to reveal further aspects of the business's performance. The following table represents the more common ones which are calculated, divided into five groups:

Group	Name of ratio	Formula
Profitability	ROCE (Return On Capital Employed)	$\frac{\text{Operating profit}}{\text{Total equity} + \text{Long} - \text{term loans}} \times 100$
	Gross margin	$\frac{\text{Gross profit}}{\text{Revenue}} \times 100$
	Mark-up	$\frac{\text{Gross profit}}{\text{Cost of sales}} \times 100$
	Net margin	$\frac{\text{Operating profit}}{\text{Revenue}} \times 100$
Efficiency	Non-current assets turnover	$\frac{\text{Revenue}}{\text{Non-current assets at net book value}}$
	Inventory turnover	$\frac{\text{Average inventory}}{\text{Cost of sales}} \times 365$
	Average collection period	$\frac{\text{Trade receivables}}{\text{Revenue}} \times 365$
	Average payment period	$\frac{\text{Trade payables}}{\text{Cost of sales}} \times 365$
Short-term solvency and liquidity	Current ratio (or working capital ratio)	Current assets : Current liabilities
	Acid test (or quick assets test)	(Current assets − Inventory) : Current liabilities
	Cash conversion cycle	(Inventory turnover + Average collection period − Average payment period)
Long-term solvency and liquidity	Gearing	$\frac{\text{Preference shares (if any)} + \text{Long-term loans}}{\text{Share capital} + \text{Reserves} + \text{Long-term loans}} \times 100$
	Interest cover	$\frac{\text{Operating profit}}{\text{Interest payable}}$
Investment ratios	EPS (Earnings per Share)	$\frac{\text{Profit for the year, after tax}}{\text{Number of equity shares issued}}$
	p/e (price/earnings)	$\frac{\text{Market price}}{\text{Earnings per share}}$

Group	Name of ratio	Formula
Investment ratios (continued)	Dividend cover	$\frac{\text{Profit available to pay dividend}}{\text{Dividends paid}}$
	Dividend yield	$\frac{\text{Dividend per share}}{\text{Market price per share}}$

Using the data form Brooklyn plc's financial summaries, the ratios are explained in sections 8.5.1–8.5.5

8.5.1 Profitability ratios

	Brooklyn plc	
Name of ratio	2014	2013
ROCE (Return On Capital Employed)	$\frac{1{,}670}{7{,}000 + 1{,}000} \times 100 = 20.8\%$	$\frac{1{,}060}{4{,}600 + 1{,}500} \times 100 = 17.38\%$
Gross margin	$\frac{2{,}370}{6{,}590} \times 100 = 35.96\%$	$\frac{1{,}530}{4{,}350} \times 100 = 35.17\%$
Mark-up	$\frac{2{,}370}{4{,}220} \times 100 = 56.16\%$	$\frac{1{,}530}{2{,}850} \times 100 = 53.68\%$
Net margin	$\frac{1{,}670}{6{,}590} \times 100 = 25.34\%$	$\frac{1{,}060}{4{,}350} \times 100 = 24.37\%$

- *Return On Capital Employed* (*ROCE*) is a fundamental measure of business performance as it compares the operating profit with the total capital used to generate that profit. Notice that we have used year-end figures for capital rather than average figures for the year, though it is permissible to use the average. A viable business should generate a considerably higher return than that available by investing in a bank or other similar interest-bearing deposits. In the case of Brooklyn plc, the return has increased slightly during the year, and is significantly higher than bank deposit rates. However, for a full assessment to be made (and this applies to all the ratios which we have calculated), we would also need to know comparative figures for other businesses operating in the same business sector. For example, if Brooklyn plc was an engineering company and other engineering business were generating only 15% ROCE, we could assume that Brooklyn was doing better than its competitors. If competitors were reporting ROCE of 27%, we might consider Brooklyn plc to be underperforming. What is certain is that we cannot make any meaningful statement about *any* ratio without having some comparable figure (previous year, competitor's results, etc.) to use as a yardstick.
- *Gross margin* shows the proportion of sales revenue which resulted in a gross profit to the company. It is affected by various factors, including changing price levels and different products being sold ('sales mix'). The margin might be reduced by aggressive companies wanting to expand their share of the market, or increased if there is reduced competition. Inaccurate inventory valuations or the theft of goods may also affect the ratio. In the case of Brooklyn plc, there has been a slight upward movement in the year, resulting in £35.96 of gross profit out of every £100 sales (previous year: £35.17 per £100).

- *Mark-up* indicates the pricing policy of the business, as it shows the percentage addition to cost price to arrive at the selling price. In 2014, every £100 of goods bought by Brooklyn plc was sold for £156.16 (previous year: £154.26).

Activity 8.3

The higher the gross margin, the higher will be the mark-up percentage. For example, a gross margin of 50% results in a mark-up of 100%, whilst a gross margin of 25% means a mark-up of 33.3%.
If a business has a gross margin of 20%, what would be the mark-up?

Answer

The mark-up is 25%.

(Revenue = 100, cost of sales = 80, gross profit = 20, therefore mark − up is $\frac{20}{80} \times 100$)

- *Net margin* shows the proportion of sales which resulted in a profit after all overheads (other than finance charges) had been deducted. In 2014, £25.34 out of every £100 sales resulted in operating profit, an increase on the previous year's £24.37. Net margin can be improved by reducing overheads, but a balance has to be achieved between cutting expenses and maintaining business efficiency.

Activity 8.4

Calculate and comment upon the four profitability ratios for the large supermarket groups Tesco plc and Sainsbury plc, from the following information:

(£m)	Tesco plc		Sainsbury plc	
	2012	2011	2012	2011
Revenue	64,539	60,455	22,294	21,102
Cost of sales	59,278	55,330	21,083	19,942
Gross profit	5,261	5,125	1,211	1,160
Total equity	17,801	16,623	5,629	5,424
Long-term loans	9,911	9,689	2,617	2,339
Operating profit	3,985	3,917	874	851

Answer

(%)	Tesco plc		Sainsbury plc	
Name of ratio	**2012**	**2011**	**2012**	**2011**
ROCE	14.38	14.89	10.60	10.96
Gross margin	8.15	8.48	5.43	5.50
Mark-up	8.88	9.26	5.74	5.82
Net margin	6.17	6.48	3.92	4.03

Comment: Without exception, the four profitability ratios have declined for the two companies between 2011 and 2012, reflecting the difficult trading experienced during a financial recession. Comparisons between the two companies show that Tesco has outperformed Sainsbury by every profitability measure. Crucially, Tesco's return on capital employed in 2012 is 40% higher than that of Sainsbury, and its net margin is 57% higher.

8.5.2 Efficiency ratios

	Brooklyn plc	
Name of ratio	**2014**	**2013**
Non-current assets turnover	$\frac{6,590}{6,200} = 1.06$ times	$\frac{4,350}{5,320} = 0.82$ times
Inventory turnover	$\frac{(2,200 + 680)/2}{4,220} \times 365 = 124.5$ days	$\frac{(680 + 640)/2}{2,820} \times 365 = 85.4$ days
Average collection period	$\frac{550}{6,590} \times 365 = 30.5$ days	$\frac{500}{4,350} \times 365 = 42$ days
Average payment period	$\frac{390}{4,220} \times 365 = 33.7$ days	$\frac{210}{2,820} \times 365 = 27.2$ days

The *non-current assets turnover* indicates that 2014 was a more efficient year than 2013 in that every £1 of non-current assets generated £1.06 of sales in 2014, but only 82p in the previous year. The more investment that is made into non-current assets, the greater should be the generation of revenue. If this isn't happening then the management must investigate and possibly sell off surplus assets. If certain assets in particular locations are being underutilised then they might consider transferring those assets to other, more productive, areas.

Inventory turnover shows the effect of the massively increased inventory at the end of 2014 as it indicates that, on average, inventory took 124.5 days to sell in 2014 but only 85.4 days in 2013. This is a significant increase and one which should cause concern to the company management. There may, however, be a rational explanation, such as a deliberate increase in the inventory at the end of 2014 to coincide with a major sales campaign at the start of 2015, or the company stocking different (and slower-moving) types of products in 2014 compared with 2013.

The *average collection period* shows an improved time period for collecting outstanding debts, down from 42 days to just over 30 days. This could be because more resources have been applied to credit control, or prompt-payment discounts have been offered. Efficient businesses collect their debts as quickly as possible.

The *average payment period* shows that the company paid its bills faster in 2014 than in 2013. This may have resulted from being offered discounts for prompt payment. It is good practice not to pay bills too quickly, as it is a form of interest-free credit to the business. However, great care must be taken not to alienate suppliers by delaying payment beyond a reasonable time.

Stop and think

Chart of shame lists time taken to settle bills

A league table charting the time every single UK public limited company takes to pay its bills was launched in 2008 in an effort to shame those companies that delay so

Scan the following QR code with your QR reader to take you to the website of the Institute of Credit Management

long in paying suppliers they place some at risk of going bust. The Institute of Credit Management said the issue of payment times would become increasingly important for business as the economy slowed. Nick Wilson, director of the Credit Management Research Centre which compiled the table, said 'when payments do not arrive, then problems with cash flow start to emerge. A lot of companies get into trouble because of managing cash flow. Trade debts are the main source of cash coming into business. If you're a small supplier, you are a lot more sensitive to payment times. It also reduces profitability. The reason for a business failure is often to do with cash flow and the time it takes to pay bills.'

The average payment time was quoted as 44 days for all plcs, but the 350 biggest companies paid within 34 days.

Activity 8.5

Calculate and comment upon the four efficiency ratios for Tesco plc and Sainsbury plc, from the following information:

(£m)	Tesco plc		Sainsbury plc	
	2012	2011	2012	2011
Non-current assets	37,918	35,167	10,308	9,678
Inventory	3,598	3,162	938	812
Trade receivables	1,848	1,416	110	93
Trade payables	5,971	5,782	1,903	1,836
Revenue	64,539	60,455	22,294	21,102
Cost of sales	59,278	55,330	21,083	19,942

Answer

(%)	Tesco plc		Sainsbury plc	
Name of ratio	**2012**	**2011**	**2012**	**2011**
Non-current assets turnover (times)	1.70	1.72	2.16	2.18
Inventory turnover (days)	22.15	20.86	16.24	14.86
Average collection period (days)	10.45	8.55	1.80	1.61
Average payment period (days)	36.77	38.14	32.95	33.60

Comment: Both companies showed a decrease in the non-current assets turnover equivalent to a drop in turnover of two pence for every one pound invested in non-current assets. Inventory turnover for the two companies again showed a worrying trend as in both companies inventory was taking longer to sell. Average collection periods are rather misleading for these two companies, as supermarkets would not have money owing to them by customers in the usual sense (customers paying immediately for the goods at the tills), so the trade receivables shown in the statement of financial position are likely to represent miscellaneous amounts due, unrelated to direct sales to customers. Average payment periods show that Sainsbury was a faster payer than Tesco, taking nearly 33 days to pay its invoices, compared with nearly 37 days for Tesco.

8.5.3 Short-term solvency and liquidity ratios

	Brooklyn plc	
Name of ratio	**2014**	**2013**
Current ratio (or working capital ratio)	3,000:1,200 = 2.5:1	1,380:600 = 2.3:1
Acid test (or quick asset test)	800[a]:1,200 = 0.67:1	700[b]:600 = 1.17:1
Cash conversion cycle	(124.5 + 30.5) − 33.7	(85.4 + 42) − 27.2
	= 121.3 days (− ve)	= 100.2 days (− ve)

[a] (3,000 − 2,200) [b] (1,380 − 680)

The ideal *current ratio* (also known as the working capital ratio) is often quoted as somewhere around 1.5:1 (that is, about one and a half times as much value in current assets compared to current liabilities), but it depends upon the type of business, and many successful companies (notably those with a high proportion of cash sales) operate on current ratios of 1:1 or less. The ratio gives a measure of the ability of a company to meet its current liabilities as they fall due so, in theory at least, having more current assets than short-term payables makes sense. In practice, efficient control of working capital will mean that:

- inventory is kept to a minimum, otherwise too much inventory may be held, resulting in high costs for storage and security, plus interest on overdrafts and loans used to pay for the inventory
- customers are encouraged to pay as soon as possible, otherwise inadequate control of invoices may result in uncollected debts
- 'surplus' cash or bank balances should be reinvested or returned to investors in the form of increased dividends
- average payables periods might be lengthened to take advantage of interest-free credit periods.

Did you know?

Current ratios can be too high as well as too low. A company with a 6:1 ratio might have too much inventory, poor credit control of receivables, or uninvested cash surpluses.

If a company (particularly a young business) expands aggressively to gain market share, it might have to invest in non-current assets such as machinery and buildings, build up inventory levels, and sell on extended credit terms, without having first built up sufficient working capital to enable it to service the finance charges on the amounts borrowed. For example, a business may get new orders beyond its existing capacity. After investing in new equipment it may have no working capital left, and have to resort to heavy borrowing and reliance on extended credit terms from suppliers. If the creditors and lenders demand payment, the company may be forced to sell its non-current assets and go out of business. This is known as *overtrading*. It would be hoped that the new orders bring in enough additional profit, cash flow and working capital to ride out the storm.

The *acid test* is the crucial measure of whether a business seems able to meet its debts in an emergency situation (e.g. if it is rumoured to be in difficulties and all or most of its creditors demand immediate payment). Quick assets are those which can be converted quickly into cash as the need arises, and it is normal to exclude inventories and work in progress from the ratio, as these assets might take many weeks or months to sell in such circumstances. The ideal ratio is often quoted as 1:1 (£1 of quick assets to every £1 of current liabilities), but look at the supermarkets' calculations below to see how viable businesses can survive on much lower ratios. In the case of Brooklyn plc, the exclusion of the high closing inventory in 2014 results in a dramatic decline in the acid test ratio, which would be of concern to the company's directors.

The *cash conversion cycle* is an indicator of the strength of the firm's working capital, and represents a practical calculation of the length of time it takes on average to convert sales into cash, compared to the time taken to pay creditors. It is in fact a combination of three of the efficiency ratios previously calculated – the inventory turnover, average collection period and average payment period. For example, if it takes 45 days from the receipt of inventory to its sale to a customer, and then the customer takes a further 30 days to pay the invoice for the sale, we can say that it is taking 75 days to convert inventory into cash. However, we can't forget the fact that the inventory has to be paid for, and if the firm pays its own bills on average 25 days after receiving an invoice, we can

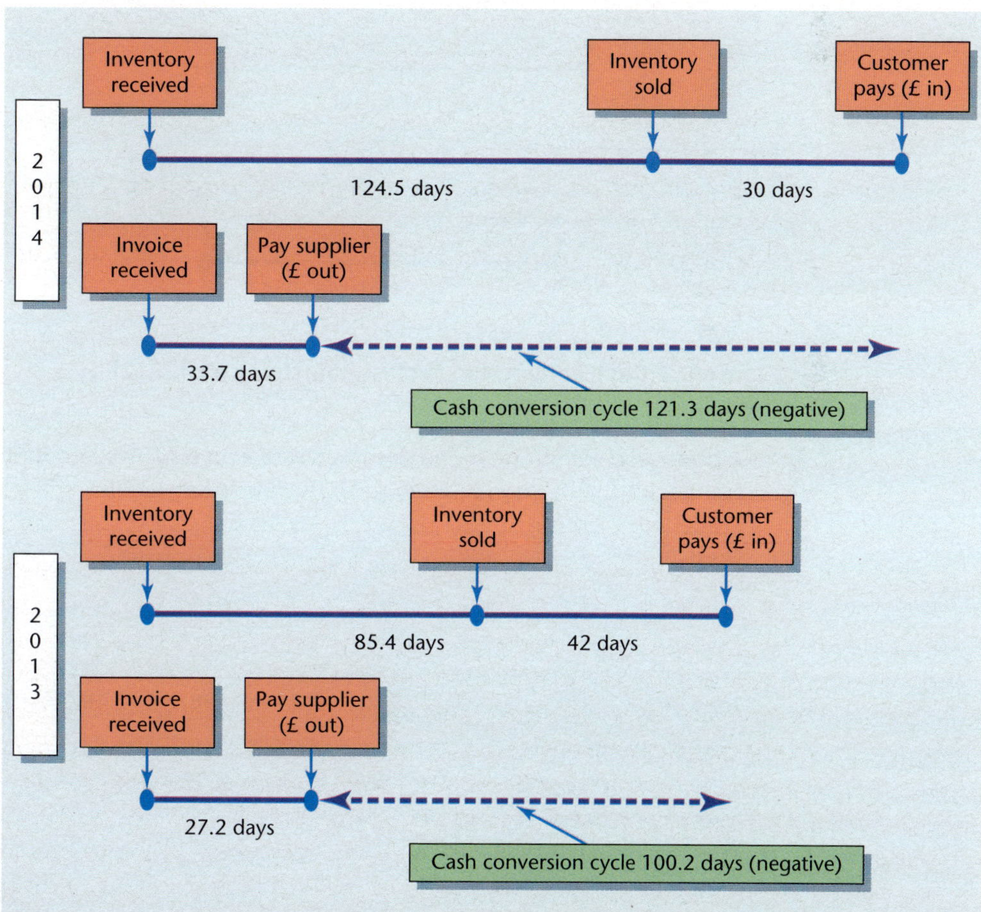

Figure 8.2 Cash conversion cycles

state that the cash conversion cycle is 50 days (i.e. 75 – 25). In fact it is a *negative* cash conversion cycle, as the cash is received from the debtor 50 days *after* the creditor is paid.

For Brooklyn plc, the cash conversion cycle has worsened in 2014, as it is taking considerably longer both to sell inventory and collect debts. The only positive note is that the company is taking an extra 6 days to pay its bills, from 27.2 days to 33.7 days. Another way of showing these trends is by drawing time lines, as shown in Figure 8.2.

We can see that the cycle worsened by over 21 days (121.3 – 100.2) in 2014.

The most efficient businesses will shorten the top timeline and lengthen the bottom timeline as far as possible to arrive at a positive cash conversion cycle. In other words it needs to sell inventory as fast as possible, get the money in from receivables as quickly as possible, and delay payments to suppliers (within reason). It could be argued that the ideal cash conversion cycle is that enjoyed by supermarket companies such as Tesco plc and Sainsbury's plc, which sell inventory in a few days, enjoy cash sales with nil or minimal collection periods, and take several weeks to pay their own suppliers! For comparison, Sainsbury plc's 2012 cash conversion cycle is (positive) 14.91 days, as shown in Figure 8.3.

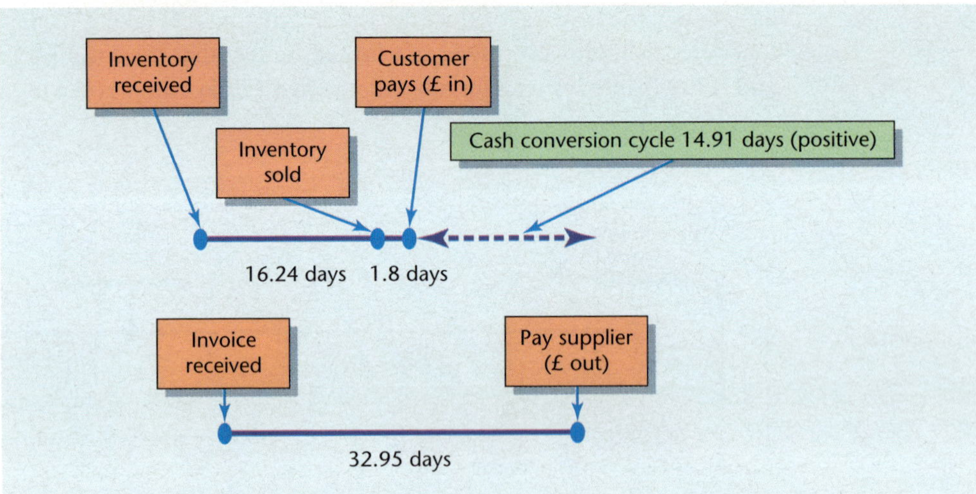

Figure 8.3 Cash conversion cycle – Sainsbury plc (2012)

Activity 8.6

Calculate and comment upon the three short-term solvency and liquidity ratios for Tesco plc and Sainsbury plc, from the following information:

(£m)	Tesco plc		Sainsbury plc	
	2012	2011	2012	2011
Current assets	12,863	12,039	2,032	1,721
Inventory	3,598	3,162	938	812
Current liabilities	19,249	17,731	3,136	2,942
Inventory turnover (days)*	22.15	20.86	16.24	14.86
Average collection period (days)*	10.45	8.55	1.80	1.61
Average payment period (days)*	36.77	38.14	32.95	33.60

* See Activity 8.5

Answer

(£m)	Tesco plc		Sainsbury plc	
	2012	2011	2012	2011
Current ratio	0.67	0.68	0.65	0.58
Acid test	0.48	0.50	0.35	0.31
Cash conversion cycle (days)	+ 4.17	+ 8.73	+ 14.91	+ 17.13

Comment: It is apparent that both companies had negative current ratios and acid test calculations. Put in simple terms, in 2012 Tesco had only 67p of current assets to meet each £1 of current liabilities. The massive cash inflows of the companies should ensure enough day-to-day liquidity to meet payables as they fall due. However, there may come a point when any company is threatened with liquidation if it cannot ensure that its creditors are paid on time. Both companies have very poor acid test ratios, though these are typical in the supermarket sector where the goods are sold quickly, customers pay at the tills, whilst suppliers have to wait several weeks to get their invoices paid. Consequently, cash conversion cycles are positive for both companies.

8.5.4 Long-term solvency and liquidity ratios

	Brooklyn plc	
Name of ratio	2014	2013
Gearing	$\frac{1{,}000}{7{,}000 + 1{,}000} \times 100 = 12.5\%$	$\frac{1{,}500}{4{,}600 + 1{,}500} \times 100 = 24.6\%$
Interest cover	$\frac{1{,}670}{60} = 27.83$ times	$\frac{1{,}670}{70} = 23.86$ times

Gearing reflects the relationship between a company's equity capital (ordinary shares and reserves) and its other forms of long-term funding (preference shares, bonds, etc.). A company may exist solely on its equity (that is, have no other long-term funding), but in order to expand it may have to issue preference shares carrying a fixed dividend rate, or borrow money on which interest must be paid. Management strategy may be to run a highly geared company, making use of a high proportion of borrowed funds to expand. This has its risks – particularly in a recession – as many companies have gone 'bust' due to borrowing money and then finding that insufficient profits are generated to repay the loans and interest. However, the rewards for ordinary shareholders can be much greater in a successful highly geared company than in its low-geared equivalent, as the increased profits, less the finance costs or fixed dividend payments, result in higher rewards to the equity shareholders. Figure 8.4 explains the advantages and disadvantages of different gearing levels.

There are a number of different ways to calculate gearing levels. In the example of Brooklyn plc, the gearing percentage can never be greater than 100% as the loans are added to the divisor in the formula. Another way of calculating gearing would be to omit the loans from the divisor, in which case the gearing could be over 100% if borrowings were greater than the equity and reserves. (For Brooklyn, the revised gearing calculation would become (1,000/7,000) × 100 = 14.3% in 2014 and (1,500/4,600) × 100 = 32.6% in 2013.) As long as the calculations are consistently made, either formula can be used. Brooklyn's gearing has halved in 2014 as a result of the stronger total net assets and the part repayment of the loan in the year.

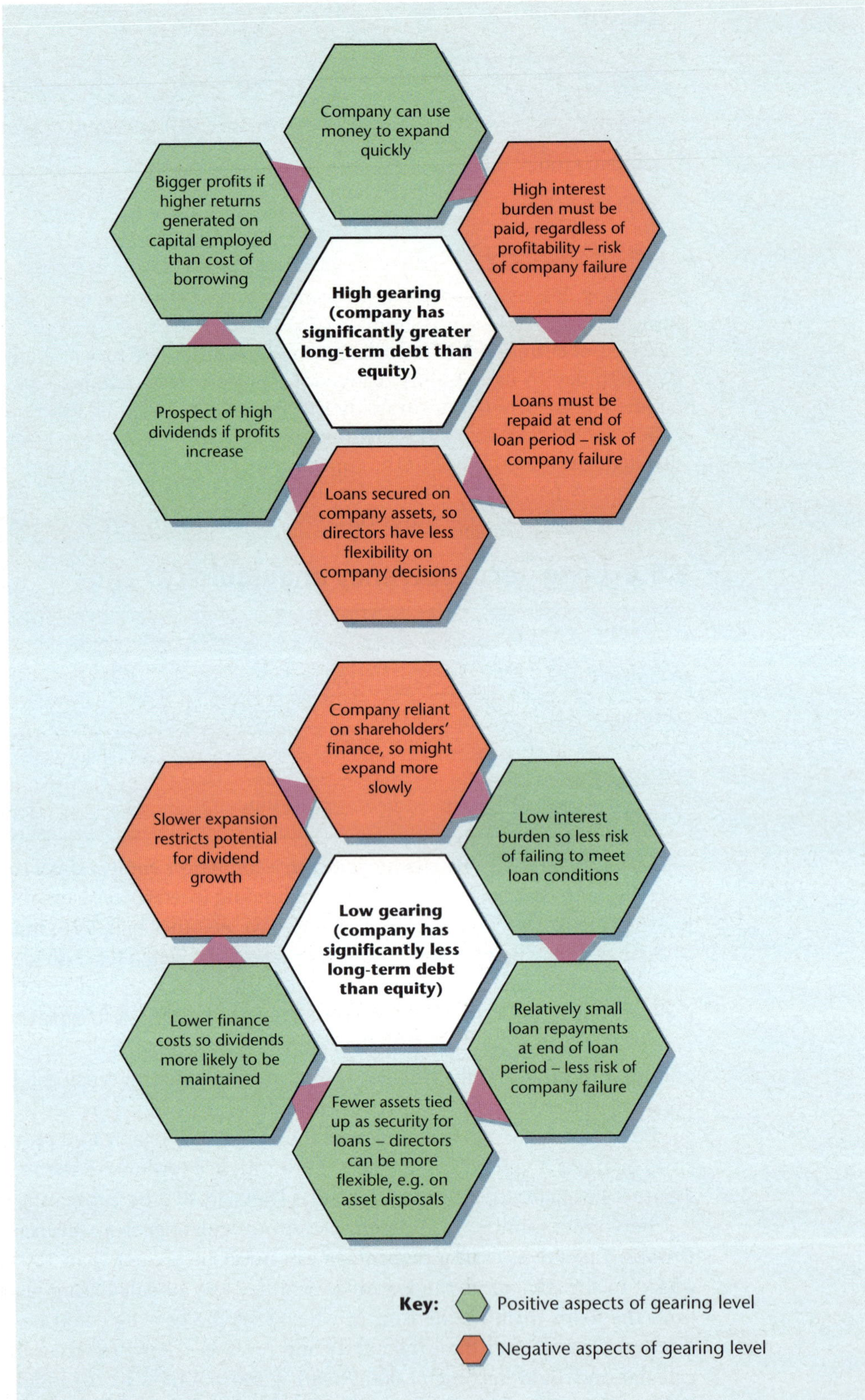

Figure 8.4 High and low gearing

Did you know?

Many companies deduct the value of 'cash and cash equivalents' from their debt totals when calculating gearing, as presumably they could be used to repay debt if required by a lender.

News clip

Football Association urged to overhaul debt levels

FT

By Ed Hammond

Football's governing body has been told it must radically overhaul the way the game is run in England or face the possibility of legislation.

In a 116-page report published on Friday, the Commons culture, media and sport select committee said the Football Association must rid the sport of its high debt levels and tackle the issue of financial instability among clubs.

The committee praised the success of the Premier League, the top division of the English and Welsh game, in terms of the quality of its football and for generating healthy returns for its member clubs.

MPs said, however, that the successes of the new domestic football model had been accompanied by financial instability and increasing levels of debt, which remained a serious problem throughout the sport.

The committee, headed by John Whittingdale, made the key recommendation of introducing a rigorous and consistent licensing model that would be imposed throughout the country's professional football clubs. The licence would promote "sustainable forward-looking business plans and underpin self-regulation measures".

On the issues of unsustainable levels of gearing among football clubs, the committee said that, while high debt was not a new issue, certain characteristics inherent in the new model had aggravated the problem. Witnesses had told the committee that the financial benefits associated with membership of the Premier League had the effect of encouraging reckless financial speculation.

"No one doubts the success of the Premier League in revitalising English Football. But it has been accom-panied by serious financial problems throughout the football league pyramid. Significant changes need to be made to the way the game is run to secure the future of England's unique football heritage, and the economic and community benefits it provides", said Mr Whttingdale.

He added that the FA was the right organisation to carry out the overhaul, but warned that is had some way to go "getting its own house in order" before it could tackle the problems in the sport.

In its report, the committee reserved particular criticism for the ownership of Leeds United. "There is no more blatant an example of lack of transparency than the recent ownership history of Leeds United," it said, before going on to urge the FA to investigate, if necessary with the assistance of HM Revenue & Customs.

The government insists it wants football to run itself and that legislation is a last resort. But it is concerned by a number of problems bedevilling the game, including the amount of debt carried by football clubs, the lack of financial transparency and the difficulty of establishing the ownership of some clubs. The sports minister, Hugh Robertson, said earlier this year: "Football is the worst governed sport in this country, without a shadow of a doubt."

Mr Whittingdale pointed out that almost all of the committee's recommendations could be achieved without legislation. "Legislation should be considered only as a last resort in the absence of substantive progress," he said.

The report went on to suggest that the 12-member board structure of the FA should be reduced to 10 and reconstructed in such a way that "vested interests do not predominate". The existing board is split 50/50 between national game and professional game representatives – a structure that has been blamed for creating deadlock in the past.

Source: *The Financial Times*, 29 July 2011

Interest cover indicates the relative safety of the interest payments by comparing the finance costs with the profit available to make the payments. Brooklyn has nearly 28 times more profits than the finance costs, which appears very safe and will give assurance to lenders that there would have to be a very dramatic decline in profit before their interest payments were threatened.

Activity 8.7

Calculate and comment upon the two long-term solvency and liquidity ratios for Tesco plc and Sainsbury plc, from the following information:

(£m)	Tesco plc		Sainsbury plc	
	2012	2011	2012	2011
Operating profit	3,985	3,917	874	851
Finance costs	417	483	138	116
Total equity	17,801	16,623	5,629	5,424
Long-term loans	9,911	9,689	2,617	2,339

Answer

	Tesco plc		Sainsbury plc	
(£m)	2012	2011	2012	2011
Gearing (%)	35.76	36.82	31.74	30.13
Interest cover (times)	9.56	8.11	6.33	7.34

Comment: Gearing levels of both Tesco and Sainsbury represent approximately one third of the total long-term capital employed, which could be regarded as a 'medium' gearing level. The interest cover shows us the extent to which each company's profits exceed the cost of finance, and in each case appears to be a satisfactory multiple. A cause for concern might be the decline in Sainsbury's cover, compared with a strengthening for Tesco in the same period.

8.5.5 Investment ratios

	Brooklyn plc	
Name of ratio	**2014**	**2013**
EPS (Earnings Per Share)	$\frac{£1{,}160{,}000}{3{,}100{,}000 \text{ shares}} = 37.4\text{p}$	$\frac{£720{,}000}{2{,}500{,}000 \text{ shares}} = 28.8\text{p}$
p/e (price/earnings)	$\frac{561\text{p}}{37.4\text{p}} = 15 \text{ times}$	$\frac{547\text{p}}{28.8\text{p}} = 19 \text{ times}$
Dividend cover	$\frac{1{,}160}{360} = 3.2 \text{ times}$	$\frac{720}{120} = 6 \text{ times}$
Dividend yield	$\frac{11.6\text{p}^{a}}{561\text{p}} \times 100 = 2.07\%$	$\frac{4.8\text{p}^{b}}{547\text{p}} \times 100 = 0.88\%$

[a] Dividends/No. of shares = £360,000/3,100,000.
[b] Dividends/No. of shares = £120,000/2,500,000.

Earnings Per Share (EPS) and the *price/earnings (p/e) ratio* are important indicators of a company's performance. The EPS is always shown at the end of a plc's income statement, its calculation being the subject of an International Accounting Standard.[1] The p/e ratio, where the market price per share is expressed as a multiple of the EPS, is the clearest indication of how the stock market rates a particular company. The higher the multiple, the greater the expectation of future profits (earnings), with investors having pushed up the market price in anticipation. A low p/e ratio results from losses or poor profits, with a depressed share price. Although Brooklyn's EPS has increased (resulting from the 61% increase in after-tax profits but only a 24% increase in share capital), the stock market appears unimpressed as the p/e ratio has slumped from 19 times to 15 times in the year. If the stock market sentiment had remained as positive in 2014 as it had been in 2013, the share price would have been 711p (19 × 37.4p) instead of 561p.

Dividend cover is similar to interest cover, in that it indicates the relative safety of the dividends for the year by comparing them with the profit available to make the payments. The increased dividends paid in 2014 have resulted in a halving of the cover, with available profit just over three times the dividend.

Dividend yield measures the actual rate of return obtained by investing in an ordinary share at the current market price. Someone buying a Brooklyn share at £5.61 would obtain a yield of 2.07%, which is a significant increase on that of the previous year.

Stop and think

Apple Inc pays a dividend after a 17 year break

The question of whether or not companies should pay dividends is one of the most difficult decisions taken by directors. If they pay nothing, can they continue to rely on shareholders' loyalty; if they pay too much, are they risking the future well-being of the business? In March 2012, the US technology company Apple Inc surprised the stock markets by announcing its first dividend (worth $45bn) after an interval of 17 years. This phenomenally successful business had hitherto ploughed all its profit back into research and development, including the creation of the iconic iPod, iPhone and iPad products. At the time of the dividend announcement, some commented that it could be a sign that the company was running out of profitable new areas in which to invest. In reality, Apple's shareholders were getting impatient for a cash return on their investment.

[1]IAS 33: Earnings per Share.

Activity 8.8

Calculate and comment upon the four investment ratios for Tesco plc and Sainsbury plc, from the following information:

	Tesco plc		Sainsbury plc	
	2012	2011	2012	2011
Earnings (£m)	2,806	2,655	608	650
Dividends (£m)	1,180	1,081	285	269
No. of shares (million)	8,045	8,061	1,929	1,921
Dividend per share (pence)	14.76	14.46	15.30	14.50
Market price (pence)*	320	440	297	369

* At 1 March 2012 and 2011

Answer

	Tesco plc		Sainsbury plc	
	2012	2011	2012	2011
EPS (pence)	34.88	32.94	31.52	33.84
p/e (times)	9.17	13.36	9.42	10.90
Dividend cover (times)	2.38	2.46	2.13	2.42
Dividend yield (%)	4.61	3.29	5.15	3.93

Comment: The raw EPS figures cannot be used for comparison between the companies as they have different numbers of shares in issue. The p/e ratios have dropped for both companies, with Tesco showing the largest decline. Share prices generally dropped sharply over the year due to macroeconomic factors rather than any specific weakness of the two companies. Dividend cover is slightly stronger for Tesco, but the decline in both companies' share price has increased the yield (the expected return from investing at the current market price) considerably in the current year.

8.6 The validity of the financial statements

In the analysis of company reports, it has been assumed that the information is accurate and reliable and provides a suitable basis for study. Whilst it is true that the published financial statements of a plc will be audited and so, with very rare exceptions, show a true and fair view according to an independent firm of qualified accountants, many objective observers have questioned the validity of financial statements for various reasons, including the following:

- Financial summaries are drawn up under the *historic cost convention*, whereby items are included at their purchase price at the time of acquisition, and *no account is taken of inflation* on the replacement price of assets such as inventory or machinery. This problem is more acute when inflation rates are high, and attempts at introducing alternative inflation-adjusted accounting methods were tried in the 1970s and 1980s when inflation rates peaked at over 25% p.a. No method was felt reliable enough to replace the traditional historic cost convention, though it was considered acceptable to allow revaluations of certain assets (notably land and buildings) where market values had changed significantly when compared with book values. The use of asset revaluation reserves to record such changes was explained earlier (in Chapter 6). In recent years, there has been an increasing trend for certain other assets to be valued at their *fair value*, which is defined by International Accounting Standards[2] as 'the amount for which an asset could be exchanged between knowledgeable, willing parties in an arm's length transaction'. Critics of this approach point out that it introduces an increased element of volatility in statement of financial position (especially in times of major economic crises) that might in fact reflect unrealistic valuations in fast-moving market conditions. The recessions of recent years have affected the values of many major financial institutions, resulting in billion-pound write-offs as 'fair' values keep falling. One chief executive, Henri de Castries, Chief Executive of Axa, a leading insurance company, remarked: 'If you are in the medical business, you want to be sure that the thermometer is the right one for benchmarking things properly. In the economy, the accounting systems are the thermometer, and I'm not sure the measurement scale is the right one.'

- The rules and regulations of accounting allow flexibility, so that companies faced with the same accounting problem may come to differing solutions. This flexibility is seen by some as strength of accounting procedures where the requirements of specific companies allow individual accounting treatments to be adopted where appropriate. An example is depreciation, where the judgement of the length of a time period over which assets should be depreciated is left to the discretion of the directors. The issuing of Accounting and Financial Reporting Standards has greatly reduced the scope for creative accounting, but unscrupulous directors will always try and find a loophole.
- Information is based on past events, but it is argued that meaningful decisions can be taken only on the basis of forecasts of future performance. Unfortunately, the future is rather harder to verify than the past, so *historical* documents are seen as a more reliable guide to future prospects than future predictions, however well researched. The ideal is perhaps a balance between the two, with a company's forecasts being published alongside the conventional historical information. However, companies are naturally reluctant to divulge information which may be of use to competitors, so the forecast information may be so vague and generalised as to be of little use to anybody.

These topics are covered in more depth later (in Chapters 15–17).

8.7 Summary

How company information can be analysed is summarised in Figure 8.5.

[2]IAS 16: Property, Plant and Equipment.

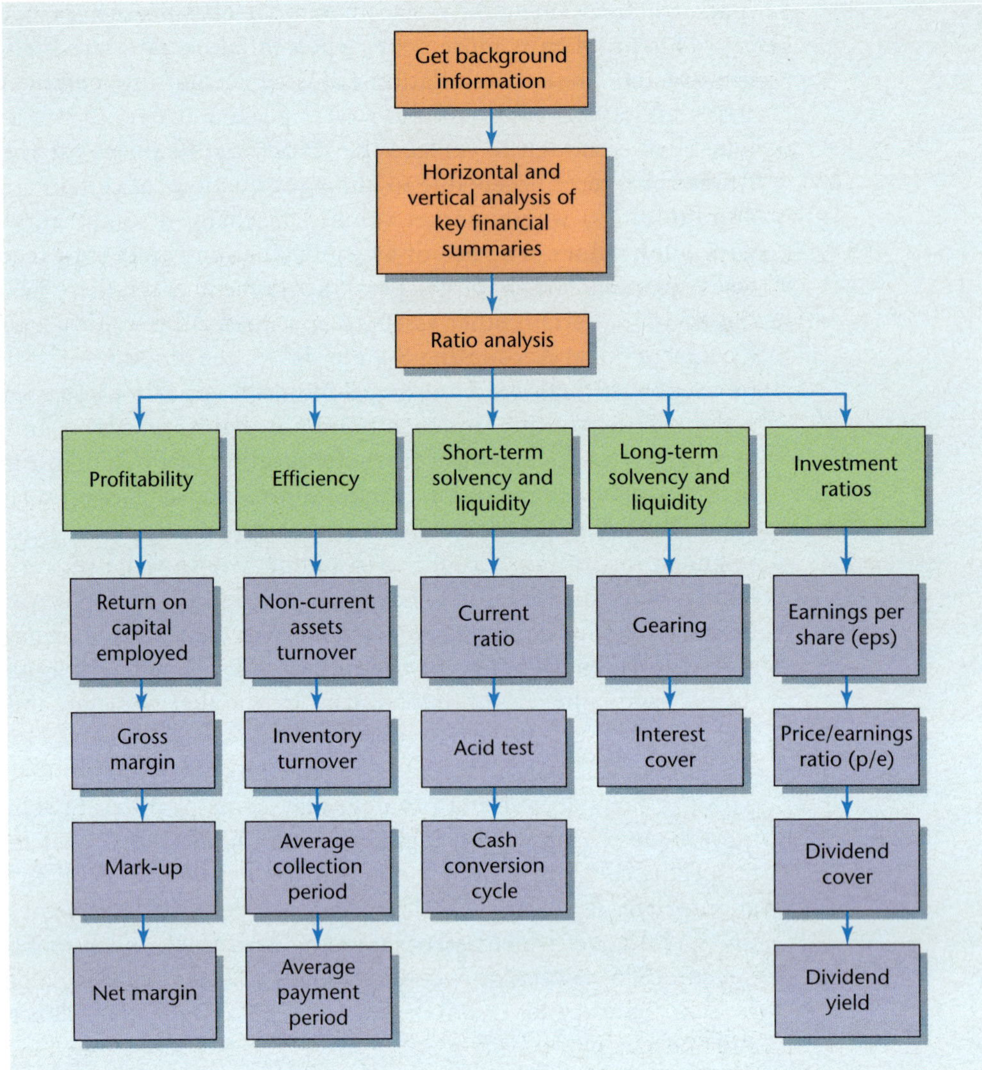

Figure 8.5 Analysing company information

8.8 Chapter glossary

Acid test The comparison between the 'quick' assets and the current liabilities (liabilities due for payment within one year).

Cash conversion cycle The time difference between receiving cash from the sale of inventory, and paying for that inventory.

Current ratio The comparison between current assets and current liabilities.

Dividend cover The ability of a company to pay its dividends, measured by expressing the profit after tax as a multiple of the dividends paid.

Dividend yield The dividend return (as a percentage) from an investment in equity shares.

Earnings Profit available to meet equity dividends.

Earnings Per Share (EPS) Earnings divided by the number of ordinary shares issued. EPS form part of the p/e ratio (see below).

Fair value The amount for which an asset could be exchanged between knowledgeable, willing parties in an arm's length transaction.

Gearing The relationship between a company's equity capital (ordinary shares) and its other forms of long-term funding (preference shares, bonds, etc.).

Gross margin Gross profit as a percentage of sales revenue.

Historic cost convention The accounting convention which values assets at their purchase price at the time of acquisition with no allowance made for subsequent inflation.

Horizontal analysis Comparison of values within financial statements by calculation of percentage changes between one year and the next.

Interest cover The ability of a company to meet its interest commitments, measured by expressing the profit before finance costs as a multiple of the finance costs.

Net margin Operating profit as a percentage of sales revenue.

Price/earnings (p/e) ratio Market price as a multiple of the latest earnings per share. Used as a relative measure of stock market performance.

Quick assets Assets which can be turned quickly into cash. Usually the current assets, other than inventory.

Vertical analysis Analysis of the relative weighting of components within financial statements by expressing them as a percentage of a key component in that statement.

Additional resources

Only accessible on Android-based devices

Now work through the various exercises and problems that you can find within the My Accounting Lab that are relevant to this chapter. Either use the QR code shown in the margin (if you use an Android-based device), or visit www.myaccountinglab.com for the log-in page.

Self-check questions

The answers to these questions are in Appendix 1.

1 Which one of the following must publish annual financial information?

(a) Limited liability companies
(b) Sole proprietorships
(c) 'Conventional' partnerships
(d) Private individuals

2 Which of the following, found within an annual report, explains the changes in shareholders' value?

(a) Auditors' report
(b) Operating and financial review
(c) Statement of accounting policies
(d) Reconciliation of movements in equity

3 Horizontal analysis is:

(a) The calculation of the relative weighting of components within a financial statement in a particular financial period
(b) The comparison of the current year's figures with the previous year's figures
(c) The comparison of one company's results with another company
(d) The comparison of the income statement with the statement of financial position

4 ROCE means:

(a) Return on current expenses
(b) Reserves of capital equity
(c) Return on capital employed
(d) Ratio of capital employed

5 If total net assets are £45,600, current liabilities £12,700, inventory £3,900 and non-current assets £29,000, what is the acid test (quick assets) ratio?

(a) 2:1
(b) 2.3:1
(c) 1.5:1
(d) 1.75:1

6 Four companies have the following p/e ratios: A 17, B 24, C 12, D 8. Which of the following statements about the companies is *incorrect*?

(a) B's share price must be twice that of C
(b) A's share price is 17 times its earnings
(c) D has the lowest share price relative to its earnings per share
(d) B has the Stock Exchange's greatest expectations for future profit growth

7 A company starts its year with inventory of £2m and ends with £3m. If it had an overall cost of sales of £12.5m, what was its inventory turnover in days?

(a) 85 days
(b) 1,825 days
(c) 73 days
(d) 7.3 days

8 Low gearing means:

(a) A company depends largely on long-term loans
(b) A company has few, if any, long-term loans
(c) A company cannot pay a dividend
(d) A company has high interest payments

9 An advantage to a company of high gearing is:

(a) The company can rely on internal funding for expansion
(b) High interest payments
(c) Lower risk of liquidation
(d) Prospect of high profits from using borrowed money for expansion

10 One of the criticisms of accounting information has been:

(a) The information is always incorrect
(b) Accountants never follow rules and regulations
(c) Inflation is not adequately reflected within the financial statements
(d) Companies should report the future instead of the past

Self-study questions

Questions marked with this symbol (#) indicate that the suggested answers are available to lecturers only – other answers are given in Appendix 2.

8.1 Obtain an annual report of a trading company (see Further research at the end of this chapter). Produce a vertical and horizontal analysis of the company's income statement, statement of financial position and cash flow statement for the current and previous years, and identify the main areas of change disclosed by the analysis.

8.2 The management of Rodington Limited pays particular attention to the ratios and percentages which they calculate from their annual accounts. For the year ended 31 December 2014, they have listed the following statistics, which they are comparing with those of another company, Sundorne Limited, shown alongside:

	Rodington Ltd	Sundorne Ltd
Gross margin	60%	5%
Net margin	20%	2%
Average collection period	30 days	5 days
Current ratio	2:1	0.4:1
Gearing percentage	20%	70%

One of the two companies is a manufacturing company, the other is a food retailer, with an expanding number of stores.

(a) Which of the two companies is the food retailer? Give two reasons for your choice.
(b) Assuming that the total cost of sales of Rodington Ltd was £200,000 in 2014, the closing cash and cash equivalents were £11,004 and the average inventory for 2014 was £40,000, calculate:
  (i) the total of Rodington Limited's trade receivables at 31 December 2014, assuming all sales were on credit terms
  (ii) the total of Rodington Limited's current liabilities at 31 December 2014.
(c) Assuming you were an equity shareholder of Sundorne Limited, what is the significance *to you* of the company's gearing percentage?

8.3 The statements of financial position of Dorrington Ltd and Rowton Ltd at 31 May 2014 were as follows:

	Dorrington	Rowton
	£000	£000
Non-current assets	125	204
Current assets:		
Inventory	85	120
Trade receivables	26	18
Cash and cash equivalents	12	39
	123	177
Less **Current liabilities**	(135)	(168)
Net current assets (liabilities)	(12)	9
	113	213
Less **Non-current liabilities**		
6% bonds	–	(100)
Total net assets	113	113
Equity		
Share capital	50	100
Reserves	63	13
Total equity	113	113

Notes:

1 The profits of Dorrington Limited are expected to continue at £40,000 p.a. The profits of Rowton Limited have averaged £40,000 before bond interest.

2 Statements of financial position at 31 May 2013 for both companies showed broadly similar figures to those for 2014.

(a) From the statement of financial position as at 31 May 2014, calculate the following ratios for both companies, and give a brief explanation of their significance: (i) Gearing ratio; (ii) Current ratio; (iii) Acid test ratio; (iv) Return on capital employed.

(b) Assume that you had been asked for advice by a cautious potential investor who has £20,000 available. Explain which of the two companies appears to represent the better choice of investment on the basis of the evidence provided.

(c) If the audit report on Dorrington's accounts had stated that the business was *not* a going concern, how would that affect your views on the company, and in particular the advice given to the potential investor in (b) above?

8.4 Uffington Limited was formed on 1 January 2014. The company's unpublished income statement for 2014 and its statement of financial position as at 31 December 2014 are as follows:

Uffington Limited
Income statement for the year ended 31 December 2014

	£	£
Revenue		670,000
Less **Cost of sales**		
Purchases	570,000	
Less Closing inventory	(90,000)	480,000
Gross profit		190,000
Administration expenses	(117,350)	
Distribution expenses	(21,600)	(138,950)
Operating profit		51,050
Finance costs		(5,600)
Profit for the year		45,450
Less Tax		(5,450)
Profit after tax		40,000

Statement of financial position as at 31 December 2014

	£	£	£
	Cost	Depreciation	Net value
Freehold land	160,000	–	160,000
Fixtures	30,000	21,000	9,000
Motor vehicles	56,000	39,200	16,800
	246,000	60,200	185,800
Current assets:			
Inventory		90,000	
Trade receivables		44,250	
Cash and cash equivalents		24,200	
		158,450	
Less **Current liabilities**			
Trade payables	73,800		
Taxation	5,450		
		(79,250)	
Net current assets			79,200
			265,000

	£	£	£
Less Non-current liabilities			
7% bonds			(80,000)
Total net assets			185,000
Equity			
Ordinary shares of £1 each			100,000
Share premium			60,000
Reserves*			25,000
Total equity			185,000

*Profit after tax £40,000 less Dividend paid £15,000.

The company is about to embark on an expansion programme which will require at least £6m for the purchase of new businesses and to support investment in increased inventory levels. The chairman of the company has called for an analysis of the 2014 figures before approaching possible sources of funding.

(a) Comment on the performance of Uffington Limited for the year ended 31 December 2014 and on its financial position at that date. Support your comments with eight relevant accounting ratios.

(b) Suggest, and comment on the suitability of, two alternative ways for the company to raise £6m.

8.5# The sales director of Kangaroo plc is an expert at selling the company's products, but at directors' meetings, he is often confused by many of the terms that the finance director uses. In brief, at a recent board meeting, he heard comments about three customers: that 'company A (a relatively new business) is over-trading, company B has a high gearing ratio, and company C has a high p/e ratio despite a low return on capital employed'.

(a) The sales director is concerned that future sales to these companies might be risky, and has asked for your advice.

(b) Explain to the sales director the significance of the comments made by the finance director.

Use the data contained within the following financial statements to answer questions 8.6–8.8 below.

Tibberton plc (summarised)
income statement for the year ended 30 September 2014

	2014	**2013**
	£000s	**£000s**
Revenue	620	540
Less Cost of sales	(240)	(280)
Gross profit	380	260
Distribution costs	(40)	(35)
Administrative expenses	(60)	(50)
Other operating income and expenditure	(20)	(10)

	2014 £000s	2013 £000s
Operating profit	300	185
Finance income	(15)	(40)
Finance costs	(35)	(10)
Net profit before taxation	280	215
Taxation	(80)	(50)
Profit for the financial year	200	165
Dividends paid (see note)	(50)	(35)
Profit retained for the financial year	150	130

Note: Dividends per share 2014: 7.14p, 2013: 5.83p

Tibberton plc
Statement of financial position as at 30 September

	2014 £000s	2013 £000s
Non-current assets		
Intangible assets	120	125
Tangible assets	1,620	1,285
	1,740	1,410
Current assets		
Inventory	80	70
Trade receivables (see note 1)	165	89
Cash and cash equivalents	30	1
	275	160
Current liabilities (see note 2)	(190)	(210)
Net current assets (2013: liabilities)	85	−50
Total assets less current liabilities	1,825	1,360
Non-current liabilities	(445)	(220)
Total net assets	1,380	1,140
Capital and reserves		
Share capital (50p nominal value)	350	300
Share premium	190	150

	2014 £000s	2013 £000s
Retained profits	840	690
Total equity	1,380	1,140

Notes:

1 Of which trade receivables:	135	85
2 Of which trade payables:	60	90
3 Long-term debt (for gearing calculation)	580	409
4 No. of equity shares issued at year-end ('000)	700	600
5 Assume stock market price (p)	135	100

Tibberton plc
Cash flow statement for the year to 30 September

	2014 £000s	2013 £000s
Cash flows from operating activities	**174**	**118**
Interest received	13	35
Interest paid	(32)	(12)
	(19)	**23**
Taxation paid	**(50)**	**(35)**
Net cash from operating activities	105	106
Cash flows from investing activities		
Purchase of non-current assets	(368)	(200)
Proceeds from sale of non-current assets	(24)	(80)
Net cash used in investing activities	**(344)**	**(120)**
Cash flows from financing activities		
Issue of equity share capital	90	20
New long-term loans	300	50
Repayments of long-term loans	(80)	(20)
Equity dividends paid	(42)	(30)
Net cash from financing activities	**268**	20
Net increase in cash and cash equivalents	29	6

8.6# Prepare a horizontal and vertical analysis of Tibberton plc.

8.7# Calculate the relevant ratios within the five groupings of: Profitability, efficiency, long-term liquidity and solvency, short-term liquidity and solvency, and investors' ratios.

8.8# Summarise your analysis of the company's results in the form of a report to a potential investor. The report should be no more than 1,500 words in length.

Case study

Esmeralda springs a surprise

On 3 July 2016, Marvin, the founder of Machiq Limited (see previous case studies), was sorting through the morning's correspondence. After reading one particular letter, he immediately summoned his fellow directors, Chiquita and Trixie, to an emergency meeting. He passed the letter round and awaited their comments. The letter read as follows:

Dear Marvin

I have not written to you since 30 June 2014, when I demanded compensation for the cruel way you sacked me and my family back in 2012. However, I realised that you would not pay me the £10m I demanded, so I devoted my energies to building a rival business. I rejoined my old employer, Kaboosh Limited, and worked so hard that I was appointed managing director. When my close friend and company chairman, Cardew Kaboosh, died two months ago, he left all his shares to me, so I now own 95% of the company. My company's performance has been so impressive that I now want to take over your company. I am enclosing a copy of the most recent income statement and statement of financial position of Kaboosh Limited for information.

Yours sincerely,
Esmeralda

After reading the letter, it was agreed that Trixie would analyse the financial summaries of Kaboosh Limited and compare them with those of Machiq Limited. She compiled the following summary:

Income statements for the year ended 30 June 2016

	Machiq	**Kaboosh**
	£	£
Revenue	705,600	1,102,500
Less **Cost of sales**	(529,200)	(661,500)
Gross profit	176,400	441,000
Less Expenses	(58,600)	(175,000)
Operating profit for the year	117,800	266,000
Less Finance costs	(1,800)	(12,000)
Profit for the year, before tax	116,000	254,000
Less Tax	(26,950)	(47,000)
Profit for the year, after tax	89,050	207,000

	Machiq	Kaboosh
	£	£
Less Dividends	(32,000)	(55,000)
Retained profit for the year	57,050	152,000
Retained profit brought forward	42,100	645,000
Retained profit carried forward	99,150	797,000

Statement of financial position as at 30 June 2016

	Machiq Limited		Kaboosh Limited	
	£	£	£	£
Non-current assets		165,980		950,000
Current assets:				
Inventory	32,650		251,300	
Trade receivables	30,950		142,500	
Cash and cash equivalents	–		36,200	
	63,600		430,000	
Less **Current liabilities:**				
Trade payables	14,080		108,000	
Tax	26,950		47,000	
Dividends approved but unpaid	32,000		55,000	
Bank overdraft	2,400		–	
	(75,430)		(210,000)	
Net current assets/(liabilities)		(11,830)		220,000
		154,150		1,170,000
Less **Non-current liabilities:**				
6% bonds				(200,000)
Total net assets		154,150		970,000
Equity				
Share capital (5p shares)		24,000		100,000
Share premium		31,000		73,000
Retained profits		99,150		797,000
Total equity		154,150		970,000

Additional information:

Inventory figures represent average values.

Price/earnings ratios for companies in the manufacturing sector average 15 times earnings.

Required

(a) Analyse each company's results into the following five groups of ratios, and comment on the relative performance of each company:
   (i) Profitability
   (ii) Efficiency
   (iii) Short-term solvency and liquidity
   (iv) Long-term solvency and liquidity
   (v) Investment ratios.

(b) Advise the directors of Machiq Limited as to whether they should agree to the company being taken over by Kaboosh Limited. State four additional items of information which they might need before they come to a final decision.

Answers are in Appendix 3

Further research

The annual report of J. Sainsbury plc: **http://www.j-sainsbury.co.uk/investor-centre/reports**

The annual report of Tesco plc: **http://www.tescoplc.com**

To download other annual reports: **www.annualreports.com**

Revision of chapters 6-8

Introduction

This section consolidates your knowledge gained so far and is structured as follows:

- Practice examination paper 1: a one-hour examination paper consisting of 40 multiple-choice questions, covering the first 8 chapters of the book.
- Practice examination paper 2: a two-hour examination paper consisting of five questions.

Answers are provided in Appendix 4.

Practice exam paper 1

Time allowed ONE hour. This question paper contains 40 multiple-choice questions. Read each question carefully and select ONE answer that you think is correct.

1 If a company is described as a 'going concern', it is:

(a) About to close down
(b) Not about to close down
(c) A company that people are concerned about
(d) A rapidly expanding company

2 A company sells £150,000 of goods during the year, having been owed £12,000 by customers at the start of the year and £18,000 at the end of the year. What revenue figure will be shown in the income statement for the year?

(a) £150,000
(b) £144,000
(c) £156,000
(d) £180,000

3 Which one of the following is a fundamental qualitative characteristic of financial statements?

(a) Comparability
(b) Verifiability
(c) Faithful Representation
(d) Timeliness

4 An owner of a business had a capital balance of £85,000 at the end of the financial year. During the year, drawings of £14,000 had been made, and the business had made an operating profit of £17,000. The owner paid in an inheritance of £40,000 into the business during the year. What was the opening capital balance?

(a) £14,000
(b) £156,000
(c) £42,000
(d) £122,000

5 In the accounting equation, assets plus expenses equals:

(a) Liabilities + Equity + Income
(b) Liabilities + Equity − Income
(c) Liabilities − Equity + Income
(d) Liabilities − Equity − Income

6 Why, if a business has money in the bank, does it appear as a debit balance in the business's ledger?

(a) It is a mistake – it should be a credit balance
(b) It is showing that the bank owes the money to the business (a business asset)
(c) As all the debits equal all the credits, there is no difference between a debit and credit balance
(d) It shows that the business is in debt to the bank

7 A business pays a cheque for £4,100 for a van, of which £150 is for road tax. What would be the correct bookkeeping entries?

(a) Dr Van £4,100, Cr Bank £4,100
(b) Dr Bank £4,100, Cr Van £3,950, Cr Motor expenses £150
(c) Dr Motor expenses £4,100, Cr Bank £4,100
(d) Dr Van £3,950 and Dr Motor expenses £150, Cr Bank £4,100

8 A cash float is:

(a) A predetermined amount of petty cash which is paid out at regular intervals
(b) Cash used only for buying non-current assets
(c) A predetermined amount needed to meet petty cash expenditure, which is topped up at intervals
(d) The amount of petty cash after all the petty cash expenditure has been deducted

9 Which one of the following is *not* a current asset?

(a) Accrual
(b) Prepayment
(c) Inventory
(d) Cash

10 A financial period:

(a) Is the same as a financial year
(b) Is the same as the date of the statement of financial position
(c) Always ends on 31 December
(d) Can be as long or as short as the business needs for a specific purpose

11 Inventory is usually valued in a statement of financial position at:

(a) Selling price
(b) Lower of cost and net realisable value
(c) Lower of cost and gross realisable value
(d) Lower of selling price and net realisable value

12 A business has a combined rent and rates account. During the year ended 31 December 2014, the business had an opening rent prepayment of £200 and an opening rates accrual of £300. During the year it paid £11,000 for rent and rates. At the end of the year, £900 had been prepaid for rates and there was an accrual of £600 for rent. What figure for rent and rates would appear in the income statement?

(a) £10,800

(b) £10,600
(c) £11,200
(d) £11,400

13 A non-current asset which cost £60,000 has been owned for three years. It is depreciated at 40% p.a. on the diminishing balance method. What is its depreciated value at the end of the third year of ownership?

(a) £21,600
(b) £8,640
(c) £12,960
(d) nil

14 Which of the following would be direct (prime) costs of a furniture manufacturer?

(a) Depreciation of woodworking machinery
(b) Wood used to make furniture
(c) Electricity used to heat the factory
(d) The rent of the factory

15 In a manufacturing business, what is work in progress?

(a) Partly completed goods
(b) Goods in transit to a customer
(c) Raw materials
(d) Work about to start on manufacturing goods

16 Assets are usually divided between:

(a) Urgent and non-urgent
(b) Current and long-term
(c) Medium-term and long-term
(d) Non-current and current

17 A car which cost £14,000 is part-exchanged for a new car exactly three years after its purchase. Cars are depreciated on the straight line basis over five years, assuming a residual value of 10% of the purchase price. If the part-exchange value of the car was £4,000, what profit or loss would be recorded in the income statement in the year of disposal?

(a) £2,440 loss
(b) £1,600 loss
(c) £440 profit
(d) £2,600 profit

18 Theoretical inventory valuation methods such as FIFO would be used where:

(a) Inventory can be priced by looking at invoices
(b) Inventory is always sold in a set order, for example oldest inventory is sold first
(c) It is difficult or impossible to match inventory with an invoiced price
(d) Inventory has not been counted at the end of the financial period

19 The trade receivables balances included within the total of current assets on a statement of financial position should be:

(a) All the balances in the Receivables Ledger
(b) Only the good debts of the business
(c) The Receivables Ledger balances, less any increase in a provision for doubtful debts
(d) All the Receivables Ledger balances except the bad debts

20 Which one of the following is a *disadvantage* of a limited liability partnership (LLP)?

(a) The LLP's members have limited liability for the debts of the partnership
(b) The LLP has to publish information about its finances
(c) An LLP does not have to pay dividends to shareholders
(d) An LLP does not have to follow Stock Exchange regulations

21 Why might a partnership charge interest on partners' drawings?

(a) Because they want to increase the money taken out by partners
(b) To deter partners from taking excessive amounts from the business
(c) To ensure that all partners take an equal amount from the business
(d) The Partnership Act 1890 states that they have to charge interest

22 A convertible loan is:

(a) A loan issued by a company which can be converted into shares at a later date
(b) Money borrowed to buy the managing director a convertible car
(c) Raw materials lent to the business which are to be converted into a finished product
(d) A loan issued by a company which can be converted into a different currency at a later date

23 A liability found in a limited company's statement of financial position but not a sole proprietorship's statement of financial position is:

(a) Corporation tax
(b) Payables
(c) Accruals
(d) Overdraft

24 A holder of a preference share has the following advantages over an ordinary shareholder:

(a) A dividend which will increase if profits increase
(b) A greater number of votes for each share held
(c) Preferential prices if buying the company's products
(d) Priority over ordinary shareholders for payment of dividends and also capital repayment if the company fails

25 A bonus issue by a company has the following effect:

(a) Existing shareholders are given more shares
(b) Existing shareholders are given the right to buy more shares
(c) Non-shareholders are invited to buy shares in the company
(d) Directors receive a salary bonus

26 A share premium is:

(a) The amount shareholders pay for a share
(b) The increase in value in a share after it is sold
(c) The difference between the stock market price of a share and the nominal value of that share
(d) The difference between the price at which a company sells a share and the nominal value of that share

27 Complete the saying 'Turnover is vanity, profit is sanity, but cash is …'

(a) Calamity
(b) Banality
(c) Reality
(d) Quality

28 Which one of the following is not a component of the working capital cycle?

(a) Share capital
(b) Trade receivables
(c) Inventory
(d) Trade payables

29 Which of the following pairs *both* result in a positive cash flow?

(a) Decrease in inventory and decrease in trade payables
(b) Increase in inventory and increase in trade payables
(c) Increase in trade payables and increase in trade receivables
(d) Decrease in inventory and decrease in trade receivables

30 If a company shows revenue £60,000 and gross profit £12,000, which of the following calculations are correct?

(a) Mark-up 20%, gross margin 25%
(b) Mark-up 400%, gross margin 5%
(c) Mark-up 33%, gross margin 50%
(d) Mark-up 25%, gross margin 20%

31 Which one of the following statements is *always* true?

(a) The directors of a company own the company
(b) The auditors of a company produce the financial statements
(c) The company's reserves are represented by bank balances
(d) The shareholders of a company own the company

32 If a company has much more borrowed capital than equity capital, which of the following statements is always true?

(a) If interest rates rise, the company will have to close
(b) The company will expand faster than a company with no borrowings
(c) The company is said to be highly geared
(d) The company is said to be low geared

33 If the directors of a plc need to raise money for the company, which of the following would *not* achieve that effect?

(a) A bonus issue of shares
(b) A rights issue of shares
(c) A new issue of shares to the general public
(d) Selling a bond

34 A company has net current assets of £20,000, including inventory valued at £22,000. The total of current assets is £60,000 and the current ratio is 1.5:1. What is the acid test ratio?

(a) 2:1
(b) 0.95:1
(c) 0.5:1
(d) 2.7:1

35 A limited company with a share capital of 500,000 ordinary shares of £1 each makes a rights issue on a '3 for 2' basis at £3 each. What effect will this have on the total equity after all the rights have been paid for by shareholders?

(a) Share capital + £1,750,000, share premium + £1,750,000
(b) Share capital + £1,000,000, share premium + £750,000

(c) Share capital + £750,000, share premium + £1,500,000
(d) Share capital + £1,500,000, share premium no change

36 What does a sole proprietor's 'unlimited liability' mean?

(a) The owner may lose his or her personal assets if the business fails
(b) The owner is not insured against the risks of running the business
(c) There is no limit to how much creditors can demand to be paid
(d) The sole proprietor is operating as a limited company

37 A limited company has a very high gearing level. If interest rates increase, but no other changes take place, which one of the following statements is certain?

(a) The company will cease trading
(b) The company's borrowings will increase
(c) The company's gross profit will decrease
(d) The company's profit for the year will decrease

38 If a company has a net margin of 20%, which of the following statements is certain about that company?

(a) The company's non-current assets exceed its current assets
(b) The company can pay all its bills
(c) The company is making a profit
(d) The company's current assets exceed its current liabilities

39 If a company's p/e ratio this year is 17, whereas last year it was 11, which of the following statements is certain?

(a) The company has made more profit this year
(b) The company's share price is higher this year than last year
(c) The stock market regards the company as a greater risk this year than last year
(d) The share price this year is a greater multiple of the reported earnings per share than it was last year

40 If a company's shares are stated to have a dividend cover of five times, which of the following statements is certain about that company?

(a) The share price is five times its dividend
(b) The dividend is five times the profits per share after tax
(c) The dividend is five times the profits per share before tax
(d) The share price is five times the dividend per share

Practice exam paper 2

Time allowed TWO hours. Answer any three out of the four questions. All questions carry equal marks.

Question 1

The trial balance of Aubrey Locke, a sole proprietor, at 31 May 2014 is as follows:

	Dr £	*Cr* £
Bank	3,840	
Cash	120	
Forklift truck: cost	20,000	
Forklift truck: depreciation to 31 May 2013		4,500
Motor cars: cost	18,000	
Motor cars: depreciation to 31 May 2013		6,000
Revenue		375,000
Purchases	195,000	
Opening inventory at 1 June 2013	62,000	
Rent	20,000	
Sales returned by customer	420	
Electricity	8,000	
Trade receivables	16,200	
Trade payables		14,600
Wages and salaries	36,820	
Provision for doubtful debts at 1 June 2013		2,640
Bad debts written off	520	
General office expenses	18,000	
Owner's drawings	18,500	
Capital at 1 June 2013		14,680
	417,420	417,420

Notes:

1. Closing stock is £50,000.
2. Electricity of £2,000 is to be accrued at the year-end.
3. Rent of £4,000 has been prepaid at the year-end.
4. Depreciation on the forklift is calculated over 4 years on the straight line method, assuming a residual value of £2,000.
5. Depreciation on the cars is calculated at 40% on the diminishing balance method.
6. The provision for doubtful debts is to be decreased by £400.

Required:

(a) Prepare an income statement for the year ended 31 May 2014 and a statement of financial position as at that date.

(b) If Aubrey Locke had been operating his business as a limited company, there are likely to be additional items of information you would expect to see when compared with the financial statement of a sole proprietor. List three additional items you would expect to include when preparing a *limited company's* statement of financial position.

Question 2

Wilma Tonbridge started a business on 1 January 2013, with her own capital of £10,000 and an interest-free long-term loan of £20,000 from a friend. Her business retails Tonies, which are luxury fluffy toys sold at £80 each. Wilma, who has little knowledge of accounting, produced the following statement of her business's financial situation at the end of her first year's trading:

Statement of Finances

	£	£
Cash received from selling 2,000 Tonies		160,000
Less Cash paid:		
Wages	56,000	
Purchases	127,200	
Rent and rates	16,000	
Office expenses	9,600	
Loan repayment	4,000	
		(212,800)
Loss		(52,800)

Wilma sent the statement to her bank manager, who immediately told Wilma to find an accountant to produce a set of financial statements drawn up according to Generally Accepted Accounting Principles. Wilma instructs you to prepare these statements.

You confirm that the amounts shown in Wilma's statements agree with details shown in the business's bank statements, but you find the following additional information:

1 A further 600 Tonies were sold in 2013, but not paid for during the year.
2 Wilma estimates that 5% of debtors are doubtful.
3 £7,000 is owed for purchases received in the year.
4 Wilma's starting capital and the loan were used to buy computers and office furniture and fittings with an estimated life of 5 years and an anticipated residual value of £5,000.
5 Wages of £1,600 and office expenses of £800 were accrued at the end of the year.
6 Inventory at the end of the year was valued at £9,200.
7 The rent and rates covered the period from 1 January 2013 to 31 March 2014.
8 The wages figure included £32,000 taken by Wilma for her own personal use.

Required:

Prepare an income statement for the year ended 31 December 2013 and a statement of financial position as at that date.

Question 3

The management of Hove Ltd has calculated the following statistics from its results for the year ended 31 December 2014. Equivalent average figures from a relevant trade association are also given.

	Hove Ltd	Trade average
Gross margin	50%	40%
Net margin	10%	8%
Return on capital employed	16%	12%
Acid test	1:1	1.5:1
Gearing	80%	30%

(a) Explain the significance of, and the basis of calculation for, each of the five statistics listed above.

(b) Explain why, if you were informed that Hove Ltd's current ratio was 6:1, compared with a trade average of 2:1, this might not indicate a satisfactory situation.

Question 4

The owner or owners of a small enterprise can choose between various forms of business organisation, including sole proprietorship and limited company status.

(a) Explain the advantages and disadvantages of sole proprietorship and limited company status in connection with the following areas:
   (i) Liability for debts
   (ii) Ability to raise capital
   (iii) Legal formality.

(b) A business is having a number of problems with customers who either cannot or will not pay their debts. For the year ended 31 December 2014, these include:
   (i) Customer A, who has died penniless, owing £800.
   (ii) Customer B, who refuses to pay a debt of £600, despite many reminders. It is believed that B has the means to pay.
   (iii) Customer C, who in July and August 2014 had paid eight amounts of £10 per week towards a total debt of £300.
   (iv) Customer D, who was a bad debtor three years ago for £500, but has come into money and has paid off his debt.

The business had total trade receivables, before any adjustments for the above, totalling £45,000. It had a provision for doubtful debts of £1,400 on 1 January 2014.

Required:

Show relevant extracts from the business's income statement for the year ended 31 December 2014 and statement of financial position as at that date relating to trade receivables after making all adjustments required by the above information.

Chapter 9

Management accounting

Objectives

When you have read this chapter you will be able to:

- Define management accounting and appreciate its scope
- Understand the classification of costs
- Analyse costs by function, type, behaviour and time

9.1 Introduction

Scan the following QR code with your QR reader to take you to the website of the Chartered Institute of Management Accountants.

The majority of the information contained in the preceding chapters of this book has been concerned with *financial accounting*, which is the branch of accounting which records, summarises and interprets financial transactions to satisfy the information requirements of the various user groups such as investors, lenders, creditors and employees. It is sometimes referred to as meeting the 'external' financial information needs of the organisation. Another major branch is *management accounting*, which concentrates on meeting the 'internal' financial information needs of the organisation, as it is designed to help managers with decision making and planning. As such, it often involves estimates and forecasts, and is not subject to the same regulatory framework (e.g. International Accounting Standards) as financial accounting. The distinction is not always clear-cut (for example, is ratio analysis the province of a management accountant or a financial accountant?). A professional organisation (CIMA) exists which promotes the interests of management accountants. Scan the QR code to take you to CIMA's website for further information.

Did you know?

One clear distinction between financial accounting and management accounting is in the field of *auditing*, where CIMA members are not permitted to act as a statutory 'external' auditor of a limited company.

9.2 Defining management accounting

According to CIMA[1], management accountants have expertise in the following areas (and see Figure 9.1):

- Designing, implementing and managing (automated) integrated information systems that combine financial and non-financial data to provide insightful (electronic) reports to assist in managing performance and inform decision making
- Designing, implementing and managing (automated) transaction processing activities, including financial accounting, payroll, purchasing and payments, often carried out in a shared service centre
- Designing, improving, measuring and managing end-to-end business processes and activities, often extending beyond the organisational boundaries, ensuring delivery of optimum efficiency and effectiveness in the use of resources
- Working as an analyst; consultant; relationship, project and change manager in support of the business; and as a business partner integrated into divisional and operational units and processes throughout the organisation, bringing commercial and strategic insight, innovative thinking and a collaborative approach
- Taking responsibility for formulating and managing organisational policy, strategy and objectives, producing business plans, forecasts, scorecards, cost/benefit analysis and budgeting information as appropriate

[1] www.cimaglobal.com/Thought-leadership/Newsletters/Insight-e-magazine/Insight-2009/Insight-June-2009/What-is-CIMAs-definition-of-management-accounting/

Figure 9.1 **Key areas of management accounting**

Source: wordle.net

- Designing and implementing excellence in corporate governance, including risk management, internal audit and controls, company secretarial, corporate social responsibility and board and stakeholder reporting
- Determining capital structure and acquiring and managing funds. Carrying out due diligence in mergers, acquisitions, business partnerships and joint ventures.

The list is deliberately all-embracing, and there are some obvious 'infringements' on what financial accountants might see as their territory. It reinforces the notion that there are overlaps between financial and management accounting, particularly in the recording, interpreting and communicating aspects.

As management accounting is not subject to a regulatory framework, the way in which information is prepared is entirely at the discretion of the users of the information. A fundamental area to explore is the level and nature of costs such as raw materials, overheads and labour. Although these are summarised by financial accountants when preparing income statements, a more detailed analysis can be of great benefit to managers.

9.3 The classification of costs

One of the key aspects of management accounting is the analysis of the organisation's costs as part of the process of identifying, presenting and interpreting information referred to earlier. When we looked at summaries produced by the financial accountant (particularly the income statement), the main criterion for cost analysis was whether a specific expense related to the *cost of sales* (in which case it was deducted in calculating the gross profit) or to a 'general' overhead expense, in which case it was deducted from the gross profit in arriving at the operating profit. However, for the management accountant, a much more detailed analysis of costs is required. There are several methods of classifying costs, each method looking at costs from a different perspective. For example, costs could be classified by:

- Function
- Type
- Behaviour
- Time.

Each of these needs to be understood before we can proceed to a consideration of the analysis techniques referred to later (in Chapter 10).

Activity 9.1

Which of the following would be considered valid reasons for analysing costs?

1 To keep costs down
2 To plan ahead
3 To establish appropriate selling prices
4 To compare with competitors' costs
5 To maximise profitability.

Answer

All of the above, except that in (4) you can only make a detailed comparison with competitors' costs by having access to that company's financial data, which is unrealistic. However, published financial information in an annual or interim report contains some cost information (see Chapter 6).

9.3.1 Analysis by function

Costs can be grouped according to the functional department which incurs them, such as production, sales, distribution and administration. Each of these would have one or more *cost centres*. Generally, a cost centre is a location, person or item of equipment – or a group of these – in relation to which costs may be ascertained and used for control purposes. Some costs, such as rent and rates, cannot be traced to one cost centre directly. These costs are gathered to an overall cost centre and are then apportioned to the other cost centres. For this reason they are sometimes known as *service centres* (see Figure 9.2).

9.3.2 Analysis by type

We have already briefly looked at direct and indirect costs in Chapter 4, but it is useful to consider their definition:

- *Direct costs* are those costs which can be readily identified with the item or service being produced, such as the raw materials and labour specific to the task. They are

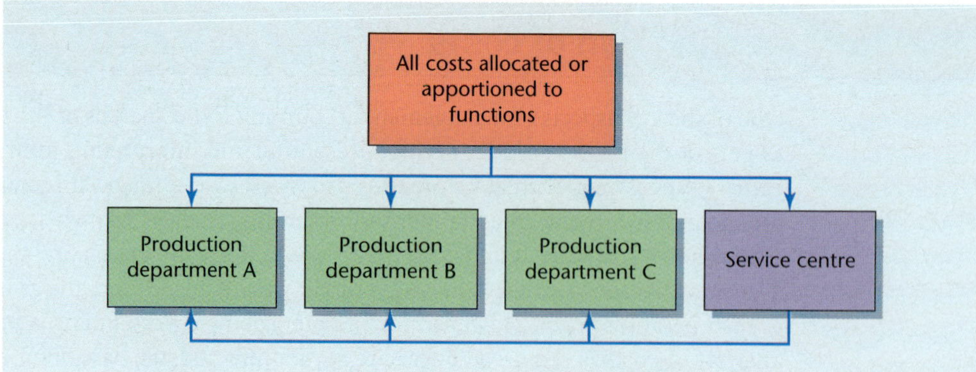

Figure 9.2 Allocation of costs to functional departments

also known as *prime costs*. An example would be the cloth used in making a dress and the machinist's time to cut and sew it.

- *Indirect costs* also known as overhead costs, are all those costs incurred in the organisation which cannot be objectively identified with a specific item or service. An example would be the cost of an advertising campaign to promote a new range of clothing.

The costs which comprise total production cost are related to the number of items which are produced: the greater the volume of production, the greater the total production cost. If a firm trebled its output, it is likely that both direct and indirect costs would be affected. If a firm enjoys economies of scale (eg negotiating discounts for bulk purchases) then costs may increase by less than the percentage change in production. If a firm suffers diseconomies of scale, costs may increase by more than the percentage change in production. Costs which relate to production in this way are sometimes called *product costs*.

Activity 9.2

Which of the formulae (a)–(d) below relate to the following?

- Total production cost
- Prime cost
- Total cost
- Total overhead cost

(a) Direct materials + Direct labour + Direct expenses
(b) Indirect material + Indirect labour + Indirect expenses
(c) Total production cost + Selling and administration overhead
(d) Prime cost + Production overhead

Answer

(a) Prime cost
(b) Total overhead cost
(c) Total cost
(d) Total production cost

9.3.3 Analysis by behaviour

Over time or over a specific range of production, some costs tend to be unaffected by the level of output, whereas others will change as output changes. In fact, overheads can be divided into three classifications, as follows:

1 *Fixed overheads,* which accrue with the passage of time, and which, within certain limits of output and turnover, tend to be unaffected by fluctuations in the level of activity. Examples are rent, rates, insurance and management salaries. Figure 9.3 shows the behaviour of fixed costs over a period.
2 *Variable overheads,* such as raw materials and packaging, which do fluctuate with the level of activity. Figure 9.4 shows the behaviour of variable costs over a period.
3 *Semi-fixed* (also known as semi-variable or 'mixed') *overheads,* which contain both fixed and variable elements and which in consequence are only partly affected by changes in the levels of activity. For example, phone charges would be part fixed rental and part based on usage. In cost analysis, such costs must be divided (however approximately) between their fixed and variable elements. Figure 9.5 shows the behaviour of semi-fixed costs over a period.

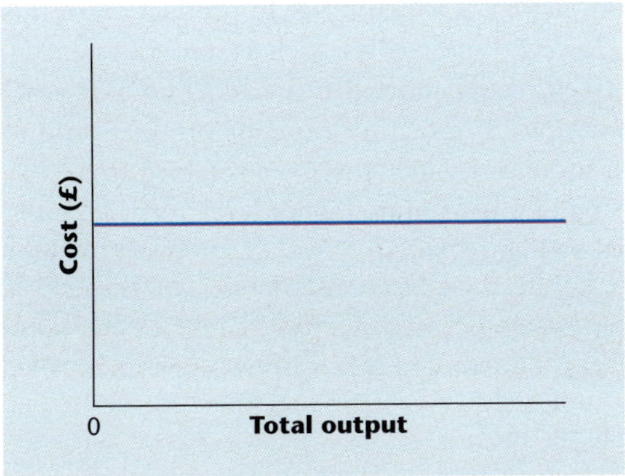

Figure 9.3 The behaviour of fixed costs over a period

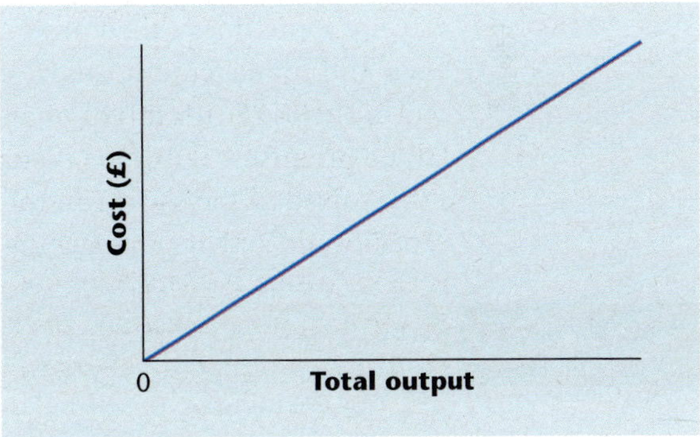

Figure 9.4 The behaviour of variable costs over a period

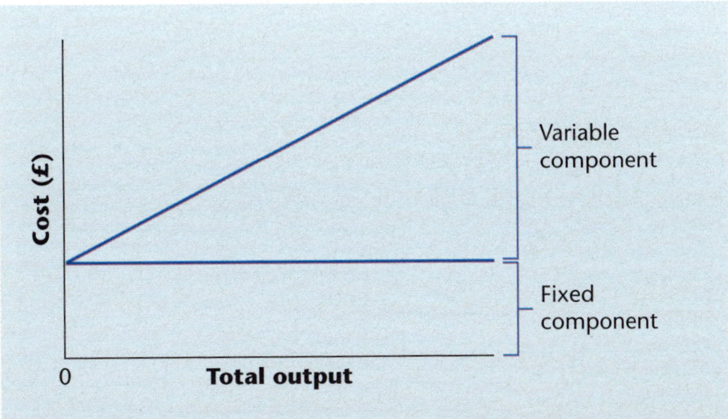

Figure 9.5 The behaviour of semi-fixed costs over a period

Activity 9.3

Are the following costs fixed, variable or semi-fixed?

(a) Metered water supply, part paid by a fixed rental, part by usage
(b) Royalties paid to an author, as a percentage of the sale price of books
(c) A flat fee paid to an author to write an article
(d) Sales commission as a percentage of sales revenue
(e) Office rent
(f) Car hire charges, part fixed rental, part based on mileage

Answer

(a) Semi-fixed cost
(b) Variable cost
(c) Fixed cost
(d) Variable cost
(e) Fixed cost
(f) Semi-fixed cost

9.3.4 Analysis by time

We have seen that the costs which comprise total production cost are related to the number of items which are produced, and that costs which relate to production in this way are sometimes called product costs. However, some costs, such as rent, rates, insurance and management salaries, will be fixed in the short run (perhaps up to a year) but in the long run might change (for example, as a factory expands production into larger premises, rent and insurance will increase). Such costs are referred to as *step costs* – fixed in the short run then increasing to one or more higher levels as production capacity and activity changes, as illustrated by Figure 9.6.

Activity 9.4

Which of the following costs would be likely to 'step up' over time?

(a) An increase in selling and distribution costs if a new product line is introduced
(b) The salary of the company's managing director
(c) Following the opening of a second factory, more supervisors are employed

Answer

(a) and (c) would step up at intervals but (b) would remain fixed.

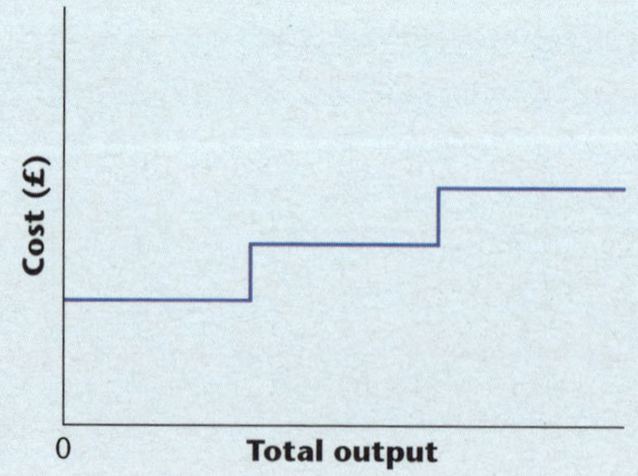

Figure 9.6 Step costs

9.4 Summary

The classification of costs can be summarised by the following table:

	Type of cost	
Cost classified by:	**Direct**	**Indirect**
Function	Allocated to production departments	Allocated or apportioned to production departments and service centre, then service centre reapportioned to production departments
Type	Direct costs, readily identified with item being produced	Indirect costs (overheads) not readily identified with item being produced
Behaviour	Variable – they fluctuate with the level of activity	Most indirect cost is fixed, but some (e.g. sales commission, power for machinery) will be variable
Time	Change in the short run	Tend to be fixed in the short run but may change in the long run (step costs)

9.5 Chapter glossary

Cost centre A location, person or item of equipment – or a group of these – in relation to which costs may be ascertained and used for control purposes.

Direct costs Costs which can be readily identified with the particular units or type of product, such as raw materials and manufacturing wages.

Fixed overheads Costs which tend to remain constant, regardless of the level of production. For example, factory insurance might remain the same whether production is high or low.

Indirect costs Expenses which cannot be directly associated with the items being produced, such as supervisors' wages, the factory canteen, and rent and rates.

Management accounting The internal financial information needs of an organisation, including planning, forecasting and budgeting for decision-making purposes.

Product costs Costs incurred in the manufacturing process.

Semi-fixed overheads Costs where part is variable and part is fixed. For example, a service contract for vans may consist of a fixed annual charge plus a variable charge based on mileage. Also known as semi-variable or mixed overheads.

Service centre Some costs, such as rent and rates, cannot be traced to one cost centre directly. These costs are gathered to a service centre and are then apportioned to the other cost centres.

Step costs Periodic increases in fixed costs caused by one or more expansions in the level of activity over time.

Variable overheads Costs which change with the level of activity. For example, a courier company uses more fuel if more packages are delivered.

Additional resources

Now work through the various exercises and problems that you can find within the My Accounting Lab that are relevant to this chapter. Either use the QR code shown in the margin (if you use an Android-based device), or visit www.myaccountinglab.com for the log-in page.

Only accessible on Android-based devices

Self-check questions

The answers to these questions are in Appendix 1.

1 Which of the following is *not* considered to be part of the role of the management accountant?

(a) Formulating strategy for management
(b) Optimising a firm's resources
(c) Acting as an auditor on behalf of shareholders in a limited company
(d) Reviewing a firm's financial systems for management

2 Which one of the following would be considered a *direct cost* of a car factory?

(a) The cost of a marketing campaign
(b) Power used to light the offices
(c) Wages paid to production line workers
(d) The salary paid to the managing director

3 Which of the following would not be considered a valid reason for analysing cost data?

(a) To help evade taxation
(b) To maximise profitability
(c) To set selling prices
(d) To help efficiency

4 Direct costs are also referred to as:

(a) Prime costs
(b) Variable costs
(c) Fixed costs
(d) Semi-fixed costs

5 Indirect costs are also referred to as:

(a) Semi-fixed costs
(b) Prime costs
(c) Overhead costs
(d) Fixed costs

6 The classification of costs according to whether they are direct or indirect is referred to as analysis by:

(a) Function
(b) Behaviour
(c) Time
(d) Type

7 The formula 'total production cost + selling and administration overhead' refers to:

(a) Total manufacturing cost
(b) Total cost
(c) Prime cost
(d) Factory indirect cost

8 Which of the following is another term for 'semi-fixed cost'?

(a) Semi-direct cost
(b) Semi-variable cost
(c) Semi-indirect cost
(d) Semi-prime cost

9 A fashion company pays a designer a royalty of 5% on the selling price of every dress based on her design. Such a cost would be classified as a:

(a) Semi-variable cost
(b) Fixed cost
(c) Semi-fixed cost
(d) Variable cost

10 Which one of the following would be considered a *step cost*?

(a) A cost which is fixed in the short term but in the long run may change
(b) A cost which does not tend to change over time
(c) A cost which changes with the level of production
(d) A cost which is incurred for one period only

Self-study questions

Questions marked with this symbol (#) indicate that the suggested answers are available to lecturers only – other answers are given in Appendix 2.

9.1 From the following forecast data for Cosysnooze, a company that makes duvets, calculate the following:

(a) Total fixed costs
(b) Total variable costs
(c) Fixed cost per duvet
(d) Variable cost per duvet
(e) Total cost per duvet.

(Forecast production: 3,481 units)

	£	% variable
Raw materials	1,505	100
Direct labour	1,161	100
Direct expenses	2,838	100
Indirect material	3,560	5
Indirect labour	3,378	7
Indirect expenses	1,544	6
Selling overhead	2,481	20
Administration overhead	2,745	5

9.2 Referring to the information in question 9.1, what do you think would be a reasonable selling price for one duvet? If Cosysnooze aims to achieve a net profit margin of 10%, what price would it charge for each duvet?

9.3# The X-Audio company manufactures digital radios. The management accountant has produced the following forecast information for the next year:

	£	% variable
Raw materials	283,420	100
Direct labour	302,100	100
Direct expenses	25,800	100
Indirect material	43,600	10
Indirect labour	84,200	15
Indirect expenses	195,600	20
Selling overhead	124,710	15
Administration overhead	95,800	5

(Forecast production: 36,800 radios)

Calculate the following:

(a) Total fixed costs
(b) Total variable costs
(c) Fixed cost per radio
(d) Variable cost per radio
(e) Total cost per radio.

9.4# Referring to the information in question 9.3, what do you think would be a reasonable selling price for one radio? If X-Audio aims to achieve a net profit margin of 40%, what price would it charge for each radio?

Case study: The great disappearing profits trick

When Trixie started to analyse the financial information of Machiq Limited (see previous case studies) following Esmeralda's takeover bid, she realised that although the company as a whole appeared profitable, no one had looked at the financial information from a management accountant's viewpoint. In particular, there had been no attempt to consider the nature of the costs incurred and how they may have affected the relative profitability of the two main divisions of the business: Performing and Retailing. After some research, Trixie produced the following analysis:

Machiq Limited: year ended 30 June 2016

	£	Notes
Revenue	705,600	30% Performing, 70% Retailing
Cost of sales	(529,200)	80% of costs are variable, divided 10% Performing, 90% Retailing
Gross profit	176,400	
Expenses	(58,600)	Overall 60% fixed, 40% variable, with 35% of the total relating to Performing, the rest to Retailing
Operating profit for the year, before taxation	117,800	

Required

Redraw the analysis to show the relevant operating profit or loss for each division.

Answers are in Appendix 3

Further research

Chartered Institute of Management Accountants: **www.cimaglobal.com** or use QR code on page 245

For more cartoons from Alex: **www.alexcartoon.com**

Chapter 10 Absorption costing and marginal costing

Objectives

When you have read this chapter you will be able to:

- Understand the principles of absorption (total) costing
- Understand what is meant by the absorption of costs and explain the difference between the allocation and the apportionment of costs
- Understand the costing method known as activity-based costing (ABC)
- Understand the principles of marginal costing and the role of the 'contribution'
- Contrast absorption and marginal costing
- Distinguish between specific order costing and operation costing
- Apply specific costing techniques to job, batch, contract, process and service costing

10.1 Introduction

In the previous chapter we saw how costs could be analysed in various ways, such as by function, type, behaviour and time. For a business to operate efficiently there must be one or more systematic methods in place to show the impact of costs on profits and to ensure that costs are reflected in an appropriate manner when evaluating the firm's output. This chapter looks at the two key methods: absorption costing and marginal costing. Absorption costing charges a share of *all* overheads to products, whereas marginal costing splits costs between variable and fixed and analyses the *contribution* which is made by products towards meeting the fixed costs of the organisation.

10.2 Absorption costing

Did you know?

The technique is also known as 'Total Absorption Costing' or 'TAC'.

Absorption costing is also called 'total costing', as it requires all costs to be 'absorbed' by the firm's output in order to establish a 'full cost' per item. This enables a selling price to be set which not only covers cost but also ensures an acceptable profit. The allocation of costs must be as fair and reasonable as possible, and this is achieved by the four-stage process described below.

10.2.1 Stage 1: Allocation of costs to cost centres

Businesses are usually divided into various functions, including production, sales, distribution and administration. Each of these would have one or more *cost centres*. Overheads which relate to specific cost centres will be allocated just to those centres. Figure 10.1 illustrates this process for a manufacturing business with three distinct production cost centres (Fabrication, Assembly and Spraying) and a service centre. It assumes that these 'specific' overheads (for example, raw materials and components used in each process) totalled £250,000, of which £100,000 related to Fabrication, £80,000 to Assembly and £70,000 to Spraying.

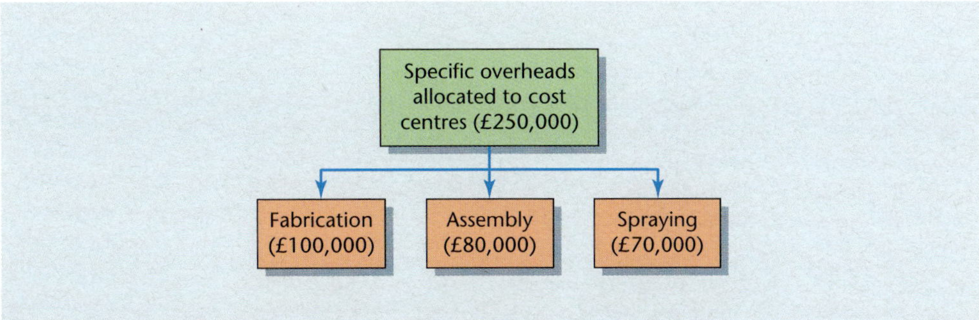

Figure 10.1 Initial overhead allocation to cost centres

Activity 10.1

Which two of the following would be reasons for allocating overheads to cost centres?

(a) To analyse the efficiency of each key section of the firm
(b) To distinguish between direct and indirect costs
(c) To establish the profitability of each key section of the firm
(d) To publish the information to shareholders

Answer

(a) and (c) are correct, as cost data is vital when assessing the profitability and efficiency of the firm; (b) is not a *reason* for allocating costs, although it is relevant when making the allocation; (d) is incorrect, as detailed cost data is not prepared for shareholders.

10.2.2 Stage 2: Apportionment of overheads

After allocating those costs that can be identified with specific cost centres, there are likely to be 'general' overhead costs that need to be apportioned on a reasonable basis between the cost centres. For example, the company in Figure 10.1 might have paid £200,000 for general overheads including insurance and security for its factory buildings and administration offices. The basis of allocation could be the value of assets used within each location. Assume that 50% of the value is within Fabrication, 25% within Assembly, 15% within Spraying and the remaining 10% is within the administration offices. Figure 10.2 shows how the overhead is apportioned, not only between the three 'productive' cost centres but also to the service centre (the administration offices).

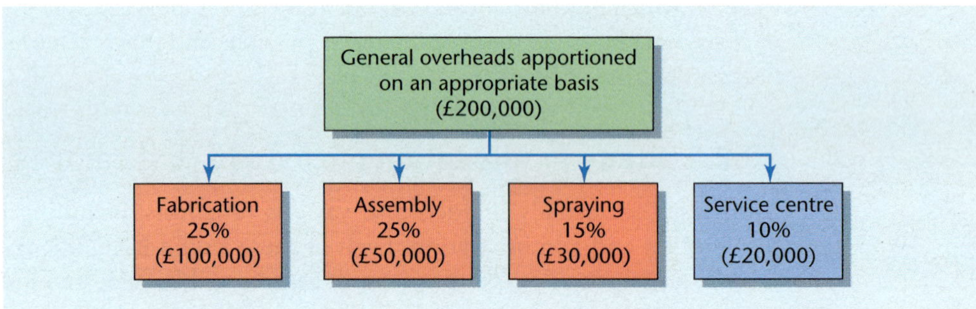

Figure 10.2 Apportionment of general overheads to all cost centres

Activity 10.2

Look at the following costs and then choose what you think would be the most suitable basis of apportionment.

Costs

(a) Rent
(b) Depreciation of computers
(c) Insurance
(d) Heating
(e) Personnel
(f) Power

Bases of apportionment

1 Machine-hours used
2 Number of employees within each cost centre

3 Floor area of each cost centre
4 Volume of buildings occupied by cost centre
5 Value of assets within each cost centre
6 Value of computers within each cost centre

Answers

(a) 3, (b) 6, (c) 5, (d) 4, (e) 2, (f) 1

10.2.3 Stage 3: Reapportionment of overheads

As all overheads must eventually be absorbed into the production output, the service centre overheads must be reapportioned to the production cost centres, again using a reasonable basis: for example, warehousing overheads could be apportioned to products depending on the volume of each product stored, or maintenance overheads according to time spent in attending breakdowns in each production area. At the end of this process, *all* overheads will have been allocated to production. For example, the company used in Figures 10.1 and 10.2 might decide to reapportion service centre overheads on the basis Fabrication 40%, Assembly 50% and Spraying 10%. Figures 10.3a and 10.3b illustrate this process.

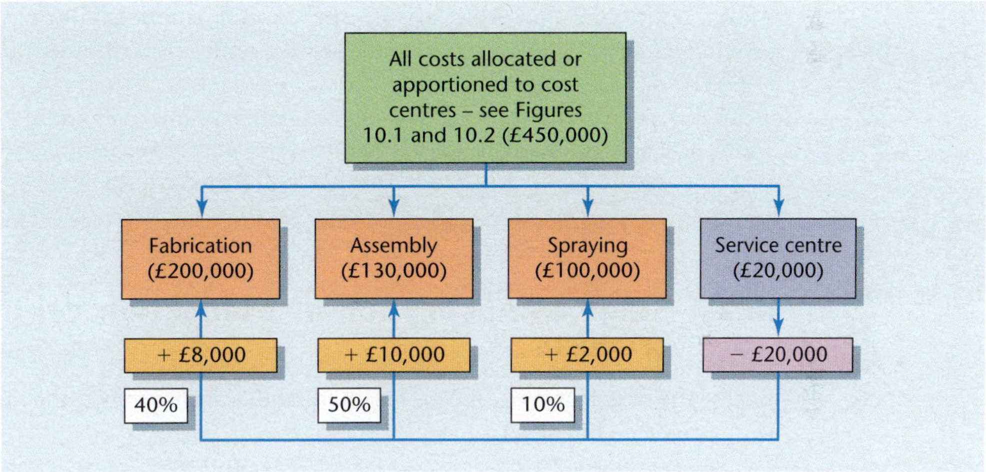

Figure 10.3a Service centre overheads reapportioned to production departments

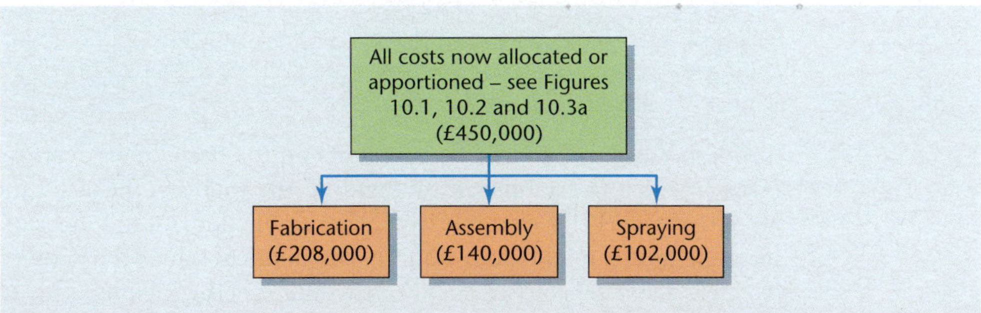

Figure 10.3b All costs allocated to the three production departments

Activity 10.3

A company with three different product lines, X, Y and Z, selling for £6, £5 and £4 each respectively, incurs a £9,000 advertising cost to get the company's name publicised. Unit sales of the products are in the proportions X 25%, Y 35% and Z 40%, and annual turnover is £242,500, split X £75,000, Y £87,500 and Z £80,000. Which of the following ratios would be a reasonable basis for reapportionment of the advertising cost?

(a) 6:5:4
(b) 25:35:40
(c) 75:87.5:80

Answer

The correct answer is (c), as this recognises both the unit costs and the number of units sold. The sales price, (a), is not relevant to the overall advertising cost, and the percentages of units sold, (b), do not take into account the relevant sales revenue per item.

10.2.4 Stage 4: Absorption of production centre costs into products

Finally, the cost centre overheads are charged to ('absorbed by') the individual cost units being produced by the cost centre.

Stop and think

A cost unit could be a tub of ice cream, an hour of an architect's time, a barrel of beer. In fact there are as many different cost units as there are types of business. You need to ask yourself 'what is being sold?' to determine the appropriate cost unit.

Overheads are absorbed by cost units on the basis of an overhead absorption rate (OAR), which is established by dividing the total overhead by the most appropriate activity level (for example, total chargeable hours, total units of production, total machine hours, total labour hours). The item chosen as the activity level will be that which is most reliable and relevant to the specific business: for example, for a car repairer it might be on the basis of the rate per labour hour charged to the customer, whereas for a pet food manufacturer it might be the rate per tonne of food produced.

The total cost per cost unit can then be found by adding together the direct materials cost, the direct labour cost and the overheads absorbed according to the OAR.

For example, if the OAR is £5 per machine-hour (that is, one machine working for one hour), a cost unit which takes 6 machine hours will absorb £5 × 6 = £30 overheads. If selling prices are determined at 80% above total cost, and assuming that direct costs are £10 per cost unit, the selling price would be 180% × (£10 + £30) = £72.

Figure 10.4 illustrates this process by again using the company shown in Figures 10.1–10.3. Assume that the most appropriate activity level here is *total machine hours*, and these are as follows: Fabrication 2,000 machine hours, Assembly 1,400 machine-hours and Spraying 1,000 machine hours. Figure 10.4 shows how the respective OAR per machine hour will be £104, £100 and £102.

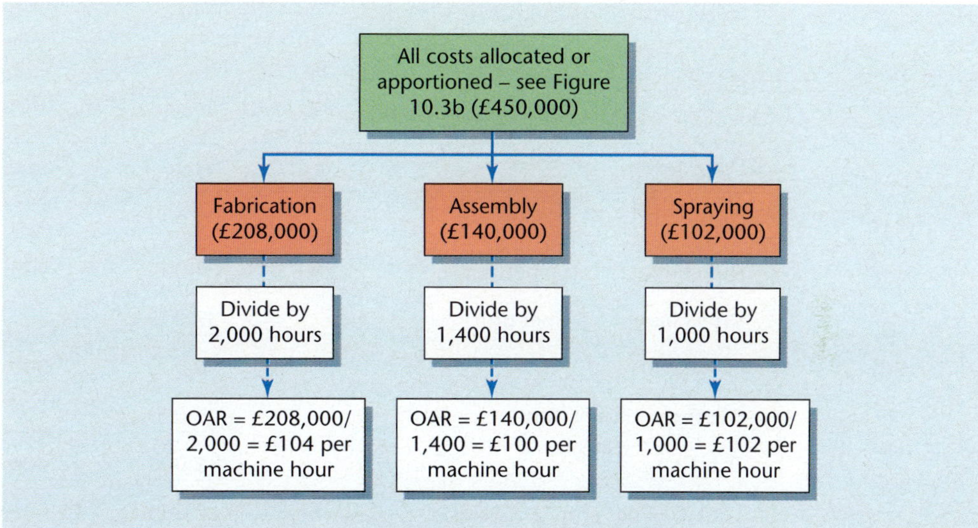

Figure 10.4 Overhead absorption rates (OARs) calculated

When a specific contract is undertaken, we can use the OAR to set a price. For illustration, assume our example company undertakes a contract which requires specific prime costs (direct materials and direct labour) of £4,000 and 17 machine hours in Fabrication, 8 machine hours in Assembly and three machine hours in Spraying. The overall contract price, assuming a mark-up of 60% will be:

Prime costs			£4,000
Overheads:			
Fabrication	17 × £104	=	£1,768
Assembly	8 × £100	=	£800
Spraying	3 × £102	=	£306
Total cost			£6,874
Mark-up (60%)			£4,124
Contract price charged to customer			£10,998*

* Probably rounded up to £11,000.

Activity 10.4

A company produces 2,000 units of Yogies and 800 units of Zeldas each month. Direct materials cost £2 per unit for Yogies and £4 per unit for Zeldas. One hour of direct labour charged at £16 per hour is needed to produce one unit of each product. The total overheads for the company are £8,400 per month.

If a mark-up of 40% on costs is required, what selling prices should be charged per unit for Yogies and Zeldas, assuming that the overhead absorption rate is based on the rate per unit? Show a cost statement explaining how you arrive at your figures.

Answer

The selling prices are: Yogies £29.40 per unit, Zeldas £32.20 per unit.

Workings

$$\text{Overhead absorption rate (OAR)} = \frac{\text{Total overheads}}{\text{Total units}}$$

$$= \frac{£8,400}{2,800} = £3 \text{ per unit}$$

Cost statement:	Yogies	Zeldas	Total
Units	2,000	800	2,800
Direct materials (£2 per Yogie, £4 per Zelda)	4,000	3,200	7,200
Direct labour (£16 per unit)	32,000	12,800	44,800
Prime costs	36,000	16,000	52,000
Overheads (£3 per unit – see above)	6,000	2,400	8,400
Total cost	**42,000**	**18,400**	**60,400**
Total cost per unit	£21.00	£23.00	
Mark-up (40%)	£8.40	£9.20	
Selling price	**£29.40**	**£32.20**	

Note: What we have seen here is the benefit of using absorption (total) costing to arrive at a realistic selling price per unit of each product.

10.3 Advantages and disadvantages of absorption costing

Absorption costing has the following advantages:

- It makes managers aware of the total costs incurred within cost centres.
- It provides full costings so that selling prices can be established by mark-up (as seen in Activity 10.4 above).
- When valuing closing inventories for the financial accounts, absorption cost methods must be used to ensure that all related production overheads are included (and therefore comply with the relevant accounting standard, IAS 2).
- The overhead absorption rate can be used when producing budgets of future expenditure: for example, if it is forecast that 10,000 direct labour hours are expected to be

chargeable next year, and the OAR is £20 per direct labour hour, budgeted overheads would be £200,000.

However, absorption costing has the following disadvantages:

- Apportionment of overheads is often made on an arbitrary basis, so total costs may in fact be unrealistic.
- Unrealistic total costs would lead to unrealistic setting of selling prices where 'mark-up on cost' is used.
- The intention is that the OAR will lead to the absorption of *all* costs into cost units. In practice, because it is usually based on *estimates* of costs and activity, there is likely to be either an *underabsorption* (leading to losses, as not all costs will be charged to customers) or *overabsorption* of overheads (leading to inflated prices and reduced sales).
- It ignores the important distinction between variable and fixed costs as discussed in the previous chapter – see 'marginal costing' below.

Activity 10.5

Acme Shirts Limited has produced the following analysis of its product range:

Shirt range				
	Formal	**Sports**	**Casual**	**Total**
	£000	**£000**	**£000**	**£000**
Revenue (A)	340	200	300	840
Direct materials	60	50	70	180
Direct labour	40	50	48	138
Variable overheads	80	60	40	180
Other factory costs (apportioned)	60	70	68	198
Total factory cost (B)	(240)	(230)	(226)	(696)
Gross profit/(loss) (A) – (B)	100	(30)	74	144
Non-production overheads (assume all fixed)				(80)
Operating profit				64

The managing director has reviewed the information and believes that the Sports shirt range should be discontinued since it appears to be making a loss. Do you agree with this course of action, and what would be its effect if implemented?

Answer

The allocation of all costs to products has resulted in a gross loss of £30,000 on the Sports shirt range, so it would appear that, by closing the division, the business's overall operating profit would increase from £64,000 to £94,000. However, this ignores the fact that some of the factory costs apportioned to the Sports division will remain, even if the division is closed. This aspect is explored in Activity 10.8 below, so we will defer a decision until that activity is completed.

10.4 Activity-based costing (ABC)

Many companies have traditionally used direct labour rates (either 'cost' or 'hours') or machine hours as the basis for their overhead absorption rates. However, with the move from labour-intensive methods of production to computer-based and robotic forms of manufacture, more relevant and up-to-date forms of costing techniques have evolved. Activity-based costing (ABC) moves away from using, for example, the number of labour hours involved in making a product as the basis for overhead absorption and instead seeks to relate costs to the *activities* which generate, or drive, the costs. These 'cost drivers' could be the key stages in the manufacturing and distribution process, such as:

- Setting up machines prior to manufacture
- Machine usage during manufacture
- Quality control tests
- Order handling.

Each cost driver would then be used as the basis for overhead absorption.

The next two activities contrast overhead absorption based, firstly, on 'traditional' absorption costing techniques and, secondly, on activity-based costing.

Activity 10.6

Lexicon Ltd manufactures two products, Gribbs and Huttles. Gribbs require 1 direct labour hour and Huttles require 2 direct labour hours in a single production cost centre. Three overhead generating activities have been identified: setting up, quality testing and order handling. The following data is available:

Overhead costs:

Setting-up costs	£60,000
Quality testing costs	£50,000
Order handling	£30,000
	£140,000

	Total	Gribbs	Huttles
Number of units	11,000	4,000	7,000
Number of direct labour hours	18,000	4,000	14,000
Number of set-ups	20	8	12
Number of quality tests	50	20	30
Orders	40	15	25

Calculate the overhead cost of one Gribb and one Huttle, using the direct labour rate as the basis for absorption.

Answer

$$\frac{\text{Overhead cost}}{\text{Direct-labour-hours}} = \frac{£140{,}000}{18{,}000} = £7.78 \text{ per labour-hour}$$

The overhead cost per unit using absorption costing is:

1 Gribb = 1 hour × £7.78 = £7.78

1 Huttle = 2 hours × £7.78 = £15.56

Activity 10.7

Using the same data for Lexicon Ltd (see Activity 10.6), calculate the product cost for Gribbs and Huttles using the activity-based costing (ABC) technique.

Answer

Overhead activity	Cost	Cost driver	Cost per cost driver
Setting up	£60,000	20 set-ups	£3,000 per set-up
Quality testing	£50,000	50 tests	£1,000 per test
Order handling	£30,000	40 orders	£750 per order

Cost absorption by products according to activity:

		Gribbs		Huttles	Total
Setting up	8 × £3,000	= 24,000	12 × £3,000	= 36,000	60,000
Quality testing	20 × £1,000	= 20,000	30 × £1,000	= 30,000	50,000
Order handling	15 × £750	= 11,250	25 × £750	= 18,750	30,000
		55,250		84,750	140,000

Therefore, overhead cost per unit is:

1 Gribb (55,250/4,000 units) = £13.81

1 Huttle (84,750/7,000 units) = £12.11

10.5 Absorption costing and activity-based costing compared

In the two activities involving Gribbs and Huttles, per unit overheads under traditional absorption costing techniques would have been Gribbs £7.78 and Huttles £15.56. Therefore, under this method, total overheads would be absorbed as follows:

Gribbs	4,000 × £7.78 =	£31,120	
Huttles	7,000 × £15.56 =	£108,920	
Total		£140,040	(£140,000 rounded)

Under activity-based costing, however, per unit overheads would have been Gribbs £13.81 and Huttles £12.11. Therefore, under this method, total overheads would be absorbed as follows:

Gribbs	4,000 × £13.81	= £55,240	
Huttles	7,000 × £12.11	= £84,770	
Total		£140,010	(£140,000 rounded)

These are very different *per unit* figures, so which ones are more reliable?

Both methods charge out *all* the overheads to products, it is just the relative proportions between the products which alter. Which looks more reasonable? Although Huttles take 3.5 times as many direct labour hours as Gribbs, they have only 1.5 times the number of set-ups and quality tests and 1.7 times the number of orders. Using the direct labour rate seems to skew the costing unfairly towards Huttles when in terms of cost-driving activities, Huttles are far less demanding. Activity-based costing appears to be the method that is more realistic. However, look at the Further research section at the end of this chapter for a reference to an article which contains a detailed criticism of the ABC approach.

10.6 Marginal costing

Marginal costing is an alternative method of costing to absorption costing and is based on the view that, in the short run, fixed costs do not alter and they have to be borne regardless of the level of production or sales in that period. The variable costs which can be accurately allocated are termed *marginal costs*. Look back at section 9.3.3, for further information on the meaning of variable and fixed costs.

In marginal costing, the calculation of the *contribution* is of vital importance. This is defined as the difference between the selling price and the variable (marginal) cost:

$$S - V = C$$

where S = sales price, V = variable (marginal) cost and C = contribution. In other words, every time a product is sold, a contribution is made towards meeting the fixed costs of the business. Once the fixed costs have been met, each contribution then represents a profit:

When Total C > Total F:

$$\textbf{Total C} - \textbf{Total F} = \textbf{Total P}$$

where C = contribution, F = fixed costs and P = profit.

When Total C < Total F:

$$\textbf{Total C} - \textbf{Total F} = \textbf{Total L}$$

where C = contribution, F = fixed costs and L = loss.

Under this method, fixed costs are not allocated or apportioned to individual cost units. Note that the term 'contribution' only becomes a 'profit' *after* the fixed costs total has been exceeded. Before that happens, the business has not reached its break-even point, and is making a loss. Figure 10.5 explains the inter-relationship between the various terms.

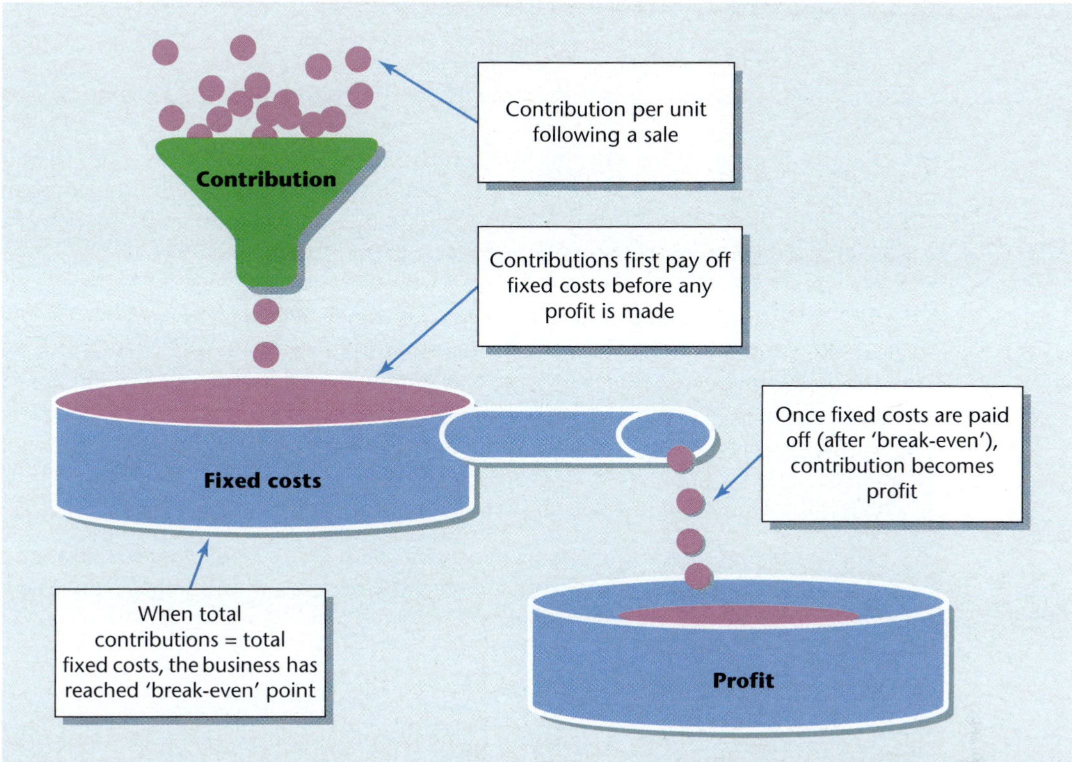

Figure 10.5 The relationship between contribution, fixed costs and profit

The best way to understand marginal costing is to work through an example.

Example 10.1

A ready-mixed concrete company has two divisions, trade (T) and domestic (D). T division delivers to professional builders whereas D division deals with the amateur 'Do It Yourself' market. Total overheads for the company for November are £100,000, which have been divided (on absorption cost principles) between the two divisions in the ratio T 65% and D 35%.

Other relevant information

	T	D
Variable cost per load	£20	£15
Selling price per load	£60	£80
Loads sold in November	2,000	400
Fixed costs (total) £54,000		

Using absorption cost principles, T's profit is £55,000 (sales 2,000 × £60 = £120,000 less £65,000 costs) whereas D makes a loss of £3,000 (sales 400 × £80 = £32,000 less £35,000 costs). The total profit is £52,000 (T's £55,000 profit − D's £3,000 loss).

To apply marginal cost principles, we can calculate the contribution made from each load in each division:

Sales − Variable Costs = Contribution

T division's contribution is therefore £40 (£60 − £20) and D's contribution is £65 (£80 − £15).

Finally, we can calculate the total contribution being made by each division towards meeting the fixed costs, and the total profit being earned by the company. T division's total contribution is £80,000 (2,000 loads × £40) and D division's is £26,000 (400 loads × £65), making a total contribution of £106,000.

Total profit = Total contribution − Fixed costs

so the profit is:

£106,000 − £54,000 = £52,000

which is the same total profit as shown under absorption cost principles.

The managing director of the company has seen D division's loss (£3,000) under absorption cost principles and wants to shut the division down. What would be the effect on total profit if this happened?

Answer

If the division was closed, *D's contribution of £26,000 would disappear*, leaving *all* the fixed costs to be borne by T division. Remember that (where TC > TF) total contribution less total fixed costs = profit, so the revised profit after shutting D division would be T's contribution less the entire fixed costs (£80,000 − £54,000) = £26,000, exactly *half* what it is with D division in operation!

Activity 10.8

Look back at the Acme Shirts Limited problem in Activity 10.5. What conclusion can be drawn regarding the Sports Shirt division if *marginal costing* techniques are used?

Answer

If the results for the period were redrawn using marginal costing techniques, the Sports Shirt division is shown as making a ***positive*** contribution of £40,000 towards meeting the fixed costs of the whole business, as shown below:

	Shirt range			
	Formal	**Sports**	**Casual**	**Total**
	£000	**£000**	**£000**	**£000**
Sales (A)	340	200	300	840
Variable costs:				
Direct materials	60	50	70	180
Direct labour	40	50	48	138
Other variable overheads	80	60	40	180
Total variable costs (B)	(180)	(160)	(158)	(498)
Contribution (C) (= A − B)	160	40	142	342

		Shirt range			
		Formal	Sports	Casual	Total
		£000	£000	£000	£000
Less Fixed costs:					
Other factory costs	(198)				
Non-production overheads	(80)				
Total fixed costs (D)					(278)
Operating profit (C − D)					64

The conclusion must be that the Sports Shirt division should *not be closed*. If it was decided to close that division, the company would be deprived of £40,000 contribution, so operating profit would *reduce* by £40,000 to only £24,000.

10.7 Using the contribution for 'what-if' calculations

Now that we know how to calculate the contribution, it is time to realise what a useful bit of management information it is. For example, what if the concrete company's managing director (see Example 10.1) was looking at December's forecasts? Cost data was unchanged from November, but he wants answers to the following questions:

- How many loads need to be delivered to make a specified profit?
- How many loads need to be delivered to break-even?
- What would be the effect on profits or losses if T division's load delivery increased by a specific percentage, but D division's declined?

All these questions can be answered by using the contribution figure.

Let's see how these calculations work. Remember from Example 10.1 that relevant figures for the two divisions in November were:

	T	D
Loads delivered	2,000	400
Contribution per load (£)	40	65
Total contribution in November (£)	80,000	26,000
Total fixed costs £54,000		
Total profit £52,000		

Specified profit calculations

Assuming demand from D division is static, how many loads have to be delivered from T division to generate an *extra* £10,000 profit?

Each T load gives a contribution of £40, so it would need a further 250 loads (250 × £40 = £10,000) to generate an extra £10,000 profit.

How many to break-even?

If D's loads remain at their November level, how many loads need to be delivered by T division to break even overall?

D's contribution in November was £26,000 towards total fixed costs of £54,000. To break even, T's contribution must exactly equal the remaining £28,000, so 700 (£28,000/£40 contribution per load) loads must be delivered by T division to break-even.

Effect on profits of changing activity levels

What would be the effect on company profits if T's deliveries were 20% higher than in November, but D's deliveries were 40% lower?

November's deliveries were: T 2,000; D 400, so December's would be: T 2,400 and D 240. Contribution would then be: T 2,400 × £40 = £96,000; D 240 × £65 = £15,600.

Total contribution = £111,600 − £54,000 fixed costs = £57,600 profit (£5,600 higher than November).

Look at the following 'Stop and think': if Mrs Brown had used marginal costing to price her products, do you think she would have signed the Groupon contract?

Stop and think

Baker gets fingers burnt as cupcake deal proves too tasty

Website discount was 'worst business decision'

Rachel Brown has been baking cakes to order for 25 years, but she bit off more than she could chew when she signed up for an offer through the discount coupon website Groupon.

Like scores of small businesses, she had hoped to attract new customers through the internet discount scheme. Mrs Brown, 50, thought she might get a few hundred extra orders for her special offer of a dozen cupcakes for £6.50, reduced from the usual price of £26.

In a normal month she bakes 100 cupcakes in addition to birthday, wedding and special occasion cakes. But she found herself with orders for 102,000 cakes when 8,500 Groupon subscribers took her up on the offer. Mrs Brown had to take on 25 agency workers in addition to her eight full-time staff. This cost her about £12,500, and this year's expected profit has been more than wiped out. It also came close to closing her business, Need A Cake, as every cake was sold at a loss. Of the £6.50 paid by customers, Groupon took £4. Mrs Brown, from Woodley, Berkshire, said she had no idea how successful the offer would be and was not prepared when orders poured in, but felt obliged to meet them because customers paid in advance.

"Without doubt it's the worst business decision I have ever made," she said. "It's been an absolute nightmare. We are still working to make up the lost money."

Source: © Simon de Bruxelles, *The Times*, 22 November 2011

10.8 Product costing

Product costing is the technique of establishing the cost of a finished item or items by combining direct costs with relevant allocated and apportioned indirect costs. The methods used will vary depending upon the custom and practice of specific industries and also the methods of production employed. In particular it is usual to classify product costing into two main groups, specific order costing and operation costing:

1 *Specific order costing* is applicable where the work consists of jobs or batches of production, and separate large-scale contracts.
2 *Operation costing* is relevant where a product or service results from a sequence of continuous or repetitive operations or processes.

Whichever approach is adopted to ascertain costs, the basic principles of determining costs (as outlined in Chapter 9) will apply. It is only the *method* of collecting and presenting cost data which differs.

10.9 Specific order costing

10.9.1 Job costing

Job costing is used where work is undertaken to a customer's specific requirements. Often a quote is given before work commences, and this can subsequently be compared with the actual costs to establish whether the work was done too cheaply and to improve future job costing. It is likely that no two jobs will be exactly the same and the job might be completed relatively quickly. Contrast a 'job' with a 'long-term contract', which normally spans at least two financial accounting periods and is of a significantly greater value than a 'job'.

Activity 10.9

Some of the following would be considered 'jobs', whereas others would be considered 'long-term contracts'. Decide which is the most appropriate category for each of the following:

(a) A routine car service at a garage
(b) A builder agreeing to construct 8,000 houses for a property developer
(c) A plumber who installs a water heater
(d) An oil rig being constructed by a shipyard
(e) An illustrator commissioned to provide a drawing for a book cover
(f) A website design company whose 20 employees will be producing a comprehensive website for an online bank over the next two years

Answer

Only (a), (c) and (e) will be regarded as 'jobs' – the rest are substantial long-term contracts.

10.9.2 Quotations and job cost sheets

Each order will be given a unique reference number and all costs relating to that job will be allocated or apportioned to that number. A job cost sheet is prepared which summarises all relevant costs of a specific job. Before a customer places an order, they may ask for a quotation (estimate of cost). Example 10.2 illustrates this process.

Example 10.2

Digitalis Ltd has been asked to quote for the design of a website by e-veg Ltd, an online greengrocer. Digitalis, which gives the reference number EV6325 to the job, estimates that special software costing £1,000 will have to be purchased for this project and that two designers will work on the website at 30 hours per week for three weeks at a rate of £40 per hour. Overheads are recovered by the direct-labour-hour method at £30 per hour. A mark-up of 40% is added to arrive at the fee payable by the customer. This is the quotation for the project:

Job No. EV6325

e-veg Ltd Quotation for website construction

Item	Estimate
Direct materials	1,000
Direct labour: (2 × 30) × 3 × £40 per hour	7,200
Overheads: 180 direct-labour-hours @ £30 per hour	5,400
Total costs	13,600
Add mark-up 40%	5,440
Price chargeable to customer	19,040

After a quotation has been given to the customer, the customer will either accept or reject it or haggle for better terms. Once the job is completed, the 'actual' costs can be compared. Assume that Digitalis Ltd has completed the design of e-veg Ltd's website. The special software cost £1,400 and the two designers worked only 26 hours per week for two weeks, but were paid at a rate of £60 per hour. Other details were as shown in the quotation. Here is the job cost sheet for the project (the 'variance' column is simply the difference between estimated and actual figures):

Job No. EV6325

e-veg Ltd Job cost sheet

Item	Estimate	Actual	Variance
Direct materials	1,000	1,400	+400
Direct labour: (actual 104 × £60)	7,200	6,240	−960
Overheads: (actual 104 × £30)	5,400	3,120	−2,280
Total costs	13,600	10,760	−2,840
Add mark-up	5,440	8,280	+2,840
Price chargeable to customer	19,040	19,040	–

Due (apparently) to efficient working, Digitalis Ltd earned £2,840 more profit than originally estimated.

10.9.3 Batch costing

Where similar or identical items are manufactured in batches, *batch costing* is used. This follows the same procedure as job costing, but the price of one unit is found by dividing the total costs of the batch by the number of units produced.

Activity 10.10

Woofer Ltd manufactures pencils in batches of 50,000. During March, Batch no. 711 was poorly finished, resulting in only 44,000 pencils being completed. The remainder were scrapped. Costs were as follows:

Raw materials	£900
Direct labour	£1,200
Overhead recovery	£660

What was the cost per pencil in Batch no. 711?

Answer

Total costs (900 + 1,200 + 660) = £2,760, divided by 44,000 = 6.3p cost per pencil.

10.9.4 Contract costing

Contracts are distinguished from 'jobs' for costing purposes, as they are of significant value and usually span more than one accounting period. Specifically, an accounting standard (*IAS 11 Construction Contracts*) gives a definition of such contracts and provides rules for determining how to treat them in the financial accounting summaries. For *management accounting* purposes, costs are allocated and apportioned to contracts in much the same way as for jobs. However, the complexity and scale of many contracts will require comprehensive cost recording systems, with 'contract accounts' being maintained to record such aspects as:

- Cost of materials sent to the construction site, less any materials returned from the site
- Labour (direct and indirect relating to the contract)
- Value of plant and machinery used on the site
- On-site costs such as security, lighting, power
- Charges by subcontractors related to the contract
- Head office costs apportioned to the contract.

With many contracts, the customer makes progress payments based on the proportion of the contract completed, as certified by an architect or surveyor. The contract may allow for 'retention money' to be withheld by the customer (for example, 10% of each stage payment) as a guarantee against defects in construction.

Profit or losses on contracts

The accounting standard relating to contracts allows companies to recognise a profit before the contract's completion. Otherwise, companies engaged in very long contracts would show 'nil' profits for several years and then have a 'bonanza' profit in the year of completion. Such a distortion goes against the accruals principle studied in earlier chapters and would result in potential investors being reluctant to invest in companies where dividends might not be paid (due to absence of profits) for many years. The downside, however, is that the standard requires that if a *loss* is forecast on the contract, the *whole* loss (that is, not just the part relating to a specific accounting period) should be recognised as soon as it is foreseen.

10.10 Operation costing

10.10.1 Process costing

In specific order costing, each job, batch or contract is costed separately. Where products are produced in a single process, or where the product of one process becomes the material of a second process, a different costing system is needed since products can no longer be identified individually. Under *process costing*, the firm is divided into departments which tend to be limited to one process or operation. Accounts are kept for each process, with materials, labour, expenses and overheads being debited to the process and scrap (materials with some recovery value) being credited (see Figure 10.6). These methods tend to be used by such industries as chemicals, distillation, steel-making and food processing.

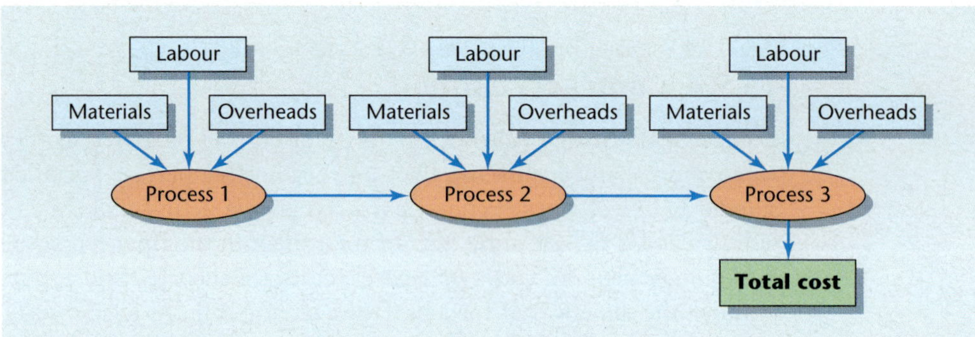

Figure 10.6 Process costing

In most processes there is a degree of wastage, but this loss might be either 'normal' or 'abnormal':

- *Normal loss* is where waste is inherent in the production process, and is seen as a legitimate expense to be borne by 'good' production.
- *Abnormal loss* is in excess of normal wastage and may be caused by inefficient working or poor materials. This is written off to the income statement. Occasionally, abnormal *gains* might be recorded where very favourable conditions have given rise to greater production than would have been expected. Such gains would be recorded separately and credited to the income statement.

Activity 10.11

Squaretree Ltd's Choc-o-crunch production line has three processes: baking, chocolate covering and wrapping. In June, 500,000 Choc-o-crunches were produced. Details of each process's costs for that month are as follows:

	Baking	Chocolate covering £	Wrapping £
Direct materials	20,000	16,000	8,000
Direct labour	4,500	5,180	1,600
Production overhead	2,500	2,620	2,600
Abnormal loss	–	3,000	–

Calculate the cost of one Choc-o-crunch.

Answer

Cost summary:	Baking	Chocolate covering	Wrapping
	£	£	£
Brought forward from previous process	n/a	27,000	47,800
Direct materials	20,000	16,000	8,000
Direct labour	4,500	5,180	1,600
Production overhead	2,500	2,620	2,600
Total costs	27,000	50,800	60,000
Abnormal loss	–	(3,000)	–
Carried forward to next process	27,000	47,800	n/a
Cost of finished goods			60,000

$$\text{Cost of one Choc-o-crunch} = \frac{£60,000}{500,000} = 12\text{p}$$

10.10.2 Service costing

The costing of specific services such as in hospitals or universities is different from costing production departments, mainly in the way cost data is collected and how costs are then allocated to cost units.

With services, cost units may be composites such as a 'patient-day' in a hospital or a 'passenger-mile' in a transport company, whereas universities might use 'full-time equivalent students'. There is no general rule – it depends on what is of most use to the organisation. Whatever cost unit is decided upon, the calculation of unit cost is similar to the calculation used in a production department:

$$\text{Cost per service unit} = \frac{\text{Total costs for the period}}{\text{Number of service units supplied in the period}}$$

Activity 10.12

A hospital has incurred costs of £3,600,000 during July and 8,000 patient-beds have been occupied during the month. What is the cost per patient bed?

Answer

$$\frac{£3,600,000}{8,000} = £450$$

Activity 10.13

Match the service industries on the left to the most appropriate service cost unit on the right:

(a) Hotel	1 Dog-days
(b) Airline	2 Meals served
(c) Caterer	3 Rooms occupied
(d) Laundry	4 Garments processed
(e) Boarding kennel	5 Passenger miles

Answers

(a) 3, (b) 5, (c) 2, (d) 4, (e) 1

10.11 Summary

Figure 10.7 shows a summary of absorption and marginal costing, while Figure 10.8 shows a summary of product costing.

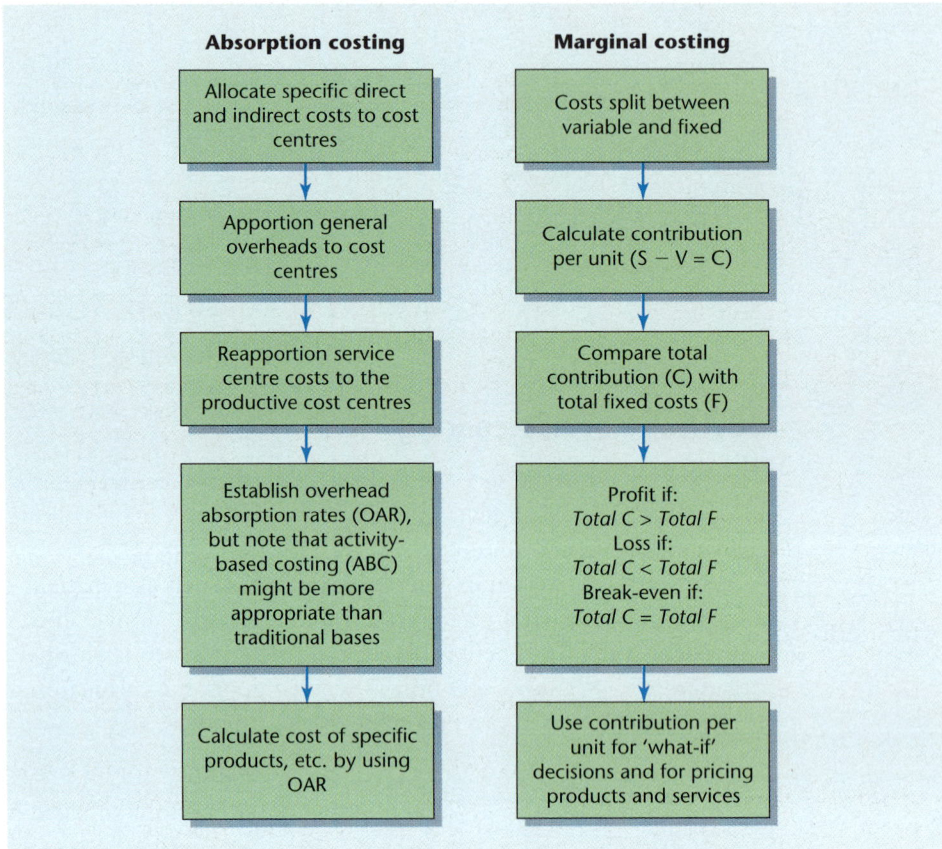

Figure 10.7 Absorption costing and marginal costing compared

10.12 Chapter glossary

Abnormal loss A loss of materials in excess of normal wastage, possibly caused by inefficient working or poor materials. The loss is not passed on to customers but is absorbed by the company.

Absorption costing A management accounting technique where costs are allocated or apportioned to various product lines to establish the profitability or overall cost of each product.

Activity-based costing (ABC) A method of cost apportionment which seeks to relate costs to the activities which generate or 'drive' the costs.

Batch costing A specific order costing system where similar or identical items are manufactured in batches.

Break-even point The point at which a business's revenue exactly meets its total costs, also where the total contribution exactly meets the total fixed costs.

Contract costing A specific order costing system for contracts of significant value and usually spanning more than one accounting period.

Contribution The difference between sales revenue and variable costs. It can be calculated either on a per unit basis (for 'what-if' and pricing calculations) or in total (to assess overall profitability).

	Specific order costing			Operation costing	
	Job costing	Batch costing	Contract costing	Process costing	Service costing
Applies to:	Work done to a customer's specific requirements, but see 'contract' definition	Similar or identical items manufactured in batches	Work of significant value usually spanning more than one financial period	One or more processes continually producing items	Service industries
Examples:	Car repairs, landscaping a garden	Pottery items such as plates, plastic components or toys	Bridge construction, building a school	Confectionery, pharmaceuticals	Universities, hospitals
Specific features:	Job cost sheet prepared with all relevant costs, possibly as a quotation (estimate of costs) for a customer	As job costing, but the price per unit is found by dividing the total batch costs by the number of items produced	Contract accounts kept for each contract. Progress payments depend on work certified. IAS 11 is relevant. Profits can be taken before contract completed, but expected losses must also be recognised	Cost of one process added to those of subsequent processes until total cost found. Unit cost found by dividing total cost by production of specific period. Losses might be normal or abnormal	Total costs found by the usual methods, but the cost unit might be a composite such as patient-day or full-time equivalent student

Figure 10.8 Product costing methods

Job costing A specific order costing system used where work is undertaken to a customer's specific requirements.

Marginal cost The extra 'variable' cost that would result from producing one extra unit.

Marginal costing A management accounting technique where costs are divided between variable and fixed, and a contribution is established by deducting the variable costs from the sales revenue.

Normal loss A loss of materials where waste is inherent in the production process, and is seen as a legitimate expense to be borne by 'good' production.

Process costing An operation costing system used where products are produced in a single process, or where the product of one process becomes the material of a second process.

Product costing The technique of establishing the cost of a finished item or items by combining direct costs with relevant allocated and apportioned indirect costs.

Service costing An operation costing system used for the costing of specific services such as hospitals or universities.

Additional resources

Now work through the various exercises and problems that you can find within the My Accounting Lab that are relevant to this chapter. Either use the QR code shown in the margin (if you use an Android- based device), or visit www.myaccountinglab.com for the log-in page.

Only accessible on Android-based devices

Self-check questions

The answers to these questions are in Appendix 1.

1 In a company manufacturing paint, which of the following would *not* be a direct cost?

(a) The cost of paint tins
(b) The cost of dyes to colour the paint
(c) The cost of advertising the paint
(d) The cost of chemicals used to make the paint

2 Another name for direct costs is:

(a) Prime costs
(b) Fixed costs
(c) Absorbed costs
(d) Overhead costs

3 A feature of absorption costing is that:

(a) The distinction between fixed and variable costs is ignored
(b) A contribution is established
(c) Only direct costs of production are considered
(d) Loss-making divisions are closed

4 Mojo Ltd manufactures pond pumps in batches of 400. During April, Batch no. 145 had a slight manufacturing fault, resulting in only 390 pumps being completed. The remainder was scrapped. Costs were: raw materials £2,000, labour and overheads £3,000. What was the cost per pump?

(a) £12.82
(b) £12.50
(c) £500
(d) £10

5 If total sales revenue for 1,000 units is £5,000 and total variable costs are £3,000, the contribution per unit is:

(a) £3,000
(b) £2,000
(c) £5
(d) £2

6 If the variable costs per unit are £6, and 500 units have been sold for £5,000, the total contribution is:

(a) £4,000
(b) £2,000
(c) £3,000
(d) £8,000

7 If total fixed costs are £12,000, the selling price per unit is £12 and the variable costs per unit are £8, the break-even point is:

(a) 12,000 units
(b) 3,000 units
(c) 1,500 units
(d) 4,500 units

8 If the break-even point is 6,000 units and the contribution per unit is £6, total fixed costs must be:

(a) £2,000
(b) £18,000
(c) £12,000
(d) £36,000

9 If fixed costs are £32,000, maximum sales are £100,000 and variable costs are £60,000 at this level, the turnover required to break-even is:

(a) £80,000
(b) £53,334
(c) £19,200
(d) £32,000

10 If fixed costs are £160,000 and the contribution per unit is £2, the number of units to be sold to achieve a profit of £60,000 is:

(a) 80,000
(b) 50,000
(c) 110,000
(d) 440,000

Self-study questions

Questions marked with this symbol (#) indicate that the suggested answers are available to lecturers only – other answers are given in Appendix 2.

10.1 Abalone operates three production departments and one service department. It estimated monthly overheads for the company at £72,600, divided as follows:

	Production departments			Service department
	A	B	C	D
	£	£	£	£
Indirect labour	20,000	16,000	8,000	7,000
Other indirect overheads	10,000	6,000	3,000	2,600
	30,000	22,000	11,000	9,600

D's overheads are to be apportioned between the production departments in the ratio: A 40%, B 40%, C 20%.

Apportion D's overheads to the production departments. If Abalone uses indirect labour hours as the basis for its overhead absorption rates (OARs), and pay rates averaged £20 per hour in Department A and B, and £16 per hour in Department C, what is the OAR for each of the three departments, A, B and C?

10.2# Boadle Limited makes five different products: Alphas, Betas, Gammas, Deltas and Epsilons. Costs per unit are: direct costs £22, £18, £35, £30 and £43 respectively, Variable overheads: £11, £9, £16, £15 and £19 respectively. Fixed expenses for a month are estimated at £8,200, which have been allocated to each unit produced as: Alphas

£17, Betas £13, Gammas £19, Deltas £15 and Epsilons £18. The company adds 20% on to the total cost of each product by way of profit.

(a) Calculate the price per unit of each product, based upon absorption (total cost) pricing.
(b) Advise the company as to which products it should produce, if selling prices are restricted to: Alphas £59, Betas £25, Gammas £80, Deltas £44 and Epsilons £92.
(c) If maximum output per product is 100 units, calculate the profit or loss for the company as a whole if it:
 (i) Produced the entire range of products
 (ii) Produced only the products you recommended in (b) above. (Assume that unused capacity cannot be used for other products.)

10.3 Complete the boxes in the following table. Assume that A and B are separate businesses.

	A	B
Sales in units		
Sales (£)	40,000	60,000
Variable costs (£)	10,000	
Contribution (£)	30,000	10,000
Contribution per unit (£)	6	0.5
Fixed costs (£)	14,400	
Profit/(loss) (£)		(5,000)
Break-even point (units)	2,400	30,000
Profit/(loss) if 3,000 units sold		

10.4# Complete the boxes in the following table. Assume that C, D and E are separate businesses.

	C	D	E
Sales in units	4,000	6,000	15,000
Sales (£)	48,000	90,000	
Variable costs (£)	32,000	54,000	30,000
Contribution (£)	16,000		75,000
Contribution per unit (£)		6	
Fixed costs (£)	7,000		50,000
Profit/(loss) (£)		12,000	
Break-even point (units)		4,000	
Profit/(loss) if 3,000 units sold			

10.5 Rumpole Ltd is proposing an expansion of their product range by manufacturing a new product. It is proposed that the new product will sell for £15 per item and will have a market of between 10,000 and 15,000 items per year. An analysis of the costs at these levels of production is:

Units:	10,000	15,000
	£	£
Materials	40,000	60,000
Labour	70,000	95,000
Overheads	50,000	55,000

(a) Calculate the variable cost per unit and the total fixed cost.
(b) Calculate how many units of the product must be manufactured to:
  (i) break even
  (ii) earn a profit of £13,000.
(c) Calculate how much profit or loss would be made if only 7,000 units were manufactured and sold.

10.6# Look back at the 'Stop and think' Case study of Mrs Brown's cake making business in section 10.7 above. Explain how a knowledge of marginal costing might have helped her to avoid the loss-making contract with Groupon. Assume that the normal variable cost of making a dozen cupcakes is 30% of the usual selling price.

10.7 Barney plc manufactures deluxe cat baskets in batches of 300. During April, Batch no. 567 took 20 hours to machine. Sixty cat baskets failed to pass an inspection, but of these, 40 were thought to be rectifiable. The remaining 20 were scrapped, and the scrap value was credited to the cost of the batch as a whole. Rectification work took nine hours. Costs were as follows:

Batch no. 567	£
Raw materials per cat basket	1.60
Scrap value per cat basket	0.86
Machinists' hourly rate	4.20
Machine-hour overhead	3.60
Setting up of machine – normal machining	21.00
Setting up of machine – rectification	18.00

Calculate:
(a) The cost of a full batch, in total and per unit, if all units pass inspection.
(b) The actual cost of Batch no. 567, in total and per unit, after crediting the recovery value of the scrapped items, and including the rectification costs.
(c) The loss incurred because of defective work.

Case study (a) Who is Mrs Eadale?

The directors of Machiq Limited (see previous case studies) decided to reject Esmeralda's takeover bid and instead devoted their talents to developing new products. Trixie, the managing director, had been sent an e-mail containing a recipe for a vanishing potion and decided to investigate the possibility of setting up a separate division to produce and promote it. The creator of the recipe, who had signed herself 'Mrs Eadale', said that the potion was totally harmless and caused only temporary invisibility. She also insisted that, as an absolute condition of her allowing Machiq Limited to use the recipe free of charge, the directors must test the potion on themselves before selling it to the general public.

Chiquita, the finance director, produced the following information:

Maximum production and sales p.a. (bottles)	**15,000**
	£
Selling price per bottle	14
Ingredients per bottle	3
Cost of bottle and label	1
Direct labour cost per bottle	2
Rent, rates and other fixed costs relating to bottling division	20,000
Portion of company's general overheads allocated to bottling division	130,000

Required

(a) Using the absorption costing technique, would the new division be viable? Show your calculations.
(b) What recommendation might have been made if marginal costing had been used to evaluate the proposed new division? Show your calculations.
(c) Using marginal costing techniques, calculate:
 (i) the break-even point (in bottles)
 (ii) the number of bottles which would have to be sold to earn £16,000 profit for the bottling division
 (iii) how much profit or loss would be made if only 4,000 bottles were sold.

A footnote

Marvin, Chiquita and Trixie set up the bottling division. They sent an invitation to Esmeralda to join them at a celebration champagne 'test the potion' party to show there were no hard feelings after her failed takeover bid. Esmeralda replied saying that she would be very pleased to watch the three directors vanish and looked forward to toasting their health in champagne beforehand. Unfortunately, a waiter hired for the occasion inadvertently poured the potion into the champagne glasses, and the directors, after raising their glasses to the toast of 'Mrs Eadale', drank the 'champagne' and promptly disappeared without trace.

(b) The antidote to the potion

The detective investigating the mysterious disappearance of the directors of Machiq Limited was searching the home of Esmeralda, the chief suspect in the case. He opened a drawer and extracted a notepad with the word 'Antidote' written on the front cover. He turned the page, and read as follows:

> *The antidote to the vanishing potion can be manufactured in 1,000 bottle batches as follows:*
>
> *Firstly, the mixing process: Combine 10 kg of Ingredient A with 5 kg of Ingredient B. One person to mix by hand for 10 hours and then transfer to the liquidising process. There the three liquidising workers will each spend 4 hours adding 14 kg of Ingredient C whilst supervising the liquidising procedure. Three-quarters of the mixture will evaporate in the liquidising process as a normal loss.*
>
> *Finally, the antidote must be bottled. This process will take 2 persons 5 hours each.*
>
> *Ingredients can all be obtained from Stoob the Chemist at the following prices: Ingredient A £80 per kg, Ingredient B £60 per kg and Ingredient C £40 per kg. The mixing operative is paid £4.50 per hour, liquidising workers are each paid £4.75 per hour and the bottling operatives are paid £5.00 per hour. Bottles cost £1 each. Other (fixed) overheads would be mixing £590, liquidising £420, bottling £380.*

Required

Calculate the cost of manufacturing one bottle of antidote.

Answers are in Appendix 3

Further research

A (very) critical appraisal of activity-based costing: **http://casparija.home.comcast.net/~casparija/dweb/l118.htm**

The website of Need A Cake: **www.need-a-cake.co.uk**

Groupon: **www.groupon.co.uk**

Synergy Business Solutions, a company that produces specialist project software: **www.synergybusiness.com**

Chapter 11

Standard costing

Objectives

When you have read this chapter you will be able to:

- Understand the principles of standard costing
- Understand what is meant by variance analysis
- Appreciate the use of variance analysis as a management tool

11.1 Introduction

In the previous chapter we looked at the two key methods of allocating overheads to products and services: absorption costing and marginal costing and their role in pricing decisions. We have been mainly concerned with the *actual* costs incurred in production: materials, labour and overheads. Standard costing, however, is concerned with what costs *ought to have been*. Standards are set in advance for levels of performance and costs of resources, and then these are compared with the actual levels of performance and the actual prices. Any differences between the standard and the actual values are known as *variances*. The benefit of standard costing is that it prompts questions to be asked as to *why* the variances have arisen. If there is a variance, then something has not gone according to plan! Even where actual costs are *less than* standard costs, this would prompt as much investigation as when the actual costs are *greater than* standard.

Standard costing also enables organisations to adopt the practice of *management by exception*, so that management's attention can be concentrated upon the key areas which materially differ from what was planned.

11.2 Variances

By determining in advance what costs should be under specific working conditions (standards) and then comparing actual costs with these standards, a number of variances can be produced which are of great value to management in terms of assessing the causes of the relative efficiencies and inefficiencies of the firm. The firm must decide in advance what costs, quantities and performance levels ought to be for each aspect of production and for each stage of production. It will therefore calculate a standard cost comprising a standard material cost, a standard labour cost and a standard overhead cost (usually split between fixed and variable). The difference between standard cost and actual cost is known as a variance, with a favourable variance existing where the actual cost or performance is less than the standard cost, and an adverse variance where the actual cost is greater than the standard cost (see Figure 11.1).

11.2.1 Setting standards

When setting standards, three alternative levels of activity can be considered as a basis:

1 *Average expected level of activity.* This standard is based upon past experience. Although it is seen as being easily attainable, it may lead to inefficient and complacent working.
2 *Maximum possible level of activity.* This is based upon the maximum levels that are theoretically possible, being related to the output of the most efficient worker, the best ever production run attained by a specific type of machine, etc. However, standards that are unlikely to be attained tend to discourage people and can bring the whole system into ridicule.
3 *Efficient working level of activity.* This standard is based upon what can be expected with efficient management. It represents a far more realistic level to aim for as it marks a standard which can reasonably be achieved.

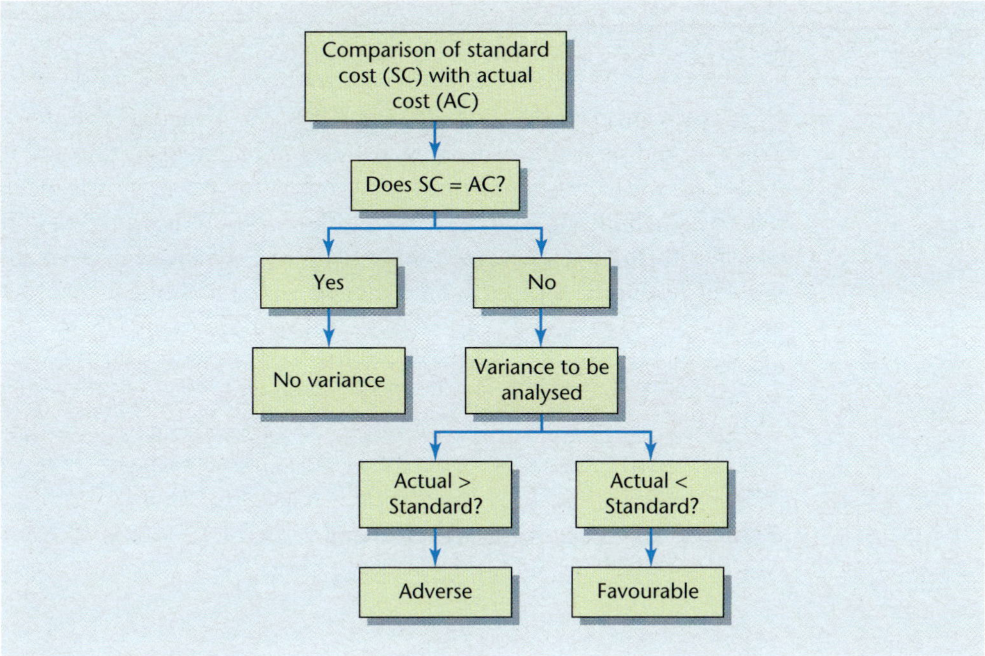

Figure 11.1 Variances

Standards will be agreed following discussions amongst key personnel within the affected departments under the headings of: direct material; direct labour; variable overheads; fixed overheads. For example, the standard materials content of a specific product will be based upon technical specifications relating to raw materials and bought-in components, and will also make allowance for normal losses such as evaporation, scrap and expected wastage.

Standard selling prices will also be set. This is usually a top management decision, based upon their view of the market, likely pricing by competitors, anticipated production costs and expected consumer demand. Information provided by the firm's salesforce will be critical. Once a standard selling price has been established for each product, the standard sales margin can be calculated as the difference between the standard price and the standard cost.

Standards should be reviewed from time to time to keep them relevant to current conditions – though small changes in wage rates, prices or materials usage are generally ignored over the short term.

11.3 Direct material variances

The overall direct material variance can be calculated by comparing the standard direct materials cost that we anticipated (standard price × standard usage) with what actually was paid (Actual price × Actual usage rate). This variance can then be analysed between *price variances* and *usage variances*. Price variances arise because the actual price paid for the material is different from the standard price. Usage variances arise where a different quantity of material has been used compared with the standard quantity. These are shown in Figure 11.2.

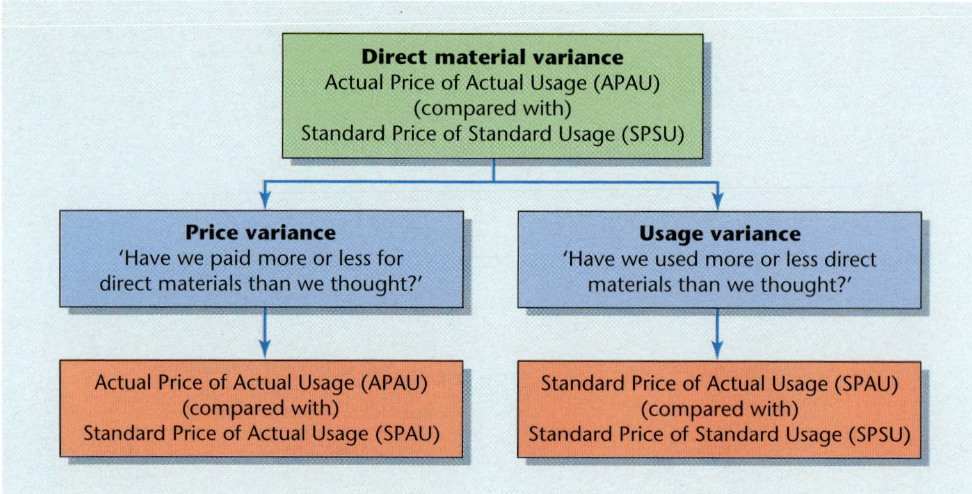

Figure 11.2 Direct material variances

Activity 11.1

Three manufacturing companies provide the following information regarding the price and usage of chemicals used to produce an identical product:

	A	B	C
Standard price per litre	£1.30	£1.20	£1.60
Standard usage (litres)	200	250	270
Actual price per litre	£1.50	£1.20	£1.40
Actual usage (litres)	200	230	280

Calculate the direct material variances for each company.

Answer

Company A's standard price of its actual usage (£1.30 × 200 = £260) was less than the actual price of its actual usage (£1.50 × 200 = £300), resulting in an *adverse* price variance of £40. However, there is no usage variance as the standard price of its standard usage (£1.30 × 200 = £260) was the same as the standard price of its actual usage (also £1.30 × 200 = £260). Overall, the total materials variance for Company A was £40 adverse (£40 adverse price variance, no usage variance).

Company B's standard price of its actual usage (£1.20 × 230 = £276) was the same as the actual price of its actual usage (also £1.20 × 230 = £276), so there is no price variance. However, as the standard price of the standard usage (£1.20 × 250 = £300) is greater than the standard price of its actual usage (£1.20 × 230 = £276), this results in a *favourable* usage variance of £24. Overall, the total materials variance for Company B was £24 favourable (no price variance, £24 favourable usage variance).

Company C has both a price variance and a usage variance. The standard price of the actual usage (£1.60 × 280 = £448) was greater than the actual price of the actual usage (£1.40 × 280 = £392), resulting in a favourable price variance of £56. The standard price of the standard usage (£1.60 × 270 = £432) was less than the standard price of the actual usage (£1.60 × 280 = £448), resulting in an adverse usage variance of £16.

Overall, the total materials variance for Company C was £40 favourable (£56 favourable price variance − £16 adverse usage variance).

The variances for the three companies are summarised in Figure 11.3.

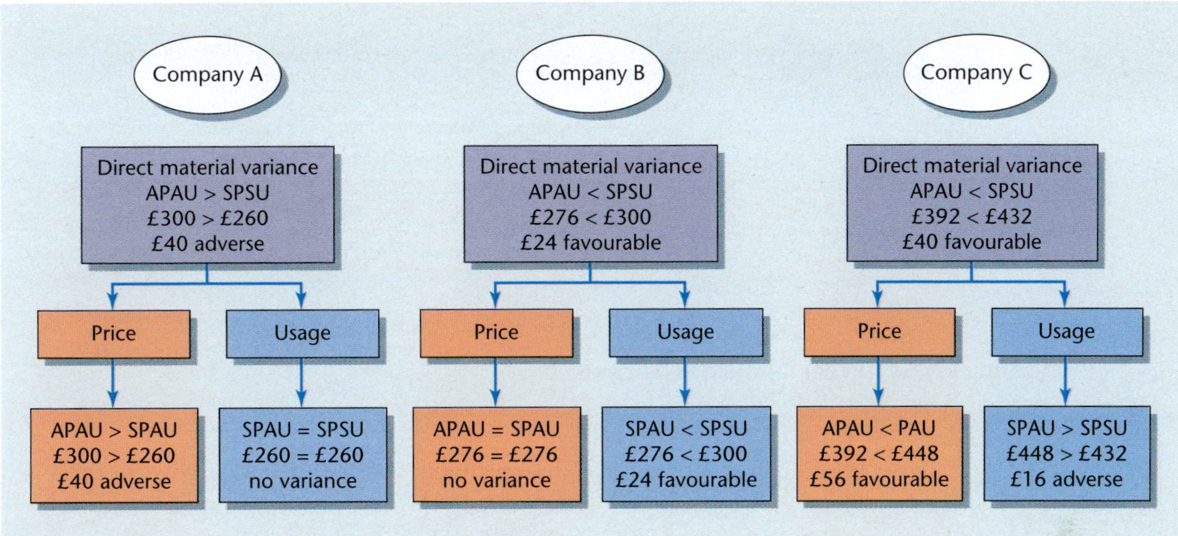

Figure 11.3 Material variances for Companies A, B and C

Direct material variances such as those seen in Activity 11.1 above enable management to focus on specific issues relating to prices and usage. Price variances may arise because the prices actually paid were different from those planned, due perhaps to general market changes or possibly because of the negotiation of quantity discounts. If such discounts were greater than anticipated then a favourable price variance would arise, but if the discounts weren't given or were less than anticipated then the price variance would be adverse. Usage variance may arise from factors such as different quality materials being used requiring greater or lesser quantities. Poor storage conditions and inadequate security may also cause an increase in material wastage which would be reflected in adverse usage variances.

11.4 Direct labour variances

The overall direct labour variance can be calculated by comparing the standard direct labour that we anticipated (standard hours × standard pay rate) with what actually was paid (actual hours × actual pay rate). This variance can be analysed between pay and efficiency (see Figure 11.4).

Pay rate variances arise because higher or lower wages were paid than were planned. There could be many reasons: for example the work may have been carried out by different grades of workers than had been intended, or perhaps unplanned overtime or bonuses were paid. Any of these would produce pay variances. The use of different grades of labour might also produce an *efficiency* variance, with employees working to a

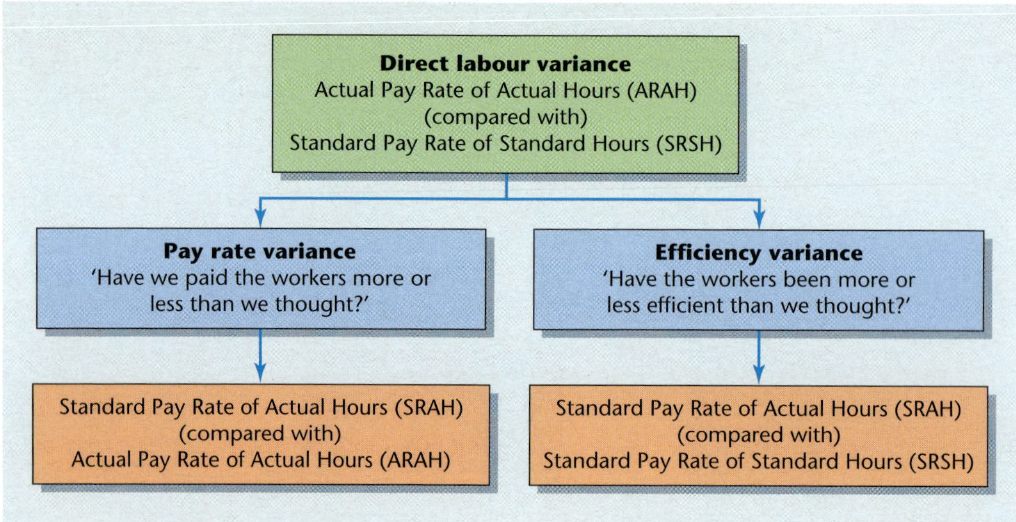

Figure 11.4 Direct labour variances

greater or lesser degree of efficiency than planned. Other reasons for adverse variances include poor supervision, machine breakdowns or poor materials requiring more time to be spent. Some things can be controlled and improved by management, but realistically other matters are outside their control, for example poor weather conditions affecting work rates.

Activity 11.2

Company D provides the following information regarding its direct labour costs:

	D
Standard hours per week	45
Standard pay rate per hour	£22
Actual hours worked in the week	50
Actual pay rate per hour	£21

Calculate the direct labour variances for the company.

Answer

If we compare the standard hours worked multiplied by the standard pay rate (45 × £22 = £990), with the actual hours worked multiplied by the actual pay rate (50 × £21 = £1,050), we see that there is an overall total direct labour variance of £60 adverse. This can be further analysed, firstly, by calculating the pay rate variance, comparing the standard pay rate of actual hours worked (50 × £22 = £1,100) with the actual pay rate of the actual hours worked (50 × £21 = £1,050), resulting in a favourable pay rate variance of £50. Secondly, the efficiency of the direct labour workforce can be assessed by calculating the efficiency variance, comparing the standard pay rate of standard hours worked (45 × £22 = £990) with the standard pay rate of the actual hours worked ($50 \times £22 = £1,100$), resulting in an adverse efficiency variance of £110. These are summarised in Figure 11.5 below.

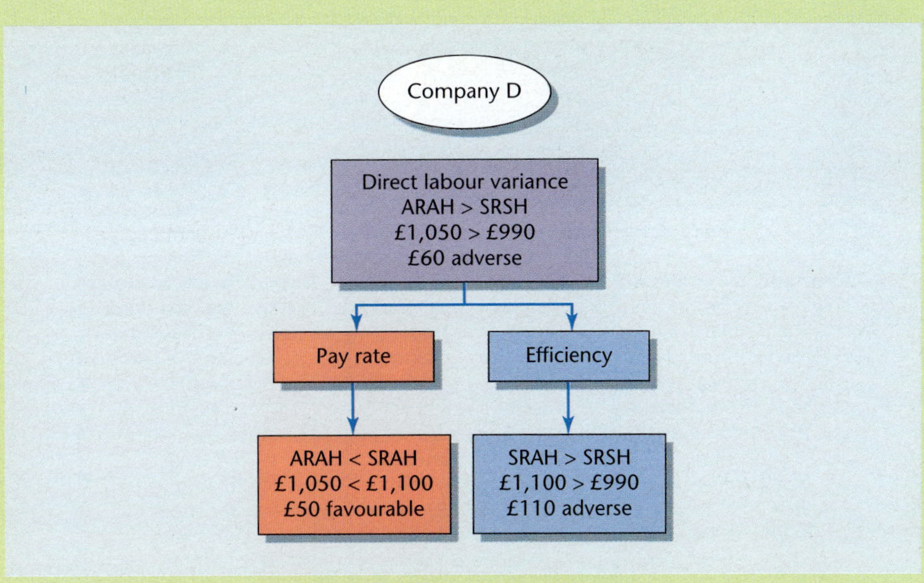

Figure 11.5 Direct labour variances for Company D

11.5 Overhead variances

Overhead variances are split between those relating to variable overheads and those relating to fixed overheads. Expenditure variances can be calculated in each case, investigating where actual cost differs from planned cost. Additionally, an efficiency variance can be calculated in respect of variable overheads – this arises due to changes in the level of activity. In the case of fixed overheads, a volume variance can be calculated which arises due to the volume of actual output being different from that which was planned. This is illustrated in Figure 11.6.

Overhead variances are slightly more complicated than material or labour variances, mainly because overheads are absorbed by means of predetermined overhead absorption rates applying to particular levels of production (see Chapter 10). In standard costing, production levels need to be expressed in terms of the measure which is common to all products: the most usual is the 'standard hour', which is the quantity of output (or the amount of work which can be performed) in one hour. It is a measure of output, not of time.

11.5.1 Variable overhead variances

As we have seen above, variable overhead variances are divided between expenditure variances and efficiency variances. Activity 11.3 (a) and (b) shows the way in which these variances are calculated.

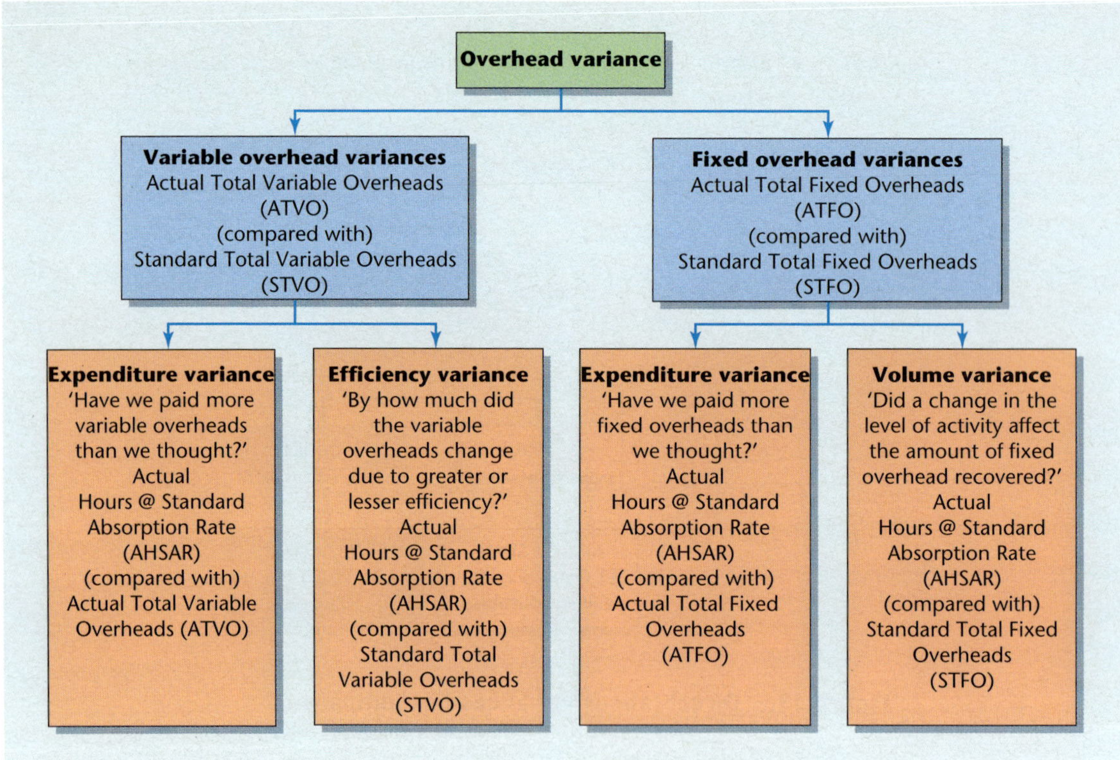

Figure 11.6 Overhead variances

Activity 11.3(a)

Variable overhead expenditure variance

Company E provides the following information relating to its variable overheads for September. Overheads are absorbed on the basis of direct labour hours:

	E
Budgeted standard total variable overhead	£200,000
Actual variable overhead	£190,000
Budgeted standard direct labour hours	5,000
Actual standard direct labour hours	4,000

Calculate the variable overhead expenditure variance for the company.

Answer

The variable overhead expenditure variance for Company E is £30,000 (adverse).

Comment:

Firstly it is necessary to calculate the standard direct labour hour rate, which is the rate at which variable overhead is incurred per standard direct labour hour. For Company E, the standard direct labour hour rate is:

$$\frac{£200{,}000}{5{,}000} = £40 \text{ per standard direct labour hour}$$

For every standard direct labour hour worked, £40 of variable overheads is incurred.

Secondly, this rate per standard direct labour hour must be applied to the actual number of direct labour hours worked, and the answer compared to the actual variable overheads in order to assess the level of variance:

	£
Actual variable overhead incurred	190,000
Actual hours at standard absorption rate (4,000 × £40)	160,000
Adverse expenditure variance	30,000

In other words, at the level of output actually achieved – 4,000 standard direct labour hours – the variable overhead incurred should have been £160,000. In fact, £190,000 was incurred, resulting in an overspending of £30,000. If overheads are recovered on a *machine hour basis*, then the calculation would be based on standard machine hours, but the method of calculation remains the same.

Activity 11.3(b)

Variable overhead efficiency variance

Using the information provided above for Company E, calculate the variable overhead efficiency variance for the company for September. Additional information is also available as follows:

Standard direct labour hours needed to produce 1 unit	0.5
Actual units produced in September	9,000

Answer

The variable overhead efficiency variance is £40,000 (favourable).

Comment:

The variable overhead absorption rate (see above) on the basis of standard labour hours is £40 per hour (£200,000/50,000). On the basis of the standard hours needed to produce one unit, a production of 9,000 units should have taken 4,500 direct labour hours (9,000 × 0.5 = 4,500). In fact the actual production took 4,000 hours. As there is a difference between the number of hours planned for production and the number of hours actually taken, a variance has resulted caused in this case by greater efficiency (fewer hours actually needed than planned).

	£
Actual hours × standard absorption rate (4,000 × £40)	160,000
Standard hours × standard absorption rate (5,000 × £40)	200,000
Favourable efficiency variance	40,000

Looking back at the information provided by Company E, the total variable overhead variance – comparing the standard cost of the variable overheads (£200,000) with the actual cost (£190,000) – is £10,000 favourable. Our calculations in Activity

11.3(a) and here have split this between a £30,000 adverse expenditure variance and a £40,000 favourable efficiency variance, as shown in Figure 11.7.

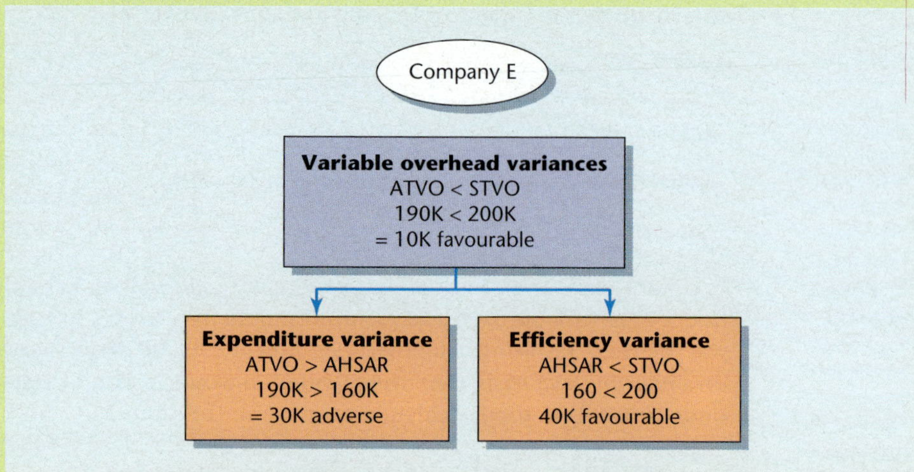

Figure 11.7 Variable overhead variances for Company E

11.5.2 Fixed overhead variances

As explained in previous chapters, certain expenses (including rents, rates and staff salaries) have all to be paid in the short-term irrespective of the level of activity, being described as 'fixed' overheads. Fixed overhead variances are divided between expenditure variances and volume variances. Expenditure variances simply compare what fixed costs we thought were likely to be absorbed compared with what fixed costs were actually absorbed. Regarding volume variances, fixed costs have to be absorbed by production and under standard costing, a standard amount of fixed overhead is assumed to apply to each unit produced. If the level of activity changes, this will affect the amount of fixed overhead recovered. The more that is produced, the more fixed overhead that is recovered, but if less is produced, less fixed overhead is recovered, resulting in a volume variance.

Activity 11.4 (a) and (b) shows the way in which these variances are calculated.

Activity 11.4(a)

Fixed overhead expenditure variance

Company F provides the following information relating to its fixed overheads for November. Overheads are absorbed on the basis of standard hours:

	F
Budgeted standard total fixed overhead	£180,000
Budgeted standard hours	10,000
Actual fixed overhead	£170,000
Actual standard hours	11,000

Calculate the fixed overhead expenditure variance for the company.

Answer

The fixed overhead expenditure variance for Company F is £28,000 (favourable).

Comment:

Firstly it is necessary to calculate the standard hour rate, which is the rate at which fixed overhead is absorbed per standard hour. For Company F, the standard hour rate is:

$$\frac{£180{,}000}{10{,}000} = £18 \text{ per standard hour}$$

For every standard hour worked, £18 of fixed overheads is absorbed.

Secondly, this rate per standard hour must be applied to the actual number of standard hours worked, and the answer compared to the actual fixed overheads in order to assess the level of variance:

	£
Actual fixed overhead absorbed	170,000
Actual hours at standard absorption rate (11,000 × £18)	198,000
Favourable expenditure variance	28,000

In other words, at the level of output actually achieved – 11,000 standard hours – the fixed overhead absorbed should have been £198,000. In fact, only £170,000 was incurred, resulting in a favourable balance of £28,000.

Activity 11.4(b)

Fixed overhead volume variance

From the information given in Activity 11.4 (a) for Company F, calculate the fixed overhead volume variance for Company F for November.

Answer

The fixed overhead volume variance is £18,000 (adverse).

Comment:

For Company F, the standard fixed overhead absorption rate is the standard total fixed overhead divided by the budgeted standard hours (£180,000/10,000 = £18 per hour). If the actual standard hours achieved was 11,000, the fixed overhead volume variance would be:

	£
Actual standard hours × standard absorption rate (11,000 × £18)	198,000
Standard total of fixed overheads (10,000 × £18)	180,000
Adverse fixed overhead volume variance	18,000

Looking back at the information provided for Company F, the total fixed overhead variance – comparing the standard cost of the fixed overheads (£180,000) with the actual cost (£170,000) – is £10,000 favourable. Our calculations in Activity 11.4(a) and 11.4(b) have split this between a £28,000 favourable expenditure variance and a £18,000 adverse efficiency variance, as shown in Figure 11.8.

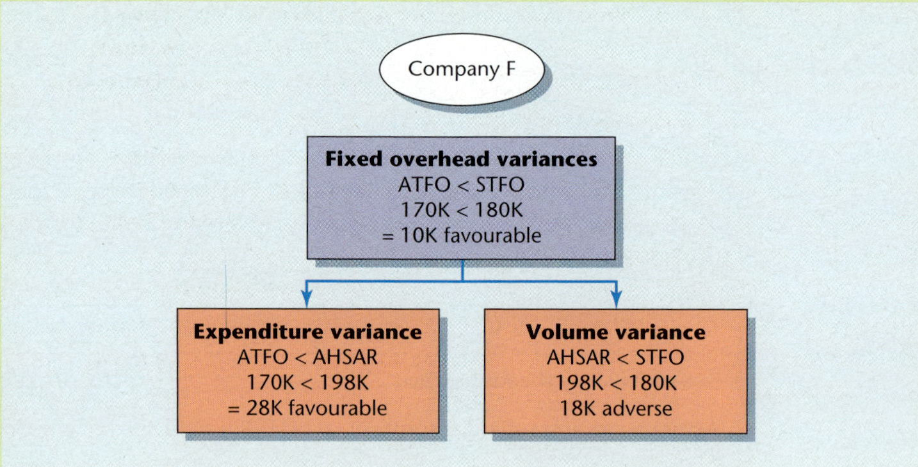

Figure 11.8 **Fixed overhead variances for Company F**

11.6 Summary

A summary of variances is shown in Figure 11.9.

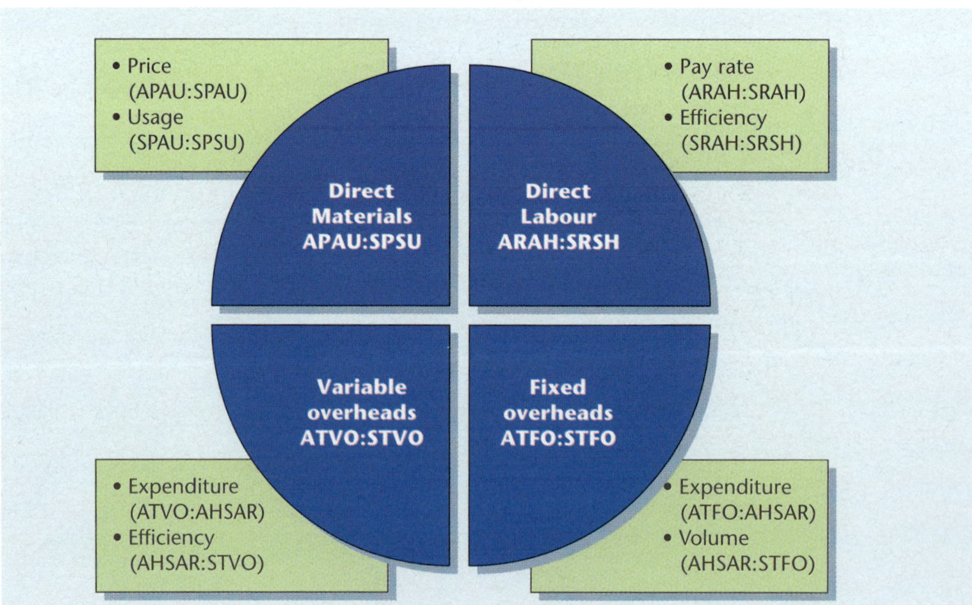

Key:

Direct materials	
APAU	Actual Price of Actual Usage
SPAU	Standard Price of Actual Usage
SPSU	Standard Price of Standard Usage
Direct labour	
ARAH	Actual pay Rate of Actual Hours
SRAH	Standard pay Rate of Actual Hours
SRSH	Standard pay Rate of Standard Hours
Variable overheads	
AHSAR	Actual Hours at Standard variable cost Absorption Rate
ATVO	Actual Total of Variable Overheads
STVO	Standard Total of Variable Overheads
Fixed overheads	
AHSAR	Actual Hours at Standard fixed cost Absorption Rate
ATFO	Actual Total of Fixed Overheads
STFO	Standard Total of Fixed Overheads

Figure 11.9 Summary of variances

11.7 Chapter glossary

Adverse variance A variance where actual cost is greater than planned.

Favourable variance A variance where planned cost is greater than actual.

Standard cost A predicted cost or performance based on an agreed level of activity.

Standard hour The amount of work that can be done at a standard level of performance.

Variance The difference between planned and actual cost.

Additional resources

Only accessible on Android-based devices

Now work through the various exercises and problems that you can find within the My Accounting Lab that are relevant to this chapter. Either use the QR code shown in the margin (if you use an Android-based device), or visit www.myaccountinglab.com for the log-in page.

Self-check questions

The answers to these questions are in Appendix 1.

1 When setting standards, which of the following levels of activity is usually considered as the most realistic to aim for?

(a) Maximum possible level of activity
(b) Minimum possible level of activity
(c) Average expected level of activity
(d) Efficient working level of activity

2 A company records the following information relating to its direct materials:

Standard price £2.40 per kg
Actual price £2.60 per kg
Standard usage 80 kg
Actual usage 78 kg

What is the company's overall direct materials price variance?

(a) £10.80 adverse
(b) £15.60 adverse
(c) £4.80 favourable
(d) £16 favourable

3 From the information in question 2, what is the company's direct materials price variance?

(a) 20p adverse
(b) £4.80 favourable
(c) £15.60 adverse
(d) £10.80 adverse

4 From the information in question 2 above, what is the company's direct materials usage variance?

(a) 2 kg
(b) £4.80 favourable
(c) £10.80 adverse
(d) £15.60 adverse

5 A company provides the following information relating to its direct labour costs:

Standard hours per week	80
Standard pay rate per hour	£16
Actual hours worked in the week	78
Actual pay rate per hour	£18

What is the company's direct labour pay rate variance?

(a) £124 adverse
(b) £32 favourable
(c) £2 adverse
(d) £156 adverse

6 From the information provided in question 5, what is the company's direct labour efficiency variance?

(a) £32 favourable
(b) £156 adverse

(c) £124 adverse
(d) 2 hours favourable

7 A company that absorbs variable overheads on the basis of machine hours provides the following information relating to its variable overheads:

Budgeted standard total variable overhead	£74,000
Actual variable overhead	£85,000
Budgeted standard machine hours	5,000
Actual standard machine hours	5,500

From the above information, what are the variable overhead expenditure and efficiency variances?

(a) Expenditure variance £3,600 favourable, efficiency variance £7,400 adverse
(b) Expenditure variance £3,600 adverse, efficiency variance £7,400 favourable
(c) Expenditure variance £3,600 adverse, efficiency variance £7,400 adverse
(d) Expenditure variance £3,600 favourable, efficiency variance £7,400 favourable

8 A company that absorbs fixed overheads on the basis of standard hours provides the following information relating to its fixed overheads:

Budgeted standard total fixed overhead	£200,000
Budgeted standard hours	8,000
Actual fixed overhead	£194,000
Actual standard hours	8,200

From the above information, what are the fixed overhead expenditure and volume variances?

(a) Expenditure variance £8,000 adverse, Volume variance £5,000 adverse
(b) Expenditure variance £11,000 favourable, Volume variance £5,000 adverse
(c) Expenditure variance £6,000 favourable, Volume variance £200 favourable
(d) Expenditure variance £10,000 adverse, Volume variance £15,000 favourable

9 Which one of the following could *not* be a reason for an adverse direct materials usage variance?

(a) Different quality materials being used than predicted
(b) Same quality materials but purchased from a different supplier at a lower price
(c) Higher rate of evaporation of materials than predicted
(d) Theft of materials

10 Which one of the following could *not* be a reason for a favourable direct labour pay rate variance?

(a) Standard number of workers paid at standard pay rates produced more work per hour
(b) Fewer qualified workers were employed than predicted
(c) Less overtime paid than predicted
(d) Unexpected redundancies amongst the workforce reduced the overall wage total.

Self-study questions

Questions marked with this symbol (#) indicate that the suggested answers are available to lecturers only – other answers are given in Appendix 2.

11.1 The Iris Company provides the following information relating to its variable overheads for October. Overheads are absorbed on the basis of labour hours:

Standard total variable overhead for October	£800,000
Standard labour hours for October	80,000
Standard hours to produce 1 unit	5
Actual units produced in the first week of October	4,000
Actual labour hours in the first week of October	18,000

Calculate the variable overhead efficiency variance for Company F for the first week of October.

11.2# Lupin and Partners provide the following information regarding its direct labour costs:

Standard hours per week	63
Standard pay rate per hour	£15
Actual hours worked in the week	70
Actual pay rate per hour	£16

Calculate the direct labour variances for the company.

11.3 Azalea Limited provides the following information relating to its variable overheads. Overheads are absorbed on the basis of direct labour hours:

Budgeted standard total variable overhead	£150,000
Actual variable overhead	£145,000
Budgeted standard direct labour hours	6,500
Actual standard direct labour hours	6,700
Standard direct labour hours needed to produce 1 unit	1
Actual units produced	7,000

Calculate the variable overhead expenditure and efficiency variances for the company.

11.4# Marigold plc provides the following information relating to its fixed overheads. Overheads are absorbed on the basis of standard hours:

Budgeted standard total fixed overhead	£360,000
Budgeted standard hours	40,000
Actual fixed overhead	£390,000
Actual standard hours	41,000

Calculate the fixed overhead expenditure variance and volume variance for the company.

11.5 A company manufactures and assembles storage units. The standard output of its employees is 16 units per person in an eight hour day. There are two production lines, A and B, each of which has 10 employees. Workers on production line A are paid £7 per hour, but the workers on production line B are paid according to how many units are produced each day at the rate of £4 per completed unit and a standard output of 20 units per person in an 8 hour day.

The company produces the following information relating to the two production lines for one day:

	Production line A	Production line B
Output (units)	220	240
Employee hours worked	98	80
Wage costs (£)	720	950

(a) For each production line calculate the overall direct labour variance, the direct labour pay rate variance and the direct labour efficiency variance.
(b) Which of the two production lines appears to be more cost efficient? Give your reasons.

11.6# Capsicum Ltd operates a standard costing system. The results for January were as follows:

Standard price of material	£6 per kg
Actual material issued to production	3,500 kg

The following two variances were also recorded:

Direct material price variance	£1,400 adverse
Overall Direct material variance	£1,100 adverse

(a) Calculate:

(i) The actual price per kg of material
(ii) The standard quantity of material used in kilograms.

(b) Suggest one possible reason for each of the two variances listed above.

Case study

Standardising the antidote

The standard costs of producing the antidote to the vanishing potion described earlier (in Chapter 10) were as follows, with the *actual* costs shown alongside:

	Standard	Actual
Number of bottles produced per batch	1,000	1,000
Direct materials per batch:		
Ingredient A – quantity	10 kg	9 kg
Ingredient A – price	£80 per kg	£82 per kg
Ingredient B – quantity	5 kg	5 kg
Ingredient B – price	£60 per kg	£59 per kg
Ingredient C – quantity	14 kg	13 kg
Ingredient C – price	£40 per kg	£40 per kg
Bottles (price per bottle)	£1	£1
Bottles used (note that 100 bottles were broken during actual production)	£1,000	£1,100
Direct labour per batch:		
Mixing hours	10	11
Mixing pay rate per hour	£4.50	£4.60
Liquidising hours	12	11
Liquidising pay rate per hour	£4.75	£5
Bottling hours	10	11
Bottling pay rate per hour	£5	£5
Other variable overheads	Nil	Nil
Total fixed overheads (absorbed on a total direct labour hour basis)	£1,390	£1,500

(a) Calculate, in as much detail as possible, the standard cost variances for direct labour, direct materials and fixed overheads.

(b) Write a brief report regarding the variance analysis.

Answers are in Appendix 3

Chapter 12

Break-even and cost–volume–profit analysis

Objectives

When you have read this chapter you will be able to:

- Prepare and interpret a break-even chart
- Prepare and interpret a profit/volume chart
- Appreciate the limitations of break-even and profit/volume charts

12.1 Introduction

This chapter explores ways of using the information generated from cost behaviour analysis in a visual format. We learn to produce charts which enable management to see at a glance such information as the profit or loss at any specific trading level, the break-even point and the activity needed to reach a target profit. The key benefit of the charts is to give a 'reasonable impression' of this information without worrying too much about the *precise* monetary amounts involved. For example, using the formulae learnt in Chapter 10, we might establish that a company would break-even next year if it sells *exactly* 25,307 units. Reading the same data from a break-even chart might however give a 'ball park' break-even target of somewhere between 25,000 and 26,000 units. This would be perfectly satisfactory from the management's viewpoint as they would know that forecast information is largely based on estimates which are subject to change, so having a 'reasonable' idea of break-even is just as valuable as having a precise number that would almost inevitably change as forecasts are revised.

12.2 Break-even charts

In Chapter 9 we looked at cost behaviour. Try Activity 12.1 to see how much you remember.

Activity 12.1

Here are two charts which show varying cost behaviour. Each has costs and revenue on the *y*-axis and output on the *x*-axis. Which graph shows:

(a) Fixed costs
(b) Variable costs?

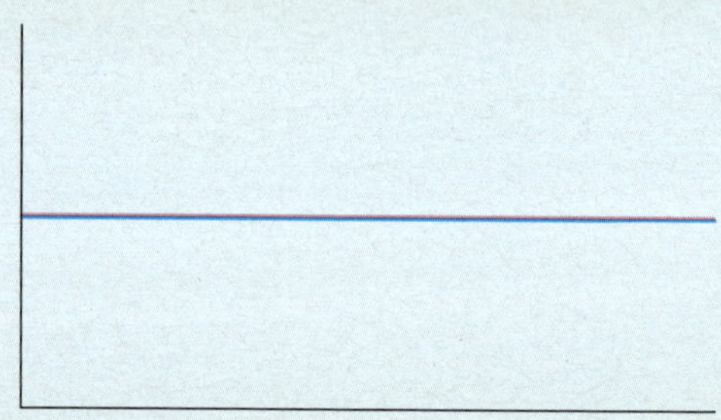

Chart 1

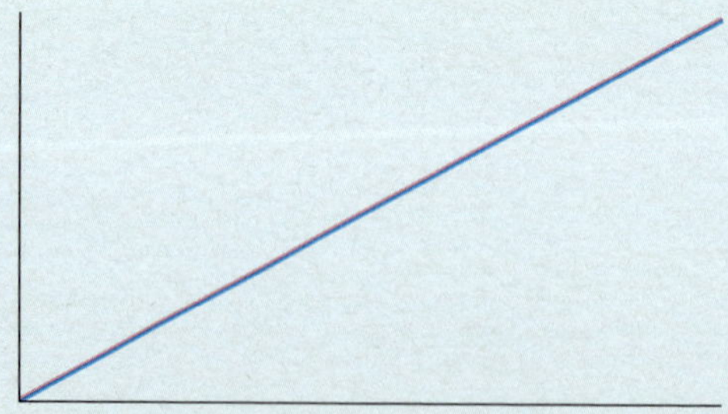

Chart 2

Answer

1 Fixed costs
2 Variable costs

12.2.1 A combination of graphs

The *break-even chart* is in fact a combination of three graphs:

- Fixed costs
- Total costs (that is, the total of both fixed *and* variable costs at each level of activity)
- Sales revenue.

Remember that any semi-fixed costs have to be split between fixed and variable before analysing cost data.

The break-even chart will, amongst other things, indicate approximate profit or loss at different levels of activity: it is based on a mixture of known and forecast information, and so gives a general idea of likely performance rather than an absolutely accurate picture.

Let's look at an example. Berwick plc, which makes one product, has forecast the following data:

Output level (units)	1,000	2,000	3,000	4,000	5,000
Sales (£)	1,200	2,400	3,600	4,800	6,000
Variable costs (£)	400	800	1,200	1,600	2,000
Fixed costs (£)	2,000	2,000	2,000	2,000	2,000

If we were producing separate graphs which plot fixed costs, total costs and revenue, they would look like Figures 12.1 to 12.3.

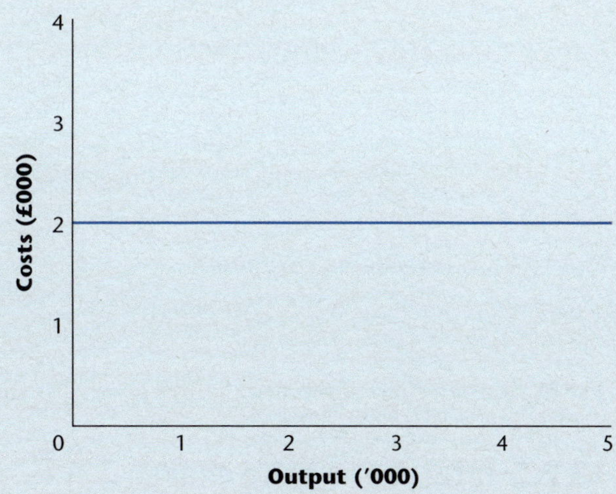

Figure 12.1 Fixed costs

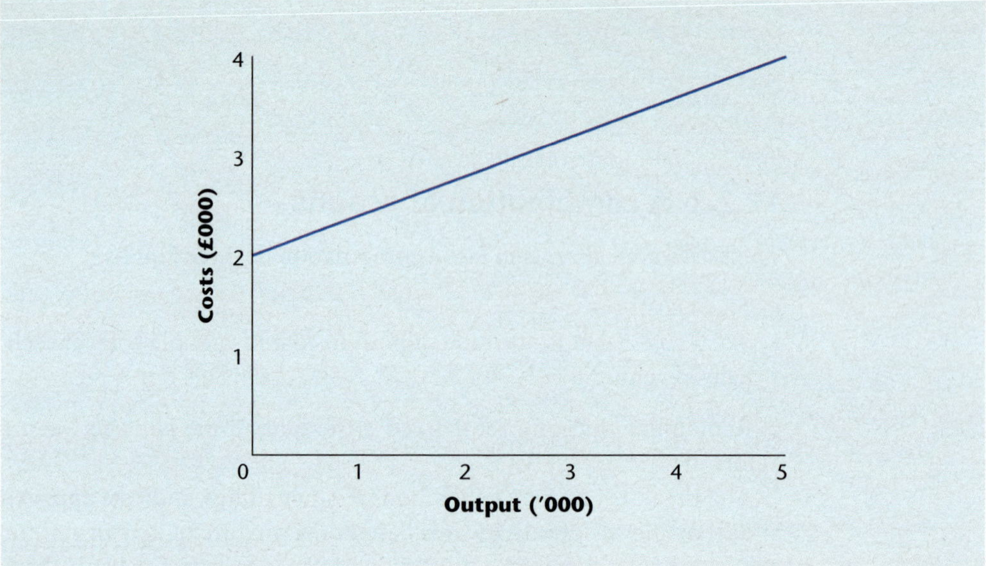

Figure 12.2 **Total costs (both fixed and variable)**

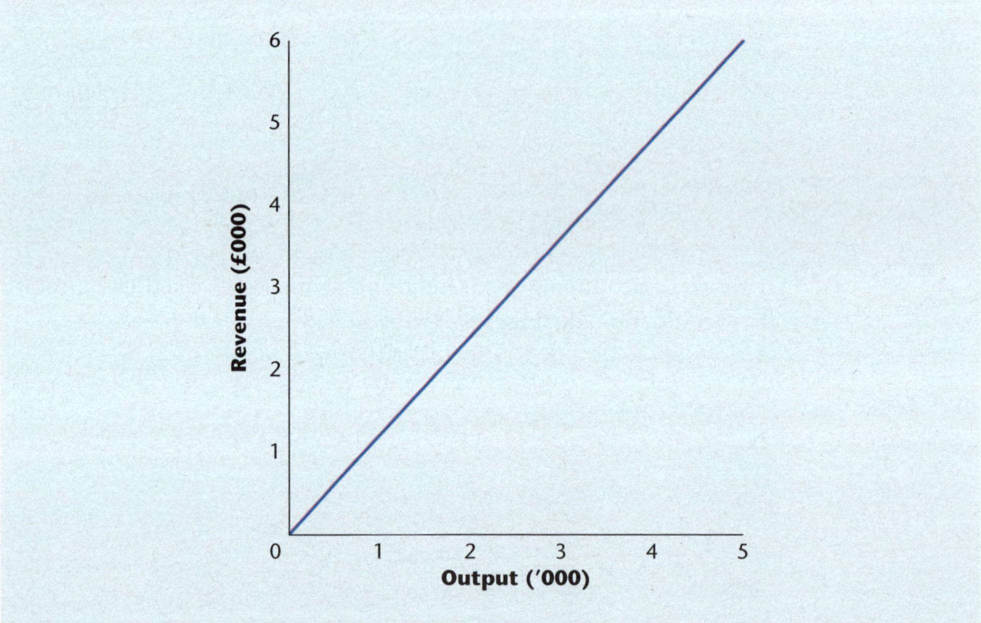

Figure 12.3 **Total sales revenue**

The break-even chart combines all three graphs, as shown in Figure 12.4:

12.2.2 Interpreting the chart

Having combined the three components (fixed costs, total costs and revenue) as shown in Figure 12.4, we can start to interpret the information, as shown in Figure 12.5.

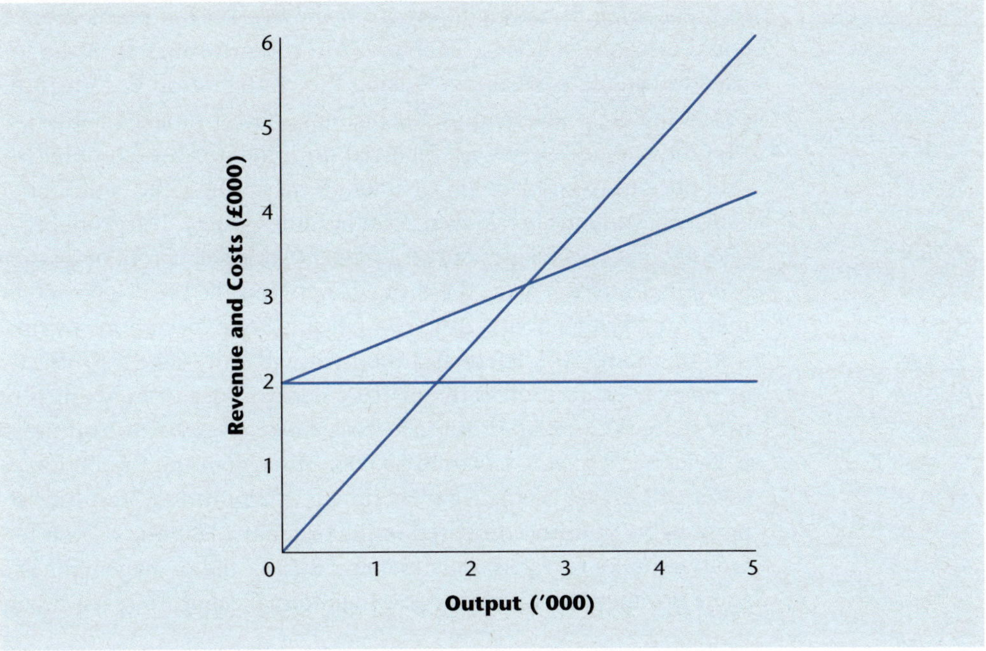

Figure 12.4 Information combined to form a break-even chart

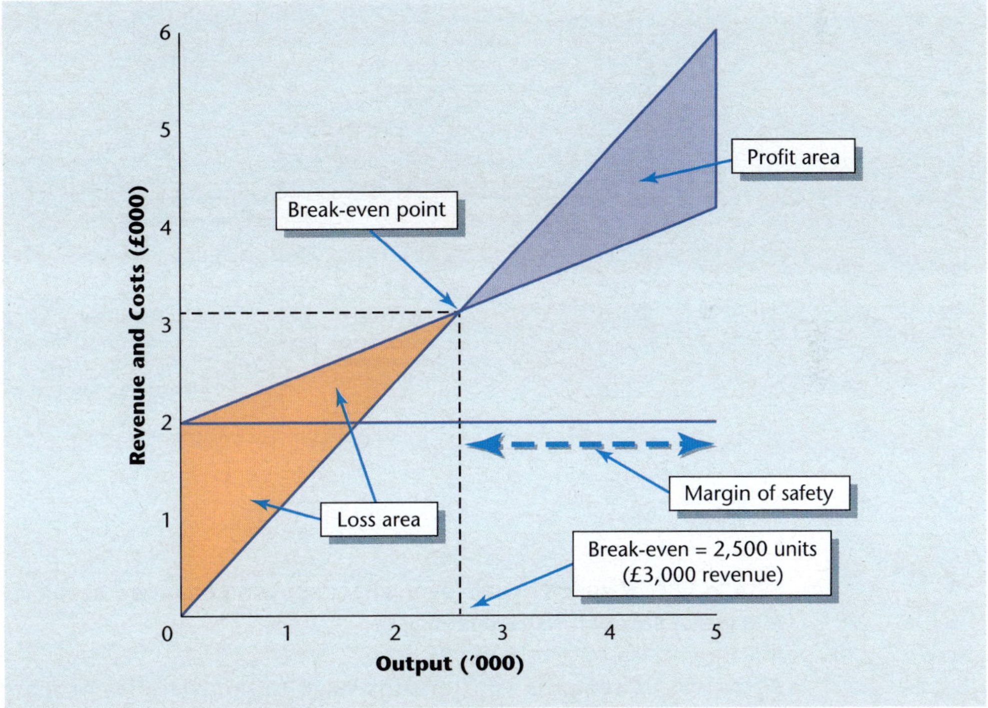

Figure 12.5 Interpretation of the break-even chart

The various elements of the break-even chart are as follows:

- *Break-even point*. This is where the sales line meets the total costs line, i.e. where sales revenue exactly matches total costs and neither a profit nor a loss is made (2,500 units in Figure 12.5). We can determine the level of sales in units needed to break-even by taking a line from the break-even point down to the x-axis. (You could also refer back to Chapter 10 to remind yourself of the formulae that can be used to calculate break-even using the contribution per unit.) As soon as the level passes the break-even point, the business starts to make profit.

- *Profit/loss areas.* Losses are incurred until the break-even point is reached. After this, profit begins to be made (in Chapter 10 we saw how the contribution from each unit of activity beyond the break-even point becomes profit). The profit becomes greater as more sales are made. Managers can see at a glance the likely profit or loss at *any* level of activity.
- *Margin of safety.* This is the distance between the break-even point and the budgeted maximum sales activity. Sales can fall short of expectations by up to (but not exceeding) the margin of safety and the firm will still make a profit. It is called a margin of *safety* because it gives the management an idea of how much remaining opportunity there is to make profit if forecasts proved to be overoptimistic. For example, if Berwick plc's fixed costs total £3,000 rather than the £2,000 forecast, the break-even point will 'travel' to the right, as shown in Figure 12.6, resulting in a new break-even point of 3,750 units compared to the original 2,500 units. Even though the margin of safety reduces to 1,250 units (5,000 – 3,750), the management knows that it still has some production available with which to make a profit (even though a reduced one).

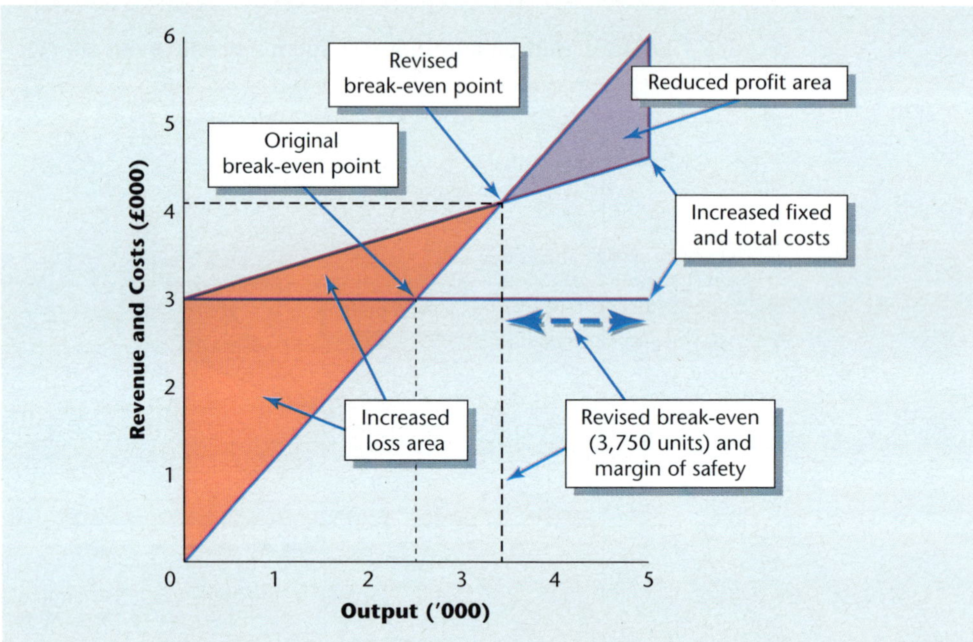

Figure 12.6 Revised break-even chart showing changed break-even point and margin of safety if fixed costs rise.

Activity 12.2 requires you to think back to your studies of marginal costing (see Chapter 10) and then prepare a break-even chart.

Activity 12.2

Appy Daze Ltd has produced a smart phone application (app) that enables users to test their blood pressure by holding their phones to their ears. The company's fixed costs, which include the development of the app, total £30,000. Users pay 50p to download the app, of which Appy Daze Ltd receives 35p after deducting the phone manufacturer's commission. There are no variable costs other than the commission.

During 2013 it expects that potential maximum downloads could be 200,000.

(a) Calculate by formula the number of downloads that must be made for the company to break even. (Hint: use the formula Fixed Costs divided by Contribution per download.)
(b) Calculate by formula the company's likely profit or loss if only 60,000 downloads are paid for. (Hint: use the formula Total contribution − Fixed costs)
(c) Calculate by formula the number of downloads that would have to be made for Appy Daze Ltd to make a profit of £50,000. (Hint: use the formula ([Fixed Costs + £50,000]/Contribution per download.)
(d) A local medical supplies company, Healthy Heart plc, has asked Appy Daze Ltd to create a variation of the blood pressure app to incorporate an advert for Healthy Heart. The extra cost to Appy Daze Ltd of creating the app would be £5,000, which would *not* be reimbursed by Healthy Heart. Users would pay only 40p to download this version of the app, and Appy Daze would receive 30p after commission from each download. Healthy Heart would pay Appy Daze Ltd 20p for every user of the modified app who clicks through to Healthy Heart's website. It is estimated that 40,000 downloads of this app will be made, and half of this total will click through to Healthy Heart's website. Advise Appy Daze Ltd (using appropriate formulae) whether they should accept the contract from Healthy Heart plc.

(Hint: calculate the total *extra* contribution generated from this app and compare it to the *additional* fixed costs).

(e) Show the information relating to the 'original' app (i.e. excluding the Healthy Heart contract) in the form of a break-even chart.

Answer

Preliminary calculation of the contribution per download:

	p
Price per download before commission	50
Less Variable costs per download (50p − 35 p)	15
Contribution per download	35

(a) To break even, the total contribution must exactly equal fixed costs. Fixed costs are £30,000 and the contribution per download is 35p, therefore the break-even point is £30,000/35p = **85,714 downloads.**
(b) If there are only 60,000 downloads, total contribution = 60,000 × 35p = £21,000. Fixed costs are £30,000, therefore the **loss** will be £30,000 − £21,000 = **£9,000.**
(c) To make a profit of £50,000, the total contribution (Profit + Fixed costs) would need to be £50,000 + £30,000 = £80,000. As the contribution per download is 35p, the number of downloads needed is £80,000/35p = **228,571**. As the maximum forecast downloads is only 200,000, this target profit is not achievable.
(d) The decision whether or not to accept the contract from Healthy Heart is based on whether it will make a positive contribution and an increased profit. The contribution per download for this app will be as follows:

	p
Price per download before commission	40
Less Variable costs per download (40p −30p)	10
Contribution per download	30

Expected downloads total 40,000, so the contribution would be 40,000 × 30p = £12,000. Additionally, the revenue generated from the click-through income would be (½ × 40,000) × 20p = 20,000 × 20p = £4,000. Total expected additional contribution therefore is £12,000 + £4,000 = £16,000. Compare this with the additional fixed costs of £5,000, and it can be seen that Appy Daze Ltd would generate a **forecast additional profit** of £16,000 − £5,000 = **£11,000** if it accepted the contract.

(e) Break-even chart

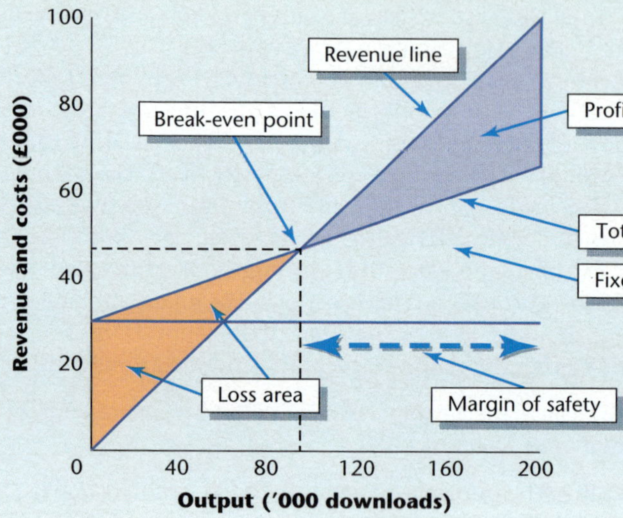

Figure 12.7 Break-even chart (Appy Daze Ltd)

Note: The *margin of safety* in Figure 12.7 indicates the number of units between the break-even point (approximately 85,000 downloads) and the maximum potential downloads (200,000 downloads). This informs management how much leeway they have if costs rise and the break-even point starts to 'travel' to the right along the total cost line.

12.2.3 Changes in costs and revenue

Clearly, if costs and revenue change, the position of the lines on the break-even chart will change, as will the break-even point and the profit/loss areas.

Activity 12.3

In each of the charts below, a change in the position of the lines is indicated. Assuming no other changes, state the effect the movement would have on profits.

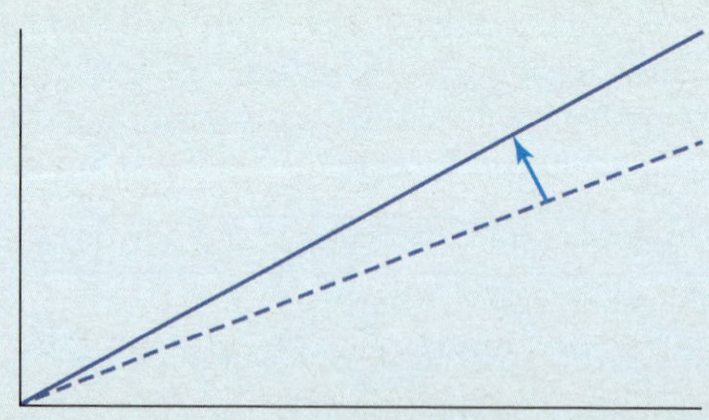

(a) Sales line

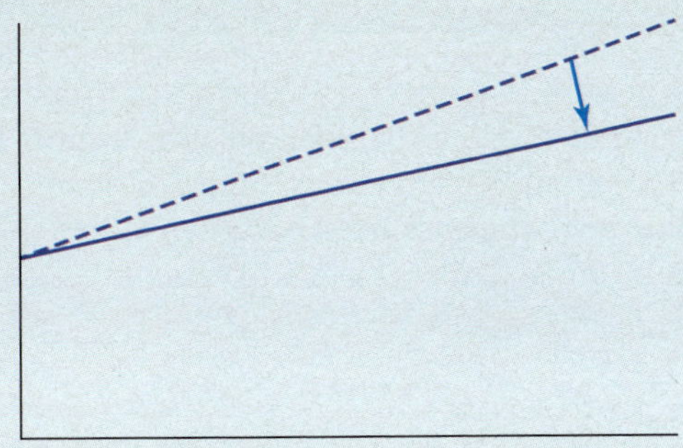

(b) Total costs line

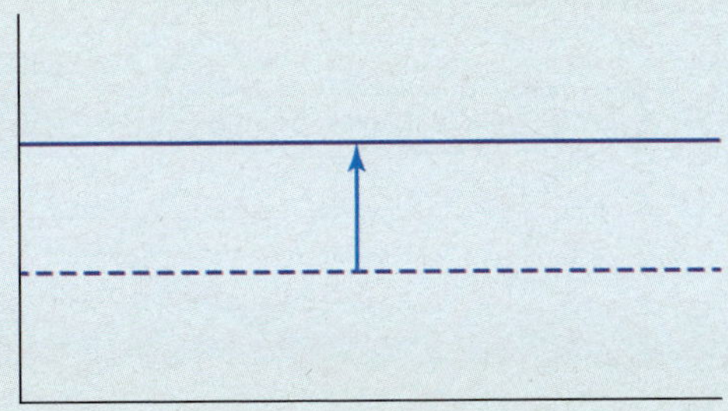

(c) Fixed costs line

Answer

(a) Increase in profits (greater sales revenue)
(b) Increase in profits (lower total costs)
(c) Decrease in profits (higher fixed costs)

12.2.4 Limitations of break-even charts

Although break-even charts have the advantage of providing a useful visual picture of a firm's predicted performance, they do have limitations, including the following:

- They are useful only in the short run where the assumptions hold true.
- The split between fixed and variable costs may have been made on inaccurate allocations
- In reality, the sales line may not be linear, as discounts may be given to encourage higher sales. For simplicity, such changes tend to be ignored when compiling the break-even chart.
- Variable costs may fall per unit, with higher production due to efficiency savings, bulk purchasing discounts, etc. Again, such changes tend to be ignored when compiling the break-even chart.
- Fixed costs may in fact change over time, so the line may need to rise in steps; for example, further factory space may have to be rented if sales output doubles.

Stop and think

An increase in fixed costs will cause a (hopefully) temporary reduction in profitability. For example, if Berwick plc (see section 12.2.1) decided to increase production to 10,000 units from the existing 5,000 units, but the only way it could achieve this would be to increase fixed costs by £1,000, the 'stepped-up' break-even chart (assuming unchanged sales prices and variable costs) would look like Figure 12.8.

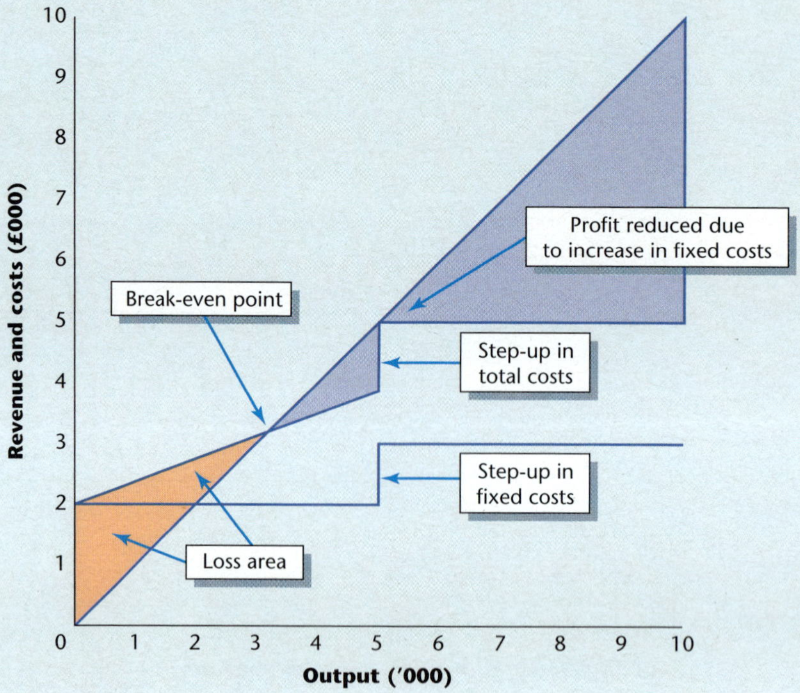

Figure 12.8 Stepped-up break-even chart

12.3 Profit/volume charts

A *profit/volume chart* (p/v chart) is a simplified version of the break-even chart, showing only the likely profit or loss at any given level of sales volume. It looks rather different because the *x*-axis splits the *y*-axis into 'profit' and 'loss' sections, as shown in Figure 12.9.

Only one line is plotted, which represents the profit or loss at each level of sales. The distance between this line and the *x*-axis represents either the total loss (below the line) or total profit (above the line). The point where the lines cross is the break-even point. To draw the line, any two coordinates can be plotted, for example:

- The fixed costs at zero activity
- The break-even point
- Total costs at maximum activity.

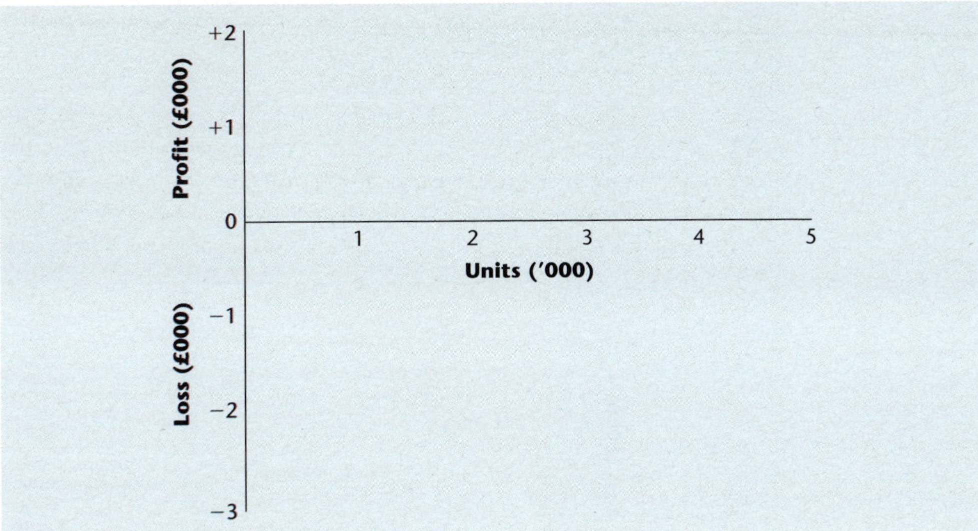

Figure 12.9 Profit/volume chart

The chart would then appear as shown in Figure 12.10 (using data from Berwick plc used earlier):

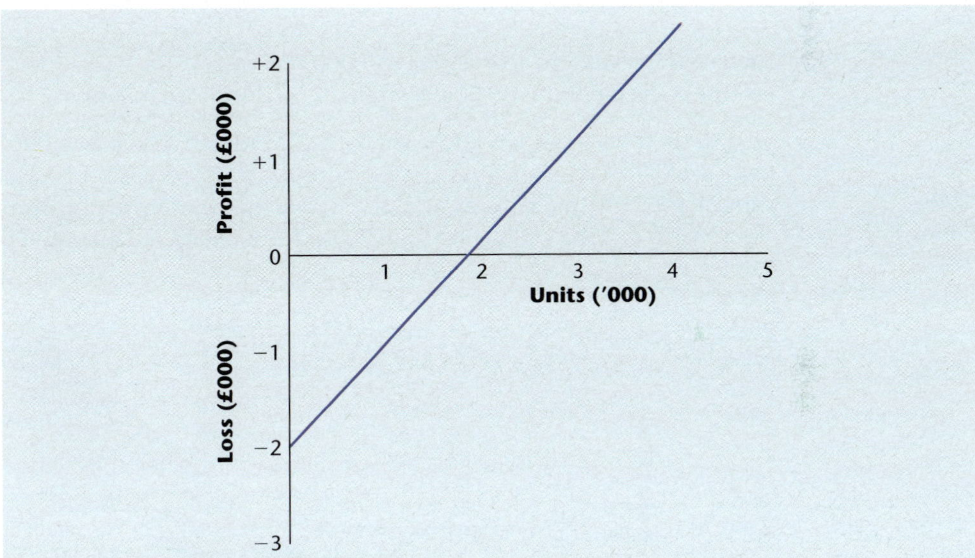

Figure 12.10 Profit/volume chart (using data from Berwick plc)

The information found within a profit/volume chart is shown in Figure 12.11.

Activity 12.4

Look back at Appy Daze Limited in Activity 12.2. Construct a profit/volume chart (without the Healthy Heart contract). Indicate the profit or loss if 120,000 apps are downloaded.

Answer

We can construct the p/v chart with two coordinates:

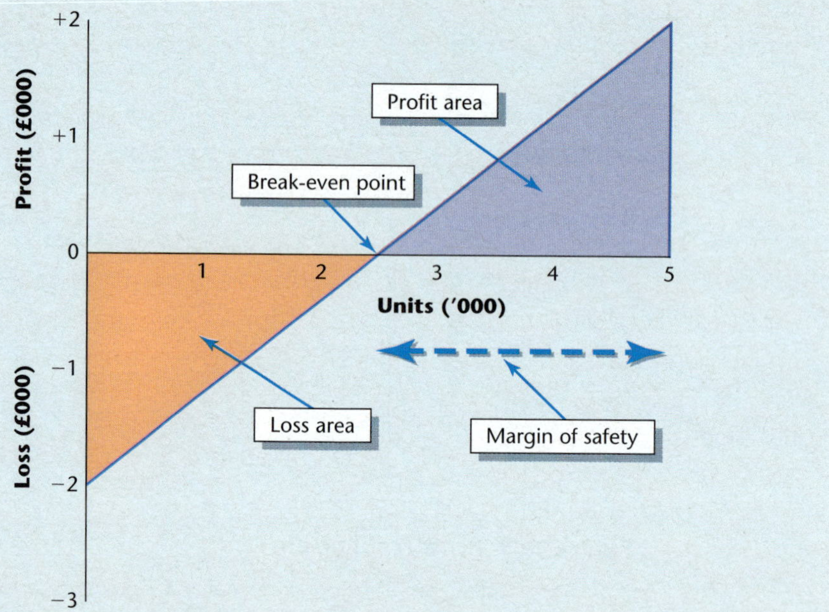

Figure 12.11 **Information within a profit/volume chart**

- Fixed costs at zero activity are £30,000
- Break-even point is 85,714 downloads (as calculated in Activity 12.2).

To draw the *x*-axis, we know that maximum activity is 200,000 downloads. For the *y*-axis, maximum loss if zero activity = fixed costs of £30,000, and maximum profit at maximum activity would be total contribution less fixed costs [(200,000 × 35p) − £30,000] = £70,000 − £30,000 = £40,000. The chart is shown in Figure 12.12.

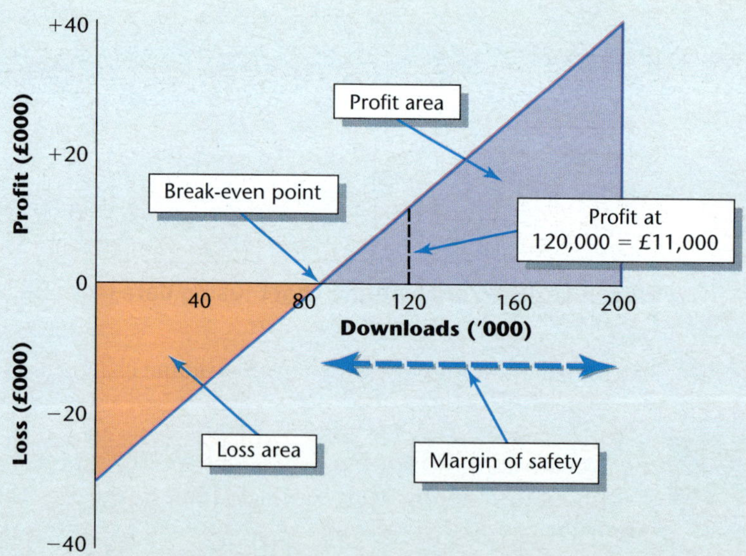

Figure 12.12 **Profit/volume chart – Appy Daze Ltd**

12.4 Summary

	Break-even charts	Profit/volume charts
y-axis (vertical)	Costs and revenue	Profits/losses
x-axis (horizontal)	Output	Output
Lines plotted	Sales, total costs, fixed costs	Profit/loss at all activity levels
Information available	Break-even point, costs and revenue at all activity levels, margin of safety, profit/loss areas	Break-even point, margin of safety, profit/loss areas
Advantages	Visual indication of potential performance. More information than profit/ volume chart	Simplicity – how much profit or loss at a specific activity level?
Disadvantages	Oversimplified information may lead to poor decisions	Limited information compared with the break-even chart

12.5 Chapter glossary

Break-even chart A graphical representation of the profits, losses, sales revenues and costs at any level of activity.

Profit/volume chart A graphical representation of profit or loss at any level of activity.

Stepped-up break-even chart A break-even chart showing increases in fixed and total costs due to such factors as additional premises to be rented due to required expansion.

Additional resources

Only accessible on Android-based devices

Now work through the various exercises and problems that you can find within the My Accounting Lab that are relevant to this chapter. Either use the QR code shown in the margin (if you use an Android-based device), or visit www.myaccountinglab.com for the log-in page.

Self-check questions

The answers to these questions are in Appendix 1

1 Which of the following *cannot* be seen on a break-even chart?

(a) Unsold inventory
(b) Fixed costs
(c) Variable costs
(d) Sales revenue

2 A break-even chart shows maximum unit sales at 300 at £500 each, maximum profit of £60,000, a break-even point of 100 units and a loss of £30,000 if no units are sold. What is the total of fixed costs?

(a) £150,000
(b) £90,000
(c) £30,000
(d) £60,000

3 Using the information given in question 2, what is the margin of safety?

(a) 600 units
(b) 100 units
(c) 300 units
(d) 200 units

4 Using the information given in question 2, what profit or loss would be earned if 150 units are sold?

(a) £75,000 profit
(b) £15,000 profit
(c) £30,000 profit
(d) £15,000 loss

5 Which one of the following is *not* a limitation of a break-even chart?

(a) Fixed costs may change over time, due, for example, to the need to rent additional premises as production increases
(b) The split between fixed and variable costs may not be clear-cut
(c) They are only useful in the short run when assumptions hold true
(d) The break-even point cannot be indicated on it

6 In a profit/volume chart, which one of the following is *not* a coordinate which could be plotted?

(a) Fixed costs at zero activity
(b) The break-even point
(c) Profit at maximum activity
(d) Variable costs at maximum activity

7 A company has maximum sales activity of 4,000 units, each with a contribution of £8. Its profit/volume chart shows a break-even point of 1,500 units and a maximum profit of £20,000. What are the total fixed costs of the company?

(a) £12,000
(b) £32,000
(c) £20,000
(d) £52,000

8 Using the information in question 7 above, how much profit would be made if 3,000 units are sold?

(a) £24,000
(b) £12,000
(c) £15,000
(d) £20,000

9 Using the information in question 7 above, what is the margin of safety for the company?

(a) 4,000 units
(b) 1,500 units
(c) 2,500 units
(d) 5,500 units

10 If the contribution per unit increases, the break-even point on a profit/volume chart will:

(a) Move to the right
(b) Be unchanged
(c) Move to the left
(d) Move downwards

Self-study questions

Questions marked with this symbol (#) indicate that the suggested answers are available to lecturers only – other answers are given in Appendix 2.

12.1 Indicate the following information on the outline break-even chart below:

- The break-even point
- The 'loss' area
- The margin of safety
- Fixed costs
- Total costs
- Sales
- The 'profit' area.

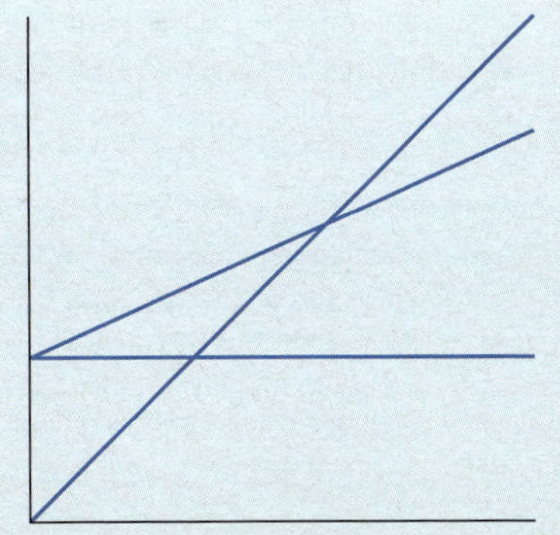

12.2# From the following information produce a break-even chart for Basil Limited:

Maximum sales and production (units)	10,000
Fixed costs (£)	18,000
Sales price per unit (£)	6
Variable cost per unit (£)	1.50

From the chart, answer the following questions:

(a) What is the break-even point in units?
(b) How much profit or loss is made if 6,000 units are sold?
(c) What is the margin of safety in units?

12.3 From the following information, prepare a profit/volume chart, and indicate the profit or loss if 6,000 units are sold:

Maximum sales (£15 contribution per unit)	10,000 units
Fixed costs	£60,000
Break-even point	4,000 units

12.4# Moolah Limited manufactures garden chairs. The company's management is preparing a budget for the next financial year and has prepared the following information:

	£
Selling price per garden chair	40
Materials per garden chair	15
Direct labour per garden chair	10
Overheads: variable per garden chair	5
Fixed overheads (total) £60,000 p.a.	

The company is planning to manufacture 12,000 garden chairs in the next year.

(a) Prepare a break-even chart showing the above information. Indicate on the chart:
  (i) The break-even point
  (ii) The margin of safety
  (iii) The profit or loss if 10,000 garden chairs are manufactured and sold.

(b) Moolah Limited is considering whether to make a de-luxe chair, which would have the same costs as the 'ordinary chair' with the exception of an additional £5 per chair for quality upholstering. An advertising campaign costing £11,000 would also be needed. The selling price could be increased to £46 per chair. This order would be within the capacity of the company. Advise the company whether the 'de-luxe' chair should be manufactured.

12.5 Read this extract and then answer the questions that follow:

> Chase Distillery is extending its product range beyond potato vodka. Apple-based vodka and gin and marmalade-flavoured potato vodka have also started rolling off the production line at a plant which to date has produced just 1,000 bottles a week. Mr Chase admits this is just a 'drop in the ocean'. But the distillery is aiming to produce 4,000 bottles a week by the end of the year. Only the high margins offered by premium brands can justify £4 a litre production costs at his distillery, which compares with 30p a litre cost of cheaper rivals. The venture, which employs six full-time staff, lost £600,000 last year, but is scheduled to break even by next year. Mr Chase concedes the real trick to creating a spirits business ... is to increase exports, particularly to North America.

Source: Adapted from 'Tyrrells founder finds vodka goes down well with crisps' by Michael Kavanagh and Harriet Styles, *Financial Times*, 26 July 2010

(a) Assuming that Chase Distillery's annual fixed costs were equivalent to the amount lost on the venture last year plus £250,000 to promote the brand in North America, and that each litre of vodka produced will sell at £10, calculate by formula the number of litres that need to be sold to break even next year.

(b) Prepare a break-even chart showing the forecast information for next year. Assume that the distillery produces vodka at 4,000 litre bottles a week for 50 weeks of the year.

(c) Assume that you are advising Chase Distillery. Explain the significance of the margin of safety as shown on the break-even chart.

Case study — Chiquita's chart

Chiquita, the finance director of Machiq Limited (see previous case studies), had, prior to her mysterious disappearance, produced a break-even chart for the new product (the vanishing potion) that the company was considering making. The information she used was as follows:

Selling price per bottle of vanishing potion	£15
Variable costs per bottle	£6
Fixed costs relating to the bottling division	£20,000

Maximum production was set at 15,000 bottles.

Required

(a) Prepare a break-even chart based on the above information.
(b) Indicate on the chart the break-even point and the areas of profit and loss.
(c) Indicate on the chart the profit or loss if 12,000 bottles were sold.

Answers are in Appendix 3

Further research

Chase Distillery: www.chasedistillery.co.uk/

Chapter 13

Business planning

Objectives

When you have read this chapter you will be able to:

- Understand the uses and benefits of budgeting and business planning
- Understand the meaning and significance of limiting and key factors
- Appreciate the different types of budgets and their use in the business planning process

13.1 Introduction

You are getting towards the end of this book. You have been working hard and you need a break. An advert on a travel website tells you that you could fly to the Bahamas next week for a seven-day holiday for only £800. You decide to book the tickets and give your credit card details. After some minutes you get a pop-up message that your card limit has been exceeded and the booking can't proceed. You know that you are up to your bank overdraft limit and are in debt to friends and family and can't ask them for any further loans. Dreams of the Caribbean are replaced by the harsh reality that you're going to have to stay at home. If only you had budgeted! Businesses need to budget as well – and in this chapter we look at the budgeting and business planning process.

13.2 Long- and short-term planning

Good management involves reviewing not only past and current performance but also the consideration of what might happen to the business in the future. The introduction of new technology to speed up manufacture, the development of new products, increased competition in a particular sector or changes in consumer buying patterns are just some of the events that would be likely to have a significant impact on the future development of a business. Effective management should anticipate and plan the future direction of their businesses, not just react to situations after they have occurred.

Organisations will tend to have two types of plan: long-term and short-term:

1 **Long-term plans** set out the strategic objectives of the firm. They consider the general growth of the market, competition in the period, anticipated profit levels, strategic acquisitions and general economic factors such as trends in interest rates. Usually they are for a period of 3–5 years from the present time, but can be of any duration that management needs to direct its future policy.
2 **Short-term plans** (usually covering the next 12 months from the present time) detail the financial and organisational objectives compatible with the achievement of the long-term plan. This will be drawn up in far greater detail than the long-term plan and is referred to as 'the budget'.

Let's consider a detailed definition of a budget:

> A budget is a quantitative expression of a plan, for a defined period of time. It may include planned sales volumes and revenues; resource quantities, costs and expenses; assets, liabilities and cash flows.[1]

The budget is a plan for action and can be used to control and organise the business's activities. It can be used to delegate responsibility to departments and allow senior management to concentrate on investigating major deviations from the plan. This is called 'management by exception' (you might recall that a previous chapter on standard costing also referred to this) and enables managers to concentrate on those aspects of the business which have not performed as planned (having performed either better or worse). At the end of the budget period, the plan is evaluated and divisional performance appraised against the agreed objectives and targets.

It should be understood that a firm may have many different plans in force at the same time, for example:

[1]CIMA official terminology.

- Plans to improve the quality of the product or service
- Plans to improve employee relations
- Plans to increase market share
- Plans to maximise the benefits of research and development.

The nature of each plan will largely depend on the subject matter – plans relating to product design will be in technical rather than monetary terms; plans to improve employee welfare will be in the language of human relations. The financial budget will be in monetary terms, and this is what we concentrate on in this chapter.

13.3 Limiting factors

For all businesses, limiting factors will cause constraints in many areas, such as the availability of raw materials or the capacity of machinery. Where there is more than one constraint, the *key factor* is the most important limiting factor at any one time, and is the one which management needs to resolve before tackling the next one to emerge. Limiting factors are also referred to as *scarce resources* and act as constraints on the activities of the firm. They differ, obviously, from business to business but may include shortages of raw materials, lack of factory capacity, restricted storage space in warehouses and a lack of skilled labour in specific regions or countries. Often the difficulty of selling all that is produced by the business becomes the most crucial factor.

Activity 13.1

Match possible limiting factors on the left to the related business activity on the right:

(a) Shortage of skilled researchers	**1** Exporting
(b) Lack of overseas representatives	**2** Product development
(c) Worn-out machinery	**3** Increasing production

Answers

(a) 2, (b) 1, (c) 3

13.4 To budget or not to budget?

In small businesses, the budgeting process may be almost non-existent, with the owner only having a vague idea of where the business is heading. Often, particularly in troubled financial periods, day-to-day survival occupies all of the owner's time and effort, with an overwhelming focus on short-term cash flow. The owner may be *forced* to consider future performance if having to renegotiate bank loans, but very often this is not a formal process, merely a 'back of the envelope' prediction of likely income flows in the forthcoming year. Even for larger businesses, there is a growing movement away from the idea of long-term planning on the grounds that attempts to predict the future will always fail and may be counter-productive: particularly in fast moving technology-driven environments. However, the majority of financial commentators would argue that *every* business needs some sort of plan, even if it has to be adapted and updated at regular intervals. Read the following 'News clip' for both sides of this argument.

News clip

When there's no Plan A

FT

By Jonathan Moules

Former US president Dwight Eisenhower famously quipped that all plans were useless, but planning was indispensable. He was talking about war. However, it is a sentiment that also applies to business-building, according to several entrepreneurs – especially in the fast-moving world of the 21st century. Dan Scarfe, chief executive of Windsor-based software development company Dot Net Solutions, boasts that he has never written a business plan for the company he founded in 2004. Now, it is one of Microsoft's five key partners in the UK and a leading player in the hot new area of cloud computing – and to Scarfe, that is proof that setting fixed objectives is a complete waste of time. "Writing software, or starting a new business, is incredibly difficult to plan for," he says. "You're effectively trying to second guess exactly what you may want down the line, based on marketing conditions and varying customer demand." Twitter, Facebook and cloud computing were not even concepts six years ago, Scarfe notes, so there would be no way he could have planned for them.

Ian Sanders, author of *Unplan Your Business*, claims that the notion of long-term planning is broken – so entrepreneurs need to trust their instincts. "We think that, by creating a plan for executing our ideas, somehow it will guarantee its success, or at least spot the potential problems," he says. "But let's be honest. We also plan because we're told that's what entrepreneurs, department heads and CEOs do."

David Hieatt, co-founder of Howies, the ethical clothing manufacturer based in Cardigan, claims that a business plan is really just a guess or a hunch. "There are some brilliant business plans written but they fail because the customer wants to do business differently," he says. "The awful truth is we don't know what will work." He claims that the secret is to be nimble – although this often takes a lot of guts. For example, in 2001, Hieatt phoned up all of Howies' retailers and said he was going to introduce organic cotton. The initial effect of this spur-of-the-moment act was disastrous. "We lost all our wholesale accounts overnight because they said nobody would pay £27 for a T-shirt," he recalls. Hieatt and his colleagues managed to rescue the situation by launching a catalogue to sell products. It proved to be a turning point for Howies. Now, the company sells 80 per cent of its products through this medium. "Losing all your shop accounts in one day is not great for business, but it's probably the best thing we did," Hieatt concludes.

Others argue that business planning is often a reason for inaction. Rajeeb Dey claims that he would have never started Enternships – a student internship matching service – if he had had to perfect his plan in a written document. "I never wrote a business plan for Enternships, I just started it," he says – although he admits that it is easier for internet-based businesses to do this.

Gary Vaynerchuk is another opponent of business plans. In 1997, he inherited a wine retail business in Springfield, New Jersey, with 4,000 square feet of space, a $3m (£2.6m, €2.4m) turnover and seven staff. He put the business online and has not looked back. "I just jumped in with no game plan, but lived it every day," Vaynerchuk says.

Wine Library turns over in excess of $60m, employs 100 people and has a spin-off video blog that is watched, according to Vaynerchuk, by 100,000 people. He says he is constantly planning, but the process is going on in his head and not on paper. This is the reason why Wine Library started accepting e-mail orders when its competitors were still using fax machines, Vaynerchek says.

Perhaps unsurprisingly, Vaynerchuk, Dey and Scarfe have all entirely self-financed their businesses. Venture capitalists and private investors do not usually approve of this cavalier attitude to planning.

To Paul Maron-Smith, managing director of Gresham Private Equity, a business plan is rather like a car's dashboard, guiding the entrepreneur along the road to success. But even he admits that problems can arise when business plans become too rigid. "The aim of a business plan is to give the stakeholders a good idea of where the business is heading," he says. "Sure, there are going to be assumptions in there that are not going to be accurate, but they are a best guess at the time."

Verne Harnish, founder of the Entrepreneurs' Organisation – a networking group of more than 7,300 entrepreneurs in 42 countries – continues the motoring analogy to analyse the likes of Scarfe. "Just like you can find people who have escaped unharmed from a motorcycle crash without wearing a helmet, you can always find someone who has succeeded without a plan," he says. "It's just the odds aren't in your favour."

This view is backed up by research by Andrew Burke, director of the entrepreneurship centre at Cranfield University. He studied a group of 422 British start-ups over a three-year period, split between those that did use business plans and those that didn't. He found that those with a business plan grew almost one-third faster in employment terms and were considerably larger than those without a business plan. However, even he admits that it is not as simple as saying that the business plan was essential. Success is also a matter of how you come to your plans and how you implement them.

"If you look at the successful new ventures, what they typically do is test the product in the market first," Burke says. "The pilot launch is also the market research that goes into the business plan."

Source: The Financial Times, 22 May 2010

For the majority of larger firms, however, budgeting is a very formal process involving many employees, only a handful of whom might be accountants. Figure 13.1 shows a typical budgeting process in such a company.

13.5 Preparing a budget

If sales are the limiting factor then budgets will be prepared by working from the sales budget. If the firm can estimate how many units of each product it can sell month by month then it can work back from this figure to estimate production and inventory levels. If more is produced than can be sold, inventory will increase, but if sales exceed production, inventories decline. Once the monthly production is estimated, further estimations can be made of plant requirements, materials, labour and overheads.

If productive capacity is the limiting factor, the sales budget will be determined by output, as will the materials and labour budgets.

Activity 13.2

Preparing a sales budget

Kumquat plc has four products: Limbards, Mintons, Nestrals and Obloids. Sales (the limiting factor) in January are expected to total 8,000 units, in the ratio 5:4:3:2 respectively. Sales in each month from February to April are expected to grow at 5% per month for each product, except Mintons which will grow by only 3% per month.

Set out in tabular form the forecast sales in units for each product in each of the four months, January to April. Work to the nearest whole number.

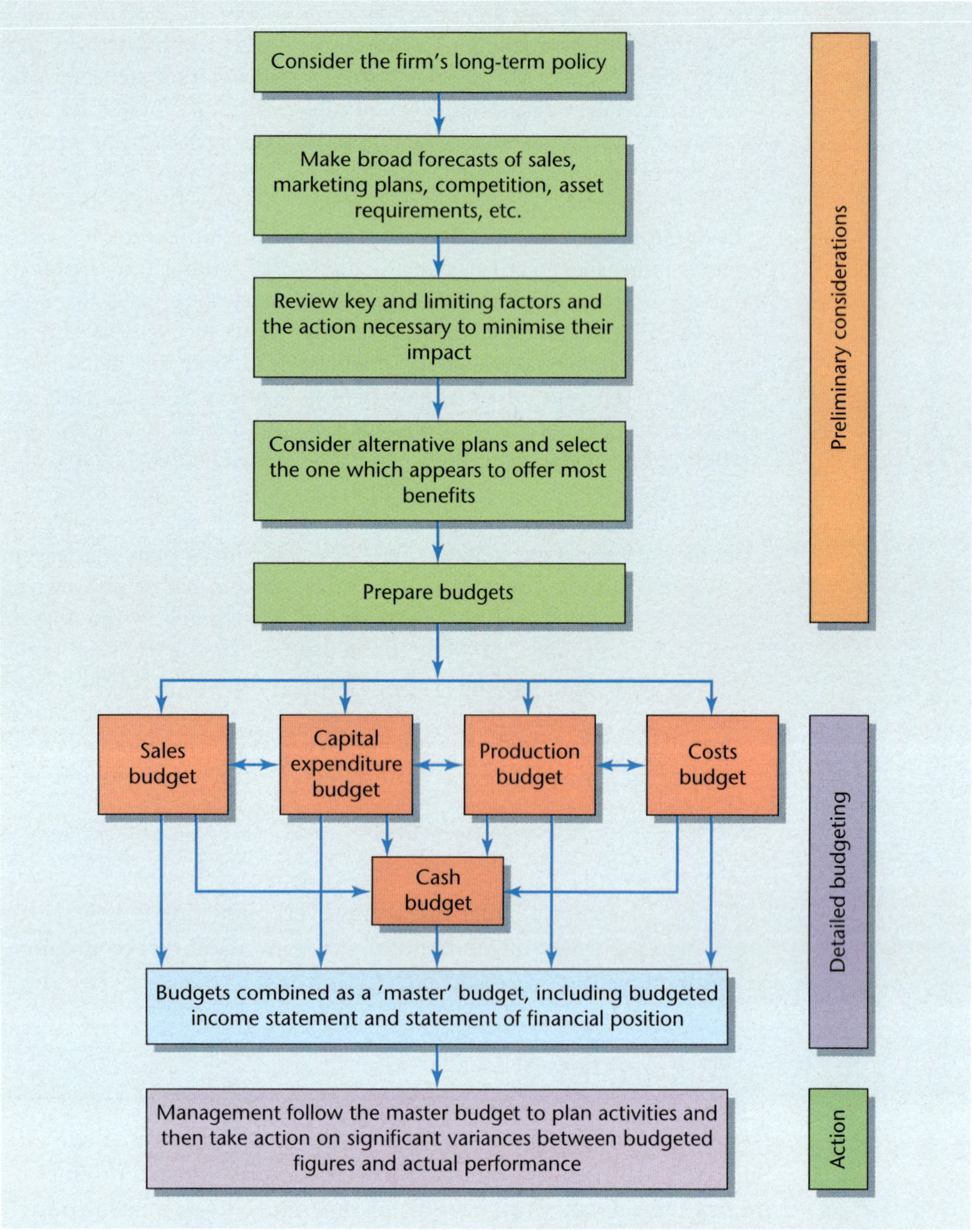

Figure 13.1 Typical budgeting process in a large company

Answer

Sales budget (units)

	January	February	March	April
Limbards	2,857	3,000	3,150	3,308
Mintons	2,286	2,355	2,426	2,499
Nestrals	1,714	1,800	1,890	1,985

	January	February	March	April
Obloids	1,143	1,200	1,260	1,323
	8,000	8,355	8,726	9,115

Workings:

	January		February		March		April	
Limbards	(5/14 × 8,000)	2,857	(Jan + 5%)	3,000	(Feb + 5%)	3,150	(Mar + 5%)	3,308
Mintons	(4/14 × 8,000)	2,286	(Jan + 3%)	2,355	(Feb + 3%)	2,426	(Mar + 3%)	2,499
Nestrals	(3/14 × 8,000)	1,714	(Jan + 5%)	1,800	(Feb + 5%)	1,890	(Mar + 5%)	1,985
Obloids	(2/14 × 8,000)	1,143	(Jan + 5%)	1,200	(Feb + %)	1,260	(Mar + 5%)	1,323
		8,000		8,355		8,726		9,115

Activity 13.3

Preparing a materials purchases budget

Kumquat plc (see Activity 13.2) uses two basic raw materials – Dructose and Zitamint – to make its products. Ingredients are mixed in the following quantities to make one unit of each product:

	Dructose kg	Zitamint kg
Limbards	2	2
Mintons	2	1
Nestrals	3	1
Obloids	1	1

Sales in January are forecast as follows:

	Units
Limbards	2,857
Mintons	2,286
Nestrals	1,714
Obloids	1,143

Opening inventories of each raw material at 1 January are Dructose 5,000 kg, Zitamint 4,000 kg. Losses by evaporation in a month are equivalent to 10% of opening inventory levels. Each kilogram of Dructose costs £6 and each kilogram of Zitamint costs £4.

Show a materials purchase budget for January only, on the assumption that opening and closing inventory levels are to be identical, and that there will be no opening inventories of completed units at 1 January.

Answer

Materials purchases budget

January	Sales/ Materials	Dructose	Sales/ Materials	Zitamint
Limbards	2,857 × 2	5,714	2,857 × 2	5,714
Mintons	2,286 × 2	4,572	2,286 × 1	2,286
Nestrals	1,714 × 3	5,142	1,714 × 1	1,714
Obloids	1,143 × 1	1,143	1,143 × 1	1,143
Total (kg)		16,571		10,857
Opening inventory	5,000		4,000	
Less evaporation (10%)	(500)	4,500	(400)	3,600
		12,071		7,257
Closing inventory level				
(same as opening inventory)		5,000		4,000
Materials to be purchased (kg)		17,071		11,257
Total materials cost (£)	@ £6	102,426	@ £4	45,028

13.6 The cash budget

We saw earlier (in Chapter 7) how important cash flow statements are when analysing a firm's performance. These are based on *past* activity, usually summarising inflows and outflows of the previous financial year. As part of the budgeting process, we need to *look ahead* as to what management thinks cash flows might be over the budget period. Detailed cash flow forecasts become part of the budgeting documentation and are vital for the planning process, in particular to:

- Ensure that sufficient cash is available when needed
- Reveal any expected cash shortage so that a loan, overdraft or other funding can be negotiated in good time
- Identify areas where payments can be delayed or inflows brought in earlier (for example, by offering cash discounts) to help cash flow
- Reveal cash surpluses which can be invested or utilised within the firm.

Figure 13.2 shows how a typical cash flow forecast might be presented. Notice the way in which the forecast data is shown on a month-by-month basis (though the time period can be adapted to whatever is relevant to the particular business), and blank columns marked 'Actual' have been provided so that, at the end of the month, the *real* cash inflows and outflows can be contrasted with those which were forecast. This then enables management to establish reasons for the circumstances where the actual performance is significantly different from what was thought likely to happen. The other point to note is how the opening forecast bank balance is adjusted by the forecast net cash flow for the month to arrive at the forecast closing bank balance, which is then transferred to the next

Cash flow forecast						
For the period from 1 January 2015 to 31 March 2015						
	Jan-15		Feb-15		Mar-15	
(£000s)	Forecast	Actual	Forecast	Actual	Forecast	Actual
Inflows						
Sales: cash	350		450		410	
Sales: invoices	1620		1200		2330	
Equity share sales	6000		0		0	
Other inflows	0		0		1000	
A: Total inflows	7970		1650		3740	
Outflows						
Purchases: invoices	2200		2000		2400	
Wages and salaries	2210		1800		2000	
Rent and rates	300		300		300	
Light, heat and power	250		260		270	
Insurance	40		0		0	
Packaging	50		45		60	
Transport	110		70		130	
Advertising	95		95		150	
Communications	30		30		40	
Professional fees	10		10		15	
Loan repayments	20		20		20	
Other	70		60		80	
B: Total outflows	5385		4690		5465	
C: Net cash flow (A - B)	2585		-3040		-1725	
D: Opening balance	65		2650		-390	
E: Closing balance (D ± C)	2650		-390		-2115	
Note: Agreed overdraft facility	0		2000		2000	

Management action needed as this would exceed agreed overdraft limit

Figure 13.2 **Cash flow forecast**

month to become the opening forecast bank balance. In the example, it is clear that, unless action is taken, the company's agreed overdraft facility will be exceeded in March 2015. Figure 13.3 shows the spreadsheet formulae used to arrive at Figure 13.2's calculations.

Activity 13.4

Preparing cash flow information

Kumquat plc (see Activities 13.2 and 13.3) allows its customers to pay in the month following sale, but pays its own suppliers two months after purchase. Relevant forecasts for January are as follows:

		Sales price per unit £
Forecast sales	**Units**	
Limbards	2,857	36
Mintons	2,286	24

	A	B	C	D	E	F	G
1	Cash flow forecast						
2	For the period from 1 January 2015 to						
3		Jan-15		Feb-15		Mar-15	
4	(£000s)	Forecast	Actual	Forecast	Actual	Forecast	Actual
5	**Inflows**						
6	Sales: cash	350		450		410	
7	Sales: invoices	1620		1200		2330	
8	Equity share sales	6000		0		0	
9	Other inflows	0		0		1000	
10	**A: Total inflows**	=SUM(B5:B9)		=SUM(D5:D9)		=SUM(F5:F9)	
11							
12	**Outflows**						
13	Purchases: invoices	2200		2000		2400	
14	Wages and salaries	2210		1800		2000	
15	Rent and rates	300		300		300	
16	Light, heat and power	250		260		270	
17	Insurance	40		0		0	
18	Packaging	50		45		60	
19	Transport	110		70		130	
20	Advertising	95		95		150	
21	Communications	30		30		40	
22	Professional fees	10		10		15	
23	Loan repayments	20		20		20	
24	Other	70		60		80	
25	**B: Total outflows**	=SUM(B13:B24)		=SUM(D13:D24)		=SUM(F13:F24)	
26							
27	**C: Net cash flow (A - B)**	=SUM(B10-B25)		=SUM(D10-D25)		=SUM(F10-F25)	
28	**D: Opening balance**	65		=SUM(B29)		=SUM(D29)	
29	**E: Closing balance (D ± C)**	=SUM(B27:B28)		=SUM(D27:D28)		=SUM(F27:F28)	
30							
31	Note: Agreed overdraft facility	0		2000		2000	

Figure 13.3 Spreadsheet formulae used to create cash flow forecast shown in Figure 13.2

		Sales price per unit £
Nestrals	1,714	40
Obloids	1,143	15

Forecast purchases	£
Dructose	102,426
Zitamint	45,028

What data relating to cash inflows or outflows will appear in Kumquat plc's cash forecasts relating to the above information?

Answer

Cash inflows from customers will appear in February's cash flow forecast (that is, one month after the sale is due to be made), as follows:

Limbards	2,857 × 36 =	102,852
Mintons	2,286 × 24 =	54,864

Nestrals	1,714 × 40 =	68,560
Obloids	1,143 × 15 =	17,145
Total		243,421

Cash outflows to suppliers totalling £147,454 (102,426 + 45,028) will appear in March's cash flow forecast (that is, two months after the purchase is due to be made).

13.7 Master budgets

When all the individual budgets have been completed, a master budget can be prepared. This is a compilation of the agreed subsidiary budgets (sales, production etc.) but also includes a set of forecast financial summaries (income statement, statement of financial position and cash flow statement) prepared for the full budget period. Usual accounting adjustments (accruals, prepayments, depreciation, etc.) are applied in the preparation of the budgeted income statement and statement of financial position, but of course it is all based on future *forecast information* rather than *actual historic data*. The master budget, as its name implies, acts as the guiding framework for the firm's future development.

13.8 Flexible budgeting

Even though the budgeting process within an enterprise might be extremely meticulous, it is virtually certain that the actual outcome of events will differ from what was planned and budgeted. The original budget that management sets is called a *fixed* budget – an informed view of future events based on a particular fixed level of activity. In order to cope with a (highly likely) situation where the actual level of activity differs from that in the original fixed budget, a variation of the original budget can be produced. This is known as a flexible (or *flexed*) budget, which shows the original budgeted figures, but adjusted, up or down as necessary, to reflect the actual level of activity. With our knowledge of the nature of costs, we should be aware that, as the level of activity changes, some costs (variable) will change whilst others (fixed) stay the same.

For example, look back at the materials purchases budget shown in Activity 13.3 above for Kumquat plc. The total materials cost budgeted for January was as follows:

Dructose	£102,426 (17,071 kg)
Zitamint	£45,028 (11,257 kg)
Total	£147,454

These totals were based on forecast sales in the same month of:

	Units
Limbards	2,857
Mintons	2,286
Nestrals	1,714
Obloids	1,143

These totals form the basis of the *fixed* budget, but when the actual performance for January is assessed by the management, the *actual* product sales may be very different from forecast, with a consequent variation in the amount of materials required. By preparing a flexed budget, management can come to a realistic assessment of performance. For example, assume that the budgeted costs of both Druktose and Zitamint for January comprised 10% fixed costs, with the remainder variable. A flexed budget for materials could then be prepared as follows (where 100% is the original fixed budget, with other percentages showing the effect of the greater or lesser level of activity):

	70%	80%	90%	100%	110%	120%	130%
Fixed costs	£14,745	£14,745	£14,745	£14,745	£14,745	£14,745	£14,745
Variable costs	£92,896	£106,167	£119,438	£132,709	£145,980	£159,251	£172,522
Total	£107,641	£120,912	£134,183	£147,454	£160,725	£173,996	£187,267

Activity 13.5

From the above flexed budget for Kumquat plc for January, if actual sales were 20% higher than forecast, and the actual material cost was £185,000, was the actual performance better or worse than budgeted?

Answer

The flexed budget shows that a 20% increase in the fixed budget should result in a total material cost of £173,996. The fact that the company actually paid £185,000 means that there was an adverse variance of £6,004 in January, so the performance was worse than that budgeted for.

13.9 Zero-based budgeting

Most budgets are produced by using the previous budget as the starting point. The danger of this is that management rarely undertakes an in-depth analysis of the financial requirements of specific departments or operations-they just rely on what has gone before and add a suitable percentage to allow for inflation. Zero-based budgeting adopts a different approach, by ignoring previous budgeting and, instead, starting from a blank sheet. Every department or operation that requires a budget is assessed in detail. Requirements are looked at objectively following detailed discussion with those affected. Although it has the advantage that a fresh appraisal is made each time the budget process is undertaken, it can be very time-consuming and therefore relatively expensive.

13.10 Summary

The key features of the budgeting process are shown in Figure 13.4.

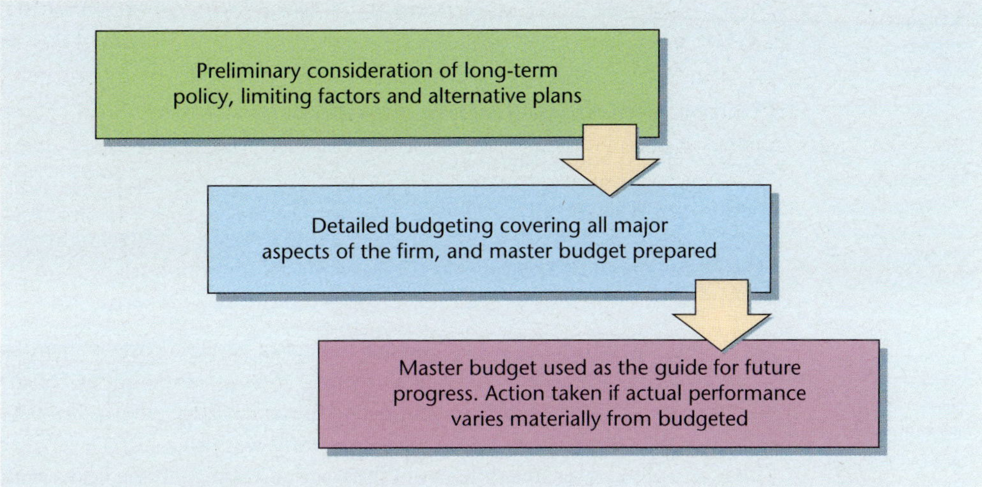

Figure 13.4 Summary

13.11 Chapter glossary

Budget A quantitative statement, for a defined period of time, prepared and agreed in advance, showing planned revenues, costs, assets, liabilities and cash flows.

Fixed budget The original budget used for comparison against actual performance.

Flexible (flexed) budget A budget showing the effect of differing levels of activity on costs.

Key factor The most pressing limiting factor at any one time.

Limiting factor Constraints on the growth of the firm.

Long-term plans Strategic objectives usually covering a period of 3–5 years from the present time, but can be of any duration that management needs to direct its future policy.

Master budget A compilation of the agreed subsidiary budgets (sales, production, etc.) including a set of forecast financial summaries (income statement, statement of financial position and cash flow statement) prepared for the full budget period.

Short-term plans Financial and organisational objectives over the next 12 months compatible with the long-term plan.

Zero-based budgeting This ignores previous budgeting and instead starts from a blank sheet. It gives the management the opportunity to thoroughly appraise the financial and other needs of each department or operation.

Additional resources

Only accessible on Android-based devices

Now work through the various exercises and problems that you can find within the My Accounting Lab that are relevant to this chapter. Either use the QR code shown in the margin (if you use an Android-based device), or visit www.myaccountinglab.com for the log-in page.

Self-check questions

The answers to these questions are in Appendix 1.

1 Zero-based budgeting:

(a) Ignores previous budgets
(b) Assumes zero inflation is to be added to last year's budget to arrive at this year's figures
(c) Uses previous budgets as the basis for the current budget
(d) Rounds all figures within the budget to the nearest zero.

2 A company produces a direct labour budget (a variable cost) for January, on the basis of an expected 5,000 hours working, showing a forecast wage bill of £60,000. The actual hours worked in January were 5,500 hours and the actual wage bill was £64,000. If the company also produced a flexed budget for January showing costs for a 110% level of activity, by how much did the actual wage bill differ from the wage cost shown in the flexed budget at that level?

(a) £4,000 adverse variance
(b) £2,000 adverse variance
(c) £2,000 favourable variance
(d) £6,000 favourable variance

3 Management by exception refers to:

(a) Management absences from work
(b) The investigation of major deviations from forecasts
(c) Exceptional management skills
(d) The preparation of the master budget

4 Which one of the following will be written mainly in financial terms?

(a) Plans for the product design
(b) Workforce requirements
(c) Planned changes to the way products will be marketed
(d) Bank borrowing requirements

5 Which one of the following would not be regarded as a limiting factor for a firm?

(a) The lack of ability of the managing director
(b) An unexpected order from an established customer
(c) A shortage of raw materials
(d) Insufficient power supplies to run machinery

6 A master budget is:

(a) Last year's budget to be used as the basis for this year's
(b) This year's actual results to be compared with the forecast results
(c) Only the cash budget, as that is the most important budget
(d) A compilation of the agreed subsidiary budgets and forecast income statement and statement of financial position

7 Ali plc has three products: K, L and M. Sales in January are expected to total 5,000 units, in the ratio 5:4:1 respectively. Sales are expected to grow at 10% per month for each product. What will be the sales of product L in March?

(a) 2,420
(b) 2,400
(c) 6,050
(d) 6,620

8 Using the information in question 7 above, if actual sales for product K in March are 2,904, what is the percentage variance from the budgeted sales for that month?

(a) − 4%
(b) + 20
(c) + 6
(d) − 25%

9 A company is preparing a cash flow forecast. In January it forecasts its net cash inflow as £90,000, but in February it forecasts a net cash outflow of £75,000. If it starts on 1 January with a bank overdraft of £50,000, what will be its forecast bank balance on 28 February?

(a) £115,000 (overdrawn) bank balance
(b) £35,000 (positive) bank balance
(c) £35,000 (overdrawn) bank balance
(d) £115,000 (positive) bank balance

10 A company is producing its forecast income statement. Which one of the following will *not* be taken into account when producing the information?

(a) Accruals
(b) Prepayments
(c) Cash flow
(d) Depreciation

Self-study questions

Questions marked with this symbol (#) indicate that the suggested answers are available to lecturers only – other answers are given in Appendix 2.

13.1 A manufacturing company makes a single product. The sales forecast for September is 11,800 units. Each unit uses 10 kg of material A and 6 kg of material B. Material A costs £6.50 per kg and B costs £9 per kg.

The anticipated inventory levels at the beginning and end of September are:

	1 September	30 September
Finished products	2,800 units	3,600 units
Unused material A	700 kg	500 kg
Unused material B	400 kg	900 kg

Produce the following budget figures for the month of September:

(a) Production of finished units
(b) Materials usage of A and B in kg
(c) Materials purchases of A and B in kg and £.

13.2 When preparing a budget, an organisation must first consider its limiting factors and key factor. Explain what you understand by the terms 'limiting factor' and 'key factor' and identify three constraints that could be a limiting factor in an organisation.

13.3 The following information relates to The Rural Art Gallery, which Gina Bruin has established to help rural craftspeople to sell their products to the tourist trade. Gina is submitting a business plan to Shire Bank plc. She has saved £4,000 as initial equity, which she would pay into the Gallery's bank account on 1 July 2015, which will be the effective starting date of the enterprise. Forecast information for the six months to 31 December 2015 is as follows:

- The landlord requires a deposit of £3,000, and rent of £1,000 per month, payable quarterly in arrears. The deposit will be paid on 1 July 2015, the first quarter's rent on 2 October 2015, the second quarter on 3 January 2016.
- Income will be generated from commissions on works of art sold through the gallery. The commission taken by the gallery will be 40%, and sales of artworks (before commission) are forecast as follows:

July	August	September	October	November	December
£8,000	£4,000	£7,000	£12,000	£18,000	£24,000

- All sales are for cash, and are banked immediately. Amounts due to artists are paid one month after the relevant sales are made.
- The Gallery will receive a one-off grant of £5,000 from the UK Tourist Board in August.
- The cost of redecorating the building will be £7,000, payable in two instalments: £4,000 in August, the balance in September.
- General overheads (including any bank interest payable) are expected to be £2,000 per month, payable one month in arrears.
- Wages to assistants will be £750 per month and are payable at the end of the month.
- Gina Bruin will draw £600 per month until December, when she will draw £900.
- Various items of equipment will be purchased for £3,000 in July, payable two months later. Depreciation for the six months will be £150.
- Initial advertising will cost £500, payable in August.

(a) Prepare a cash flow forecast (there is no need to include 'actual' columns) for The Rural Art Gallery for the six months to 31 December 2015.

(b) Comment on the forecast, and state whether you think that the project appears feasible.

13.4# Talbot plc manufactures car alarms, and its trading results for the year ended 31 October 2014 are as follows:

	£000	£000
Revenue (800,000 alarms)		7,200
Costs:		
Materials: direct, variable	1,600	
Labour: direct, variable	960	
Labour: indirect, fixed	280	
Other production overheads: variable	400	
Other production overheads: fixed	640	
Selling overheads: variable	480	

	£000	£000
Selling overheads: fixed	360	
Distribution overheads: variable	280	
Distribution overheads: fixed	120	
Administration overheads: fixed	600	
		(5,720)
Operating profit for the year		1,480

Talbot Ltd is planning next year's activity and its forecasts for the year ended 31 October 2015 are as follows:

1 A reduction in selling price per car alarm to £8 per alarm is expected to increase sales volume by 50%.
2 Materials costs per unit will remain unchanged, but 5% quantity discount will be obtained.
3 Hourly direct wage rates will increase by 10%, but labour efficiency will be unchanged.
4 Variable selling overheads will increase in total in line with the increase in sales revenue.
5 Variable production and distribution overheads will increase in line with the 50% increase in sales volume.
6 All fixed costs will increase by 25%.

(a) Prepare a budgeted profit statement for the year to 31 October 2015 showing total sales and marginal costs for the year and also contribution and net profit per unit.
(b) Calculate the break-even point for the two years and explain why the break-even point has changed. Comment on the margin of safety in both years.
(c) Calculate the sales volume required (using the new selling price) to achieve the same profit in 2015 as in 2014.
(d) A director comments that: 'With these figures, all we have to do to work out our budgeted profit is to multiply the net profit per unit by the units we want to sell.' Why is this statement incorrect?

Case study

Reappearance, followed by glowing and floating . . .

The directors of Machiq Limited (see previous case studies) staged a miraculous reappearance after vanishing at a product test organised by their arch business rival, Esmeralda (a.k.a. Mrs Eadale). Antidote had been sprayed liberally around the company's headquarters, and this had had the desired effect of neutralising the vanishing potion. Esmeralda also returned and, as an act of repentance, decided immediately to give up the business world and devote herself to charitable work.

Realising that the business had (almost literally) been left floating in thin air, the three directors, Marvin, Chiquita and Trixie, decided to plan ahead. In particular, they wanted to consider reopening a manufacturing division to make two products: Glow Gel and Floating Juice, both to be sold in 1 kg tubs.

They decided to produce a budget for the year ending 30 June 2017 relating to these two products. The following information is available:

- Both products use the same raw materials, Luminos and Schlepp. One kilo of Glow Gel uses 6 litres of Luminos and 8 litres of Schlepp. One kilo of Floating Juice uses 10 litres of Luminos and 4 litres of Schlepp.
- Forecast sales are 16,000 kg of Glow Gel and 12,000 kg of Floating Juice.
- The company plans to hold inventories of 1,200 kg of Glow Gel and 800 kg of Floating Juice on 30 June 2017, and at the same date forecasts inventories of raw materials as 15,200 litres of Luminos and 9,200 litres of Schlepp.
- Due to environmental factors beyond the company's control, it is forecast that there will be losses of items in store as follows:

Glow Gel	100 kg
Floating Juice	200 kg
Luminos	1,000 litres
Schlepp	400 litres

- The cost price of one litre of Luminos is £4, and one litre of Schlepp costs £2.50.

Required

Prepare a materials purchase budget for the two products for the year to 30 June 2017.

Answers are in Appendix 3

Further research

Business planning and budgeting software is available from a number of websites, including: **www.planware.org**
Scan the QR code with your QR reader to take you to the website of planware.org

Chapter 14

Investment appraisal

Objectives

When you have read this chapter you will be able to:

- Understand the term 'investment appraisal'
- Understand the meaning of the 'time value of money'
- Evaluate alternative projects using a variety of investment appraisal techniques, including net present value, internal rate of return and payback methods
- Appreciate the advantages and disadvantages of each method

14.1 Introduction

Businesses often have to make choices between different projects in which to invest. Many of these are for the long term, and represent significant strategic decisions. They might result in the future success or failure of the company. At their simplest, choices of investment may be made on subjective criteria. For example, if a company's car fleet manager knows how many cars are needed within a specific price range, the decision will probably be taken on the basis of the different build quality, specification and fuel consumptions of several car models. Once investment decisions become more complex, various techniques would be needed to assess them. What if the car fleet manager is faced with a bewildering choice of payment methods over differing time periods?

When deciding whether to commit finances to a long-term investment, the firm's management must consider the following:

- How costs, revenues and interest rates are likely to change over time.
- How technology is likely to develop.
- What risks the firm is prepared to take.
- What are the alternative opportunities for investment.

It is wrong to assume that a company will always choose to invest in the least expensive option available to it. For example, cheaper machinery may be of poorer quality and may demand greater maintenance than more costly equivalents. The process of evaluating capital projects and of estimating costs and revenues associated with them is known as *investment appraisal.*

14.2 Present values and future values

One of the basic concepts of investment appraisal is that of the *time value of money*, which, in simple terms, tells us that money received at a future date is worth less than the same amount of money received today. Conversely, money received today is worth more than the same amount of money receivable at a future date. The key reason for this is that money received today can be invested to accumulate interest, so that, for example, if £100 is invested for a year at 5% compound interest per annum, it will have grown to £105 at the end of the first year [£100 + (5% × £100)], £110.25 at the end of the second year [£105 + (5% × £105)], etc.

14.2.1 From present values to future values

When considering investment appraisal techniques, the initial £100 investment (from the previous example) would be referred to as a *present value*, whereas the amounts as

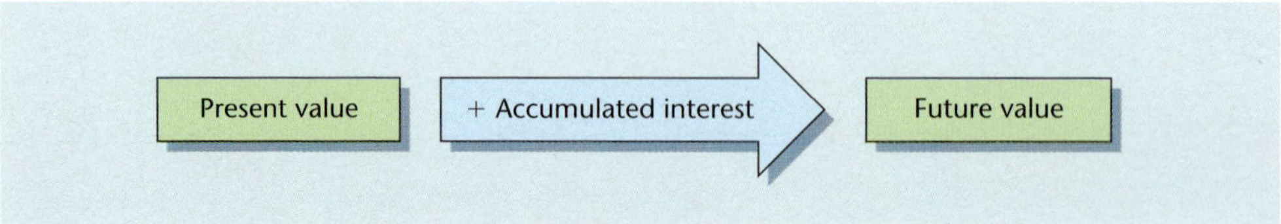

Figure 14.1 From present value to future value

increased by interest (£105 and £110.25) are referred to as *future values*. This change is shown diagrammatically in Figure 14.1.

Activity 14.1

Your employer gives you a bonus of £1,000 and you decide to invest it at 3% p.a. compound interest. What is the *present value* of the bonus, and what will be that bonus's *future value* in three years' time?

Answer

The present value is £1,000. The future value in three years' time is £1,091.89.

Workings:

	£
Initial value of gift (present value)	1,000.00
First year's interest at 3%	30.00
	1,030.00
Second year's interest at 3%	30.09
	1,060.09
Third year's interest at 3%	31.80
Value at the end of three years (future value)	1,091.89

14.2.2 From future values to present values

We have seen in section 14.2 how a present value of £100 invested at an interest rate of 5% p.a. has a future value of £105 in one year's time and £110.25 in two years' time. With this information, we can also say that if interest rates are 5% p.a., an investor can regard £105 receivable in one year's time as being equivalent to £100 now, or £110.25 receivable in two years' time as being equivalent to £100 now. This process of converting a future money value into a present value equivalent is referred to as *discounting*. It is shown diagrammatically in Figure 14.2.

To convert future values into present values, individual calculations could be made of accumulated interest which could then be deducted from the 'future' amounts. However, this could be very complicated when dealing with many different interest rates over many different time periods. To simplify the process, tables can be used that provide *discount factors*. These are decimals which, when applied to future values, convert them into present values. A discount factor table is shown in Figure 14.3.

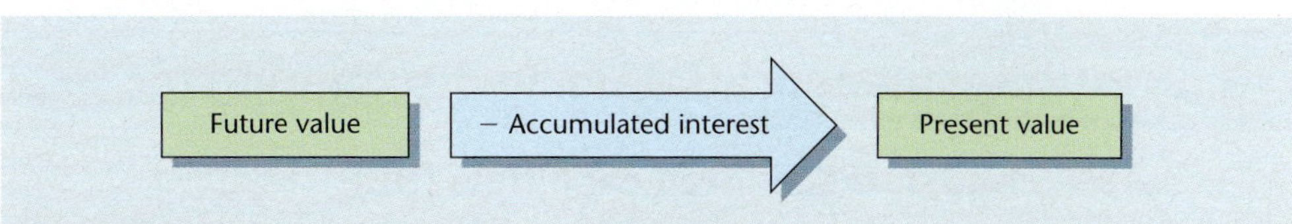

Figure 14.2 From future value to present value

	Interest rates									
Years	1%	2%	3%	4%	5%	6%	7%	8%	9%	10%
1	0.990	0.980	0.971	0.962	0.952	0.943	0.935	0.926	0.917	0.909
2	0.980	0.961	0.943	0.925	0.907	0.890	0.873	0.857	0.842	0.826
3	0.971	0.942	0.915	0.889	0.864	0.840	0.816	0.794	0.772	0.751
4	0.961	0.924	0.888	0.855	0.823	0.792	0.763	0.735	0.708	0.683
5	0.951	0.906	0.863	0.822	0.784	0.747	0.713	0.681	0.650	0.621
6	0.942	0.888	0.837	0.790	0.746	0.705	0.666	0.630	0.596	0.564
7	0.933	0.871	0.813	0.760	0.711	0.665	0.623	0.583	0.547	0.513
8	0.923	0.853	0.789	0.731	0.677	0.627	0.582	0.540	0.502	0.467
9	0.914	0.837	0.766	0.703	0.645	0.592	0.544	0.500	0.460	0.424
10	0.905	0.820	0.744	0.676	0.614	0.558	0.508	0.463	0.422	0.386
11	0.896	0.804	0.722	0.650	0.585	0.527	0.475	0.429	0.388	0.350
12	0.887	0.788	0.701	0.625	0.557	0.497	0.444	0.397	0.356	0.319
13	0.879	0.773	0.681	0.601	0.530	0.469	0.415	0.368	0.326	0.290
14	0.870	0.758	0.661	0.577	0.505	0.442	0.388	0.340	0.299	0.263
15	0.861	0.743	0.642	0.555	0.481	0.417	0.362	0.315	0.275	0.239

Figure 14.3 Discount factor table

Activity 14.2

Using the discount factor table, convert the following future values into present values:

(a) £5,000 receivable in 11 years' time (8% interest rate)
(b) £3,000 receivable in 4 years' time (5% interest rate)
(c) £10,000 receivable in 1 year's time (10% interest rate)
(d) £1,000 receivable in 2 years' time (7% interest rate)

Answer

The present values are:

(a) £2,145 (£5,000 × 0.429)
(b) £2,469 (£3,000 × 0.823)
(c) £9,090 (£10,000 × 0.909)
(d) £873 (£1,000 × 0.873)

Note that, in all cases, the present value is a lower amount than the future value, and the greater the interest rate and the longer the time period, the smaller the present value will be.

14.3 Investment appraisal using discounting techniques

14.3.1 Discounted cash flow (DCF)

When a firm has a choice of projects in which to invest, a thorough evaluation would include not only the initial cost of the alternatives but also the future cash flows that each will generate over its life. For example, assume a company has a choice between two machines, A and B, each costing £100,000. Each machine has an estimated life of three years with no scrap value. Machine A is expected to generate yearly earnings of £30,000, £60,000 and £95,000, whereas machine B has estimated yearly earnings of £80,000, £65,000 and £35,000. If the machines are to be compared in terms of their earning power, it is not sufficient simply to choose Machine A on the basis of the total earnings (A = £185,000, B = £180,000), since we know that money received in the future is worth less than the same amount of money received now. In order to find each machine's *true* comparative value, the income flow must be converted into *present value* terms, a process known as 'discounting the cash flow'. Using the discount factor table in Figure 14.3, and assuming an interest rate of 8%, the discounted cash flow (DCF) calculations can be set out as follows:

Year	*Machine A*		*Machine B*	
	Future value × Discount factor	*Present value*	*Future value × Discount factor*	*Present value*
1	£30,000 × 0.926	27,780	£80,000 × 0.926	74,080
2	£60,000 × 0.857	51,420	£65,000 × 0.857	55,705
3	£95,000 × 0.794	75,430	£35,000 × 0.794	27,790
Discounted cash inflow		154,630		157,575

According to the calculations, machine B has a higher discounted cash inflow than machine A. Remember that the forecast *undiscounted* future cash flows for machine A were £5,000 higher than for machine B.

Did you know?

If managers are comparing projects with different degrees of risk, they might apply a higher discount rate to the riskier project as a way of making a more balanced assessment. For example, if Machine B in the example was using an untried technology, the interest rate used might be increased to 10% rather than the original 8%.

Another use for the DCF investment appraisal method arises when a firm is comparing future cash *outflows*. For example, there might be a choice of financing the purchase of two identical vehicles, C and D. Vehicle C can be bought with an initial deposit of £20,000 followed by two annual payments of £15,000 (total £50,000). Vehicle D can be purchased over a slightly longer period, with an initial deposit of £5,000 followed by four annual payments of £12,000 (total £53,000). Interest rates are 6% p.a. Using the discounted cash flow table (Figure 14.3), we can evaluate the two purchase methods, as follows:

Year	Vehicle C		Vehicle D	
	Future value × Discount factor	Present value	Future value × Discount factor	Present value
0		20,000		5,000
1	£15,000 × 0.943	14,145	£12,000 × 0.943	11,316
2	£15,000 × 0.890	13,350	£12,000 × 0.890	10,680
3			£12,000 × 0.840	10,080
4		———	£12,000 × 0.792	9,504
Discounted cash outflow		47,495		46,580

Vehicle D shows the *lowest* discounted cash outflow, so it appears that this vehicle's method of financing is preferable to that of vehicle C. Note that the initial deposits (shown as 'Year 0' in the above table) required at the start of the financing period are already 'present' values that do not require discounting.

Activity 14.3

Using the discounted cash flow table (Figure 14.3), evaluate two identical projects, E and F, each of which require the payment of an initial deposit of £10,000. Project E is financed by three equal annual instalments of £30,000; project F is financed by two equal annual instalments of £45,000. Assume a 5% p.a. interest rate.

Answer

Year	Project E		Project F	
	Future value × Discount factor	Present value	Future value × Discount factor	Present value
0		10,000		10,000
1	£30,000 × 0.952	28,560	£45,000 × 0.952	42,840
2	£30,000 × 0.907	27,210	£45,000 × 0.907	40,815
3	£30,000 × 0.864	25,920		———
Discounted cash outflow		91,690		93,655

As project E has the lower discounted cash outflow, this would appear to be preferable to project F.

14.3.2 Net present value (NPV)

In addition to using the DCF investment appraisal technique to evaluate projects that have *either* cash inflows or cash outflows, there are many situations where there is a mixture of inflows and outflows that have to be considered. For example, a firm might be considering a new project (G) that requires an initial payment of £100,000, followed by a further payment one year later of £50,000. The project is forecast to generate three annual cash inflows at the end of years 2, 3 and 4 of £60,000 each, and at the end of the project (end of year 4) assets related to the project are expected to be sold for £30,000.

Assume a 9% p.a. interest rate. To evaluate this project we use the DCF technique seen earlier to convert future cash outflows to present values, but we also factor in the present values of the cash inflows to arrive at the *net present value* (NPV), as follows (cash outflows are shown in brackets):

Year	*Future value × Discount factor*	*Present value*
0		(100,000)
1	(£50,000) × 0.917	(45,850)
2	£60,000 × 0.842	50,520
3	£60,000 × 0.772	46,320
4	£60,000 × 0.708	42,480
	£30,000 × 0.708	21,240
	NPV	+ 14,710

The project is recording a *positive* NPV of £14,710 (discounted cash inflows exceed discounted cash outflows). When assessing an investment project, the general rule is that projects with a positive NPV are acceptable, those with negative NPVs are not. Projects with higher NPVs are preferable to those with lower NPVs.

Stop and think

A quick way of calculating the discounted value where the same future values are receivable (or payable) each year for several years is to add together the individual discount factors for each year and then multiply the 'annual' monetary amount by that one factor. For example, in project G above, we made three separate calculations to establish the present value of £60,000 received each year for three years (£50,520 + £46,320 + £42,480 = £139,320). We would have reached the same result if we had added the three factors (0.842 + 0.772 + 0.708 = 2.322) and multiplied the result by £60,000 (£60,000 × 2.322 = £139,320).

Activity 14.4

A firm has the choice of three machines, H, I or J, but it can afford only one. Interest rates are 10% p.a. Machine H costs £10,000; machine I costs £13,000; machine J costs £15,000. Forecast cash inflows are as follows (£):

Year	H	I	J
1	3,000	4,000	5,500
2	4,000	6,000	6,500
3	5,000	7,000	8,200

Calculate the NPV of each machine using the discount factor table (Figure 14.3).

Answer

The NPVs of the three machines can be calculated as follows:

Year	Discount factor	Machine H		Machine I		Machine J	
		Cash flow	Present value	Cash flow	Present value	Cash flow	Present value
0		(10,000)	(10,000)	(13,000)	(13,000)	(15,000)	(15,000)
1	0.909	3,000	2,727	4,000	3,636	5,500	5,000
2	0.826	4,000	3,304	6,000	4,956	6,500	5,369
3	0.751	5,000	3,755	7,000	5,257	8,200	6,158
NPV			− 214		+ 849		+ 1,527

Machine H has a negative NPV, so this would be unacceptable. Both of the other machines have a positive NPV, and since machine J's NPV is greater than that of machine I, machine J would be chosen.

14.3.3 Internal rate of return (IRR)

When we found the net present value for machines H, I and J in the previous activity, we used an interest rate – known as the *cost of capital* or *discount rate* – of 10%. Machine H's NPV was negative but machines I and J's were positive. Another method of comparing alternative projects is to establish the *specific* discount rate that, if applied to the cash flows relating to that project, would reduce the NPV to zero. We call the rate of discount that makes NPV = 0 *the internal rate of return* (IRR), or 'yield' of the project. The IRRs of different projects can easily be compared against each other (the highest being preferred), and also against the firm's average cost of capital (see the 'Did you know?' box below). Projects that would earn a lower IRR than the cost of capital would be rejected in favour of those that earned an IRR in excess of the cost of capital.

The IRR is found by discounting the net cash flows at different rates – by trial and error – until the NPV is zero (or near to zero).

Activity 14.5

Project K costs £10,000 and has expected net annual cash flows of £3,000 at the end of year 1, £4,000 at the end of year 2 and £4,300 at the end of year 3. By a process of trial and error using interest rates of 5%, 6% and 7%, establish the internal rate of return for the project.

Answer

The IRR is 6%, as shown in the following table:

		5%		6%		7%	
Year	Net cash flows	Discount factor	Present values	Discount factor	Present values	Discount factor	Present values
	£		£		£		£
0	(10,000)		(10,000)		(10,000)		(10,000)
1	3,000	0.952	2,856	0.943	2,829	0.935	2,805
2	4,000	0.907	3,628	0.890	3,560	0.873	3,492
3	4,300	0.864	3,715	0.840	3,612	0.816	3,509
NPV			+ 199		+ 1		− 194

As the NPV at 6% is (almost) zero, the IRR for the project is said to be 6%. If the cost of capital is greater than 6%, then the project is unlikely to be worthwhile.

Did you know?

A firm's *cost of capital* depends on its sources of long-term finance and the returns expected by lenders and shareholders. For example, consider two separate companies A and B, both with total long-term investment of £1 million. A is financed only by ordinary share capital (shareholders expect a return of 10%), whilst B is financed by a combination of £400,000 ordinary share capital (also with a return of 10%) and £600,000 secured bonds on which it pays 5%. The cost of capital of Company A is obviously 10%, but Company B's cost of capital needs to be weighted between the equity capital and loan capital as follows:

Equity	400,000 @ 10%	= 40,000
Bond	600,000 @ 5%	= 30,000
	1,000,000	70,000

$$\text{Cost of capital} \quad \frac{70{,}000}{1{,}000{,}000} \times 100 = 7\%$$

It can be seen that Company B's weighted average cost of capital is less than Company A's.

If a new project required additional funding, then the cost of capital might be specific to that project. For example, if Company A required a long-term loan carrying a 6% interest rate in order to embark on a particular investment, then the discount factors for the project would be based on 6% rather than the previously calculated 10%.

14.3.4 Using spreadsheets to calculate NPV and IRR

Excel spreadsheet models can be used to calculate both NPV and IRR. For example, assume a project requires an initial investment of £40,000, followed by annual cash inflows of £17,000, £15,000, £12,000, £8,000 and £7,000. The cost of capital for the NPV calculation is 8%.

The data can be input as shown in Figure 14.4:

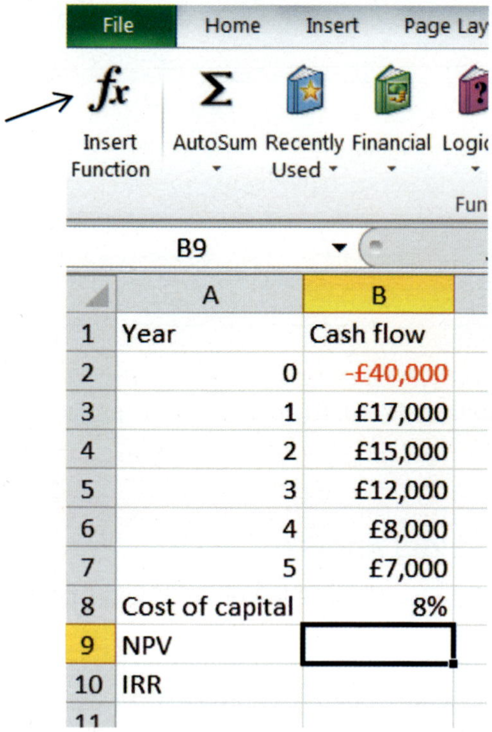

Figure 14.4 Input of data

After clicking the insert function button, the NPV formula can be found, as shown in Figure 14.5:

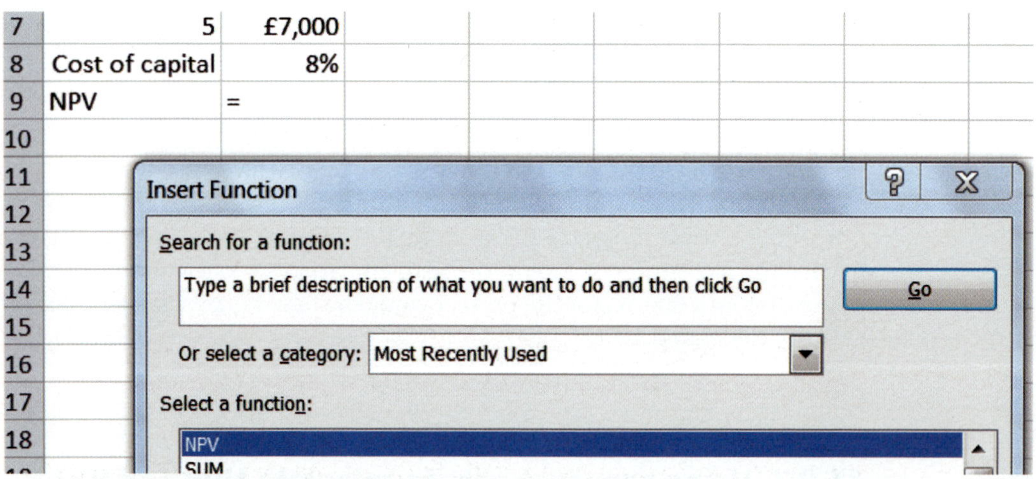

Figure 14.5 Selecting the NPV function

Data is then selected as shown in Figure 14.6:

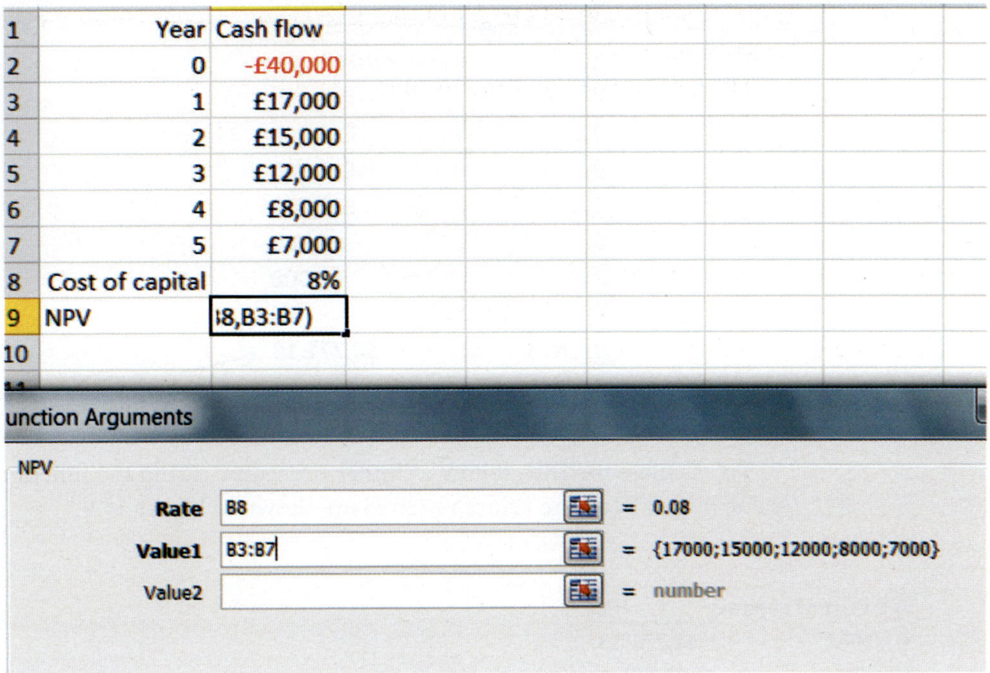

1	Year	Cash flow
2	0	-£40,000
3	1	£17,000
4	2	£15,000
5	3	£12,000
6	4	£8,000
7	5	£7,000
8	Cost of capital	8%
9	NPV	‡8,B3:B7)
10		

Figure 14.6 Inserting data into the function

The formula must be adjusted to include the initial investment (Cell B2 in this example), as shown in Figure 14.7:

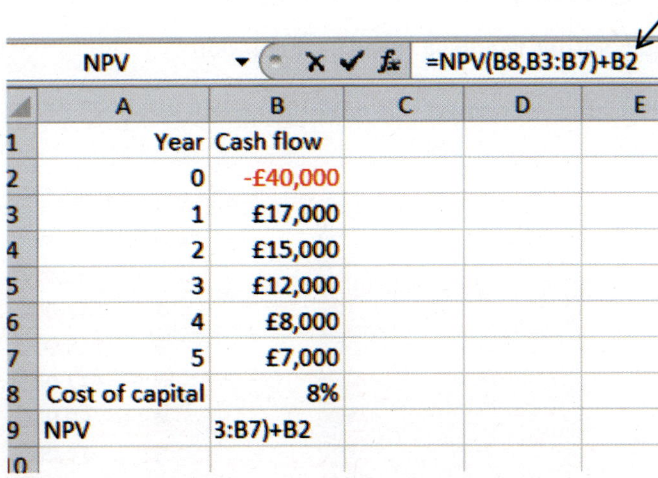

NPV =NPV(B8,B3:B7)+B2

	A	B	C	D	E
1	Year	Cash flow			
2	0	-£40,000			
3	1	£17,000			
4	2	£15,000			
5	3	£12,000			
6	4	£8,000			
7	5	£7,000			
8	Cost of capital	8%			
9	NPV	3:B7)+B2			
10					

Figure 14.7 Adjusting the formula for the initial investment (Cell B2)

The NPV value will appear in Cell B9 as shown in Figure 14.8:

	A	B
1	Year	Cash flow
2	0	-£40,000
3	1	£17,000
4	2	£15,000
5	3	£12,000
6	4	£8,000
7	5	£7,000
8	Cost of capital	8%
9	NPV	£8,771.13

Figure 14.8 NPV calculated

To calculate the IRR, follow a similar procedure, using the function IRR to provide a value in Cell B10. The values required are shown in Figure 14.9:

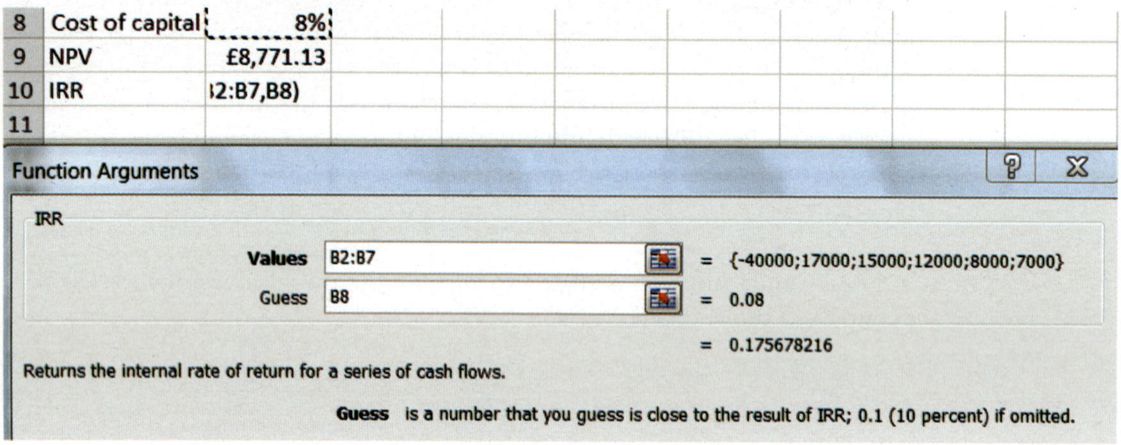

Figure 14.9 Values required for IRR calculation

In the example, this results in an IRR value of 18%, as shown in Figure 14.10:

	A	B
1	Year	Cash flow
2	0	-£40,000
3	1	£17,000
4	2	£15,000
5	3	£12,000
6	4	£8,000
7	5	£7,000
8	Cost of capital	8%
9	NPV	£8,771.13
10	IRR	18%

Figure 14.10 IRR calculated

14.4 Investment appraisal using non-discounting techniques

Methods of investment appraisal that consider the time value of money rely heavily upon the following estimates:

- The life of the project
- The cost of capital that will be appropriate throughout its life
- The level of future net cash flows.

Each of these estimates demands an ability to forecast; and the further into the future one goes, the greater is the risk of the forecasts being wrong. Because of this, and the complexities of discounting techniques, many firms still prefer methods that ignore time values. These are called *non-discounting methods*, and the most common of these is called the 'payback period' method.

14.4.1 Payback period

The payback period approach ignores interest rates and time values altogether, and looks solely at how *long* the investment takes to pay for itself (the 'payback period'). Although unsophisticated, it is useful where there is uncertainty about the forecasts – perhaps economic circumstances are unclear – as the investment decision is taken simply on the basis of which project is fastest at repaying its initial investment. Any cash flows occurring after the payback is achieved are ignored – the critical information is how quickly the cash flowing from the investment covers the outlay.

Activity 14.6

A firm has a choice of three projects, L, M and N. Each requires an investment of £15,000, and forecast cash flows are as follows:

Year	L	M	N
	£	£	£
0	(15,000)	(15,000)	(15,000)
1	3,000	4,000	2,000
2	4,000	5,000	4,000
3	5,000	6,000	9,000
4	6,000	6,000	7,000
5	10,000	6,000	7,000
6	16,000	6,000	7,000

Calculate each project's payback period. On the basis of this appraisal technique, which project would be recommended?

Answer

The payback periods of each project are as follows:

Project L $= 3\frac{1}{2}$ years $\left[3{,}000 + 4{,}000 + 5{,}000 + \left(\frac{1}{2} \times 6{,}000\right) = £\,15{,}000\right]$

Project M = 3 years (4,000 + 5,000 + 6,000 = £ 15,000)

Project N = 3 years (2,000 + 4,000 + 9,000 = £ 15,000)

It would appear that M and N would be equally preferred. However, if one looks closely at project N, it is seen that over half of the required earnings (£9,000) arise in the third year – the *discounting* methods of investment appraisal have told us that the value of money declines the further into the future it is received. Also, looking beyond the payback period, we can see that project N goes on to earn a further £21,000 in the final three years, whereas project M earns only £18,000. (See Figure 14.11) The payback method completely ignores earnings that occur after the payback period. Project L, which was originally rejected, is projected to earn £29,000 after the payback period of 31/2 years – perhaps project L should have been chosen after all?

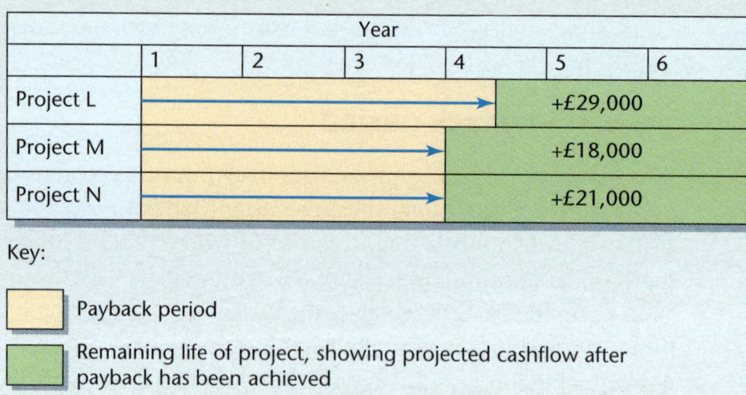

Figure 14.11 Projects L, M and N – payback periods and cash flows after payback

14.4.2 Accounting rate of return (ARR)

The accounting rate of return (ARR) technique establishes the percentage annual return generated by a project over its life. It compares the non-discounted *profit* flows with the capital to be invested in the project. 'Profit' for this purpose is usually defined as net profit before interest and taxation. For example, a project costing £250,000 that generates net profits before interest and taxation of £500,000 over a 10-year period would have an accounting rate of return of 20% p.a., based on the following formula:

$$\text{APR} = \frac{\text{Average annual net profit before taxation and interest}}{\text{Capital employed}} \times 100\%$$

$$\frac{(\pounds 500{,}000/10)}{\pounds 250{,}000} \times 100\% = 20\%\text{p.a.}$$

This method provides a percentage that can be compared with the percentage rates of return of other potential projects and also the percentage cost of capital. Like the payback method, it ignores the time value of money, and the relative proportions of profit received earlier or later in the project's life are not taken into consideration. A project that is forecast to earn the bulk of its profits in the first few years would normally be preferable to another where most profits are earned near the end of the project's life, due to the inherent uncertainty of forecast data.

Activity 14.7

Calculate the ARR of a project that requires an initial capital investment of £4m and is estimated to return net profits before interest and taxation totalling £1.6m over a five-year period.

Answer

The ARR is 8%, calculated as follows:

$$\frac{\text{Average annual net profit before taxation and interest}}{\text{Capital employed}} \times 100\%$$

$$\frac{(\pounds 1.6\text{m}/5)}{\pounds 4\text{m}} \times 100\% = 8\% \text{ p.a.}$$

14.5 Summary

The features of the various methods are as follows:

		Advantages	Disadvantages
Discounted cash flow (DCF)	Converts future cash flows into present values by using discount factors	Considers the time value of money. Looks at the whole life of projects	Discount rate chosen might be unrealistic. Need to use discount tables. Future cash flows might be difficult to predict with any accuracy. Not as easy to understand as non-discounting techniques
Net present value (NPV)	Converts both cash inflows and outflows relating to a specific project into present values, the end result being a 'net' present value	As DCF, but takes both cash inflows and outflows into consideration	As DCF
Internal rate of return (IRR)	Establishes the discount rate that, if applied to the cash flows relating to a specific project, would reduce the NPV to zero. This enables competing projects to be compared in terms of the percentage return they would earn after discounting	As DCF, but evaluation can be achieved on the basis of comparative percentage returns	As DCF
Payback	Evaluates competing projects solely by reference to the speed with which the initial investment is repaid	Simple to use and understand. Useful as an additional appraisal method where forecasts are particularly uncertain	Ignores time value of money. Ignores cash flows after pay-back period is reached

		Advantages	Disadvantages
Accounting rate of return (ARR)	The percentage return per annum generated by a project over its lifetime	Simple to use and understand. Uses profit as the basis for the calculation rather than cash flows, which ties in with other accounting ratios	Ignores time value of money and when profit is earned

14.6 Chapter glossary

Accounting rate of return The percentage annual return generated by a project over its life, calculated by comparing the non-discounted profit flows with the capital to be invested in the project

ARR *See* Accounting rate of return.

Cost of capital The cost of financing a specific project, or the weighted average cost of capital of a firm based on existing equity and loan investment

Cumulative discount factor Combined discount factors used to facilitate the calculation of present values when the same sum is to be received or paid over several successive periods.

DCF *See* Discounted cash flow.

Discount factor The decimal used to convert a future value into a present value.

Discount rate The rate of interest used in the discounting process – *see* Cost of capital.

Discounted cash flow Future cash flows converted to present values by the use of discount factors.

Discounting The process of converting future values into present values.

Future value The present value plus accumulated compound interest up to the time when the cash flow occurs.

Internal rate of return The discount rate which results in a zero net present value. It is used to compare alternative projects (that with the highest IRR is chosen) and/or to evaluate a project's rate of return with the firm's cost of capital.

Investment appraisal The process of comparing two or more potential investment projects to establish which is more favourable to the firm.

IRR *See* Internal rate of return.

Net present value The difference between a project's discounted cash outflows and inflows.

NPV *See* Net present value.

Payback The point when a project's cash flows match the cost of the project.

Payback period The time taken for a project to repay its original investment, using non-discounted cash flows.

Present value A cash flow occurring at the start of a project, or a 'future' cash flow discounted to the equivalent value if it had been received or paid at the start of a project.

Only accessible on Android-based devices

Additional resources

Now work through the various exercises and problems that you can find within the My Accounting Lab that are relevant to this chapter. Either use the QR code shown in the margin (if you use an Android-based device), or visit www.myaccountinglab.com for the log-in page.

Self-check questions

The answers to these questions are in Appendix 1.

1 What is the future value in exactly three years' time of an investment of £1,000 received today and invested at 5% compound interest?

(a) £1,215.50
(b) £1,157.63
(c) £1,150
(d) £1,102.50

2 A two-year project is being evaluated using a discount rate of 7% p.a. It is expected to have a cash inflow of £40,000 at the end of its first year and £60,000 at the end of its second year. What is the present value of the future cash flows if the discount factors are: year 1: 0.935 and year 2: 0.873?

(a) £100,000
(b) £89,780
(c) £91,020
(d) £72,320

3 If two projects have different levels of risk, what can managers do to make their investment appraisal more realistic?

(a) Apply a lower discount rate to the riskier project
(b) Not consider the riskier project
(c) Apply a higher discount rate to the riskier project
(d) Ignore any cash inflows occurring after the first three years

4 Under which one of the following circumstances could a cumulative discount factor be used?

(a) Where the same future values are receivable or payable each year for several years
(b) Where different future values are receivable or payable each year for several years
(c) Where the payback period method of investment appraisal is being used
(d) Where the accounting rate of return method of investment appraisal is being used

5 Which one of the following could be considered as a benefit of using the payback period method of investment appraisal?

(a) Both present and future values are being considered
(b) The time value of money is considered
(c) All cash flows arising on the project are brought into the calculation
(d) It is simple to calculate

6 As a result of using various investment appraisal techniques, a firm has established that machine A has a payback period of 4 years, machine B has a negative internal rate of return of 6%, machine C has a net present value of £50,000 and machine D has an accounting rate of return of 8% p.a. Based on this information alone, which one of the machines would appear to be the *least* favoured investment?

(a) Machine A
(b) Machine B
(c) Machine C
(d) Machine D

7 Which one of the following methods of investment appraisal requires a trial-and-error approach for its calculation?

(a) Internal rate of return
(b) Payback period
(c) Accounting rate of return
(d) Net present value

8 A company is evaluating two alternative projects, X and Y, each of which will cost £50,000. Project X is expected to generate £20,000 p.a. for three years and project Y is expected to generate £15,000 p.a. for four years. At the end of each project, assets will be sold for £10,000 relating to project X and £15,000 relating to project Y. The discount rate is 5% and relevant discount factors are: year 1: 0.952, year 2: 0.907, year 3: 0.864 and year 4: 0.823. What is the net present value of each project?

(a) Project X £4,460, project Y £3,190
(b) Project X £20,000, project Y £25,000
(c) Project X £13,100, project Y £15,535
(d) Project X £63,100, project Y £65,535

9 Using the information contained in question 8, what is the payback period for each project?

(a) Project X 3 years, project Y 4 years
(b) Project X 2 years, project Y $2^1/_3$ years
(c) Project X $2^1/_2$ years, project Y $3^1/_3$ years
(d) Project X $1^1/_2$ years, project Y $2^1/_3$ years

10 Which one of the following is an acceptable definition of the internal rate of return?

(a) The annualised profits as a percentage of the amount invested
(d) The discounted cash flows as a percentage of the amount invested
(c) The time it takes to repay the initial investment
(d) The discount rate that results in a zero net present value for a project

Self-study questions

Questions marked with this symbol (#) indicate that the suggested answers are available to lecturers only – other answers are given in Appendix 2.

14.1 A project (A) costs £3,000 today and is expected to generate a cash flow of £10,000 in a year's time, whereas an alternative project (B) costing £4,000 today is forecast to generate £12,000 in two years' time. Calculate the net present value of each project, and state which project appears to be preferable.

Use a 10% p.a. discount rate. Relevant discount factors are:

Year 1	0.909
Year 2	0.826

14.2# Using the net present value method of investment appraisal, contrast two projects, C and D. Project C will cost £10,000 and will generate £9,000 p.a. for three years. Project D will cost £12,000 but will generate £7,000 p.a. for four years. The discount rate is 6% p.a. Relevant discount factors are:

Year 1	0.943
Year 2	0.890
Year 3	0.840
Year 4	0.792

14.3 Two projects, G and H, cost £20,000 and £30,000 respectively. Project G is estimated to produce annual cash flows of £4,000 for 10 years whereas project H is estimated to produce annual cash flows of £5,000 for eight years.

Which project would be chosen, using the payback method?

14.4# Using a range of discount rates between 5% and 8% p.a., establish by trial and error the internal rate of return of the following project:

Year 0	Cash outflow	£20,000
Year 1	Cash inflow	£6,700
Year 2	Cash inflow	£8,600
Year 3	Cash inflow	£8,100

Relevant discount factors are:

Year	Discount rate			
	5%	6%	7%	8%
1	0.952	0.943	0.935	0.926
2	0.907	0.890	0.873	0.857
3	0.864	0.840	0.816	0.794

14.5 A private hospital needs to equip an operating theatre by installing new medical equipment. The equipment costs £700,000 to buy outright, and is expected to require continuing maintenance costs of £30,000 p.a. for five years. At the end of five years it is expected to have a scrap value of about £100,000. With the benefits deriving from the new equipment, the hospital can expect to generate extra income of about £300,000 p.a. for the first three years, falling to an additional £200,000 p.a. for the remaining two years.

An alternative is to lease slightly more advanced equipment, which would require an initial deposit of £400,000, followed by five annual end-of-year payments of £120,000 each. The lessor will maintain the equipment and will reclaim the equipment at the end of Year 5. Income is expected to increase by £300,000 p.a. over the entire five-year period.

Assume that the cost of capital is 8% p.a.

Discount factors at 8% p.a. are:

Year	Discount factor
1	0.926
2	0.857
3	0.794

Year	Discount factor
4	0.735
5	0.681

Should the hospital buy or lease, and what additional information might be needed before a final decision is taken?

14.6 Catalysts plc is planning the installation of a new processing plant. It currently has two alternatives under consideration:

Project Alpha:	The capital cost of this plant is £10 million.
Project Beta:	This plant would cost £20 million.

Forecast information for each of the alternatives is as follows:

£m	Project Alpha		Project Beta	
	Revenue	Payments	Revenue	Payments
Year 1	7.6	4.0	13	5.8
Year 2	10.2	5.2	14.4	6.2
Year 3	12.8	7.8	18.6	9.6
Year 4	13.8	9.4	19.8	10.4
Year 5	16.2	10.4	12.8	11.6

The company's cost of capital is 8 % per annum, and the relevant discount factors are shown below:

Year 1	0.926
Year 2	0.857
Year 3	0.794
Year 4	0.735
Year 5	0.681

On the basis of the net present value of the alternative projects, make a recommendation to the management of Catalysts plc as to which of the two projects should be chosen.

14.7# Allerton plc is considering investing in a new capital project and has a choice of three alternatives, only one of which can be implemented. The following data is available (assume that capital outlays occur immediately and net cash flows occur at each year-end):

£m	Project 1	Project 2	Project 3
Initial outlay	400,000	460,000	360,000
Project life:	5 years	5 years	4 years

£m	Project 1	Project 2	Project 3
Net cash inflows:			
Year 1	160,000	200,000	110,000
Year 2	140,000	140,000	120,000
Year 3	130,000	100,000	190,000
Year 4	120,000	100,000	150,000
Year 5	110,000	100,000	–
Residual value	20,000	30,000	16,000

The company's cost of capital is 7% and the relevant discount factors are shown below:

Year 1	0.935
Year 2	0.873
Year 3	0.816
Year 4	0.763
Year 5	0.713

Project 2 has a higher labour content than the other two projects. Project 1 is powered by fossil fuel whereas projects 2 and 3 use solar power.

(a) Calculate the net present value of each project and evaluate the three alternatives based purely on this method.
(b) Calculate the payback period of each project and evaluate the three alternatives based purely on this method.
(c) Identify three other factors which might influence the management's decision.

Case study

Answers are in Appendix 3

Machiq Limited's bid for world domination

Marvin and Chiquita (see previous case studies) had seen their business, Machiq Limited, change considerably over the years to a point where its brand name was recognised throughout the country. However, the two directors were very ambitious and believed that there was a worldwide market for the company's products if only they could achieve global brand awareness. To this aim, they decided to investigate the cost of launching their own television channel (Machiq TV) to broadcast advertisements for Machiq Limited's products 24 hours a day, seven days a week to the northern hemisphere. Alternatively, they intended to consider a joint venture with Kaboosh Limited to launch a satellite (Matrix 1) that would enable the whole world to receive advertisements for both company's products.

Available data is as follows:

Machiq TV:

Initial set-up costs: £250m
Annual running costs: £100m
Estimated life of project: 5 years
Value of assets released at the end of the project: £40m
Increased sales as a result of advertising products: £60m in the first year, growing cumulatively by 50% each year for the following four years.

Matrix 1 satellite:

Initial set-up costs: £700m
Annual running costs: £50m
Value of assets released at the end of the project: £10m
(Note: all the above to be shared 50/50 with Kaboosh Limited)

Estimated life of the project: 6 years
Increased sales for Machiq Limited as a result of advertising products globally: £80m in the first year, growing cumulatively by 20% each year for the following five years.
Funding for both projects would be at a cost of capital of 6%.
Relevant discount factors at 6% p.a. are:

Year	Discount factor
1	0.943
2	0.890
3	0.840

Year	Discount factor
4	0.792
5	0.747
6	0.705

Required

Using the net present value method of investment appraisal, critically evaluate the two proposals.

Answers are in Appendix 3

Further research

You may want to read a journal paper describing the development of discounted cash flow techniques:

Dulman, S. (1989). 'The development of discounted cash flow techniques in US industry', *Business History Review*, 63(3)

Revision of Chapters 9–14

Introduction

This section consolidates the knowledge gained on several of the management accounting topics contained in Chapters 9–14 by providing an examination paper consisting of four questions. Answers are provided in Appendix 4.

Practice examination paper 3

Time allowed THREE hours. Answer all four questions. All questions carry equal marks.

Question 1

Spectacular plc is a company that manufactures computer equipment. It has three production departments and a service department, and has produced the following budgeted cost of production for the year ended 31 March 2016:

		£	£
Production cost	Direct materials	240,000	
	Carriage inwards	10,000	
	Direct wages	200,000	
			450,000
Indirect wages	Department P	8,000	
	Department Q	12,000	
	Department R	18,300	
	General service department	6,700	
			45,000
Other costs	Consumable stores	32,000	
	Rent	21,000	
	Light and heat	14,000	
	Power	36,000	
	Depreciation (20% × cost)	80,000	
	Insurance: machinery	2,000	
			185,000
			680,000

The following data relates to the physical and performance aspects of the company:

Department	Area m^2	Cost of plant £	Stores requisitions	Power consumption kW	Direct labour hours	Direct-labour cost	Machine hours
P	15,000	140,000	180	80	100,000	50,000	70,000
Q	22,500	180,000	120	100	80,000	60,000	90,000
R	20,000	10,000	100	5	220,000	90,000	10,000
Service	12,500	70,000	–	15	–	–	–

The general service department is apportioned to the production departments on the basis of direct labour cost.

(a) Prepare an overhead analysis for the departments, showing clearly the basis of apportioning costs to departments.

(b) Prepare a computation of hourly cost rates (direct labour hours or machine hours) of overhead absorption for each production department.

(c) Critically assess the two overhead absorption rates calculated in (b) above.

Question 2

Fripple Limited manufactures coats. The company's management is preparing a budget for the next financial year and has prepared the following information:

	£
Selling price per coat	100
Materials per coat	25
Direct labour per coat	30
Overheads: variable per coat	5
Fixed overheads (total) £240,000 p.a.	

The company is planning to manufacture 16,000 coats in the next year.

(a) Calculate by formula, showing your workings:

   (i) The maximum profit if all coats are sold
   (ii) The break-even point (number of coats)
   (iii) The margin of safety (number of coats)
   (iv) The profit or loss if 11,000 coats are manufactured and sold.

(b) Prepare a cost/volume chart showing all the information calculated in (a) above.

(c) A supermarket chain has approached Fripple Limited with a view to placing a special order for 5,000 coats bearing a prominent advertisement, but is only prepared to pay £70 per coat. The additional cost of embroidering the advertisement would be £6 per coat. This order would be within the capacity of the company and fixed costs would remain unchanged. Should Fripple Limited accept the order?

Question 3

Humbug Ltd manufactures artificial Christmas trees in batches of 600. During October, batch no. 701 was manufactured at the rate of 12 per hour. Ninety of the trees failed quality tests, but of these, 50 were thought to be rectifiable. The remaining 40 were scrapped, and the scrap value was credited to the cost of the batch as a whole. Rectification work took 6 hours. Costs were as follows:

Batch No. 701	£
Raw materials per tree	2.40
Scrap value per tree	0.75
Machinists' hourly rate	4.80
Machine-hour overhead	5.30
Setting up of machine: normal machining	15.00
Setting up of machine: rectification	10.00

(a) Calculate the cost of a full batch, in total and per unit, if all units pass inspection.
(b) Calculate the actual cost of batch no. 701, in total and per unit, after crediting the recovery value of the scrapped trees, and including the rectification costs.
(c) Calculate the loss incurred because of defective work.

Question 4

Appraise plc is considering manufacturing and developing a new product requiring a £2m investment. The following are estimates of costs and revenues for the first five years of the product's life:

1 Forecast sales:

Year	Quantities sold units	Selling price £ per unit
1	5,000	250
2	15,000	230
3	22,000	200
4	15,000	200
5	5,000	200

2 New machinery will be bought at the start of the project at a cost of £2m. It is expected to have a resale value of £150,000 at the end of five years.
3 Labour costs will be £40 per unit in year 1, rising by £2 per unit in each succeeding year.
4 Materials costs will be £80 per unit for the first two years of production, rising by 10% in year 3, and by a further £6 in each of years 4 and 5.
5 Other costs will be £25 per unit. These are forecast to remain unchanged over the life of the project.
6 The cost of capital to the company is 6% p.a.

Relevant discount factors are:

Year	Discount factor
1	0.943
2	0.890
3	0.840
4	0.792
5	0.747

(a) Evaluate the project by calculating the:
  (i) Net present value
  (ii) Payback period.

(b) Advise the company whether it should proceed with the new product.

(c) If the company decides to manufacture the new product, it intends to use standard costing techniques as an aid to efficient management. Explain how these may be of benefit in controlling a company's performance.

Chapter 15

Decision-making

Objectives

When you have read this chapter you will be able to:

- Understand the scope and importance of decision-making for an organisation
- Outline the different types of decision-making
- Be aware of the different classifications of costs for decision-making purposes
- Evaluate shut-down or continuation decisions
- Incorporate cost and financial data into various decision-making situations

15.1 Introduction

This chapter reviews the decision-making process from the perspective of management and examines the financial and non-financial factors that should be considered by managers when making decisions. In our day-to-day life we are accustomed to making decisions all the time, some more important than others, but often as inconsequential as deciding whether to have pizza or pasta for dinner. However, in a business context, when resources are limited, the implications of a particular decision may be extremely far-reaching, perhaps affecting the lives of thousands of people. Judgements must be made as to the relative importance of immediate and longer-term returns: for example, a decision to expand to new international markets may be at the expense of investment in research and development.

Of course, when facing such decisions, financial data cannot be considered in isolation from other non-financial factors. Imagine the owner of a call centre who desperately needs to cut costs. His or her first thought might be to make a percentage of the staff redundant, thereby achieving the immediate goal of reducing expenditure. However, if those same redundancies lead to a decline in service levels and, ultimately, the loss of contracts and a reduction in revenue, what might have seemed a financially prudent decision may turn out to have been imprudent or even foolhardy.

15.2 The background to decision-making

The manager must review a wide range of information and scenarios before taking a decision, as indicated in Figure 15.1.

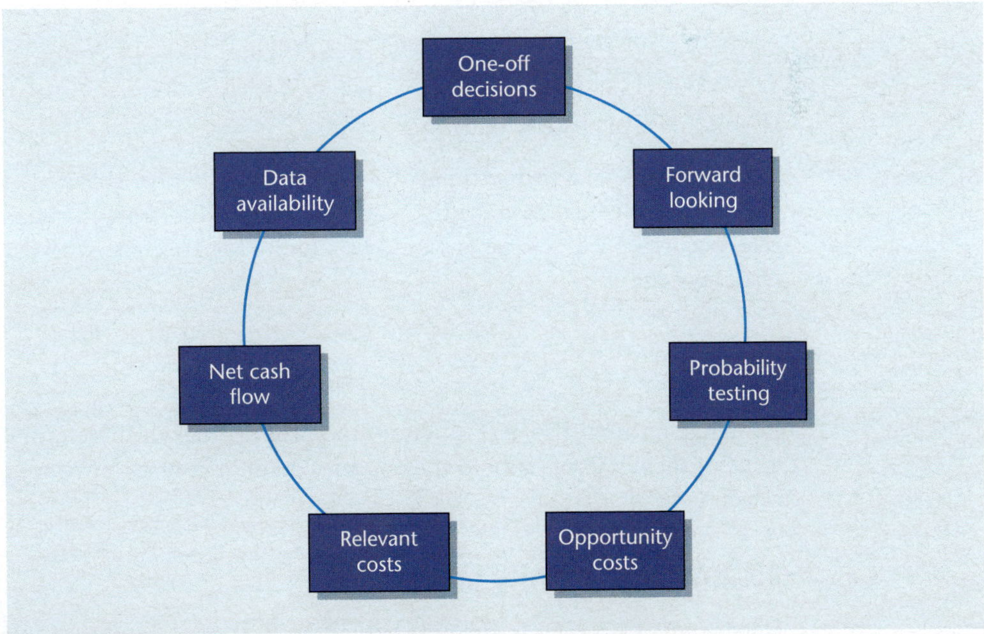

Figure 15.1 Background to decision-making

15.2.1 One-off decisions

Some decisions are non-recurrent, such as whether to repair or salvage an asset. To perform such *one-off decisions*, information must be gathered which is specifically related to that one unique issue. When BP experienced a major oil spill in the Gulf of Mexico in April 2010, it had to make an immediate decision in terms of allocating up to $10 billion for emergency clean-up operations in the areas affected.

15.2.2 Forward-looking information

To make well-founded decisions, it is essential to look at both past performance and future business conditions. *Forward-looking* information can help to predict both future opportunities and challenges. Procter and Gamble had announced in 2010 that its objective was to add a billion new customers by 2015, a 25% increase. However, unlike its great rival, Unilever, it had been slower to diversify its operations away from recession-hit Europe and the US and slower to move towards the less expensive brands favoured by increasingly cost-conscious consumers. The outcome was a record low share price in June 2012 for Procter and Gamble and a record high share price for Unilever.

15.2.3 Probability testing

Important business decisions are often based on hypotheses about the future. *Probability testing* may be used to help managers identify the likelihood of various outcomes, in order to choose between alternatives. This introduces the idea of an *expected value* of an event, which is defined as 'the sum of the probability of each possible outcome multiplied by the value (impact) of each outcome'. This can be evaluated by the formula:

$$\text{EV} = \sum_{i=1}^{n} p_i x_i$$

where p_i = probability of outcome i (as a decimal)

x_i = value of outcome i

n = number of possible outcomes

For example, if a firm estimated a 60% probability of a 'strike' type of labour dispute occurring (in which case profits would be £20m) and a 40% probability of a 'work to rule' occurring where profits would be £40m, the expected value (EV) should a labour dispute occur is:

$$\begin{aligned} \text{EV(£m)} &= (0.60 \times 20) + (0.40 \times 40) \\ &= \text{£28m} \end{aligned}$$

A change in the firm's assessment of the probabilities of these events occurring or the value of their impacts should they occur would, of course, influence the expected value calculation.

15.2.4 Opportunity costs

Opportunity costs refer to the next best alternative use of resources which have been sacrificed as a result of a business decision. When IKEA announced in June 2012 that it would spend \$1.9bn opening its first 25 stores in India, the opportunity cost might well have been the stores it would otherwise have opened in its next most favoured location.

15.2.5 Relevant costs

Sometimes referred to as differential or incremental costs, *relevant costs* are the costs that are specific to a particular course of action. They relate to the future, not to the past, and may differ from option to option. Focusing on relevant costs can help to eliminate unnecessary information that may complicate the decision-making process. Relevant costs usually include *variable costs*, and may also include *opportunity costs.*

15.2.6 Net cash flow

Used as an indication of available funds, *net cash flow* – or, sometimes, simply cash flow – is the profits of a business plus non-cash expenses. In order to pay suppliers, wages or rent, a business needs a healthy *net cash flow*. Thus, when making a decision, managers need to take into account the effect of the various options on net cash flow.

15.2.7 Data availability

Some decisions can be made based on information from the cost accounting system, but others require further information to be extracted from other sources. *Data availability* may be an issue, and new information may need to be acquired. Such information may already be published in *secondary sources of data* such as international or national economic surveys or other official publications. However, sometimes new information may need to be generated by the business itself as *primary sources of data.* Such 'primary' or original sources of data may require the use of carefully designed pilot studies or questionnaire surveys by the firm's own marketing department or by external marketing consultants.

15.3 Cost classification

Earlier we showed that, depending on their purpose, costs and revenues can be put into various categories. While a categorisation into direct and indirect costs is useful when evaluating issues involving inventory holding and the costing of products, it may be less useful when making decisions.

In the following section, we look at a variety of cost categories which may be relevant for business decision-making.

15.3.1 Fixed and variable costs

Fixed costs are unaffected by the level of business activity. Insurance, property tax or rent, for example, remain unaltered whatever the volume of goods or services produced. Since these costs are unaffected regardless of the course of action taken, they are often given little attention as regards the decision-making process. By contrast, *variable costs* do change according to the volume of production, rising when production levels increase and falling when they decrease. Expenditure on labour or materials are examples of variable costs.

However, the time period is important here. The long-run is defined as that period of time in which *all* factors of production can be varied, and for which all costs are arguably variable. It may take 10 years to plan and build a new power station, but only one year to plan and build a new office. We would say the long-run time period is 10 years for building power stations and one year for building offices. In the long-run, for each activity, all costs must be covered, both fixed and variable. Indeed a 'normal' profit return on capital invested will be expected for various sectors of economic activity. This also could be regarded as a variable cost in the long-run, since if such a return is *not* forthcoming, then resources will be moved into the next best alternative activity.

15.3.2 Relevant and non-relevant costs

As previously noted, decision-making involves an analysis of relevant costs. While fixed costs stay the same, and therefore are often neglected when making a decision, variable costs are usually given careful attention. Hence, fixed costs are sometimes seen as an example of *non-relevant costs* while variable costs can be considered to be *relevant costs.*

However in the long-run time period, *all costs* are, arguably, relevant costs, including fixed costs, variable costs and 'normal profit', since unless all these are covered, resources will be allocated elsewhere in the long-run time period when all factors of production can be varied.

15.3.3 Avoidable and non-avoidable costs

Costs that are dependent on the course of action taken – that is, they will only be incurred if a particular decision is made – can be classified as *avoidable costs.* Variable costs are avoidable: if an extra unit is *not* produced, the cost of its production will not be incurred. Manufacturers are often keen to drop underperforming product lines in order to avoid the cost of their production.

Fixed costs are often regarded as *unavoidable* and will be incurred irrespective of the course of action chosen. However, in the long-run time period all factors of production can be varied, and so arguably even fixed costs are avoidable over that time period.

15.3.4 Sunk costs

Sunk costs are based on past decisions and cannot be recovered. Since they remain unaffected by any decisions undertaken, they are often disregarded in the decision-making process. For example, suppose a pharmaceutical company invests £100,000 into the research and development of a new drug. Although the drug has not yet been developed, the money must be considered to be sunk, since it cannot be regained.

The company must decide whether continuing the research will help to recoup the sunk funds or whether the project should be left incomplete to avoid incurring further costs.

15.3.5 Committed costs

Committed costs can be seen as investments that a business has already made, or is obliged to uphold, and thus cannot be recovered. Since committed costs will be incurred irrespective of specific management decisions, they can be seen as irrelevant for the decision-making process. For example, if a company buys a £15,000 machine, signing a maintenance contract worth £3,000 per annum over a period of four years, it has committed costs of £27,000.

15.3.6 Opportunity costs

As previously noted, when facing a decision, managers have to consider the *opportunity costs* – or benefits sacrificed as a result of any particular decision. For example, the opportunity cost of sending staff for training may involve the lost working time, which would have added value to the business. However, this must be considered against the benefits of a well-trained workforce, whose skills will contribute to long-term business success.

Activity 15.1

Janet works as a door-to-door salesperson for a vacuum cleaner producer. She has to decide whether to spend her hard-earned money on a new car, or an all-inclusive cruise around Asia with a friend.

Tickets for the cruise are £2,000, and include food, accommodation and all on-board services. Janet loves sightseeing, but excursions are not included in the price, so she plans to do only five excursions, costing £30 each. She also calculates that she will need £50 for souvenirs at each of the five destinations.

Janet has always dreamed of going to Asia. Her friend will be getting married soon, so this may be their last chance to travel together.

However, Janet's car is vital for her job. It has broken down several times recently, and really needs to be replaced. A suitable car will cost £2,500, and she can sell her old car for approximately £500.

What opportunity costs should Janet consider to help her make her decision?

Answer

To find the opportunity cost of each decision, Janet needs to first calculate the financial cost.

Asia cruise	£
Tickets	2,000
Excursions (5 × £30)	150
Souvenirs (5 × £50)	250
Total	**2,400**
New car	£
New car	2,500
Sale price of old car	– 500
Total	**2,000**

The cruise will cost Janet £400 more than the new car. Thus, one of the opportunity costs of the decision to go on the cruise is the £400 lost. However, to give a complete picture, the non-financial opportunity costs should also be considered.

Since Janet's car is essential for her to work, the opportunity cost of taking the cruise is the possibility of losing business, or even her job, if the old car breaks down again. Losing business would result in a loss of future earnings, making it more difficult for Janet to save for the cruise later on.

Since Janet has always dreamed of travelling to Asia, an opportunity cost of the decision to buy the car is her unfulfilled dream. She would also sacrifice the pleasure of sightseeing, and possibly the final opportunity to travel with her friend.

Whilst it is easy to calculate the financial opportunity costs of each decision, it is much more difficult to see the non-financial costs. Both decisions involve sacrifices, so the decision ultimately rests on which opportunities Janet prefers to forgo.

15.4 Types of decision

Having looked at the main characteristics of information required for decision-making and introduced the main cost classifications, it will be useful to examine more closely the various types of decisions managers must make (see Figure 15.2).

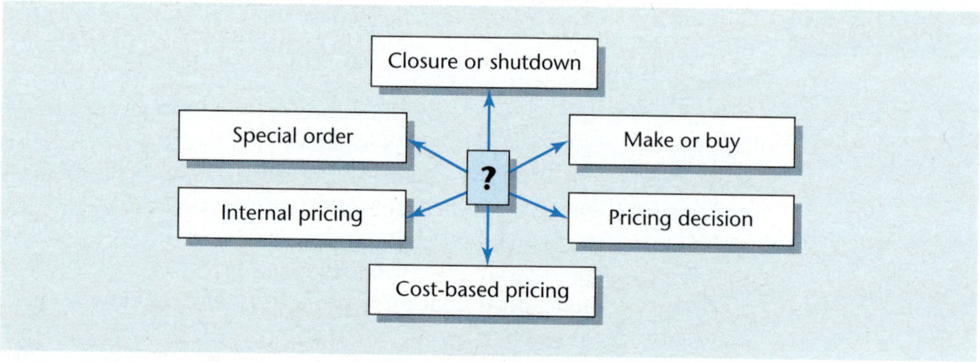

Figure 15.2 Types of management decisions

15.4.1 Closure or shut-down decision

If a product line, department or factory is making a loss or is too expensive to run, managers may be forced to decide whether to close it or to shut it down. In this context, *shutdown* means that a business line is made temporarily inactive, since managers expect it to become profitable again in the future. *Closure* means that management sees no potential for recovery and decides to abandon it permanently in order to save annual operating costs and to use its fixed assets in more beneficial projects.

When making a shutdown or closure decision, a thorough analysis of all the financial aspects is needed, with careful consideration of the implications – both financial and non-financial – of each decision. A department closure, for example, may save the company £60,000, but may result in £75,000 of redundancy payments, ultimately causing a loss.

In addition, some areas may not seem to show high profit margins, but they may make an important non-financial contribution, since they provide vital services for other, high-profit activities.

Furthermore, a product or activity may be unprofitable yet still make a contribution towards fixed costs, which makes its closure or shutdown questionable.

15.4.2 Make or buy decision

Managers may also need to decide whether to produce an item internally or buy it from an outside supplier. This is known as a *make or buy* decision.

This dilemma may arise when a company has trouble with its existing supplier or encounters a diminishing capacity. An airplane manufacturer, for example, may have to decide whether to produce its own components or buy them from a supplier, instead focusing its efforts on assembly.

Should the company decide to purchase from a supplier rather than produce the item itself, it is engaging in an outsourcing decision. This may be an attempt to reduce costs and to stay competitive. Other reasons for outsourcing might involve reducing risk by having a multiple-source policy, lack of expertise, brand preference or simply the belief that a company should specialise on what it is best at, which means concentrating on its core competencies.

However, some items may be regarded as critical aspects of the activities of the company and as key to its having a competitive advantage. Hence, they may need to be manufactured in-house in order to maintain quality control and design secrecy. Other reasons to avoid outsourcing and subcontracting may be concern as regards disruptions in supply, and shortages of suppliers for certain products.

Indeed the Japanese tsunami of 2011 and associated impacts on the Japanese economy caused major disruption to the component supply chain of car manufacturers who had become overly dependent on that source (see the 'News clip' below). Moreover, outsourcing to low cost countries may bring about reputational damage to companies if their suppliers infringe human rights, or cause severe environmental pollution, as Nestlé found in 2011 with negative blogs and adverts exposing links between chocolate production for its *KitKat* bars and associated deforestation in Indonesia.

Usually, a make or buy decision cannot be made by considering costs in isolation. Since it is often a strategic decision, various other factors need to be taken into consideration, such as an analysis of future market trends or of the competitive landscape.

News clip

Supply chain: tsunami, floods and storms move logistics up the agenda

FT

By Robert Wright

When a tsunami triggered by a vast earthquake crashed over sea walls on Japan's east coast on March 11 last year, some tiny ripples from the vast tragedy made themselves felt as far away as England's West Midlands. Disruption to Japanese electronics makers because of the tsunami led to shortages of key electronics components at British car factories, including Jaguar Land Rover's Castle Bromwich plant in Birmingham. There was yet further evidence of the vulnerability of global supply chains in November, when floods in Thailand inundated areas that account for 45 per cent of the world capacity to manufacture computer hard disk drives. In between, destructive storms in the US's Tennessee Valley in April caused severe disruption to some US domestic supply chains.

The spate of disasters has raised serious questions about how far retailers and manufacturers will be able to pursue the outsourcing to Asia that has transformed the world economy over the last decade. Increasing numbers, according to executives who organise large companies' logistics, are pondering the risks inherent in relying on a single supplier thousands of miles from their core operations. Those worries have heightened the concerns about supply chain issues that many companies have felt ever since many found themselves holding too much stock following the 2008 economic crisis. Inflexible supply chains kept delivering goods after the downturn hit in volumes that proved impossible to sell profitably.

The question is how quickly the new concerns will produce an anticipated shift of some manufacturing activity away from Asia towards Turkey, Mexico or other low-cost countries that will allow manufacturers and retailers to shorten their supply chains. Mark Parsons, a senior executive in the UK and Ireland supply chain business of DHL, the logistics operator, says supply chain risk – which senior executives never used to raise as a concern – is now a regular topic of conversation with top-level managers. The only question is how quickly that concern converts itself into real changes in sourcing patterns.

"It will take a little bit of time for the buyers to reflect what may be currently a board level issue," Mr Parsons says.

Steven Gold, an experienced supply chain officer who now works for Alvarez & Marsal, the consultancy, says that individual decisions will come down to the characteristics of demand for particular products.

Mr Gold, based in the United States, says clothes makers and electronics companies – both of whose products are subject to sudden, fashion-driven demand swings – as those most likely to move production to Mexico, from where lead times are far shorter than from Asia.

"The consumer is moving very, very quickly," Mr Gold says. "The need to respond very quickly is becoming imperative."

Bruno Sidler, chief operating officer for Ceva Logistics, the Netherlands-based logistics company, says the push towards shorter supply chains fits in with the trend since the late 2008 downturn for companies to try to cut down the amount of stock they hold. For the many companies still undertaking most of their manufacturing in Asia, that has meant trying to apply over the long distances of seaborne or airborne supply chains the "just-in-time" techniques originally designed to ensure factories sited near each other held only minimal stock.

"I believe that we have an ongoing evolution from production based on a forecast to on-demand production," Mr Sidler says. "People are trying very, very hard to keep as little inventory as possible."

The challenge, however, is to find the optimum balanced for each set of products between the strengths and weaknesses of the different approaches.

Companies' desire to hold minimal stock, for example, can present severe challenges for the shipping lines and air freight operators that move the goods. The "slightest movement" in consumer demand has an immediate effect on demand in supply chains when stock levels are so low, Mr Sidler says.

"That has an immediate effect on carriers," he says. "The airlines and shipping lines, because they have assets that they need to fill, they're really suffering from this volatility."

Near-shoring also potentially increases the costs of transporting goods, even though they are travelling a shorter distance. The vast container ships that bring most goods from Asia to Europe and the United States offer very cheap transport even in normal times – and severe overcapacity at present has sent prices to move containers on some routes down to negligible levels.

"The cost of moving stuff from the far east is still going to be relatively cheap in the greater scheme of things," Mr Parsons says.

Mr Sidler also points out that the shift towards Asian manufacturing is unlikely to be swiftly reversed.

"If you take certain types of technology, the outsourcing has been done to an extent that today the entire supply business, whether it's components or cables and semi-conductors, are all in Asia," he says. "It's not something where you can say tomorrow, 'I want to do it in eastern Europe'."

Mr Gold agrees, pointing out that changes of strategy on supply chain issues are expensive. "You don't do these on a turn of a dime," he says.

Yet there has also been a change of mood. After a decade when the overriding consideration was to reduce costs by outsourcing to Asia, there has been a decisive change in the factors companies take into account.

"This is the year of supply chains," Mr Gold says. "There are going to be a lot of companies trying to rethink and review these questions. Companies are starting to adopt these ideas."

Source: *The Financial Times*, 24 January 2012

15.5 Pricing decisions

The question of pricing is crucial for any business, even for organisations that are not-for-profit. This is because pricing decisions must take into account the cost element, in order to ensure that the selling price exceeds or is equal to the average unit cost in order to make a profit or break-even.

When shopping at a retailer, the customer usually encounters set prices, but the way these prices are calculated depends on managerial pricing decisions, based on factors such as competition, product quality and manufacturing costs. Strategic objectives – such as market share or profit maximisation – also play a vital role in a company's pricing strategy.

Generally, pricing decisions can be placed into two categories: external or internal pricing. *External pricing* relates to goods and services sold to external customers and clients. *Internal pricing* relates to charges made to another department or business segment within the same company and is also referred to as *transfer pricing*.

15.5.1 External pricing

Cost-based pricing

As the name suggests, this method bases the selling price on the cost to the company. A business can choose to what extent it covers variable and total costs, depending on what it is trying to achieve with its pricing strategy. For example, if a business has a product that cost £100 and the business wishes to make 50% profit, then the cost-based pricing will be £100 + (50% × £100) = £150.

Cost-plus pricing

A percentage of the total product cost, or a fixed sum, is added to the cost of the product to determine the selling price (known as a 'mark-up'). This allows the company not only to cover all variable and fixed costs, but also to generate some profit in order to sustain and grow the business. For example, imagine a business wishes to make an additional £300 of profit on top of the unit cost of production which is £1,000, then the business should sell its product for £1,000 + £300 = £1,300. This is equal to a mark-up of 30% (i.e. the cost price of £1,000 plus a profit of 30% × £1,000).

Total cost pricing

A total cost strategy allows a company to cover not only all product-related fixed and variable production costs, but also fixed costs related to other product lines within the company. There is, however, no contribution to profit, so this strategy is mostly used in order to survive during a recession. For example, if a company produces product A and B, which have the following costs:

	A	B
Variable costs	10	8
Fixed costs	30	20
Total costs	40	28

If demand for product A is good, but product B's demand is falling, the selling price for product A could be set at £45, resulting in a £35 contribution (i.e. £45 selling price – £10 variable costs = £35) towards A's fixed costs of £30. The surplus of £5 can then contribute to the fixed cost of product B and product B could then be sold for only £23 (i.e. Total cost of B = £28, less A's contribution £5 = £23), which is less than cost.

Total production cost pricing

A product's total production cost comprises all product-related fixed and variable production costs. The company is not able to cover fixed costs related to other product lines. This strategy is used to create demand for a specific product when sales fall below expectations. Using the same example above, the company will sell product A for £40 (covering its total costs), leaving no contribution towards the fixed costs of product B.

Variable cost pricing

Variable costs are taken as a cost base, while all fixed costs are excluded. Thus the product does not generate any profit and is principally used to outsell the competition or to launch a new product line. For example, if the total variable cost of one unit of production is £100 and a mark-up of 50% is added, the selling price as determined by this method would be £150. If the fixed costs per unit is estimated at £30, then the profit per unit would be £20.

Loss leaders

Alternatively, a low price may be used to attract customers, who are then expected to buy other goods as well. This is known as a 'loss-leader' and is rarely used as a long-term strategy, since it does not contribute towards profit, and other product lines have to contribute towards the coverage of total fixed costs. For example, a store sometimes sells 12 bottles of water for £1.99 (the same as its own purchase price from the supplier). Its reasoning is that most customers are unlikely only to purchase bottled water from the store, they will also purchase other items. The overall profit made during this promotional period must cover the losses incurred on the bottled water. This is a good strategy to attract new customers, get a reputation as a low-cost provider or get rid of slow-moving product.

Below variable cost pricing

If a company sets its price *below* the variable cost of its product, it incurs a loss. So why should such a strategy be adopted? This method may be used to gain customers' attention at the launch of a new product, or to outsell rivals if a competitor is trying to eliminate competition. However, since it does not contribute towards profit, below variable cost pricing is rarely pursued as a long-term strategy (see Figure 15.3).

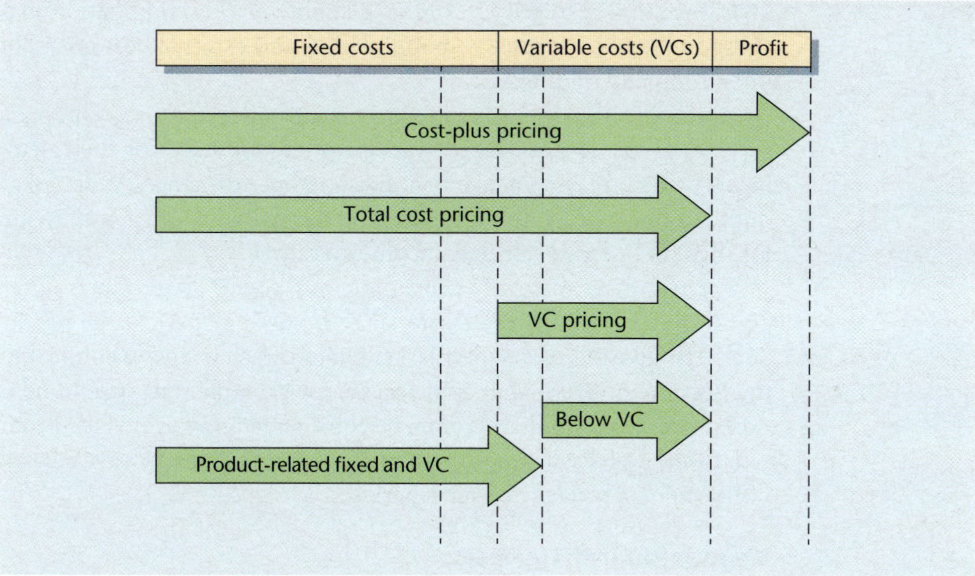

Figure 15.3 Pricing decisions

Stop and think

Wal-mart was founded in 1962 in Arkansas. In 1979, it had an annual turnover of $1bn. By 1993 it was achieving the same turnover on a weekly basis; by 2001, it was reaching that figure every day. The company seemed unstoppable.

However, in 1997, Wal-mart entered the German retail market, acquiring Wertkauf and Interspar (both local German retailers). In the US, Wal-mart's motto was 'Everyday low prices' and 'We sell for less – always', but in Germany this approach did not work.

Wal-mart's policy of aggressively low pricing was the wrong strategy for the German market. In addition to that, due to German law, Wal-mart could not act in the same way as it did in the US, and unfavourable press coverage made it very difficult for the company to achieve sustainable growth, and even forced it to close some of its stores.

Wal-mart's failure in Germany demonstrates the importance of choosing the appropriate strategy for the particular market, as well as carefully considering the various influencing factors.

15.5.2 Internal pricing

As previously noted, internal pricing (or transfer pricing) refers to prices charged between divisions of the same organisation. Many companies have divisions which trade among each other – such as a parent company trading with its subsidiaries, or subsidiaries buying and selling from each other – leading to inter-company pricing arrangements.

Setting an appropriate transfer price is important, since subsidiaries of major companies are free to buy from the supplier that offers the best deal. Thus, they are able to purchase products from an external supplier offering a competitive price, even if those products are supplied by another segment of the same company. Equally, supplying divisions are free to sell to external customers. This competition makes it important to charge an attractive price to both internal and external customers, in order to promote inter-company trading.

Moreover, transfer prices are important in decentralised companies where divisions serve as profit centres. Here, transfer prices are used for the calculation of divisional profits, which play a vital role in divisional performance evaluation. Additionally, since multinational companies transfer products across countries, these prices are important for them in order to calculate income taxes[1].

Internal prices may vary depending on whether the products purchased by a division are destined for immediate sale, or to be used as part of the production process. If a Southern division of a supermarket chain transfers apples to the Northern division for the purpose of producing apple sauce, for example, they would be part of the production process and would therefore be considered an intermediate product.

However, just as with external pricing, there are many ways by which a company may decide upon a product's internal price.

Negotiated transfer prices

If transfer prices are not imposed by senior management, they may be subject to negotiation between divisional managers, and the buyer and seller will agree on a price that offers mutual benefits. This has the advantage of creating a free market between divisions, which may encourage them to trade with each other, rather than with external partners, thus raising corporate profit.

Cost-based transfer prices

Just as with external pricing, divisions may use costs as a basis for pricing decisions, and so may also choose to adopt cost-plus, total cost or variable cost pricing.

Cost-plus pricing

Cost-plus pricing may provide an incentive for the selling division to trade internally, since it not only covers costs, but also allows for generation of profit. As long as this price is lower than the external market price, it should not discourage the buying division from purchasing internally.

Total cost

When pricing at *total cost*, direct costs are covered, but also part of the production and non-production overheads. Since there is no profit margin, this pricing method diminishes the incentive for the selling division to trade internally while encouraging the buying division to pursue internal trade.

Variable cost

This approach is very advantageous for the buying division, since the price will most certainly lie below the market price. It does not, however, cover any of the fixed costs, so the selling division may add a small charge to the variable cost, in order to receive a contribution towards fixed costs.

[1] The role of transfer pricing in helping multinationals to avoid taxation was brought into sharp focus in the UK in late 2012, when companies including Starbucks, Amazon and Google were accused by a parliamentary committee of manipulating transfer prices to minimise their tax payments (see Further research on page 387).

15.5.3 Other internal pricing strategies

Opportunity cost-based prices

In addition to the internal pricing methods already discussed, a division can elect to price its products based on its opportunity costs. In this case, it must state the standard variable costs, as well as the opportunity costs that this transaction will bring about. Clearly, this can be problematic, since the opportunity costs of a transaction can be difficult to determine.

Market price and adjusted market price based pricing

When pricing products for inter-company trade, the supplying division may decide to use the market price of similar products as a benchmark, but this approach offers little economic incentive for divisions to trade internally. The supplying division may therefore adjust the market price to reflect savings made by trading internally, such as a reduced spend on marketing, administration or delivery.

15.6 Special orders

While a company may have orders which it fulfils routinely, from time to time it may also receive special orders: a customer or a potential customer may place a special production request and the company then has to decide whether to accept and, if so, how to price it.

The decision to accept the order may largely be based upon the company's ability to complete it without expanding its operations, but the relationship between *incremental revenues* – the additional revenue generated by the order – and *incremental costs* – the additional costs incurred – should also be considered.

Generally, a company is likely to accept a special order if it has the capacity to fulfil it, the marginal (incremental) costs it incurs are lower than the incremental revenue and its decision does not affect present sales. Look back at the discussion of marginal costing (in Chapter 10) for further details.

Once the company decides that it has the capacity to handle the order, it must decide how to price it, ensuring that the minimum price covers the variable cost. It may also consider setting the price higher than the variable costs, to ensure a contribution towards product-related and non-product-related overheads. However, this strategy may deter the customer from pursuing the order and negatively affect customer retention.

There are, however, some occasions when a company may decide to price below variable cost – when trying to avoid a shutdown, for example, or when trying to undercut competitors. Undercutting the competition may allow the company to gain future orders from a lucrative client, thus making profit in the long-run.

Activity 15.2

The ice-cream business is highly seasonal. A German ice-cream producer finds that in autumn, it encounters spare capacity due to low demand. However, it then receives a special order from an expanding food retailer in Italy, requesting a special consignment of ice-cream.

What factors should the ice-cream producer take into account when deciding whether or not to accept this special order? How should the order be priced?

Answer

When deciding whether or not to accept the special order, the following aspects should be considered:

- Does the company have spare capacity? Can the order be completed without expanding operations?
- What variable costs would be incurred? Will they be inferior to the incremental revenue generated?
- Will the special order affect present sales?

When deciding upon a pricing strategy, the manufacturer should consider the benefits of accepting the order:

- Ice-cream is a seasonal business and sales are low in Germany in autumn. Supplying to an Italian customer may raise sales considerably, since Italy enjoys a warmer climate at this time of year.
- The retailer is expanding, so this order may offer future business potential in new markets.

Thus, the behaviour of competitors should be considered alongside production capacity, variable costs and revenues when deciding whether to accept a special order and how to price it.

Behaviour of competitors should also be considered. If the company is keen to retain the customer, it may decide to price at variable costs. However, if competition is fierce, this special order may be priced below variable costs in order to undercut the competitors.

Although the information provided gives no clues to the current financial situation of the ice-cream manufacturer, if it is trying to avoid a shutdown, it may also decide to price below variable cost.

If, however, the company is satisfied with its current situation, it may not be interested in expanding to other markets, or in supplying the Italian retailer long-term. In this case, it may fix a price point that is higher than its variable costs, thus making a contribution towards fixed costs and generating some profit.

15.7 The Balanced Scorecard

The Balanced Scorecard is a tool used by businesses, industries, governments and different institutions for the purpose of strategic planning. It aligns the business activities with the strategic vision of an organisation, seeks to improve the internal and external communications and more effectively monitor and control business activities.

In 1990, David Norton and Robert Kaplan conducted a study to develop a new performance measurement model. The findings of their study were published in the Harvard Business Review in January 1992 proposing the new measurement system known as the Balanced Scorecard. It was developed to give managers an overall view which includes a non-financial as well as various financial and other performance measures. It proposed four perspectives (see Figure 15.4).

15.7.1 The learning and growth perspective

In order for companies to survive in periods of intense global competition they have to remain competitive. Companies can remain competitive through the continuous

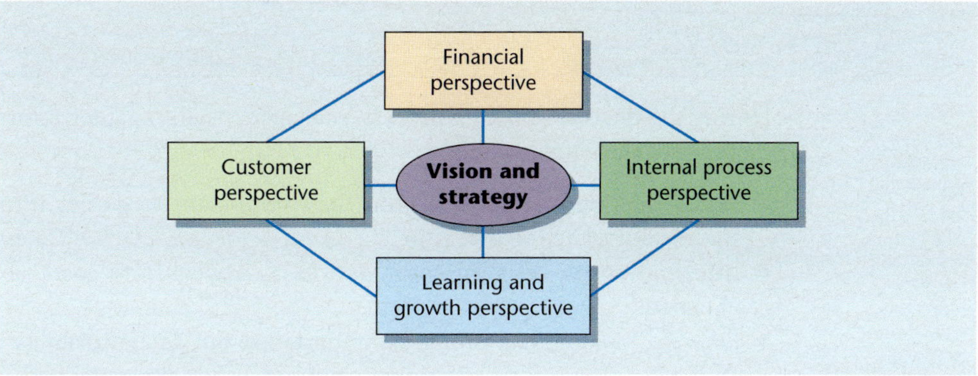

Figure 15.4 The Balanced scorecard

development and improvement of their employees. This perspective emphasises the learning and development of employees and corporate self-improvement. Currently, technology is fast moving and employee knowledge is widely regarded as a key source of success for an organisation. This perspective of the Balanced Scorecard can be useful for managers in allocating their training funds where they can have the greatest impact.

15.7.2 The business process perspective

This perspective refers to the internal business processes that have the greatest impact on customer satisfaction. It is important for managers to know how well their business is running and whether they are meeting their logistical requirements and fulfilling their customer orders, both in terms of quality and timeliness.

15.7.3 The customer perspective

In order for organisations to retain their customers, managers have to keep their customers satisfied, hence, managers have to measure customer experience and ensure that customers are satisfied with the goods and services they are receiving. If customers are not satisfied they may switch to other suppliers, resulting in a future decline in sales, despite the fact that the current financial indicators might appear positive. This perspective of the Balanced Scorecard deals with the factors that matter to customers and ensures that managers have enough information to make decisions on areas that require improvements.

15.7.4 The financial perspective

Traditionally, companies used to focus on the financial measures and ignore the non-financial ones. Even though the non-financial indicators are now more widely appreciated, the financial perspective of the Balanced Scorecard remains crucial for managers. Indeed financial indicators are a crucial measure as to whether the company's strategy, its implementation and execution are contributing to the overall profitability of the company and creating value for its shareholders.

15.8 Summary

During the decision-making process, managers need to gather information that allows them to see the whole picture:

- When making one-off decisions, it is important to gather information which is specifically related to that issue.
- Information on relevant costs, as well as opportunity costs, should normally be obtained.
- Forward-looking data is of great importance, but data availability may sometimes be an issue. Some information may need to be specially generated to facilitate the decision in hand.
- The effect of the decision on net cash flow should be considered.
- Probability testing can help to identify the likelihood of a specified event's occurrence, and may be of great assistance when choosing between alternative projects.

So as to better understand what costs a decision may incur, managers should take cost classifications into consideration:

- Fixed/variable costs
- Relevant/non-relevant costs
- Avoidable/non-avoidable costs
- Sunk costs
- Committed costs
- Opportunity costs.

Managers may encounter various kinds of decisions:

- **Closure or shut-down.** Should an underperforming business line be made inactive only temporarily or permanently abandoned?
- **Make or buy.** Should an item be produced internally or bought from an outside supplier?
- **Pricing decisions.** External and internal (transfer) pricing, using a variety of methods such as cost-based pricing, market price-based pricing etc. need to be made.
- **Special orders.** The decision to accept or decline a special order, and how to price it, will depend on factors such as: spare production capacity; incremental revenues; incremental costs; and competitor behaviour.

15.9 Chapter glossary

Avoidable costs Costs that will only be incurred if a particular decision is made. Variable costs are an avoidable cost.

Balanced Scorecard A management tool used to measure both the financial and non-financial performance of the company. It assists management to obtain a more balanced view and make informed strategic decisions.

Committed costs Costs will be incurred irrespective of specific management decisions.

Decision The selection between two or more alternatives.

External pricing Related to goods and services sold to external customers and clients.

Fixed cost Costs that are unaffected by the level of business activity.

Forward-looking Anticipating future opportunities and challenges.

Internal pricing Relates to charges made to another department or business segment within the same company (also called transfer pricing).

Net cash flow The profit of the business plus non-cash expenses.

One-off decision Non-recurrent decision.

Opportunity costs These refer to the next best alternative use of resources which have been sacrificed as a result of a business decision.

Probability test Helps to identify the likelihood of various outcomes, in order to choose between alternatives.

Relevant costs Costs that are specific to a particular course of action

Sunk costs Costs are based on past decisions and cannot be recovered.

Variable costs Costs that change according to the volume of production, rising when production levels increase and falling when they decrease.

Additional resources

Only accessible on Android-based devices

Now work through the various exercises and problems that you can find within the My Accounting Lab that are relevant to this chapter. Either use the QR code shown in the margin (if you use an Android-based device), or visit www.myaccountinglab.com for the log-in page.

Self-check questions

The Answers to these questions are in Appendix 1

1 Which one of the following items is *least* useful for decision-making?

(a) Relevant costs
(b) Accruals and prepayments
(c) Net cash flow
(d) Opportunity costs

2 Decision-making can be defined as

(a) Planning
(b) Choosing between alternatives
(c) Developing alternative courses of action
(d) Monitoring and control

3 Which one of the following items refers to past costs that cannot be recovered?

(a) Opportunity cost
(b) Sunk cost
(c) Committed cost
(d) Avoidable cost

4 Which one of the following items is normally ignored when deciding whether or not to close a factory for a short period?

(a) Fixed costs
(b) Opportunity costs
(c) Total costs
(d) Variable costs

5 What is the minimum cost a company must be able to cover if it is to continue production even in the short-run?

(a) Variable cost
(b) Total cost
(c) Below variable cost
(d) Between variable cost and total cost

6 Transfer price refers to:

(a) Charges made internally
(b) Charges made externally
(c) Market price
(d) Price of outsourcing

7 A Balanced Scorecard is:

(a) A management tool that measures the financial aspects of the business
(b) A management tool used for strategic planning
(c) A management tool used for measuring non-financial aspects of the business
(d) None of the above

8 The long-run is a period of time in which:

(a) The firm is able to maximise total profit
(b) The firm may want to build a bigger plant, but cannot do so
(c) The firm can hire all the workers that it wants to employ, but it does not have sufficient time to buy more equipment
(d) The quantities of all inputs can be varied.

9 If there is a 30% probability of an investment giving a return of £40m and a 70% probability of the investment giving a return of £50m, what is the expected value of the investment?

(a) £12m
(b) £47m
(c) £35m
(d) £55m

10 If data availability requires new data to be generated by a questionnaire, we call this:

(a) Secondary data
(b) Tertiary data
(c) Primary data
(d) Quaternary data

Self-study questions

Questions marked with this symbol (#) indicate that the suggested answers are available to lecturers only – other answers are given in Appendix 2.

15.1 WV is a car manufacturer. It is currently deciding whether to buy in car doors for a particular model rather than continue to manufacture them. The estimated costs for one door are as follows:

Direct materials	£70
Direct labour	£80
Total fixed costs applicable to car door production*	£100,000
Units of production*	10,000
* per year	

An external supplier offers a price of £140 per door. Should WV choose the external supplier or continue to produce the doors itself? Discuss your answer.

15.2# Senior Ltd is thinking about launching a new product. The marketing department estimated, based on market research, that the expected sales and respective probabilities are as follows:

Revenue	Probability
2,000	45%
2,500	25%
3,200	20%
4,000	10%

Calculate the expected value of launching a new product.

15.3 Sabine entered her second year of business. She makes product A, which takes 3 hours using a basic machine. The marginal (variable) cost and selling price are £50 and £62 respectively. Component B, which is used in the manufacturing process of product A, could be made on the same machine in 1 hour with a marginal cost of £10. The best price for product B that Sabine managed to get from an external supplier is £12.

Sabine has to decide on whether to make or buy component B. Note that the machine currently is working at full capacity. Explain whether she should make or buy the component.

15.4# What is meant by the Balanced Scorecard? What are its four perspectives?

15.5# British Foam Group (BFG) Ltd makes and sells packaging solutions products. The material cost is £15 per packaging solution which requires $1\frac{1}{2}$ hours of skilled labour at £10 per hour.

BFG Ltd has no variable overheads but has fixed overheads of £10,000 per month, each packaging solution sells for £42, and there is a heavy demand on the product throughout the year.

A one-off contract has been offered to BFG Ltd to supply a different packaging solution as compared to its standard product.

(a) The labour time for the one-off contract would be 110 hours.
(b) The material cost would be £700 plus the cost of additional special components
(c) The special components could be purchased from an outside supplier for £180 or could be made by BFG Ltd for a material cost of £110 and labour time of four hours.

You are required to give BFG Ltd advice on:

(i) Whether the special component should be manufactured by BFG Ltd or purchased from the outside supplier
(ii) Whether BFG Ltd should accept the one-off contract
(iii) How much should be charged to the client to enable BFG Ltd to make a 30% mark-up on the cost of the one-off contract.

Case study: Marvin balances his business

Marvin was so pleased at the growth of his business that he applied to his bank manager for further funding to enable him to expand over the coming years of operation. He particularly wanted to invest in extra assistants when performing, more business support staff, more modern vehicles for transport and additional stage props.

He had discussed his growth plans and financial needs with his bank manager but was puzzled when he was asked to produce a 'Balanced Scorecard'! However, he knew how difficult it was for companies to raise funds, so he thought he had better find out what he would need to provide when he next met the bank manager.

Marvin reckoned that the extra funding would improve his marketing, enable him to perform his shows more frequently, give better customer experience, travel to more distant destinations and make his business more efficient and sustainable.

He eventually put together the information in the box below.

Marvin's Balanced Scorecard

	Current year	Following year (after investment)
1. Variable costs per performance	£850	£1,200
2. Number of performances per year	100	180
3. Overhead costs (interest payments, office and administration)	£40,000	£55,000
4. Revenue per performance	£2,500	£4,000
5. Improved seating and viewing of performance using height adjustable chairs		
6. Development of 'fan club' using new website		
7. Improved programmes with extra information, new photographs and better quality print		
8. New training programme for assistants		
9. Perform at extra venues beyond 100 miles from the 'home base'		
10. Explore bringing in new partner to support and help fund business development		
11. Change role of part-time business manager to full-time business manager		
12. Improved booking and enquiries		

Questions

- Has Marvin produced a genuine 'Balanced Scorecard'? Explain your reasoning.
- What aspects of his 'Balanced Scorecard' might the bank manager want to explore further with Marvin?

Answers are in Appendix 3

Further research

A short film clip showing Dr Robert Kaplan, the co-creator of the Balanced Scorecard, can be found at: **http://www.youtube.com/watch?v=oJldZvX_jbQ or use the QR code.**

A BBC article on the role of transfer pricing in avoiding taxation by multi-national companies:

Chapter 16 Contemporary issues in finance

Objectives

When you have read this chapter you will be able to:

- Explain what is meant by 'Integrated Reporting' and the advantages and disadvantages of this approach
- Understand issues related to executive compensation, governance and shareholder 'democracy'
- Review developments in accounting standards, particularly relating to 'fair value' and pensions
- Examine the financial implications and relevance to business of changes in sovereign debt and credit ratings

16.1 Introduction

In the previous chapter we considered the decision-making process from the manager's perspective, the different types of cost classifications, and strategic support for decision making such as the use of the Balanced Scorecard to give an overview of financial as well as non-financial data when measuring company performance. This chapter will further examine aspects of financial and non-financial information and data that companies report to their stakeholders through what is called 'Integrated Reporting'. In the past four decades, companies have become more environmentally and socially conscious, with large organisations increasingly using the framework of their annual reports to state both their financial and non-financial contributions to stakeholders and the wider community. This integration of financial information with issues of sustainability, governance and ethics is increasingly seen by a wide range of stakeholders as essential to the long term viability of the business. The concept of 'corporate social responsibility' is sometimes used interchangeably with that of 'Integrated Reporting'. Technological advances, the internationalisation of production, population growth and increased mobility have all contributed to a globalised business climate, resulting in new risks, new opportunities and new interdependencies. Stakeholders, including governments, are also continually imposing new expectations on businesses, in terms of additional regulations, standards, codes and ethical guidelines. It is therefore evident that a new approach to reporting and analysing information and data is required, placing each element in a more holistic and global context and acknowledging the various synergies.

News clip

No easy formula for success as companies face scepticism

FT

By Sarah Murray

Today, few leading companies would dispute the need to embrace corporate responsibility and environmental sustainability. Topics such as labour and human rights, climate change and resource management have made their way on to the boardroom agenda. But while companies' efforts to become good citizens have become more broadly recognised by consumers, businesses still face a sceptical element of public opinion that is prepared to take to the streets to oppose their activities.

Source: The Financial Times, 29 May 2012

16.2 What is Integrated Reporting?

Integrated reporting considers an organisation's performance – both financial and non-financial – in the context of the commercial, social, and environmental climate in which it operates. This integration enables investors, stakeholders and the wider community to understand how the company is performing. An organisation called the International Integrated Reporting Council (IIRC) was established in October 2011 to promote the

Scan the following QR code with your QR reader to take you to the website of The International Integrated Reporting Council.

development of integrated reporting, and its website (www.theiirc.org) contains much useful information, including the following definition:

> Integrated Reporting is a new approach to corporate reporting that demonstrates the linkages between an organization's strategy, governance and financial performance and the social, environmental and economic context within which it operates. By reinforcing these connections, Integrated Reporting can help business to take more sustainable decisions and enable investors and other stakeholders to understand how an organization is really performing.

It is a way of consolidating existing reporting protocols, whilst at the same time emphasising a wider range of considerations to more accurately assess corporate value. Integrated Reporting looks beyond the present financial picture of the company and attempts to address the longer-term financial and non-financial consequences of corporate decisions. It recognises that an organisation's ability to create and sustain value is increasingly measured through factors such as:

- Environmental concerns
- Concerns over current and future scarcity of resources
- Demand for corporate transparency
- Contributions to corporate and social responsibility (CSR).

16.3 The International Integrated Reporting Framework

The International Integrated Reporting Framework, developed by the International Integrated Reporting Committee (IIRC), aims to provide an international standard, outlining parameters for policy-makers and regulators, and ensuring consistent reporting. The standardised information will help companies to align and simplify their internal and external reporting and create a more consistent and efficient means of communication with various stakeholders.

16.3.1 Key principles

According to the IIRC, the following key principles underpin the preparation of a successful report:

- **Organizational overview and business model**

What the organization does and how it creates and sustains value in the short, medium and long term

Highlights the organization's mission, principal activities, markets, products and services; its business model, value drivers and critical stakeholder dependencies; and its attitude to risk.

- **Operating context, including risks and opportunities**

Operational circumstances, key resources, relationships, risks and opportunities

Identifies commercial, social and environmental context; resources and relationships that are key to the organization's success, including key stakeholders and their expectations; and the availability and affordability of relevant resources.

- **Strategic objectives and strategies to achieve them**

Where the organization wants to go and how it will get there

Describes the factors that drive and protect the value of the organization, including risk management arrangements and sustainability considerations.

- **Governance and remuneration**

The governance structure, how it supports strategic objectives and how it relates to organizational remuneration

Explanation of leadership and strategic decision-making processes; how leaders influence strategic direction, including its culture, ethical values and stakeholder relationships; and how the remuneration of leaders is linked to performance.

- **Performance**

Measures performance against strategic objectives and related strategies

Provides qualitative and quantitative data on key performance indicators (KPIs) and key risk indicators (KRIs); positive and negative impact on resources and relationships; and external factors affecting performance. Information should be concise and connected, with links between past and current performance and future outlook made clear.

- **Future outlook**

Opportunities, challenges and uncertainties and their implications for future performance

Attempts are made to outline the implications of these principles on the future direction and policies of the organisation.

Source: The International Integrated Reporting Council, © 2011, www.theiirc.org

16.4 Socially responsible investing

As the global appetite for Socially Responsible Investing (SRI) continues to grow, increasing numbers of investors are considering non-financial themes such as environmental, social and governance (ESG) factors in investment decisions. According to the research paper *Responsible Investing: A Paradigm Shift*, published by Robeco and Booz and Co. (see Further Research at the end of the chapter), by 2050 SRI will reach \$26.5tr (approx. £17tr), representing over 15% of total global Assets Under Management (AUM). Since 2003 the SRI market has grown at an annual rate of 22%, whilst global AUM growth rates covering all assets have grown much less quickly at around 10% per annum. Integrated reporting helps the trend towards SRI in the following ways:

- **Increases transparency:** Integrated Reporting supports SRI by increasing transparency and considering a wider range of Key Performance Indicators (KPIs) and Key Risk Indicators (KRIs), demonstrating an organisation's use of financial, manufactured, human, intellectual, natural and social capital. The increase in corporate transparency through Integrated Reporting will improve the relationship and credibility between the company and the key stakeholders. This is a very important step for building a long-term sustainable business.
- **Improves performance:** By providing a broader description of performance than traditional reporting methods, Integrated Reporting stimulates greater consideration of an organisation's long-term business model and strategy, its ability to meet the needs of stakeholders and its allocation of resources

- **Other advantages:** In addition to the above, Integrated Reporting:
  - Helps businesses to be more responsive to opportunity, risks, internal and external drivers through a focus on longer-term business impact
  - Provides insights into linkages between executive pay and company performance
  - Achieves a competitive advance through cost savings, operational efficiencies, brand differentiation and innovation
  - Embraces communicating more clearly with the wider community
  - Manages shareholder expectations and addressing their needs
  - Improves compliance with the existing guidelines, ethics procedures, regulations and corporate governance requirements.

16.5 Executive pay, remuneration policy and shareholder 'democracy'

Whilst touched upon by Integrated Reporting, this is a key area of financial concern in its own right. There has been much debate about excessive Chief Executive Officer (CEO) compensation across leading companies over the past decade, with director remuneration rising much faster than average employee earnings across those companies. There has been a major change from a situation where the average CEO salary of 'Top 100' companies was 75 times the average employee's salary in 2001, but 128 times that salary in 2011.

Table 16.1 gives data over a 11-year time period for the FTSE 100 (the UK's largest companies by stock market value):

The data suggest that the variation in salaries between average CEO earnings and average employee earnings has vastly widened between 1998 and 2011. In other words,

Table 16.1 Compensation in the FTSE 100 companies

Year	Average CEO earnings (£)	Average employee earnings (£)
2001	1,812,750	24,170
2002	2,587,474	24,182
2003	2,773,904	24,767
2004	3,121,435	25,955
2005	3,312,285	27,254
2006	3,339,421	30,828
2007	3,935,820	25,677
2008	3,950,642	30,994
2009	3,710,440	32,521
2010	3,940,822	32,896
2011	4,210,422	32,984

the average director's remuneration rose much faster than average employee earnings. The average CEO salary was 47 times the average employee's salary in 2001, but 128 times that salary in 2011.

This situation has serious potential implications for CSR since directors should, arguably, be aiming to increase shareholder wealth and respond to shareholder needs rather than act in their own best interest. It is this kind of development that is leading to shareholder displeasure at annual general meetings and has led to, for example, recent changes in UK government regulations relating to shareholders voting on executive pay increases.

The 'News clip' below usefully captures aspects of this debate.

News clip

Barclays suffers executive pay backlash

FT

Nearly a third of Barclays shareholders failed to support the bank's pay report during a fiery annual meeting in April 2012 at which the bank's chairman apologised for its "poor communication" on executive pay – as many as 26.9 per cent of shareholders opposed the Barclays pay plan and a further 4.6 per cent abstained, marking another signal of investor discontent in what is being dubbed a "shareholder spring".

Chairman Marcus Agius and Alison Carnwath, who chairs the bank's remuneration committee, also pledged to cut bankers' pay and boost shareholder payouts in future: "The balance of rewards between shareholders and employees has to change in favour of shareholders," Ms Carnwath said to enthusiastic applause from shareholders.

The Barclays vote comes after all-out opposition to Citigroup's pay report and the departure of AstraZeneca's chief executive in the UK, both in April 2012. Also, in the same month, Credit Suisse directors faced a similar rebellion, as 32.4 per cent of shareholders refused to back the Swiss bank's pay report. The rebellion would have constituted a formal defeat for the bank under proposals which would force a binding vote on pay with a "super-majority" approval threshold of 75 per cent. Vince Cable, Business Secretary, welcomed what he said was shareholders "doing what they are supposed to do, which is holding executives to account".

Dominic Rossi, head of equities at Fidelity Worldwide, said: "[Bank boards] must respond to the fundamental shift which has taken place in the status of banks, which now increasingly resemble low return, highly regulated, capital intensive public utilities. In these sectors the executives earn less, yet the returns on equity are higher."

The Barclays row has been brewing for weeks, after the bank's 2011 executive pay plans revealed Bob Diamond, chief executive, and Chris Lucas, finance director, had been awarded annual bonuses close to the maximum defined by the bank even though the share price slumped by a third, dividends stagnated and profits fell. There had also been shareholder anger at a £5.75m "tax equalisation" deal for Mr Diamond, paid to compensate him for duplicate tax liabilities in the US and UK.

Almost 1,000 largely retail investors, assembled at London's Royal Festival Hall, heard Mr Agius apologise for the way the pay issue was handled. "Evidently we've not done enough [to communicate with share holders]," he said. "And for this I apologise." His remarks still drew a sprinkle of boos and heckles from his audience, as did Ms Carnwath for her role in overseeing last year's pay deals.

Source: *The Financial Times*, 27 April 2012

Activity 16.1

Remuneration around the world

Look carefully at the data in Table 16.2 and then answer the question that follows.

Table 16.2 Structure of CEO remuneration packages around the world

Country	Base salary (%)	Cash bonus (%)	Incentive plan compensation (%)
United States	23	17	60
Brazil	27	41	32
Germany	39	47	14
United Kingdom	40	38	22
France	44	25	31
Ireland	44	43	13
Hong Kong	51	19	30
Netherlands	51	28	21
Belgium	52	26	22
Italy	52	29	19
Japan	71	12	17

Note: Only includes companies with revenues between $1bn and $3bn.

Source: Adapted from Watson Wyatt Worldwide (2009) *Executive pay practices around the world*

What does the data suggest? What implications might this have for policy making aimed at improving corporate social responsibility?

Answer

The Data shows that CEOs in Japan have the highest base salary, with relatively little coming from bonuses or other incentives whereas in the United States, only a quarter of the remuneration paid to CEOs is in the form of a base salary, with the remainder being bonuses and incentives. This could lead to excessive risk-taking by US executives as their remuneration is highly geared to company performance (which could be measured by KPIs such as profitability and share price). Japanese managers might take a more cautious approach as their personal pay is only marginally increased by reaching similar targets. This applies in varying proportions to the other countries listed, with an inverse relationship between base salary and risk-taking.

Activity 16.2

Read this article and then answer the questions that follow.

Vince Cable's new executive pay rules branded a 'climbdown'

By Rajeev Syal

New rules which will force publicly listed companies to give shareholders three-yearly votes on executive pay have been announced by the business secretary Vince Cable. The changes announced in June 2012 have been criticized for failing to live up to previous government promises made in the wake of the so-called "shareholder spring" revolt against excessive pay.

Currently, shareholder votes are advisory, which means companies can ignore them. While there will now be a binding vote on pay, this will only take place every three years rather than annually, unless a company makes a 'material change to a director's deal'.

The business secretary noted that "For the first time there will be a real, lasting and binding vote on a company's pay policy including their exit payments." He went on to say that binding votes on pay would require the support of a majority of shareholders. Once a policy is approved, companies would not be allowed to make payments outside its scope, he added. Companies will also be required to explain their policy on pay-offs to shareholders, which will also be subject to a binding vote. When a director leaves, the company will be told to publish all payments.

All firms will have to report a single figure for the total pay directors receive every year and this will cover all rewards received, including bonuses and long-term incentives. They will also have to report details of whether they met performance measures and a comparison between company performance and chief executives' pay.

Critics of the proposals have called for employee representatives on remuneration committees and for firms to publish the ratio of the average pay of a worker to that of the highest paid executive.

Source: Guardian, 20 June 2012
© Guardian News & Media Ltd 2012

1 Why have some praised these new rules as increasing shareholder power?
2 Why have some criticised these new rules as not being sufficiently strong to achieve their objectives?

Answer

1 There has been praise because until the change the shareholders' votes were only advisory, which meant that companies could ignore them, whereas the new rules will give shareholders power to determine the pay policy every three years unless a company makes a 'material change to a director's deal'.
2 There has been criticism because many companies will only have to have a binding vote every three years rather than every year and there is no requirement for employee representatives on remuneration committees as had been proposed originally. Also there was no requirement for firms to publish the ratio of the average pay of a worker to that of the highest paid executive.

16.6 Accounting standards, 'fair value' and pensions

The International Accounting Standards Board (IASB) aims to harmonise international accounting practices in order to make it easier to compare the financial health of different companies based in different countries. Its rules are known as International Accounting Standards (IASs) or International Financial Reporting Standards (IFRSs), and deal with key issues such as: disclosure of information; presentation of information in the financial statements; assets valuation; and profit measurement. All these rules will have different impacts on the companies, directors' remuneration, pensions and investors.

For example, the International Accounting Standards Board has sought a global convergence on an agreed standard for accounting for pensions – with some of its proposals based on rules introduced in the UK. FRS 17, as the UK rule is known, was agreed when Sir David Tweedie (who became Chairman of the IASB) was head of the

UK Accounting Standards Board and some companies have cited that standard as their reason for forcing the closure of their relatively generous defined benefit ('final salary') pension schemes. Like the IASB's standard on financial instruments, the International Accounting Standard (IAS 19 Employee Benefits) puts a heavy emphasis on 'fair value' accounting. Under the standard, the measurement of the assets in a defined benefit pension scheme should reflect their fair or market value. The standard also tells accountants how to arrive at the present value for future liabilities; it adds them up and discounts back at an interest rate equal to that on AA-rated corporate bonds. Credit ratings agencies are responding to the pension standard by downgrading the debt of companies where they have concerns about pension deficits. Many employers, however, argue that the standard on pensions is misleading: although a pension shortfall is presented as a liability, it is not one about to come due in full any time soon.

More than 110 countries, including most of Europe and Asia, use the International Financial Reporting Standards drawn up by the IASB. US companies continue to report under Generally Accepted Accounting Principles while its regulators consider whether to endorse IFRS.

The activity below indicates the impacts of accounting conventions on business, using the issues raised by the collapse of Lehman Brothers in 2008, which many saw as further deepening the 'credit crunch' in the following years, with global adverse impacts.

Activity 16.3

Read this article and then answer the questions that follow.

Accounting: Fooled again

By Jennifer Hughes

In the wake of revelations on how Lehman flattered its balance sheet, questions are arising about how such techniques became possible and what can be done to curb them. On March 18 2008, Erin Callan, Lehman Brothers' chief financial officer, told a conference call that the bank was 'trying to give the group a great amount of transparency on the balance sheet' by providing more details. Analysts on the line even thanked her for it. But what Ms Callan did not tell them is that Lehman had shifted $49bn (€36bn, £32bn) off its balance sheet in the quarter just ended, using a process it nicknamed Repo 105. That was expressly to help bring down the bank's reported leverage – or the ratio of assets to equity – the very reduction of which she was promoting to the analysts.

That and other similar deals came to light in March 2010 in a 2,200 page report by Anton Valukas, the bankruptcy court-appointed examiner. With little or no economic rationale they are simply a form of the age-old accounting wheeze of window-dressing the books to look better temporarily. What has grabbed attention two years on is the matter-of-fact way the arrangements were discussed inside the bank by senior executives and were accepted by its counterparties – other financial groups with which Lehman did business before its collapse that September.

Yet even inside Lehman, not everyone saw the mechanism in so benign a way. Bart McDade, who became chief operating officer in June 2008, called Repo 105 'another drug we [are] on' in an e-mail and planned to slash its use, amid howls of protest from some departments. Martin Kelly, global financial controller, warned his bosses about the 'headline risk' to Lehman's reputation if the deals were to become public.

The process even cost the bank money. As one e-mail from another staffer put it: 'everyone knows 105 is an off-balance sheet mechanism so counterparties are looking for ridiculous levels [of prices] to take them.' But the pressure to do more of the deals grew in 2008, as did the outside world's obsession with the bank's precarious finances, particularly its leverage. Internal e-mails exhorted managers to work harder to get assets off the books.

Among the questions the Valukas report raises about the appropriateness of the accounting – and the auditing conducted by Ernst & Young – lies a bigger issue: how did this sort of financial engineering come to be considered a legitimate business tool and what, if anything, can be done about it?

Window-dressing the accounts is not new and can take many forms. In manufacturing companies, for example, a manager might engage in 'channel stuffing' – shifting products just before quarter-end, even if they have not been expressly ordered – to help meet targets and boost reported revenues.

Sean FitzPatrick resigned in 2010 as chairman of Dublin-based Anglo Irish Bank following the revelation that he had for years concealed personal loans worth up to €87m ($119m, £77m). He did so by transferring them to another bank just before his bank's year-end, then returning them after the balance sheet date.

Two years before Mr Fitzpatrick's departure, the US Securities and Exchange Commission forced a group of Puerto Rican banks to restate their accounts following its investigation into several misdemeanours, including managing earnings through a series of simul-taneous purchase and sale transactions with other banks.

The practice is hardly recent: in 1973, the UK's London and County Securities collapsed after a government-initiated credit squeeze helped fulfil widespread market suspicions about its rocky finances. On unpicking L&Cs accounts, the liquidators found, among many sharp practices, a window-dressing system involving a ring of banks that deposited funds with each other just before year-end to boost their reported liquidity.

How Repo worked

Banks use repurchase agreements, known as repos, all the time for short-term financing. One borrows cash and gives the other securities, such as government bonds, as collateral. Both agree to unwind the arrangement on a set date. The deals, which usually run only for days or weeks, are accounted for as financings, and remain on the books with banks recording an asset – the cash – and a matching liability in the promise to buy back the collateral.

Lehman's 105 was different – instead of handing over securities equivalent to the cash it received, the bank gave more than was necessary. The point was to exploit a loophole allowing such over-collateralised deals to be accounted for as true sales. Lehman then reported its obligation to repurchase the securities at a fraction of the full cost, and used the cash it had received to pay off its liability, thereby 'shrinking' its balance sheet.

Use of Repo 105 peaked sharply at the end of each accounting quarter – more so in 2008 as pressure grew on Lehman to reduce its leverage – and fell just as dramatically soon after the new accounting period began, as deals were unwound.

Source: Financial Times, 19 March 2010 (adapted)

1 What do you understand by 'off balance sheet' accounting (remember that the balance sheet is the same as the *statement of financial position*)?
2 How did such practices contribute to the collapse of Lehman Brothers?

Answers

1 These are arrangements involving transactions that do not appear in full on the company's published balance sheet. In fact the arrangements are structured ('financial engineering') to give the published balance sheet an appearance that is actually misleading to many investors who are unaware of these arrangements,

e.g. Repo 105. The term 'window dressing' is often applied, i.e. making the various accounting ratios which involve the balance sheet, and which are used to evaluate the financial health of companies, seem much more positive than is actually the case.

2 Lehman Brothers were heavily involved in such 'off balance sheet' accounting', especially the use of Repo 105 transactions. These distorted the situation at Lehman's, making it look as though the leverage and gearing ratios were more favourable than was actually the case. In other words, there was a higher ratio of liquid assets to total liabilities than was actually the case. This gave investors and others greater confidence in the business activities of Lehman's senior management than they should have had, so that 'corrective actions' did not occur, i.e. to develop a more sustainable business in Lehman's. When reality was eventually exposed at Lehman, the situation had become so serious that collapse of the bank, rather than incremental improvement, was the actual outcome.

16.7 Credit ratings and financial implications

There has been much criticism of credit rating agencies who gave high (known as 'triple A') ratings to financial institutions that were subsequently found to be 'anything but' credit worthy as events in the sub-prime market unfolded. Investors who later lost huge amounts of money complained that they had been misled by the AAA ratings that the agencies had handed out on complex packages of mortgage-related debt. The critics further argued that there was a clear conflict of interest when the credit rating agencies are themselves paid by the issuers to assess their bonds and other debt instruments.

Investor attention has now shifted to 'sovereign debt risk'. This involves bonds issued by a national government, in a different currency, to finance the issuer's debt, which is a risky investment for those purchasing the bonds because of the possibilities of default and of fluctuations in exchange rates. The three big credit rating agencies (Fitch, Moody's and Standard & Poor's) again found themselves at the centre of attention because of their role in setting the level of risk for those lending to the various countries. Sovereign debt rating upgrades actually exceeded downgrades in every year between 1999 and 2007, but that changed as a result of the financial crisis and over the period 2008–11when sovereign debt downgrades exceeded upgrades by a ratio of 7:1, the exact reverse of previous experiences.

The workings of the financial system make these ratings even more important; for example should any EU country be downgraded below A−, then that country's bonds become ineligible for use as collateral by the European Central Bank (ECB) under the tighter ECB rules since the end of 2010. This concern has been a key factor in persuading the various EU governments to accept austerity measures as a condition for support for their currencies from the EU and IMF.

Over the long term the ratings of most developed nations have been remarkably stable. No country rated AAA, AA or A by Standard and Poor's has subsequently defaulted within a 15-year period. Indeed, nearly 98% of countries ranked AAA were either at that rating, or at the AA level, 15 years later. That stable record may not persist. Investors have been buying government debt for years in the belief it is 'risk-free', almost regardless of the economic fundamentals. But if they lose faith in a government's policies, the situation can change very quickly. Such concerns are especially true since sovereign debt has increased from 62% of World GDP in 2006 to over 85% in 2011.

The Eurozone problems over the period 2010–12 have led to downgrading of many countries, not just Portugal, Italy, Greece and Spain, but also France and other major EU countries. Some, however, argue that governments and investors place too much importance on credit rating. Canada lost its AAA rating in the 1990s, but then regained it during the past decade, while Japan managed to keep borrowing at a cheap rate, despite losing its triple AAA rating. However there is certainly evidence that countries under pressure from the credit rating agencies have to pay at or above the 7% rate for borrowings over 10-year period, which is widely regarded as an unsustainable rate if debt is ever to be repaid!

The agencies are well aware that ratings changes are highly sensitive. Decisions are therefore made by committee, rather than by an individual, to reduce the scope for outside pressure. Consensus is generally sought before a downgrade is made. The agencies also seek to protect themselves from criticism by being as transparent as possible

A number of factors help determine whether a country's AAA status can be maintained, including economic and institutional strength, the government's finances and susceptibility to specific shocks. Others argue that the key ratio is not debt-to-GDP but interest payments as a proportion of government revenues. Once that gets beyond 10%, a government may face difficulties.

That does not mean a downgrade is inevitable, however. If the government is implementing a credible plan to cut its deficit, then it may maintain its AAA status. Agencies may also have to make qualitative judgements about a range of other factors, e.g. the willingness of Eurozone countries to bail out countries such as Greece when they enter financial difficulties!

From the above it is clear that credit rating is important for a country as well as businesses. If a downgrade took place in a country it will become more difficult and more expensive for businesses in that country to borrow money from banks and other financial intermediaries. This will eventually lead to less liquidity available for businesses to use for investment and therefore there will be reduced growth and innovation.

16.8 Summary

- Integrated Reporting demonstrates the linkages between an organisation's strategy, governance and financial performance and the social, environmental and economic context.
- Some benefits of the Integrated Reporting include:
  - communicating the financial and non-financial indicators to different stakeholders
  - helping organisations to consolidate their reporting into one concise report that conveys the value creation to different stakeholders
  - increasing CSR
  - helping organisations make successful long-term decisions.
- Excessive executive remuneration has been identified by measures such as a sharply increasing ratio between top executives' pay and average employee pay.
- Attempts are being made to increase 'shareholder democracy' by giving binding votes to shareholders on proposed remuneration packages. A major objective is to reduce the disconnect between executive pay and corporate performance.
- 'Fair value' accounting is having major implications for corporate reporting and for pension provision. Critics suggest it is a key cause of a fall in final salary pensions.

- The credit rating agencies are an increasingly important factor in determining borrowing costs for governments and businesses

16.9 Chapter glossary

Corporate Social Responsibility Company's sense of responsibility towards the wider community and environment in which it operates.

Integrated Reporting New approach to corporate reporting that demonstrates the links between an organisation's strategy, governance and financial performance and the social, environmental and economic context within which it operate.

Off-balance-sheet accounting Financial transactions that are designed to minimise transparency within published financial reports, often resulting in misleading profit or asset values.

Pension Post-retirement benefit that an employee might receive from an employer.

Remuneration Executive pay and other compensation.

Scarcity of resources Limited resources such as water, land and capital.

Socially Responsible Investing (SRI) More investors considering non-financial factors such as the environment, society and governance in investment decisions.

Social P&L Includes social impact such as fair wages; freedom of association, health; security and stability; empowerment; community cohesion; human capital; and gender equality.

Window-dressing Manipulating financial statements (usually in contravention of generally accepted accounting principles) so that a company reports misleading results. For example, a company might make a significant sale of its products just before its financial period ends (thereby boosting profits), only to accept the return of those products when the new financial period starts.

Additional resources

Now work through the various exercises and problems that you can find within the My Accounting Lab that are relevant to this chapter. Either use the QR code shown in the margin (if you use an Android-based device), or visit www.myaccountinglab.com for the log-in page.

Only accessible on Android-based devices

Self-check questions

The answers to these question are in Appendix 1.

1 Any group or individual who can affect or is affected by the achievement of an organisation's purpose can be called a:

(a) Profit maximiser
(b) Stakeholder
(c) Director
(d) Coalition

2 Integrated reporting and CSR are positively correlated with revenue and profit because:

(a) Consumers respond positively to links between the organisation and ethical and environmentally acceptable outcomes
(b) Consumers do not respond positively to links between the organisation and ethical and environmentally acceptable outcomes
(c) An increase in demand will reduce revenue and profitability
(d) Being ethical costs money

3 The ratio of the highest to the lowest paid in an organisation has:

(a) Risen sharply over recent years
(b) Decreased sharply over recent years
(c) Remained static over recent years
(d) None of the above

4 Integrated Reporting demonstrates the linkages between:

(a) Revenue and cost to the organisation
(b) The strategy, governance, opportunities and the social, environmental, economic and financial context
(c) The highest and lowest paid members of the organisation
(d) None of the above

5 Integrating reporting considers an organisation's performance in the context of:

(a) Contributions to corporate and social responsibility (CSR)
(b) Concerns over current and future scarcity of resources
(c) Environmental concerns
(d) All the above

6 The International Integrated Reporting framework aims to:

(a) Identify financially insolvent companies
(b) Control excessive executive remuneration
(c) Provide an international standard to ensure consistent reporting
(d) Maximise profit

7 The FTSE quoted company Barclays lost a shareholder vote in April 2012 because investors were angry at:

(a) Poor share performance
(b) A decision to withhold dividends
(c) A clear disconnect between executive pay and corporate performance
(d) Lack of transparency in the annual report

8 Downgrading a country's credit rating is likely to result in:

(a) More rapid economic growth
(d) Higher costs for future borrowings
(c) Increased investment in plant and machinery
(d) Increased export earnings

9 Fair value accounting has been criticised for:

(a) Increasing the proportion of final salary pensions
(b) Decreasing the proportion of final salary pensions
(c) Increasing earnings per share
(d) Giving a more accurate version of the true value

10 A reduction in the ratio of national debt to GDP is likely to result in:

(a) A fall in a country's credit rating
(d) Higher borrowing costs
(c) Lower borrowing costs
(d) Less credit being available to the country

Self-study questions

Questions marked with this symbol (#) indicate that the suggested answers are available to lecturers only – other answers are given in Appendix 2.

16.1 If reporting in the past did not seem to influence corporate behaviour, why are companies now focusing on developing Integrated Reporting?

16.2# Outline the arguments for and against regulating the pay of executives.

16.3 Read the following article, then answer the question that follows:

UK retreat on accountancy standards

By Simon Mundy

UK accountancy regulators have rowed back from a proposal to impose international disclosure standards on 'publically accountable' non-listed companies, after complaints that it would impose unnecessary costs on building societies and credit unions. Under the Accounting Standards Board's original plans, published in October 2010, entities deemed 'publicly accountable' – usually taken to mean companies that lent money to individuals – would have had to use European International Financial Reporting Standards from 2013.

Auditors criticise the vague definition of public accountability and said that many companies would be forced to incur unacceptable costs by producing accounts with an unnecessary level of detail.

The ASB – part of the Financial Reporting Council – yesterday said that it had dropped the proposals after complaints that 'the cost to certain entities could not be justified by the benefits'. The regulator will now move forward with reforms to the UK's existing accounting standards, although there will be a further delay to their implementation. The details will be published in mid-2013, with the rules coming into effect in January 2015 – years after the ASB began consulting on the reforms.

The new standards, known as FRSME, are expected to be a fifth of the length of the existing rules – which run to 2,000 pages – and more in line with IFRS, the international standard. A person close to the ASB said that while there had been complaints about some details of the proposals, companies and auditors accepted the need to update current standards, which take insufficient account of innovations.

Auditors welcomed the change of heart. Ian Selfridge, a partner of PwC, said that the decision 'will not impede the quality of financial reporting [but] will provide welcome relief for many companies in this economic climate, given the time and cost burden of producing accounts under full IFRS for the first time.'

Other changes also found a warm reception. The ASB said that subsidiaries of listed companies could use IFRS with reduced disclosure – a 'real advantage [that] will enable more consistent reporting within many UK and global groups, whilst mitigating the volume of disclosures that would be mandated under EU-endorsed IRFS', said Andrew Davies, leader of the financial accounting advisory team at Ernst & Young.

However, some industry figures were more cautious Nigel Sleight-Johnson, head of the financial reporting faculty at the Institute of Chartered Accountants in England and Wales, said that there was still 'a lack of certainty over what will happen to the reporting requirements for small companies', pointing to the European Commission's planned simplified regime for smaller enterprises.

Source: Financial Times, 31 January 2012

Consider the advantages and disadvantages to business of this so-called 'retreat' on accountancy standards.

16.4# Suggest how the downgrading of a country's credit rating might impact on business activity in that country.

Case study

Is it adiós to Marvin?

Marvin (see previous case studies) has received an offer to take his show to Spain for a three-month tour, with all costs met by a Spanish entrepreneur. However, he has just heard that the various credit rating agencies have downgraded Spain's credit rating as shown below:

Moody's	From A3 to Baa3
Standard & Poor's	From A to BBB+
Fitch IBCA	From AA to BBB

Marvin decides to find out what these credit ratings mean before taking a decision, and discovers the following table of credit risk assessments:

	Moody's	Standard & Poor's	Fitch IBCA
Highest credit quality; issuer has strong ability to meet obligations	Aaa	AAA	AAA
Very high credit quality; low risk of default	Aa1	AA+	AA
	Aa2	AA	
	Aa3	AA−	
High credit quality but more vulnerable to changes in economy or business	A1	AA+	AA
	A2	AA	
	A3	AA−	
Adequate credit quality for now, but more likely to be impaired if conditions worsen	Baa1	BBB+	BBB
	Baa2	BBB	
	Baa3	BBB−	
Below investment grade, but good chance that issuer can meet commitments	Ba1	BB+	BB
	Ba2	BB	
	Ba3	BB−	

	Moody's	Standard & Poor's	Fitch IBCA
Significant credit risk, but issuer is presently able to meet obligations	B1	B+	B
	B2	B	
	B3	B−	
High default risk	Caa1	CCC+	CCC
	Caa2	CCC	CC
	Caa3	CCC−	C
Issuer failed to meet scheduled interest or principal payments	C	D	DDD
			DD
			D

Question

What impacts might these downgrades have on Marvin's decision? Explain your reasoning.

Answers are in Appendix 3

Further research

The research paper referred to in section 16.4 can be found at http://www.booz.com/media/uploads/Responsible-Investing-Paradigm-Shift.pdf or by using this QR code.

Chapter 17

Environmental accounting

Objectives

When you have read this chapter you will be able to:

- Explain what is meant by 'environmental accounting'
- Understand how 'environmental accounts' are constructed
- Understand the purpose of 'environmental accounting' and its relevance to management decision making
- Identify the different types of 'environmental accounting'

17.1 Introduction

In the previous chapter, we looked at various contemporary issues involving business finance, including Integrated Reporting, executive pay and remuneration, accounting standards and 'fair value' accounting, pensions and the financial implications of changes in national and corporate credit ratings.

In this chapter we will consider how *environmental data* is incorporated into an 'environmental accounting' framework. The chapter will explain the meaning and the purpose of 'environmental accounting' and its relevance for management decision making. As we have seen, it is very important for companies to be socially responsible and to consider the impact of their policies on such matters as climate change, pollution, 'carbon footprint', waste, greenhouse gas emissions, energy and water usage. Increasingly, investors and other stakeholders take these non-financial elements into account when making their investment decisions. Efforts are also underway to develop an international standard for environmental accounting.

17.2 What is environmental accounting?

Environmental accounting is an approach that seeks to measure and evaluate the contribution of the natural environment within each country's economy.

Whilst organisations already use traditional accounting and financial tools to measure the environmental impacts of their business practices and decisions, these are often seen as failing to capture the true costs and benefits to the organisations or to society in general. Environmental accounting seeks to help organisations and governments to improve their approach to measuring environmental impacts and thereby take decisions that will be more environmentally sustainable.

Also known as 'green', 'sustainable' or 'integrated economic and environmental' accounting, this is a way of measuring the social costs and benefits of using natural resources and assets, as well as allocating resources to their protection and management.

Table 17.1 outlines the components of the environment which are seen as requiring new approaches if they are to be appropriately measured and valued.

Table 17.1 Environmental components

Physical environment	Components
Air and atmosphere	Air quality; 'greenhouse gases'; ozone layer
Water resources	Water quality and quantity
Soil and geology	Nutrients, erosion, contamination
Flora and fauna	Plants and vegetation; birds, mammals, fish, etc.
Human beings	Health and well-being
Landscape	Characteristics and quality of landscape
Cultural heritage	Conservation areas; historic and archaeological sites and buildings; other material assets
Climate	Temperature, rainfall, wind, etc.
Energy	Fossil fuels; renewable and non-renewable energy.

17.3 How does environmental accounting work?

Scan the following QR code with your QR reader to take you to the website of The United Nations Statistics Division for more information regarding the SEEA:

Every country uses a System of National Accounts (SNA) to track its economic activity. Data from the SNA is typically used to calculate key economic indicators, such as Gross Domestic Product (GDP), Gross National Product (GNP) and savings rates. This data is produced regularly, and in a standard format, according to a framework produced by the United Nations Statistical Division (UNSTAT). This allows international comparison, and provides a consistent portrayal of each country's economic development, in a global context.

Environmental accounting modifies the SNA to include the value, use or depletion of natural resources. The System of Environmental-Economic Accounting (SEEA) contains the internationally agreed standard concepts, definitions, classifications, accounting rules and tables for producing internationally comparable statistics on the environment and its relationship with the economy. To access more information on SEEA, go to https://unstats.un.org/unsd/envaccounting/seea.asp or use the QR code shown in the margin.

However, as we shall see in section 17.5, there is some way to go before a unified and fully audited global system can be said to exist!

17.4 What is environmental accounting used for?

Countries are using data from their SEEA to track performance across key areas, such as:

- Pollution
- Consumption of natural resources
- Expenditure on environmental protection.

The environmental accounts also play a significant role in policy analysis and decision-making. For example, Australia has used environmental accounting data to assess how water is being used nationwide and how that has changed over time, whilst Namibia has made changes to its quota level fees on fish catches after analysing data from its environmental accounts.

Scan the following QR code with your QR reader to take you to the website of The Prince's Accounting for Sustainability Project:

Environmental accounting has also been identified as an important way of monitoring climate change, as well as energy usage, fisheries, forests, minerals, air pollutant emissions and water usage. In the UK, an 'Accounting for Sustainability' project (A4S) was established in 2004 at the initiative of the Prince of Wales to provide organisations with the appropriate tools, applications and methodologies to enable them to embed sustainability into day-to-day operations and decision-making processes and thereby to report more effectively and consistently on their sustainability performance. It was widely accepted that sustainability should be connected with an organisation's strategy and financial performance. To access more information on A4S, go to www.accountingforsustainability.org, or use the QR code shown in the margin.

As part of the A4S project, a 'Connected Reporting Framework' was also developed as a result of a wide range of consultations with large public companies, Non-Governmental Organisations (NGOs), standard setters, different accounting bodies and others. The main aim of the framework is to ensure that sustainability aspects of financial performance are reported in ways which demonstrate their strong interdependence.

Environmental accounting can help decision makers at the organisational level to:

- Manage resources more effectively
- Identify methods of sustainable development
- Evaluate environmental pressures
- Highlight the implications of regulations, taxes and consumption patterns on environmental sustainability.

Activity 17.1 looks at the importance of environmental accounting for organisations.

Activity 17.1

Read this article and then answer the questions that follow.

US companies urged to put natural capital in accounts

By Mike Scott

Last week's Rio+20 summit was, essentially, all about the importance of environmental, social and governance (ESG) issues to governments, businesses, investors and consumers.

But for investors, one of the main problems about these issues is that there is not enough information about them and what there is varies so much from one company to another that meaningful comparison is difficult. At the same time, businesses often provide too much information that is irrelevant to the main challenges that they face.

A new organisation aims to change this – in the US at least. The Sustainability Accounting Standards Board has been set up, and named, to stand as a companion to the Financial Accounting Standards Board, the body that 40 years ago established the Generally Accepted Accounting Principles on behalf of the Securities and Exchange Commission.

"FASB has created very robust, trustworthy markets in the US, but a lot has changed in the last 40 years," says Jean Rogers, chief executive of the new body. "There is an entire class of information that is increasingly relevant to businesses and investors and that information is not flowing freely. It's in tot`ally different formats, it's not standardised, it's not in a digestible format and investors cannot compare and they cannot benchmark."

Corporate growth and success are no longer constrained solely by the availability of financial capital, SASB believes.

Rather, global resource constraints and management of environmental and social issues are integral to the long-term success and sustainable value creation of companies.

Issues such as climate change, population growth, urbanisation and shortage of raw materials will have a growing impact on company performance, but because these externalities are inadequately priced, the view that investors have of the performance of resource intensive companies is skewed.

"Forty years ago, companies competed on how well they used financial capital. Now other forms of capital are recognised as important too," Ms Rogers says. "We cannot have companies that maximise one form of capital at the expense of other assets such as natural capital. Value creation cannot be sustainable if the underlying capital is being depleted."

ESG information is reported to some degree, but it is not comprehensive and it is not comparable, she adds. And while initiatives such as the Global Reporting Initiative have started to raise awareness about the importance of ESG issues, uptake in the US has been extremely slow. Out of 35,000 listed companies, in

2010 just 183 US groups reported to GRI standards.

"There are very few GRI reporters – and they are the leaders in their fields. Far fewer US companies consider sustainability risks and opportunities than in the rest of the world," Ms Rogers states. "We want to set a floor, a minimum set of standards for everyone that creates a level playing field."

In contrast to the GRI, which is an independent body outside of the financial regulatory system, SASB aims to create a new standard for companies that sits inside the existing system.

At the heart of the filing requirements for US listed companies is Form 10-k, a mandatory disclosure form that companies must file with the SEC. Among the issues that must be included is one on risk factors and it is here that SASB hopes to make its mark.

"We are designing standards that should fit right into Form 10-k," says Ms Rogers. "We hope that every company in a particular industry will know what to disclose so that analysts have enough information to be able to start benchmarking sectors."

To do this, SASB, which like FASB is a private sector not-for-profit body, is looking at 102 industries, starting with a review of the importance of various ESG issues to different sectors to create a "materiality map".

"This deliberately narrows our field of vision to the most indisputable issues, so that no one can argue that these factors should not be in Form 10-k," Ms Rogers adds. "Materiality comes from the perspective of the 'reasonable investor'. We believe that the reasonable investor wants to know about these things."

Once these issues have been identified, SASB will work out how to measure, recognise and account for them. The organisation will also look at the links between the factors and value drivers such as growth, return on capital and management quality.

Source: *The Financial Times*, 24 June 2012

1 Why is a new approach to environmental accounting seen as necessary?
2 What are the essential requirements for companies to be able to use such an approach?

Answers

1 The current approach emphasises financial capital but fails to capture information and data on all the forms of capital now in use, especially natural or environmental capital. Although attempts are being made in this direction (e.g. the Global Reporting Initiative), relatively few companies have taken part in such voluntary reporting schemes which are outside the official financial regulatory systems in the US and elsewhere.
2 Many believe that it is essential to have a mandatory scheme with carefully defined reporting requirements (e.g. Form 10-k for the SASB scheme). The information required on natural capital and other environmental, social and governance issues should be that which the 'reasonable investor' would expect to be there. The reporting requirements may need to be 'tailored' to the different sectors of economic activity. Precise metrics must be developed for measurement and reporting purposes. The new approach must incorporate the whole infrastructure of standards, audit and supervision that currently exists for financial data.

As we can see in the News clip below, sustainability and environmental accounting are rising up the corporate agenda, supported by the stock exchanges of many countries.

News clip

Calls for corporate disclosure of social impact

FT

By Ed Crooks

"What gets measured gets managed," said Peter Drucker, the business guru, and it is even more true when the measurements are reported to regulators and investors. That is the thinking behind the pressure from some investors, governments and campaign groups for companies to improve their reporting of their environmental and social impact. By disclosing their results in areas such as water and energy use, waste and workplace safety, businesses will be encouraged to improve their performance.

Governments and stock exchanges around the world are coming out in support of "sustainability reporting", as it is known, driving the most significant changes to corporate disclosure since the move towards international accounting rules a decade ago.

The Sustainable Stock Exchanges Initiative, a UN-backed group, has held conferences in recent years with exchanges including Nasdaq OMX from the US, Bovespa from Brazil, and the Istanbul Stock Exchange, requesting more disclosure of sustainability information from companies as part of their listing standards. The model for campaigners on this issue is the Johannesburg exchange, which since 2010 has required every listed company to publish what is known as an integrated report, including environmental and social data alongside their financial results.

Source: *The Financial Times*, 24 June 2012 (adapted)

A further example of the importance of environmental accounting at the corporate level becomes clear from Activity 17.2, which relates to Puma, the world's third largest sports business.

Activity 17.2

Read the article and answer the questions that follow.

Puma releases 'true' carbon emission cost

By Peter Marsh

Puma has become one of the first global companies to release what it thinks is the true cost of its carbon dioxide emissions. The company says the cost is more than three times higher than the current price for permits under European environmental legislation.

The disclosure by the German company – the world's third biggest sportswear business and majority-owned by the French luxury group PPR – could prompt similar disclosures by other leading manufacturers.

Jochen Zeitz, Puma's chief executive, who is also chief sustainability officer at PPR, said publication of the data was a useful step to "providing transparent benchmarks" about emissions of carbon dioxide and related gases, such as methane, that are associated with global warming.

Findings by consultancies PWC and Trucost show that the true cost of the company's emissions of greenhouse gases is at €66 ($93) a tonne.

Compare this with the current price of carbon dioxide permits under the European emissions trading scheme of €17.

Professor Alyson Warhurst, chief executive of Maplecroft, an environmental consultancy, said the figures showed that the cost of carbon dioxide permits "did not reflect the true cost" of emissions when global warming was taken into account.

The €66-a-tonne figure is the consultancies' estimate of the cost to the world economy of future damage such as hurricanes and other unusual weather events that are likely to be caused by climate change sparked by rising concentrations of greenhouse gases.

Emissions of carbon dioxide and related gases that were produced last year from the manufacture of Puma products reached 717,000 tonnes or a "true cost" of €47m, said the consultancies.

They also said that the amount of water used to make Puma products last year was 77m tonnes or a total cost of €47.4m.

Most of the greenhouse gas emissions and water use were not from the direct operations of Puma but from the activities of several hundred suppliers around the world, mainly in Asia.

The consultants also provided emissions and water use data of companies in the Puma supply chain.

These figures included emissions and water use in farms, which produce cotton for Puma's sports shirts, and cattle ranches, which supply the hide for Puma leather shoes.

Alan McGill, a partner at PWC, said: "More companies may need to consider disclosures of this kind, as a result of the legislation that is under consideration in a number of companies that could make the publication of this kind of data mandatory."

Source: Financial Times, 17 May 2011

If the disclosures of such details became mandatory, what implications will this have for companies?

Answer

If the disclosure of such details became mandatory, businesses will have to consider which of their activities will harm the environment and which are considered to be environmentally friendly. Conventionally, business, financial and accounting practices used to focus solely on financial performance, and on activities which maximise shareholders' value. Investors have, however, started to consider non-financial indicators for their investments such as environmental and social practices, aware that negative publicity in these areas is likely to damage the business in which they have invested. Managers have to be more proactive than reactive to such legislation.

Of course there will be a need to comply with the legislation and to record environmental outcomes as required, which will impose a resource cost on the company. Nevertheless, such environmental accounting can help decision-makers to manage resources more effectively using the availability of quantitative and qualitative data of this kind.

17.5 Types of environmental accounting

The International Organisation of Supreme Audit Institutions (INTOSAI) produced a report on Environmental Accounting in 2010, which listed four main types of environmental accounting: natural resource asset; pollution and material physical flow; monetary and hybrid; and environmentally-adjusted macroeconomic aggregates. The full report can be downloaded at www.environmental-auditing.org or by using the QR code shown on page 413.

17.5.1 Natural resource asset accounts

Primarily concerned with stocks of natural resources, accounts focus on changes due to economic activity (e.g. mining minerals) or natural processes (e.g. 'births' and 'deaths' of trees in a forest).

Scan the following QR code with your QR reader to enable you to download INTOSAI's report on Environmental Accounting:

Typical considerations include changes to the stock of agricultural land, fisheries, forests, minerals and petroleum, and water. Accounts usually show physical assets and monetary assets:

- Physical asset accounts can be used to show the effects of policy on quantities of resource stocks, thus providing an information basis which can help resources to be managed more effectively.
- Monetary asset accounts can provide a monetary value for a resource, helping to determine more accurately a country's total wealth, and highlighting assets that are vulnerable to exhaustion or depletion.

However, whilst tracking the market value of resources is relatively simple, changes in stock values can be due to physical changes in the resource or to fluctuations in the market price, making it difficult to establish their value.

The importance of natural resource asset accounts is usefully illustrated by the dilemma facing Puma over the use of leather in its sports products, as shown in the 'News clip' below.

News clip

Puma to kick leather into touch

FT

By Pilita Clark

Puma will have to stop using leather in its famous football boots and trainers because it is such an environmentally damaging product, the sportswear company's executive chairman has said.

"I think eventually we'll have to look at alternative materials, there's no question about it," Jochen Zeitz told the *Financial Times* in an interview at the UN Rio+20 earth summit. "We should eat less meat, all of us, and we should use less leather, I mean that's reality . . . We all know that cattle and beef are among the biggest contributors to carbon emissions."

Mr Zeitz is regarded as a pioneer of environmentally sound business practices and says he has cut his own meat consumption by 80 per cent in recent years.

He has also introduced "meat-free Mondays" in office canteens at Puma, whose shoes have clad the feet of some of the world's best known athletes, from Argentine footballer Diego Maradona to Jamaican sprinter Usain Bolt.

The company unveiled an "environmental profit and loss account" last year that valued the environmental impact of its operations and supply chain at €145m. In the first quarter of 2012 Puma's sales were €821m.

The measure showed the production and processing of raw materials was the biggest contributor to Puma's environmental footprint, said Mr Zeitz, "with leather being the biggest impact driver".

That is partly because cattle ranching soaks up water supplies and requires land to be cleared, which can affect plant and wildlife species, and also because of the chemicals and contaminants associated with leather tanneries.

That means footwear has the biggest environmental footprint of Puma's products, said Mr Zeitz, explaining innovative ways of tackling the problem had to be found. "It may sound crazy, but maybe there's an economic way of producing a leather-like product in the laboratory," he said. "We have to find alternative ways of producing our raw materials without asking nature to do it for us."

Source: *The Financial Times*, 22 June 2012

17.5.2 Pollution and material physical flow accounts

This kind of data reports the *quantity* of resources (e.g. energy, water and materials) used in economic activities, as well as the quantity of residuals generated by these activities (e.g. solid waste, air emissions and waste water)

Did you know?

The National Accounting Matrix including Environmental Accounts (NAMEA), created by the Netherlands, identifies pollutant emissions by economic sector. The system is now commonly in use in the EU to determine the cost of environmental degradation and the costs and benefits of environmental protection.

It is not only governments that are interested in pollution and material physical flow accounts. Dyson Ltd, the UK-based manufacturer of electronic products such as bagless vacuum cleaners, is making full use of independent 'life cycle assessments' for the environmental impacts of its *Airblade* hand dryer in its promotion and marketing campaigns. A study it commissioned with the Massachusetts Institute of Technology (MIT) showed that the hand dryer generated only 30% of the carbon emissions of rival products such as paper towels and conventional warm-air hand dryers.

Interface Inc. is the world's largest carpet tile maker and is another company which has shown how important it regards the environment. For the past decade it has been a leader in using environmental standards as a way to sell more products. Of the company's $1bn sales in 2011 roughly 90% came from carpet tiles sold with an 'environmental product declaration' which assessed the environmental factors linked to the product's manufacture, such as energy use, production of waste and greenhouse gases. In fact a range of 'Kitemarks' exist for firms to certify that their product is derived from environmentally acceptable practices, such as the 'Forestry Stewardship Council' mark which certifies that wood is derived from sustainable forestry extraction methods (see Figure 17.1).

Figure 17.1 Example of a sustainability 'kitemark'

17.5.3 Monetary and hybrid accounts

These accounts focus on expenditure and taxes related to protecting the environment, and the economic contribution of environmental service industries. They can help to assess issues such as the cost of environmental regulation and the impacts of eco-taxes ('green' taxes). They may include government-imposed charges for the use of resources such as minerals or fisheries, or money spent on water treatment.

Activity 17.3 emphasises the use of expenditure by governments on subsidies (positive incentives) and the use of 'green taxes' as important policy instruments linked to these types of account.

Activity 17.3

Read this article and then answer the questions that follow.

Forestry and environmental decision making

The vital contribution of forests to a sustainable global environment has long been recognised, especially their ability to give out oxygen and absorb and store carbon. Of course destroying forests for wood, for increased plantation or cattle rearing, works in reverse – with around half the dry weight of a tree consisting of stored carbon, much of which is released into the atmosphere when trees are burned or left to rot. In fact around half the earth's total forest area has been cleared by man-made interventions in the past 10,000 years, and today continued deforestation contributes some 15–17% of the world's annual emissions of carbon dioxide (CO^2). Forest clearance does still more damage than this, with the loss of plant sources of many modern medicines and animal species, as well as threatening the habitats and livelihoods of some 400 million of the world's poorest people, and resulting in increased flooding as bare hillsides fail to absorb rainfall as effectively as in the past.

The increasing emphasis of the media on such environmental issues has increased pressures on corporations and governments to advance more 'responsible' approaches to forests and their many products and uses. A UN supported organisation, The Economics of Ecosystems and Biodiversity (TEEB), has estimated that negative externalities from forest loss and degradation cost between $2tr and $4.5tr each year!

The prominence given to the important role of forests in 'sustainability' related concerns is providing both positive and negative incentives for corporations to adopt policies consistent with increased environmental responsibility.

Positive incentives: On the positive side, governments and environmental agencies are providing incentives of various kinds to encourage a more responsible corporate attitude towards forestry. For example agricultural companies and farmers are benefitting from incentives in the form of *Payments for Ecosystem Services* (PES) to reforest agricultural land – in China farmers in the vicinity of the Yangzi River are paid $450 a year per reforested hectare, in an attempt to lessen flooding damage. Costa Rica offers $45–163 per reforested hectare.

Negative incentives: On the negative side, *failure* to support sustainable forestry can result in serious damage to corporate profitability. Nestlé has been targeted by Greenpeace with negative blogs and adverts exposing links between the production of chocolate for *KitKat* bars and associated deforestation in Indonesia; around half of the forest areas cleared for crops in Indonesia are used for oil palms, mainly for chocolate production. The impact of such negative publicity was deemed so severe by Nestlé that it ceased buying palm oil from its main Indonesian supplier, Sinar Mas, and promised to remove from its supply chain any producer of palm oil linked to deforestation.

Governments are also using 'green taxes' as a further negative incentive to companies to discourage them from activities which damage the environment. Tax on fuel in the UK accounts for over 62% of the total price of petrol and is raised regularly by governments to discourage road transport with its relatively high emissions of CO^2 per kilometre travelled, as well as its contribution to road congestion and accidents.

1 How might the 'positive incentives' for forestry in China influence the environment?
2 How might the 'negative incentives' for Nestlé influence the market for its chocolate-related products?
3 How might 'green' taxes influence the environment?

Answers

1 These will encourage reforestation, with all the benefits to forests of reducing CO^2 and retaining important plant and animal species.
2 Unless Nestlé pays attention to the adverse publicity and improves its environmental practices as regards it supply chain, there are likely to be sharp falls in the demand for its chocolate products.
3 'Green' taxes will tend to raise the price of the environmentally damaging goods and services and thereby restrict their use.

17.5.4 Environmentally-adjusted macroeconomic aggregates

Using the data from the previous types of account, aggregates are used to gain an overview of each country's environmental status and economic progress by correcting the GDP to include the monetary value of decline or depletion of stocks, or the cost of environmental degradation due to polluting economic activities.

There is growing interest amongst governments to adjust the GDP figure to account for environmental impacts, as shown in the 'News clip' below.

News clip

Environment and the economy

FT

Britain informed the 'Rio+20' Summit that it will move away from using Gross Domestic Product (GDP) as its sole measure of economic progress by 2020 and adopt one that includes the value of 'natural capital'. Calling for a new global measure of 'GDP' the Deputy Prime Minister of the UK said that 'for too long we have valued the wrong things and undervalued the damage to natural resources.'

Environmental economists have long argued that GDP, which looks at the value of goods and services produced in a country, is not a true indicator of wealth. A country might get temporarily rich by cutting down its trees, but the corresponding loss of the trees as future assets is not captured in the GDP figures.

The UK's Deputy Prime Minister called for a new global measure of GDP, arguing that for far too long the UK has undervalued the damage to natural resources in the official national income accounts.

17.6 Problems with environmental accounting

As a developing discipline, environmental accounting faces certain challenges – not least varying approaches to its application. In addition:

- There is currently no international consensus on methodology.
- Evaluation of natural assets is problematic, particularly where those assets are not priced in markets (e.g. clean air and water).
- The availability and reliability of data is often inconsistent.

17.7 Summary

By giving environmental goods and services a more meaningful value, environmental accounting helps policy-makers to manage resources better, assess different types of environmental pressures, and identify the implications of different regulations, taxes and consumption patterns on environmental sustainability. In these ways environmental accounting helps governments, companies and policy-makers identify paths to sustainable economic development.

One of the main reasons that environmental accounting is required is because of the existence of *externalities*. An externality exists when the *private cost* to the decision maker does not measure the *social cost*, i.e. the resource cost to society from that activity. For example when a firm or an individual makes a decision that increases pollution, and damages the health or well-being of others, then there is a cost to society. However if the individual firm or individual does not have to pay for that damage, then the private cost is zero even though the social cost is not zero.

'Green' taxes are a policy instrument to help correct this type of environmental externality. Of course if the firm or individual takes a decision that benefits the health or well-being of others, then there is a case for a 'green' subsidy or payment to encourage such socially responsible decision making.

Investors and managers are increasingly aware of the importance to the reputation and success of the organisation of 'sustainable' behaviour. Indeed environmental accounting will assist managers to embed strategic sustainable objectives into their annual reporting in a meaningful and robust manner.

17.8 Chapter glossary

Environmental accounting An approach to capture better the 'true' value of the use of natural resources and the emission of pollution for the economy and the individual organisation.

Gross Domestic Product (GDP) The measure of the market value of all finished goods and services produced within a country in a given period of time.

Externality Where the private cost of an activity differs from the social cost of that activity.

Negative externality Where the social cost is greater than the private cost.

Positive externality Where the social benefit is greater than the private benefit (or social cost is smaller than the private cost).

The Accounting for Sustainability project A project set up by the Prince of Wales to provide organisations with the appropriate tools, applications and methodologies to enable them to embed sustainability into day-to-day operations and decision-making processes and to report more effectively and consistently on their sustainability performance.

The System of Environmental Economic Accounting (SEEA) SEEA contains the internationally agreed standard concepts, definitions, classifications, accounting guidelines and data for producing internationally comparable statistics on the environment and its relationship with the economy.

System of National Accounts (SNA) Every country uses SNA to track economic activity. Data from SNA is typically used to calculate key economic indicators, such as Gross Domestic Product (GDP), Gross National Product (GNP) and savings rates.

Additional resources

Only accessible on Android-based devices

Now work through the various exercises and problems that you can find within the My Accounting Lab that are relevant to this chapter. Either use the QR code shown in the margin (if you use an Android-based device), or visit www. myaccountinglab.com for the log-in page.

Self-check questions

The answers to these questions are in Appendix 1.

1 An externality is said to exist when:

(a) Private cost is the same as social cost
(b) Private benefit is the same as social benefit
(c) Private cost is different from social cost
(d) None of the above

2 Which one of the following is an example of applying the principles of environmental accounting?

(a) The Index of Sustainable Economic Welfare
(b) The Retail Price Index
(c) The Index of Industrial Production
(d) None of the above

3 Environmental accounting can help policy makers and decision makers to:

(a) Manage employees more effectively
(b) Pinpoint the advantages and disadvantages of using certain accounting and economic data
(c) Highlight the implications of regulations, taxes and consumption patterns on environmental sustainability
(d) Identify the company's financial position and its future expansion plans

4 Natural resources asset accounts are primarily concerned with:

(a) The expenditure and taxes related to protecting the environment, and the economic contribution of environmental service industries
(b) Reporting the quantity of resources used in economic activities, as well as the quantity of residuals generated by these activities
(c) Reporting on the usage of energy and water
(d) Stocks of natural resources

5 Pollution and material physical flow accounts are primarily concerned with:

(a) Reporting the quantity of resources used in economic activities, as well as the quantity of residuals generated by these activities
(b) The expenditure and taxes related to protecting the environment, and the economic contribution of environmental service industries
(c) Reporting on the usage of energy and water
(d) Stocks of natural resources

6 Monetary and hybrid accounts are primarily concerned with:

(a) Stocks of natural resources
(b) Reporting the quantity of resources used in economic activities, as well as the quantity of residuals generated by these activities
(c) Reporting on the usage of energy and water
(d) The expenditure and taxes related to protecting the environment, and the economic contribution of environmental-related activities

7 Environmentally-adjusted macroeconomic aggregates are primarily concerned with

(a) The expenditure and taxes related to protecting the environment, and the economic contribution of environmental service industries
(b) Reporting the quantity of resources used in economic activities, as well as the quantity of residuals generated by these activities
(c) Reporting on the usage of energy and water
(d) Correcting the GDP measure to provide a more accurate value of economic activity when environmental-related activities are involved, such as the cost of environmental degradation due to polluting economic activities

8 The term 'carbon footprint' usually refers to:

(a) Impacts of an organisation on carbon emissions throughout its supply chain
(b) Impacts of an organisation on land use
(c) Impacts of an organisation or carbon emissions from its own production only
(d) None of the above

9 Which one of the following is *not* regarded as a problem related to environmental accounting?

(a) Data is often unreliable or unavailable
(b) Difficulty of evaluating natural assets such as clean air
(c) Unwillingness of governments to discuss environmental topics
(d) Lack of international consensus on methodology

10 When a government announces a higher fuel tax to discourage the use of road transport, it is said to be imposing:

(a) A 'green' tax
(b) A 'green' subsidy
(c) A new regulation
(d) An antisocial tax

Self-study questions

Questions marked with this symbol (#) indicate that the suggested answers are available to lecturers only – other answers are given in Appendix 2.

17.1# Read the following article and then answer the question.

Apple agrees to China pollution audit

By Chris Nuttall

Apple has agreed to a jointly monitored audit of pollution controls at a supplier's factory in China, in what activists see as a breakthrough in their efforts to persuade the world's most valuable company to address environmental concerns.

A maker of printed circuit boards for the Silicon Valley company is due to be inspected in the next few weeks by auditors, with Apple and the China-based Institute of Public and Environmental Affairs (IPE) jointly monitoring their efforts.

Last month, Apple backed a report by the Fair Labor Association that recommended improvements in working conditions at three Foxconn factories in China where its products are made. Environmental issues now appear to be getting the same level of attention.

It has held lengthy talks in recent months with the IPE, a non-governmental organisation that has amassed a database of 97,000 environmental violations in China from official data.

Apple was the only one of 29 companies that failed to respond to a 2010 report by an IPE-led environmental coalition on hazardous wastes from suppliers causing pollution and health problems in China.

Ma Jun, IPE director, told the *Financial Times* that Apple's attitude changed in September 2011, two weeks after a second report said pollution discharges were expanding and spreading in Apple's supply chain.

Talks with the IPE began in Beijing and led to a series of other discussions culminating in a five-hour meeting at Apple's Cupertino headquarters at the end of October.

"One Apple vice-president said that transparency was needed and I felt that was the moment they decided they wanted to change the way they were doing things," he said.

Apple had been insisting earlier that details about its suppliers and its own audits of them were private.

"But it's now become about validation, we keep telling them that you can't just say that everything's fine – we need proof."

It met the IPE-led coalition in China in November and told it an outside specialist firm had been engaged to carry out inspections of environmental practices.

The IPE hopes that the first jointly monitored audit will act as a pilot for others to take place at 13 more factories where Apple has been carrying out its own environmental checks.

An Apple spokesperson declined to comment on the matter.

As the world's most valuable company, with a $564bn market capitalisation, activists hope its responsiveness to their concerns will also influence others to take action.

Ma Jun cited Taiwan's HTC, Sweden's Ericsson and Japan's Canon as laggards in responding to pollution problems highlighted in their supply chains.

Source: Financial Times, 15 April 2012

Explain why Apple has changed its mind and is now cooperating with independent audits of its supply chain in China.

17.2 Read the following article and answer the questions that follow.

Putting a value on wildlife

A number of case studies and investigations have involved contingent valuations. In a widely reported study, Bandara and Tisdell (2004) used a sample of 300 residents in the Sri Lankan capital of Colombo to establish their willingness to pay for the survival of the elephant population in Sri Lanka. Background information was given to all respondents as regards the current threats facing the elephants, and details were also provided of a proposed conservation strategy.

The following question was then asked: 'For the next five years would you be willing to pay *z* rupees per month to establish the proposed Trust Fund . . . . to conserve the elephants in the country?' Various values were then listed to represent *z* rupees.

The results suggested that 93% of respondents were willing to make some payment, with 89% willing to pay (WTP) 25 rupees or more, 50% willing to pay 100 rupees or more, and 9% willing to pay 500 rupees or more. The average WTP was 110 rupees per month (around $2), some 1% of the average respondent's monthly income. These results suggested that the urban population of Sri Lanka as a whole were willing to pay $90 million per year for elephant conservation, much more than the $11 million estimated annual damage caused by elephants to crops and property in rural areas of Sri Lanka.

Source: adapted from Bandara and Tisdell (2004), 'The net benefit of saving the Asian elephant: a policy and contingent valuation study; *Ecological Economics*, vol. 48, pp. 93–107.

(a) What issue is this case study addressing as regards putting a value on an environmental asset such as wildlife?

(b) What solutions are being suggested?

17.3 Discuss what environmental accounting can be used for.

17.4# Select a company from *one* of the following industries:

- Chemicals
- Cosmetics
- Furniture retailing.

Conduct your own research (for example, looking at the company's latest annual report) to find out the extent to which they are involved in environmental accounting. Make your own recommendations as to how your chosen firm can develop/improve its environmental accounting.

Case study

Marvin's big footprint

Marvin (see previous case studies) has been delighted at the growth of his business and the beginnings of his internationalisation strategy. However, he was rather surprised when his bank manager, who has provided important new funding for his business, asked him about his 'environmental footprint'! The bank manager had told him that being 'environmentally friendly' was important to the future of Marvin's business and that, in the future, Marvin may have to include information on his business's environmental activities, as 'environmental accounting' was something the government had promised to introduce.

Questions

1 What did the bank manager mean by 'environmental footprint'?
2 Why has the bank manager suggested that Marvin should start to think about his 'environmental footprint'?
3 What kind of information would Marvin need in order to assess the 'environmental footprint' of his business?

Answers are in Appendix 3

Further research

In addition to those referred to in the chapter, there are many organisations concerned with sustainability and general environmental issues, including:

www.climatecare.org

www.environmental-finance.com

www.sustainability.co.uk

Appendix 1 Answers to self-check questions

Chapter	Question									
1	1d	2a	3c	4b	5a	6b	7c	8c	9d	10a
2	1c	2d	3a	4c	5b	6c	7d	8a	9c	10b
3	1b	2c	3c	4c	5c	6d	7a	8a	9c	10d
4	1c	2b	3a	4d	5a	6c	7b	8c	9d	10a
5	1c	2a	3d	4b	5a	6d	7b	8c	9a	10c
6	1c	2d	3d	4a	5b	6b	7a	8c	9c	10d
7	1d	2d	3a	4d	5b	6c	7c	8a	9c	10a
8	1a	2d	3b	4c	5a	6a	7c	8b	9d	10c
9	1c	2c	3a	4a	5c	6d	7b	8b	9d	10a
10	1c	2a	3a	4b	5d	6b	7b	8d	9a	10c
11	1d	2a	3c	4b	5d	6a	7c	8b	9b	10a
12	1a	2c	3d	4b	5d	6d	7a	8b	9c	10c
13	1a	2c	3b	4d	5b	6d	7a	8a	9c	10c
14	1b	2b	3c	4d	5d	6b	7a	8c	9c	10d
15	1b	2b	3b	4a	5a	6a	7b	8d	9b	10c
16	1b	2a	3a	4b	5d	6c	7c	8b	9b	10c
17	1c	2a	3c	4d	5a	6d	7d	8a	9c	10a

Appendix 2 Answers to self-study questions

Chapter 1

1.1

	Assets	Liabilities	Equity
	£	£	£
1	25,630	14,256	11,374
2	39,156	23,658	15,498
3	619,557	352,491	267,066
4	69,810	54,947	14,863
5	57,058	21,596	35,462
6	36,520	12,010	24,510
7	151,632	65,342	86,290
8	114,785	17,853	96,932
9	212,589	65,769	146,820
10	265,108	63,527	201,581

Note that Assets − Liabilities = Equity.

1.2 (a)

	Assets	Liabilities	Equity
	£	£	£
1 Owner starts business with £10,000 paid into a business bank account on 1 May	+£10,000 Bank		+£10,000 Capital
2 Business buys furniture with a cheque for £2,500 on 2 May	+£2,500 Furniture −£2,500 Bank		
3 Business pays £600 by cheque for a photocopier on 4 May	+£600 Photocopier −£600 Bank		
4 Business receives an invoice on 5 May from Chambers Ltd for £2,000 for inventory	+£2,000 Inventory	+£2,000 Payables	
5 Also on 5 May, the business buys inventory with a cheque for £600	+£600 Inventory −£600 Bank		

	Assets	Liabilities	Equity
	£	£	£
6 Owner takes £400 from bank for personal spending money on 6 May	−£400 Bank	−£400 Equity	
7 On 7 May, the business pays the invoice received from Chambers Ltd on 5 May	−£2,000 Bank	−£2,000 Payables	
8 On 8 May, the business receives an invoice for £4,000 for a motor van	+£4,000 Motor van	+£4,000 Payables	
Summary (overall change)	**+£13,600**	**+£4,000**	**+£9,600**

(b) From the above table, complete the following equation:

Overall change in assets	13,600
Less Overall change in liabilities	4,000
Overall change in equity	9,600

(c) The formula Assets − Liabilities = Equity is known as the *statement of financial position equation.*

1.3 (a) 'Going concern' is one of the two underlying assumptions when preparing financial statements. It assumes that the business can continue to trade for the foreseeable future. If it did not apply then that would indicate that the business had a very uncertain future, with a real possibility of failure.

(b) *Accruals.* When calculating the profit or loss of an organisation, all income and related expenditure for a specified period should be included, not simply money paid or received.

Comparability. Accounting procedures used should normally be the same as those applied previously for similar items. This allows comparability of financial summaries over time. By following GAAP a business can ensure comparability between its own financial statements and those of other entities that also follow GAAP.

(c) The qualitative characteristic of 'faithful representation' refers to the need for the financial statements to show, as far as possible, completeness, neutrality and freedom from errors.

Chapter 2

2.1

1 Adequate accounting records must be kept that are sufficient to explain the company's transactions and to disclose with reasonable accuracy at any time the financial position of the company. In particular, the accounting records must contain entries from day to day of all money received and expended with details of transactions, and a record of assets and liabilities.

A full and properly operated double-entry bookkeeping system will ensure that 'proper accounting records' are maintained.

2 The company refers to 'reasonable accuracy' rather than 'total accuracy' due to the fundamental quality characteristic of *faithful representation.* Although the

overall aim of financial statements should be to present complete, neutral and error-free information, a *reasonable* attempt at this is acceptable. In any case, *total* accuracy might be impossible to achieve, particularly in trying to assess a current value for assets such as land, buildings, machinery and inventory.

3 The directors of the company manage the business on behalf of the shareholders. As such, they are responsible for the good management of all aspects of the company's finances. Part of this duty is to ensure that the group's assets are not wasted or lost due to theft, fraud, or 'other irregularities'.

2.2

(a) First, re-arrange the balances according to whether they are debit or credit balances, as follows:

Name	Debit	Credit
Receivable: J. Petrov	650	
Rent and rates	6,400	
Machinery	25,680	
Equity		?
Wages	18,630	
Purchases	14,560	
Advertising	1,500	
Payable: P. Pavlov		960
Accountancy fees	350	
Sales		32,510
Bank	5,000	
Payable: L. Grigorvic		250
	72,770	33,720

The double-entry equation tells us that the sum of the debit balances must equal the sum of the credit balances. Therefore, the equity account balance must be the amount which, when added to the credit total, makes the credit column equal the debit column. 72,770 − 33,720 = **39,050.**

(b) and (c)

Name	Assets	Expenses	Liabilities	Equity	Income
Receivable: J. Petrov	650				
Rent and rates		6,400			
Machinery	25,680				
Equity				39,050	
Wages		18,630			
Purchases		14,560			
Advertising		1,500			
Payable: P. Pavlov			960		
Accountancy fees		350			
Sales					32,510

Name	Assets	Expenses	Liabilities	Equity	Income
Bank	5,000				
Payable: L. Grigorvic			250		
	31,330	41,440	1,210	39,050	32,510

Assets 31,330 + Expenses 41,440 = **72,770**

Liabilities 1,210 + Capital 39,050 + Income 32,510 = **72,770**

2.3

Cash Book							
		Bank account			**Cash account**		
Date	**Details**	**Debit**	**Credit**	**Bank Balance**	**Debit**	**Credit**	**Cash Balance**
1 October	Rachel Roberts: Equity	9,000		9,000 Dr	100		100 Dr
	Purchases		4,000	5,000 Dr			
	Stationery					60	40 Dr
2 October	Sales	600		5,600 Dr	280		320 Dr
3 October	Advertising		30	5,570 Dr			
	Printing		45	5,525 Dr			
4 October	Rent		100	5,425 Dr			
5 October	Sales	700		6,125 Dr	130		450 Dr
6 October	Drawings		400	5,725 Dr			
	Wages					260	190 Dr
7 October	Sales returns		40	5,685 Dr			

General Ledger

Rachel Roberts: equity account				
Date	**Details**	**Debit**	**Credit**	**Balance**
1 October	Bank		9,000	9,000 Cr
	Cash		100	9,100 Cr

Purchases account				
Date	**Details**	**Debit**	**Credit**	**Balance**
1 October	Bank	4,000		4,000 Dr

Stationery account				
Date	**Details**	**Debit**	**Credit**	**Balance**
1 October	Cash	60		60 Dr

Sales account				
Date	Details	Debit	Credit	Balance
2 October	Bank		600	600 Cr
	Cash		280	880 Cr
5 October	Bank		700	1,580 Cr
	Cash		130	1,710 Cr

Advertising account				
Date	Details	Debit	Credit	Balance
3 October	Bank	30		30 Dr

Printing account				
Date	Details	Debit	Credit	Balance
3 October	Bank	45		45 Dr

Rent account				
Date	Details	Debit	Credit	Balance
4 October	Bank	100		100 Dr

Wages account				
Date	Details	Debit	Credit	Balance
6 October	Bank	260		260 Dr

Drawings account				
Date	Details	Debit	Credit	Balance
6 October	Bank	400		400 Dr

Sales Returns account				
Date	Details	Debit	Credit	Balance
7 October	Bank	40		40 Dr

Trial balance as at 7 October		
Details	**Debit**	**Credit**
Cash Book:		
Bank account	5,685	
Cash account	190	
General Ledger:		
Equity		9,100
Purchases	4,000	
Stationery	60	
Sales		1,710
Advertising	30	
Printing	45	
Rent	100	
Wages	260	
Drawings	400	
Sales returns	40	
Totals:	10,810	10,810

2.5 Tariq Ahmad's business

Purchases Day Book		
Date	**Details**	**£**
1 May	C. Moss	630
	J. Carter	419
	A. McKeane	330
3 May	A. Iqbal	560
	A. McKeane	210
		2,149

Sales Day Book		
Date	**Details**	**£**
2 May	K. Palfreyman	199
	L. Patel	870
		1,069

Purchases Returns Day Book		
Date	**Details**	**£**
4 May	J. Carter	80
7 May	A. Iqbal	40
		120

Sales Returns Day Book		
Date	**Details**	**£**
5 May	L. Patel	62
		62

Payables Ledger

C. Moss account				
Date	Details	Debit	Credit	Balance
1 May	Invoice		630	630 Cr

J. Carter account				
Date	Details	Debit	Credit	Balance
1 May	Invoice		419	419 Cr
4 May	Purchases returns	80		339 Cr
6 May	Bank	339		—

A. McKeane account				
Date	Details	Debit	Credit	Balance
1 May	Invoice		330	330 Cr
3 May	Invoice		210	540 Cr

A. Iqbal account				
Date	Details	Debit	Credit	Balance
3 May	Invoice		560	560 Cr
7 May	Purchases returns	40		520 Cr

Receivables Ledger

K. Palfreyman account				
Date	Details	Debit	Credit	Balance
2 May	Invoice	199		199 Dr

L. Patel account				
Date	Details	Debit	Credit	Balance
2 May	Invoice	870		870 Dr
5 May	Sales returns		62	808 Dr
6 May	Bank		808	–

General Ledger

Bank account				
Date	**Details**	**Debit**	**Credit**	**Balance**
6 May	L. Patel	808		808 Dr
	J. Carter		339	469 Dr

Sales account				
Date	**Details**	**Debit**	**Credit**	**Balance**
7 May	Sales Day Book (total invoices)		1,069	1,069 Cr

Purchases account				
Date	**Details**	**Debit**	**Credit**	**Balance**
7 May	Purchases Day Book (total invoices)	2,149		2,149 Dr

Purchases Returns account				
Date	**Details**	**Debit**	**Credit**	**Balance**
7 May	Purchases Returns Day Book (total returns)		120	120 Cr

2.6

Date	Details	Debit	Credit	Balance	Cleaning	Travel	Postage	Other
14 October	Opening float	200		200 Dr				
	Travel expenses		26	174 Dr		26		
15 October	Window cleaning		14	160 Dr	14			
16 October	Train fares		18	142 Dr		18		
17 October	Dog kennel		40	102 Dr				40
	Dog food		19	83 Dr				19
18 October	Postage		3	80 Dr			3	
19 October	Loan to Hiram Decker		10	70 Dr				10
20 October	Window cleaning		24	46 Dr	24			
	Transfer: Cash Account	154		200 Dr				
					38	44	3	69

2.8 Paul Pascoe's journal

			Dr	Cr
			£	£
(a)	Debit	Andrew Young's Receivables ledger account	400	
	Credit	Andrew Cheung's Receivables Ledger account		400
	– Correction of misposting to A. Young's account			
(b)	Debit	Stationery	80	
	Credit	Bank		80
	– Correction of reversed entries (£40 to cancel incorrect entry, plus £40 for correct entry = £80)			
(c)	Debit	Purchases	200	
	Credit	Dingle Dynamics' Payables Ledger account		200
		– Correction of omitted entry		

Chapter 3

3.1

(a) Unsold inventory is never normally valued at selling price, as this assumes – possibly incorrectly – that they will be sold at a profit. The normal valuation will be based on cost price (even though this may have to be calculated on a theoretical basis such as *FIFO – First In First Out*). Occasionally, inventory has deteriorated, gone out of fashion or otherwise been devalued so that its anticipated selling price is actually less than its cost price. Only in these circumstances can the inventory be valued at what it could be sold for, less any expenses needed to be incurred to make it saleable (also known as the 'net realisable value').

(b) The usual method of inventory valuation is 'at the lower of cost and net realisable value'. In the case of the Tablet computers, the selling price is lower than cost, and additional costs will need to be incurred to sell them. Their valuation will therefore be:

Anticipated selling price	20 × £350	£7,000
Less Upgrade costs	20 × £75	£1,500
		£5,500

With regard to the laptops, as the cost is less than the 'net realisable value', they must be valued at cost price: 10 × £400 = £4,000.

3.2

(a) Depreciation is defined by *International Accounting Standard 16: Property, Plant and Equipment* as 'the systematic allocation of the depreciable amount of an asset over its useful life'. The *depreciable amount* refers to the loss of value that the asset suffers due to factors such as wear and tear, passage of time and obsolescence due to changes in technology.

(b) Depreciation is charged under the straight line method:

$$\text{Annual depreciation} = \frac{\text{Cost} - \text{Estimated residual value}}{\text{Estimated useful life}}$$

$$= (£200{,}000 - £24{,}400)/10 = £17{,}560 \text{ pa}$$

(c) The depreciation charge for the first three years under the diminishing balance method at 19% per annum will be:

Year ended 31 December 2011 £200,000 × 19% = £38,000
Year ended 31 December 2012 (£200,000 − £38,000) × 19% = £30,780
Year ended 31 December 2013 (£200,000 − [£38,000 + £30,780]) × 19% = £24,932

The effect on the operating profit is shown in the table below:

Year ended 31 December	Original profit after depreciation (straight line method)	Straight line depreci- ation (see (b) above)	Original profit before depreciation	Diminish- ing balance depreciation (see above)	Revised profit after depreciation if diminish- ing balance method had been used
2011	**£160,000**	£17,560	£177,560	£38,000	**£139,560**
2012	**£190,000**	£17,560	£207,560	£30,780	**£176,780**
2013	**£230,000**	£17,560	£247,560	£24,932	**£222,628**

If the diminishing balance method is used, high depreciation is charged in the early years but this progressively reduces over the life of the asset. This has the effect of a greater reduction in profit in the early years when compared to the straight line method, but a lower charge in the later years. For example, depreciation under the diminishing balance method in the eighth year of ownership of the machinery is only £8,693 compared to the £17,560 under the straight line method.

3.3

(a) Accruals are additional expenses incurred during the financial period which have neither been invoiced nor paid by the end of that period. They do not include 'trade payables' which would have been invoiced in the normal way.
(b) The total rent shown as part of the expenses in the income statement is 12 × £2500 = £30,000.
(c) In the statement of financial position, current liabilities will include an accrual for £2,500, being the one month's rent owing at the end of the year.

Chapter 4

4.1

Business 1: Amber
Income statement for the year ended 30 April 2014

	£	£
Raw materials		
Opening inventory at 1 May 2013	8,320	
Add Purchases of raw materials	52,450	
	60,770	
Less Closing inventory at 30 April 2014	(9,641)	
Cost of raw materials		51,129

	£	£
Other direct costs:		
Production labour		47,653
Prime cost of production		98,782
Indirect factory costs:		
Factory expenses (excluding depreciation)	89,322	
Depreciation of factory	6,000	
		95,322
		194,104
Add Opening work-in-progress	35,620	
Less Closing work-in-progress	(32,040)	
		3,580
Total cost of manufacturing		197,684
Revenue		253,620
Less Cost of sales		
Opening inventory at 1 May 2013	12,634	
Add Cost of manufacturing (see above)	197,684	
	210,318	
Less Closing inventory at 30 April 2014	(13,671)	
		(196,647)
Gross profit		56,973
Less Expenses		
Office expenses	34,600	
Depreciation	3,600	
		(38,200)
Operating profit		18,773

Business 2: Blue
Income statement for the year ended 31 May 2014

	£	£	£
Revenue			184,162
Less Cost of sales			
Opening inventory at 1 June 2013		12,700	
Add Purchases		65,210	
		77,910	
Less Closing inventory at 31 May 2014		(10,700)	
			(67,210)
Gross profit			116,952

	£	£	£
Less Expenses			
General office expenses (excluding depreciation)		54,923	
Depreciation: office		2,300	
			(57,223)
Operating profit			59,729

Business 3: Cerise
Income statement for the year ended 30 June 2014

	£	£
Fees from clients		85,400
Less Expenses		
General office expenses	21,500	
Depreciation: office	1,600	
		(23,100)
Operating profit		62,340

4.2

Wesley Timpson
Income statement for the year ended 30 November 2014

	£	£	£
Revenue			245,610
Less Cost of sales			
Opening inventory at 1 December 2013		15,684	
Add Purchases		124,100	
		139,784	
Less Closing inventory at 30 November 2014		(16,822)	
			(122,962)
Gross profit			122,648
Less Expenses			
Wages and salaries		47,231	
Depreciation: office furniture		2,500	
computers		900	
motor cars		4,500	
Postage and stationery		2,710	
Sundry office expenses		3,571	
Communication charges		1,499	
Light and heat		5,230	
			(67,331)
Operating profit			55,317

4.3

Betta Buys
Income statement for the year ended 28 February 2014

	£	£	£
Revenue			425,000
Less Cost of sales			
Opening inventory at 1 March 2013		90,000	
Add Purchases		204,000	
		294,000	
Less Closing inventory at 28 February 2014		(70,000)	
			(224,000)
Gross profit			201,000
Less Expenses			
Wages and salaries		62,000	
Rent (£15,000 − £3,000)		12,000	
Electricity (£4,000 + £1,000)		5,000	
Depreciation: shop fittings (£30,000 − £4,000)/5		5,200	
Depreciation: car 40% × (£12,000 − £4,800)		2,880	
			(87,080)
Operating profit			113,920

Betta Buys
Statement of financial position as at 28 February 2014

	£	£	£
	Cost	**Total depre-ciation**	**Depreciated value**
Non-current assets			
Shop fittings	30,000	15,600	14,400
Motor car	12,000	7,680	4,320
	42,000	23,280	18,720
Current assets			
Inventory		70,000	
Trade Receivables		35,200	
Prepayments		3,000	
Bank		960	
Cash		250	
		109,410	
Less Current liabilities			
Trade payables	27,600		
Accruals	1,000		
		(28,600)	
Net current assets			80,810

	£	£	£
	Cost	**Total depre-ciation**	**Depreciated value**
Total net assets			99,530
Equity			
Opening balance, 1 March 2014		10,610	
Add Operating profit		113,920	
		124,530	
Less Drawings		(25,000)	
Closing balance at 28 February 2014			99,530

4.4

Helen Thorne
Income statement for the year ended 31 May 2014

	£	£
Revenue		325,340
Less Cost of sales		
Opening inventory at 1 June 2013	35,750	
Add Purchases	168,220	
	203,970	
Less Closing inventory at 31 May 2014	(27,880)	
		(176,090)
Gross profit		149,250
Less **Expenses**		
Wages	33,100	
Insurance	7,420	
Telephone and e-mail (£5,200 + 200)	5,400	
Light and heat	6,230	
Security guards' wages (£12,400 + £400)	12,800	
Repairs to premises	3,970	
Amortisation of leasehold premises (£60,000/20)	3,000	
Depreciation of safe (40% × (£12,000 − £4,800))	2,880	
Depreciation of shop fittings (10% × £34,000)	3,400	
Rent and rates	17,000	
Website maintenance charges (£1,430 − (7/12 × £900))	905	
Publicity and advertising	9,740	
Sundry expenses	3,940	
		(109,785)
Operating profit		39,465

Helen Thorne
Statement of financial position as at 31 May 2014

	£	£	£
	Cost	**Total depreci-ation**	**Depreciated value**
Non-current assets			
Leasehold premises	60,000	21,000	39,000
Safe	12,000	7,680	4,320
Shop fittings	34,000	13,600	20,400
	106,000	42,280	63,720
Current assets			
Inventory		27,880	
Trade receivables		3,400	
Prepayments		525	
Cash		520	
		32,325	
Less Current liabilities			
Trade payables	19,670		
Accruals	600		
Bank overdraft	2,380		
		(22,650)	
Net current assets			9,675
			73,395
Less Non-current liabilities (loan)			(20,000)
Total net assets			53,395
Equity			
Opening balance, 1 June 2013		38,630	
Add Operating profit		39,465	
		78,095	
Less Drawings		(24,700)	
Closing balance at 31 May 2014			53,395

Chapter 5

5.1

Income statement for the year ended 31 December 2014 (extract)

	£
Expenses include:	
Depreciation on vessels	240,000
Loss on disposal of vessels	152,500

Statement of financial position as at 31 December 2014 (extract)

	Cost	Total depreciation	Depreciated value
	£	£	£
Vessels	1,600,000	645,000	955,000
Note:			
Vessels	£		
Cost at 1 January 2014	1,950,000		
Add Additions in year	700,000		
	2,650,000		
Less Disposals at cost	(1,050,000)		
Cost at 31 December 2014	**1,600,000**		
Depreciation at 1 January 2014		1,102,500	
Add Charge for the year		240,000	
		1,342,500	
Less Depreciation on disposals		(697,500)	
Depreciation as at 31 December 2014		**645,000**	
Depreciated value as at 31 December 2014			**955,000**
Depreciated value as at 1 January 2014			847,500

Workings (figures in £000):

	Vessel				
	Invisible	**Submersible**	**Outrageous**	**Implausible**	**Total**
Depreciation p.a.	$\frac{£450 \times 75\%}{5}$	$\frac{£600 \times 75\%}{5}$	$\frac{£900 \times 75\%}{5}$	$\frac{£700 \times 75\%}{5}$	
	= 67.57	= 90	= 135	= 105	
Depreciation to 1 January 2014	67.5 × 5 = 337.5	90 × 4 =360	135 × 3 = 405	(none)	1,102.5
Depreciation for 2014	(none)	(none)	135	105	240
Depreciated value at disposal	450 − 337.5 = 112.5	600 − 300 = 240	n/a	n/a	
'Proceeds' of disposal	nil	200	n/a	n/a	
Loss on disposal	112.5	40	n/a	n/a	152.5

5.3 (a) This is the application of the faithful representation principle to inventory valuation in order to ensure that asset values are not overstated. Cost represents all those costs incurred in the normal course of business in bringing the product to its present location and condition. Net realisable value is the estimated proceeds from the sale of items of inventory less all further costs to completion and less all costs to be incurred in marketing, selling and distributing directly related to the items in question.

(b) *Orange Lace*

Cost £9,000
Net realisable value £2,000 – £500 = £1,500
Therefore, valued at the lower figure, £1,500.

Saltypigs
Cost £16,000
Net realisable value £4,000 – (2,750 + 2,650) = £1,400 loss
Therefore, it would be omitted from the inventory calculation (inventory written down to zero) as it is likely that the inventory would be thrown away rather than be exported at a loss.

5.5 (a) Bad debts occur when a customer has bought goods or services and does not pay for them. The company selling the goods or services has given up trying to recover the debt, and accepts that it has lost money on the transaction.

Doubtful debts occur when there is an element of doubt as to whether a customer will pay for goods or services, but it has not reached the stage where the company is prepared to write off the debt as bad.

(b)

Bickley Brothers
Income statement (extract) for the year ended 31 May 2014

	£	£
Expenses include:		
Bad debts written off		2,400
Increase in provision for doubtful debts		500

Statement of financial position (extract) as at 31 May 2014

	£	£
Current assets include:		
Trade receivables	11,125	
Less Provision for doubtful debts	(3,500)	
		7,625

Bickley Brothers
Income statement (extract) for the year ended 31 May 2015

	£	£
Added to gross profit:		
Decrease in provision for doubtful debts		300
Expenses include:		
Bad debts written off		600

Statement of financial position (extract) as at 31 May 2015

	£	£
Current assets include:		
Trade receivables	17,030	
Less Provision for doubtful debts	(3,200)	
		13,830

(c) When Robin Taylor's debt was written off as bad in the year ended May 2014, the customer's account in the receivables ledger would have been closed. In the following year, the receipt of the amount owing is taken as additional income straight to the income statement – described as 'bad debt recovered'. There are no relevant entries in the statement of financial position.

Closing balance at 31 December 2008	12,560

Chapter 6

6.1 A partnership is not a collection of sole proprietors, as the partners run the business in the knowledge that they will be *sharing* the risks and rewards. They would usually have signed a partnership agreement to acknowledge this fact. Although sole proprietorship suits many people, it can be very helpful to be able to draw on the expertise of others. Sharing of problems and the ability to discuss business possibilities are also very positive aspects of a partnership. It is very difficult to expand a business with only one owner, and bringing in partners can draw in finance which is otherwise unavailable.

6.2

Disraeli and Gladstone
Income statement (appropriation section)
for the year ended 31 December 2013

	£	£
Net profit for the year		40,000
Less Salary to Disraeli		(9,000)
		31,000
Less Interest on capital		
Disraeli (5% × £20,000)	1,000	
Gladstone (5% × £15,000)	750	
		(1,750)
		29,250
Disraeli: share of profit ($\frac{2}{3}$ × £29,250)	19,500	
Gladstone: share of profit ($\frac{1}{3}$ × £29,250)	9,750	
		29,250

Disraeli and Gladstone
Statement of financial position as at 31 December 2013

	£	£	£
Total net assets			**43,000**
Capital accounts	Disraeli	Gladstone	
Opening balance, 1 January 2013	20,000	15,000	
Add Salary	9,000		
Interest on capital	1,000	750	
Share of profit	19,500	9,750	
	49,500	25,500	

	£	£	£
Less Drawings	(18,000)	(14,000)	
Closing balance, 31 December 2013	31,500	11,500	**43,000**

6.4 Question

Morse Ltd
Income statement for the year ended 31 December 2013

	£	£
Revenue		462,600
Less Cost of sales		
Opening inventory at 1 January 2013	14,900	
Add Purchases	140,800	
	155,700	
Less Closing inventory at 31 December 2013	(17,650)	
		(138,050)
Gross profit		324,550
Less Expenses		
Directors' salaries	59,200	
Salesforce wages	65,230	
Office salaries	34,900	
Advertising and website charges (15,300 – 160)	15,140	
Sales delivery costs	632	
Bad debts	750	
Depreciation on delivery vehicles		
[30% × (143,600 − 27,800)]	34,740	
Office expenses (33,897 + 800)	34,697	
		(245,289)
Operating profit		79,261
Finance costs		(2,502)
Profit before tax		76,759
Less Taxation		(24,000)
Profit for the year, after tax		52,759
Less Dividend paid		(5,000)
Retained profit for the year		47,759

Morse Ltd
Statement of financial position as at 31 December 2013

	£	£	£
	Cost	**Total depreciation**	**Depreciated value**
Non-current assets			
Delivery vehicles	143,600	62,540	81,060
Current assets			
Inventory		17,650	

	£	£	£
Trade receivables		64,100	
Prepayments		160	
Cash and cash equivalents		11,500	
		93,410	
Less Current liabilities			
Trade payables	32,711		
Accruals	800		
Taxation	24,000		
		(57,511)	
Net current assets			35,899
			116,959
Less Non-current liabilities			
Bond (repayable 2020)			(11,600)
Total net assets			105,359
Equity			
Share capital			25,000
Share premium account			15,000
Retained earnings:			
Balance at 1 January 2013		17,600	
Retained profit for the year		47,759	
			65,359
Total equity			105,359

6.6 (a) **Pembroke Limited**

Statement of financial position as at 30 September 2013 (Total Equity section only)

	£
Capital and Reserves	
Called up share capital (120,000 shares of 50p nominal value)	60,000
Share premium account	12,000
Retained earnings	82,000
Total equity	154,000

(b) A bonus issue is a free issue of shares given to existing shareholders pro rata to their current holdings. The issue does not affect the company's value; all that happens is that some or all of the reserves are 'capitalised', i.e. transferred into the share capital of the company. For example, a company with 10,000 ordinary shares of £1 each and £120,000 accumulated in its retained earnings may decide to make a bonus issue on a 5 for 1 basis in order to reduce the amount of the company's distributable reserves. After the bonus issue, the share capital will have increased by £50,000 to £60,000, and the balance on the retained earnings will have reduced from £120,000 to £70,000. The statement of financial position's total remains unchanged at £130,000. There are a number of reasons why a company might make a bonus issue including:

- If the company wants to restrict potential future dividend payouts, a bonus issue out of retained profits converts *distributable* reserves into *non-distributable* reserves. This reduces the pressure on directors from shareholders wanting increased dividends.
- A high stock market price may act as a deterrent to potential investors. As a bonus issue increases the number of shares traded, the price per share will decrease to a more realistic level.
- Stock exchanges might link bonus issues with 'good news' from profitable companies, leading to an increase in share prices.
- Over time, a company might accumulate many different reserves; distributable and non-distributable. A bonus issue serves as a convenient way of tidying up the balance sheet by transferring some or all of the reserves into share capital.

Chapter 7

7.1 A: £10,080 B: £22,570 C: £(7,930) D: £(6,270).

7.2 Cash is vital for a business to survive, as without it businesses would be unable to pay their liabilities. This would lead to creditors forcing the company into liquidation. Profit is also vital for a business's survival as profitable businesses are able to reinvest and expand whilst rewarding shareholders with appropriate dividends. Profitability does not necessarily equate to healthy cash flows, as acquisitive, profit-generating businesses are often using cash balances in replacing non-current assets, buying other businesses, etc.

7.3 The answer depends upon the reasons for continual cash outflows: some are unavoidable, such as taxation payments or loan repayments, others indicate expanding, aggressive businesses using cash resources to invest in non-current assets or take over other businesses.

Net cash outflows resulting from poor trading conditions are the most worrying sign, and continual net cash outflows might cause liquidity problems, so must be monitored closely.

The cashflows should be considered in conjunction with other financial indicators such as profitability, return on capital employed and the strength of working capital.

7.6

Asterix plc
Cash flow statement for the year ended 31 May 2013

		£000
Cash flows from operating activities (see Note 1)		28,800
Interest paid		(1,200)
Taxation paid		(4,000)
Net cash from operating activities		**23,600**
Cash flows from investing activities		
Purchase of non-current assets	(22,000)	
Proceeds from sale of non-current assets	1,800	
Net cash used in investing activities		(20,200)
Cash flows from financing activities		
Proceeds from issue of share capital	1,100	
Dividends paid	(13,000)	

	£000
Net cash used in financing activities	(11,900)
Net decrease in cash and cash equivalents	(8,500)
Cash and cash equivalents at beginning of period	2,800
Cash and cash alternatives at end of period	**(5,700)**

Note 1: Reconciliation of operating profit to cash flows from operating activities

	£000
Operating profit before interest	25,900
Depreciation charges	6,000
Loss on sale of non-current assets	3,200
Increase in inventories	(1,000)
Increase in receivables	(1,500)
Decrease in payables	(3,800)
Cash flows from operating activities	**28,800**

Chapter 8

8.1 There is no set answer to this question.

8.2 (a) Sundorne Limited is likely to be the food retailer, for the following reasons: Food retailing produces a small gross profit margin, but the fast turnover ensures that profit is earned much faster than in a manufacturing business. Very few retail food sales are made on credit terms, so the year-end receivables figure will be very low. Due to the fast inventory turnover, trade payables totals might be twice as much as inventory, giving rise to the negative current ratio for Sundorne Limited of 0.4:1.

(b) (i) *Trade receivables:* Rodington Limited's sales can be calculated as £200,000 × 100/40 (because the gross margin of 60% means that cost of sales must be 40% of the sales figure). If the average collection period is 30 days, then the trade receivables total is 30/365 of the sales figure: (30/365) × £500,000 = £41,096.

(ii) *Current liabilities:* The current ratio (current assets: current liabilities) is 2:1. Current assets for Rodington Limited are:

	£
Inventory	40,000
Trade receivables (as calculated above)	41,096
Cash and cash equivalents	11,004
	92,100

Therefore, current liabilities are 1/2 × £92,100 = £46,050.

(c) Sundorne Limited is highly geared, which indicates that the company has significant long-term debt. As an equity shareholder, you would need to be satisfied that the company can repay the interest due on such loans and that the return generated by the borrowed capital is greater than the cost of financing it. Highly geared companies carry more risk than low-geared companies, but can produce higher returns if the company and its profits expand as a result of the borrowings.

8.3 (a)

		Dorrington	Rowton	Comments
(i)	Gearing	Nil	$\frac{100}{100 + 113} = 47\%$	Gearing for Rowton is a high 47%, whereas Dorrington has no fixed return borrowings
(ii)	Current ratio	123:135 = 0.9:1	177:168 = 1.05:1	Both companies have low working capital ratios, Dorrington worse than Rowton
(iii)	Acid test	38:135 = 0.28:1	57:168 = 0.34:1	Both companies are exposed to liquidity ratio problems if creditors start demanding payment
(iv)	ROCE	$\frac{40,000}{113,000} = 35.4\%$	$\frac{40,000}{113,000 + 100,000} = 18\ 8\%$	Dorrington has almost twice the ROCE of Rowton. Are they in comparable business sectors?

(b) Rowton is more vulnerable due to high gearing and lower ROCE. Both companies show poor acid test ratios, but this may be a feature of their type of trade (for example, supermarkets).

If Dorrington would be prepared to issue a bond secured on its assets, then the investor might be better off with Dorrington, though again the lack of liquidity would be worrying. Neither seems suitable for a cautious investor.

(c) If the going concern principle (see Chapter 1) was not applicable, then Dorrington would be about to fail, with asset values (almost certainly) being downgraded, and provisions being made for the likely costs of liquidation.

The advice to the potential investor in that situation would be to steer clear of the company.

8.4 (a) Any eight of the following ratios:

From the income statement:

Mark-up	190/480 × 100	39.6%
Gross margin	190/670 × 100	28.4%
Net margin	51,050/670,000 × 100	7.6%
ROCE	51,050/265,000 × 100	19.3%
Earnings per share	40,000/100,000	40p
Interest cover	51,050/5,600	9.1 times
Dividend cover	40,000/15,000	2.7 times

From the statement of financial position:

Asset turnover	670,000/185,800 × 100	360.6%
Current ratio	158,450/79,250	2:1
Acid test	68,450/79,250	0.86:1
Gearing	80,000/(185,000 + 80,000) × 100	30.2%
Inventory turn	90,000/480,000 × 365	68.4 days
Average collection period	43,650/670,000 × 365	23.8 days
Average payment period	48,000/570,000 × 365	30.7 days

Comment: One year's figures should never be taken by themselves as a measure of a company's performance, as other figures are needed for comparison, for example, those of previous years or competitors. With this major proviso, we can see that the company had a strong current ratio, a seemingly healthy ROCE (when compared with what we know of prevailing interest rates), a good safety level for interest payments (profit available being 9.1 times the finance costs) and realistic collection and payment periods. Gearing is on the high side, but as we have seen, the interest is covered strongly.

(b) £6m is a significant amount for a company which made only £40,000 profit after taxation. However, possibilities for raising capital include:

- A rights issue (but it is a new company, so would shareholders put in so much more capital so quickly?)
- Loans (but existing bonds might be secured on assets, so it is unlikely that there would be enough security available for more loans).

Note that, as a private limited company, it could not sell its shares to the general public.

Chapter 9

9.1 (a) Total fixed costs £12,568.
(b) Total variable costs £6,644.
(c) Fixed cost per duvet £3.61.
(d) Variable cost per duvet £1.91.
(e) Total cost per duvet £5.52.

Workings:

	£	% variable	% variable	£ variable	£ fixed
Raw materials	1,505	100	0	1,505	0
Direct labour	1,161	100	0	1,161	0
Direct expenses	2,838	100	0	2,838	0
Indirect material	3,560	5	95	178	3,382
Indirect labour	3,378	7	93	236	3,142
Indirect expenses	1,544	6	94	93	1,451
Selling overhead	2,481	20	80	496	1,985
Administration overhead	2,745	5	95	137	2,608
Total	19,212			6,644	12,568
Cost per duvet (3,481 produced)	£5.52			1.91	3.61

9.2 The company must charge a price in excess of the total cost of £5.52 in order to make a profit.

If the company hopes to make a net profit margin of 10%, it would charge:

$$£5.52 \times \frac{100}{(100 - 10)} = £6.13 \text{ per duvet}$$

Chapter 10

10.1

	Production departments			Service department
	A	B	C	D
	£	£	£	£
Indirect labour	20,000	16,000	8,000	7,000
Other indirect overheads	10,000	6,000	3,000	2,600
	30,000	22,000	11,000	9,600
Department D's overheads	3,840	3,840	1,920	(9,600)
Total	33,840	25,840	12,920	–

	Production departments			Service department
	A	B	C	D
	£	£	£	£
Indirect labour hours	1,000	800	500	
OAR	£33.84	£32.30	£25.84	

10.3

	A	B
Sales in units	**5,000**	**20,000**
Sales (£)	40,000	60,000
Variable costs (£)	10,000	**50,000**
Contribution (£)	30,000	10,000
Contribution per unit (£)	6	0.5
Fixed costs (£)	14,400	**15,000**
Profit/(loss) (£)	**15,600**	(5,000)
Break-even point (units)	2,400	30,000
Profit/(loss) if 3,000 units sold	**3,600**	**(13,500)**

10.5 (a)

	10,000 units	15,000 units	Change +5,000 units
	£	£	£
Total costs	160,000	210,000	+ 50,000

Therefore, variable costs = £50,000/5,000 units = £10 per unit Variable costs @ £10 per unit: 100,000 for 10,000 units; 150,000 for 15,000 units
Answer: fixed costs = **£60,000**

(b) Break-even = Fixed costs/contribution per unit
Contribution per unit = Selling price (£15) – Variable cost (see (a) above) (£10) = £5
Therefore the break-even point = £60,000/£5 = 12,000 units.
To earn a profit of £13,000, total contribution must be:
Fixed costs £60,000 + Profit £13,000 = £73,000
As contribution per unit is £5, they must sell £73,000/5 = **14,600 units.**

(c) If only 7,000 units were manufactured and sold, the total contribution would be 7,000 × £5 = £35,000, which is £25,000 less than the fixed costs of £60,000. Therefore, **a loss of £25,000** is made.

10.7 (a)

	Unit	Cost Total
	£	£
Raw materials (1.60 × 300)	1.60	480
Wages (£4.20 × 20 hours)	0.28	84
Overheads (20 × £3.60)	0.24	72
Setting-up costs	0.07	21
Cost of full batch	**2.19**	**657**

(b)

	£	£
Cost of full batch		657.00
Add Rectification costs		
Wages (9 hours × £4.20)	37.80	
Overheads (9 hours × £3.60)	32.40	
Setting-up costs	18.00	
		88.20
		745.20
Less Income from scrapped components 20 × £0.86		(17.20)
Total cost of 280 cat baskets		728.00
Cost of batch per unit £728/280		2.60

(c)

	£
280 units should have cost 280 × £2.19 (see (a) above)	613.20
Actual cost (see (b) above)	728.00
Loss	114.80

Chapter 11

11.1 The variable overhead efficiency variance is £20,000 (favourable).

Workings

The variable overhead absorption rate on the basis of standard labour hours is £10 per hour (£800,000/80,000). On the basis of the standard hours needed to produce one unit, a production of 4,000 units should have taken 20,000 labour hours (4,000 × 5 = 20,000). In fact the actual production took 18,000 hours. As there is a difference between the number of hours planned for production and the number of hours actually taken, a variance has resulted caused in this case by greater efficiency (fewer hours actually needed than planned).

	£
Actual hours × standard absorption rate (18,000 × £10)	180,000
Standard hours × standard absorption rate (20,000 × £10)	200,000
Favourable efficiency variance	20,000

11.3 The variable overhead expenditure variance for Azalea Limited is £9,616 (favourable). The variable overhead efficiency variance is £4,616 (adverse).

Workings

The standard direct labour hour rate is:

$$\frac{£150{,}000}{6{,}500} = £23.077 \text{ per standard direct labour hour}$$

This rate per standard direct labour hour is then applied to the actual number of direct labour hours worked, and the answer compared to the actual variable overheads in order to calculate the variance:

	£
Actual variable overhead incurred	145,000
Actual production at standard absorption rate (6,700 × £23.077)	154,616
Favourable expenditure variance	9,616

On the basis of the standard hours needed to produce one unit, a production of 7,000 units should have taken 7,000 direct labour hours. In fact the actual production took 6,700 hours. An adverse efficiency variance has resulted, calculated as follows:

	£
Actual hours × standard absorption rate (6,7000 × £23.077)	154,616
Standard hours × standard absorption rate (6,500 × £23.077)	150,000
Adverse efficiency variance	4,616

We can check that the above variances are correct by comparing them with the overall overhead variance, calculated by comparing the standard total variable overheads (£150,000) with the actual total variable overheads (£145,000). This results in an overall favourable variance of £5,000, which agrees with our calculations of the expenditure variance of £9,616 (favourable) less the efficiency variance of £4,616 (adverse)

11.5 (a)

Production line A

Overall direct labour variance = £50 (favourable)

Calculation:

Standard pay rate of standard hours ([220 × 0.5 hours] × £7 = £770) compared with actual pay rate of actual hours (£720)

Direct labour pay rate variance = £34 (adverse)

Calculation:

Standard pay rate of actual hours (£7 × 98 = £686) compared with actual pay rate of actual hours (£720)

Direct labour efficiency variance = £84 (favourable)

Calculation:

Standard pay rate of actual hours (£7 × 98 = £686) compared with standard pay rate of standard hours ([220 × 0.5 hours] × £7 = £770)

Production line B

Overall direct labour variance = £310 (adverse)

Calculation:

Standard pay rate of standard hours (80 hours/10 employees = 8 standard days × 20 units per day = 160 units @ £4 per unit = £640) compared with actual pay rate of actual hours (£950)

Direct labour pay rate variance = £10 (favourable)

Calculation:

Standard pay rate of actual hours (£4 × 240 = £960) compared with actual pay rate of actual hours (£950)

Direct labour efficiency variance = £320 (adverse)

Calculation:

Standard pay rate of actual hours (£4 × 240 = £960) compared with standard pay rate of standard hours (80 hours/10 employees = 8 standard days × 20 units per day = 160 units @ £4 per unit = £640)

(b) The cost per unit of production line A is £3.27 (wage costs of £720 divided by output of 220 units), compared to a cost per unit for production line B of £3.96 per unit (wage costs of £950 divided by output of 240 units). On this basis, production line A is clearly more cost efficient. Investigation of the variances show that whilst there was a small adverse pay variance for production line A there were efficiency savings of £84, giving an overall direct labour variance of £50 favourable. In contrast, although there was an insignificant favourable pay rate variance (£10) there was a large adverse efficiency variance (£320). Management would have to investigate this further, as it might have been caused by specific factors e.g. machine breakdowns, which were out of the control of the workforce. If that was not the case then it would appear that the standard output of 20 units per day is not achievable. Either this has to be reconsidered and a new standard set, or else production line B's workforce should be remunerated on the same basis as production line A.

Chapter 12

12.1 Break-even chart

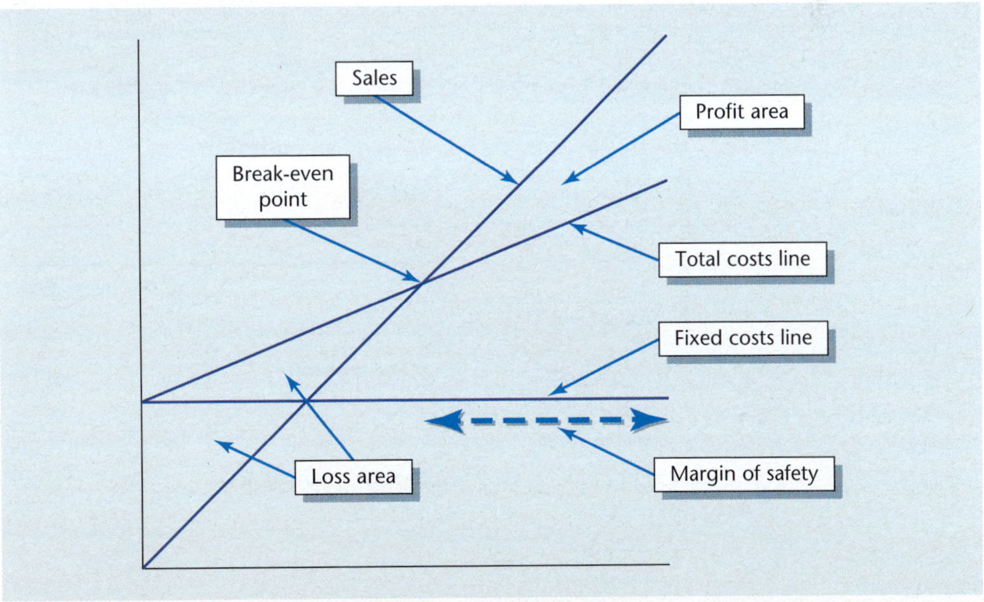

12.3 Profit/volume chart

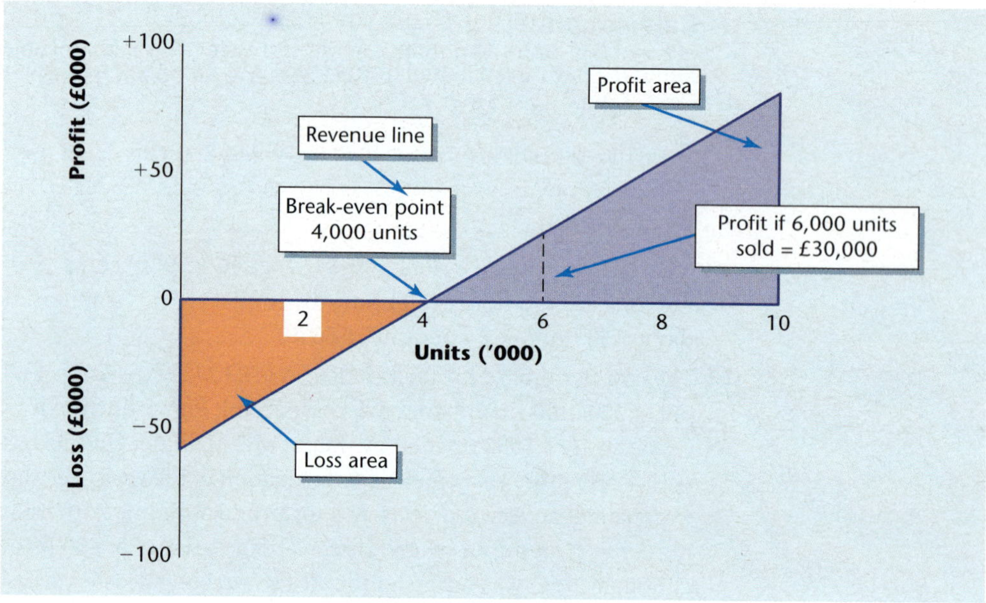

12.5 (a) The contribution from each litre of vodka is £6 (selling price £10 – production cost £4 = £6). The fixed costs are forecast at £850,000, so the break-even sales calculation is Fixed Costs ÷ Contribution per litre = 141,667 litres (£850,000/£6).

(b)

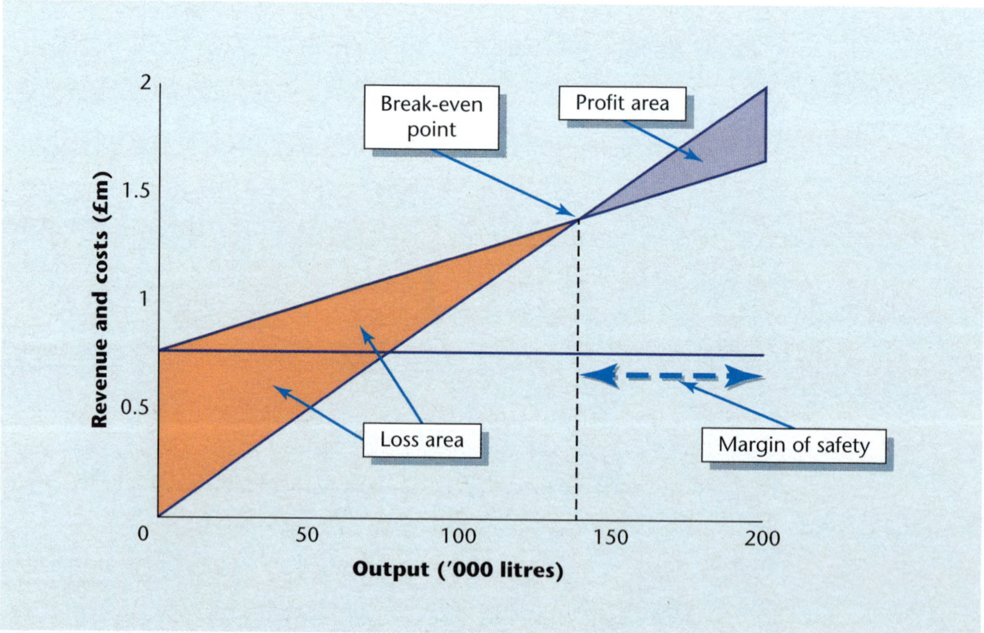

(c) The margin of safety as shown on the break-even chart is just less than 60,000 litres. The forecast production is 200,000 litres, so 70% of production needs to be sold to reach the break-even point, with 30% being profitable production after that point. Another way of expressing this is that if sales fall by 30% then the company will *not* make a profit, so they have to be very confident in entering the North American market. The other factor is that if costs increase which cannot be passed on to customers then the break-even point moves along the output line, leaving even less of a safety margin. Ideally, the company should try and reduce the break-even point as far as possible by increasing the sales price or reducing both variable and fixed costs.

Chapter 13

13.1 (a)

	Units
Sales forecast:	11,800
Less Opening inventory	(2,800)
	9,000
Add Closing inventory	3,600
Production required	12,600

(b) Materials usage:

Material A: 12,600 × 10 kg = 126,000 kg

Material B: 12,600 × 6 kg = 75,600 kg

(c) Materials purchases:

	Material A	Material B
	kg	kg
Usage (see (b) above)	126,000	75,600
Less Opening inventory	(700)	(400)
	125,300	75,200
Add Closing inventory	500	900
Materials to be purchased	125,800	76,100
Value per kg (£)	6.50	9.00
Total value	£817,700	£684,900

13.2 Limiting factors are areas within the business which restrict the growth of that business. At any one time, there will be a key factor which needs to be addressed before the business can make progress. Examples include:

- Shortage of adequately trained workers
- Unreliable supplies of raw materials
- Unavailability of spare parts to repair machinery.

13.3 (a)

Gina Bruin: The Rural Art Gallery cash flow forecast from 1 July 2015 to 31 December 2015

£	July	August	September	October	November	December
Inflows						
Sales: cash	8,000	4,000	7,000	12,000	18,000	24,000
Equity invested	4,000	-	-	-	-	-
Other receipts: grant	-	5,000	-	-	-	-
A: Total Inflows	12,000	9,000	7,000	12,000	18,000	24,000
Outflows						
Due to artists	-	4,800	2,400	4,200	7,200	10,800
Wages	750	750	750	750	750	750
Deposit to landlord	3,000	-	-	-	-	-
Rent	-	-	-	3,000	-	-
Redecorating premises	-	4,000	3,000	-	-	-
General overheads	-	2,000	2,000	2,000	2,000	2,000
Gina's drawings	600	600	600	600	600	900
Equipment	-	-	3,000	-	-	-
Advertising	-	500	-	-	-	-
B: Total outflows	4,350	12,650	11,750	10,550	10,550	14,450
C: Net cash flow (A - B)	7,650	-3,650	-4,750	1,450	7,450	9,550
D: Opening bank balance	-	7,650	4,000	-750	700	8,150
E: Closing bank balance (D ± C)	7,650	4,000	-750	700	8,150	17,700
Note: Agreed Overdraft Facility	(None)	(None)	(None)	(None)	(None)	(None)

(b) The forecast appears to show a healthy business, with the closing bank balance reaching £17,700 by the end of the year. However, payments in January 2016 (not shown within the six-month cash flow forecast period) are forecast to reach £19,400 (rent, general overheads and the 60% of December's sales due to artists). No overdraft limit has been agreed, so Gina would have to convince the bank that her business can survive into the following year. She would also need a temporary overdraft for September 2015 (£750) and at least £1,700 in January (£19,400 – £17,700 forecast bank balance on 1 January 2016). The worrying aspect of the business is that it may be seasonal, so the overdraft might have to rise sharply in the first quarter of 2016.

Chapter 14

14.1

Year	Future value × Discount factor	Project A	Future value × Discount factor	Project B
0	n/a	(3,000)	n/a	(4,000)
1	0.909 × £10,000	9,090	–	
2			0.826 × £12,000	9,912
NPV		6,090		5,912

Project A has a higher net present value, so would be chosen, on this basis, in preference to project B.

14.3 Project G pays back its initial investment in 5 years (£4,000 × 5 = £20,000), whereas project H pays back its initial investment in 6 years (£5,000 × 6 = £30,000). Project G has a shorter payback period, so would be chosen, on this basis, in preference to project H. Note that cash flows arising after the payback period has been reached are ignored, as is the time value of the money.

14.5 Buy the equipment option

Year		Future value × Discount factor*	Present value
0	Cost		(700,000)
1–5	Maintenance	£30,000 × 3.993	(119,790)
5	Scrap value	£100,000 × 0.681	68,100
1–3	Income	£300,000 × 2.577	773,100
4	Income	£200,000 × 0.735	147,000
5	Income	£200,000 × 0.681	136,200
NPV (positive)			304,610

* cumulative factors shown where same amount received or paid each year over several years

Lease the equipment option

Year		Future value × Discount factor*	Present value
0	Deposit		(400,000)
1–5	Lease payments	£120,000 × 3.993	(479,160)
	Income	£300,000 × 3.993	1,197,900
NPV (positive)			£318,740

* Cumulative factors shown where same amount received or paid each year over several years

Analysis

Buying the equipment outright appears to be the cheaper option by just over £14,000. However, it should be borne in mind that buying the equipment requires an immediate payment of £700,000 compared with a deposit to the lessor of only £400,000. If there is uncertainty surrounding the potential income generation, then leasing might have its advantages, as payback is reached in just over two years (income of £600,000 in two years nearly matches the lease payments of £640,000 in the same period). Total payments in the first two years when buying the equipment (including maintenance) are £760,000, but income in that period is only £600,000.

Other considerations would be the relative quality of the equipment (note that the leased equipment is slightly more advanced than that purchased outright), its relative reliability, and the status of both the lessor and the supplier of the equipment. The latter point is particularly important as the hospital will require continuing maintenance for the five-year period, either paid for annually in the case of the equipment being purchased outright, or as part of the leasing package.

14.6 Catalyst plc: evaluation of alternative investment possibilities

Project Alpha

£m	Discount factor	Net cash flow	Discounted cash flow
Year 0	1	(10.0)	(10.000)
Year 1	0.926	3.6	3.334

£m	Discount factor	Net cash flow	Discounted cash flow
Year 2	0.857	5.0	4.285
Year 3	0.794	5.0	3.970
Year 4	0.735	4.4	3.234
Year 5	0.681	5.8	3.950
Net Present Value			**8.773**

Project Beta

£m	Discount factor	Net cash flow	Discounted cash flow
Year 0	1	(20.0)	(20.000)
Year 1	0.926	7.2	6.667
Year 2	0.857	8.2	7.027
Year 3	0.794	9.0	7.146
Year 4	0.735	9.4	6.909
Year 5	0.681	1.2	0.817
Net present value			**8.566**

On the basis of the net present value of each project, Project Alpha is recommended as its net present value is over £200,000 greater than Project Beta.

Chapter 15

15.1 The company's production costs are £160 per door. Based on the financial facts, it would be reasonable to choose the external supplier, since their doors are £20 cheaper. However, some important non-financial facts should be considered:

- Accuracy of data: How reliable is the data? How it was collected? Have all costs been considered for calculation?
- Reliability of external supplier: Is the external supplier a new or an established company? How reliable it is in terms of delivery and quality? How much control will the company have over the production? How can product quality be assured?
- Cost: Is the price for the doors fixed or flexible? Can the supplier cope with increased demand? If demand decreases, is the company obliged to purchase a minimum number of doors?

15.3

Contribution of product A	= £62 − £50 = £12
Contribution per hour of use of the machine	= £12/3 = £4

If component B is made in 1 hour then 1 × £4 = £4 which means £4 contribution would be lost. Opportunity cost plus marginal cost = £4 + £10 = £14 which is greater than the best price £12 that Sabine managed to get. Therefore it is better for Sabine to buy component B rather than make it.

Because the machine is working at full capacity we had to calculate the opportunity cost of lost production. However, if the machine is idle for a significant amount of time there would be no loss of contribution. The only cost of making component B is its marginal cost of £10 which is *less* than the best price of £12 that Sabine managed to get.

Chapter 16

16.1 Reporting has a strong influence on corporate behaviour. Integrated reporting links environmental, social and governance issues which are increasingly seen as at the core of the business. Integrated Reporting will itself cover many of the issues at the heart of the corporate social responsibility debate for an organisation. It is therefore seen by many as supporting the organisation's value creation strategy. Integrated Reporting recognises that an organisation's ability to create and sustain value is increasingly measured through factors such as:

- Environmental concerns
- Concerns over current and future scarcity of resources
- Demand for corporate transparency
- Contributions to corporate and social responsibility.

Therefore, Integrated Reporting is an important mechanism for influencing corporate behaviour.

16.3 Advantages:

- More in line with IFRS
- Shorter and more concise
- Support from companies and auditors which have accepted the need to update current standards, seen by many as taking insufficient account of innovations
- PwC welcomed the proposal
- Increased subsidiaries disclosure
- More consistency within many UK and global groups.

Disadvantages:

- Imposing unnecessary cost on building societies and credit unions
- Imposing unnecessary cost on many companies which would be forced to incur additional costs by having to produce accounts with an unnecessary level of detail. Therefore, the cost to certain entities could not be justified by the benefits.
- A lack of certainty over what will happen to the reporting requirements for small companies.

Chapter 17

17.2 (a) The issue is that many environmental services are provided for free and therefore it is difficult to find a market value to represent their worth to individuals, organisations or society.

(b) The solutions suggested involve using questionnaires and surveys to find out what people are willing to pay to receive the benefits of the environmental activity – here the availability of wildlife.

17.3 First, environmental accounting can help policy-makers and decision-makers to manage resources more effectively through the availability of quantitative and qualitative information that assist in making more sustainable decisions. Second, it can help identify the appropriate methods and applications that lead to long-term sustainable development for national and organisational decision-makers. Third, evaluating environmental pressures through estimating the value of environmental impacts, such as the greenhouse gas emissions of businesses, the usage of energy and water, and how these relate to global warming, can provide useful measures to be used as a basis for decision making. Fourthly, having mandatory and consistent reporting of environmental impacts results in transparency for governments and organisations when seeking comparisons with other governments and organisations. Finally, using environmental accounting techniques helps awareness of the implications of regulations, taxes and consumption patterns on environmental sustainability, which will help policy-makers to make more informed regulations.

Appendix 3 Answers to case study questions

Chapter 1

(a)

Income in week ending 7 July:	£
Fee for National Magic Show appearance	750
Less Travel expenses	(20)
Profit	730

(b)

Non-current assets	£	£
Costume		3,000
Magic book		2,000
Cards		400
		5,400
Current asset		
Bank account	750	
Less Current liability		
Creditor (Kazam Limited)	(400)	
		350
Total net assets		5,750

Because of the accounting equation (Assets − Liabilities = Equity), Marvin's equity at 7 July was £5,750.

Proof

Marvin paid for the costume, the book and the travel expenses out of his own private resources (£3,000 + £2,000 + £20 = £5,020), and the business made a profit during the week of £730 which increased the value of his equity to £5,750.

Chapter 2

(a) and (b)

Cash Book							
		Bank account			Cash account		
Date	Details	Debit	Credit	Bank Balance	Debit	Credit	Cash Balance
7 July	Fee	750		750 Dr			
10 July	Fee				100		100 Dr
10 July	Travel					15	85 Dr
11 July	Cleaning		18	732 Dr			
12 July	Fee	120		852 Dr			
12 July	Travel					9	76 Dr
14 July	United Rabbit Corporation		240	612 Dr			
14 July	Kazam Ltd		400	212 Dr			

General ledger

Marvin's equity account				
Date	Details	Debit	Credit	Balance
1 July	Costume		3,000	3,000 Cr
2 July	Magic book		2,000	5,000 Cr
7 July	Travel		20	5,020 Cr

Costume account				
Date	Details	Debit	Credit	Balance
1 July	Marvin's equity account	3,000		3,000 Dr

Magic book account				
Date	Details	Debit	Credit	Balance
2 July	Marvin's equity account	2,000		2,000 Dr

Playing cards account				
Date	Details	Debit	Credit	Balance
3 July	Kazam Ltd	400		400 Dr

Fees account				
Date	Details	Debit	Credit	Balance
7 July	Bank		750	750 Cr
10 July	Cash		100	850 Cr
12 July	Bank		120	970 Cr
13 July	Mr and Mrs Peter		250	1,220 Cr

Travel expenses account				
Date	Details	Debit	Credit	Balance
7 July	Marvin's equity account	20		20 Dr
10 July	Cash	15		35 Dr
12 July	Cash	9		44 Dr

Rabbits account				
Date	Details	Debit	Credit	Balance
8 July	United Rabbit Corporation	240		240 Dr

Rabbit food account				
Date	Details	Debit	Credit	Balance
8 July	Amalgamated Carrots	250		250 Dr

Cleaning account				
Date	Details	Debit	Credit	Balance
11 July	Bank	18		18 Dr

Purchases returns account				
Date	Details	Debit	Credit	Balance
14 July	Amalgamated Carrots		60	60 Cr

Payables ledger

Kazam Ltd account				
Date	Details	Debit	Credit	Balance
3 July	Playing cards		400	400 Cr
14 July	Bank	400		-

United Rabbit Corporation account				
Date	Details	Debit	Credit	Balance
8 July	Rabbits		240	240 Cr
14 July	Bank	240		-

Amalgamated Carrots plc account				
Date	Details	Debit	Credit	Balance
8 July	Rabbit food		250	250 Cr
14 July	Purchases returns	60		190 Cr

Receivables Ledger

Mr and Mrs Peter account				
Date	Details	Debit	Credit	Balance
13 July	Fees	250		250 Dr

(c)

Marvin the Magician Trial balance as at 14 July		
	Debit	**Credit**
Cash Book:		
Bank	212	
Cash	76	
General Ledger:		
Equity		5,020
Costume	3,000	
Magic book	2,000	
Playing cards	400	
Fees		1,220
Travel expenses	44	
Rabbits	240	
Rabbit food	250	
Cleaning	18	
Purchases returns		60
Payables Ledger:		
Amalgamated Carrots plc		190
Receivables Ledger:		
Mr and Mrs Peter	250	
Totals:	6,490	6,490

Chapter 3

Marvin the Magician Income statement for the six months ended 31 December

	£	£
Sales of novelties (2,500 + 350)		2,850
Less Cost of sales		
Opening inventory at 1 July	–	
Add Purchases	1,700	
	1,700	
Less Closing inventory at 31 December	(80)	
		(1,620)
Gross profit on sales of novelties		1,230

	£	£
Add Appearance fees as entertainer		18,320
		19,550
Less Expenses		
Wages (1,200 + 100)	1,300	
Travel (2,600 − 50)	2,550	
Rabbit expenses	430	
Cleaning	140	
Depreciation – magician's equipment	540	
Depreciation – disappearing lady apparatus	400	
		(5,360)
Operating profit		14,190

Statement of financial position as at 31 December

	£	£	£
Non-current assets			
Magician's equipment, at cost (3,000 + 2,000 + 400)		5,400	
Less Depreciation (20% for half-year)		(540)	
			4,860
Disappearing lady apparatus		2,000	
Less Depreciation (40% for half-year)		(400)	
			1,600
			6,460
Current assets			
Inventory		80	
Trade receivables		350	
Prepayment – travel		50	
Cash equivalents (Bank)		120	
Cash		560	
		1,160	
Less Current liabilities			
Trade payables (Kaboosh Ltd, 1,700 − 1,500)	200		
Accrual – wages	100		
		(300)	
Net current assets			860
Total net assets			**7,320**

	£	£	£
Equity			
Opening balance (as calculated in case study in Chapter 2)		5,020	
Add Operating profit		14,190	
		19,210	
Less Drawings		(11,890)	
Closing balance at 31 December			**7,320**

Chapter 4

Income statement for the year ended 30 June 2012

	£	£
Raw materials		
Purchases of raw materials (note: no opening inventory)	15,621	
Less Closing inventory at 30 June 2012	(6,320)	
Cost of raw materials		9,301
Other direct costs:		
Production labour		5,820
Prime cost of production		15,121
Indirect costs:		
Rent and rates	3,600	
Light and heat	2,500	
Other workshop expenses	4,100	
Depreciation of workshop machinery	500	
		10,700
Cost of manufacturing		**25,821**
Revenue		45,821
Less Cost of sales		
Purchases (note: no opening inventory)	3,400	
Cost of manufacturing (see calculation above)	25,821	
	29,221	
Less Closing inventory at 30 June 2012	(2,400)	
		(26,821)

	£	£
Gross profit		19,000
Add Appearance fees as entertainer		34,500
		53,500
Less Expenses		
Assistant's wages	12,400	
Travel	5,510	
Rabbit expenses	430	
Cleaning	280	
Depreciation – magician's equipment	1,080	
Depreciation – disappearing lady apparatus	800	
		(20,500)
Operating profit		33,000

Statement of financial position as at 30 June 2012

	£	£	£
Non-current assets			
Magician's equipment, at cost		5,400	
Less Depreciation		(1,080)	
			4,320
Disappearing lady apparatus		2,000	
Less Depreciation (40%)		(800)	
			1,200
Workshop machinery		3,600	
Less Depreciation		(500)	
			3,100
Depreciated value of non-current assets			8,620
Current assets			
Inventory (6,320 + 2,400)		8,720	
Trade Receivables (Tanya Turner)		200	
Prepayment – rent and rates		600	
Bank		660	
Cash		40	
		10,220	

	£	£	£
Less Current liabilities			
Trade Payables (Kaboosh Ltd)	240		
Accruals (£200 + £100)	300		
		(540)	
Net current assets			9,680
Total net assets			**18,300**
Equity			
Opening balance (as per case study in Chapter 2)		5,020	
Add Operating profit		33,000	
		38,020	
Less Drawings		(19,720)	
Closing balance at 30 June 2012			**18,300**

Chapter 5

(a)

	£
Cost of the equipment	2,000
Depreciation to 30 June 2012	800
One month's depreciation to disposal date:	
$\frac{1}{12} \times [40\% \ (2{,}000 - 800)]$	40
Total depreciation to date of disposal	(840)
Depreciated value at date of disposal (2,000 − 840)	1,160
Proceeds	1,000
Loss on disposal	160

(b) The £200 bad debt will be written off to the income statement, thus reducing operating profit. Trade receivables (current assets) also decrease by £200.

Doubtful debts do not affect the receivables ledger as the account is kept alive as long as there is a glimmer of hope of payment. However profits are set aside from the income statement to ensure that all the doubtful debts are covered by a provision. The total provision is then deducted from the total trade receivables (after any bad debts have been deleted). The effect on profits depends on whether the provision is being created, increased or decreased:

- Created: the full amount of the provision comes out of profit (shown as part of 'expenses').
- Increased: only the extra amount needed comes out of profit (shown as part of 'expenses').
- Decreased: the surplus provision is added back to increase the profit.

Revision (page 127)

Marvin's second birthday

Income statement for the year ended 30 June 2013

	£	£
Revenue		35,900
Less Cost of sales		
Opening inventory at 1 July 2012	2,400	
Add Purchases	15,600	
	18,000	
Less Closing inventory at 30 June 2013	(2,500)	
		(15,500)
Gross profit		20,400
Add Appearance fees as entertainer		45,200
		65,600
Less Expenses		
Assistant's wages	24,600	
Travel (£6,220 – prepaid £450)	5,770	
Bad debt	200	
Increase in provision for doubtful debts (5% × £2,600)	130	
Cleaning	1,570	
Depreciation – magician's equipment	1,300	
Depreciation – 'saw the lady in half' prop [(£3,000 – £600)/4]	600	
Loss on disposal of disappearing lady apparatus	160	
		(34,330)
Operating profit		31,270

Statement of financial position as at 30 June 2013

	£	£	£
Non-current assets			
Magician's equipment, at cost		7,700	
Less Depreciation (1,080 + 1,300)		(2,380)	
			5,320

	£	£	£
'Saw the lady in half' equipment		3,000	
Less Depreciation		(600)	
			2,400
			7,720
Current assets			
Inventory		2,500	
Trade Receivables	2,600		
Less Provision for doubtful debts	(130)		
		2,470	
Prepayment – travel		450	
Bank		5,160	
		10,580	
Less Current liabilities			
Trade payables	480		
Accruals	250		
		(730)	
Net current assets			9,850
Total net assets			17,570
Equity			
Opening balance, 1 July 2012		18,300	
Add Operating profit		31,270	
		49,570	
Less Drawings		(32,000)	
Closing balance at 30 June 2013			17,570

Chapter 6

(a)

Machiq Partners
Income statement (appropriation section) for the year ended 30 June 2014

	£	£
Operating profit for the year		58,800
Divided as follows:		
Marvin: share of profit (60% × £58,800)	35,280	

	£	£
Chiquita: share of profit (40% × £58,800)	23,520	
		58,800

Machiq Partners
Statement of financial position as at 30 June 2014

	£	£
(Total net assets)		**35,000**
Marvin's Capital Account		
Opening balance, 1 July 2013	17,570	
Add Share of profit	35,280	
	52,850	
Less Drawings	(32,850)	
Closing balance, 30 June 2014		20,000
Chiquita's Capital Account		
Opening balance, 1 July 2013	10,000	
Add Share of profit	23,520	
	33,520	
Less Drawings	(18,520)	
Closing balance, 30 June 2014		15,000
		35,000

(b)

Machiq Limited
Income statement for the year ended 30 June 2015 (extract)

	£
Operating Profit for the year, before tax	92,000
Less Taxation (20% × £92,000)	(18,400)
Profit for the year, after tax	73,600
Less Dividend (£2.25 × 14,000 shares)	(31,500)
Retained profit for the year	42,100

Machiq Limited
Statement of financial position as at 30 June 2015 (extract)

	£
Equity	
Share capital (£1 shares)[1]	14,000
Share premium account[2]	21,000

	£
Retained earnings:	
Retained profit for the year	42,100
Total equity	77,100

Notes:

[1] The balances transferred from Machiq Partners (see above) were Marvin £20,000, Chiquita £15,000 (ratio 4:3), so the share capital of £14,000 is allocated as follows: Marvin (4/7) = 8,000 shares, Chiquita (3/7) = 6,000 shares.

[2] The partners' balances totalled £35,000, so the share premium must be £35,000 less the nominal value of £14,000 = £21,000.

Chapter 7

(a)

Machiq Limited
Cash flow statement for the year ended 30 June 2016

		£
Cash flows from operating activities		120,060
Interest paid		(1,800)
Taxation paid		(18,400)
Net cash from operating activities		**99,860**
Cash flows from investing activities		
Purchase of non-current assets	(97,000)	
Net cash used in investing activities		**(97,000)**
Cash flows from financing activities		
Proceeds from issue of share capital	20,000	
Dividends paid	(31,500)	
Net cash used in financing activities		**(11,500)**
Net decrease in cash and cash equivalents		**(8,640)**
Cash and cash equivalents at beginning of period		**6,240**
Cash and cash equivalents at end of period		**(2,400)**

Note:

	£
Operating profit	117,800
Depreciation	5,060
Increase in inventory (32,650−17,370)	(15,280)

	£
Decrease in receivables (39,560 – 30,950)	8,610
Increase in payables (14,080 – 10,210)	3,870
Net cash inflow from operating activities	120,060

(b) The cash flow statement clearly shows the main cause of the decrease in cash for the year: the purchase of the two luxury cars for Marvin and Chiquita. If more modest vehicles costing, say, £15,000 each had been purchased, there would have been a positive cash flow of nearly £60,000. If Trixie can curb the extravagance of her fellow shareholders then the company can both be profitable and have strong liquidity.

Chapter 8

(a) Ratio analysis:

Group	Name of ratio	Machiq Limited	Kaboosh Limited
(i) Profitability	ROCE	76.4%	22.7%
	Gross margin	25%	40%
	Mark-up	33.3%	66.7%
	Net margin	16.7%	24.1%
(ii) Efficiency	Non-current assets turnover	4.25 times	1.16 times
	Inventory turnover	22.5 days	138.7 days
	Average collection period	16 days	47.2 days
	Average payment period	9.7 days	59.6 days
(iii) Short-term solvency and liquidity	Current ratio (or working capital ratio)	0.84:1	2.05:1
	Acid test (or quick assets test)	0.41:1	0.85:1
	Cash conversion cycle (negative)	28.8 days	126.3 days
(iv) Long-term solvency and liquidity	Gearing	nil	17.1%
	Interest cover	65 times	22 times
(v) Investment ratios	eps (earnings per share	18.6p	10.35p
	p/e (price/earnings)	(assume) 15	(assume) 15
	Dividend cover	2.78 times	3.76 times
	Dividend yield	2.4%	1.77%

Comments:

(i) *Profitability*: We are comparing just one year's results for each company, so we must be cautious in drawing conclusions, as trends may show an improvement or decline when compared with previous years. With this proviso, Machiq Limited's ROCE is impressively high compared with Kaboosh's, indicating that Machiq is operating profitably from a relatively low capital base. It could also mean that Kaboosh has been investing in new non-current assets, and expects profitability to increase significantly as a result.

Kaboosh's margins are higher than Machiq's. If we assume that the companies are selling the same type of goods, then Machiq could seemingly raise its prices without affecting sales. Another interpretation is that Kaboosh is controlling its buying prices and costs much more efficiently than Machiq.

(ii) *Efficiency*: In terms of efficiency, in all respects Machiq is performing better than Kaboosh. Non-current assets are producing over three times as much sales, inventory is sold every 22.5 days (compared with a lengthy 138.7 days) and debts are being collected three times as quickly. The only surprise is that creditors are paid so fast – it would be more efficient to take advantage of interest-free credit and pay creditors after approximately 30 days. Kaboosh's inventory turn is very worrying – why has it let inventory build up to such an extent? Is part of the inventory unsaleable and perhaps overvalued?

(iii) *Short-term solvency and liquidity*: Kaboosh has a good current ratio, though the acid test could be slightly stronger. Machiq's ratios are very low, and the acid test shows only 41p of quickly realisable assets for every £1 of current liabilities. Machiq's management should reassess the dividend levels to improve the current and acid test ratios. Kaboosh has a worryingly high negative cash conversion cycle.

(iv) *Long-term solvency and liquidity*: Machiq has no long-term borrowings, so the gearing is zero. Kaboosh is low-geared at 17.1%. Neither company has any problems over safety of interest payments, with cover of 65 and 22 times respectively.

(v) *Investment ratios*: Neither company would have a stock market price (not being listed plcs), so the p/e ratio may not be a realistic comparison. However, the dividend yield has been calculated on the basis of a share price 15 times the eps. Both companies have reasonable safety of dividend, though Machiq's generous dividend policy results in a higher yield than that of Kaboosh.

(b) Purely on the basis of the ratio comparison with Machiq Limited, the key concerns within Kaboosh Limited's financial statements are:

- Low return on capital employed
- Poor working capital control, especially inventory

Within Machiq Limited's statements, the key concerns are:

- Lower profit margins
- Poor liquidity.

The poor liquidity, if uncorrected, could prove fatal to Machiq Limited, so the directors need to address this problem urgently. Once they can overcome this, they may feel that they do not need to sell out to Kaboosh Limited, especially in view of Machiq's massively higher return on capital employed. Before a decision can be taken, the following further information is needed:

- How much is Kaboosh Limited offering for the shares in Machiq Limited?
- What steps is Kaboosh Limited taking to overcome its poor working capital control?

- What plans does Kaboosh Limited have for improving its return on capital employed?
- What roles will the three directors of Machiq Limited have in the new company, and are they acceptable? What salaries would they be paid?

Chapter 9

		Total		Performing division		Retailing division
	£	£	£	£	£	£
Revenue		705,600		211,680		493,920
Less Cost of sales:						
Variable (80%)	423,360		42,336		381,024	
Fixed (20%)	105,840		10,584		95,256	
		(529,200)		(52,920)		(476,280)
Gross profit		176,400		158,760		17,640
Less expenses:						
Variable (40%)	23,440		8,204		15,236	
Fixed (60%)	35,160		12,306		22,854	
		(58,600)		(20,510)		(38,090)
Operating profit (operating loss)		117,800		138,250		(20,450)

Summary: The Performing division appears to have made an operating profit of £138,250 but the Retailing division appears to have made an operating loss of £20,450.

Chapter 10

Part (a)

(a) Using absorption costing principles, the bottling division would 'absorb' all the relevant costs, as follows:

	£	£
Forecast sales revenue (15,000 × £14)		210,000
Direct costs (15,000 × £6)	90,000	
Fixed costs of bottling division	20,000	
		(110,000)
Gross profit		100,000

	£	£
Company costs absorbed by division		(130,000)
Net loss		(30,000)

(b) Using marginal costing techniques, the information would be redrawn as follows:

	£
Forecast sales revenue (15,000 × £14)	210,000
Less Variable costs (15,000 × £6)	(90,000)
Contribution	120,000
Less Fixed costs of division	(20,000)
Profit of division	100,000

On this basis it can be seen that the bottling division would make a positive contribution of £120,000 to meeting the general costs of the business as a whole.

(c) The answers to the questions are as follows:

(i) The contribution per bottle is £14 − £6 = £8, so to meet the fixed costs of £20,000 (that is, the break-even point), **2,500 bottles** must be sold (£20,000/£8).

(ii) To earn £16,000 profit for the division, total contribution would need to be £36,000 (P + F = C). At a contribution of £8 per bottle, **4,500 bottles** would need to be sold.

(iii) If 4,000 bottles were sold, total contribution would be £32,000. After deducting fixed costs of £20,000, profit would be **£12,000**.

Postscript: Did you notice that 'Mrs Eadale' is an anagram of the name 'Esmeralda'?

Part (b)

	Mixing £	Liquidising £	Bottling £
Brought forward from previous process	n/a	1,735	2,772
Materials:			
Ingredient A 10 kg @ £80	800		
Ingredient B 5 kg @ £60	300		
Ingredient C 14 kg @ £40		560	
Bottles (1,000 × £1)			1,000
Labour:			
Mixing 10 hours × £4.50	45		
Liquidising 3 × (4 hours × £4.75)		57	
Bottling 2 × (5 hours × £5)			50
Other overheads	590	420	380

	Mixing	Liquidising	Bottling
	£	£	£
Total costs	1,735	2,772	4,202
Carried forward to next process	1,735	2,772	–
Cost of finished production			4,202
Cost per bottle			**£4.20**

Note: The normal loss caused by evaporation is a cost to be borne by the remaining production.

Chapter 11

(a) Variance analysis

Direct materials

1. Overall variance	**Actual Price of Actual Usage (APAU)**		**Standard Price of Standard Usage (SPSU)**		**Variance**
Ingredient A	9kg @ £82	£738	10kg @ £80	£800	£62 Fav
Ingredient B	5kg @ £59	£295	5kg @ £60	£300	£5 Fav
Ingredient C	13kg @ £40	£520	14kg @ £40	£560	£40 Fav
Bottles		£1,100		£1,000	(£100) Adv
		£2,653		£2,660	£7 Fav

2. Price variance	**Actual Price of Actual Usage (APAU)**		**Standard Price of Actual Usage (SPAU)**		**Variance**
Ingredient A		£738	9kg @ £80	£720	(£18) Adv
Ingredient B		£295	5kg @ £60	£300	£5 Fav
Ingredient C	(as above)	£520	13kg @ £40	£420	(£100) Adv
Bottles		£1,100		£1,100	–
		£2,653		£2,540	(£113 Adv)

3. Usage variance	**Standard Price of Actual Usage (SPAU)**		**Standard Price of Standard Usage (SPSU)**		**Variance**
Ingredient A		£720		£800	£80 Fav
Ingredient B		£300		£300	–
Ingredient C	(as above)	£420	(as above)	£560	£140 Fav
Bottles		£1,100		£1,000	(£100) Adv
		£2,540		£2,660	£120 Fav

Direct labour

1. Overall variance	Actual Pay Rate of Actual Hours (ARAH)		Standard Pay Rate of Standard Hours (SRSH)		Variance
Mixing	11 × £4.60	£50.60	10 × £4.50	£45.00	(£5.60) Adv
Liquidising	11 × £5	£55.00	12 × £4.75	£57.00	£2.00 Fav
Bottling	11 × £5	£55.00	10 × £5	£50.00	(£5.00) Adv
		£160.60		£152.00	(£8.60) Adv

2. Pay rate variance	Actual Pay Rate of Actual Hours (ARAH)		Standard Pay Rate of Actual Hours (SRAH)		Variance
Mixing	(as above)	£50.60	11 × £4.50	£49.50	(£1.10) Adv
Liquidising		£55.00	11 × £4.75	£52.25	(£2.75) Adv
Bottling		£55.00	11 × £5	£55.00	–
		£160.60		£156.75	(£3.85 Adv)

3. Efficiency variance	Standard Pay Rate of Standard Hours (SRSH)		Standard Pay Rate of Actual Hours (SRAH)		Variance
Mixing	(as above)	£45.00	(as above)	£49.50	(£4.50) Adv
Liquidising		£57.00		£52.25	£4.75 Fav
Bottling		£50.00		£55.00	(£5.00) Adv
		£152.00		£156.75	(£4.75) Adv

Fixed overheads

1. Overall variance	Actual Total of Fixed Overheads (ATFO)		Standard Total of Fixed Overheads (STFO)		Variance
		£1,500		£1,390	(£110) Adv

2. Expenditure variance	Actual Total of Fixed Overheads (ATFO)		Actual Hours @ Standard Absorption rate (AHSAR)		Variance
note: Standard Absorption Rate = £1,390/32 = £43.44		£1,500	33 × £43.44	£1,433.52	(£66.48) Adv

3. Volume variance	Actual Hours @ Standard Absorption rate (AHSAR)		Standard Total of Fixed Overheads (STFO)		
	33 × £43.44	£1,433.52		£1,390	(£43.52) Adv

Summary of variances

	Direct Materials		
	Price	**Usage**	**Overall**
Ingredient A	(£18) Adv	£80 Fav	£62 Fav
Ingredient B	£5 Fav	–	£5 Fav
Ingredient C	(£100) Adv	£140 Fav	£40 Fav
Bottles	–	(£100) Adv	(£100) Adv
Overall			£7 Fav

	Direct Labour		
	Pay rate	**Efficiency**	
Mixing	(£1.10) Adv	(£4.50) Adv	(£5.60) Adv
Liquidising	(£2.75) Adv	£4.75 Fav	£2.00 Fav
Bottling	–	(£5.00) Adv	(£5.00) Adv
Overall			(£8.60) Adv

	Fixed overheads		
	Expenditure	**Volume**	**Overall**
	(£66.48) Adv	(£43.52) Adv	£110.00 Adv

(b) Report: The variances relate to the production of a batch of 1,000 bottles. Regarding the Direct Materials, it can be seen that the overall variance is £7 favourable (less than one pence per bottle), but on investigation the main variances are the usage of Ingredient C (£140 favourable) and the £100 adverse variance relating to the number of bottles used, caused by breakages. Both these should be investigated by management: firstly to see whether the standard cost of Ingredient C was unrealistic and should be changed, and secondly, regarding the bottle breakages, to see the causes of the breakages and what measures can be implemented to minimise such problems in the future.

The direct labour variances are all relatively minor in terms of the values involved, but they should still be investigated so that management understands why more or fewer hours were required than the standard and also why different rates of pay (other than for the bottling process) were paid. In terms of efficiency, those working in the liquidising process recorded a favourable variance but the other two processes have adverse variances. Again, this should be investigated by management to ensure that the standard costs have been set at a realistic level.

Finally, the actual total fixed overheads were £110 greater than standard, of which £66.48 related to expenditure with the balance of £43.52 relating to a difference between the actual hours worked at the standard absorption rate compared with the standard total fixed overheads. Again, management should check that the standards have been set at a reasonable level.

Chapter 12

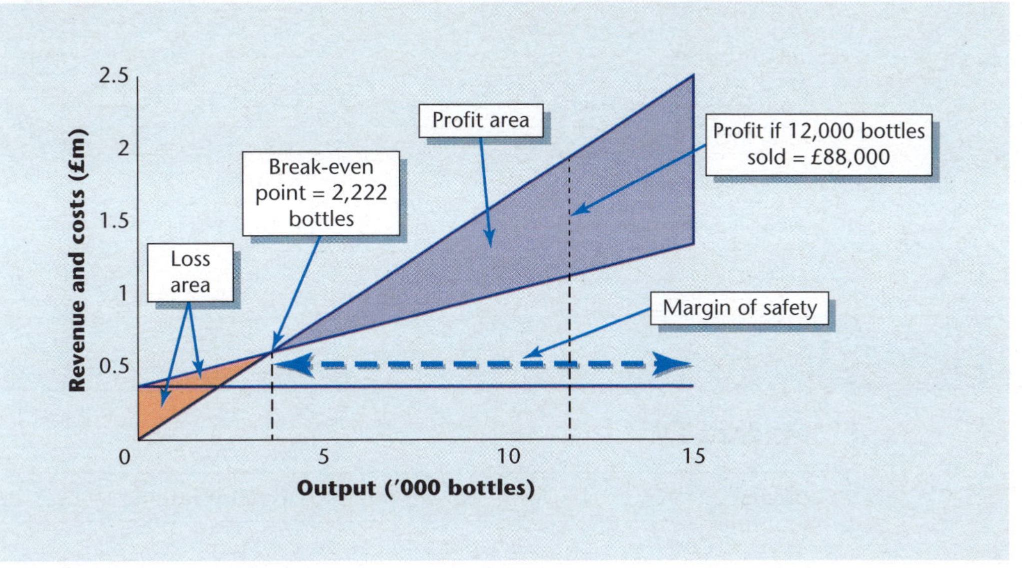

Chapter 12 Case study answer

Chapter 13

	Glow Gel	Floating Juice
	kg	*kg*
Revenue	16,000	12,000
Provision for losses	100	200
Closing inventory	1,200	800
Production budget	17,300	13,000

	Luminos	Schlepp
	litres	*litres*
Materials needed to produce:		
17,300 kg of Glow Gel	103,800	138,400
13,000 kg of Floating Juice	130,000	52,000
Usage budget	233,800	190,400
Provision for losses	1,000	400
	234,800	190,800
Closing inventory	15,200	9,200
Materials purchase budget (A)	250,000	200,000

	Luminos *litres*	Schlepp *litres*
Cost per litre (B)	£4	£2.50
(A) × (B)	£1m	£0.5m
Total cost of materials	**£1.5m**	

Chapter 14

Machiq TV

Year		Future value × Discount rate	Present value £
0	Cost	n/a	(250,000,000)
1–5	Running costs	£100m × 4.212*	(421,200,000)
5	Assets released	£40m × 0.747	29,880,000
1	Income	£60m × 0.943	56,580,000
2	Income	(150% × £60m = £90m) × 0.890	80,100,000
3	Income	(150% × £90m = £135m) × 0.840	113,400,000
4	Income	(150% × £135m = £202.5m) × 0.792	160,380,000
5	Income	(150% × £202.5m = £303.75m) × 0.747	226,901,250
NPV (negative)			(3,958,750)

*Cumulative factor shown as same amount paid each year over several years

Matrix 1 satellite

Year		Future value × Discount rate	Present value £
0	Initial set-up ($^1/_2$ × £700m)	n/a	(350,000,000)
1–6	Running costs	($^1/_2$ ×) £50m × 4.917*	(122,925,000)
6	Assets released at end of project	($^1/_2$ ×) £10m × 0.705	3,525,000
1	Income	£80m × 0.943	75,440,000
2	Income	(120% × £80m = £96m) × 0.890	85,440,000
3	Income	(120% × £96m = £115.2m) × 0.840	96,768,000
4	Income	(120% × £115.2m = £138.24m) × 0.792	109,486,080

Year		Future value × Discount rate	Present value £
5	Income	(120% × £138.24m = £165.888m) × 0.747	123,918,336
6	Income	(120% × £165.888m = £199.066m) × 0.705	140,341,530
NPV (positive)			161,993,946

*Cumulative factor shown as same amount paid each year over several years

The net present value of the TV channel option is negative whereas the satellite option is positive. On this basis alone, the satellite option would be chosen. In reality, a full appraisal would be taken of the relative merits of each proposal (not just in financial terms). For example, how realistic are the income forecasts, who would provide the significant capital involved, what management structures would be put in place to cope with such a massive project, etc?

Chapter 15

1 The table produced by Marvin actually does represent many of the ideas behind the Balanced Scorecard even though it does not use the conventional headings of:

- Financial perspective
- Customer perspective
- Internal process perspective
- Learning and growth perspective

Items 1 to 4 in Marvin's table represents key aspects of the *financial perspective*, providing useful information and data to assess revenue and profit potential after the new investment.
Items 5, 6, 7 and 12 certainly help with the *customer perspective*, improving customer experience.
Items 10 and 11 and possibly items 8 and 12 have the potential to help with the *internal process perspective*, improving management co-ordination and control.
Items 8, 9, 10 and 11 also have potential for increasing organisational capacity and thereby supporting the learning and growth perspective

2 The bank manager will certainly be interested in emphasising further the financial perspective of Marvin's business. The bank manager may well wish to know more about the following:

- How much profit will Marvin make?
- When will Marvin be able to pay back his loan?
- How much risk is involved, e.g. is there any collateral to help secure the loan?
- What is the return on capital employed?
- What is Marvin's operating profit margin?
- What is Marvin's sales forecast?

The bank manager may also wish to explore further the aims, objectives and strategies of the business.

Chapter 16

There will be serious possible implications for Spanish organisations and the Spanish government, and possibly for those entities dealing with Spain. A downgrading of the credit ratings of either private company or government bonds in Spain can have serious implications for the issuer. Lenders will insist on higher interest rates on any future loans to that company or government in order to cover the increased risks of making such loans. This is likely to raise the costs of borrowing and reduce the likelihood of being able to access funds even at higher interest rates. It is therefore likely to depress the Spanish economy even further.

If Spanish businesses and consumers have less income then they are less likely to pay to attend Marvin's shows in the numbers he might have expected. This is likely to reduce his revenue and profit below that forecast. There is also a greater risk for Marvin as the Spanish entrepreneur may now have difficulties in paying Marvin and funding the Spanish tour.

Chapter 17

1 He meant the total impact on the environment of all Marvin's activities, not only his own direct environmental impact but also that of the supply chain that provides the transport, the materials and the props that go into his performances.
2 The bank manager knows that being 'environmentally friendly' is important to the profile and future success of Marvin's business. The bank manager is also aware that the government is moving towards making all businesses provide annual information on their environmental impact. Even the amount of tax Marvin will have to pay in the future may depend on this.
3 Marvin will need to work out details such as the total number of miles travelled by him and by those providing support and materials for his act, the type of transport (road, rail, air) the energy used in each performance (electricity, gas, etc.) both directly and indirectly in his supply chain. There is expected to be a standardised form which will require specific answers to specific questions, but which will be attempting to find the impacts of Marvin's activities on CO_2 and other greenhouse gas emissions, amongst a range of other defined environmental impacts.

Appendix 4 Answers to revision sections

Revision of Chapters 1–5 (p. 127)

Section 1

Multiple choice questions

1a	**2**c	**3**b	**4**d	**5**a	**6**a	**7**c
8b	**9**d	**10**b	**11**a	**12**b	**13**d	**14**a
15c	**16**b	**17**b	**18**c	**19**a	**20**a	**21**c
22c	**23**d	**24**a	**25**b	**26**b	**27**c	**28**c
29a	**30**b	**31**c	**32**a	**33**a	**34**d	**35**b

Questions

(Note: For the first of the three questions in this section, the full methodology of the answer is explained.)

Question 1

Methodology

Before constructing the income statement and statement of financial position we need to follow a series of steps.

Step 1

Read through the trial balance items, making a mental note of possible problem areas – these could include the treatment of the loan interest and the provision for doubtful debts. This enables you to get an overall 'feel' of the problem.

Step 2

Read through the notes, and write in the adjustments needed for notes 3, 4 and 5 against the relevant trial balance items. These will appear as follows:

	£	£
Revenue (−£2,000)		626,220
Depreciation on motor cars, at 1 June 2013 (−£3,840)[a]		26,800
Electricity (+£1,300)	6,420	
Insurance (−£200)	2,640	
Loan interest (half-year) (+£2,400)	2,400	
Motor cars (cost) (−£6,000)	65,920	
Provision for doubtful debts at 1 June 2013 (+£500)		2,000

[a] The depreciation on the car that was sold: first year £2,400, second year £1,440.

Step 3

Using the information in notes 2 and 3, calculate the year's depreciation charge and the loss on disposal of the car. The calculations are as follows:

Motor cars:	£	£
At cost as shown in trial balance		65,920
Less Cost of car sold		(6,000)
		59,920
Depreciation at 1 June 2013	26,800	
Less depreciation on car sold	(3,840)	
		22,960
'Diminished' value to be depreciated at 40%		36,960
Depreciation for the year (40% × £36,960)		14,784
Total depreciation (for statement of financial position) (£22,960 + £14,784)		37,744
Profit or loss on disposal of car		£
Cost of car sold		6,000
Less Depreciation to date of sale		(3,840)
Depreciated value at date of sale		2,160
Proceeds of sale		(2,000)
Loss on disposal		160

Fixtures and fittings:

Depreciation for the year 10% × £24,210 = £2,421

Total depreciation (for statement of financial position) £6,503 + £2,421 = £8,924

Step 4

Draw two columns each about 3 cm wide on the right-hand side of two sheets of A4 paper. Write in the heading and then start compiling the first part leading to the gross profit (no *cost of manufacturing* is required in this question). Continue with the rest of the income statement, leading to the operating profit or loss, making sure that all the adjustments previously noted have been made. Then complete the statement of financial position.

Note: The heading of the income statement should contain the 'Three W's': Who, What and When. Who – the business name; What – the name of the statement (income statement); When – the financial period (year ended 31 May 2014).

The answer

Aneka Patel
Income statement for the year ended 31 May 2014

	£	£
Revenue		624,220
***Less* Cost of sales**		
Opening inventory at 1 June 2013	87,355	
Add Purchases	482,230	
	569,585	

	£	£
Less Closing inventory at 31 May 2014	(84,800)	
		(484,785)
Gross profit		139,435
***Less* Expenses**		
Wages and salaries	64,551	
Advertising	18,563	
Bad debts written off	5,835	
Bank interest paid	5,231	
Depreciation on fixtures and fittings	2,421	
Depreciation on motor cars	14,784	
Electricity	7,720	
Increase in provision for doubtful debts	500	
Insurance	2,440	
Loan interest	4,800	
Loss on disposal of motor car	160	
Rent and rates	5,900	
Telephone	11,240	
Sundry expenses	13,700	
		(157,845)
Operating loss		(18,410)

Aneka Patel
Statement of financial position as at 31 May 2014

	£	£	£
	Cost	**Total Depreciation**	**Depreciated value**
Non-current assets			
Motor vehicles	59,920	37,744	22,176
Fixtures	24,210	8,924	15,286
	84,130	46,668	37,462
Current assets			
Inventory		84,800	
Trade receivables	16,540		
Less Provision for doubtful debts	(2,500)		
		14,040	
Prepayments		200	
Cash		650	
		99,690	
***Less* Current liabilities**			
Trade payables	24,510		
Accruals	3,700		
Bank overdraft	14,852		
		(43,062)	

	£	£	£
Net current assets			56,628
			94,090
***Less* Non-current liability**			
6% Loan (repayable 2019)			(80,000)
Total net assets			**14,090**
Equity			
Opening balance, 1 June 2013		100,000	
Less Operating loss		(18,410)	
		81,590	
Less Drawings		(67,500)	
Closing balance, 31 May 2014			**14,090**

Question 2

Felicity Frankton
Income statement for the year ended 30 September 2014

	£	£
Revenue		105,800
Less Cost of sales		
Opening inventory at 1 October 2013	16,520	
Add Purchases	32,410	
	48,930	
Less Closing inventory at 30 September 2014	(14,560)	
		(34,370)
Gross profit		71,430
Less Expenses		
Wages and salaries	18,500	
Bad debts	500	
Light and heat	2,200	
Provision for doubtful debts (1,210 − 800)	410	
Rent and rates (3,200 + 600)	3,800	
Sundry office expenses (10,200 − 200)	10,000	
Loss on sale of car[1]	400	
Depreciation on car[2]	4,200	
Depreciation on computer[3]	722	
		(40,732)
Operating profit		30,698

Notes:

[1] (7,900 − 6,000) − 1,500.

[2] 60% × [(16,500 − 7,900) − (7,600 − 6,000)].

[3] 3,610/5.

Felicity Frankton
Statement of financial position as at 30 September 2014

	£	£	£
	Cost	**Total depreciation**	**Depreciated value**
Non-current assets			
Computers	3,610	2,572	1,038
Motor cars	8,600	5,800	2,800
	12,210	8,372	3,838
Current assets			
Inventory		14,560	
Trade receivables	24,200		
Less Provision for doubtful debts	(1,210)		
		22,990	
Prepayments		200	
Bank		2,350	
		40,100	
Less Current liabilities			
Trade payables	13,600		
Accruals	600		
		(14,200)	
Net current assets			25,900
Total net assets			29,738
Equity			
Opening balance, 1 October 2013		15,940	
Add Operating profit		30,698	
		46,638	
Less Drawings		(16,900)	
Closing balance at 30 September 2014			29,738

Question 3

Patrick Cooper
Income statement for the year ended 31 December 2013

	£	£
Revenue (289,512 – 100)		289,412
Less **Cost of sales**		
Opening inventory at 1 January 2013	5,820	
Add Purchases	132,950	
	138,770	
Less Closing inventory at 31 December 2013	(4,900)	
		(133,870)
Gross profit		155,542

	£	£
Less expenses		
Wages and salaries	39,540	
Bad debts written off	250	
Bank interest	950	
Administration expenses (55,500 − 150)	55,350	
Increase in provision for doubtful debts	250	
Selling expenses (37,790 + 300)	38,090	
Depreciation on equipment[1]	2,680	
Loss on sale of equipment[2]	140	
		(137,250)
Operating profit		18,292

Notes:

[1] 20% × (14,000 − 600).
[2] Cost − Depreciation to date of sale = 600 − (60% × 600) = 240.
Loss = 240 − 100 proceeds = 140.

Patrick Cooper
Statement of financial position as at 31 December 2013

	£	£	£
	Cost	**Total depreciation**	**Depreciated value**
Non-current assets			
Equipment	13,400	4,670	8,730
Current assets			
Inventory		4,900	
Trade receivables	6,300		
Less Provision for doubtful debts	(550)		
		5,750	
Prepayments		150	
Cash		140	
		10,940	
Less Current liabilities			
Trade payables	5,210		
Accruals	300		
Bank overdraft	1,600		
		(7,110)	
Net current assets			3,830
Total net assets			12,560
Equity			
Opening balance, 1 January 2013		16,268	
Add Operating profit		18,292	
		34,560	
Less Drawings		(22,000)	
Closing balance, 31 December 2013			12,560

Revision of Chapters 1–8 (p. 235)

Section 2

Exam paper 1 (multiple choice)

1b	11b	21b	31d
2a	12b	22a	32c
3c	13c	23a	33a
4c	14b	24d	34b
5a	15a	25a	35c
6b	16d	26d	36a
7d	17a	27c	37d
8c	18c	28a	38c
9a	19b	29d	39d
10d	20b	30d	40b

Exam paper 2

Question 1(a)

Aubrey Locke
Income statement for the year ended 31 May 2014

	£	£
Revenue	375,000	
Less Sales returns	(420)	
		374,580
Less Cost of sales		
Opening inventory at 1 June 2013	62,000	
Add Purchases	195,000	
	257,000	
Less Closing inventory at 31 May 2014	(50,000)	
		(207,000)
Gross profit		167,580
Add Decrease in provision for doubtful debts		400
		167,980
Less Expenses		
Wages and salaries	36,820	
Rent	16,000	
Electricity	10,000	
Bad debts written off	520	
General office expenses	18,000	
Depreciation on forklift truck [(20,000 − 2,000)/4]	4,500	
Depreciation on cars [40% × (18,000 − 6,000)]	4,800	
		(90,640)
Operating profit		77,340

Aubrey Locke
Statement of financial position as at 31 May 2014

	£	£	£
	Cost	**Total depreciation**	**Depreciated value**
Non-current assets			
Forklift truck	20,000	9,000	11,000
Motor cars	18,000	10,800	7,200
	38,000	19,800	18,200
Current assets			
Inventory		50,000	
Trade receivables	16,200		
Less Provision for doubtful debts	(2,240)		
		13,960	
Prepayments		4,000	
Bank		3,840	
Cash		120	
		71,920	
Less **Current liabilities**			
Trade payables	14,600		
Accruals	2,000		
		(16,600)	
Net current assets			55,320
Total net assets			73,520
Equity			
Opening balance at 1 June 2013		14,680	
Add Operating profit		77,340	
		92,020	
Less Drawings		(18,500)	
Closing balance at 31 May 2014			73,520

Question 1 (b)

A limited company's statement of financial position contains: taxation liabilities; share capital; share premium; reserves.

Question 2

Wilma Tonbridge
Income statement for the year ended 31 December 2013

	£	£
Revenue		208,000
Less Cost of sales		
Add Purchases	134,200	
Less Closing inventory at 31 December 2013	(9,200)	
		(125,000)
Gross profit		83,000

	£	£
Less Expenses		
Wages and salaries	25,600	
Rent and rates	12,800	
Provision for doubtful debts	2,400	
Office expenses	10,400	
Depreciation on computers, etc.	5,000	
		(56,200)
Operating profit		26,800

Wilma Tonbridge
Statement of financial position as at 31 December 2013

Non-current assets	**Cost** £	**Total depreciation** £	**Depreciated value** £
Computers, etc.	30,000	5,000	25,000
Current assets			
Inventory		9,200	
Trade receivables	48,000		
Less Provision for doubtful debts	(2,400)		
		45,600	
Prepayments		3,200	
		58,000	
Less Current liabilities			
Trade payables	7,000		
Accruals	2,400		
Bank overdraft	52,800		
		(62,200)	
Net current liabilities			(4,200)
			20,800
Less Non-current liabilities (loan)			(16,000)
Total net assets			4,800
Equity			
Opening balance at 1 January 2013		10,000	
Add Operating profit		26,800	
		36,800	
Less Drawings		(32,000)	
Closing balance at 31 December 2013			4,800

Question 3(a)

Gross margin	(GP/Sales) × 100	Hove Ltd's margin is higher than average. Possible reasons include lack of competition, better buying policies, errors in inventory counts

Net margin	(Operating profit/ Sales) × 100	Hove Ltd's margin is higher than average. Possible reasons include greater control of expenses, more automation (lower wage costs)
ROCE	Operating profit/ Capital employed (total net assets + loans) × 100	Hove Ltd's margin is higher than average. Possible reasons include greater efficiency overall, less competition
Acid test	Ratio of (current assets − inventory): Current liabilities	Hove Ltd's margin is lower than average. Possible reasons include better use of interest-free credit from suppliers, fewer credit sales than average
Gearing	Fixed % borrowing/ Capital employed or Fixed % borrowing/ Capital employed + Fixed % borrowing	Hove Ltd's margin is much higher than average. Possible reasons include past expansion financed by borrowings, or borrowing in anticipation of future expansion

Question 3(b)

A current ratio of 6:1 might indicate too much inventory being carried, poor control of debtors, or surplus bank balances not being reinvested into non-current assets. It is not normally seen as a positive indicator, though it could indicate just a temporary situation which could be altered as soon as the surplus inventory is sold (or used to manufacture), a customer pays a large outstanding debt or surplus cash is used to reinvest, or in other ways such as paying dividends or staff bonuses.

Question 4(a)

(i) Liability for debts:

- Sole proprietor: unlimited liability for the debts of the business.
- Limited company: shareholders' liability is limited to the value of the share capital invested or agreed to be invested in the company.

(ii) Ability to raise capital:

- Sole proprietor: restricted to loans from family, friends, acquaintances and banks.
- Limited company: a private limited company cannot issue an invitation to the general public to invest, but ownership is split into shares, so investment becomes more attractive to friends, family and other acquaintances who then become part-owners rather than creditors.

  Public limited companies can sell their shares to the general public and have the potential to raise much more than any other type of business organisation.

(iii) Legal formality:

- A sole proprietor is the most informal form of business organisation, with few specific rules and regulations to follow. They do need to inform government authorities if taxable profits are made.
- Limited companies are subject to company legislation, which requires the companies to publish accounts, file an annual report and keep share- holders informed, among other things. Public limited companies may also have to follow Stock Exchange regulations.

Question 4(b)

Income statement for the year ended 31 December 2014 (extract)		
Income includes:		
Bad debt recovered (Customer D)	500	
Decrease in provision for doubtful debts		
(Customers B and C doubtful at year-end)	580	
[brought forward 1,400 – carried forward (600 + 220)]		
Expenses include:		
Bad debt written off (Customer A)	800	
Statement of financial position as at 31 December 2014 (extract)		
Receivables (Customer A written off) (£45,000 – £800)		44,200
Less Provision for doubtful debts		(820)
		43,380)

Revision of Chapters 9–14 (p-362)

Question 1

(a) Spectacular plc: Overhead analysis sheet

Overhead	Basis of apportionment	P	Q	R	Service
Indirect wages	(Actual)	8,000	12,000	18,300	6,700
Consumable stores	Requisitions	14,400	9,600	8,000	–
Rent	Area	4,500	6,750	6,000	3,750
Light and heat	Area	3,000	4,500	4,000	2,500
Power	kW	14,400	18,000	900	2,700
Depreciation	20% × cost	28,000	36,000	2,000	14,000
Insurance: machinery	Cost of plant	700	900	50	350
		73,000	87,750	39,250	30,000
Service	Direct labour cost	7,500	9,000	13,500	(30,000)
		80,500	96,750	52,750	–

(b) Computation of hourly rates of overhead absorption

Basis	P	Q	R
Direct-labour-hours	$\frac{80{,}500}{100{,}000}$ = £0.805	$\frac{96{,}750}{80{,}000}$ = £1.209	$\frac{52{,}750}{220{,}000}$ = £0.24 = £0.24
Machine-hours	$\frac{80{,}500}{70{,}000}$ = £1.15 = £1.15	$\frac{96{,}750}{90{,}000}$ = £1.075 = £1.075	$\frac{52{,}750}{10{,}000}$ = £5.275 = £5.275

(c) Labour hour rates are applicable if work is labour intensive. They relate to time, and overcome fluctuating wage rates and different grades of worker. A disadvantage could be the time and cost of maintaining labour records. Machine hour rates are applicable where work is capital intensive. They also relate to time and can be analysed by individual machine or group of machines. A disadvantage could be the reliability of the data and the time and cost of collecting it.

Question 2

(a) (i) Contribution = £100 − (£25 + £30 + £5) = £40, so maximum profit is:

Total contribution	16,000 × £40 =	£640,000
Less Fixed costs		(£240,000)
Maximum profit		**£400,000**

(ii) Break-even point = Fixed costs/contribution per coat:

£240,000/£40 = **6,000 coats**

(iii) Margin of safety = Maximum production less break-even point

16,000 − 6,000 = **10,000 coats**

(iv) If 11,000 coats are sold, contribution = 11,000 × £40 = £440,000. Fixed costs are £240,000, so profit = £440,000 − £240,000 = **£200,000.**

(Alternative calculation: 11,000 coats = 5,000 more than the break-even point; 5,000 × £40 contribution = £200,000).

(b)

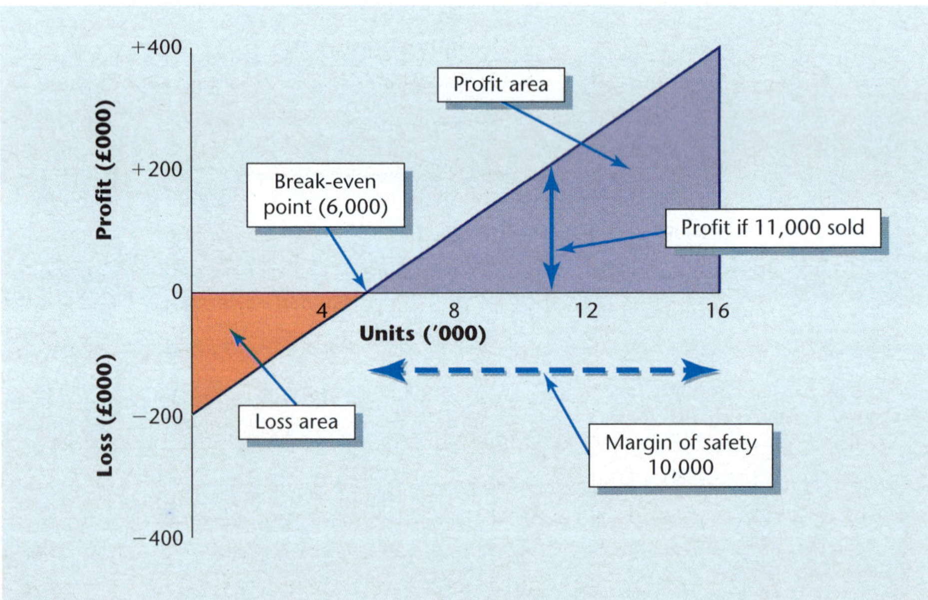

(c) The contribution from the special order will be £70 − (25 + 30 + 5 + 6) = £4. Total additional contribution = 5,000 × £4 = £20,000 with no additional fixed costs, so the order should be accepted, provided that it does not cause disruption to existing production.

Question 3

(a)

	Cost per Unit	Total
	£	£
Raw materials (2.40 × 600)	2.400	1,440
Wages (£4.80 × 50 hours)	0.400	240
Overheads (50 hours × £5.30)	0.442	265
Setting-up costs	0.025	15
Cost of full batch	3.267	1,960

(b)

		£
Cost of full batch		1,960.00
Add Rectification costs		
Wages (6 hours × £4.80)	28.80	
Overheads (6 hours × £5.30)	31.80	
Set-up costs	10.00	
		70.60
		2,030.60
Less Income from scrapped trees 40 × £0.75		(30.00)
Total cost of 560 trees		2,000.60
Cost of batch per unit £2,000.60/560		3.57

(c)

	£
560 units should have cost 560 × £3.267 (see (a) above)	1,829.52
Actual cost (see (b) above)	2,000.60
Loss	171.08

Question 4

(a) (i) Net present value is (positive) £1,027,000 (workings below).

(ii) The payback period is reached after $2\frac{1}{4}$ years. The net cash flows (undiscounted) as shown in the workings table below are: year 1 £525,000, year 2 £1,245,000, total £1,770,000. The additional £230,000 needed to match the £2m investment is reached roughly one-quarter of the way through year 3's net cash flow of £946,000.

(b) The project is forecast to generate a positive NPV, and the payback is reached after less than half of the project's total anticipated life. On each of these criteria, it would appear that the project is worth proceeding with. One point to query is whether it is realistic for 'other costs' to remain at £25 per unit over the project's life.

(c) In standard costing, standards are set in advance for levels of performance and cost of resources, and then these are compared with the *actual* levels of performance and the actual prices. Any differences between the standard and the actual values are known as *variances*. The benefit of standard costing is that it prompts questions to be asked as to *why* the variances have arisen. If there is a variance, then something has not gone according to plan. Even where actual costs are *less than* standard costs, this would prompt as much investigation as when the actual costs are *greater than* standard. Standard costing also enables organisations to adopt the practice of *management by exception*, so that management's attention can be concentrated upon the key areas which materially differ from what was planned.

Workings:

Year	Units	Labour	Materials	Over-heads	Total cost	Sales	Net cash flow	Discount factor	PV
		£000	£000	£000	£000	£000	£000		£000
0					(2,000)		(2,000)	n/a	(2,000)
1	5,000	200	400	125	(725)	1,250	525	0.943	495
2	15,000	630	1,200	375	(2,205)	3,450	1,245	0.890	1,108
3	22,000	968	1,936	550	(3,454)	4,400	946	0.840	795
4	15,000	690	1,410	375	(2,475)	3,000	525	0.792	416
5	5,000	240	500	125	(865)	1,000	135	0.747	101
							150	0.747	112
NPV									1,027

Index